The Hippie Dictionary:

A Cultural Encyclopedia (and Phraseicon) of the 1960s and 1970s

written and compiled by
John Bassett McCleary

edited by
Joan Jeffers McCleary

Ten Speed Press
Berkeley / Toronto

1⊜

Ten Speed Press
P.O. Box 7123
Berkeley, California 94707
www.tenspeed.com

Distributed in Australia by Simon and Schuster Australia, in Canada by Ten Speed Press Canada, in New Zealand by Southern Publishers Group, in South Africa by Real Books, in Southeast Asia by Berkeley Books, and in the United Kingdom and Europe by Airlift Book Company.

Text Designer: John McCleary
Cover Designer: Paul Kepple @ Headcase Design

Library of Congress Cataloging-in-Publication Data

McCleary, John Bassett, 1943-
    The hippie dictionary : a cultural encyclopedia of the 1960s and 1970s / written and compiled by John Bassett McCleary ; edited by Joan Jeffers McCleary.
        p. cm.
    ISBN: 1-58008-355-2
    1. Hippies--United States--Dictionaries. I. McCleary, Joan Jeffers. II. Title.

HQ799.7 .M28 2002
305.5'68--dc21

                                                                2002018062

First printing, 2002
Printed in Canada

1 2 3 4 5 6 7 8 9 10 — 06 05 04 03 02

"I learned how to spell respect from Aretha Franklin and encyclopedia from Mickey Mouse."
JBMc

Contents

Apologies

I may have overlooked some events, people or terms of the era, and for this, I apologize. Some "facts" may be missing or questionable due to a lack of resources, and for that, I apologize. I do not consider this book to be the last word on every subject of the hippie era, yet I do believe it is the best overview of the entire era yet compiled. There are many other books focusing more closely on individual aspects of the period. I think I have covered self-gratification pretty well, but if one wants to study the subtleties of joint rolling or grock the inner workings of a Volkswagen carburetor, there are other sources to peruse. Many of these sources are noted in "Books of and About the Era" in lists at the back of this book.

Even though this is a reference book intended as a scholarly observation of a period of history, I am not ignoring the free spirit of the era. If I were merely objective and technically pedantic in the creation of this book, I would be missing the true value of the hippie era to our society and ignoring the lessons that period of time contributed to history. In the spirit of adventure and experimentation evoked by the 1960s and 70s, I am breaking some rules, taking liberties with the English language and even creating new words to communicate new ideas and concepts.

From this point on in my writing, "they" and "their" will be used to represent singular as well as a plural. Example: "Each person has **their** own fork," and "someone who is trying to be what **they** are not." These words have been used this way in verbal conversation for a long, long time, by almost everyone (except my wife). This change to the English language will help to alleviate the problem of "his or her" and the constant debate about creating new words, such as "hesh" or "hirsh" to produce a gender-neutral, singular designation. "Hesh" or "hirsh" sounds funny, "his and/or hers" is awkward, and, to be politically correct, which should come first, she or he? I want to get over this debate and on with writing.

In this book I concentrated primarily on the counterculture of America, yet I know that there were and are hippies and people of that spirit in all countries of the world. I also relied heavily on California definitions, institutions and activities; that is because I believe, if the hippie culture had a center, it was most likely the West Coast of America. This is not to say that I have ignored other states of the union or other countries. Whenever I was aware of a variation in definition, I included it.

No Apologies

Some critics might say that, since this is a reference book, opinions of the writer should not be voiced; yet I am editorializing at times in this dictionary because the era was a very opinionated period of time, and certain attitudes that I express represent, I believe, typical hippie philosophy.

In the spirit of better communication and understanding, I have created a new form of dictionary and coined a new word to describe it. On the title page, in the subtitle of this book, one will find the new word *"Phraseicon"*; this is a new concept in dictionaries. As one will soon discover within this book, a large portion of the entries are phrases composed of several words. This is a unique development in dictionaries; I have included a higher percentage of phrase entries in this publication than appear in previous reference books.

In a standard dictionary, approximately 1 in 25 entries is a multiword offering; in slang dictionaries prior to this book, the ratio has been about 5 in 25 entries; while in this dictionary, the percentage is almost 50 percent phrases. I have done this because the language of today consists of more than merely several syllable grunts as it was back in the 1950s. Abstract communication requires multiple words. Feelings and philosophies demand phrases, contractions, prefixes and suffixes. Very few new words are actually created each day or even within each era, but many new concepts based on existing words are being developed. Combining existing words to create new meanings is a process I have addressed in this book. I have also created several new words in the writing of this book as new concepts arose. These new words are marked with *** (three asterisks).

This dictionary was a monumental undertaking; it has consumed much of my interest for over eight years. When I started, the Internet was not readily available to me, and I got most of my information, facts and figures the old way—by reading, listening and searching libraries. As I approach the completion of this book, the Internet is available, yet still convoluted and confusing. Although I have employed computer references at times, I find that old "hard copy" is still the best way to get most of the information I need. Another advantage to going to the library is that it gives one a social life. Sitting at a computer all day and night is no proper life for a human being. There are people at the library and opportunities for social exchange. Trips to the library have also enabled me to maintain a healthy skin color through continuous, regular exposure to the copy machine lamps.

**In memory of my mother, Pauline Meeks McCleary,
and my mother-in-law, Frances Wheeler Jeffers,
two bohemian spirits.**

Acknowledgments

I want to thank my wife, Joan Jeffers McCleary, who is also my editor. Not many editors will reheat your coffee and kiss the nape of your neck as you hunch over your computer monitor.

I also want to thank Janis Joplin, Ravi Shankar and Country Joe McDonald. If I hadn't experienced their performances at the Monterey Pop Festival, I might never have known that there was an alternative to Patti Page, Rev. Billy Graham and Mr. Cleaver. A special tribute to Blake, Byron, Darwin, Emerson, Goethe, Rimbaud, Shelley, Wilde and Whitman.

I wish to thank the staff members at the reference desks of my local libraries in Monterey and Pacific Grove, in particular Victor Bausch, Rosy Brewer, Jean Chapin, Tamara Hennessy, Douglas Holtzman, Joe Johnson, Janis Rodman and Stephen Parker. Without these people, my task would have been impossible. Visit your library; it is still the best place to improve your life.

Also, to the creators of the personal computer, I offer my #*x@x+x> gratitude, specifically Steve Wozniak and Steve Jobs for their wonderful Macintosh.

At the back of this book, along with photo credits, is a list of other people who have helped in the creation and completion of this project.

Introduction

Why a Hippie Dictionary?

Because some of us were there, but can't remember it.

Because some of us were living in the Midwest and missed it.

And because some of us have found beads and bell-bottoms in the back of our parents' closet and want to know what it was all about.

There are those who will consider the phrase "Hippie Dictionary" to be an oxymoron, implying that hippies were not scholarly enough to warrant a dictionary. I beg to differ, and once you stick your curious, though skeptical, noses into this book, you will understand why.

I contend that the hippie era was the intellectual renaissance of the 20th century. I believe it came about because of an emotional rebellion against the mindless direction in which our world was headed. I believe the hippie era gave this world and human society a reprieve. Without the new emotions and outlook of the hippie era, the world would be a dull place today. Without the philosophies and ideals espoused during the hippie era and expressed in books like *Nobody Knows My Name, On The Road, Silent Spring* and *1984*, then 1984 would have become a reality. The 60s counterculture postponed the oppressive police state that was overtaking society. Now many people feel that, unless we have another intellectual rebellion, 1984 and its political oppression will indeed happen sometime in the 2020s. That is the reason for this dictionary; that is why I am reacquainting you with the counterculture of the 1960s and 1970s.

Subcultures and countercultures recur throughout history. There have always been small segments of society that rebel against the norm. There are countercultures existing now, and new ones will appear tomorrow. However, within recent history, no other counterculture has had as much effect upon our lives and our vocabulary as has the hippie culture. Without passing judgment on whether it was good or bad, one must admit that the 1960s and 70s greatly influenced what exists today. If nothing else, it was a thought-provoking time.

After a brief review of this book, one might ask why so much of the counterculture vocabulary was related to sex, drugs and rock & roll. The simple answer is that it was what was happening at the time. The profound answer is that the hippie movement was a revolution rejecting the excesses of the straight society, and what better way to confront the excesses of the establishment than to display the opposite excesses?

Countercultures often seem to take the repressions of the establishment and throw them back in its face. It is fortuitous that those repressed activities also often happen to be fun.

My feeling is that all the noise that the church, media and government make about sex, drugs and rock & roll is just a smoke screen to divert attention from all the really nasty and truly immoral things that governments and the military-industrial complex are doing around the world. Which is worse, getting stoned and making love or killing Indians in the rain forest to get their land to raise beef for fast-food restaurants?

The hippie era was a time of excesses: The Vietnam War was excessive, corporate arrogance was excessive, racial violence was excessive. Hippies demonstrated against the Vietnam War, corporate greed and racial intolerance, and they often did it to excess.

True, hippies overindulged in sex, drugs and rock 'n' roll, yet they also took a deeper look at religion than had been taken for some time. Civil rights and ethnic intolerance were major issues during the era as well. New areas of importance, such as ecology, were brought to prominence, and concerns about physical health and mental well-being were expanded. All of these brought new words to our vocabulary.

The words in this dictionary span a kaleidoscope of interests, such as religion, metaphysics, social concern, political rebellion and, of course, sex, drugs and rock 'n' roll. Some of the words defined in this book may seem too arrogant, violent or politically incorrect for a hippie dictionary, and yes, they would be if we were dealing only with the hippie culture. However, this book is also a "cultural encyclopedia of the 1960s and 70s," and it deals with all of the attending words and attitudes of that period.

In this book, you will be confronted with many "politically incorrect" terms; however, you must remember that the term "politically correct" itself had not yet been coined. We were experimenting with correctness at the time. Men were reevaluating their relationships with women, and women were beginning to demand their rightful place; all people were questioning prejudices and hatreds.

As a messenger, to be true to the era, I have had to delve into some subjects with which I myself do not agree, but to omit them from this book would be academically incorrect. I will not defend the vulgarity or naiveté of the era, except to say that we were experimenting and learning what might work in the future for human beings.

I do not care for the words "nigger," "cunt" or "turd burglar." I do not think that heroin, methamphetamines or cocaine are reasonable things to put into one's body. Self-destruction and bigotry are not my way of life, yet to forget that these things exist is to perpetuate ignorance and to prolong their existence. Not all of the words in this dictionary exemplify the true hippie value system; many of these terms were merely present during the era and had some influence on the events of the time.

I believe that the majority of people possess a common sense mechanism in their minds. That spot is in there waiting for the information necessary to process each situation and make the right decisions.

I will go so far as to say that even lies or incorrect information serve a purpose and must be available as a comparison to the truth. Give people good information, and they will come up with good solutions. Ignorance keeps us from perfection, and information is the cure for ignorance.

Keep in mind that I am not advocating any of the drug-taking or sexual behavior described in this book, nor am I condemning it, though I may give a warning from time to time. People will do what they want to do, and I believe that is their prerogative as long as they are not directly harming others. However, I also feel that people should be aware of the facts, good and bad, about any indulgence they plan to pursue, and that is one of the reasons for this book.

To write off this book as a mere self-indulgence about an obscure period of time would be a mistake. Thinking that because the word "hippie" appears in the title, it is relevant only to those who were hippies would also be short-sighted. The "hippie era" was filled with new thoughts and ideas as well as the reevaluation of old thoughts and ideas. We, both hip and straight, still benefit today from many of the developments of that era, and we will continue to be affected by many concepts begun at that time.

Some folks out there may not agree with romanticizing, or even publicizing, the hippie era. They may argue that a time that produced rampant free sex and drug usage and contributed to the breakdown of conservative family values does not deserve a place in our history. Yet, if one dissects any time of history, a double-edged sword can be found. All eras had positive contributions as well as negative influences.

If one agrees, as do many scholars, that being able to think, reason and adapt to one's changing environment are human beings' most important attributes, then one must agree that the 1960s and 70s were an important period for mankind. The most prominent aspect of the hippie era was the emergence of new ideas and experimentation on social, political, religious and environmental issues.

Nothing produced by humans is ever completely new. Everything we create is assembled from things or concepts that were previously available. This can be said of inventions or ideas and most surely of words.

Many of the entries in this book are not exclusive to the hippie period. A good number of them were in use earlier, and some are universal; however, my objective is to place them in the context of the time. Many of the words and phrases herein are still in use today. Some are used as they were then, some are changed, and some, built upon. In some cases, a word with which one is familiar may have had a different connotation in the hippie era.

The vocabulary of the hippie generation comes, in large part, from the beat generation, jazz and blues music, African-American culture, Eastern religions and the British musical invasion of the early 1960s. Yet that is only the beginning of the story.

One category of words that evolved greatly during the hippie era was that which previously described physical things or actions, but began to take on emotional, psychological or even metaphysical connotations. Examples: **hang** in there, get **down**, keep on **trucking**. Other examples: **deep** and **heavy.** "Falling into that *deep* well created **deep** metaphorical questions regarding mortality." "He took the job moving *heavy* rocks in order to give himself space to think about the **heavy** conflicts in his life."

Another aspect of the vocabulary of the hippie era was the way in which previously established words began to posses more qualities or dimensions. For example, a word like "**head,**" which previously described a part of the body, but eventually evolved into a state of being: A "**head**" is someone who takes psychedelic drugs. A "**head**" is a person who "knows what is happening." A "**head** case" is a crazy person. These new definitions deal with what goes on *inside* the "**head.**"

Most of the words that became prominent during the hippie era had at least some previous usage, yet they were changed to describe formerly unfamiliar situations or used uniquely in old situations.

Do you know the philosophical relevance of the word "**maintain,**" or the social value of "**cool**"? Can you pick out a "**cat**" in bunch of "**dogs**" at a party attended only by people? Are you "**bad**" when you're "**good**" or "**good**" when you're "**bad**"?

This is a dictionary, yet it is also a history book. It is a dictionary of a period that is past; therefore, a 1970 definition will be a 1970 definition forever. Yet this book will never become outdated; history is always a current subject. This book chronicles a period of time that means a great deal to the development of our present and our future.

To understand a period of time completely one must know its slang vocabulary. To know how someone "feels," one must know their colloquial communication; the formal vocabulary seldom expresses true emotions. *The Hippie Dictionary* gives a deeper insight into a period that was much more historically pivotal and socially interesting than many eras before or since.

Some of you may be offended by some of the words included here. My answer is that words are only a description of actions or attitudes. We should not be afraid of the words themselves. It is the actions described by those words that must concern us, and we cannot solve a problem if we are afraid to discuss it. We must have the proper words to converse intelligently about a subject.

People often utter words when they are ignorant of the true meaning of those words; if they knew the reality of their words, they might not be so quick to speak them. Only after fully understanding the meaning of a word can someone decide whether they agree with what it stands for or are willing to experience its consequences. If it is possible to teach the harsh reality of certain deeds and attitudes through a book like this, it is important to try. The alternative is for everyone to experience every situation firsthand, and people often will not survive that kind of education.

We will never change improper actions and bad attitudes until we understand their consequences. A dictionary that is totally candid can expose all manner of things, good and bad, for what they are. Hopefully, this book will keep some people from making experimental mistakes. But for those of you who must always do it on your own, may your God be with you.

Enjoy this dictionary, laugh at those terms that are fun and frivolous, but also learn from the serious and important words and people of the time.

Look for these prominent people and terms marked by asterisks:
*One of the 100 most prominent words or phrases that evolved out of the hippie era into continual use today.
**One of the 35 most influential people of the hippie era.

A

A *drugs* abbreviation for **amphetamines** or for **acid**, depending on which drug crowd one "**hangs** with." In the drug culture, conversations are often cryptic and abbreviated for purposes of concealment. Talking that way also sounds real **cool**. The growth of language has two different directions, expansion and contraction. Expansion involves grouping more words together into phrases and also creating longer words to expand a thought. The contraction of our language is the process of shortening these words and phrases after everyone knows their meaning. (See: **amphetamines** and **acid**)

a *interjection* used to emphasize a point, it is the abbreviation for **ass**. Example: "Fucking **a**, he's a hot guitar player!"

A&R and **A&R man** Artist and Repertory. Having to do with the promotion of songs or musicians. A salesman of music or talent. A music industry term that came into use in the 1960s and 70s. It acquired a negative connotation because A&R men were often considered "sleazy," materialistic, non-artistic members of the industry and because of the association of such people with the payola scandal. (See: **payola** and **Allen Freed**)

Abba *disco, pop, rock & roll* a Swedish band formed in 1971 whose members were Benny Andersson, kybd., synth., voc.; Bjorn Ulvaeus, gtr., voc.; Agnetha "Anna" Fältskog, voc.; Anni-Frid "Frida" Synni-Lyngstad-Fredriksson-Andersson, voc. The most commercially successful musical group in the 1970s, yet it was dismissed by most of the **counterculture** as "bubblegum" music.

Abbey, Edward (1927-1989) a radical environmentalist and author of the 1975 book, *The Monkey Wrench Gang*. The book chronicles a fictional group of **environmental** commandos who plan to blow up the controversial Glen Canyon Dam. Abbey is responsible for the word **monkeywrenching**, the act of physically disrupting a company involved in activity that is considered environmentally objectionable, such as dam construction and logging. Abbey and his book influenced Dave Foreman and other leaders of the **Earth First!** movement.

Abbots *drugs* **Nembutal** pills, the brand name **barbiturate** produced by Abbot Laboratories. A **downer**.

Abernathy, Rev. Ralph David (1926-1990) *social issues* Baptist minister, civil rights leader, a founder and eventual president of the **Southern Christian Leadership Conference (SCLC)** after the death of **Martin Luther King, Jr.**, on April 4, 1968. One of King's most trusted associates who was with him when he was assassinated. Rev. Abernathy led the **Poor People's March**

on Washington, DC, in 1968. He is reportedly the first person to use the word **pig** in reference to the police. He used the term in a speech about the police riots in Chicago during the **Democratic National Convention** in August, 1968.

A-bomb *drugs* a combination of drugs smoked together, usually **marijuana** or **hash** mixed with **heroin** or **opium**.

abortion a disaster. Example: "That party was an **abortion**." During the hippie era, a number of words that had previously defined physical actions began to be used to describe psychological, emotional or intangible situations.

abraxas *occult* a **magic** word, said to be the name of a god. In **numerology** these seven letters form the number 365, the number of days in the year. This word engraved on a gem or stone is considered by occultists to constitute a very potent charm. (See: **numerology**)

absofuckinglutely *interjection* without a doubt. Example: "That is **absofuckinglutely** the best concert my ears have suffered through!" It is a strange compound created from the words "absolutely" and "fucking." The profanity, as usual, is employed for emphasis.

Abzug, Bella (1920-1998) *social issues* attorney, politician, civil rights advocate and **women's rights leader. As a White female lawyer from the north, in 1951, she defended Willie McGee, a Black man charged with raping a White woman in Mississippi. It was a pivotal trial in the effort to bring equal legal rights to the African American community in the Southern United States. Abzug was elected to the US House of Representatives from New York City in 1971, serving four terms. She was the primary officer of the national commission presiding over the historic International Women's Year conference in Houston, Texas, in November, 1977. Bella Abzug wrote the book *The Gender Gap,* published in 1984.

academic freedom the existence of **free speech** within educational institutions. The principle of academic freedom suggests that, in a free society, teachers and students have the right to express unpopular ideas, or even unproven theories, in the classroom without repercussions from the school administration. This was at the core of most of the college campus unrest, particularly at Columbia, **UC Berkeley** and the **University of California, Santa Barbara (UCSB)**, in 1969-70. For example, at the University of California, Santa Barbara, in February, 1970, Assistant Professor of Anthropology **William Allen** was dismissed because of the content of his lectures. This fermented student unrest and led to the burning of the **Isla Vista branch of the Bank of America**.

Acapulco Gold *drugs* a particularly popular and reportedly potent strain of **marijuana**. The name alone warranted a higher price. If marijuana had come in packs with brand names, this would have been the most popular label. The leaf was usually golden brown. It was reportedly grown in the Acapulco area of Mexico, but since, at the street level, it was almost impossible to verify where marijuana was grown, I suspect that much of the "Gold," as it was called, came from Northern California and was dried under heat lamps to give it that golden color.

AC/DC *sex* **bisexual** activity. **Going both ways**, being attracted to or indulging in intimacy with both sexes. Originally from electrical terminology meaning "alternating current" and "direct current," the two forms of electricity. a.k.a. **bisexual, bi, switch hitter**.

AC/DC *rock & roll* a **heavy-metal** band formed in 1973 in Sydney, Australia. The group became one of the major metal bands of the 1980s and 90s. Led by two Scottish brothers, lead guitarist Augus Young and Malcolm Young. Augus is famous for mooning audiences and for wearing British public school attire, shorts and cap, on stage. Their 1980 hit, "You Shook Me All Night Long," is an anthem of sorts for **headbangers** and those who find it necessary to sing about sex in double entendre.

Ace n.   a name used instead of someone's real name in a confrontation. Example: "Back off, **Ace**; hit me again and I'll bleed all over you."

ace adj.   a person, place or thing of the highest value (contrary to the previous definition). Example: "He's an **ace** dude." Probably derived from the fact that the ace is the highest playing card in the deck.

ace n. *drugs* a **marijuana** cigarette.

***ace(d)** v.   completed to perfection. Examples: "Did he **ace** the test?" "He **aced** the written exam, but was too **stoned** to negotiate the driving test."

aced out v.   defeated, outmaneuvered, replaced or overlooked. Example: "I was **aced out** of the job by a guy with the same last name as the owner."

ace in v.   to maneuver into an advantageous position or lucrative situation. **2.** to understand or become aware.

a charge   excitement or stimulation. Something like **kicks** or a kick in the ass.   Related to getting an electrical shock sent through the body. Examples: "Wow, I got **a charge** from that dance!"

acid *drugs* **lysergic acid diethylamide (LSD)**, the primary **psychedelic** drug used by the hippie culture. a.k.a. **LSD, instant zen, vitamin A**. (See: **LSD** in alphabetical listings and in **Drugs of the Era** in **Lists** at the back of this book)

acid casualty *drugs* someone who has supposedly sustained long-term ill effects from the use of **LSD** or other **hallucinogens**. This term is often directed toward latter-day hippies who still exhibit a disdain for straight society or ignore modern realities. Contrary to popular belief, **acid** created very few irretrievable casualties. Yet, there were some who made irreversible decisions while under its influence, such as the Harvard student who jumped off a building or someone who stepped in front of a car thinking they were immortal. Among those who took acid, there were fewer casualties than the same number of beer drinkers would have created. Acid did push some folks over the edge into insanity or phobias, but those individuals would probably have found their way there anyhow. Actually, acid created a great number of very curious, tolerant, and profound people.

acid flash or **flashback** *drugs* a vision or feeling supposedly recurring from a past **acid trip**. To be a true flashback, it would have to occur when one's system was completely free from the chemical influence of **LSD**. It is very rare, and I know of only a few neurotic people who will swear to having had such an occurrence under those conditions.

acid freak *drugs* someone who takes a lot of **acid**. **Freak** used in this case means someone who likes something to obsession, and not that they are more strange under its influence. Example: "She's an **acid freak**; careful or she'll sponge all your windowpane."

acid funk *drugs* an **LSD**-induced depression.

acid head *drugs* someone mentally diminished or numbed by too much **LSD**. Acid heads, it is said, walk around in a **purple haze**. This state is most often temporary and wears off with time and abstinence from the source.

acid pad *drugs* a place where **LSD** is consumed. a.k.a. **launching pad**.

acid rain precipitation from the sky containing particles of chemical dust or compounds that are harmful to plants, animals and humans. The most common cause of this phenomenon is industrial waste released into the atmosphere through smokestacks. Other causes include large forest fires and volcanic eruptions. Acid rain can cause the suffocation of plants and animals, pollution of water and a chemical etching reaction to such surfaces as auto body paint finishes.

acid rock *rock & roll* a form of music that evolved from traditional rock and roll after the introduction of psychedelic drugs. Also known as **psychedelic music.** It was either created by musicians under the influence of psychedelics, meant to be compatible with psychedelic drug use or produced to create and enhance the feeling of being on psychedelics. The **Jefferson Airplane** and **Jimi Hendrix** were the major creators of the genre. "**In-A-Gadda-Da-Vida,**" by Iron Butterfly, 1968, is recognized as the best example of this music. Much of the tonality and personality of this music

photo by John McCleary ©

form was borrowed from Asian cultures and music. This is one of the reasons Ravi Shankar was so well-received by hippie audiences at **Monterey Pop** and **Woodstock.** When Jorma Kaukonen, Jefferson Airplane's lead guitarist and a primary innovator of psychedelic music, was asked which came first, psychedelics or the psychedelic guitar riffs, he said, "Without psychedelics, things wouldn't have developed the way they did. We all know that's a fact; it certainly changes the way we looked at things. My mind was open; I didn't have any preconceptions as a guitar player coming in. A lot of our stuff really came out of left field, and we were very fortunate that it was able to coalesce into a music form. I listened to a lot of stuff; my dad was in the service overseas, and we lived in the Indian subcontinent, and I heard different things, like the veena. It emerged in odd ways, and when I couldn't think of a more traditional rock and roll solo, I wouldn't hesitate to play some weird thing that was lurking in my mind." (See: **veena**) Before the widespread availability of headphones, it was a common experience to get **stoned** on drugs, lie on the floor, and listen to "In-A-Gadda-Da Vida," the Airplane or

Hendrix at high volume through full-size speakers placed on either side of the head.

acid test *drugs* a party or gathering where **LSD** is ingested in some form of ritual. The **acid** is often consumed in food or drink. The term and activity originated with **Ken Kesey** and the **Merry Pranksters**. The first acid test and **Trips Festival** was hosted by Kesey on January 21-23, 1966, at the Longshoremen's Hall in San Francisco. **The Grateful Dead** played. **2.** in some places this meant the redecorating of an environment to enhance the atmosphere for taking acid. Example: "Let's **acid test** this place with some black light posters." (See: **Ken Kesey, Merry Pranksters** and **Trips Festival**)

ACLU (See: **American Civil Liberties Union**)

*a clue understanding, wisdom or awareness. Example: "After all these years, Bob still doesn't have **a clue** about women."

action the energy or activity that makes a place or occasion exciting; **sex, drugs or rock and roll** are action. Example: "Check out the girl **action** over to your right."

activist someone who performs acts of defiance in support of a cause or organization. Definitions of this word do not distinguish between violent or nonviolent, offensive or defensive action; sometimes peace demonstrators were considered activists. It was a word used by politicians and the press to insinuate that such people were violent and acting outside the law. In truth, most "activists" were just American citizens lobbying for their civil rights.

acupuncture an Oriental form of healing and preventive medicine using needles to activate energy points in the human body. Especially designed, ultra-thin needles are inserted into designated areas, thus triggering the body's self-healing mechanisms. Acupuncture points are specific locations along the meridians of the body, and each point has a predictable effect upon the energy that passes through it. Modern science has measured electrical impulses at these points, thus corroborating the locations of the meridians that were mapped by ancient practitioners. There is a continuous clinical history of acupuncture for thousands of years. Acupuncture, **herbalism** and numerous other forms of Oriental medical treatment are deemed outside the norm of Western culture. Many of these practices and disciplines were developed in Asia centuries ago and have been proven, with modern testing, to be true preventive measures. The American Medical Association (AMA) and the Federal Drug Administration (FDA) fought what they called **alternative medicine** throughout the 1960s, 70s and 80s. Not until recently have some of these medical practices, such as acupuncture, been accepted as valid forms of therapy. The AMA and FDA are particularly sceptical where preventive medicine is concerned. Many proven preventive measures were considered "alternative" during the hippie era, and most are still under suspicion by the established medical community.

Adam *drugs* one of the names for **MDA** or **ecstasy**, an early form of the **designer drugs** that arrived on the scene in the latter 1970s. a.k.a. **love drug, vitamin E, vitamin X, X, XTC**. (See: **ecstasy** or **MDA**)

adam kadmon Hebrew name for primeval man. The Kabbalistic name for humanity, the "Heavenly Man," before falling into sin. (See: **Kabbalah**)

Adamson, Joy (1910-1980) a British naturalist and author who lived and worked in Africa, studying the big cats of that continent. Working in Kenya with endangered lions, cheetahs and leopards, she wrote about her experiences. Adamson's books, including the popular 1960 *Born Free,* were worldwide best-sellers and contributed to the public's awareness of the plight of Africa's big game. Joy Adamson was found dead on the Shaba Lion Preserve north of Nairobi, Kenya, on January 4, 1980. Though officials tried to blame lions for her murder, it was later determined that she had been brutally stabbed with a native knife in such a way as to make it appear that her beloved animals were responsible for her death. Since her preservationist activity was in direct conflict with local native poachers, it is assumed that she was killed for her efforts to protect the animals.

addiction *drugs* a medical and emotional problem, not a drug problem. The availability of drugs is not an issue; someone with an addictive personality will find a way to become addicted. A drug addiction may start just as well with a beer as with a marijuana joint. Anything that lowers someone's inhibitions may lead to an addiction. No matter what the introduction is, people will find their drug of choice; it is in their nature, the beer or marijuana is not at fault. An addictive person must somehow learn to stay away from drugs; this requires a medical and educational solution, not a legal action. Prohibiting and criminalizing drugs does not solve the problem if the legal system and society are not willing to

discuss the medical and educational options. Remember, alcohol is still by far the most addictive drug in our society and every other culture on earth.

Adler, Lou one of the major forces in popular music entertainment from the late 1950s into the mid-70s. A partner with **Herb Alpert** in the late 1950s, managing rock-and-roll acts such as Jan & Dean. Adler also wrote songs, including **Sam Cooke**'s "Only Sixteen." Some of his composition he wrote under the name Barbara Campbell. Adler started Dunhill Productions in 1964 and managed such talent as Shelley Fabares (whom he married in 1964), **Carole King, The Mamas and the Papas**, Barry McGuire and Johnny Rivers. He sold Dunhill to ABC in 1966 and was involved in producing the **Monterey Pop Festival** in 1967. That same year he started the Ode record label, whose first hit was Scott McKenzie's "San Francisco (Be Sure To Wear Flowers in Your Hair)," and later, Carole King's album *Tapestry* in 1971.

advanced soul *occult* in **occult** philosophy, a person whose spiritual development has exceeded that attainable by his fellow man.

advertising it *sex* the act of flaunting sexuality. Example: "Check out Kerry's see-through blouse; she sure is **advertising it** tonight."

Afghani black particularly strong hashish produced in Afghanistan using an ancient middle-Eastern process. Distributed primarily on the East Coast of the US during the hippie era.

Afro- *prefix* a prefix indicating something of African heritage or influence. Example: **Afro-**American man, **Afro-**Cuban music, **Afro-**hair.

Angela Davis

Afro n. a hairstyle adopted by people of African heritage or anyone with very thick, curly hair. The hair was left to grow long and natural until it produced a round, thick "helmet" appearance. **Civil rights** activist **Angela Davis** sported one of the most prominent examples of the style.

Age of Aquarius an astrological era of 2,000 years that is expected to start some time around 2060 A.D. Lyrics of a song in the rock opera "**Hair**" stated, "This is the dawning of the **Age of Aquarius**." The age is said to be a time of the decline of institutions and religions and the rebirth of enlightenment, **self-awareness** and **brotherhood of man**.

Agent Orange a chemical **defoliant** used extensively by the US Army in **Vietnam** to kill plants and trees, thus exposing the enemy. Agent Orange was not its real name, but the chemical came in 50-gallon metal drums with orange stripes, thus the name. It was produced by **Dow Chemical Company** and seven smaller companies. Soldiers exposed to Agent Orange and other defoliants containing dioxin have developed extreme, sometimes deadly, symptoms. Dow knew in the mid-60s that dioxin in its pesticides could cause

sickness and death, but continued to produce the products. Dow was also the major producer of **napalm** during the **Vietnam War**.

aggression therapy emotional therapy in which aggression is allowed to surface in a safe, controlled environment in order to release frustrations and suppressed hostility. Elements of this type of therapy may include screaming and pillow abuse, in which a subject is encouraged to beat an object aggressively for emotional release. Aggression therapy incorporates some of the same elements as **encounter** or **marathon group** therapy and **sensitivity training**, based on the theory that confrontations and interplay among unrelated people enable one to open up to positive change and **self-realization**. The process often consists of getting a group of people together for an intense two- or three-day period to break down walls and inhibitions through something like exhaustion therapy. People are encouraged to express their prejudices about other members of the group and to verbalize their own fears and hatreds. **Native American** tribes of the South West indulge in similar "therapy" as part of their **peyote** rituals. During the peyote-induced "trip," tribal members are allowed to speak out their gripes and complaints about other members without the fear of retaliation. (See: **group therapy, gestalt, Esalen Institute, marathon group** and **peyote ceremonies**)

agnosticism the belief that not enough knowledge exists to make a religious commitment. In essence, agnostics are members of the largest religion in the world, the congregation of those who are not willing to make a dogmatic choice in a matter that has little or no facts to support it. Agnostic is created from the word **gnosis**, the Greek word for knowledge. Originally a generic term for knowledge in the first and second centuries A.D., it came eventually to mean **esoteric** knowledge of higher religious philosophy acquired only by an elite group of intellectuals. Agnosticism comprises the largest religious group of people in the world. Agnostics have not seen proof that any one doctrine is the true religion, and, although they may be spiritual people, they are not willing to devote their total spiritual energy to one religion.

a-go-go a **discotheque** or club for **rock-and-roll** dancing. **Whiskey-a-go-go** on Sunset Boulevard in Hollywood was the most famous. Originally, the term was French, "a gogo," meaning loosely "galore." There was once a Parisian club called "Whiskey a Gogo."

agricultural astrology a type of **astrology** concerned with the planting and harvesting of crops.

a grip, grip or **get a grip** self-control. Comes from "get a hold of yourself" or "get a grip on yourself." One of many abbreviated terms created and used extensively by the hippie culture. Examples: "Snookie doesn't have **a grip** on his excesses." "Snookie has no **grip** on reality." "So Snookie left you; **get a grip**, life goes on."

*a handle understanding, **awareness** or control. Examples: "J can't get **a handle** on the theory of sobriety, let alone relativity."

a-head *drugs* an **amphetamine** user. Amphetamines are **speed** or **pep pills**. **Speed freak** is a more common term.

a-head *drugs* **acid head**, habitual acid taker.

a-hole an **asshole**. Derogatory oath directed metaphorically at a person. Used by people who don't really "approve" of profanity or by someone in a public forum where they wish to be more circumspect. It was not used by **true hippies**, who felt suppressing emotions or evading reality was hypocritical.

Aikido (Aiki-do) a Japanese martial discipline, the only non-aggressive **martial art/way**. It is almost always practiced with a partner, and its purpose is to achieve harmony with the universe. To an observer, it is like a dance with fluid movements and steps. These movements have names, stories and traditions. The martial disciplines are divided roughly into *ways* (do) and *arts* (jutsu). The prime purpose of a *way* is other than battle; the prime purpose of an *art* is battle. Examples of martial *arts* are Jujitsu and Karate. Examples of *ways* are Aikido, **Tai Chi**, Tai Kwon do, Judo and Kudo (archery). With the exception of Aikido, most ways are practiced as sports. During the idealistic hippie era, it was widely believed that the martial arts (disciplines) were an attempt to divert negative energy in order to achieve peace. This attitude has had an effect on the way in which they are taught in America, and now the martial disciplines are considered a balance of body and mind control for the use in self-improvement as well as physical confrontations. (See: **Martial Arts** and **Tai Chi Chaun**)

ain't no great shakes someone or something that is less than impressive. Example: "Don't make fun of her; you **ain't no great shakes** yourself."

ain't shit of no value, worthless, useless. The implication is that the recipient of the oath is of less value than excrement. Example: "He **ain't shit** in my book."

airhead a silly, dumb, or empty-headed person. Having no brains, just air in the head. The term is usually directed at a woman. a.k.a. **bimbo**.

air signs of the zodiac: Aquarius, Gemini, Libra; mental, communicative and intellectual.

a job, do a job or **to do a job on** a physical or psychological violation of someone. An unkind act. Example: "He did **a job** on her, so her boyfriend proceeded to **do a job** on him, putting him in the hospital." Similar usage as **a number**, yet **"a job"** can denote something a little more violent in nature.

album a **vinyl** long-playing record album. (See: **LPs** and **vinyl**)

Alcatraz Island in November, 1969, 78 **Native Americans** from 50 tribes, "Indians of All Tribes," took over Alcatraz Island in San Francisco Bay. They occupied the former prison until June, 1971. The action was taken to draw attention to the dissatisfaction Native Americans felt with government treatment of their race.

alchemy the occult science dealing with decomposition and recomposition of elements of nature in an effort to increase their value or importance. Alchemy employs philosophy and spirituality, whereas chemistry deals mainly with matter.

Alembic "Guitar" Company *rock & roll* a company started in the 1960s by Rick Turner, a guitar maker and electric "pick-up" specialist. Also involved in the company were **Augustus Owsley Stanley III**, **LSD** chemist; and Ron Wickersham. Some of Owsley's LSD proceeds, it is said, went to producing

a sound system for **The Grateful Dead**, and that was the start of Alembic. The organization functioned as engineers

John Entwistle and his Alembic bass

for the Dead, and manufactured custom guitars and sound systems. Jack Casady of **Jefferson Airplane** used their instruments, and **the Who**'s bass player, John Entwistle, played a futuristic bass by Alembic. The company was very much a **counterculture** entity in San Francisco. As of the publication of this book, they are still producing public address systems.

alfalfa *drugs* (See: **marijuana**)

Alfalfa a person with freckles and unruly hair or someone who looks and acts like a hick. From the character of that name in the "Our Gang" movie comedies of the 1930s.

Ali, Muhammad (b. Cassius Marcellus Clay, 1942-) Olympic Gold Medalist, World Heavyweight Boxing Champion, **Black Muslim and **anti-war draft resister**. As Cassius Clay, he won the light heavyweight gold medal in the 1960 Olympics. Clay beat Sonny Liston for the World Heavyweight title in 1964 and was World Heavyweight Champion three times between 1964 and 1979. Cassius Clay changed his name to Cassius X Clay in 1964 and then to Muhammad Ali in 1965. He was stripped of his title in April, 1967, for refusing to be inducted into military service, claiming exemption as a Black Muslim minister. At the time Ali said, "I ain't got no quarrel with them Viet Congs." Ali was convicted of **draft evasion** in May, 1967. He was given the maximum sentence of a $10,000 fine and five years in prison because he was being used as an example by the courts. Unlike other, poorer resisters, he was able to fight the conviction, and it was overturned in 1970. His decision to resist the draft greatly damaged his fighting career, but it made him a hero in most peoples' eyes. Ali eventually regained his boxing title. Muhammad Ali is one of the most respected athletes of the 1960s and 70s, living or dead.

Alice B. Toklas brownies *drugs* brownies baked with **marijuana** in them. Said to be made by Alice B. Toklas, Gertrude Stein's lover, and described by Stein in her book, *The Autobiography of Alice B. Toklas*. Another account of this story is that Toklas never intended to make marijuana brownies, but that it was a recipe sent to her by a friend which she inadvertently published in a cook book. Alice reportedly made hers from scratch, but the following is a recipe for "Cop-Out Brownies" found in the book *A Child's Garden of Grass* by Richard Clorfene and Jack S. Margolis, published in 1969:
1 16-oz. package of Betty Crocker Fudge Brownie Mix
1/2 cup of grass
2 eggs
1/2 cup of nuts or ground macaroons
Follow the directions on the box for cake-like brownies rather than fudge brownies. Warning: concocting the above mixture will create a product construed by most law enforcement agencies and dietitians as an illegal confection.

Alice B. Toklas Club (Alice for short) the name of the **Homosexual** Democratic Club in San Francisco founded in December, 1971, by Jim Foster. It was the first **gay** Democratic Party club in the nation.

Alicia Bay Laurel author of *Living on The Earth*, a book about living a simpler lifestyle, published in 1971. www.aliciabaylaurel.com

a life meaningful activity. A useful existence. Something someone is lacking if they are unproductive. Example: "Get **a life**; turn off the soap opera and create some turmoil of your own!"

a little on the side *sex* sex outside of an established relationship.

"A little warms the heart, too much burns the soul." *drugs* the effects of **marijuana**. This message was written on packages of high-potency **skunk weed** seeds from **Sacred Seeds**, a small underground company that sold or sometimes distributed free, small packets of marijuana seeds. Remember, listen to the muse, don't destroy it. The **true hippie** used **sex, drugs & rock and roll** to brighten life, not to dull it.

Allah the name of God in **Islam**.

Allen, William *social issues* Assistant Professor of Anthropology, **University of California, Santa Barbara**, whose dismissal over **academic freedom** was to ferment student unrest and lead to the burning of the **Isla Vista branch of the Bank of America** on February 25, 1970.

Alles, Gordon the UCLA researcher who discovered the **amphetamine** chemical compound in 1927, and later, in the early 1950s, recognized the psychedelic effects of **MDA (methylene-dioxy amphetamin)**.

alley cat someone, usually a man, who is continually seeking **action**, parties and sex. **2.** to search for action, parties and sex.

all hang down or **let it all hang down** to be unrestrained, to show one's inner self and emotions. It could mean sexual expression, yet just as often, **soul** exposure. Evolved from **let it all hang out**, yet not as widely used. Most recognized usage was in **Eric Clapton**'s 1970 hit song, *After Midnight*.

all hang out or **let it all hang out** to be unrestrained, to show one's inner self and emotions. Though many thought that this phrase was sexual in nature, it most often alluded to unashamed self-expression or exposure of the **soul**. As with many other words and phrases of the hippie era, this sometimes had a nonspecific meaning and was often used only as punctuation to a conversation.

photo by John McCleary ©

alligator clip *drugs* a **marijuana roach holder** named for its resemblance to an alligator's jaws. The device was adapted from another use; originally, it was manufactured to clamp "hot" wires together to conduct electricity.

Allman Brothers Band, The *rock & roll* formed in 1968 in Macon, Georgia, its members included Duane Allman (b. Nov, 20, 1946, Nashville, Tenn.; d. Oct., 29, 1971, Macon, Ga.) gtr.; Gregg Allman (b. Dec. 8, 1947, Nashville, Tenn.) kybds., gtr., voc.; Berry Oakley (b. Apr. 4, 1948, Chicago, Ill.; d. Nov.

11, 1972, Macon, Ga.), bass; Dickey Betts (b. Dec. 12, 1943, West Palm Beach, Fla.), gtr., voc.; Jai Johanny Johanson, a.k.a. Jaimoe (b. John Lee Johnson, July 8, 1944, Ocean Springs, Miss.), drums; Butch Trucks (b. Jacksonville, Fla.), drums. A number of personnel changes took place over the years, but this was the major format. One of the most influential country-blues-rock bands of the era. Duane Allman's death in a motorcycle accident in 1971 was one of the great losses of the musical era. Dicky Betts on guitar and Gregg Allman on keyboards are two of the best musicians to come down the groove. Inducted into The Rock and Roll Hall of Fame in 1995.

all-out full speed, using all resources. Example: "Mannie went **all-out** to win Sadie's affection, but, being a dog of distinction, she rejected the chew toy he brought her."

all over or **all over that** to want, show interest in, or desire. Examples: "I was **all over that** the moment she walked in the door." "He was **all over** the idea to cook up a stir fry."

all right! interjection an approval, greeting, or exclamation of admiration. Emphasis is on the "right," and "right" is sometimes used alone. It is related to "right on." Examples: "**All right**! What's happening? That's an **all right** hat. See ya' later, **right**?"

all she wrote the end, all that's left, finished. Example: "His van hit the wall, and that was **all she wrote** for the tape deck."

all shook up distracted or confused. Sexually aroused. **2.** The title of one of **Elvis Presley**'s songs, 1957.

all the right moves all the right social skills to attract the opposite sex. The ability to do something skillfully.

all-time the **ultimate**, the best. Sometimes used as a modifier of the best. Examples: "He's **all-time**." "It's his **all-time** best."

a load a lie. Example: "That's **a load**. He can't really play the harmonica with intestinal gas!" This term is short for and comes from **a load of shit**.

a load or **a load of that** look at or observe. Example: "Get **a load of that** girl."

a load off sit down, relax. Example: "Get **a load off**. You must be tired holding that **yoga** position for three hours." This term is short for and comes from "get **a load off** your feet."

a lock on skills or knowledge of something. Having an exclusive on something. Examples: "He has **a lock on** that guitar riff." "You think you have **a lock on** her? Think again, Gonzo's been there too."

Alpert, Herb (b. March 31, 1935, Los Angeles, Calif.) *Mexican American, jazz and rock music* Hispanic trumpet player, producer and music executive. The most popular creator of **Ameriachi music**, Mexican music played with an American jazz flavor. His Tijuana Brass hits in the 1960s made him the most successful producer of instrumental music in history. In 1962, along with Jerry Moss, he founded A&M Records, which became the nation's largest independent record company, recording many great musicians and producing numerous important hits during the 1960s and 1970s.

Alpert, Richard, PhD (See: **Dass, Ram**)

Altamont an automobile racetrack near a town of the same name just northeast of San Francisco, where, at a **free concert** by **The Rolling Stones** on December 6, 1969, the **Hells Angels**, who were hired to be provide security, stabbed to death Meredith Hunter, a Black member of the audience. Some reports indicated that Hunter was brandishing a gun. It was one of the tragic events that occurred within a few short years, tainting the **counterculture** and giving the "hippie" existence a bad name. The Chicago **demonstrations** in August, 1968; the **Manson Family** murders in August, 1969; **Jimi Hendrix's** drug-related death on September 18, 1970; **Janis Joplin's** drug overdose on October 4, 1970; and **Angela Davis's** involvement in an attempted jail break in 1970 all contributed to disillusionment of the era.

Altair 8080 *computer revolution* "the people's computer," one of the first popular hobbyist computers (**personal computer** or **microcomputer**). It was a kit produced and sold by Micro Instrumentation and Telemetry Systems (MITS), a company owned by Ed Roberts. MITS was the first company in the US to build calculator kits. When MITS began producing the Altair 8080 in 1974, it used an Intel 8080 chip and ran a **BASIC** operating system programmed by Bill Gates, Paul Allen and Monte Davidoff. The Altair kit sold for $397. Altair was named by a twelve-year-old girl after the forbidden planet to which the Starship Enterprise was heading in "**Star Trek**." When members of the **Homebrew Computer Club** obtained an early Altair, their first and only success was coaxing it to play the tune "Daisy." You know, "Daisy, Daisy, give me your answer do...." (See: **Computer Revolution Milestones,**

Companies and Leaders starting on page 626 in Lists at the back of this book)

altered state of consciousness (ASC) *drugs/religion* an **elevated** mental experience. An occasion when a person's thinking processes have reached a place beyond the normal, everyday concerns of the **ego**. Used to describe either the meditative or drug-induced state of mind.

photo by John McCleary ©

alternative lifestyle a social, moral, or economic style of living that deviates from the norms of established society. **Communal households**, multiple sex partners, and **recreational drug** use are examples.

alternative medicine acupuncture, herbalism, homeopathy and numerous other forms of medical treatment that are considered outside the norm of Western culture. Many of these practices and disciplines were developed in Asia centuries ago and have since been proven, with modern testing, to be true preventive measures. The American Medical Association (AMA) and the Federal Drug Administration (FDA) fought what they called "alternative" medicine throughout the 1960s, 70s and 80s. Not until recently have some of these medical practices, such as acupuncture, been accepted as valid forms of therapy. The AMA and FDA

are particularly sceptical and combative where preventive medicine is concerned. Many proven preventive measures were considered "alternative" during the hippie era, and most are still under suspicion today by the established medical profession.

Alto *computer revolution* the first actual **personal computer (PC)**, created in the early 1970s by Xerox Corporation's Palo Alto Research Center (PARC.) It was primarily made for executives at PARC where it was in use as early as 1974. Only 1,500 were built, and some went to associates at Stanford Research Institute, Stanford **Artificial Intelligence** Laboratory, the US Congress and White House staff. It had most of the elements of the PC of today, including a **bit-mapped**, high-resolution screen and a **mouse pointing device**. (See: **Computer Revolution Milestones, Companies** and **Leaders** starting on page 626 in **Lists** at the back of this book)

amanita mushrooms *drugs* **psychedelic mushrooms** (fly agaric). Active ingredient: ibotenic **acid**, muscimole; street name: **shrooms, soma**. Warning, many mushrooms are deadly; please be sure of what you are eating for food or pleasure.

ambrosia the **food of the gods** in Greek mythology. Some forms of **psychedelics** were called this; particularly **psychedelic mushrooms**.

amen *occult* Hebrew word, used today to mean "verily, I say." Consider by occultists to be a mystic word related to the **Sanskrit** "**om**."

ambidextrous *sex* **bisexual**, able to go both ways. A sexual euphemism employing the conventional term that means to be able to use either the right or left hand.

Ameriachi Mexican music played with American **jazz** flavor or American music played with a mariachi flavor.

"American Bandstand" TV rock and roll show, first on the air as "Bandstand" in 1952 in Philadelphia, hosted by Bob Horn. **Dick Clark**, a **disk jockey**, began hosting the show in 1956, and it became "American Bandstand," syndicated by ABC on August 5, 1957. It is the grandfather of all TV music shows and the precursor of all the shows that popped up in the 1960s and 1970s. Although "American Bandstand" continued during the hippie era, it was considered too "pop" for most hippies; yet it was fun to get **stoned** in the afternoon and watch the girls dance in big hair and hot pants. Other music and dance shows that followed "Bandstand" were the likes of "**Hullabaloo**," "Hollywood a Go Go," "**Shindig**," "**Soul Train**," "Where The Action Is" and "Happenin' 68," which was filmed on the beach. All the TV music shows of the era experimented with different formats, some live, some pre-taped, some with professional dancers, some with non-professional audience members dancing, some live music, some with guest artists "**lip-synching**" their hit songs. Many videos of 1960s performers come from these TV series. "American Bandstand" was considered different from most other shows because it was a daytime show. (See: **"Hullabaloo," "Ready, Steady, Go!," "Shindig," "Soul Train"**)

American Civil Liberties Union (ACLU) *social issues* founded in 1920 by Jane Addams, Roger Baldwin, Clarence Darrow, John Dewey and Helen Keller. An organization of lawyers presumed and often accused of being **liberal**, whose main function is to protect the **First Amendment** rights of the people of America. The ACLU is arguably the most American and patriotic of all institutions in this country since it believes passionately that our freedoms should be granted equally to all people regardless of whether or not one agrees with their ideology. The ACLU will supply legal aid in cases of **civil rights** violations to any party, whether a member of the **KKK**, the **NAACP**, the **Communist Party**, the **John Birch Society**, **anti-abortion** or pro-abortion movements. Now that is true adherence to the Constitution of the United States of America. (See: **Civil Rights Events, Groups and Leaders** starting on page 546 in **Lists** at the back of this book)

American dream the perfect life, exemplified by a married couple, he gainfully employed, she a housewife, with two healthy kids, preferably a boy and a girl, living in a nice, pink house with a white picket fence in a quiet, tree-shaded neighborhood, with a car for him, a station wagon for her, a dog named Spot, and cat named Puff.

American Indian Movement (AIM) *social issues* a **Native American civil rights** and advocacy organization founded on July 28, 1968, in Minneapolis, Minnesota, by **Dennis Banks** and George Mitchell. Other leading members have been Clyde Bellecourt, Pat Ballanger, Edward Benton-Banai, Russell Means, John Trudell and Leonard Peltier. AIM was formed to draw attention to Native American issues and promote better treatment for Indian peoples. The organization is responsible for the occupation of **Alcatraz Island** in 1969 and the takeover of **Wounded Knee** in 1973. (See: **Wounded Knee** and **Alcatraz Island**)

Amerika the alternative spelling of America, using German spelling evoking Nazi activities. This spelling was used in the writings of many radical leaders of the era, including **Jerry Rubin**. It was also used in the documentary "Don't Bank on Amerika," produced by students at the **University of California, Santa Barbara**, and in editorials referring to the riots in **Isla Vista** and the burning of the local **Bank of America branch** on February 25, 1970.

amnesty a pardon by a legislative authority that expunges not only the punishment but its cause as well, therefore forbidding any new prosecution for the offense. **President Gerald Ford** declared an amnesty in 1970, offering to release **Vietnam War draft evaders** from their military obligation in exchange for two years of community service.

Amnesty International *social issues* a nonpolitical humanitarian organization headquartered in London, created on October 15, 1962, by British lawyer **Peter Benenson**. Consisting of over 700 groups, each is required annually to select three victims of racial, religious or political persecution, one each from the **communist**, **capitalist**, and uncommitted world, and work for their release by exposing the injustice. The organization also observes and sends missions to countries, and, when human rights violations are found, it reports the de-

tails to the UN and the Council of Europe. Amnesty International was awarded the Nobel Peace Prize in 1977.

Amorphoria: The Cannabis Cooperative an organization started in California to legalize **marijuana**, formed in the early 1970s by Blair Newman and Mike Aldrich. Newman was the creator of the **Acapulco Gold** rolling papers. Amorphoria lobbied for free, legal backyard marijuana cultivation.

amp *drugs* short for **ampoule**, a small glass or plastic container used to hold or dispense drugs. a.k.a. **ampoule, jug**.

amp or **amps** *rock & roll* short for amplifiers, electrical gadgetry used to project sound. Large and powerful ones were used by musicians of the hippie era to produce a physical, as well as audible, effect from their music.

amped up at maximum sound or power. At high speed. **2.** On speed or drugs of some kind.

amphetamines *drugs* synthetic stimulants similar in effect to **cocaine**, yet longer lasting and less expensive. Most brand name prescription drugs of this compound were originally created for weight loss. Some prominent brand names include **Methadrine**, **Benzedrine** and **Dexedrine**. After the Controlled Substance Act of 1970, the illegal production of amphetamines began. Prominent street names of the 1960s and 1970s were **crosstops, whites, black beauties, bennies, pep pills, beans, dexies, speed, meth, crystal, crank** and **ice**. Although usually swallowed during the hippie era, the current powered forms are now snorted, shot and smoked. Making this drug at home has become a cottage industry, and many of the manufacturers are not very good at it. There are inherent dangers with this drug and worse consequences from taking bad doses. Most recommendations are to stay away from this drug; it will kill you prematurely. Remember, all things in moderation; thinking people use their drugs, foolish people use drugs that will kill them.

ampoule *drugs* a small glass or plastic container used to hold or dispense drugs. a.k.a. **jug, amp**.

amp out to the extreme, to go crazy, to blow a fuse; amp refers to electrical sound amplifiers. Example: "**Amp out**, turn that volume to eleven!" This word has some of the same usage as **max out**.

amulet an object worn to bring luck. Something on which a charm is written or over which a spell was said, worn by an individual to protect against danger, disease, ghosts or evil magic.

amy *drug* nickname for **amyl nitrite**.

amyl *drugs* abbreviation for **amyl nitrite**.

amyl nitrite (nitrate) *drug* a chemical compound originally prescribed for the treatment of angina pectoris, heart pain caused by poor blood flow to the heart. When inhaled, it produces a short spurt of energy. Legally sold in **poppers**, vials broken open and snorted as a party enhancer. Said to be sexually stimulating and widely used in the gay community.

anal uptight. Short for the more clinical psychological term **anal retentive**. (See: **anal retentive**)

anal retentive uptight. Compulsive, meticulous behavior, often with a rigid, suppressed sexual lifestyle. Similar usage as **retentive**. During the hippie era, this term was used to describe some-

one conservative, close-minded or incapable of having fun. In **Gestalt** therapy, it is believed that rigid thinking impedes the cure of neuroses and psychoses. Anal retentives are theorized as being in danger of exploding in a violent outburst because of their inability to release tensions periodically. (See: **Gestalt therapy**)

anal sex *sex* penetration of the anus with the penis. Contrary to conservative religious spokesmen, this term was not invented in San Francisco by homosexuals, but has been with us as a bisexual form of intercourse for thousands of years. It is practiced widely in strict Christian societies in order to preserve the virginity of young, unmarried females.

analog computer *computer revolution* a computing device that used mechanisms or rotating rods to control electrical impulses, rather than switches, as in **digital computers**. Analog computers are easy to build, yet often inaccurate. (See: **Computer Revolution Milestones, Companies and Leaders** starting on page 626 in **Lists** at the back of this book)

ananda the **Sanskrit** word for joy, happiness, bliss.

Ananda Cooperative Community a **commune** formed in 1967 on two parcels of 70 and 270 acres near Nevada City, California. It was started by **Swami Kiyananda**, a disciple of **Paramahansa Yogananda**, who founded the **Self-Realization Fellowship**. (See: **Self-Realization Fellowship** in alphabetical listings. See also: **Gurus, and Religious Leaders** on page 648 in **Lists** at the back of this book)

anarchist and **anarchy** from the Greek word meaning someone who wants no ruler above him. The word anarchy has come to mean chaos, but, in essence, it means freedom from oppressive rule.

anatomy is not destiny implies that to be a woman does not mean that one must become a wife and mother exclusively. A **women's liberation** slogan that came from **Simone de Beauvoir** in her rebuttal to **Freud**'s theories on sexual roles.

an attitude self-centered, exhibiting an arrogant demeanor toward others.

Andelson, Sheldon *social issues* a **gay** Beverly Hills lawyer who supported and defended **homosexuals** arrested on morals charges. A millionaire with investments in real estate and an occasional gay bathhouse, he became one of the major political powers in the nation's gay community, giving support and money to Democratic candidates and **liberal** causes. Along with Don Kilhefner and Morris Knight, Anderson helped start The Gay Community Service Center in Los Angeles in October, 1971, one of the first homosexual health clinics.

angel dust *drugs* a street name for **PCP**. (See: **PCP**)

angle an ulterior motive or less than pure desire. Example: "I don't know what his **angle** is, but I wouldn't trust him with a penniless virgin nun."

animal a crude, disgusting, or dangerous person. It was considered complimentary to those who cultivated the bad-boy image and was often used to describe someone possessing an overactive sexual appetite.

animal house a place in which crude, disgusting, or dangerous people live. It can be a fun place depending on what kind of a crowd one hangs out with. **Zoo** has similar usage. "Animal House" or, to be precise, "National Lampoon's Animal House," was a 1978 movie produced by the *National Lampoon* magazine, directed by John Landis and staring John Belushi, among others. A must-see movie. (See: **Movies** in **Lists** at the back of this book)

animal magnetism according to schools of **mysticism, occultism** and **esoteric philosophy**, this is a force that causes energy to emanate from humans, animals and or objects as an **aura** or as a form of light. Some people, it is said, can emit this from their eyes or the tips of their fingers for purposes of healing.

Animals, The *rock & roll* a **British invasion** band formed in Newcastle-Upon-Tyne, England, in 1962, most notable for their lead singer Eric Burdon, and for a number of really interesting hits in the mid-1960s that made them sound more like an American band than an English one. Some of their most popular hits were "The House of the Rising Sun," 1964; "San Francisco Nights," 1967; and "Monterey," 1968. Inducted into The Rock and Roll Hall of Fame in 1994.

animal tranquilizer *drugs* one of the many names used to describe **PCP**. a.k.a. **angel dust, crystal, fairy dust,**

hog and **tranq**. It was a misnomer in that PCP (active ingredient phencyclidine) was originally a human tranquilizer eventually used on animals. Also sometimes called an **elephant tranquilizer**, but whether or not it was ever used on elephants is debatable. The indication in the use of the word elephant is that it was very powerful, which it was. Because of PCP's problems, it has been dropped from all legal usage. Sometimes, people looking for **methamphetamine** will be sold PCP instead, often with damaging results. (See: **PCP**)

animism *occult* the belief in spirits in nature and that humans and other objects are animated by spirits. Some people believe that all creatures and even inanimate objects, such as rocks and trees, possess humanlike mental processes equal to those of man.

ankh the Egyptian cross, the symbol for immortality and sometimes prosperity. Often pictured with Egyptian pharaohs in hieroglyphics. It resembles a cross with an oblong loop over the horizontal arms. Reproductions of the ankh were worn by many hippies because of a belief in its power.

antediluvian "in the time of Atlantis." From Latin, meaning "before the flood." In stories, songs and folklore of the hippie era, the antediluvians were considered the keepers of all **cosmic** knowledge and predecessors of the enlightened hippie.

anti-capitalist philosophy *social issues* the philosophy that opposes unrestricted and oppressive capitalistic activity that enslaves the working class by means of monopoly, price fixing and suppression of labor negotiations. Most anticapitalists do not oppose free enterprise, and they are not communists, although they support some socialist institutions to balance capitalism and protect the poor and working class.

anti-establishment the **counterculture**. Those individuals in any society who are unwilling to accept meekly the indignities forced upon them by a government or employer. I prefer to hyphenate this word to accentuate the importance of the "anti-."

antifreeze *drugs* heroin.

anti-nuke anything relating to the opposition to nuclear energy or nuclear armament.

anti-war *social issues* against war. That should be obvious, yet spelling and language sometimes serve to obscure the emotions and true meanings of an idea. This hyphenated word has become a joined word lately in dictionaries and spell checks, but I prefer to emphasize the "anti-" by keeping it separate. Anti-war is one of the most poignant issues of the hippie era; it goes to the depth and emotions of a group of people, misunderstood and maligned, who truly believed in peace and the "Golden Rule."

anti-war movement *social issues* the efforts of a group of individuals and organizations that opposed the **Vietnam War**. Though it was spoken of in terms of a movement, it had little organized cohesiveness and was never the insidious, anti-American conspiracy that conservatives feared. It was often just small groups of individuals who gathered to demonstrate against the war. Some groups had their own agendas, but mostly it was just Americans disagreeing with their government's policies. (See: **Anti-War Events, Groups and Leaders** starting on page 562 in **Lists** at the back of this book)

antsy nervous, jumpy or bored. Coming from having "ants in the pants."

a number, do a number or **to do a number on** a physical or psychological violation of someone. An unkind act. Example: "She did **a number** on his head, so he did **a number** on her bank account." Close in usage to **a job**, which can denote something a little more violent in nature.

any *sex* another nondescript word that is sometimes used to indicate sexual intercourse. Example: "Are you getting **any**?"

ape or **ape-shit** crazy or out of control. Examples: "He got stoned and went **ape**." "She got drunk and went **ape-shit**."

aphrodisiac any food, drug, drink, or situation that stimulates or enhances sexual desire. Many drugs of the hippie era were thought to be aphrodisiacs; for example, **MDA**, the **love drug**. For the most part, these drugs simply reduced inhibitions, which enabled people to enjoy sex more, and in that way they did work as aphrodisiacs.

apocalypse prophecy concerning the end of the world. It is misunderstood by many to mean the end itself, but it is just the prophecy of the end. Biblical prophecies mention many debaucheries and conflicts that seem to point to the hippie era and the **Vietnam War**. This caused many religious people to believe that the 1960s were

the coming of the end. The 1979 movie by Francis Ford Coppola, "Apocalypse Now," fed this belief.

Apple I *computer revolution* one of the first ready-made **personal computers** available to the public, introduced in April, 1976. The keyboard and monitor were not supplied, yet connectors were present. For the hobbyists of the time, it was a unique toy. Its reliability gave Apple a reputation to start with and helped to launch that company when it introduced the much more **user-friendly Apple II**. (See: **Computer Revolution Milestones, Companies and Leaders** starting on page 626 in **Lists** at the back of this book)

Apple II *computer revolution* the first completely self-contained, ready-to-use, **user-friendly**, **personal computer**. Introduced to the public in 1977, it had a **bit-mapped** monitor, 8K of memory, expansion card, Microsoft **BASIC** 6502, weighed 12 pounds and cost $1,350. It was convenient, had a modular design, pleasant appearance and low price. (See: **Computer Revolution Milestones, Companies and Leaders** starting on page 626 in **Lists** at the back of this book)

apples testicles. Sometimes, small breasts. As with all round fruits, these metaphors are obvious and numerous.

apple sauce that which holds the world together. It can mean existence, **magic** or cosmic energy. The invisible and largely indescribable energy that flows throughout the world and our lives. Examples: "There is cosmic **apple sauce** around us that we can never understand." "...the blood that was available to him in intercourse...made us believe he was in the **apple sauce** for twenty years...." (A passage from **Tom Wolfe's** 1968 book about **Ken Kesey** and the **Merry Pranksters,** *The Electric Kool-Aid Acid Trip*.) a.k.a. **cheese, chi, glue, ether, pudding,** or **sauce.** (See: **ether** or **chi**)

Aquarius astrological sign, January 20 to February 19, eleventh house of the **zodiac,** fixed air sign, symbolized by the water bearer. Traits: knowledge, understanding. Self-perception: I know.

arathwa *drugs* an Amazonian **hallucinogen.** It is used by native **shaman** to induce delusions of being a wild animal, such as an eagle, jaguar or python. Effects last 36 hours. a.k.a. **arasqua.**

Archie Bunker a bigot. Named after a lower-middle-class, bigoted character in the TV series, "All in the Family." Example: "My girlfriend's father is an **Archie Bunker.** I have to prove I'm Anglo-Saxon every time I pick her up."

are you for real? a comment questioning a person's reasoning, stability or sincerity. Similar to questions, such as: "Are you serious?" "Do you really mean that?"

*****"are we having fun yet?"** the favorite question of **Zippy the Pinhead,** a pointy-headed cartoon character in a clown suit with a naive, though profound sense of the world, drawn by cartoonist Bill Griffith. This question has become one of the most quoted phrases of the hippie era and is still used daily into the 21st Century. (See: **Zippy the Pinhead**)

Aries astrological sign, March 20 to April 20, 1st house of the **zodiac,** cardinal fire sign, symbolized by the ram. Traits: innocence and impulsiveness. Self-perception: I am.

armpit an unpleasant place to be. Found in the expression "the **armpit** of the universe" and related to "the asshole of the universe."

around the bend (to go) to go crazy or become strange.

around the block having a lot of experience. Example: "She's been **around the block**; she won't date someone as shallow as I am."

around the world *sex* the act of kissing, sucking and licking the penis, testicles and anus. A request commonly made to prostitutes, it is not considered a normal activity in romantic sexual unions.

ARPAnet *computer revolution* the predecessor of the Internet. Developed in the mid-1960s by Advanced Research Project Agency (ARPA), which was created in 1961 by the **Kennedy** Administration and funded by the Defense Department Advanced Research Project Agency to advance America's defense-related technologies. ARPA, run by Jack Ruina, J. C. R. Licklider and Bob Taylor, made human–computer symbiosis a national goal. They bypassed the normal government peer review process and put research administrators in direct contact with researchers. Licklider, as director, started funding unrestricted research at 13 different universities and labs, including MIT, UC Berkeley, UCLA, UC Santa Barbara, USC, Carnegie-Mellon University, University of Utah, Stanford Research Institute, System Development Corporation and Rand. ARPAnet was developed as the link among these locations. (See: **Computer Revolution Milestones, Companies** and **Leaders** starting on page 626 in **Lists** at the back of this book)

arse the British form and spelling of ass. It has all the accompanying litany of terms: arsehole, arse-licker, arse-man, etc.

article a strange or annoying person. Example: "He's a real **article** of hysterical interest." Same usage as **piece of work**.

artificial intelligence (AI) *computer revolution* computer-enhanced intelligence. A term probably first used in the 1950s, but not widely circulated until the 1960s and 70s.

artificial leather a synthetic petrochemical leather introduced to the public in 1964.

artificial tanning cream a formula applied to the skin that colors the body to look as if the wearer has spent hours basking on the beach in Hawaii. Introduced to the American public in 1960.

artillery *drugs* needles, syringes and **paraphernalia** used by **drug addicts**. Related to the term to **shoot up**, in a place called a **shooting gallery**. a.k.a. **kit, fit**.

artist someone who is good at a task. Example: "He is a real **artist** with a shovel." Can also be a derogatory description, such as: "rip-off **artist** or bullshit **artist**."

Aryan Nation *social issues* a **brotherhood** of individuals who believe in the supremacy of the White, or Caucasian, race. Sometimes called skinheads. A violently racist group that was bred primarily in the prison system during the 1960s and 1970s, where gangs of White, Black and Hispanic inmates fought for dominance. Sometimes called "The Order." Many people in the organization have no idea with what they are aligning themselves when they call themselves Aryan. Originally, Aryans were followers of Arius of Alexandria, a Libyan churchman (most likely a Black man), who lived from 280 to 336 A.D. He and his followers were among the first heretics when they preached that Christ was not divine. The Church of the Germanic tribes was Aryan until the 7th century A.D. That is why WWII Germans use the word Aryan to describe themselves and why racist groups adopted the word. I think it is humorous that such groups have adopted a term that originally meant African, anti-Christian philosophy when they profess White supremacy and Christian chauvinism.

ASC (See: **Altered State of Consciousness**)

Asher, Peter (1944-) singer, music producer and talent manager. Member of the singing group Peter and Gordon, formed in London in 1963 with Gordon Waller (1945-). Asher later became the **A&R (artist and repertory)** man for **The Beatles'** Apple label and eventually the manager/producer for such talent as **James Taylor**, **Linda Ronstadt**, **Carole King**, **Joni Mitchell**, **Randy Newman** and Warren Zevon. A Grammy-winning producer, he is still directing talent.

Hindu lotus symbol

ashram the **Hindu** name of a settlement of disciples living with or around a **guru** (spiritual leader or teacher). During the hippie era, it became a gathering place for followers of any guru or Eastern religious discipline.

ass an all-purpose intensifier that alludes to a body part, yet encompasses much more. Examples: bad **ass**, stupid **ass**, bet your sweet **ass**. Can be an adjective. Examples: bad-**assed**, tight-**assed**.

ass or **piece of ass** *sex* an inanimate description of a faceless object of lust. A derogatory name for a woman and an insensitive description of the act of sexual intercourse.

ass rear end, backside, butt, buttocks and all its accompanying derogatory commentary.

ass backwards turned around either physically, in speech or philosophy. Example: "Your thinking is **ass backwards**, and so is your underwear."

asshole an anus or anal passage. During the hippie era, it was used as a derogatory description of a person. Like many other "Anglo-Saxon" words, it was reintroduced and brought back to America by soldiers during and after WWII. Like fart, shit, dick and cunt, it had evolved into a pronoun describing a person rather than just a noun describing a body part or body function. During the hippie era, these words found expanded usage, yet still remained unacceptable in "polite society" or in more conservative atmospheres.

ass in an uproar mad. The ass is not literal, and other parts of the body can be used, such as **balls**, head, etc. Example: "He got his **ass in an uproar** over some stupid thing she said, like good-bye."

ass-kicker a strong, stimulating or powerful person, place or thing. Example: "That club is an **ass-kicker**, their drinks are **ass-kickers**, the guitar player is an **ass-kicker,** and the bouncer **kicks ass**."

All related to kicking ass. Other variations are: "That club is a **kick in the ass**, their drinks will **kick ass**, the guitar player **kicks ass,** and if you don't **cool** it, the bouncer can **kick your ass** out the door."

ass-kisser someone who flatters or grovels before (or behind) a person to get favors or recognition. a.k.a. **ass-licker, brown nose, kiss-ass**.

ass-licker same as ass-kisser.

ass-man a man who is attracted to women primarily by the appearance of their **ass**.

ass-master *sex* a homosexual. **2.** a successful heterosexual seducer.

ass off an all-purpose intensifier. Example: "He can work his **ass off**."

ass-wipe toilet paper. **2.** a disgusting person.

astral *occult* having to do with the stars and space, yet not as much with their physical reality as their aspect of existence outside human physical reality. That area outside of our physical reality.

astral body *occult* in **occult** terminology, man's ethereal counterpart or replica of the physical body (**gross body**). More subtle than the physical body and in a constant, sensitive state of vibration. (See: **gross body**)

astral plane *occult* in **occult** terminology, the first plane or "world" of existence after the death of the physical body (**gross body**). The place of non-material existence, as opposed to the **material plane**. In **dreams**, it is the residence of the soul when outside the body. (See: **mental plane** and **gross body**)

astral projection *occult* in **occult** terminology, the partial or complete separation of the **astral body** from the physical body. To visit another locality. Said to occur in sleep, but, as a general rule, the person does not recall the experience upon awakening. Believed by some people to be a state in which the **soul** leaves the physical body, in past, present or future. Some believers use it to mean traveling at will outside one's body and being able to see the place traveled in one's mind. Some think it is actual physical travel. Someone proficient in occult art or science (called an **adept**) can direct his astral body to travel wherever he desires in order to investigate or observe.

astrology the study of the influence on human beings of **cosmic** forces coming from the stars. A person's **astrological sign** is determined by the position of the constellations at the time of his or her birth. The attributes of the **zodiac** sign or constellation under which a person is born are then said to affect the personality of that individual. The attributes of each sign of the zodiac have been unscientifically determined, but many people believe in their reality. The earliest evidence of astrology dates back to 15,000 B.C. Mesopotamia. It is the forefather and predates the true science of **astronomy** by many centuries. Determining and reading horoscopes is done by astrologers, people with many hours of education and a good knowledge of mathematics. However, reading horoscopes and astrology, is considered a pseudo-science, unlike the science of astronomy.

astrology machine an early computer device created in 1975 by Ben Cooper and Gary Kildall, maker of the CP/M operating system and founder of Digi-

tal Research. These devices were placed at various San Francisco locations, and for 25 cents, people could enter their birth dates and get a printout of their astrological charts. The dials were complicated, and the paper often jammed; so goes another cosmic money-making endeavor.

Astrological signs: **Aries**, March 20 to April 20; **Taurus**, April 20 to May 21; **Gemini**, May 21 to June 21; **Cancer**, June 21 to July 22; **Leo**, July 22 to August 23; **Virgo**, August 23 to September 23; **Libra**, September 23 to October 23; **Scorpio**, October 23 to November 22; **Sagittarius**, November 22 to Dec. 21; **Capricorn**, December 21 to Jan. 20; **Aquarius**, January 20 to February 19; and **Pisces**, February 19 to March 20.

AstroTurf a synthetic plastic grass manufactured to create a durable and weather-resistant playing field for sporting events. It was developed in 1960 and installed in the Astrodome in Houston, Texas, the home of the Houston Astros baseball team in 1965. It was named after the place and the team. AstroTurf was used in industry and in private homes to create a carpetlike surface for outside environments or areas of heavy use. It was used in the Astrodome because it was a covered and enclosed ball field in which real grass would not grow.

as we speak at this moment. Example: "My beard is turning gray **as we speak**."

ate it to be **damaged**, wounded or killed. Example: "His car hit the wall and he **ate it**." Comes from "ate the big weenie."

ate the big weenie (weeny) or **ate the big one** to be **damaged**, wounded or killed. To fail. Examples: "His skateboard threw a wheel and he **ate the big weenie**." "She **ate the big one** on that test." The sexual connotation of "weenie" or "one" prevails here as the male genitals, but it is a confusing since there is no inference of homosexuality when a man eats the weenie. Just as when a man **screws the pooch** (messes up), bestiality is not inferred; it is merely a humorous phrase.

a thing about an intense feeling about something, either positive or negative. Examples: "I have **a thing about** broccoli; I hate the color."

a thing for an attraction to someone or something. Example: "Don't tell her, but I have **a thing for** her cat."

at it *sex* another euphemism for having sex: Example: "River and Sage are **at it** again."

Atkinson, Ti-Grace (1939-) *social issues* president of the New York **NOW** chapter in 1967, one of the most **radical feminists** of the time. She was part of the **lavender menace** of **lesbian feminists** forced to leave NOW in 1970. Atkinson helped to force the passage of the New York State abortion law in 1970 and founded a radical feminist group in 1971 called *The Feminists*. At one time Atkinson advocated abolishing the institution of marriage and suggested raising children **communally**.

-attack *suffix* an addition to the end of a word, indicating an obsession, need or hunger for something. Examples: sack-attack or rack-attack, the need for sleep; snack-attack, food hunger or the **munchies**. Possible modern usages: crack-attack, either a desire for **cocaine** or sex; Mac-attack, the need for one's computer terminal or a quarter pounder.

Attica Prison *social issues* a maximum security prison in upstate New York where, on September 9, 1971, more than 1,200 inmates rioted against poor conditions, gained control of the facility and took 50 hostages. Four days later after unsuccessful negotiations, a force of 1,000 well-armed New York State police officers and National Guardsmen attacked and regained control of the prison. During the retaking of the prison, nine hostages and 32 prisoners were killed. Only one hostage was actually killed by the prisoners, probably unintentionally when he was beaten during the initial prison riots. The prisoners had rioted only after getting no satisfaction from their peaceful protests against prison conditions. With hostages as leverage, the inmates negotiated for 28 demands with authorities and Governor of New York Nelson A. Rockefeller. Correctional officers and civilian employees taken hostage were beaten by prisoners. One of the demands was for amnesty for the crimes they committed during the takeover of the prison, but when the officer died of injuries inflicted by the prisoners, amnesty was ruled out and the prison retaken. Most of the prisoners and hostages who died were victims of gunshot wounds, including six correctional officers; since no inmates had guns during the engagement, it is assumed that the victims were shot by the police and National Guard. The aftermath and investigations brought about criticism of the penal system in New York and the rest of the nation and helped to create badly needed prison reforms.

attitude a dangerous disposition; an obnoxious or self-centered opinion of oneself. Examples: "She's got a real

attitude; watch out for her." "He's got a real **attitude**; he thinks he's God."

Auger, Brian (b. July 18, 1939, London, England) *jazz, fusion, rock, music* British keyboardist who helped create **jazz fusion**. Has played with many important musicians throughout the years and developed many musical nuances.

Augustus Owsley commonly used, but incorrect name for **Augustus Owsley Stanley III**, the King of **LSD** and the unofficial mayor of San Francisco in the 60s. He is sometimes erroneously called Augustus Owsley or Augustus Stanley Owsley and most often described as just "Owsley." (See: **Stanley, Augustus Owsley III**)

aunt emma *drugs* morphine.

auntie an aging homosexual.

Aunt Jemima a subservient Black woman who accepts unequal treatment based on her race. The female equivalent of **Uncle Tom**.

aura in metaphysical teaching and some Eastern religions, it is thought to be a field of energy surrounding and radiating from a person, expressing moods, attitudes, personality or physical health. The **aura** supposedly manifests itself in colors. Some of the colors and their reported meanings are: **Black**—death, **Brown**—apathy, **Pea Green**—boredom, **Green**—adjustment, **Medium Blue**—enthusiasm, **Turquoise**—amusement, **Yellow**—interest, analysis, **Orange**—healing, vitality, **Peach**—feminine healing, **Red**—passion, anger, **Rose**—self-love, **Pink**—love, affinity, **Violet**—joy, bliss, **Gold**—compassion and **White**—prayer, meditation.

autumnal equinox autumn equal night. A day of the year on or around September 23; one of the two times of the year when day and night are equal in lengths. The other is the **vernal equinox** on or around March 21. These days, along with the winter and summer solstices, have been celebrated by farmers and agrarian peoples for thousands of years due to their importance to the growing cycle. Because of the hippie culture's attraction to the spiritual activities of such ancient cultures as the **Druids**, many equinox and **solstice** parties, festivals, and gatherings took place during the 1960s and 1970s. (See: **solstice** and **vernal equinox**)

Avalon Ballroom (April, 1966- November, 1968) *rock & roll* 1268 Sutter Street in San Francisco, California. The Avalon, the psychedelic epicenter of the world, was originally the Puckett Academy of Dance, built in 1911. Music promoter **Chet Helms** converted it to a **rock and roll** dance hall in 1966. As one of the first and most popular **psychedelic** dance halls, it vied with **Bill Graham's Fillmore Auditorium** as the home of local bands, such as **The Grateful Dead**, **Jefferson Airplane**, **Moby Grape**, Bozz Scaggs, **Quicksilver Messenger Service**, **Big Brother and the Holding Company**, **Country Joe and the Fish**, **Canned Heat**, etc. It was here that **Janis Joplin** made her first public appearance with Big Brother and the Holding Company in June, 1966. The Avalon was closed in November, 1968, due to complaints about noise and was converted into a cineplex during the 1970s. The Avalon Ballroom and the concerts Chet Helms produced were considered by many to be the real hippie happening, more so than the Fillmore Auditorium.

Avatar the **Sanskrit** word meaning an incarnation of **Vishnu** in Hindu theology. Vishnu is one of the three gods of the Hindu trinity (**Brahma**, the Creator; **Vishnu**, the Preserver; and **Shiva**, the Destroyer).

awareness one of the many conventional words that acquired new dimensions during the hippie era. Awareness often related to a spiritual or cosmic dimension, such as **self-awareness**, God-awareness, belly-button-lint-awareness.

*****awesome** something of great wonder, magnitude, or beauty.

A.W.O.L., pronounced "a-wall," or spelled out **awol,** missing or gone, having fled to avoid a responsibility. **Ab**sent **W**ith **O**ut **L**eave, a military term that came into common usage in the **counterculture**. In the military it referred to desertion from duty. Because of the pressures of the **Vietnam War**, military desertion reached record levels during that conflict. In the counterculture, A.W.O.L. was used to describe someone who was "gone" or "missing," mentally or physically. It can also be written as a word, awol.

ax or **axe** a musical instrument; any tool of a person's trade. From **blues** and **jazz** slang. The possible evolution of this word is intriguing. Often, during the period of slavery in this country, Blacks were not allowed to possess musical instruments, and so slaves may have called instruments "axes" in order to camouflage their existence. In the hippie era, an ax became any tool of someone's interest or work. Example: "His camera is his **ax**."

Ayahuasca *drugs* **Vine of Souls**, *Banisteriopsis caapi*. The name of the **psychotropic** plant found in South America and the beverage made from it.

Ayers, Bill (b. William Charles Ayers, Dec. 26, 1944) *social issues* originally a member of VOICE at University of Michigan, arrested in Ann Arbor at draft board **demonstrations**; early member of SDS with Tom Hayden. Revolutionary Youth Movement leader and founding member of the **Weathermen**. He was underground for ten years and was wanted by the FBI. Bill Ayers is now a

Distinguished Professor of Education at the University of Chicago, Illinois, and is married to **Bernardine Dohrn**, also a former member of the **SDS** and the Weathermen.

B

B *drugs* street term for **Benzedrine**.

Baba a teacher, benevolent friend or respected person. In India and some Middle Eastern cultures, this means father. If a person is considered a worthy teacher or spiritual leader, Baba is placed before their name as a sign of respect. Examples: "**Baba** Ram Dass"

Baba Ram Dass (See: **Ram Dass**)

babe an impersonal name for a woman, sometimes derogatory, but most often benevolent. Usually an attractive woman. Example: "She's a real **babe**."

baby or **babe** a term addressing someone, regardless of age or gender, across social or political lines, with positive or negative intent. Examples: "Burn, **baby**, burn." "Stay cool, **babe**." "Keep the faith, **baby**!"

Babylon the African American and **Rastafarian** name for any place that is an exile away from Africa. America is called Babylon, the place of prejudices, temptations and excesses.

Bacchus Roman god of wine and fertility. Same as the Greek god **Dionysus**. Some feel that he is the **spirit** of the **true hippie**. Many men of the hippie era imagined themselves as Bacchus, and many assumed the appearance with long, flowing hair, beards, and as little clothing as possible. Also associated with the same theme as the **Satyr** or seducer of women. Thomas Bulfinch (1796 -1867), in his definitive books on Greek and Roman mythology first printed in 1855, says of Bacchus and Dionysus, "He represents not only the intoxicating power of wine, but its social and beneficent influences likewise, so that he is viewed as the promoter of civilization, and a lawgiver and lover of peace."

back at you or **back at ya'** a statement of reciprocation. Response to a positive comment. Example: To a positive statement, "You're **cool**, man!" Response, "**Back at ya'**, guy." **2.** a statement of confrontation. Response to a negative comment. Example: to a negative statement, "You're sperm bankrupt, and your family reads *The Digest*!" Response, "**Back at ya'**." The hippie era was a time when media and electronic communications advanced so quickly that language from different cultures and geographic areas began to clash and overlap, often causing conflicting definitions of the same words and phrases.

back door a euphemism for anal intercourse, **homosexual** or **heterosexual**.

back door man a woman's secret lover.

back off *interjection* a demand, ordering someone to quit bothering or confronting. Related to **get out of my face**. Example: "**Back of**f! I don't want you in my face."

photo by John McCleary ©

back-to-the-earth a movement adopted by many hippies. The desire to simplify life, become farmers, and supply one's needs from nature and the toil of one's own labors.

bad meaning good. Depending on the situation and vocal inflection, bad meant good. Bad was often used to compliment something that was unappreciated by straight society. Example: "That was a **bad** concert, man." Clarence Major, in his *Juba to Jive, A Dic-*

tionary of African-American Slang, says that "bad used this way has its roots in several African languages and means a reversal of the white standard."

bad meaning BAD.

badass someone dangerous who may inflict physical harm.

badge a policeman or authority figure.

bad hair day a day when a person's hair is unattractive or unkempt. It is usually due to being slept on, smashed under a hat or not properly attended to after a shower. It also became an indication of the person's mood. The inference was that, if someone had bad hair, it was because they were out of sorts and inattentive to their appearance.

bad karma adverse fate brought on by a negative incident, action or attitude. Something that has to be worked off or resolved by a positive counteraction. (See: **karma**)

bad news a name given someone who is trouble. Example: "She's **bad news**; she'll wreck your bed and in the morning kick you in the head."

bad ounce *drugs* a 3/4 ounce bag of cheap, Mexican **marijuana**. Also called a **can**, and on the West Coast called a **lid**.

bad scene an unpleasant place or occurrence. Example: "He's bad news, and everywhere he goes it's a **bad scene**."

bad sign (born under a) an unlucky **astrological sign**; a date of birth resulting in perpetual bad luck. Related to the signs of the **zodiac**. Although no one sign of the zodiac is considered totally unlucky, the combination of some sun and moon signs together is

believed to be inauspicious. "Born Under a Bad Sign" is a song written by Booker T. Jones and William Bell and recorded by many, most notably, Albert King and **Cream**.

bad trip an unpleasant experience, often drug-related.

Baez, Joan Chandos (b. Jan. 9, 1941, Staten Island, NY) folksinger/songwriter, **anti-war and **civil rights activist**. daughter of a Mexican father, Albert Baez, and Scottish mother, Joan Bridges. Her family moved to California before she was five years old, and as a teenager she began playing and singing folksongs in the family coffee house and other places along the Monterey-Big Sur coast.

photo by John Jeffers ©

While attending Boston University in the late 1950s, she performed in Boston area, Chicago and New York City coffee houses, evolving into a politically motivated folksinger. Baez appeared at the 1959 Newport Folk Festival and recorded her first album in 1960 (Vanguard) entitled *Joan Baez*. With that and several other early albums, she became a primary spokesperson of the hippie era. To many, she was the first **hippie chick**. Joan Baez is the flower of the hippie **counterculture**; she represents its most beautiful faces and most intelligent minds. Her songs are piercing rhapsodies and whispered threats. Her causes are political and ethereal. If anyone ever questions the value of the era, one needs only say, "Joan." An avid and outspoken advocate of nonviolence and human rights, Baez has supported and helped create many organizations devoted to peace and people. In 1964, she began refusing to pay taxes for war support, and in 1967, she was arrested for **civil disobedience** while opposing the war in Vietnam. Since the 1970s, Joan Baez has continued to be politically active and performs and records her music on a regular basis. Along with all of her many other activities, she is also involved in Bread and Roses, a charitable organization started with her late sister **Mimi Fariña** to provide entertainment to children and people institutionalized in prisons and hospitals. (See: **Mimi Fariña** and **Richard Fariña**)

bag job, interest or hobby. Example: "Music is his **bag**."

bag to catch or take. Often sexual. Example: "Did you **bag** her?"

bag or **baggy** *drugs* a container of **dope**. Usually a transparent plastic sandwich bag.

baggage a psychological problem carried around from a bad experience in the past. A term used a lot by such **self-help** cults as **EST**, but it may originally have come from street usage. Example: "He carries a lot of **baggage** from a bad childhood."

baggies loose, oversized shorts worn by surfers. Example: "We'll be wearin'

our **baggies**, huarache sandals, too," *(Surfin' USA,* **The Beach Boys**, 1963).

bag it quit. To stop what you're doing.

bag man *drugs* someone who sells or carries drugs.

Baha'i faith *religion* followers of Baha'ullah, born in Persia (now Iran) (1817-1892). His teachings include: oneness of God; common foundation of all religion; oneness of humanity; individual search for truth; elimination of prejudice of all kinds; equality of men and women; elimination of extremes of wealth and poverty; universal peace upheld by world government; and protection of cultural diversity. In 1867, he wrote to all the kings and rulers of the world outlining the requirements for lasting peace among nations. He called for countries to relinquish some of their sovereignty in order to form a world government to enforce peace. On the 100th anniversary of this letter in 1967, this message was again presented to all governments by the Baha'i community.

bail to leave in a hurry. Comes from to bail out of an airplane. Example: "Hey, I don't **dig** this place; let's **bail**."

bait an underage sexual partner or potential partner. Short for **jailbait**. An attractive young woman or girl under the age of consent, which is normally 18 years.

Baja Bug a customized **Volkswagen Bug** designed to go off road and into the desert. A Volkswagen Bug is the small, round, dumpy, but beloved Volkswagen passenger car. Baja refers to Baha, California, the area of Mexico where surfers used these types of vehicles to get to good surfing spots where no roads existed. (See: **Volkswagen Bug, Bug,** and **Beetle**)

baksheesh money, a bribe, tip or payment. Derived from the Middle Eastern word "bakshish" meaning something given.

ball n. a good time; uninhibited fun, as in a party. Example: "Last night's jam was a **ball**."

ball or **balling** v. *sex* to have sexual intercourse; a very derogatory term indicating the least sensitive form of lovemaking. This one didn't last too long during the hippie era; there was an unsettling segment in the movie **Woodstock** where a young, innocent looking couple used the term to describe their lovemaking, which, I believe, negatively affected even the most **hard-core** supporter of **free love**.

ball-breaker or **ball-buster** an aggressive or demanding woman, sexually or socially.

balloon *drugs* an ordinary toy balloon used for storing or carrying **heroin**.

balls a man's testicles. Also, it means to have guts. Example: "He's got **balls**, jumping out of that tree, but not too many **smarts**."

balls in an uproar mad. The balls are not literal, and other parts of the body can be used, such as **ass**, head, etc. Example: "He got his **balls in an uproar** over the tofu I slipped into his scrambled eggs."

balls to the wall to go all out in some effort. Example: "When he drives his car, he goes **balls to the wall**." My only source indicates this may originally be a surfer term referring to facing a wall of water and exposing oneself to danger. The balls referred to are assumed to be the male testicles.

ballsy having guts, courage or, naturally, **balls**. Example: "Dorothy's a

ballsy chick; even without testicles, she carries the aggressive hormone." This term began to appear in 1967, yet, as with many **counterculture** words and phrases, it was used for several years in the **underground** before being seen in the general public.

bam *drugs* a drug mixture containing both a stimulant and a depressant. **2. amphetamines**.

bam! an exclamation verbalizing a surprise thought or unexpected occurrence. Used in comic books to indicate the sound of a collision or arrival of some surprise. Example: "I was thinking of her and, **bam!** there she was." Similar usage as **shazam** or **wham**.

banana this was one of the most outrageous hoaxes of the era, rating along with the reported death of **Paul McCartney**. In a **Donovan** song, "**Mellow Yellow**," November 19, 1966, the lyrics mentioned "e-lec-tri-cal banana." The outcome was a dramatic increase in banana sales across the United States. In the next six months, experimentation into the different ways one could ingest, insert or inhale the banana reached epidemic proportions. Everyone thought that the banana possessed some **psychedelic** qualities. It was eventually determined that the best way to enjoy a banana was to peel it, eat it and savor the taste.

Band, The *folk, country, rock & roll* formed in 1967 in Woodstock, New York, James Robbie Robertson (b. July 5, 1944, Toronto, Can.), gtr.; Richard Manuel (b. Apr. 3, 1945, Stratford, Can.; d. Mar. 4 1986, Winter Park, Fla.), piano, voc.; Garth Hudson (b. Aug. 2, ca. 1943, London, Can.), organ, sax; Rick Danko (b. Dec. 29, 1942, Simcoe,

Can.; d. Dec. 10, 1999, Woodstock, NY), bass, viola, voc.; Levon Helm (b. May 26, 1940, Marvell, Ark.), drums, voc., mandolin. Most notable for their association with **Bob Dylan**, whom they backed on tour and played with on recordings that were later released in 1975 as *The Basement Tapes*. Their debut album on their own, the 1968 *Music from Big Pink,* was a revolutionary piece that has influenced many musicians in the area of **folk rock**. They have continued to play and record to good purpose for years and were inducted into the Rock and Roll Hall of Fame in 1994.

band aid a **groupie**. 2. drugs or anything that helps a **rock and roll** band make it throught the night.

photo by John McCleary ©

bandanna one of the most common **fashion** statements of the era, the old cowboy standby, a blue or red bandanna. On some occasions, it was the only clothing, in contrast to a totally brown, totally nude body. All the most style-conscious **hippie** dogs wore them. Bandannas could be seen as **halter tops** on nubile nymphs and **headbands** on sweaty dancers. In the 1960s and 70s, the bright bandannas were a flag of the peace and love generation; today they are gangbanger attire for which children are **shot down** in the streets.

band rat a **groupie**, someone who follows a rock band for the express purpose of having sex with the members.

bang or **banging** *sex* sexual intercourse; a less than sensitive description of lovemaking. Examples: "Did you **bang** her?" "He was busy **banging** his ol' lady."

Bangladesh, The Concert for one of the very best and very first benefit concerts, August 1, 1971. Organized by Beatle **George Harrison** to benefit Bangladesh refugees and held at Madison Square Garden, NY. Performing were Harrison, **Eric Clapton**, Leon Russell, Billy Preston, **Ringo Starr** and **Bob Dylan**. Bangladesh was once the eastern portion of Pakistan, a country split in two by the borders of northern India.

bang on correct or accurate. Same as **right on**, **dead on** or **dead bang on**. Examples: "You're **bang on** about the taste of bean curd." A **British invasion** term.

bang to rights correct or accurate. Example: "She's sexy; you got that **bang to rights**."

bang-up job a good job, a job well done. One of those phrases that is hard to date, but it was often used in the 1960s and 1970s by straight and **counterculture** people alike.

banish his ass a sarcastic implication that someone should be told to leave.

banish the thought a sarcastic way of admitting interest in something while professing indifference. Example: "Who me, hot for Judy? **Banish the thought!**" The term used to be perish the thought, but it somehow got changed during the era.

bank v. to trust or rely on. Introduced as a verb in 1962.

Bank of America branch burning in Isla Vista on February 25, 1970 *social issues* when **University of California, Santa Barbara**, Assistant Professor of Anthropology **William Allen** was dismissed over **academic freedom**, members of the student body went on strike. Eventually, because of this and further disagreements with the University administration, riots broke out on the campus and in **Isla Vista**, the housing community adjacent to the campus. On the

photo by John McCleary ©

night of February 25, 1970, students, **free-speech** and **anti-war** demonstrators burned the Bank of America branch in Isla Vista.

Banks, Dennis (1937-) *social issues* a **Native American**, Chippewa, co-founder and one-time director of the **American Indian Movement (AIM)**.

banzai! an exclamation of joy or fear when surfing, jumping into the water or generally doing something exhilarating or dangerous. A bastardized version of the Japanese war cry supposedly used by Kamikaze pilots.

bar *drugs* **marijuana** or **hashish** mixed with water and honey or sugar so it will harden into a solid block for shipping and storage. a.k.a. **brick**.

Baraka, Amiri (b. Nov. 7, 1934, Newark, New Jersey) the name adopted by **LeRoi Jones** in 1967 because of his Muslim beliefs. A **Black** poet, writer, **political activist** and teacher. Member of the beat literary community in New York and San Francisco to which **Allen Ginsberg, Jack Kerouac, William Burroughs, Lawrence Ferlinghetti**, George Corso, **Gary Snyder, Diane di Prima** and Frank O'Hara belonged. As a poet and playwright, he is one of the first modern proponents of Black political literature. His life and work represent a strong connection among the Black community, the beat generation and hippie culture. There is strong support to placing him among the two or three most important Black literary figures of the twentieth century. A 1953 Graduate of Howard University, he published his first major book of poetry, *Preface to a Twenty Volume Suicide Note*, in 1961. He founded Totem Press in 1958, and published works by Kerouac, Ginsberg and others of the time. Baraka's play, *Dutchman*, which opened off-Broadway to critical acclaim, contains an encounter between a Black intellectual and a White woman that graphically expresses the hostility Black Americans feel toward the dominant White culture. In 1965, Baraka founded the Black Arts Repertory Theatre in Harlem, and in 1968, the Black Community Development and Defense Organization, a Muslim group committed to Black culture and political power. Amiri Baraka teaches at the university level and continues to write today.

barb *drugs* short for **barbiturate**. A **Downer**.

barb a verbal attack or harsh word.

barbarian someone who is unencumbered by the use of social graces. Because of the era's rejection of established etiquette, this description was used in a more positive or endearing manner than it had been before or since. Example: "**Barbarians** have all the fun."

Barbie or **Barbie doll** a derogatory name for a woman who is considered shallow. A female who is overly concerned with **fashion** and personal appearance rather than intellect. Named for the Mattel doll created in 1959.

barbiturates *drugs* drugs that depress the central nervous system. Any number of **sedative-hypnotics** or **downer** drugs. Examples: Amytal, Darvon, **Nembutal, Quaaludes**, Seconal, **Tuinal**. (See: **downers**)

barf vomit or to vomit. A 50s term that grew in use in the hippie era.

barf bag a disgusting person. **2.** a small bag found on commercial airplanes for use by passengers when they become airsick.

barf city a disgusting place or function. Example: "That party was **barf city**; everyone there was a **loser** except you and me."

Barnard, Christiaan (b. 1922, Beaufort West, South Africa; d. 2001) surgeon who graduated from Cape Town, South Africa medical school. In the mid-1950s, he studied and conducted research in America before returning to Cape Town in 1958 to work on open-heart surgery and organ transplantation. On December 3, 1967, at Groote Schuur Hospital in Cape Town, he performed the first successful human heart transplant. The recipient, Louis Washkansky, died of pneumonia after 18 days due to infection brought on by anti-tissue rejection medication. The second patient, Philip Blaiberg, operated on in January of 1968, survived for 594 days.

Barney's Beanery *social issues* a chili restaurant on Santa Monica Boulevard in Hollywood that had a large after-hours clientele in the late 1960s. Even though many **homosexuals** frequented the place and were never discriminated against, there was a sign on the wall that read "Fagots Stay Out " [sic]. The homosexual community finally decided to make an example of the restaurant and began picketing it in January of 1970. After three months, the owner finally removed the sign. (See: **Gay & Lesbian Movement Events, Groups and Leaders** starting on page 601 in **Lists** at the back of this book)

base *drugs* **freebase cocaine**. Freebase is cocaine from which the hydrochloride has been removed. The process makes the drug more potent. Making this drug at home has become a cottage industry, and many of the manufacturers are not very good at it. There are inherent dangers with this drug and worse consequences from taking bad doses. Most recommendations are to stay away from this drug; it will kill you prematurely. Remember, all things in moderation; thinking people use their drugs, foolish people use drugs that will kill them.

bash a party, a good party, a very good party.

bash or **bashing** to say derogatory things about someone. Examples: "I was having fun until Judy found me with Suzi and dispensed a verbal **bashing**." **2.** physical violence, most often a social or hate crime. Examples: **gay bashing**, granny bashing, Pak bashing. A **British invasion** term.

BASIC (1964) *computer revolution* **B**eginner's **A**ll-purpose **S**ymbolic **In**struction **C**ode, one of the earliest "simple" computer languages. Developed by two Dartmouth College professors, John Kemeny and Thomas Kurtz, through a grant from the National Science Foundation to teach their students an easier way to use computers. BASIC was used in the early hobbyist, **personal computers**. In 1975, Bill Gates, Paul Allen and Monte Davidoff wrote a BASIC program for the **MITS Altair 8080**. They wrote it while students at Harvard, on a PDP-10 computer funded by taxpayers' money through the Defense Advanced Research Projects Agency. (See: **Computer Revolution Milestones, Companies and Leaders** starting on page 626 in **Lists** at the back of this book)

basing *drugs* smoking **freebase cocaine**.

basket case someone who is helpless, stupid or consumed by drugs.

Bates, Daisy Gaston (1920-1999) *social issues* Black **civil rights activist**; President of the Arkansas **NAACP**, 1953-1961; a leader in the 1957 effort to integrate Little Rock Central High School; author of a 1962 book, *The Long Shadow of Little Rock*; publisher of the Arkansas State Press until her retirement in 1987.

bathroom walls the media and music were important to the development and spread of counterculture language, but few people realize the invaluable contribution that the bathroom walls of coffee houses, dance clubs and gas stations played in the proliferation of language during the 1960s and 70s. The counterculture of that period was very transient, traveling for excitement and curiosity. Jokes, political satire and philosophy crisscrossed the United States, moving from public bathroom wall to public bathroom wall, thus helping to spread ideas and language.

bazooka *drugs* a large **marijuana joint**. a.k.a. **bomber, zepplin**.

bazookas, bazumas, bazungas female breasts. There are many forms of this word play, most derived from the word "bosom."

Beach Boys, The *rock & roll* California surf music band formed in 1961 in Hawthorne, California. **Brian Wilson** (b. June 20, 1942, Hawthorne) primary songwriter, voc., bass, kybds.; Dennis Wilson (b. Dec. 4, 1944, Hawthorne; d. Dec. 28, 1983, Marina del Rey, Calif.) voc., drums; Carl Wilson (b. Dec. 21, 1946, Hawthorne; d. Feb. 6, 1998. Los Angeles) voc., gtr.; Mike Love (b. March 15, 1941, Los Angeles) voc., perc.; Al Jardine (b. Sept. 3, 1942, Lima, Ohio) gtr., voc. The Beach Boys were not a hippie **rock and roll** band by any stretch of **psychedelic** imagination, yet they hold a warm place in the hearts of anyone who lived during the 1960s. They are sometimes the brunt of jokes, referred to as a decadent, apolitical group, but their music gave great pleasure, especially if one were caught in a blizzard in Fargo, North Dakota. To be truthful, Brian Wilson is considered by other musicians to be one of the pure musical geniuses of the era, and The Beach Boys' 1966 album, *Pet Sounds*, is touted as one of the records that ushered in the psychedelic era. Inducted into The Rock and Roll Hall of Fame in 1988,

beached whale an overweight person lying on the beach in the sun.

beaded curtain a number of strings of beads hanging from the door frame, covering the opening, creating unrestricted passage, yet visual privacy and atmosphere. An interior decoration in many hippie homes borrowed from Middle Eastern cultures.

beads the most common adornment of the hippie era. Usually, a necklace of inexpensive beads worn by men and women alike. The beads were often just colored glass or plastic, but **puka shells** and **Venetian-made African trading beads** were highly prized.

beanbag chair a chair with the shape and appearance of a large bag filled with beans. Actually, they are usually filled with much lighter styrofoam pellets. Invented in Italy in 1968 by Piero Gatti, Cesare Paolini and Franco Teodoro.

beans money.

beans *drugs* tablets of brand name **Dexedrine**.

bean sprouts a food source high in fiber and reportedly good for cleansing the colon, which is supposedly good for a person's health. Many hippies grew them at home. The process involves placing dried beans or peas in a tray with water until they sprout a short root or stem, which is harvested and used in salads or as a condiment on food. Today's interest in health food and healthy lifestyles began with the hippie movement's concern with eating natural, unprocessed foods.

bear a police officer. A term used by **citizens band radio (CB radio)** operators to warn other drivers. CB radios are used by truckers and other drivers to communicate personal messages as well as road information. (See: **citizens band radio**)

bear a difficult person or situation. From the fact that a bear can be a difficult animal. Examples: "That test was a **bear**." "My father's a **bear**. If I fail that class, he'll kill me."

bearded clam *sex* female genitalia. Get it? It's a visual thing.

beast or **the beast within us** some people say that within each of us is a primal person who is more animal than human. The beast within each of us who sometimes comes out to act in antisocial ways. The party animal.

beast with two backs *sex* a couple making love.

***beat** tired.

beat a member of the **beat generation**, a **beatnik**. Predecessor of the hippie. A **hipster** term said to have been introduced to **Allen Ginsberg, Jack Kerouac and William Burroughs** in the mid-1940s by Herbert Huncke, a junkie friend of Burroughs. **Lawrence Ferlinghetti** suggests that it was a term given to **Jack Kerouac** by Gertrude Stein when she said to him, "You are a beat generation." The term can equate to the condition of being beaten down, downtrodden or poor. It is also said to relate to the word beatitude, or holiness. Thus, the righteous poor.

"It's the **Beat** generation. It's Be-At. It's the beat to keep. It's the **Beat** of the heart. It's being **beat** and down in the world and like old time low down. And like in ancient civilizations the slave boatman rowing galleys to a **Beat** and servant spinning pottery to a **Beat**."

Jack Kerouac

beat a retreat to leave somewhere under pressure.

beaten with an ugly stick ugly.

beat feet to leave in a hurry.

beat generation a term coined by writer **Jack Kerouac**, or, as some say, Gertrude Stein and first published by John Clellon Holmes in his 1952 article for *The New York Times Magazine*, "This is the Beat Generation." The generation just before the hippie, born in the 1920s and 1930s. A relatively small group of individuals residing primarily in urban and academic atmospheres, coming into their awareness in the period of time between WWII and the hippies of the 1960s. I have included beatniks and the beat generation in this dictionary because of their importance to the development of the hippie **counterculture**. The beats, by expressing their distaste and distrust of American hypocrisy and **materialism**, made the hippie era possible. Their philosophies would become the basis of the rebellions of the 1960s and 1970s. **2**. "The Beat Generation" was a three-act play written by Jack Kerouac in 1957.

Beatle boots pointed-toed, high-heeled, ankle-high boots with elastic sides or zippers on the inside of the foot. They were basically the Cuban style boot with a high, Cuban heel. Stylish footwear worn mostly by **mods** and by **The Beatles** early in their career. Sometimes called **fruit boots** or **winkle pickers**. (See: **fruit boots, winkle pickers** and **mods**)

Beatlemania fanatical behavior directed at the British rock group, "**The Beatles**."

Beatles, The *rock & roll* musical group formed in 1959 in Liverpool, England. Originally named the Quarrymen. **John Lennon** (b. John Winston Lennon, Oct. 9, 1940, Liverpool; d. Dec. 8, 1980, New York City, NY) gtr., voc.,

harmonica, kybds.; **Paul McCartney** (b. James Paul McCartney, June 18, 1942, Liverpool), bass, voc., gtr., kybds.; **George Harrison** (b. Feb. 25, 1943, Liverpool; d. Nov. 29, 2001, Los Angeles, Calif.) gtr., voc.; **Ringo Starr** (b. Richard Starkey, Jr., July 7, 1940, Liverpool), drums, perc., voc.; Stu Sutcliffe, bass, and Pete Best, drums,

photo by Lisa Law ©

were members of the band before fame struck. Sutcliffe died in 1962, and Best was replaced in 1962 by Starr. Brian Epstein, their early manager, and **George Martin**, their producer (sometimes called the fifth Beatle), both influenced their rise to popularity, but it was their music, personal chemistry and the writing of McCartney and Lennon that made The Beatles the most popular rock and roll band of the era. The magic was created by the personalities and talents of the four musicians together. John and George's social concerns, Paul's musical genius and Ringo's whimsy were a combination of the right elements at the time. To try to describe the influence The Beatles have had on our culture would be like trying to evaluate music itself. For those who do not understand their influence, it is suggested that you view The Beatles' movie, "A Hard Day's Night." No one, young or old, can deny the appeal of those boys in that film. After watching the movie, listen to their albums, *Revolver, Sgt. Pepper's Lonely Hearts Club Band, Abbey Road*, and

Let It Be, and then you will have some idea of the influence The Beatles had on our lives. Inducted into The Rock and Roll Hall of Fame in 1988.

beatnik someone following the **beat** lifestyle. The predecessor of the hippie, widely considered to be personified by an unkempt appearance, poetry reading and bongo playing. The "nik" was added to the root word "beat" by the journalist Herb Caen. Supposedly relating to a Russian or **communist** influence. The term was then adopted by the beats in a self-directed sarcasm meant to rub it in the face of **straight** society. Many of the same social issues engrossed the **bohemians** of the 1920s, the beatniks of the 1950s, and the hippies of the 1960s and 1970s. In the hippie era, the term beatnik became almost derisive, meaning someone who was behind the times, yet most beatniks became hippies in essence as the two eras overlapped each other.

beat off or **beat one's meat** to masturbate (male usage). Many phrases and words have been used for each sexual activity, and they are often regional. Male **masturbation** has more than its share of euphemisms: **whipping the dog, jerkin' the gherkin, choking the chicken, flogging the lizard, hand jive, loving the one you're with, palm aid**, etc.

beats me I don't know. Comes from **beats the hell out of me**.

beats the hell out of me I don't know. I think it comes from "you could beat me and I still wouldn't know."

beat (one's) **time** to get the girl. To outdo someone in a romantic competition. Examples: "I **beat his time** with the new girl down the street." "She **beat my time** with the girl up the street."

beat to the punch to accomplish something before another person.

beaucoup a lot. A French word most likely brought into the culture by soldiers returning from **Vietnam**, where many of the population spoke French. Example: "Don't worry, I have **beaucoup** bucks."

beautiful exclamation of approval. During this period, the word acquired a more cosmic connotation, and it was not reserved only for physical, musical or creative endeavors. Examples: "He has a **beautiful** soul." "She has a **beautiful** strength."

beautiful people hippies, friendly people.

Beautiful People **fashion**-conscious, wealthy people. **Jet setters**.

photo by John McCleary ©

Beautify America, get a haircut! a billbord slogan displayed throughout America by an outdoor advertising company. Another failed attempt by the conservative population to ridicule the hippie culture. Reactionaries have yet to learn that they cannot throw words at an intellectually based **counterculture** without having those same words come back to haunt them. This phrase, originally meant to embarrass the hippie, became an anthem of the counterculture when it was added as a caption to a picture of George Washington showing his normal, long hair cut into a flat-top.

beaver the female genitals. Relating to the supposed resemblance between the hairy animal and that area of a woman's body.

beaver shot a glimpse of a woman's crotch or underwear permitted by a short skirt and the way she is sitting. The view of a woman's **vagina**, crotch or underwear offered when she wears a short dress and reclines in a revealing manner. **2.** a photograph of a woman's vagina with her legs spread. This type of photo is taken for the express purpose of creating sexual excitement. Same as **spread beaver** and **split beaver**.

Beck, Jeff (b. June 24, 1944, Surrey, England) *rock & roll* one of the most influential guitarists in rock music. He has played with everyone and influenced many.

beef a fight, complaint or grudge. Example: "They got into a **beef** over vegetarianism."

Bee Gees, The *rock & roll/disco* Australian disco and soft rock musical group formed in 1958 in Brisbane, Australia. Barry Gibb (b. Sept. 1947, Manchester, Eng.) gtr., voc.; Maurice Gibb (b. Dec 22, 1949, Isle of Man) voc., bass, kybds.; Robin Gibb (b. Dec 22, 1949, Isle of Man) voc. The Bee Gees are notable for recording some of the most popular disco songs and being involved with the 1977 "**Saturday Night Fever**" soundtrack. Their classic disco songs on the soundtrack are "Staying Alive," "Night Fever" and "How Deep is Your Love?" Inducted into the Rock and Roll Hall of Fame in 1997.

beehive hairdo a woman's coiffure that is backcombed, stacked up high and coated with lacquer hair spray to keep it tall and indestructible. Introduced into American culture in 1960. a.k.a. **big hair**.

been had taken advantage of, cheated. Example: "I've **been had**; the guy at the vegetarian hot dog stand gave me change for a five and I gave him a ten."

Beetle a Volkswagen passenger car. (See: **Volkswagen Bug** and **Baha bug**)

be here now concentrate on the moment at hand; from the 1971 book, *Be Here Now*, by **Baba Ram Dass**, a.k.a. Richard Alpert, PhD. *Be Here Now* was a very popular book that helped to define the spiritual philosophy for many young people of the time. Alpert was a philosophy professor at Harvard in the 1960s when he began research in **consciousness** with **Timothy Leary** and Ralph Metzner. This research included studying the effect on humans of **LSD** and other drugs. Alpert and Leary were eventually fired from Harvard in 1963 for LSD experimentation involving undergraduates. They continued their experiments from a mansion in upstate New York and became, in essence, the fathers of the 1960s psychedelic revolution. In 1967, Alpert went to India to find drug-free enlightenment and became a follower of the late Indian guru Neem Karoli Baba. Neem Karoli Baba gave Alpert the name Ram Dass, which means servant of god. Because of Ram Dass's status as a religious teacher, he was granted the honorary title of **Baba**.

behind about or with. Example: "James has a problem **behind** Laura's seeing other men." An African American term before it gained popularity during the hippie era.

behind it to be engrossed or involved. In agreement with something.

"Behind the Green Door" a 1972 X-rated movie that became the first of the new wave of "sex flicks" which actually featured "attractive girls from next door." It starred, performing sexual acts, Marilyn Chambers, whose previous job had been as the "Ivory Snow Girl" in advertisements for the conservative soap manufacturing company.

be-in a gathering of people for creative expression. Originating in San Francisco's **Golden Gate Park**, these **happenings** often involved drugs, theatrical performances and music, and sometimes took on the appearance of large **dada** art objects. **Bill Graham**, of later music promotion fame, was an actor and producer of plays performed by the **Mime Troupe** and **Artists' Liberation Front** at the first be-ins. A notable example was the **Human Be-in Gathering of the Tribes** held at the Polo Fields in San Francisco's Golden Gate Park on January 14, 1967, in observance of the day **LSD** became illegal in California. Present were **Jerry Rubin, Timothy Leary, Richard Alpert, Gary Snyder, Allen Ginsberg** and 50,000 other people. "Etiquette in Public Places," *Emily Post's Tenth Edition Blue Book*, published in 1960 by Funk & Wagnall, states, when throwing a party, "The first rule is to avoid crowding." **Wavy Gravy**, Woodstock, 1969, said, "Get closer to your neighbor, it conserves body heat."

being the part of a person's soul that is seen by the world, the moral **essence** of a person exposed to society. Example: "He is a beautiful **being**."

being there experiencing something to the fullest. Observing the present with all of one's senses. **2.** the book *Being There* (1970) by Jerzy Kosinski.

bell bottoms one of the most endearing, yet potentially embarrassing, clothing styles of the 1960s and 1970s. The style started probably when some hippies went to a military surplus store and purchased Navy sailors' pants. They were constructed with flared bottoms so that, if a sailor found himself in the ocean, the pants could be removed, the legs tied together and filled with air, thus creating a life preserver. When the hippies wore the Navy bell bottoms out of the store, some ingenious **fashion** designer saw them, went back to his studio, and a **fad** was born. **Rudi Gernreich** comes to mind as one of the designers who expanded the **style**.

belly of the beast a bad place to be. A tough spot. Comes from the fact that a person who is eaten by a beast is not in a very good situation. This is an older term that came back to life during the hippie era, which was the intellectual renaissance of the twentieth century.

Belushi, John (1949-1982) comedian, actor. Born in Chicago, Illinois, and raised in Wheaton, he played football, acted in a student variety shows and was homecoming king during his senior year at Wheaton Central High. Attended the University of Wisconsin, dropped out, and formed an improv comedy troupe called the West Compass Players, which led to his being accepted into the Second City comedy troupe in 1971. In 1973, he joined the cast of the off-Broadway rock musical "National Lampoon's Lemmings," which led to a 1974 writing job for the "National Lampoon's Radio Hour" (later the "National Lampoon Show"). In 1975, he joined the cast of television's new comedy series "**Saturday Night Live**." His costars included Dan Akroyd, Steve Martin, Bill Murray and Gilda Radner. For the next five years, Belushi portrayed numerous characters on "Saturday Night Live" and became one of the country's most revered comedians. Belushi also made several films during this period, including "National Lampoon's Animal House" in 1978, "The Blues Brothers" in 1980 and "Continental Divide" in 1981. Belushi was always considered a self-indulgent risk taker, and few people were surprised when on March 5, 1982, he was found in his room at a Hollywood hotel, dead of a drug overdose.

benny or **bennies** *drugs* tablets of brand name **Benzedrine** and other manufactured **amphetamine** sulfate doses used legally as diet pills or illegally as a **recreational drugs**. **Uppers**.

Benenson, Peter a British lawyer and founder of **Amnesty International** in 1962. Amnesty International is an apolitical, humanitarian organization headquartered in London, consisting of over 700 groups. Each is required to select three victims of racial, religious or political persecution annually, one each from the **communist**, **capitalist**, and uncommitted world, and work for their release by exposing the injustice. The organization also observes and sends missions to countries, and, when human rights violations are found, it reports the details to the UN and the Council of Europe. Amnesty International was awarded the Nobel Peace Prize in 1977.

bent crazy. **2.** dishonest.

bent out of shape mad. Example: "Don't get **bent out of shape**, but I just smoked the last." Same usage as **out of shape, out of sorts, torqued**.

Benzedrine *drugs* a brand name tablet of **amphetamine** sulfate manufactured by Smith, Kline, French Laboratories. The pill creates an artificial feeling of excitement and surge of power, inhibiting sleep. It is an **upper**. Used legally as a diet pill or illegally as a **recreational drug**. a.k.a. **pep pill, bean, benny, goofball, hi-ball, benz**.

Berkeley, University of California the Berkeley campus was a center for the **academic-freedom** movement, the **free-speech movement**, and the protest against on-campus military and military-industrial recruiting.

Berrigan, Fathers Daniel and Philip *social issues* Roman Catholic priests and leading **anti-war** activists. On October 27, 1967, Father Philip Berrigan and three others poured blood on Selective Service files in the Baltimore, Maryland, Custom House. On May 17, 1968, Daniel and Philip burned draft board records they liberated from the Cantonsville, Maryland, board. Sentenced to prison terms, the Berrigans went **underground**, but eventually were captured and imprisoned. Daniel was the first priest on the FBI's Ten Most Wanted List. (See: **Anti-War Events, Groups and Leaders** starting on page 562 in **Lists** at the back of this book)

Berry, Chuck (b. Charles Edward Anderson Berry, Oct. 18, 1926, San Jose, Calif.) Black **rock & roll** singer/songwriter/guitar player.   One of the most influential musicians of the 1950s, who had an effect on the 1960s and 1970s. Berry wrote "Johnny B. Goode," "Sweet Little Sixteen," "Rock & Roll Music" and at least half a dozen songs that every musician must know and play in order to be called a rock and roll musician. Inducted into The Rock and Roll Hall of Fame in 1986.

best shot your best. Example: "Don't hold back; give it your **best shot**."

bet your ass, bet your sweet ass or **bet your bippy** a statement of agreement or affirmation. Any number of phrases starting with "bet your," that show agreement. Examples: "**Bet your sweet ass** I'll be there." "You can **bet your bippy** he loves Mississippi."

bfoq an acronym meaning **bona-fide occupational qualifications. (See: bona-fide occupational qualifications)**

Bhagavad Gita (BAH-guh-vahd GEE-tuh) *religion* **Sanskrit** for Son of the Divine One. A portion of the sacred books of **Hinduism,** the epic poem containing a dialogue between **Krishna** and the Indian hero Arjuna, which states the relationship between morality and ethical values in Hindu philosophy. It also can mean "the song of God."

bhakti yoga the **yoga** of love. The quest for a union with the Divine Spirit through the *bhakti-marga,* the harmonizing of the nature of man with the purity and Divine Love of the Creator.

bhang *drugs* a Middle Eastern word for **marijuana**. (See: **marijuana**)

bi *sex* short for **bisexual**. Interested in sexual activity with both males and females.

biblical something of monumental spiritual proportions or widespread religious value. This is what **Jerry Garcia** called **Woodstock**.

big bang theory the theory that our Earth, our Moon, Sun and all the planets were created and placed in their positions by a huge explosion of a larger mass. This theory and the term were introduced into use in 1966.

Big Blue a nickname for the IBM company. It was so named because its logo is composed of the large block letters "IBM" in blue.

Big Brother a character in **George Orwell**'s book, *1984,* published in 1949. In general usage, it has come to mean an authority figure who watches society and disciplines those who break the "rules."

Big Brother and the Holding Company *rock & roll* **Janis Joplin**'s band for her first **albums** and her appearance at the **Monterey Pop Festival** in June, 1967.

big brown eyes female breasts.

big chief, the *drugs* mescaline, an **hallucinogenic. 2. lysergic acid diethylamide (LSD).**

big D   *drugs* **lysergic acid diethylamide (LSD).**

big deal   something important. Examples: "His habit ain't no **big deal**; just give him a candy bar and a pep pill at midnight." Often used sarcastically to mean the opposite of something important. Example: "So you got your first hickey, **big deal**!?"

biggie   something important. Short for big deal. Examples: "Winning that talent contest is a **biggie**; it means we can move out of the garage."

big gun or **big guns**   an important person, the best or most effective people for a job. **2.** In surfing terminology, it means a big surfboard.

big H *drugs* **heroin.**

big John   policeman.

big man on campus   a pejorative reference to an individual who thinks and acts as if he is an important person. May or may not relate to a literal school campus situation. Hippies often took terms that had positive definitions in the straight society and turned them into sarcasm, i.e., **cowboy**, gentleman, **lady**, the boss, **Mr. Clean**, etc.

Big Sur Coast   an area of perhaps eighty miles along the central California Coast. The Big Sur coast offered the **Esalen Institute**, infinite beauty to the soul, a place away from the materialistic, militaristic vibrations of the world and plenty of land to grow great marijuana. Big Sur was as important to the counterculture evolution as were the university communities, **Haight-Ashbury** in San Francisco, California, and **Greenwich Village** in New York City.

photo by John McCleary ©

Big Sur was featured prominently in **beat** and hippie literature and became a place through which kids **on the road** had to pass in order to absorb the **vibe** of **peace, freedom and love**. At one time, that area of the California coast had its own variety of gonorrheal venereal disease. (See: **Esalen Institute**)

big ticket item   a very expensive product. In reference to a large number that appears on the price tag or "ticket."

big time   prominent or large scale. Example: "He's a **big-time** beansprout dealer."

Big Top   the Capitol building in Washington, DC. A **Weathermen** term as related by **Bill Ayers** in his 2001 book *Fugitive Days: a memoir*, published by Beacon Press. On March 1, 1971, the Weather Underground planted a package of **"ice cream"** at the **Big Top**; the resulting explosion blew a door off its hinges, broke some windows, injured no one, but made a statement. (See: **Bill Ayers, ice cream** and **Weathermen**)

bike   a motorcycle.

biker   a motorcycle rider, most often a member of a motorcycle gang.

Billboard #1records for the years of:
1960 "The Theme From A Summer Place," Percy Faith
1961 "Tossin' and Turnin,'" Bobby Lewis

1962 "I Can't Stop Lovin' You," Ray Charles
1963 "Sugar Shack," Jimmy Gilmer & the Fireballs
1964 "I Want To Hold Your Hand," The Beatles
1965 "Yesterday," The Beatles
1966 "I'm A Believer," The Monkees
1967 "To Sir With Love," LuLu
1968 "Hey, Jude," The Beatles
1969 "Aquarius/Let the Sun Shine In," The 5th Dimension
1970 "Bridge Over Troubled Water," Simon & Garfunkel
1971 "Joy To The World," Three Dog Night
1972 "The First Time Ever I Saw Your Face," Roberta Flack
1973 "Killing Me Softly With His Song," Roberta Flack
1974 "The Way We Were," Barbara Streisand
1975 "Love Will Keep Us Together," Captain & Tennille
1976 "Tonight's The Night (Gonna Be Alright)," Rod Stewart
1977 "You Light Up My Life," Debby Boone
1978 "Night Fever," Bee Gees
1979 "My Sharona," The Knack

bimbo an attractive, yet silly or empty-headed woman who is easily taken advantage of sexually. A male chauvinist term, reportedly a derivative of the Italian word for baby, "bambino." At one time, it designated a clumsy or stupid man, but in 1950s mystery novels, it evolved into the description of a flashy, loose and available woman.

bindle *drugs* a package of illicit drugs. Of no specific designated weight or volume, it usually consisted of a small amount of **powder** for **snorting** or **shooting**. The word comes from the bundle of bedding, "bindle" that "bindlestiffs," or hobos, used to carry.

bint a girl or young woman. The Arabic word for a girl or daughter, it traveled to England with colonial soldiers and then to America with the 1960s **British invasion**. This term, as with many of the communications among men about women, is suggestive of sexual intent or chauvinism.

biodegradable *the environment* the ability of a man-made object or chemical to break down (decompose) into its original, natural form and once again become a useful part of the earth. Many man-made objects and substances are altered so drastically that they are incapable of decomposing into the environment and once again being safe for ingestion by other organisms. Beginning in the 20th century, particularly in the petrochemical industry, scientists began to alter the molecules of many elements, thus producing substances, such as polyurethane, which are not acceptable into the earth's natural evolutionary chain. This means that valuable elements necessary to the continued existence of our planet are being chemically changed into unusable blobs, thus taking them away from our limited store of resources, polluting the environment and killing other organisms at the same time. A term introduced to the public in this definition in 1965. Similar usage to **degradable**.

biofeedback a process whereby a person's own brain waves can be fed back to them so that they can learn to control such things as stress, pain, and anxiety. Electrodes are placed on the skin of the head and body, picking up electronic impulses, which are displayed on a screen or played through headphones to the patient. The patient can then learn to control the bodily functions that create these patterns. First developed in the 1940s by Yale psychologist Dr. Neal Miller, it evolved into something of a parlor trick in the 60s, but is now recognized as a valuable physical and psychological therapy tool.

biorhythms a system of charting one's capabilities and weaknesses at any given time. Based on the belief that each person has a vacillating rhythm of mental abilities, physical abilities, and emotional states. It is believed that each of these human elements has a different rhythmic time line and is independent of the others. The rhythms range from positive efficiency to negative efficiency over a time period similar to a woman's menstrual cycle. To learn one's state of mind or abilities at a given time, one determines the location of these three elements on a printed chart based on the person's birth date.

bird a girl or young woman, not necessarily derogatory. **British invasion**.

bird dog *sex* to follow or seek out, usually the search for a sexual partner. Coming from the dogs that seek out game birds for hunters. Example: "He's a **bird dog** for girls with curls."

Birmingham Sunday *social issues* September 15, 1963, the day on which the Sixteenth Street Baptist Church in Birmingham, Alabama, was bombed, killing four young Black girls and injuring 20 others. The girls were: **Addie Mae Collins, 14; Denise McNair, 11; Carol Robertson, 14;** and **Cynthia Wesley, 14. Robert Edward Chambliss, "Dynamite Bob,"** a member of the 13th Klavern of the Alabama **Ku Klux Klan,** was convicted in 1977 of the bombing. Three other men were also sus-

pected in that bombing, yet Chambliss was the only one convicted at the time.

Addie Mae Collins   Denise McNair

Carol Robertson   Cynthia Wesley

Also suspected were Thomas Blanton, Jr., Bobby Frank Cherry and Herman Cash. Cash died without ever being charged, but after the turn of the century, new trials were opened against Blanton and Cherry. Blanton was finally convicted on May 1, 2001, and Cherry is under indictment, yet has not been tried as of this publication due to his medical condition. "Dynamite Bob" died in prison in 1985. (See: **Chambliss, Robert Edward, "Dynamite Bob"**) (See also: **Civil Rights Events, Groups and Leaders** starting on page 546 in **Lists** at the back of this book)

birth control *sex* contraception in its many forms. **Margaret Sanger** coined the term in 1914 in a pamphlet entitled *Family Limitations.* Abstention was almost unheard of during the hippie era. Enovid, the original oral birth control pill, was introduced in 1960. Over a period of time, other brand names were developed. The **Pill** was an accessible, inexpensive, fairly safe, almost totally effective form of birth control, and it greatly contributed to the **sexual revolution**. Drawbacks were weight gain and hormonal problems for some women. New **intrauterine devices** (I.U.D.s) were also available during the era. They promised a carefree sex life, yet proved to be somewhat less effective or safe and have now almost totally disappeared. The **diaphragm** flew in, and, of course, prophylactics have been around for quite a while. Women have continually argued that most contraceptive devices are developed and marketed by men and that women should be allowed to have a try at developing them. Add to this a strong religious backlash against teaching effective contraception, and a situation still exists in the year 2002 where the unwanted birth rate is unacceptably high, and women must sometimes rely on abortion as a form of birth control. It is amazing, but some people still think that it is possible to legislate or religiously prohibit human sex drives. Make birth control available and inform young people about it; that is how to reduce unwanted pregnancies. Unwanted children often become problems to their families, society, and before God. (See: **Margaret Sanger)** **Failure rates of the various contraceptive techniques are as follows:** Abstention (the Rhythm method): 90 pregnancies per 100 women per year. Spermicide: 20 pregnancies per 100 women per year. Condoms: 12 to 14 pregnancies per 100 women (from improper use). Diaphragm: 12 per 100 (from improper use). I.U.D.: 3 per 100. The Pill: 3 per 100 (from improper use).

bisexual, bisexuality *sex* having an interest in sexual relations with both genders. A phenomenon, not new, yet introduced to many in the 60s. Along with new sexual freedoms came experimentation, and with the feelings of benevolence toward sex on the whole, many people tried it. Some would find that it was not for them and return to or turn to homosexual or heterosexual status exclusively.

bit an activity, often a theatrical exhibition. Example: "He's doing his guru **bit**."

bit *sex* intercourse, sexual activity. Example: "He's getting a **bit** on the side."

bit *computer revolution* a basic measure of information in a computer. It is also defined as a computer decision. Devised by Claude Shannon of MIT and Bell Laboratories, based on his work on the mathematical foundation of information theory during and after WWII.

bitch a negative term that is not gender related and can also describe inanimate objects. Examples: "This cold's a **bitch**." "He's a **bitch** to work with."

bitch an unpleasant woman. In the 1960s, this word was reserved for an individual, unlike the 1990s, when it became a generic term for women.

bitching or **bitchin'** fine or extraordinary. Example: "I liked the dildo-shaped cookies at your **bitchin'** party."

bite me more of an oath than a challenge, it means something like **fuck off**.

bit-map *computer revolution* refers to each dot of light on the computer monitor as being connected to one bit of information in the computer's memory. This allows the cursor to affect the computer memory by clicking on or off the dots on the screen; by turning on or off bits in the computer, the image on the screen is changed. This process, using the mouse and keyboard, gives the computer user an automatonic connection to the computer. This is the symbiotic foundation upon which the success of the personal computer is based. Allen Keys, a Xerox consultant and member of the original team at Palo Alto Research Center, was a prime figure in the concept and development of bit-mapping in the early 1970s.

bit of fluff a woman who is decorative and not to be taken seriously. A **British invasion** term.

bizarre strange or odd. Example: "I liked the dildo-shaped cookies at your **bizarre** party."

bizarro an expanded form of the word **bizarre** with a pseudo-exotic twist.

black *drugs* **hashish**.

black *drugs* **opium** one of the many underground names from different regions of the country where it is smoked and different parts of the world where it is grown. Also called black stuff or black pill from the look of the round pellet of opium that is placed in a pipe for smoking.

Black a term for **African Americans** that grew in popularity in the early 1960s to replace the word Negro, which had taken on a subservient connotation. The word Black was adopted by African Americans because it portrayed a stronger, self-reliant image. Used in this book because it was appropriate during this time.

Black activist a term created by politicians and the press to infer that such people were somehow outside the law.

In truth, most Black **"activists"** were merely American citizens lobbying for their civil rights.

black and tan *drugs* a capsule of Durophet-M.

black and white a police car. Some cities, such as Los Angeles, have police cars painted black and white. Even where cars are not painted in this way, they are often called black and whites.

black and white *drugs* a capsule of Biphetamine or **amphetamine**. Some are both black and white, some are all black and some are all white. **Uppers**.

black beauties *drugs* Biphetamine capsules of **amphetamine**. Some are all black, some are both black and white. **Uppers**.

black bomber *drugs* a 20-mg Biphetamine capsule of **amphetamine**. An **upper**.

black box similar to the **blue box**. (See: **blue box**)

black hole "...a region (in space) where matter is so condensed, and hence gravity so strong, that nothing—not even light—can escape. Black holes can form as the result of the catastrophic collapse of matter," wrote Michael Hawkins. The term was coined in 1969 by American scientist John Wheeler, yet it has been a theory for at least 200 years. It was studied and written about extensively during the 1970s by Isaac Asimov and Stephen Hawking.

black hole a failed social situation or a boring place.

Black is Beautiful the expression of pride in African American heritage. For generations, African Americans were made to feel inferior, and during the 1960s and 70s the quest for self-esteem spawned interest in many things, such as Afro clothing, hairstyles, Black history and **ethnic studies**. The term, Black is Beautiful, was echoed in celebration of this newfound pride. **Malcolm X** and others spoke of how much more attractive skin of color was than the pale, white, pigmentless skin of the Caucasian.

black light an ultraviolet light source with a purple tint that makes many white objects glow in the dark. In the hippie era, it was very popular in dance clubs to add a **psychedelic** atmosphere. The poster industry created black light posters that produced a florescent glow when exposed to black light. I can still close my eyes and see Jimi Hendrix in orange and green swirls of color.

black magic the use or abuse of supernormal powers for selfish purposes, such as sorcery, necromancy (communicating with the dead), raising the dead or placing spells on enemies.

black mote *drugs* **marijuana** that has been cured in honey or sugar and buried in darkness to strengthen its potency and lengthen its effectiveness.

Black Muslims a.k.a. **Nation of Islam** or **Lost-Found Nation of Islam** (See: **Nation of Islam**)

Black Nationalist Party *social issues* an offshoot of the **Black Muslims** created by **Malcolm X**. He formed this new organization in March, 1964, because of dissatisfaction with the Muslims' nonviolent approach and **Elijah Muhammad's** personal sexual transgressions. Malcolm X moved his followers to a position of active self-defense against **White supremacists**, stating that "there can be no revolution without bloodshed and it is nonsense to describe the **Civil Rights Movement**

as a revolution." Malcolm X was killed by gunmen from a rival religious faction on February 21, 1965. (See: **Malcolm X** in alphabetical listings) (See also: **Civil Rights Events, Groups and Leaders** starting on page 546 in **Lists** and **Revolutionary Groups** on page 585 in **Lists** at the back of this book)

Black Panther Party *social issues* an organization created and dedicated to policing the police in the ghettos, ethnic self-defense, and Black community **self-help**, co-founded by **Huey P. Newton** and **Bobby Seale** in October, 1966. Other prominent members were **Eldridge Cleaver, Fred Hampton, Stokely Carmichael**, Bobby Rush, Rufus Walls and Jewel Cook. "The Panthers" created free children's breakfast programs and free health clinics; they taught political education classes and conducted a community police control project, which monitored the actions of police in Black ghettos to keep them from violating the **civil rights** of citizens. The Panthers were greatly feared, misunderstood, and persecuted because of the formidable appearance of their uniform of black beret and leather jacket and because they often carried weapons openly, which was legal in many parts of the US. All members were hounded, even Whites who displayed Panther stickers, and party members were involved in a number of shoot-outs with police. On December 4, 1969, Chicago police raided the Black Panthers' Illinois Headquarters and killed Illinois Chairman **Fred Hampton** and party member Mark Clark. In all, about 28 party members and 14 police officers died in various Panther-police conflicts. Bobby Seale was eventually accused of executing a dissident party member, and Newton was tried and convicted of the murder of a policeman on August 9, 1968. (See: **Huey P. Newton** and **Bobby Seale** in alphabetical listings) (See also: **Civil Rights Events, Groups and Leaders** starting on page 546 in **Lists** and **Revolutionary Groups** on page 585 in **Lists** at the back of this book)

Black Power an attitude more than an organized movement, with many adherents within all **civil rights** and Black political groups. The term was coined by **Stokely Charmichael**. At the Mexico City Olympics on October 18, 1968, **Tommie Smith**, gold medal winner in the 200-meter run, and bronze medal winner **John Carlos** were suspended from the games for displaying the Black Power salute while wearing black gloves and scarves. Three others, Lee Evans, Larry James and Ron Freeman, also demonstrated but were not disciplined.

Black Pride the expression of pride in African American culture and heritage. For generations, African Americans were made to feel inferior, and during the1960s and 70s the quest for self-esteem spawned interest in many things, such as Afro clothing, hairstyles, Black history, and **ethnic studies**.

Black Student Union (BSU) *social issues* a Black student organization that started in the mid-1960s on many high school and college campuses. BSU's purpose is to promote the welfare of Black students and encourage classes and programs that study Black culture.

black tar or **tar** *drugs* Mexican black tar **heroin**, the most common street supply in the US. It is up to 80 percent pure. As opposed to the dry, white powdered form, tar is sticky and black with more plant impurities than the more refined Asian variety.

Blackwell, Chris *reggae/rock & roll* owner of Island Records in Jamaica, the label of artists including **Jimmy Cliff** and **Bob Marley**. A member of the British White aristocracy of Jamaica who became intrigued by the Black music of the islands and helped to introduce it to the rest of the world. Inducted into the Rock and Roll Hall of Fame in 2001.

blackxploitation the practice in the film industry of the 1970s of using Black stereotypes to capitalize on the Black culture in America. A genre of films exploiting Black culture to sell movies. Movies like the **"Shaft"** series with actor Richard Roundtree in 1971, '72 and '73 are the best examples. Pam Grier also starred in a series of Black action movies. Her character, Foxy Brown, could be called the queen of blackxploitation, as Roundtree's Shaft would be the king of the genre. **Gordon Parks** was the director of "Shaft."

blahs emotional or mental fatigue. A term introduced into popular use in 1970.

blast something that is exciting or fun. Example: "That Fellini film was a **blast**."

blast *drugs* to smoke **marijuana** or **hash**. Example: "Stop bragging about the THC content; let's just **blast** that sucker." **2.** a stream of marijuana smoke blown by someone into the nose of another from a pipe called a **steamboat** or the mouthpiece of a regular pipe.

blasted extremely effected by drugs or alcohol.

blast from the past a former lover.

bleeding heart or **bleeding heart liberal** someone who is "soft" on human frailties and permissive concerning social issues, such as welfare, personal freedoms and prison reform. A term created by conservatives as a derogatory name for people with liberal ideals. Meant to be derisive, it is actually a compliment to someone who cares about mankind. After all, the opposite of a bleeding heart is a hard heart.

bleep or **bleeping** to censor. Example: "Don't you dare **bleep** my passionate language from this manifesto." **2.** a word used in place of a profanity or obscenity. Most often used in sarcasm or humor. Examples: "Get the **bleep** out of here, and take your **bleeping** false morality with you."

Blind Faith *rock & roll* British group formed in London in 1969, Steve Winwood (b. May 12, 1948, Birmingham, Eng.), kybds., gtr., voc.; **Eric Clapton** (b. Eric Clapp, March 30, 1945, Ripley, Eng.), gtr., voc.; Ginger Baker (b. Aug. 19, 1939, Lewisham, Eng.), drums, voc.; Rick Grech (b. Nov. 1, 1946, Bordeaux, France; d. Mar. 17, 1990), bass, violin. This "supergroup" stayed together for one long, sold-out tour, which was performed before they even recorded their one and only album, the 1969 *Blind Faith*. The album was memorable for two songs, Winwood's "Can't Find My Way Home" and Clapton's "Presence of the Lord," and a flip side that contained just two

songs, one of which jammed for 15 minutes. Drugs and a long touring schedule ended this band.

bliss spiritual serenity or sexual ecstasy. Another word that has always meant the same thing, but came into broader and more profound use during the 60s. Examples: "She's in **bliss** over my **bliss** about the **bliss**."

blissed-out in extreme bliss. Example: "She's **blissed-out** by that guy."

blitzed drunk or under the influence of drugs. From the German term *blitzkrieg* (lightning-war), loosely meaning taken by surprise.

block *drugs* a quantity of compressed **hashish**.

block an interruption of the normal energy flow of the body.

blocks psychological or physical restrictions to normal bodily functions or emotions. A term from Reichian therapy. **Wilhelm Reich**, a break-away disciple of **Freud**, worked with therapy and massage to dissolve the tensions (blocks) that produce muscular constrictions (body armor) which some people have due to repressed emotions. Reich believed, as do many massage therapists, that these "blocks" exacerbate repressed emotions, and dissolving these "blocks" will cure emotional problems in many people.

Blondie *rock & roll* a chick-led New York **punk** band formed in New York in 1975. Deborah Harry (b. July 1, 1945, Miami, Fla.), voc.; Chris Stein (b. Jan. 5, 1950, Brooklyn, NY), gtr., voc.; Clem Burke (b. Nov. 24, 1955, New York City), drums; Jimmy Destri (b. Apr. 12, 1954, Brooklyn, NY), kybds.; Gary Valentine, bass, replaced in 1976 by Frank Infante, who switched to guitar in 1977 on the arrival of Nigel Harrison (b. Apr. 24, 1951, Stockport, Eng.), bass. Primarily of importance because they represented the New Wave and illustrated how well a woman could front a band. Later, the band experimented in Black sounds, covering the reggae song, "The Tide Is High," in 1980. In 1981, they produced "Rapture," one of the very first rap songs commercially released to the White public. Deborah Harry is very decorative, but more than that, she was a trend maker with a presence that exemplified the punk movement.

blood an African American term for another African American, a close friend.

Blood, Sweat and Tears *jazz, rock & roll big band* a band formed by **Al Kooper** in New York City in 1967. It was an experiment by Kooper to produce a large group that would encompass many styles of music. Al Kooper left the band within a year, but BST went on to record a number of good songs with David Clayton-Thomas as lead singer. Their hits included "You've Made Me So Very Happy," "Spinning Wheel" and "And When I Die," all of which reached #2 on the charts in 1969.

Bloody Sunday March 7, 1965. The beginning of the first **civil rights** march from Selma to Montgomery, Alabama. Marchers were halted by 200 state troopers at the Edmund Pettus Bridge and were attacked with tear gas and nightsticks. (See: **Civil Rights Events, Groups and Leaders** starting on page 546 in **Lists** at the back of this book)

Bloomfield, Michael (b. July 28, 1944, Chicago, Ill.; d. Feb. 15, 1981, San Francisco, Calif.) *blues, rock & roll* a White blues and rock guitar player who learned by watching and listening as a teenager to **Muddy Waters**, Albert King and others in clubs in Chicago. One of the most influential White blues players to record and perform, he played and recorded with almost everyone at one time or another. Early on, he played with **Paul Butterfield**, Charlie Musselwhite and Nick Gravenites. It is his electric guitar on **Bob Dylan**'s classic recording, "Like a Rolling Stone," and he played on Dylan's album, *Highway 61 Revisited*. Bloomfield was in the groups Electric Flag and **Al Kooper**'s Super Session, and lent his talent to scoring movie sound tracks, such as "Medium Cool," "Steelyard Blues," and Andy Warhol's "Bed." His death from an accidental overdose was one of music's great losses.

BLOSSOM (Basic **L**iberation **o**f **S**mokers and **S**ympathizers **o**f **M**arijuana) an organization formed in 1970 in Washington State that worked to legalize **marijuana**. Its leader was Steve Wilcox. Most of the members lived on a commune near Olympia, Washington. The majority of the group were **vegetarians** to whom smoking marijuana was a sacrament. They reportedly followed a ritual of continually passing a lighted marijuana joint as if it were an eternal flame.

blotter acid *drugs* liquid **LSD** dropped on small squares of **blotter** paper for easy transport, sale and ingestion. A person would merely swallow the small piece of paper. There was a story, not substantiated, yet quite possible, that someone produced a psychedelic poster with a drop of **acid** absorbed into one corner.

blow n. *drugs* (See: **cocaine**) **2**. also a verb, to snort cocaine or to smoke **marijuana**.

blow v. to leave. One of the standard beatnik words that continued in use during in the 1960s and 70s. Example: Beatnik, "Let's **blow** this crazy pad." Hippie, "Yeah, let's **blow** this scene."

blowback *drugs* a method of enhancing the intake of **marijuana** by blowing the smoke into someone's mouth or nose. The "shooter" puts the lighted end of a **joint** in his mouth and blows out through the other end into the mouth or nose of the recipient. Also known as a **shotgun**.

blowin' and a goin' moving at high speed, getting something done quickly, doing a job well. Example: "Get out of her way, she's **blowin' and a goin'**."

blow it off or **blow (someone) off** to forget something, to take something lightly, to ignore someone. Example: "I'm serious, don't **blow it off**, you must keep your acupuncture appointment."

blow it out to do something without restrictions. To drive quickly. Examples: "We'll **blow it out** tonight, go dancing and prancing!" "Accelerate, **blow it out**, let's feel the wind in our hair!" In the automotive references to speed, it means to open up the carburetor, let the air flow through, go fast and clean out the carburetor jets at the same time.

blow it out your ass a rejection. A phrase telling someone that you don't want to deal with them or what they have to say.

blow job *sex* **fellatio**, oral stimulation of the penis. A form of copulation involving oral manipulation of the male genitalia. It can be a **homosexual** or heterosexual act. Distinguished from **cunnilingus**, which is the oral stimulation of the female sexual organs, the **clitoris** and vulva (vaginal opening). This is a term conceived not in the hippie era, but in the 1940s and 50s; most likely, it came back with soldiers from the Second World War. a.k.a. **head job, hum job, suck off**.

blow off to ignore or abandon. Example: "Don't **blow off** your acupuncture appointment."

blowout a big party or big occasion.

blow snow *drugs* to snort **cocaine**.

blow up your TV and **kill your TV** a common suggestion expressing the rebellious feelings of the time. TV represented then, and to many still does today, the worst of the materialistic, shallow and overly commercial aspects of modern life. The first widespread use of the phrase was in the a 1971 **John Prine** song. The saying began to appear on bumper stickers and eventually evolved to "Kill Your TV," seen on car bumpers in the 1990s.

blow your cool to make a fool of yourself, let down your guard or lose the facade of perfection. A very **beatnik** phrase that experienced continued use in the 1960s and 70s.

blow your mind or **blowing your mind** to be amazed by something. **2**. to be high on drugs.

blue angel, blue bullets, blue dolls, or **blue devils,** *drugs* pills or capsules of the **barbiturate**, brand name Amytal.

blue balls *sex* extreme male sexual frustration. Relates to the pressure of unreleased sperm or the accumulation of blood in the testicles, which is assumed to cause a change of color. Pain, real or imaginary, is sometimes felt in the testicles when a man is aroused, yet unfulfilled.

blue box an illegal, homemade device that produced the proper tones in a telephone to eliminate long-distance charges. This invention was created, most sources say, by John Draper also called **Captain Crunch**. Some of the first **computer programmers** were first telephone "**hackers**," or "**phone phreaks**" including **Steve Wozniak** of **Apple Computer**. (See: **Captain Crunch** and **phone phreaks**)

blue box an **IBM** computer. Thus named because the IBM logo is blue.

blue cheer *drugs* **LSD (lysergic acid diethylamide)**. Related to the name of a commercial soap product. Liquid **acid** appears light blue in color, and some popular forms of LSD tablets were blue.

Blue Cheer *heavy-metal/rock & roll* one of the first **heavy-metal** rock bands, formed in 1967 and named after an **LSD** tablet. Their 1968 rendition of Eddie Cochran's "**Summertime Blues**" was considered by many to be the first popular heavy-metal song.

blue dot *drugs* a drop of blue liquid **LSD** on a tablet or a piece of white **blotter** paper.

blue-eyed soul brother a White male who supported African American causes and/or socialized with Blacks.

blue-eyed soul sister a White female who supported African American causes and/or socialized with Blacks.

blue heaven *drugs* amobarbital, sodium **amytal**, a **barbiturate**. Brand name Amytal. **2. morphine**.

blue light or **grow lamp** *drugs* a florescent lamp that gives off a blue, ul-traviolet light essential for growing **marijuana** indoors.

Blue Meanies strange little characters who disrupted the tranquility of Pepperland and were vanquished by the **Beatles** as *Sergeant Pepper's Lonely Hearts Club Band*. This was the scenario in "**Yellow Submarine**," the 1968 animated film based on the Beatles' music, produced in England and directed by Gordon Douglas. The movie featured **psychedelic** visual effects and cartoon characters.

photo by John McCleary ©

Blue Meanies Alameda County Sheriff's Deputies. During the **free-speech, anti-war** and **People's Park** marches, these deputies, who wore bright blue uniforms, were called in to help quell **demonstrations** in **Berkeley, California**, when the local authorities felt they needed reinforcements. These sheriffs were particularly "forceful" in the performance of their duties, thus earning them this nickname that came from the militant little characters in the **Beatles**' 1968 movie, "**Yellow Submarine**." (See: **People's Park** and "**Yellow Submarine**")

blues sorrow or melancholy. States of mind that normally carry negative connotations, yet they also possesses positive, "emotive" values. The blues are usually described as a courageous resignation to the tribulations or life. They are considered primarily an African American slave emotion related to the trials of prejudice and poverty. The blues are primarily expressed through music. **2.** longing, the feeling of missing someone or something. Example: "He's got the 'Joan **blues**' again tonight." **3.** depression.

blues *music* a type of music. The emotions of sorrow or melancholy expressed through music. Considered the first truly American form of music and accepted as the precursor of **rock and roll**. Blues are always played and sung as if they were a badge of perseverance and a cosmic/comic acceptance of the problems of life. The blues are considered primarily an African American slave emotion and a form of music related to the trials of prejudice and poverty. The major blues artists are: Willie Dixon, Son House, **Robert Johnson**, **John Lee Hooker**, **B. B. King**, Blind Lemon Jefferson, Big Mama Thornton and **Muddy Waters**. It's hard to be White and pull off the blues, but a few who have managed to accomplish it are: **Michael Bloomfield**, **Paul Butterfield, John Hammond, Janis Joplin, John Mayall**, Charlie Musselwhite, **Bonnie Raitt** and **Johnny Winter**.

Blues Project, The *blues, rock & roll* formed in New York City in 1965, it was notable for **Al Kooper**'s involvement and its contribution to the revival of blues. Along with the **Paul Butterfield** Blues Band, **The Blues Project** is responsible for introducing blues to an attentive new, young, White audience that would take this influence on into **rock and roll**, creating aesthetic,

historic **roots** for the evolution of music.

blue velvet *drugs* an injected mixture of **opium** and antihistamine that reportedly had a "smooth effect" on the user. Related to the smoothness of the fabric and the 1963 song, "Blue Velvet," by Bobby Vinton.

blunt a **marijuana** cigarette. The term has also been associated with **cocaine**, "**coke** blunt." In some regions of the US, it means a **joint** of marijuana and cocaine mix.

"Bob and Carol and Ted and Alice" a 1969 movie breakthrough in the examination of human interpersonal and sexual relationships. It dealt with the **swapping** of marital partners and other taboos of our society. The movie featured scenes at a group therapy retreat patterned after the **Esalen Institute** on the **Big Sur**, California coast. The story suggests that abandoning conservative sexual inhibitions will improve emotional stability and increase happiness. This theory was a prominent belief of the hippie culture, and its practice was a major activity of the time. The movie starred Elliott Gould, Dyan Cannon, Natalie Wood and Robert Culp. It was Paul Mazursky's directorial debut.

bod short for body. Used when complimenting or lusting after someone. Example: "What a beautiful **bod** she has, and so does her 6' 8" boyfriend."

bodacious outrageous, impressive or arrogant. Example: "She has **bodacious** breasts." Its origin is clouded; it was used in the American South, prevalent in Black conversation, and appears to have roots in the French language and Cajun dialect.

bodhisattva *religion* **Sanskrit** for "existence in wisdom." In **Buddhist** terminology, one who has gone through the ten stages to spiritual perfection and is qualified to enter **Nirvana** and become a Buddha, but prefers to remain a Buddha-to-be in order to work for the salvation and deification of all beings. In Tibetan, "a master" or "great soul." During the hippie era, there were many self-proclaimed Bodhisattvas running around using their "powers" to obtain sex, drugs and rock & roll. (See: **Buddhism** and **Nirvana**)

bodhidharma Tibetan word for "**dharma** path," the "**wheel of life**" or "great wheel."

body armor a term for muscular constrictions caused by tension **(blocks)** referred to in Reichian therapy. From theories on human behavior by **Wilhelm Reich**, a break-away disciple of **Freud**. Reich worked with therapy and massage to dissolve the tensions that create **body language** which interferes with human personal relationships. (See: **Wilhelm Reich** and **body language**)

body art tattoos, scarification, earrings, nose rings and chains. In the United States until the hippie era, women were almost never tattooed, and a man would never be caught dead wearing an earring. The 60s **spirit** of rebellion caused a blossoming of **anti-establishment** body art. Many of the **fads** were garnered from other cultures throughout the world as young people became more international in their scope and travel. The nose ring came from India; decorative tattoos, from the Orient and South Sea Islands; and ear-

rings for men, from the Middle East and India, where men had worn them for centuries. Scarification is the creation of designs on the skin by cutting the flesh. (See: **tattooing**, **body piercing** and **Skin Brothers**)

body language nonverbal communication, either intended or inadvertent, expressed by the way one holds and moves his or her body. The term was introduced around 1971. Tied closely to the theories on human behavior by **Wilhelm Reich**. Most often, body language is interpreted in sexual terms or as an indication of how socially aggressive or timid a person might be. A basic observation is that if a woman slouches, she is either ashamed of or embarrassed by her breasts. A man who holds his hand or arm over his crotch is either ashamed of or embarrassed by his penis. (See: **Wilhelm Reich** and **body armor**)

body painting employing a human body as a canvas, thus making it an art object. It popped up anew in north America around 1965, although aboriginal peoples around the world have practiced it for thousands of years as part of their religious or sexual rituals. As distinguished from **tattooing**, it was a temporary form of adornment. It should also be distinguished from painting *with* bodies, a late-1950s and early-60s art form in which the artist (for example, Yves Klein) applied paint to a nude body, which was then rubbed or rolled on a surface to produce an impressionistic image.

body piercing common fashion for centuries in the Middle East, India, Southeast Asia and Africa. The 1960s spirit of rebellion caused a blossoming of **anti-establishment** body art. Many of the fads were garnered from other cultures throughout the world as young people became more international in their scope and travel. After a time, the earring on men became a statement of sexual orientation. In the 1970s, wearing a ring in the left ear began to mean heterosexual, and the right ear meant homosexual. But the most extreme, and still to this day the least talked about or seen, are **Skin Brothers**. Skin Brothers wear chains, rings, even nuts and bolts, attached to the genitalia. This is largely a **homosexual** activity, but it is also practiced by some straight men and women, usually in **biker** culture. (See: **Fakir Musafar** and **Skin Brothers**)

body stocking a tight-fitting nylon or wool knit garment similar to pantyhose, but covering the body and sometimes the arms and legs. It was adapted from the leotard originally worn by dancers. **Mary Quant**, the British **pop fashion** designer, is often associated with popularizing it in the late 1960s.

boff *sex* a humorous or derogatory term for the act of lovemaking.

bog British slang for toilet or bathroom. Bog as a toilet most likely came from the original English description, which was a damp patch of ground. A number of British words and phrases were adopted by the **counterculture** because of the music invasion and a fascination with England. The strange thing about this was that most British songwriters used American English words and terms in their songs because of the huge market of record buyers in America.

bogart to monopolize or hoard, usually a **marijuana** cigarette. To fail to share with the next person. Example: "Don't **bogart** that joint, my friend."

bogus something unreal or incorrect. Originally used in this form in nineteenth century America to describe counterfeit money. The word tantrabogus was used in Colonial New England to denote something odd looking, and it may have derived from the Devonshire, English word for devil, Tantrabob.

bohemians an artistic, **liberal**, socially conscious group of people during the 1920s, congregating primarily in Berlin and Paris. The predecessors of the **beatniks** of the 1950s and the hippies of the 1960s. In France, "bohemian" came to mean vagabond or **gypsy** since gypsies were thought to have come from the central part of Europe near Bohemia in Czechoslovakia.

bold daring, flamboyant or sometimes arrogant. Another word that has always meant the same thing, but came into broader and more profound use during the 1960s.

bomb or **bombed** a failure or to fail. Examples: "His concert was a **bomb**." "She **bombed** the audition."

bomb or **bomber** *drugs* a big, thick **marijuana** cigarette. a.k.a. **zeppelin, bazooka**.

bombed extremely effected by drugs or alcohol.

"...bomb them back into the Stone Age" a threat made in 1965 by member of the US Joint Chiefs of Staff Curtis LeMay (1906-1990), in reference to the North Vietnamese.

bona-fide occupational qualifications (bfoq's) a law stipulating that an employer cannot be required to give both sexes equal consideration if a job genuinely needs to be filled by one sex rather than the other; for example, a movie director cannot be required to hire a female to play a male role. **Flo Kennedy**, "Ol' Black Flo," **civil rights** lawyer and feminist activist, once said, "There are very few jobs that actually require a penis or a **vagina**."

Bond, Horace Julian (1940-) *social issues* Black **civil rights** leader, writer, educator and politician. A co-founder of and the communications director for the **Student Nonviolent Coordinating Committee (SNCC)**, 1961-66. Elected to the Georgia State House of Representatives in 1965, but barred from taking his seat because of his **anti-war** politics. He was reinstated on the grounds that his expulsion was unconstitutional. He was re-elected several times, and in 1975 was elected to the Georgia State Senate. Since the end of the 1970s, Bond has been a visiting professor, teaching history and politics at numerous universities, including Harvard, University of Virginia and Williams College. He narrated Parts 1 and 2 of the PBS TV documentary "Eyes on the Prize" in 1987. A board member and advocate of many funds and projects aimed at racial equality, economic and cultural development, Julian Bond is one of the most widely respected and articulate representatives of his race and this country.

boner a male **erection**.

boner a mistake. Widely used in the 1950s with some resurgence in the 1960s.

boning or to **bone** *sex* another insensitive, semi-humorous term for sexual intercourse.

bong or **bhong** *drugs* a device used for smoking **dope**, usually a cylinder with a hole in it to hold a joint or a bowl for **weed** or **hash**. Most often, it has a **carburetor**, which is a hole that allows the smoker to control the air-to-smoke proportion. The simplest bong was made from a toilet paper roll. There is some dispute as to whether a bong must also be a **water pipe**. In some regions this is the case, but in most street language a bong can be a any simple, cylindrical pipe. The word comes from the Thai term *"bhaung."*

bonk *sex* humorous term for sexual intercourse.

bonkers crazy.

boo *drugs* **marijuana**, one of the more than 40 names for this most prevalent hippie culture indulgence. Clarence Majors in *Juba to Jive* says that this is a corruption of an African word for marijuana, "jabooby." (See: **marijuana**)

boob a stupid, gullible or socially inappropriate person. Comes from a word coined by H. L. Mencken, **booboisie**, his term for middle-class shortsightedness in moral, religious and political issues.

boobs breasts.

boogaloo to dance **2.** to go or to leave.

boogie to dance. To have fun. Related to **boogie woogie** and **boogaloo**. **2.** to go or to leave. **3.** an earlier term for sexual intercourse.

boogie down to dance or have fun. Related to **boogie woogie** and **boogaloo**.

boogie man a person of bad disposition and/or terrifying appearance.

book to leave, to leave in a hurry.

Book of Changes, The a collection of possibilities and explanations used in **divination** (fortune telling), written in China by various authors at different times up to the latter part of the third century B.C. Also called **I Ching**. (See: **I Ching**)

book of the dead both ***The Egyptian Book of the Dead*** and ***The Tibetan Book of the Dead*** were read and studied by the hippie culture. The Egyptian book, often illustrated, is a collection of spells sometimes buried with the dead in ancient Egypt to lead their souls through judgment. *The Tibetan Book of the Dead* contains instructions and preparations for death and rites to be performed for the dying. In Tibetan **Buddhism**, the dying must train in order to avoid rebirth or at least to ensure rebirth in human form.

boo-koo a lot. A strange spelling of the French word, **beaucoup**.

boom box a large portable radio or tape player. The boom represents the loud sound it makes as some teenager carries it through your neighborhood. a.k.a. **ghetto blaster** or **ghetto box**. (See: **ghetto blaster**)

boom shacka lacka lacka *rock & roll* memorable lyrics from the 1969 song, "I Want To Take You Higher," by **Sly & The Family Stone**. In 1970, Ike & **Tina Turner** recorded it and took it on the road where Tina elevated those lyrics to a new level of sexuality.

boonies or **boondocks** out in the bushes. A military term that crept into **counterculture** usage. From the Philippine Tagalog language word, *bundok*, meaning mountain area.

boost to steal. From the terms **heist** or **lift**. Saw some use in the hippie era in certain regions of the US.

bootie or **booty** *sex* ass, buttocks or gluteus maximus. Example: "What a nice **bootie** he's got." **2.** sexual intercourse, itself. Example: "I'd like to get some of that **bootie**."

Boots, Gypsy (1910-) health food advocate and personality of the counterculture. His mantra is "Bare Feet and Good Things to Eat." He could be called a comedian, entertainer, writer or nutritionist, and he was a regular on "The Steve Allen Show" on television in the 1960s.

Boozefighters MC the name of the first California rebel motorcycle club. MC stands for Motorcycle Club. The predecessors of the **Hell's Angels**. Comprised primarily of World War II veterans and crew members of combat airplanes. This club and others like it began to appear in 1947 in and around El Cajon, California, where rootless, disenfranchised vets started riding **Harley Davidsons**, congregating and drinking at places like the All-American Bar. There were other motorcycle clubs, with names such as Desert Donkeys, Galloping Gooses and Moonshiners. It was not the Hell's Angels, but the Boozefighters and these other early clubs that invaded Hollister, California, for the July 4, 1947, weekend motorcycle rally on which the 1954 movie "The Wild One" with Marlon Brando was based. It was this movie that started the biker image off in a rebellious direction. (See: **Hells Angels**)

bop or **bop around** to dance or to run around at a fast pace.

bop v. to go or leave. Example: "Let's **bop** outta' here."

bopper short for **teenybopper**.

bopper someone who likes to **party**.

boss (bauss) very nice, attractive. Often used in a carnal way. Example: "She's a **boss** chick."

Boston Women's Health Book Collective, The *social issues* a **feminist** organization founded in 1969 by Nancy Hawley and a group of women in Boston, Massachusetts. In 1970, the group compiled and published the influential health book for women, *Our Bodies, Ourselves*, which is still being revised and reprinted today.

both ways (to have it) to be able to pick what you want. To be spoiled.

both ways, to (have or get) it *sex* to have both vaginal and **anal sex**. To have both vaginal and **oral sex**. **2.** to have both hetero- and homosexual tendencies.

bottleneck a guitar playing technique in which the player slides the neck of a bottle or some other hard, smooth surface along the strings of the guitar to achieve a desired sound. The bottleneck sound is a crying, siren's wail that emotes a freight train's lonely passage through a dark, Southern night.

bottom line the basic facts. The most important element or fact in a situation. Example: "The **bottom line** is, we don't think the government knows what it's doing with our lives."

Bower, David Ross (1912-) *social issues* one of the world's leading con-

servationists since the early 1950s. He was the developing founder and long-term director of the Sierra Club from 1952 to 1969. In 1969, he also founded **Friends of the Earth** and served as its president until 1979.

Bowie, David (b. David Robert Jones, Jan. 8, 1947, London Eng.) *rock & roll* British rock singer/songwriter. First recorded in 1967. Notable for starting the **glam rock** movement in 1972, with his alter ego personality, Ziggy Stardust. Bowie, ever changing, continually advancing, has been one of the musicians of the hippie era who has been able to make it in a new era on his new material and not just on his nostalgia value. Inducted into the Rock and Roll Hall of Fame in 1996.

bowl the part of a **pipe** that holds the **dope** when smoked.

photo by John McCleary ©

bowl a **pipe** in which to smoke **dope**. Example: "Do you have a **bowl** to light this in?"

bow legged *sex* a term used to imply that a woman is a nymphomaniac, meaning, of course, that her legs are spread wide from habit. **2.** a term used to imply that a man has a big penis, meaning that his big **member** forces his legs wide apart.

box a **vagina**, the female sex organ.

box lunch *sex* **cunnilingus**. **Box** is a woman's **vagina**. (See: **cunnilingus** for more graphic details)

boy! *interjection* an exclamation verbalizing an inner realization. Not gender specific. Example: "**Boy**, what a beautiful girl you are!"

boy scout a young man who follows all the rules. Someone who is too proper to be any fun. **2.** a policeman.

boy toy *sex* a man who is the object of someone's sexual favor. It suggests that this man is available for casual sex, just like a woman who is called a **plaything**. This term can be used in **heterosexual** or **homosexual** circumstances.

bozo a clown, a foolish person, an awkward person. From the circus personality called Bozo the Clown. Bozo means "lump" or "bump" in Italian.

bra-burners a term used by some to describe **feminists**. It was first coined by the media in the fall of 1968 during the Miss America pageant in Atlantic City, New Jersey, when 200 **women's liberation** demonstrators invited women to discard "objects of female torture" like hair curlers, girdles, bras and high heels. Later, there were some **demonstrations** in which bras where burned, but many feel that these demonstrations, though dramatic, merely detracted from the real issues of the women's movement.

bragging rights the privilege to take credit for something. Advantage gained by prevailing in a competition.

Brahma the Creator of Hindu **mythology** and **occult** philosophy. One of the three aspects of Ishwara, the Personal God.

Brahman the Absolute in Hindu **mythology** and **occult** philosophy.

brain change drugs (See: **educational drugs**)

brain fart a lapse in good thinking. A mental mistake.

brainfuck, brainfucker or **brainfuckers** a person, place, thing or situation that is confusing or confounding. Something that messes with one's head or baffles the mind. A major problem.

brainpan the skull and its contents. It emerged in the 1960s in general usage to mean the head or the thinking organ of a person.

braless without a bra. One of the prominent female **fashion** statements of the 1960s. To some women, it represented a rejection of society's roles forced on them; to some, a statement for sexual freedom; and to others, merely comfort.

Brand, Stewart (b. Dec. 14, 1938, Rockford, Ill.) *social issues* founded, edited, and published the original **Whole Earth Catalog** from 1968 to 1972. Graduated in Biology from Stanford University in 1960. A US Army officer on active duty from 1960-62, he qualified for the Airborne and took up skydiving. Taught basic infantry training and worked as a photojournalist with the Pentagon. Between 1962 and 1968, Brand was involved in producing multimedia performances and events, such as "America Needs Indians," "War: God," "**Trips Festival**," "Whatever It Is" and "World War IV." He also collaborated on museum exhibits entitled "Astronomia" and "We Are All 1." In 1966, he conceived the idea for, and sold buttons reading, "Why Haven't We Seen A Photograph of the Whole Earth Yet?" Legend has it that this prompted NASA to produce good color photos of the Earth taken from outer space during the Apollo program. The ecology movement is said to have begun in 1968-69 in part as a result of those photos. (See: **Whole Earth Catalog**)

bread money. Another term adopted from the beatnik period. Evolved from the time when money was called "dough."

break or **give me a break** relief, an opportunity, a pause in any activity. Examples: "The band took a **break** and gave us a **break** from their noise."

break (one's) **balls** to exert pressure on someone. Example: "Don't **break my balls** over something I can't do anything about." It can also mean to work hard. Example: "He **broke his balls** to get the job done." Balls refer to testicles.

break dancing part acrobatic, part pantomime dance form developed on the streets of New York City in the mid-1970s by young Blacks. It is characterized by floor back spins, leg splits and many dance steps that originated from jump rope and double-Dutch moves. The dancers, called b-boys and fly girls, performed to **disco** music from musicians like **James Brown**, **Funkadelic** and **Sly and the Family Stone**. These street dancers listened to early rap from disc jockeys like Kool Herc, Afrika Bambaataa and Pete "**DJ**" Jones.

breast-man or **tit-man** a man who is attracted to women primarily by the appearance of their breasts.

Breatharian someone who lives on air alone. It was likely a hoax, but there were people who reportedly lived for long periods of time, some said indefinitely, on breath alone. **Dick Gregory** was a proponent for a period, while he was fasting against violence. (See: **Dick Gregory**)

breath of fire a breathing technique employed in meditation and **yoga** exercise. Normally performed in the seated yoga position, with legs crossed under the body and the back straight. The breaths are taken rapidly, in and out through the nose in a determined number. Nine or numbers divisible by nine might be appropriate since it is an auspicious number in yoga and the Hindu culture. After breathing, the hands and arms are raised above the head, where thumbs touch, and then lowered upon releasing the last breath. Breath disciplines are important in cleansing the blood and bringing a more oxygenated flow to the brain and body. Rapid breathing also causes lightheadedness, and therefore simulates a spiritual or **psychoactive** experience.

breeder someone who has children. A **homosexual** term for a **heterosexual**.

brew beer.

brew a mixture or combination of drugs that creates strange visions. Song lyrics from **Cream**, "Strange **brew**, see what's inside of you."

brewski a humorous term for beer.

brick a **kilogram** of **marijuana**, 2.2 pounds, which often came in a pressed, **brick**-shaped block.

bring (someone) **down** to depress someone or to introduce them to harsh reality. Examples: "Don't **bring me down** with your persimmons of pessimism."

bringdown a disappointment or awakening to reality. Example: "The invoice from her ex-lover was a real **bringdown**."

bring it on I'm ready. I'm prepared for whatever you confront me with.

bring it to me I'm ready. Give me your best shot.

British invasion the predominance of British music and culture that hit the United States in the mid-1960s. It was initiated by the popularity of **The Beatles** and sustained by other British musical groups, such as **The Rolling Stones** and **The Who**.   A number of British words and phrases were adopted in the **counterculture** because of the music invasion and a fascination with England. The strange thing about this was that most British songwriters used American English words and terms in their songs because of the huge market of record buyers in America.

bro' a male greeting to a good friend. Short for brother.   Not necessarily directed at a true sibling.   Example: "What's happening, **bro'**?"   Originally an African American slang term.

broad a derogatory term for a woman. It most likely comes from the fact that the female body is generally broader in the hips than a man's body. Anatomically, this is to accommodate childbirth.

broke-ass or **brogass** in bad shape. It can also mean to be without money, but it became a broader term during the hippie era to indicate a variety of troubles. Often pronounced "bro-gas." Example: "His woman left him and he's **broke-ass**." An African American slang term.

Bronner's Soap or **Dr. Bronner's Soap, All-One** pure-castile soap marketed by Dr. E. H. Bronner (1908-1997), a third-generation master soap maker.   His family's soap business originated in Heilbronn, Germany in the mid-19th century.   Dr. Bronner's life is summarized by the words on his gravestone: *A Life Dedicated To God, Mankind & Spaceship Earth.* Bronner spent much of his life searching for "God and Full Truth" and passed on these wisdoms in his own eccentric writings on the labels of his soap. Dr. Bronner saw his soap as a messenger for his vision of truth and morality. His spiritual messages on the soaps were neither understood nor agreed with by everyone who bought them, yet his product was used religiously by many members of the **counterculture**.   The smell of his peppermint castile soap was nearly as prominent at **Grateful Dead** concerts as was **marijuana** or **patchouli oil**. Dr. Bronner was one of the original **environmental** businessmen of the last century. The labels of his pure-castile soaps became a medium for his vision of global unity and peace. After Bronner's death, his family pledged to continue to produce the fine, ecological soaps he had made for 50 years and to share profits with employees and other worthwhile causes.

brother a close male friend, or someone of like mind, no blood relation necessary. Began as a Black term for other Blacks, but was adopted by the hippie culture.

brotherhood the brotherhood of motorcycle riders, most often refers to **Harley-Davidson** club riders.

Brotherhood of Eternal Love (BEL) a religious group created by John Griggs and friends. They started a **head shop** called Mystic Arts World on Pacific Coast Highway near Los Angeles, California. **Timothy Leary** sympathetically called them a **cult** of **dope dealers**. BEL was started on the inspiration of Leary's book, *Start Your Own Religion.*

brothers' handshake a handshake between close friends. Originally a Black counterculture gesture, which was adopted by hippies. It is accomplished by griping the thumb of another person, bringing palms together. The hands are often held to the chest, bringing the two friends closer together.

brought down depressed or saddened by the words or actions of another person. Example: "Ruffin was **brought down** by Star's 'get lost' ultimatum."

Brower, David Ross (1912- 2000) one of the world's leading conservationists from the early 1950s. The architect and director of the **Sierra Club** from 1952 to 1969, and founder of **Friends of the Earth** in 1969, of which he served as president until 1979.

brown, brown powder or **brown stuff** (See: **heroin**)

brown acid the **acid** that one of the announcers told the crowd to avoid at **Woodstock**, 1969. Brown acid was actually most often mescaline, which is synthesized peyote.

Brown Berets a pro-Mexican-American militant organization similar to the **Black Panthers**.

Brown, H. Rap (b. Hubert Gerold Brown, 1943-) (has since changed his name to Jamil Abdullah Al-Amin) *social issues* a **militant civil rights** leader and chairman of the **Student Nonviolent Coordinating Committee (SNCC)**, 1967-68. He later served as the **Black Panthers'** minister of justice. In 1967, he was arrested and later convicted of

inciting to riot in Cambridge, Maryland. Upon failing to appear for trial in 1970, Brown was placed on the FBI's Ten Most Wanted List. He was shot and captured by New York City police in 1971, found guilty of armed robbery and sentenced to 5 to 15 years. Brown was released from prison in 1977 and converted to the Darul Islam **(Black Muslim)** movement. As of 2002, he is in prison in Atlanta, Georgia, on trial for allegedly killing a sheriff's deputy. Al-Amin also is the leader of a **mosque** and owns a grocery store in Atlanta.

**Brown, Helen Gurley (1922-) *social issues* author of the 1962 book, *Sex and the Single Girl*. It was a real opening salvo in the feminist fight by advocating more sexual freedom for women. Brown was eventually rejected by many feminists as being too "giggly and male-flattering." She was the editor of *Cosmopolitan* magazine from 1965 to 1997.

Brown, James, "The Godfather of Soul," "The Hardest Working Man in Show Business," "Soul Brother Number One" (b. May 3, 1933, Barnwell, SC) *soul, blues, rock & roll* one of the best known and most successful Black artists of the 1960s and early 1970s. He has never had a number one hit, yet only two acts charted more top-forty songs in the 1960s and 1970s than Brown with 43. **Elvis** had 69, and **The Beatles**, 47. Brown has worked hard on stage and off to create an image, some of which is not so savory, while other parts are saintly. One of his songs, **"Say It Loud, I'm Black and I'm Proud,"** was an anthem for the Black Pride movement. He has sponsored youth programs in ghettos, invested in Black businesses, performed for troops in Vietnam, and appeared on television to speak out against violence following **Martin Luther King**'s assassination. In the 1970s, Brown promoted himself as "The Original **Disco** Man," a claim many agree with. In recent years, he has even embraced rap. Without James Brown, the world would be less exciting, and disco would be without **soul**. Inducted into The Rock and Roll Hall of Fame in 1986.

Brown, Jerry (b. Edmund Gerald Brown, Jr., 1938-) *social issues* a political maverick and son of former California governor Edmund G. "Pat" Brown, he himself was the Democratic Governor of California from 1975 to 1983. A Jesuit novice, attorney and California Secretary of State from 1970 to 1974. After his governorship, he studied Zen Buddhism in Japan and was a candidate for President of the United States in 1976 and 1992. Called **Governor Moonbeam** because of his liberal and counterculture activities. Brown became Mayor of Oakland, California, in 1998.

Brown, Rita Mae (1944-) *social issues* writer, editor and outspoken **lesbian**. Author of *Rubyfruit Jungle* in 1973. Active in the **National Organization of Women (NOW)**, she served as editor of the New York chapter newsletter in 1969. Brown was first to raise the lesbian question within NOW. Resigned from NOW in 1970 during the first lesbian purge. (See: **Women's Movement Events, Groups and Leaders** starting on page 591 and **Gay and Lesbian Movement Events, Groups and Leaders** on page 601 in **Lists** at the back of this book)

Browne, Jackson (b. Oct. 9, 1948, Heidelberg, West Germany) *rock & roll* White rock and sociopolitical singer/songwriter. Played backup for

Tim Buckley in the late 1960s and wrote songs for **The Eagles**, **The Byrds**, **Bonnie Raitt** and **Linda Ronstadt**. Brown's first three albums, *Jackson Browne: Saturate Before Using* in 1972, *For Everyman* in 1973 and *Late for the Sky* in 1974, provided an emotional direction for many of us during that time. *Saturate Before Using* is one of the most spiritually moving records ever produced.

browned off mad.

brownie-hound a **homosexual** male. From a perverted comparison between feces and chocolate and the practice of homosexual **anal sex**.

Brownie Mary (b. Mary Jane Rathbun, 1922-1999) a volunteer for **AIDS** patients at San Francisco General Hospital for over 17 years and during the height of the epidemic in the late 1980s. She was a superb baker and eventually began dispensing baked goods laced with **marijuana**, which relieved AIDS victims' nausea and pain. It is not known exactly when Rathbun started to incorporate marijuana into her brownie mix; even though she most likely began in the 1980s, she is still a product of and important to the hippie era influences today. Mrs. Rathbun, along with Dennis Peron, founded the San Francisco **Cannabis** Buyers' Club, which provided marijuana for medicinal purposes. Her hospital dispensing and involvement with the Cannabis Club resulted in Rathbun's being arrested several times. One prosecutor warned, "Bringing to trial a grandmother who bakes pot brownies would attract too much sympathy," but the authorities still pursued prosecution. Mrs. Rathbun received only a minimal sentence of community service (which she served at the hospital); yet, as predicted, Brownie Mary became a national figure and her notoriety helped lead to the legalization of medicinal marijuana in California in 1996. The hospital where Mary dispensed her "goodies" designated $1 million for research into the benefits of medicinal marijuana, and similar studies have since been established elsewhere in America. In her earlier years, Rathbun had campaigned for miners' rights and abortion rights, and she often call herself an anarchist.

brownie points credit for a job well down. Originally derived from the points that girls accumulated to reach levels of achievement in the "Brownies," a club to which younger girls belonged before entering Girl Scouts. It also indicates achievement in competition for romance. Example: "He lost **brownie points** for that belly flop on the bed." Also related to brown-nosing or kissing someone's ass to achieve a place of status.

brown-nose n. a person who flatters others for dubious reasons. An **ass kisser**.

brown-nose v. to flatter someone or (figuratively) **kiss someone's ass**.

brown rice the basis for the Zen **macrobiotic** diet. It became a joke that living on brown rice was necessary for membership into the hippie culture. It stopped being a joke when people began to die from following strict macrobiotic diets. Unlike Asian cultures that were accustomed to such diets, the previously meat-eating hippie was vulnerable to sickness and even death from deficiencies in a strictly brown rice and vegetable diet. Vegetarian diets can be beneficial to most people, but one should begin them with a basic knowledge of nutrition. Brown rice is a very healthy food and an excellent source of fiber.

Brown Shoes agents of the Federal Bureau of Investigation (FBI). A **Weathermen** term as related by **Bill Ayers** in his 2001 book *Fugitive Days: a memoir*, published by Beacon Press. It was eventually shortened to "**Shoes.**" Referring to the nondescript brown shoes worn by FBI agents and also to the earlier term gumshoe. (See: **Bill Ayers** and **Weathermen**)

brown sugar or **brown stuff** an African American woman. Normally used in sexual connotations. Brown stuff is the more derogatory term; brown sugar can be a compliment. **2.** The title of a 1971 **Rolling Stones'** hit song "Brown Sugar."

Bruce, Lenny (b. Leonard Alfred Schneider, Oct. 13, 1925, Mineola, New York; d. Aug. 3, 1966, Los Angeles, Calif.) *social issues* comedian, social commentator. Born into a burlesque and comedian family, he was a US navy recruit at 16 and saw action during WWII. After the war, he began a career as a standup comedian in all the seedy nightclubs across the United States. In his notorious rise to fame, he attacked all the hypocrisy, bigotry and greed of America's conservative establishment. As a **heroin** addict, starving entertainer and beat generation icon-to-be, he associated with all the leading **counterculture** malcontents of the era; through his cutting social commentary, he influenced every **liberal** and **anti-establishment** spokesperson to come. Arrested at least 20 times on obscenity charges for his standup comedy routines. Jailed, harassed, bankrupt, close to eviction, he died of a drug overdose in the bathroom of his home.

No other person was a louder voice against American hypocrisy than Lenny Bruce. "I'm not a comedian. And I'm not sick. The world is sick and I'm the doctor. I'm a surgeon with a scalpel for false values. I don't have an act. I just talk. I'm just Lenny Bruce...."

BS short for **bull shit**. Bull shit is a lie, an exaggeration or fabrication.

B.S.U. (See: **Black Student Union**)

bubba a sarcastic term for a large, awkward person. It sometimes had racial connotations. Considered a Southern expression. **2.** slowly, it gained use as a sarcastic form of endearment for a friend or acquaintance. The amount of endearment depended on the person or situation.

bubblegum someone or something juvenile or childish. Example: "That party was **bubblegum**."

bubblehead someone dumb. A term usually reserved for a not-so-intelligent, woman.

buck a strong, young Black male. It can be a complimentary, but sometimes it is offensive and derogatory as in the **Redneck** term "buck Nigger."

buck (ass) **naked** without clothing. Rural Southern colloquialism.

Buckley, Lord (b. Richard Buckley in California) (1906-1960) standup comedian and **jazz** club owner. Legend has it that he was a marathon dancer in the 1920s and traveled with carnivals. During the Depression, he had a jazz club in Chicago, the Suzie Q, where bizarre ceremonies of his Church of the Living Swing took place, with belly dancers replacing choirboys. At this time, he appointed himself Lord. "People should worship people," was his gospel. A White man with the voice and hip vocabulary of the Black ghetto. "Negroes spoke a language of such power, purity and beauty that I found it irresistible," Lord Buckley said of himself, "I couldn't resist this magical way of speaking." He learned the street talk of the Black musicians with whom he shared the stage. Buckley could do 10-minute monologues with jazz-like rhythm and tempo improvisations. Some say that his speech was raw, yet intimate, the way Charlie Parker played. Buckley was a comic who made people laugh, but he was more of a storyteller, discussing supermarkets, the bomb and historic events. When Lord Buckley died in a hotel room in 1960, his jazz friends, Dizzy Gillespie and Ornette Coleman, played at his memorial service.

Buckley, Tim (b. Feb. 14, 1947, Washington, D.C.; d. June 29, 1975, Santa Monica, Calif.) White **folk** and early **rock** singer/songwriter. One of the late folk musicians who influenced many rock musicians into becoming more social and political in their music.

Buckley, William F. Jr. (1925-) journalist, author, political conservative, son of a wealthy oilman. A graduate of Yale University in 1951, he founded the conservative *National Review* magazine in 1955 and served as its editor until 1990. Buckley hosted the political issues discussion television program "Firing Line" beginning in 1966. His books include a series of popular spy novels. He has been called a conservative intellectual, the only person to be so named. A conservative intellectual is actually an economist. It *is* an oxymoron to be intellectual and conservative. Pedantic and erudite, Buckley's communiques are often impossible to comprehend, yet as the Republican poster boy, he receives the approval of most conservatives, regardless of whether or not they understand him. I keep expecting William F. Buckley, Jr., to wake up one morning and look in the mirror and say, "Oh my God, what have I done? Due to what others perceive that I have said, this world is going to destruct in a conflagration of arrogance, greed and poverty-driven anarchism." But Buckley will probably never recant; it is for history to condemn him.

Bucky Fuller (See: **Fuller, Buckminster**)

bud *drugs* the **flower** bud of the **marijuana** plant that contains the more potent **resins**. The most sought after part of the plant, yet, throughout much of the 1960s and 70s, most people smoked only the leaf and seldom saw the flowers.

bud short for buddy. Example: "Hey, you're my **bud**. Don't worry, I wouldn't hit on your chick."

Buddha an **enlightened** and wise individual who has attained perfect wisdom. Specifically, **Gautama Siddhartha**, founder of **Buddhism** in the sixth century B.C. (See: **Gautama Siddhartha**)

Buddha head a derogatory name for a person of Asian descent.

Buddha nature the spiritual personality of a human being.

Buddha stick or **Buddha Thai** *drugs* (See: **Thai stick**)

Buddhi Sanskrit word meaning Universal Mind.

Buddhism *religion* East Asian religion founded on the teachings of **Gautama Buddha**, 563 B.C.-483 B.C. Born Prince **Gautama Siddhartha** in what is now

Nepal, he was a pampered member of the ruling class, who chose at 29 years of age to give it up to become a poor

philosopher. **Buddhism** deals mainly with "four noble truths": addressing suffering, the cause of suffering, the way to cease suffering and the way to ease suffering. Thus, Buddhism emphasizes spiritual and physical discipline to attain a state of liberation from the conflicts of life. (See: **Gautama Siddhartha, Mhayana, Theravada and Bodhisattva**)

buff physically well-shaped (female) or muscular (male). It is a term and way of life that evolved in the 1970s, particularly in the male homosexual world, yet it really came into its own in the **me generation** of the 1980s.

buff someone who is extremely interested and knowledgeable about a particular subject. Example: "He's a car **buff,** she's a guys-who-are-interested-in-cars **buff**."

Buffalo Springfield *rock & roll* a band formed in Los Angeles in 1966, Stephen Stills (b. Jan. 3, 1945, Dallas, Tex), gtr., kybds., bass, voc.; **Neil Young** (b. Nov. 12, 1945, Toronto, Can.), gtr., voc.; Richie Furay (b. May 9, 1944, Dayton, Ohio), voc., gtr.; Dewey Martin (b. Sept. 39, 1942, Chesterville, Can.), voc., drums; Bruce Palmer (b. 1946, Liverpool, Can.), bass. Even though it was short lived, this band influenced many musicians, introduced country rock to many fans and spawned the most popular super group of the era, *Crosby, Stills, Nash and Young*. Their one top-40 hit, "For What It's Worth" in 1967, is one of the classic songs of that revolutionary time. Inducted into the Rock and Roll Hall of Fame in 1997.

Buffett, Jimmy (b. Dec. 25, 1946, Pascagoula, Miss.) *rock & roll* this singer/songwriter is in a class by himself; he is personally responsible for the now monumental popularity of tequila and the margarita with his 1977 hit single, "Margaritaville." Irreverence is his territory with song titles like "Why Don't We Get Drunk (and Screw)" and "My Head Hurts, My Feet Stink and I Don't Love Jesus." He is the head beach bum and drunken sailor. Buffett started churning them out in 1970 and hasn't stopped yet.

Bug a Volkswagen passenger car. The small, round, dumpy, lovable car also called a "Beetle." (See: **Volkswagen Bug** and **Baha bug**)

bug n. an enthusiast. Synonymous with **buff**. Example: "He's a car **bug,** she's a bug in his rug."

bug v. to bother or annoy. Probably comes from the annoyance created by insects. Example: "You **bug** me; bug off!"

bugger *sex* in many forms, it relates to the practice of anal sex. Reportedly derived from the name of heretics from Bulgaria called *Bogomil* (lovers of God) who were said to indulge in "unnatural acts," such as sodomy.

bug off go away, leave me alone. Example: "You bug me; **bug off!**"

bug out to go or leave in a hurry.

built physically strong or well-developed. Can be directed toward males or females. Often relates to a woman with large breasts.

built-in obsolescence (See: **planned obsolescence**)

bull or **bullshit** lies or deceit.

Bull Connor (See: **Connor, Bull**)

bull dyke or **bulldyke** a **lesbian**, most often used as a derogatory term. The more masculine or dominant female in a lesbian relationship. **Fem** is the term for the more feminine member of a lesbian relationship.

bull or **bulls** the police.

Bullroarer the English name for an instrument of **magic** and defense used by Australian **aborigines** and Navajo Indians. It is whirled through the air, around the head, making a sound like thunder, which is believed to frighten away evil spirits.

bum n. British term for buttocks. Adopted by **counterculture** America along with many other British words and **fads**.

bum v. to beg or borrow.

bummer "Too bad." A bad occurrence, a bum trip.

bump heads to fight or argue.

bumping bellies, bumping tummies or **bumping bones** *sex* sexual intercourse.

bum rap an accusation of which one feels he or she is innocent. A bad situation or mistaken suspicion. **Bum** is synonymous with **bad**. The term bum meaning bad was an old usage, revitalized by the hippie culture.

bum trip a bad drug experience. A bad occurrence.

bunny a sexually promiscuous female.

"bunny law" *social issues* the **Civil Rights Act of 1964** has an amendment sometimes called the bunny law. Michigan Democratic Congresswoman **Martha Griffiths** suggested that the word "sex" be added to **Title VII** of the Civil Rights Act of 1964, thus prohibiting discrimination on the basis of gender in employment, public accommodations, publicly owned facilities, union membership, and federally funded programs. This addition to the Act raised the question of **bona-fide occupational qualifications (bfoq's)**, which stipulates that an employer cannot be required to give both sexes equal consideration if a job genuinely needs to be filled by one sex rather than the other; for example, a movie director cannot be required to hire a female to play a male role. This dilemma also raised the question of whether the Playboy Clubs would be required to hire male "bunnies." The press immediately dubbed the sex amendment the "bunny law." The Playboy Clubs did eventually hire male "bunnies," but not because of this law. (See: **Title VII**) (See also: **Women's Movement Events, Groups and Leaders** starting on page 591 in the **Lists** at the end of this book)

buns the posterior or **ass** of a person. Refers to the two, round buttocks.

burn to cheat or steal. **2.** bogus substances purchased as drugs.

burn or **burned** a social embarrassment. An example of one-upmanship. Examples: "What a **burn** asking Bob for a date in front of John, while sitting on Gary's lap."

burn to light and smoke **dope**. Example: "Let's **burn** a bowl of your new shit?"

"burn, baby, burn" the battle cry of **radical** political **demonstrators** or rioters. Thought to refer to the fires of Watts, Los Angeles, during the race riots of August, 1965.

burned mad.

*burned cheated. Examples: "He got **burned** investing in a nauga ranch."

burned arrested.

Burning Spear (b. Winston Rodney, March 1, 1945, St. Ann's Parish, Jamaica) *reggae* one of the most respected Black **Rastafarian** musicians. His music has always been about Black freedom, pride and history.

burnout n. someone who is **destroyed** by **drugs**.

burn out v. to reach a saturation point with something. To get tired of something. **2.** to be destroyed by drugs.

Burroughs, William S. II (alias Doctor Benway) (b. Feb. 5, 1914; d. Aug. 2, 1997) beat poet and outspoken **homosexual**. One of the major forces in the **beatnik movement**, along with **Allen Ginsberg, Jack Kerouac, Lawrence Ferlinghetti, Gary Snyder, LeRoi Jones, Diane di Prima**, Frank O'Hara and a few other poets, writers and artists. Burroughs and his friends verbalized the unspoken thoughts of intellectuals and many people of the **working class**. By expressing their distaste and distrust of American hypocrisy and **materialism**, they made the hippie era possible. Their philosophies would become the basis of the rebellions of the 1960s and 1970s. William Burroughs' grandfather, who shared his name, invented the adding machine and founded the company that bears his name, yet William Burroughs II chose poetry as his expression and his force. Burroughs, by virtue of his age and longevity, could be considered a father of the beat generation and grandfather of the hippie culture. He is credited by many with

William Burroughs

introducing **psychedelics** into our culture, at one time consulting with **Timothy Leary** in 1960-1961 about his experiences with **yage** and other **hallucinogenic** drugs. Burroughs is also credited with coining the term **heavy metal**, which he used in *The Naked Lunch*. Because of its explicit sex and violence, *The Naked Lunch* was the subject of a pivotal obscenity trial. His publications include *Junkie* (as William Lee), 1953; *The Naked Lunch*, 1959; *The Soft Machine*, 1961; *The Yage Letters* (with Allen Ginsberg), 1963; *and Queer*, written in 1953, first published in 1985.

Burton, James *rock & roll* one of the most influential, yet unheralded, guitar players of **rock and roll**. He was the lead guitar player for Ricky Nelson in

the 1950s, played with **Elvis Presley** for years, and has backed up numerous other artists, such as **Jerry Lee Lewis, Aretha Franklin, Emmylou Harris** and **The Mamas and the Papas**. Inducted into the Rock and Roll Hall of Fame in 2001.

bus invariably a **Volkswagen**, a house on wheels, sometimes known as the **sin bin** because of the activity that often took place inside. A common sign found on buses was, "**If you see it rockin', don't come knockin'**."

bush pubic hair. Most often related to a woman's anatomy.

business used in the **counterculture** to mean anything to do with selling or negotiating for **dope**. Example: "I got to go down the street and do some **business**."

business deception or **flim-flam**. Example: "He gave me the **business** and got all my money."

businessman's special *drugs* **dimethyltryptamine (DMT)**, a short-acting hallucinogen that can be either a synthetic or extracted from **yopo beans**, epená or Sonoran Desert toad. Active ingredient, dimethyltryptamine; street names, businessman's trip or **cohoba snuff**. Called this because, theoretically, a businessman can use it for a short period during the day and return to work. (See: **cohoba snuff, yakee** or **dimethyltryptamine**)

busing *social issues* the effort to redistribute the ethnic balance within schools by transporting Blacks out of ghettos into White schools and Whites into Black ghetto schools. This was done in an effort to improve the quality of education and teach ethnic diversity and communication between the races. It was an experiment that had a great deal of opposition in both ethnic cultures, and, in the long run, it caused a great deal of violence with the value of its effectiveness still in question. (See: **Civil Rights Events, Demonstrations and Legislation** in **Lists** at the back of this book)

bust to arrest. To catch someone in an embarrassing or compromising situation.

bust chops or **bust my chops** to bother or pressure someone. From **jazz** language in which **chops** are musical notes played on an instrument (or **ax**), and busting is interrupting the music.

*busted arrested, caught.

busted broke, without money.

bust my hump or **bust** (one's) **hump** to work hard, to exert effort.

busting heads hitting someone over the head. Occasionally done by law enforcement officers when dispersing **civil rights** and **anti-war demonstrators**.

butch a strong, assertive person. Most often used to describe the more masculine or dominant member of a **gay** or **lesbian** relationship.

Butterfield, Paul (b. Dec. 17, 1942, Chicago, Ill.; d. May 4, 1987, North Hollywood, Calif.) *blues, rock & roll* a White **blues** and **rock** singer and harmonica player who influenced many with his passion for the blues. He learned his craft from the greats in Chicago's South Side clubs when he was a teenager, eventually working his way up on the stages to jam with the likes of Buddy Guy, Howlin' Wolf, Little Walter and Otis Rush. Later, after forming his **Paul Butterfield Blues Band**, he played and recorded with many of the best artists of the time, working with **Bob Dylan**, **Muddy Waters**, Rick Danko and others. Butterfield's alcohol-related illness and death in 1987 cut short a talented career.

Butterfield Blues Band, Paul *blues, rock & roll* formed in Chicago, Illinois, in 1963, **Paul Butterfield** (b. Dec. 17, 1942, Chicago; d. May 4, 1987, North Hollywood, Calif.), voc., harmonica; **Michael Bloomfield** (b. July 28, 1944, Chicago, Ill.; d. Feb. 15, 1981, San Francisco, Calif.), gtr.; Elvin Bishop (b. Oct. 21, 1942, Tulsa, Okla.), gtr.; Mark Naftalin, kybds.; Jerome Arnold, bass; Sam Lay, drums. A mostly White **blues** band, it was the first important group in the blues revival. Along with **The Blues Project**, it was responsible for introducing blues to adventurous young musicians and new White audiences, thus laying the groundwork for sophisticated, future **rock and roll**. The band dissolved in 1972.

buttfuck, butt-fuck or **buttfucker, butt-fucker** a male **homosexual**. **2.** A detestable person, not related to homosexuality or **sodomy**. Example: "She's a **buttfuck**."

buttfuck, butt-fuck or **buttfucker, butt-fucker** to **sodomize**, **heterosexual** or **homosexual** activity. To do something detestable to another human being unrelated to homosexuality or sodomy.

button *sex* an endearing name for the **clitoris**.

button, to push someone's to get someone annoyed or mad, to start someone's anger.

buttoned-down mind conservative. Someone who is closed-minded to new ideas and emotions. From a reference to buttoned-down collars on conservative dress shirts worn by "business type" people in the 1960s and 70s. Example:

"He has a **buttoned-down** mind, and he's too straight to understand that's not a compliment."

buttons *drugs* a name for the round **top** of a **peyote cactus**, which is ingested for its **hallucinogenic** properties.

butt out mind your own business.

butt ugly very ugly, resembling someone's rear end. It originally was a cowboy term. How it made the transition from the cowboy culture to the hippie culture is a mystery since not a lot traveled between those two lifestyles during that period.

buy *drugs* to buy **drugs**. Example: "Did you make a **buy**?"

buy into to accept as fact or to agree with something. Originally a physical action that became an emotional concept during the hippie era. It possibly came from "I don't buy it."

buy off to bribe someone with money or goods.

buy the farm to die. From the fact that many farmers have life insurance policies to pay the debt on their farm at their death.

buzz something happening. Example: "What's the **buzz**?"

buzz or **buzz on** something exciting. Something uplifting that affects a person either physically or emotionally. Often pertains to the effects of **drugs**. Similar usage as **zing**. Examples: "I got a **buzz** from that dance." "I got a **buzz on** from her love in."

buzz off interj. don't bother me.

B.Y.O.B. acronym for **B**ring **Y**our **O**wn **B**ottle. There were many variations during the hippie era, such as bring your own **bud** (**marijuana**), bring your own **body** (**sex partner**).

Byrds, The *rock & roll* a Los Angeles band formed in 1964 that pioneered **folk rock** and **country rock**. The group had a number of solid hits, including **Dylan's** "**Mr. Tambourine Man**" and **Pete Seeger's** treatment of a biblical passage set to music, "Turn! Turn! Turn!" The band is most notable for its musicians who went on to do other things. **David Crosby** (b. David Van Cortland, Aug. 14, 1941, Los Angeles, Calif.), gtr., voc., went on to join Crosby, Stills, Nash and Young. Roger McGuinn (b. James Joseph McGuinn III, July 13, 1942, Chicago, Ill.), gtr., voc., had been a member of the Limelighters and The Chad Mitchell Trio and backed up **Judy Collins**. McGuinn later played with many people and had a solo career of some note. The Byrds recorded two albums in 1968, *The Notorious Byrd Brothers* and *Sweetheart of the Rodeo*, which greatly influenced later folk rock and country rock groups, such as Tom Petty, **Fleetwood Mac** and **The Eagles**. Inducted into The Rock and Roll Hall of Fame in 1991.

byte *computer revolution* a unit of computer information equal to approximately 8 **bits**. A bit is a decision in the computing process of a computer. A computer is a tool like a hand. A hand has five fingers; a computer can have millions of bytes. The number of bytes depends on the power of the computer and also determines the power of the computer.

Byte Shop *computer revolution* one of the world's first computer stores. Located in Mountain View, California, and owned by Paul Terrell. Terrell was the first person to place an order for the first **Apple computer** (**Apple 1**). He bought fifty units in July, 1976, after a barefoot **Steve Jobs** walked in to make a sales call.

C

C street term for **cocaine**. (See: **cocaine**)

C and H *drugs* a mixture of **cocaine** and **heroin**.

C and M *drugs* a mixture of **cocaine** and **morphine**.

cactus *drugs* **peyote**, a small **psychedelic** plant used as a sacrament in **Native American** religious ceremonies and eventually used as an educational and **recreational drug** by hippies. (See: **peyote**)

Cadillac *drugs* an ounce of **heroin**.

California Cooler, wine cooler or **wine spritzer** a mixture of cheap, red wine and 7-Up. A drink originally concocted in the 1960s by surfers and volleyball players on the beaches of Southern California. It was an effort to dress up bad wine, giving it a refreshing taste and "fruity bouquet."

California Marijuana Initiative (CMI) *drugs* a group that tried in the early 1970s to get an initiative legalizing **marijuana** on the California ballot. They patterned the restrictions, taxing and sales regulations after the already established liquor controls in the state. CMI was formed in early 1972 by Leo Paoli, John Kaplan and Robert Ashford. Unsuccessful in getting legalization on the ballot in 1972 and 1975, they lobbied and finally convinced the State of California to decriminalize possession of small amounts of marijuana in 1975.

California neon dust pointillist particles, **psychedelic** decor, **eyelid movies**, **hallucinogenic** visual stuff. **Tom Wolfe** wrote about it in his 1968 book, *Electric Kool Aid Acid Test*.

call or **call** (someone) **on** (something) to confront or challenge someone on the validity of information. Example: "If I were you, I'd **call him on** that story of accidently running into your wife at the motel."

calling card something left behind showing that someone was there. Not literally a business card in this context. Example: "Your dog left his **calling card** on my front lawn." **2.** needle marks or tracks made by intravenous drug injection.

Cambridge, Massachusetts the location of Massachusetts Institute of Technology (MIT) and Harvard University. Similar to **Berkeley, California**, it was a **liberal** student community from which a great deal of **anti-war** protest and **counterculture** activity grew.

camp or **campy** something considered silly by the **counterculture** that is popular with the decadent upper or upper-middle class. Examples: convertible cars are camp, paper dresses are camp, racketball is camp. A term introduced into **mainstream** American culture in 1965, it was originally an English theatrical term describing young, male actors dressed as women. **2.** in the late 1970s, this word began to be used to describe **ultracool** fads or counterculture spoofs on straight society. Pink flamingos are camp, beat up old convertibles are camp, wearing a prom dress to a barbecue is camp.

can *drugs* a 3/4 ounce bag of cheap, Mexican **marijuana**. Also called a **bad**

ounce, and on the West Coast called a **lid**.

Cancer astrological sign, June 21 to July 22, fourth house of the **zodiac**, cardinal water sign, symbolized by the crab. Traits: sensitivity and possessiveness. Self-perception: I feel.

candy *drugs* any number of illegal drugs, most notably **cocaine** and **heroin**. Liquid **LSD** dropped on a **sugar cube**.

candy ass a **wimp**, a weak or easily frightened person. **2.** something cheap, ineffectual or worthless.

candy man *drugs* a drug **dealer** or **pusher**.

can it save it for someone else or some other time. Comes from, I believe, "Put it in a can and preserve it for later."

cannabinoids *drugs* the different compounds found in **cannabis** that cause the **psychoactive** effects that make it popular to smoke or ingest.

cannabis *drugs* Moraceae, a genus of widely cultivated annual plants. Also called **hemp**. The stem fiber of the plant is used to make twine, rope and coarse fabrics. Cannabis is also a drug with many medicinal uses. In America, the leaf and flower of this plant are called **marijuana** and are smoked for their euphoric qualities. A stronger narcotic is made from the oils of the plant, and this is called **hashish**. THC (tetrahydrocannabinol) is the chemical substance in this plant that creates the **psychoactive** state. Euphoric drugs derived from cannabis have been illegal in America since the uncontested passage by Congress of the Marijuana Tax Act of 1937. (See: **marijuana**)

Cannabis indica *drugs* one of the major varieties of **cannabis**. It is primarily native to Afghanistan and is sometimes called *Cannabis afghanica*.

cannabis oil *drugs* a liquid concentrate of **cannabis** made by dissolving **marijuana** in organic solvents, such as alcohol or ethers, to extract the **THC**. Cannabis oil is used like hashish or mixed with some form of tobacco and smoked. Hash oil is similar, except the extract comes from already processed **hashish**.

Cannabis sativa *drugs* one of the major varieties of cannabis. It is considered to be native to India. The most popular smoke among connoisseurs.

Canned Heat *blues/rock & roll* a California band formed in 1965, whose classic hits of the era included "On the Road Again" and "Going Up the Country." It burst on the scene at **Monterey Pop**, played at **Woodstock** and was featured at the beginning of the "Woodstock" movie. In 1970, co-founder Al Wilson died, and in 1981, co-founder and lead singer Bob Hite ("Bear") died, but the other members carried on with various personnel changes. Guitarist Harvey Mandel was a member for a while. One memorable album was the 1989 collaboration with bluesman **John Lee Hooker** called *Hooker and Heat*.

cap *drugs* a capsule of drugs. The growth of language has two different directions, expansion and contraction. Expansion involves grouping words together into phrases and creating longer words to expand a thought; contraction is the process of shortening these words and phrases after their meanings are well established.

cap to kill someone. To verbally humiliate someone.

capeesh? do you understand? A perversion of the Italian word *capisci*, meaning to understand.

capitalist someone who lives off the proceeds of their capital, which is invested money. The meaning of this term has evolved during the last 50 years due to changes in the economy. Now one of the basic definitions is "a greedy person." The hippie definition would be someone who lives off the blood, sweat and tears of other people. True capitalists need not work to maintain their lifestyle, because their money is working for them. Very few people are technically capitalists, since most individuals must work for others in order to receive a salary. Not all business owners are capitalists since they must physically work to maintain their business and income. A large number of business people think they are capitalists and act like capitalists, therefore, they warrant the negative capitalist label. Many people strive to become capitalists, and that is why they vote Republican, thinking the other capitalists will help them to obtain wealth. In the philosophy of the **true hippie,** there is nothing actually wrong with being a capitalist. The problem is that many capitalists have little or no respect or compassion for the people who contribute to their wealth, and they are sys-tematically enslaving the lower classes and destroying the environment. America was founded on the concept of free enterprise, not capitalism. Capitalism is similar to the feudal system from which people were fleeing when they emigrated to America. Many business people take advantage of the benevolent ideals of free enterprise to enslave the working class, and the **counterculture** feels that this is very anti-American behavior. Most intelligent people of the counterculture realize that free enterprise is a valuable and essential element to this world. They don't want to destroy free enterprise, but they would like to educate capitalists to be a little more benevolent in their dealings with the "common" people and the world in which they live. Just as there should be a reasonable minimum wage, there should also be a reasonable maximum profit for any endeavor.

Captain Beefheart (b. Don Van Vliet, Jan.15, 1941, Glendale, Calif.) *rock & roll* a child-prodigy sculptor, Van Vliet met **Frank Zappa** at a young age and moved into music. It is said that Zappa gave him the name Captain Beefheart. Beefheart's irregular and surreal music was an education in what, for good reason, had not been done before. He and Zappa gave a generation of musicians a license to experiment.

Captain Crunch a whistle toy included in Captain Crunch cereal boxes in the late 1960s, which, when blown into a telephone, could clear the phone line, permitting free long-distance calls. **2.** a nickname given to John Draper, a particularly creative "**phone phreak**" in the late 1960s. Draper's creation, the **blue box,** was an illegal, homemade device that produced the proper tones in a telephone to eliminate long-distance charges. (See: **blue box** and **phone phreak**)

Capricorn astrological sign, December 21 to January 20, tenth house of the **zodiac**, cardinal earth sign, symbolized by the ram. Traits: structure and response. Self-perception: I use.

carburetor *drugs* a small hole in a bong, or smoking pipe, that allows the smoker to control the mixture of air and smoke with the touch of a finger. Sometimes the entire pipe with such a hole was called a carburetor.

cardinal signs of the zodiac the four signs that begin each season: **Aries**—spring, **Cancer**—summer, **Libra**—autumn, **Capricorn**—winter.

Carlin, George (b. May 12, 1937, Bronx, New York) comedian, social commentator, actor, writer. Carlin attended parochial school, and much of his negative religious sentiment stems from his experience as a Roman Catholic altar boy. Carlin dropped out of high school after only two years. At age 17, he joined the US Air Force as a computer mechanic. In 1959, Carlin teamed up with Texas newscaster Jack Burns. They collaborated on a radio show in Fort Worth before going to Hollywood, where they met legendary comedian **Lenny Bruce**. Bruce helped Burns and Carlin get appearances on Johnny Carson's "The Tonight Show." The duo eventually split up, and over the next few years Carlin continued to make appearances on "The Tonight Show" and "The Merv Griffin Show." In the early 1960s, Carlin worked standup comedy in Las Vegas and on TV, enjoying moderate success. Then, in the mid-70s, he recreated his image to a more radical approach. Carlin's

routines began to express his disillusionment with the world, exploring more sensitive issues, such as Vietnam and free speech. One of his standup characters was Al Sleet, the Hippy-Dippy Weatherman. In July, 1972, Carlin was arrested for obscenity for his routine, "Seven Words You Can Never Say on Television." Because of his atheist views and **cocaine** use, Carlin received a great deal of ridicule from the establishment, but his outspoken voice for freedom and equality has earned him a following in the **counterculture**. Carlin was the first host of the revolutionary and controversial "Saturday Night Live" TV show, which premiered on October 11, 1975.

Carlos, John *social issues* the Olympic 200-meter dash, bronze medalist at the Mexico City Olympics on November 18, 1968. He and **Tommie Smith,** the gold medalist, displayed the **Black Power** salute upon receiving their awards. They were harshly reprimanded and banned from the remainder of the games. (See: **Black Power** in alphabetical listings) (See also: **Black Power Events and Demonstrations** on page 585 in **Lists** at the back of this book)

Stokely Carmichael speaking at a Black Power rally

Carmichael, Stokely (1941-) *social issues* has since changed his name to **Kwame Ture.** Black **civil rights activist**; chairman of **Student Nonviolent Coordinating Committee (SNCC)**

1966-67. In 1966, Carmichael coined the phrase "Black Power." In 1968, he married South African singer Miriam Makeba. He was prime minister of the **Black Panther Party**, 1968-69. In 1969, Carmichael resigned from leadership of the Black Panthers over differences in the party's principles and went into self-imposed exile in Guinea, where he still resides.

Carnaby Street, London   an obscure alley behind the grand shopping thoroughfare of Regent Street.   In the late 1960s with its wild boutiques and informal **fashions**, Carnaby Street became the most popular retail clothing area of London, producing many of the **mod** fashions of the 1970s.

carnal knowledge sexual experience. If one has carnal knowledge of someone else, then they have had sexual intercourse.   A biblical term that came back into popular use during the hippie era, in part due to the 1971 movie, "Carnal Knowledge."

carrying *drugs* having drugs on your person. Example: "If you're **carrying,** tell me so I can get out of the car."

Carson, Rachel (1907-1964) *social issues* marine biologist, ecologist, teacher and author of the 1962 book, *Silent Spring*, which was one of the most important books of the ecology or "green" movement. *Silent Spring* revealed the dangers of **DDT** and started many people thinking about what we were doing to our **environment**. She also wrote *The Sea Around Us* in 1951.

Carter, James Earl Jr., "Jimmy" (b. October 1, 1924 in Plains, Georgia) Democrat,   the 39th President of the United States from 1977-81.   Graduated from the US Naval Academy in

1946. Served as Governor of Georgia from 1971 to 1975.

cartoons *drugs* drug-induced **hallucinations**.

cartoons (See: **comix**)

cartwheels *drugs* **Benzedrine** or Dexamyl tablets or capsules. **Amphetamine. Uppers**.

case attraction or "infection." Not an actual disease, but a positive attraction to a person, place or situation. Example: "I've got a bad **case** of California."

case a strange person, someone who is a dilemma.   Example: "He's a real **case**." "She's a **case** for serious study."

case *sex* gonorrhea, a sexually transmitted disease. Short for "case of the **clap**." Example: "Be careful what you wish for; you could get a **case** from that girl of your dreams." (See: **clap**)

case v. to inspect someplace. To check out a location, often for some nefarious activity.

Cash, Johnny (b. February 26, 1932, Kingsland, Arkansas) *country rock* one of the major crossover country to rock and roll artists. Along with **Willie Nelson**, **Waylon Jennings** and **Kris Kristofferson**, he is responsible for loosening up the country and western music industry, forcing it to take itself less seriously. A bad boy, but a prolific songwriter, he has inspired a generation of outcasts to dream of better things.

Cassady, Neal (b. 1926; d. February 4, 1968) one of the **beat generation**'s leading names, along with **Allen Ginsberg, Jack Kerouac, William Burroughs** and **Ken Kesey**. Neal was the model for Jack Kerouac's character, Dean Moriarty, in *On the Road*, 1957. Neal's lifestyle alone was more of an influence on the era than anything he wrote or created himself. Through his friendships, and some say love affairs, with several of the best beat writers, he reached a form of immortality. Although a very good corespondent who aspired to be a writer, he never published anything of great importance. In retrospect, he falls somewhere between a **working class** hero and a restless, tortured spirit. Neal suffered a very severe childhood and was more likely to be found at a stock car race than a college lecture forum. When he died in San Miguel de Allende, Mexico, of undetermined drug- and alcohol-related problems, Neal Cassady was described in his obituary as a former railroad conductor.

Castaneda, Carlos (b. December 25, 1931, Sao Paulo, Brazil or 1925, Cajamarca, Peru; d. 1999) author and cultural anthropologist. Educated at the University of California at Los Angeles, receiving a BA in 1962 and a PhD in 1970. Published *The Teachings of Don Juan: A Yaqui Way of Knowledge* in 1968, which he claimed was based on a five-year apprenticeship with a Yaqui Indian sorcerer. The Yaqui live in northwestern Mexico, bordering the United States. This book was hugely popular with the **counterculture** because of its mystical content and primitive wisdom. Because of Castaneda's evasiveness, the fictional quality of the book and its status as part of a cultural fad, many anthropology professionals doubted its authenticity. Castaneda continued publishing a series of popular books, including *A Separate Reality* (1971) and *Tales of Power* (1975). The debate continues as to how much of his writing was true anthropology and how much was based on his own imagination; yet, as spiritual illumination and mystical empowerment, his works are valuable contributions to the era.

Castle, The a large stone castle-like house in the Los Feliz Hills of Los Angeles, California. In 1966, it was a gathering place for members of the **beat** and hippie movement as well as musical and art luminaries, such as **Bob Dylan**, **Andy Warhol**, **Lou Reed**, Nico, **David Crosby** and Robbie Robertson. Owned by John Phillip Law, Tom Law and Jack Simmons, it was the home of future members of the **Hog Farm**, including photographer Lisa Law. Many well known rock artists' photographs were taken at The Castle.

casualty someone who has been psychologically damaged. A person who has been hurt by a social situation. Another word that originally related to a physical situation, but was expanded during the hippie era to encompass emotional or psychological aspects of life as well. **2.** someone who is damaged by drug or alcohol use.

cat a young man; usually a positive term denoting someone who is **cool** and contemporary.

catch an attractive or desirable person.

catch "someone" up, to to expose someone in a lie. To reveal an untruth. Example: "If I **catch him up** telling that story about the cat eating my **stash**, I'll make him smoke the cat."

catch some Z's to sleep. Example: "I got to **catch some Z's** before I get too old."

catnip *drugs* weak **marijuana**. Occasionally, real catnip was sold as marijuana to an unsuspecting buyer or used to **cut** marijuana.

cave or **cave in** to quit or give-in. From "cave in," relating to the collapse of a mining cave.

CB citizens band radio. (See: **citizens band radio**)

CBGB *rock & roll* New York City **punk** club opened in 1973, originally intended to be a **C**ountry, **B**lue**G**rass, **B**lues club from which the acronym comes. It eventually became a punk club and featured such groups as **Blondie**, **Patti Smith**, The Ramones, Mink deVille and Talking Heads.

cell a small group or faction of an organization. It originally came into the American English lexicon from Communist Party terminology. Before and during the Second World War, and until **Joseph McCarthy's** and **Richard Nixon's** accusations, the Communist Party, along with the blue-collar workers' unions, was actually considered a viable and valuable part of American society. This is one of the words that emerged from that era.

centered comfortable with one's identity and beliefs. Focused. An indication of being self-confident and well balanced. Examples: "No one can change her mind; she's **centered** in her beliefs." "He's **centered**; you can't spook him."

chain a series of incidents of similar nature or similar subject matter.

chakra a **Sanskrit** term meaning wheel. In Eastern religions, chakras are the centers of energy of the human body. There are seven chakras within the body and five outer chakras radiating from the body. The primary, or body chakras, are: **1.** Muladhara, root (base center), at the base of the spine (survival) **2.** Swadisthana, spleen, located three fingers below the navel (sexual energy) **3.** Manipura, solar plexus, at the navel (energy distribution & power) **4.** Anahata, heart, at the sternum (love & affinity) **5.** Vishuddhi, throat, at the cleft of the throat (communications & creativity) **6.** Ajna, brow, between the brows (**clairvoyance**) **7.** Sahasrara, crown, at the top of the head (spirituality)

Chambers Brothers, The *gospel, funk and rock* a Black band comprised of four brothers, formed in Los Angeles in 1961. They eventually crossed over from gospel and became **psychedelic** innovators when they recorded the classic 1968 **acid** sound hit, "Time Has Come Today."

Chambliss, Robert Edward "Dynamite Bob" *social issues* a member of the 13th Klavern of the Alabama **Ku Klux Klan**. Is said to have been the bomber of many Black homes and businesses in the **Dynamite Hill** area of Birmingham during the early 1960s. In 1977, Chambliss was convicted of the September 15, 1963, bombing of the Sixteenth Street Baptist Church in Birmingham, Alabama. The date of the bombing is known as the infamous **Birmingham Sunday**. Four young Black girls were killed and 20 others wounded. Three other men were also suspected in that bombing, yet Chambliss was the only one convicted at the time. After the turn of the century, new trials were opened against the two suspects still alive. "Dynamite Bob" died in prison in 1985. (See: **Birmingham Sunday**) (See also: **Civil Rights Events** starting on page 546 in **Lists** at the back of this book)

THE FBI IS SEEKING INFORMATION CONCERNING THE DISAPPEARANCE AT PHILADELPHIA, MISSISSIPPI, OF THESE THREE INDIVIDUALS ON JUNE 21, 1964. EXTENSIVE INVESTIGATION IS BEING CONDUCTED TO LOCATE GOODMAN, CHANEY, AND SCHWERNER, WHO ARE DESCRIBED AS FOLLOWS:

ANDREW GOODMAN　　JAMES EARL CHANEY　　MICHAEL HENRY SCHWERNER

Goodman　　Chaney　　Schwerner

Chaney, James Earl (1943-1964) *social issues* Black **civil rights** activist; a native of Meridian, Mississippi, where in 1963 he became a **Congress of Racial Equality (CORE)** worker. In 1964, he helped other CORE workers, **Michael Schwerner** and his wife Rita, establish a field office in Meridian. On June 21, 1964, Chaney; Michael Schwerner, a White man; and another White CORE worker, **Andrew Goodman** were murdered by Klansmen with the help of local sheriff's deputies. As of 2001, the murderers have not yet been brought to justice. (See: **Civil Rights Events, Groups and Leaders** starting on page 546 in **Lists** at the back of this book)

*changes significant episodes in a person's life.

Changing Woman the most beloved deity of the Navajo Indians; mother of Monster Slayer and Child of the Water, who slew the monsters that threatened mankind.

channel or **channeler** n. in **occult** beliefs, a person through whom the dead are able to speak or who possess psychic powers to facilitate communication with the dead.

channel v. to focus one's energies into doing something properly. It can be as mundane as taking out the trash.

Chapin, Dwight L. (1940-) *politics* President **Nixon**'s appointment secretary, organized "dirty tricks." Named executive director of the home office of United Airlines in Chicago after the crash of Flight 553. Convicted of perjury, 1974. (See: **dirty tricks** and **plumbers** in alphabetical listings) (See also: **Nixon's Watergate Conspirators** on page 582 in **Lists** at the back of this book)

charas *drugs* **hashish**, the **resin** from **cannabis**. A Hindi word. **2. marijuana**.

charge, charged or **charged up** excited, uplifted or energized by something. Relates to getting an electrical shock from something. Example: "I got a **charge** out of watching Blair folk dance."

charisma an uncommon attraction or impressive personality possessed by some people. It is not a word exclusive to or new in the 1960s, but is thousands of years old in almost the same form. The Greek root means basically "gift of grace from God." The 1960s seemed to have an unusually large number of charismatic people: **John F. Kennedy, Rev. Martin Luther King, Jr.,** Marilyn Monroe, **The Beatles**, Mick Jagger and yes, even Jimmy Hoffa, William F. Buckley, and Henry Kissinger are examples.

Charlatans, The *folk, blues, jug band* formed in San Francisco, California, in 1964, they were initially an amateur group said to be the original **Haight-Ashbury** band. Many feel that they were the first **acid rock** band. George Hunter, voc.; Mike Wilhelm, gtr.; Richard Olson, bass; Michael Ferguson, piano; Sam Linde, drums; and Dan Hicks, drums, gtr.   In the summer of 1965, they played at the **Red Dog Saloon** in Virginia City, Nevada, where many of the hippie "hijinks" and traditions originated, including rock posters, **psychedelic light** shows and the **happening** phenomena.   During the birth of psychedelic music at **The Fillmore**, the **Avalon Ballroom** and other dance halls in San Francisco, The Charlatans played many of the same **gigs** as **The Jefferson Airplane** and **The Grateful Dead** (then called **The Warlocks.**) The Charlatans recorded only one album, *The Charlatans,* in 1969 and then disbanded.   George Hunter and Dan Hicks were also members of **Family Dog**, the commune and music promotion "gang."

Charles, Ray (b. Ray Charles Robinson, September 23, 1930, Albany, Georgia) *blues, jazz, rock* blind, Black and orphaned in his teens, Ray Charles still became one of five or six most influential musicians of the century. A keyboardist, singer, songwriter and musical arranger who contributed so much to the atmosphere of our lives throughout the 1960s and 1970s.

chart in **astrology**, it means generally the same as the word **horoscope**. It shows the placement of a person's stars and their bearing on the life of that individual.

chart *rock & roll* sheet music giving the arrangement for musicians to read and play.

chase the dragon *drugs* to smoke **heroin**.

chauvinist pig an insensitive man or one who believes in the superiority of male over female. A chauvinist is someone who is excessively loyal to a person, place or cause. The word chauvinist is French, derived from the name of Nicholas Chauvin, a soldier who was such an enthusiastic follower of Napoleon that his name eventually came to mean overzealous support of any cause.

Chávez, César Estrada (1927-1993) *social issues* founder and leader of The **United Farm Workers' Union (UFW)** from its beginning in 1962 until his death in 1993. The union was formed to represent California's field workers, comprised largely of naturalized Mexican-Americans. The UFW began to demonstrate and strike in 1965 and boycotted California grape growers in 1966. They also struck and boycotted the lettuce industry, eventually gaining better pay and conditions for union workers. Chávez fasted several times in protest of workers' compensation and working conditions. The **fasting** damaged his health, and he died shortly after his last fast in 1993. (See: **United Farm Workers Union**) (See also: **Minority Rights Groups** starting on page 609 in **Lists** at the back of this book)

cheap tight with money. **2.** low-class or in bad taste.

***cheap shot** a snide or derogatory comment, often unfounded and possibly untrue. Example: "Telling everyone she snores was a **cheap shot**"

cheaters sunglasses. Usage probably came from the fact that one can't see a person's eyes behind sunglasses, and therefore can't determine whether they are telling the truth. The term was used in card playing, where sunglasses would aid a person in maintaining a good "poker face."

***check it out** or **check out** look at or pay attention to. This appears to have originated as an Hispanic street term. Example: "**Check it out;** they have veggieburgers on the menu."

cheeba *drugs* (See: **marijuana**)

cheese   the nebulous element that holds life together. (See: **chi**)

cheeseburger   the epitome of twentieth century bad eating habits. The bane of all **vegetarians**. A word used to describe the decadence of the **fast food** culture that sprung up in the 1950s and expanded throughout the rest of the century. Examples: "He's a real **cheeseburger**, and look at the striped tie!" A conversation between Flower and River: "I saw Gondolf downtown eating a **cheeseburger**." "No, how gross!" "And he had to put on shoes to go in the place!" "God, what is this commune coming to?"

cheesy of low quality or poor taste.

chemicals *drugs* drugs that are made by a chemical process. **LSD** or powders like **cocaine**, **mescaline** and **methamphetamines**.

*****cherry** good, **cool** or the best. Example: "Your new pipe is **cherry**." An evolution of the word cherry as a virgin.

cherry new, uninitiated, unused. A virgin. Example: "I've got a **cherry** new pipe. Do you want to burn the first bowl with me?" The cherry fruit has been used for centuries to indicate the maidenhead of a virgin female.

Chess, Leonard (b. Mar. 12, 1917, Poland; d. Oct. 16, 1969, Chicago, Ill.) *blues, R&B, rock & roll* record producer and record company owner, along with his brother Phil, of Chess Records, a label that featured the cream of the blues and the first blues/rock crossover musicians, such as **Muddy**

Waters, Howlin' Wolf, Sonny Boy Williamson, Etta James and **Chuck Berry**. Inducted into The Rock and Roll Hall of Fame in 1987.

chew (someone's) **ass** or **chew** (someone) **out** to reprimand or chastise.

chi Chinese for force or **spirit**. In **esoteric** terminology, understood as breath or vital fluid. Also known as the name for the Spirits of Earth: the gods of the ground, grain, mountains, rivers and valleys. A very important Chinese character found in many words depicting life and nature; for example, in **Tai Chi**, the Eastern exercise meditation. Among the intellectual hippie culture, ch'i was used to describe the inexplicable **essence** of life. A number of other more mundane or humorous words were sometimes used. Examples: **apple sauce, cheese, ether, glue, pudding** and **sauce**. A common greeting among the more esoteric hippies was to ask, "How's your **chi**, man?"

chiba shop or **smoke shop** *drugs* a store that sold **marijuana** under the counter. A shop disguised as a reputable business, yet offering illegal drugs on the side.

Chicago *big band /rock & roll* formed in Chicago in 1967, it was a very successful rock and roll band with a horn section.

Chicago Democratic National Convention, anti-war demonstrations and police riots *social issues* during the week of August 24 through 29, 1968, the Democratic National Convention was held in Chicago. **Anti-war** rallies were conducted by various groups, and police brutality occurred. **Vietnam War** protesters demonstrated and were beaten and maced outside the Convention Center. It was widely agreed that

Mayor **Richard Daley**'s police force overreacted with totalitarian gestapo tactics. Mayor Daley was recorded saying, "The police are not here to create disorder, but to preserve disorder," an obvious mistake in words thought by many to reveal his true nature. **Hubert Humphrey** was nominated as the party's presidential candidate. He was defeated by **Richard Nixon** in November of the same year. During the convention week, 668 demonstrators were arrested, 101 hospitalized and 1,025 treated for minor injuries, including those caused by tear gas or mace, on the street or in the seven medical facilities set up by the Medical Committee of Human Rights. 192 police officers were injured. (See: **Anti-War Events, Groups and Leaders** starting on page 562 in **Lists** at the back of this book)

Chicago Eight (See: **Chicago Seven**)

Chicago Green dark green **marijuana** popular in the Chicago, Illinois, area. (See: **marijuana**)

Davis, Hoffman, Weiner, Dellinger, Froines, Rubin, Hayden

Chicago Seven, The *social issues* **Rennie Davis, David Dellinger, John Froines, Thomas Hayden, Abbie Hoffman, Jerry Rubin** and **Lee Weiner**, **anti-war** leaders who were arrested and tried as co-conspirators for crossing state borders to incite to riot during the 1968 **Democratic National Convention** in Chicago. **Bobby Seale** was originally included in the trial, making it the **Chicago Eight**;

he was so disruptive in his political zeal that the courts had him shackled and gagged at times, and his case was eventually separated from the others.

Chicago Seven trial *social issues* the prosecution of seven **anti-war** leaders who were arrested and tried as co-conspirators for crossing state boarders to incite demonstrators to riot during the 1968 **Democratic National Convention** in Chicago. The trial of **Rennie Davis, David Dellinger, John Froines, Thomas Hayden, Abbie Hoffman, Jerry Rubin** and **Lee Weiner** was one of the most controversial examples of our judicial system. The courts disregarded the defendants' personal freedoms and stretched laws to the breaking point. The defendants used the trial as a platform to inform the public about the inequities and inconsistencies of the courts as related to political activism. Because of their outspoken dissent and the disrespect they showed for the courts, the defendants were issued a large number of contempt citations. As Tom Hayden later wrote in his 1970 book *Trial*, "When the courts are turned into a weapon against change, trials must be turned into an attack on the courts. Make it known that American citizens are being jailed because of their political attitudes or in our case, for their 'state of mind' by a state that cannot reconcile its pledge of a fair trial with its stake in preserving the status quo." The Judge was Julius J. Hoffman. Prosecuting attorneys were Thomas Foran and Richard Schultz. Defense lawyers were William Kunstler and Leonard Weinglass. The trial lasted from September of 1969 to February of 1970. The defendants were out on bail and made public appearances during the trial. John Froines and Lee Weiner were acquitted; the others were convicted and sentenced to five years, and all of them received contempt of court sentences as well. Eventually, the convictions were overturned because of Judge Hoffman's gross misbehavior during the trial.

chick a girl or young woman. Thought by many women to be a derogatory or demeaning term, yet most men used it with less complicated intent. To most guys, it was considered an endearing term. This brings up one of the more interesting and complex elements of vocabulary. The two sexes at times have different understandings of the same word. The male personality often uses cruel humor or sarcasm as a form of romantic communication. This tradition may not always be appropriate, but it should be recognized for what it is, and that is a basic male sexual insecurity stemming from the double standard. These misunderstood words and seemingly misogynistic activities are largely responsible for the initiation and growth of the women's movement.

chicken out to refuse to do something because of fear.

chicken shit someone who is afraid. Something of little value or of low quality.

chief, the chief *drugs* one of the more obscure names for **LSD**.

chill or **chill out** calm down, stop what you're doing. This term is thought to have ethnic roots, but it has been a part of the **beat** and **hippie** vocabulary from the beginning. It may have connections in **blues** and **jazz** music culture.

chillin' relaxing. A late 1970s evolution of the term to **chill out**.

chilly a heartless act, without remorse or conscience. Most likely, it came originally from "cold hearted." Example: "That was **chilly**! He put purple food dye in her bean sprouts."

chillum *drugs* a tube made of clay, wood or metal in which to smoke **dope**. Sometimes a chillum is merely constructed using a cone of two or more smoking **papers**. It is the traditional method of smoking **ganja** (**marijuana**) or **charas** (**hashish**) in India and Nepal.

chin to talk.

China *drugs* related to **heroin**. China white, China brown, Chinese rocks, all forms of heroin.

chinos (chee-nos) loose-fitting, **khaki** pants worn by many members of the **beat generation**. During the **hippie** era, they were worn only when one really wanted to dress up. There is some question as to the origin of the word. Some people feel that it came from the pre-WWI US Army summer uniform, which was made in China; others feel that the name is derived from the Spanish root *chino*, meaning rough, coarse or mixed. The color is also thought to be responsible for the name, since, in several languages, the word brown is pronounced similarly to chino.

chip (See: **silicon chip**)

chipper *drugs* a person who uses illicit **drugs** occasionally, not an **addict**.

chippie or **chippy** *sex* a prostitute or promiscuous woman.

chipping *drugs* using illicit **drugs** only occasionally.

Chisholm, Shirley (b. Anita St. Hill, 1924-) *social issues* Black **civil rights** and **women's rights** leader. In 1968, she became the first Black woman elected to the US Congress when she won a seat in the House of Representatives for the 12th Congressional District in Brooklyn, New York. In 1972, Chisholm ran in the New York Democratic primary for President of the United States, thus becoming the first Black woman to run for president. She worked vigorously for civil rights, women's rights and the environment. After retiring from Congress in 1982, she took a position teaching Politics and Women's Studies at Mount Holyoke College in Massachusetts.

chocolate bandit *sex* male **homosexual**. In regard to homosexuality, all references to something brown relate to excrement and the practice of **sodomy**. Along with other similar terms, such as **brownie hound** and **turd burglar**, this is among the most offensive references, used only by offensive people.

choirboy a naive young man, uninitiated in sex or other vices of the world. Can be a derogatory term and used sarcastically to describe someone who is feigning purity.

*choke to make a mistake under pressure. Related to getting "all choked up."

choke (the/one's) **chicken** *sex* to masturbate (male usage). Many phrases and words have been used for each sexual activity, and they are often regional.

cholo a derogatory name for a person of Mexican heritage. A Spanish word related to another Spanish word, *pachuco*, meaning a young Mexican-American, usually a gang member, who dresses and grooms in a particularly rebellious style.

Chomsky, (Avril) Noam (1928-) linguist, social/political theorist. Born in Philadelphia, the son of a distinguished Hebrew scholar, he was educated at Harvard and the University of Pennsylvania, where he received his PhD in 1955. Chomsky had a long teaching career at the Massachusetts Institute of Technology. He is known as one of the principal founders of transformational-generative grammar, a system of linguistic analysis that challenges traditional linguistics and encompasses philosophy, logic and psycholinguistics. His 1957 book, *Syntactic Structures*, was credited with revolutionizing the discipline of linguistics. Chomsky's theory suggests that every human utterance has two structures: a "surface structure," the superficial combining of words; and a "deep structure" of universal rules and mechanisms. In more practical terms, the theory argues that the means for acquiring language is innate to all humans and is triggered as soon as an infant begins to learn the basics of a language. Chomsky expressed radical criticism of American politics and economics, particularly of American's foreign policy as influenced by the conservative establishment and presented by the media; he was outspoken in his opposition to the **Vietnam War**. His published works in this area include *American Power and the New Mandarins* in 1969, and *Human Rights and American Foreign Policy* in 1978.

chop an insult. Example: "Stealing his falsies was a cruel **chop**."

chopped hog a motorcycle that has been customized. **Hog** almost always refers to a big **Harley Davidson**. Usually, the front wheel forks were lengthened, handlebars redesigned, and gas tank and seat reshaped. Derived from the 1950s term when cars had sections "chopped" out of them to make them more streamlined.

photo by John McCleary ©

a motorcycle that has been customized, usually a **Harley Davidson**. **2**. During the **Vietnam War**, helicopters were also called choppers, which came from a combination of the sound the machine made and a shortening of the word helicopter to copter.

chops skills or abilities. Any creative activity. Same usage as **moves**. Examples: "That keyboard player has great **chops**." "Garth's got his **chops** down when it comes to gardening." **2**. musical notes or musical ability. From **ax**, referring to a musical instrument, and chops being what the ax produces. (See: **ax**)

chow down to eat. a.k.a. **scarf**, **munch**.

chris or christina *drugs* **methamphetamine** in **crystal** or powered form.

Christian, Charlie (b. 1919, Dallas, Texas; d. March 2, 1942, New York City) *music/jazz* a Black **jazz** guitarist credited with elevating the guitar from its place as a rhythm instrument into the position of a solo instrument. Inducted in to the Rock and Roll Hall of Fame in 1990 as an early influence.

Christian Science *religion* a religion and philosophy founded in 1875 by Mary Baker Eddy, based on the following teachings: "God, the universal mind, is the only existing reality; man is God's

spiritual idea and belongs by right to an order in which there is no sickness, sin, sorrow or death; all such things are errors of man's mortal mind and have no reality for man except when he admits them; if man denies them, they cease to exist." Sometimes called **Western yoga** because of its esoteric involvement.

Christmas tree *drugs* a **Tuinal** capsule. Named for the red and green or red and blue coloring of the capsule. **Downer**.

chuck to get sick and vomit. Short for upchuck.

chuck it get rid of it. From "to throw" something away.

chucks the craving for sweets experienced by a drug **addict** while **withdrawing** from drugs.

chuck you, Farley! *exclamation* a humorous variation of **fuck you, Charley**! Fuck you, Charley, was an expletive directed at someone whose name one didn't know. The name Charley was often used as a generic term, but it was also a name used to describe North Vietnamese soldiers. "Fuck you, Charley" was also a cartoon by **R. Crumb** in Head Comix, 1968.

chug or chug-a-lug to drink something down quickly, usually alcohol. Same use as **pound** or **pounding**.

chump a loser, a naive person, or victim.

ciao a greeting or parting salutation. Originally Italian, it was adopted by the **counterculture** along with similar greetings from other countries, such as "aloha" from Hawaii or "hola" (o'la) from Mexico.

circle jerk sex men in a circle masturbating each other. Or men in a circle masturbating themselves to see who can ejaculate first and/or farthest. *God, what some people will do for entertainment!*

citizens band radio (CB radio) a radio frequency designated for the general public to use to communicate with each other over short distances. On the nation's highways in the 1970s, many truckers and car travelers used CB radios for communication. One of the major pastimes was warning fellow drivers of the authorities so that travelers could slow down in order to avoid speeding tickets.

city *intensifier or suffix* a suffix indicating a multitude of something. A congregation of anything. Examples: "Dork-**city**: a lot of guys in polyester," "God squad **city**: a church convention," "butt-crack **city:** a bunch of overweight ditch diggers."

City Lights Books America's first all-paperback bookstore. Founded in San Francisco's **beatnik** North Beach area by **Lawrence Ferlinghetti** and Peter Martin. Opened in 1955 to fill the poetry needs of the beatnik generation, it soon became the hippie **counterculture's** favorite source for rebellious literature as well. It is the West Coast's intellectual mecca and possibly the most famous bookstore in America. staff@citylights.com (See: **Lawrence Ferlinghetti**)

Civil Disobedience a book by Henry David Thoreau in which he wrote, "I think that we should be men first, and subjects afterwards. It is not desirable to cultivate a respect for the law, so much as for the right."

civil disobedience *social issues* the practice of questioning authority and conducting disturbances in order to bring attention to inconsistencies in laws and government activities. In the 1960s and 70s, it usually meant blocking government facilities or university offices with sit-ins and creating a nuisance on public streets with marches and **demonstrations**. In that era of **social consciousness**, it was considered

photo by John McCleary ©

the participants to be the proper way in which to bring awareness to a problem. Occasionally, it became violent, but the usual intent was to take the legal, peaceful right of assembly to a point where it pushed the authorities to overreact, thus bringing one's cause to the attention of the public. The issue of breaking the law and restricting other people's **civil rights** in order to force changes in laws or civil rights was a moral concern then, and still is today in such cases as antiabortion demonstrations. (See: **Civil Rights Events, Groups and Leaders** starting on page 546 in **Lists** at the back of this book)

civil liberties *social issues* the rights to freedom of thought, expression and action, and the protection of these rights from government restriction and interference. The Bill of Rights and the **First Amendment** guarantee freedom of assembly, press, religion and speech.

civil rights *social issues* the basic foundation upon which the United States of America is founded. The Constitution, The Bill of Rights, and Constitutional Amendments are concerned primarily with stating and preserving these rights. The **essence** of being a good American is realizing that these rights are for everyone, even those with whom one does not agree, and the duty of every good American is to defend these rights for everyone.

civil rights (See: **Civil Rights Events, Groups and Leaders** starting on page 546 in **Lists** at the back of this book)

civil rights and anti-war *social issues* after **Dr. Martin Luther King, Jr.'s** acknowledgment of and entry into the **anti-war movement** in 1967, the Black community began to demonstrate for both civil rights and anti-war causes. Since an inordinate proportion of soldiers sent to Vietnam were poor Black men, the civil rights and anti-war movements had many of the same interests. It became obvious that economic circumstances often determined whether a young man was drafted. Due to college deferments and family pressures on local draft boards, affluent White boys were slipping through the cracks, whereas the poorer minorities, such as Hispanics and Blacks, were being drafted at higher rates. Both anti-war and civil rights issues were related in the student demonstration at the predominately Black, **Jackson State College** in Mississippi. On May 14, 1970, during several days of campus **demonstrations**, two Black students, James Earl Green, a high school student; and Phillip Gibbs, a 20-year-old college student and father of an 18-month-old son, were shot and killed by Mississippi State patrolmen and/or Jackson City police. Twelve others were wounded.

clairvoyance *occult* sight with the inner eye. The ability to foresee events; a gift of spiritual sight. An **occult** term unrelated to drug-induced insight. However, throughout history, chemical enhancement has been responsible for clairvoyance; for example, the **Oracle** of Delphi sat over a fissure in the ground from which gases seeped, producing a drug-like trance.

clap *sex* the slang term for **gonorrhea**, a common **venereal disease** of the hippie era. Symptoms include a burning sensation when urinating. Usually treated with penicillin.

Clapton, Eric (b. Eric Clapp, March 30, 1945, Ripley, England) *rock & roll* British guitar player, singer/songwriter who first performed and jammed with many yet to be famous musicians in London in the early 1960s. Clapton worked with **John Mayall**, Jack Bruce, Ginger Baker, **Steve Winwood** and Duane Allman in such groups as the Bluesbreakers, **Cream**, **Blind Faith** and Derek and the Dominos. His work and his lifestyle defined the hippie-era guitar virtuoso. Inducted into the Rock and Roll Hall of Fame in 2000.

clarabelle *drugs* **tetrahydrocannabinol (THC)**, synthetic **marijuana**. From the name of the clown on the "Buffalo Bob" TV show of the 1950s.

Clark, Dick (b. Nov. 39, 1929, Mount Vernon, New York) *rock & roll* radio and TV music show host. The unbelievably clean-cut vision seen introducing songs and musicians on the "**American Bandstand**" network TV show from 1957 to 1988. Always politically correct, impeccably dressed and an unofficial arbiter of style for the nation of teenagers. Somehow, he was able to integrate Black, hippie and even gender-confused music into his shows without passing judgment or getting fired. This was his contribution to mankind. Although the hippie **counterculture** often poked fun at him, we were all influenced by his contribution to music.   Inducted in to the Rock and Roll Hall of Fame in 1993.

Clark, Ramsey (1927-) *politics* Attorney General under **President Lyndon Johnson**, 1967-69. Considered by many to have been the last people-friendly attorney general in this country. Since his time, the position has been held primarily by people committed only, it seems, to the **military-industrial complex**, often ignoring the interests of the majority.

Clash, The *rock & roll* the definitive **punk rock** group formed in 1976 in London, England. Mick Jones (b. Michael Jones, June 26, 1955, London), gtr., voc.; Paul Simonon (b. Dec. 15, 1955, London), bass; Joe Strummer (b. John Graham Mellor, Aug. 21, 1952, Ankara, Turkey), voc. gtr.; Tory Crimes (b. Terry Chimes, London), drums, replaced in 1977 by Nicky "Topper" Headon (b. May 30, 1955, Bromley, Eng.), drums. Although most **punk rockers** were anti-hippie in their outlook, the appearance of punk music was an exciting twist to rebel music and was accepted and embraced by many hippies. At least it wasn't drum machines and **disco** beats!

Class A narcotics Federal Bureau of Narcotics' category of addictive narcotics, i.e., **opium** and its derivatives. A designation used in prescribing and manufacturing such drugs.

Class B narcotics Federal Bureau of Narcotics' category of drugs that are almost nonaddictive, i.e., codeine.

Class M narcotics Federal Bureau of Narcotics' category of nonaddittive drugs.

Class X narcotics Federal Bureau of Narcotics' category of drugs containing very small amounts of narcotics combined with nonnarcotic medications, i.e., codeine cough syrups.

class act an impressive person. Example: "Whitey's a **class act** until he starts to dance or play basketball."

class struggle *politics* revolution, the struggle of poor and oppressed people to rise above servitude and gain dignity and enough prosperity to have some control of their own future.

classy chassis the body of a beautiful woman.

clay *drugs* **tetrahydrocannabinol (THC)**, synthetic **marijuana**.   a.k.a. **clarabelle**.

Clay, Cassius the birth name of **Muhammad Ali** (See: **Ali, Muhammad**)

clean having no drugs on one's person, the state of being without drugs. Example: A policeman might say, "He's **clean**, but I arrested him for poor taste in **bell-bottoms**." **2.** not taking drugs.

clean out of sight the description of an impressive person, place or thing. Example: "His polka-dot bell-bottoms were all right, **clean out of sight**." (See: **out of sight**)

clean or Mr. Clean a sarcastic description of someone who is too perfect, as was Paul's father in the **Beatle's** "**A Hard Day's Night**." Example: "He's a **clean** old man, but there's something nasty going on behind that immaculate smile."

clean up your act get straightened out; often, it means to get off drugs.

clear free of emotional or psychological obstacles or **baggage**. A psychological term rather than a physical description. Another one of those words that is not unique to the hippie era, but which took on more profound dimensions and subtle, new usage. Example: "Jody is emotionally **clear**, but I wish she'd shave her legs." "Greg has a **clear** sense of self, but a cloudy view of self-indulgence."

clear and present danger *politics* dangerous use of freedom of speech. If someone encourages others to be destructive, to inflict pain, or to take away another's rights, then that individual is in violation of **free-speech** limitations. For example, no one has the constitutional right to yell "fire" in a crowded theater when there is no fire because that action could pose a "clear and present danger" to public safety. Originally used by Oliver Wendell Holmes in his arguments in the 1919 court case of *Schenck v. United States*.

Cleaver, (Leroy) Eldridge (1935-) *social issues* **Black Panther Party** leader. His collection of essays written while in prison was published as the 1968 book, *Soul on Ice*. Presidential candidate in 1968, running with **Dick Gregrory** on the **Peace and Freedom** ticket. On April 6, 1968, he was arrested after a gun battle with the Oakland, California, police. In July, 1969, Cleaver violated his parole and took refuge in Cuba, Algeria and France. Re-turning to America in 1975, he struck a deal and avoided prison. Joining the Republican Party, he ran unsuccessfully for the US Senate in 1986.

click to get along, to have a good relationship. Example: "My new roommate and I **click** on everything except dirty dishes."

click one mile. Adopted into **counterculture** use from the military where the odometers on military vehicles clicked over to mark every mile. Many terms came back from Vietnam, and in a strange, satirical twist, the hippie culture adopted them almost as a confrontation with the military and in reaction to the war.

Cliff, Jimmy (b. James Chambers, April 1, 1948, St. James, Jamaica) *reggae* one of the first **reggae** stars to be heard outside Jamaica. Cliff was the star and performed many of the songs in the unique and musically important 1973 movie, "The Harder They Come," which introduced the Jamaican island culture and its music to the rest of the world. Jimmy Cliff was best known as a songwriter. "Vietnam," Cliff's **anti-war** song, was declared by **Bob Dylan** to be "the best protest song ever written."

climax *sex* an orgasm. The moment of sexual fulfillment for either male and female.

climb into a bottle to get drunk and stay that way for a long time.

clip *drugs* short for **roach clip**, a device for holding the last remaining end of a **marijuana** cigarette. (See: **roach clip**)

clit short for **clitoris**. The tiny **button** of flesh just above the opening of a woman's **vagina**. It is the part of a woman's sexual anatomy that transmits the majority of feelings of sexual arousal to the brain; that is, of course, if it is properly caressed during intercourse or **foreplay**. Most men don't know a clit from a cloud in the sky. Recognize it, men, get to know it, it is your best friend. If you can reach a place of appreciation and proper treatment of this little, erogenous spot, women will flock to you, love you...not just put up with you.

close enough for government work means the job doesn't have to be perfect. Refers to the popular belief that the government does shoddy work. Not a very obvious **counterculture** comment, but it came into use during the 1970s in reference to a growing disillusionment with the government. It was common among hippie construction workers, of whom there were many. Carpentry was a particularly attractive occupation for hippies because it was creative, physical, and could be done part-time, leaving time for sex, drugs, rock and roll or an occasional religious pilgrimage to India or a **Grateful Dead** concert.

closet secret or hidden. Examples: **closet** liberal, **closet** queen, **closet** fascist. Attached to someone who is ashamed of their activities or afraid of the repercussions of discovery.

closet homosexual, closet queen *sex* a **homosexual** male who, due to shame or fear of repercussions, prefers to remain unrecognized as **gay**. Coming out of the closet is the act of acknowledging one's homosexuality to the general public, and sometimes it is the act of admitting it to oneself as well.

clue understanding. The opposite of ignorance. Comes from police and mystery novel jargon, meaning the indication of an answer to a puzzle.

clueless ignorant, unaware of the "mysteries" of life. Uninformed. Considered a **Valley talk** term, but it originated with the hippie **counterculture**. (See: **Valley talk**)

clyde someone who doesn't appreciate **rock and roll** music. A **British invasion** term.

C.O. (See: **conscientious objector**)

coast or **coasting** to proceed, mentally or physically, without effort or confrontation. To do something with ease. Examples: "Dave can **coast** through the day without having to work, think or act." "She's **coasting** with a theme; stay out of her way and pick up the pieces."

coca *drugs* (See: **cocaine**)

cocaine *drugs* an alkaloid extracted from coca leaves. Coca is a native plant of Bolivia and Peru. Usually, the end product is a **white powder** that, when ingested by eating, snorting, smoking, or shooting, can create a heightened sense of physical and emotional well-being. In the hippie era, until cocaine came along, the use of drugs was an effort to improve oneself by expanding one's horizons. Most drugs during this time were taken for intellectual experimentation. Cocaine, on the other hand, belonged in the self-indulgent category with alcohol. Cocaine is bad for the soul. I have a saying about the stuff, "Coke doesn't make you feel like the best person in the world; it makes you feel like the *only* person in the world." There are inherent dangers with this drug and worse consequences from taking bad doses. Most recommendations are to stay away from this drug; it will kill you prematurely. Remember, all things in moderation; thinking people use their drugs, foolish people use drugs that will kill them. a.k.a.

blow, C, coca, coke, Colombian marching powder, girl, gold dust, happy dust, joy powder, Lady Snow, the leaf, magic dust, marching powder, nose candy, snow, snuff, star dust, toot, vitamin C, white, white lady. (See also: **cocaine** in **Drugs of the Era** in **Lists** at the back of this book)

cocaine slut a person who will do anything for **cocaine**. Originally, it was directed at a woman who would have sex with any man in exchange for cocaine. But, since many **homosexual** men would do the same and most **heterosexual** men would sleep with any woman for far less, I don't think that women should be singled out.

cock *sex* the male sex organ. It is uncertain which came first, cock, meaning the dominant male chicken in the barnyard, or cock as a penis. a.k.a.: **penis, dick, prick, jones**, a.k.a. in erect position: **erection, boner, hard-on, shaft**. **2**. in some Southern states, this word was used to describe exactly the opposite, meaning the woman's **vagina**. Example: A Southern man might say, "I'm going down town and get some **cock** tonight."

cock-rock *rock & roll* a form of **rock and roll** that employed self-indulgent lyrics, loud, driving beats, and tight-pantsed, oversexed lead singers. **Led Zeppelin, Steppenwolf, The Who, The Doors** and **The Rolling Stones** started the genre, but their lyrics were generally more thought provoking than most of the latter proponents of the "art," such as **Deep Purple**, Def Leppard, Judas Priest, Nazareth, **Blue Cheer**, Black Sabbath and **Van Halen**.

cocktail *drugs* a mixture of pills or drugs concocted to create various physical or mental effects.

cock-tease or **cock-teaser** *sex* a woman who frustrates men with flirtation, yet has no intention of granting sexual favors. A little less offensive form of the term prick-teaser.

cocky arrogant or self-important. From the term **cock**, meaning the dominant male chicken in the barnyard. Also related to "cock of the walk."

codeine *drugs* methylmorphine, derivative of morphine. Swallowed or injected with an active duration of approximately four hours. Used medically as a treatment for severe coughs or as a local anesthetic. a.k.a. **school boy, cubes**.

coffee house an establishment that serves primarily coffee and provides a venue in which students and intellectuals gather to discuss revolution and listen to **folk music** and poetry. A phenomenon that evolved from the student bistros of Paris in the early part of the century into the beatnik spots in New York's **Greenwich Village** and San Francisco's North Beach in the 1950s. They proliferated in the late 1950s, became music or comedy clubs in the 1960s, and **trendy** restaurants in the 1970s. Some of the most famous were The Other End and Gertie's in New York City and The Hungry I in San Francisco.

Coffee Mate a powdered, imitation milk product introduced in 1961. Created to offer a nonperishable product that would make coffee look and "taste" as if cream were added.

Cohen, Leonard (b. Sept. 21, 1934, Montreal, Canada) *music* White folksinger/songwriter. First recorded his own songs on the 1967 album, *Songs of Leonard Cohen*. Cohen was a noted poet and novelist before turning to music in the 1960s. Many of his songs have been recorded by others, and his ethereal, poetic style of writing influenced many rock and roll songwriters of the hippie era.

Cohn-Bendit, Daniel (Danny the Red) (b. April 4, 1945, Montaubanin, South of France) *social issues* French-born of German parents, as a student at the **Sorbonne** in Paris, he led the May, 1968, student revolts against university totalitarian rules in an effort to achieve more **academic freedom**. Eventually, hundreds of thousands of French workers joined the students' protest and struck against the de Gaulle government, bringing the country to a standstill. The resulting concessions were considered a victory for the struggles of the common man. Daniel Cohn-Bendit was denounced as a "German anarchist" and expelled by the French government. "Danny the Red" entered politics and become a Frankfurt city councilman and an elected member of the European Parliament, representing the German Green party. (See: **Sorbonne demonstrations**)

cohoba snuff (yakee, yato or **epená)** *drugs* a South American snuff derived from the **yopo bean**, a legume with **psychedelic** properties whose active ingredient is **dimethyltryptamine (DMT)**. DMT was one of the very first **psychoactive** creations of modern man and his knowledge of chemistry. It was found in "European" snuff during the turn of the century. South American indigenous peoples call the snuff by various names, such as **yakee**, yato, cohoba and epena. DMT may also be found in the Syrian rue herb in China and the venom of a Sonoran Desert toad. a.k.a. **businessman's special** or **businessman's trip**. (See: **yakee** or **di methyl tryptamine**)

coil an intrauterine contraceptive device that must be inserted by a doctor and is designed to remain in place for a semi-permanent length of time. a.k.a. **intrauterine device (IUD)**. (See: **contraceptives** and **intrauterine device (IUD)**)

coin money. Not just change; may also indicate paper money.

cojones (ko-ho-nes) guts or courage. From the Spanish slang word for balls. A macho-related term.

coke *drugs* abbreviation for **cocaine**. (See: **cocaine**)

cokehead *drugs* habitual **cocaine** user.

cokie *drugs* a term used by non-users to describe a **cocaine** user.

cold cock to knock someone out. Possibly from the fact that an unconscious man has a "cold" penis and will be dysfunctional. **2.** a psychological attack that leaves a person incapacitated and without a response.

cold or **cold shot** heartless, an action without remorse or conscience. Examples: "Man, that was **cold**, hiding her Kahlil Gibran under the bean sprouts." "What a **cold shot**, switching her K-Y jelly with toothpaste."

cold turkey *drugs* a manner of quitting a habit abruptly, without the assistance of alternative drug therapy. May apply to any **addiction**, indulgence or habit, for example, to food, another person, or television.

collateral damage unintended destruction and death of civilian noncombatants as a result of a military action. It filtered into the vocabulary of the **counterculture** after returning with **Vietnam War** veterans. Used sarcastically since the hippie culture considered any expedient violence against innocent people to be deplorable. **2.** used in social situations during the era to indicate unavoidable emotional pain inflicted on someone due to fickle romantic activity.

collective a group of people who form an association to pool resources for financial benefit or to further mutual interests. A **commune** can be called a collective, as can a **food co-op** or a group of friends who buy a truck together. Originally a communist term, many people believe it is the same as communism; in reality, it is an ancient form of mutually beneficial social behavior. Tribes, extended families, churches, social clubs, small towns and farming communities have been and continue to be forms of collectivism. (See: **List of Communes** on page 642 in **Lists** at the back of this book)

collective unconscious a theory by **Carl Jung** that memories or mental patterns are shared by all people. This can be somewhat substantiated by the fact that disconnected people around the world often invent or think of the same things simultaneously. This precept is a basic belief of the hippie culture, which uses the idea to advance the concept that all people are brothers and sisters.

Collins, Judy (b. May 1, 1939, Seattle, Washington) White folk/rock singer who first recorded in 1961. Judy was one of the original **hippie chick** singers, along with **Joan Baez** and **Joni Mitchell**. We all wanted to sing with them; the guys all wanted to sleep with them. Her 1967 *Wildflowers* is on many people's top ten hippie album list.

Coltrane, John (1926-1967) jazz saxophonist and composer. One of the leaders in music innovation at the beginning of the hippie era. He was one of the first American composers to incorporate African, East Indian and Asian themes and sounds into his music. Although he was primarily a jazz musician, his influence on all musicians of the time helped to infuse elements of jazz into rock and roll, thus giving it more depth and diversity. Had he not died at age 41, given his nature of experimentation and the revolutionary period in music, he would have contributed even more to the era.

colors the jacket worn by **Hell's Angels bikers**. It is normally a **Levi's** or **jeans** jacket with the sleeves cut off. Club insignia are usually on the back, and other patches express the interests or philosophies of the wearer.

Colombian marching powder *drugs* **cocaine**. Much of the cocaine supply comes from Colombia, and it gives a user energy to march. (See: **cocaine**)

Columbia University student takeover *social issues* located on Manhattan Island in New York City and surrounded by the influences of a socially elite population and the unrest of an urban **folk** culture, Columbia became a cauldron of **civil rights** and **anti-war** protests in the 1960s and 70s. In April, 1968, students seized and occupied campus buildings, including the president's office. The **demonstrations** were led by **Students for a Democratic Society (SDS)** member **Mark Rudd**. (See: **Students for a Democratic Society** and **Mark Rudd** in alphabetical listings) (See also: **Anti-War Events, Groups** and **Leaders** starting on page 562 in **Lists** at the back of this book)

come or **cum** n. *sex* semen, the male sexual secretion carrying the sperm that fertilizes the female's egg.

come v. *sex* to have an orgasm.

come across *sex* to grant sexual favors, usually after an initial reluctance.

come across to give something, usually after an initial reluctance.

comedown the descent from a drug high. A physical or mental depression following the elation of an **amphetamine** or **cocaine** high. **2.** the descent from any exciting experience. The mental depression following the elation of any exciting experience.

come off to return to normal behavior after a drug experience. To experience a physical or mental letdown after a drug high.

come off it stop, change your direction. Possibly a derivative of "Come down off your soap box."

come on or **come onto** *drugs* to begin to experience the effects of a drug.

*come on strong to be pushy or arrogant, often, but not exclusively, in the effort to gain sexual favors.

come onto *sex* to proposition or flirt with someone.

come out *sex* short for **come out of the closet**, meaning to acknowledge one's **homosexuality** to the general public.

come out of the closet *sex* to acknowledge one's **homosexuality** to the general public.

comes (or goes) with the territory what you get as part of the bargain, something endemic to a situation. Examples: "Crabs **come with the territory** if you sleep around." "Regrets

come with the territory if you don't sleep around." In this usage, "territory" is more of a situation or a mental state than a physical place. Another example of a word once used only in the physical realm, expanding during the hippie era to describe a state of mind or emotional place.

come together originally the title of a 1969 **Beatles'** song, it became a **counterculture** anthem and major theme suggesting that people cooperate with one another.

come to the table to get together for negotiations or the discussion of a divisive subject.

coming at you, coming at ya' or **comin' at cha'** a greeting or a warning of impending communication.

*coming from the foundation of a position or point of view. Example: "I am deeply sacrilegious. That's where I'm **coming from**."

comix comic books. During the hippie era, **underground** comic books were plentiful. Second only to recorded music, they were one of the most prolific means of expressing and absorbing **counterculture** philosophy, art and humor. They were most often drawn while the artist was under the influence of drugs or from **stoned** experiences and were expected to be read while stoned. In fact, when read or viewed while straight, most of the "message" was missed. It would take a whole book to do justice to the art form as it was created during the 1960s and 1970s. For more information about the art form, see *A History of Underground Comics* (Ronin, 1987) and *The New Comics* (Berkeley, 1988). (See: **Comix Publishers, Comix & Underground Cartoon Strips** and **Comix Artists of the**

Hippie Era starting on page 640 in **Lists** at the back of this book)

Committee, The a theater troupe that performed for years around San Francisco, California, during the 1960s and 70s. Its members were deeply involved in the **beat** and hippie movements and used their performances to express social dissent and contempt for **uptight** society. Many people passed through the ranks of performers, notably, **Mimi Fariña** and Howard Hesseman.

Committee to Re-elect the President (CRP) (pronounced **CREEP**) President Richard **Nixon's** 1973 re-election organization, whose illegal activities caused his eventual resignation.

common man, the the uncomplicated, **working-class** members of society.

communards members of a commune.

photo by John McCleary ©

commune a group of unrelated people with mutual interests, living together in cooperation for mutual gain. A root form of the word communist. In the hippie era, it was often an arrangement enabling a number of people to live less expensively and to experience common social activities together. Most tribes in primitive cultures and villages in second- and third-world countries function using communal activities and

philosophies. All of the original villages, towns and colonies in America had to rely on communal cooperation to survive. America was originally founded more on communism (cooperation) than capitalism (individual gain). During the hippie era, there were many Christian-influenced communes, as well as **Buddhist**, **Taoist** and some from self-created religions. Political and religious similarities were not always the glue, but many communes sprang up dedicated to issues and lifestyles. A commune can be composed of as few as three or more unrelated people all the way to hundreds, as with **Stephen Gaskin's** Farm in western Tennessee and **Synanon** in the Central California foothills. (See: **Communes of the Hippie Era** on page 642 in **Lists** at the back of this book)

compact car a small, economical automobile introduced to the American public in 1960 by many of the automobile manufactures.

compadre friend. A Spanish word meaning friend adopted by the **counterculture**.

Compleat Idiot's guide the nickname for the book, *How To Keep Your Volkswagen Alive: A Manual of Step by Step Procedures for the Compleat Idiot*. A must-have maintenance manual for any Volkswagen owner of the era, written and first published by John Muir in 1969.

compost n. decaying **organic** matter.

compost heap n. a pile of decaying **organic** matter.

composting v. OK, you asked for it! Composting is a basic **back-to-the-earth** ecological way to reuse food scraps and yard cuttings to reclaim the earth and produce healthy fertilizer. It consists of piling together "dead" plant life and/or clean organic kitchen scraps (vegetables) and letting them decompose into earth. No meat products or oils need apply. The pile is kept damp, covered with something like black plastic, and turned over once a week or so. When this salad is decomposed, it is put into the garden as new, very healthy dirt. One can get fancy by having two or three piles decomposing with older and newer organic material and by building special bins. Spontaneous combustion can occur, so the piles should be in a safe place in the back of the yard. This is also advisable because of the unique perfume of decomposing matter. Composting, just as **brown rice** and bell bottoms, was an integral part of the hippie culture. To those who do not understand the **spirit** of the period, such things as **tarot cards**, composting, and incense are incomprehensible. The era was a time of searching for knowledge and a longing for purity. Even though many of us who lived the life of that time will admit today to some embarrassment for some of the things we did, we will still, almost to a person, say that our efforts were sincere. Many of the things we did then have proven to be of great value and are still in use today. Composting is one of them.

computer chess *computer revolution* the first chess playing computer was **MacHack**, created around 1960 by Richard Greenblatt while working at MIT's multiaccess computing (MAC) project.

computer dating a computerized system used to select a compatible mate for a social event from a data bank of possible choices. First introduced to the public in 1965.

computerize to input information into an electronic, digital storage unit, a computer. The process involves breaking down our elements of communication, our alphabet and our numbering system, into a series of zeros and ones and using that recording tool to save information for retrieval, use and manipulation at a later date. First introduced to the public in 1965.

computer language *computer revolution* the unique set of codes, rules and vocabulary used to program a computer to perform a function. Also called a **programming language**. (See: **Computer Revolution Milestones, Companies and Leaders** starting on page 626 in **Lists** at the back of this book)

computer revolution the development of electronic augmentation of the human brain and the creation of symbiotic interaction between man and computer. The computer revolution started in the 1960s with the development of **integrated circuits**, **silicon chips**, graphic displays, **bit-mapping** and the **mouse**. These and other developments of the era enabled the creation of the **personal computer (PC)** in a size, price and simplicity that enabled ordinary individuals to buy them for home use. Many people think that the computer industry is a prime example of commerce, industry and greed, but they are mistaken. The computer revolution was actually a creative explosion that also had collateral commercial and economic repercussions on our society; yet, it was not greed, but art, that brought this new tool to life. No one could honestly believe that thousands of imaginative young people joyously worked millions of hours just so others could watch pornography on home screens, trade disappearing stocks, or steal money from others thousands of miles away! Education and sharing information were the major stimuli and the real justification for the computer revolution. There is also a close tie to the availability of **marijuana** and psychedelic drugs at the time of the creation of the PC. Many of the best new creations come from environments nurturing freedom of expression and from circumstances that stimulate unconventional experimentation. The hippie era was the intellectual renaissance of the twentieth century. (See: **Computer Revolution Milestones, Events, Companies, Agencies, Groups, and Leaders** starting on page 626 in **Lists** at the back of this book)

Computer Space *computer revolution* the first commercially oriented computer game. Introduced in 1970, developed by Nolan Bushnell from the original non-commercial **Spacewar**. An arcade game distributed by a firm called Nutting Associates. Bushnell later invented **Pong** and founded Atari. (See: **Pong**, **Spacewar** and **video games**)

con a scheme to obtain money, things or favors from someone. Short for confidence. Comes from the term "confidence man," a person who gains one's confidence in order to steal money from them. a.k.a. **hustle**. **2.** to defraud.

conformity being like everyone else, doing what everyone else is doing. Usually, an effort to achieve social acceptance. May be a sign of weakness of character or merely a lack of imagination. Not always a negative, but if the group to which one conforms is not really appropriate to one's personality,

it is hypocritical and can be self-destructive.

photo by Jerry Takigawa ©

confrontation a political demonstration that becomes hostile or even violent. During the **civil rights**, free speech and **anti-war** demonstrations of the hippie era, it became evident that getting arrested was a good way to gain attention for a particular cause. Eventually, political action groups learned to take the legal, peaceful right of assembly to a point at which it pushed the authorities to overreact, thus bringing one's cause to the attention of the public. The issue of breaking the law and restricting other people's civil rights in order to force changes in laws or civil rights was a moral concern then, and remains so today in such cases as antiabortion **demonstrations**.

Confucianism worship of Confucius, an ancient Chinese philosopher. Once the state religion of China before being suppressed by Communism. Based on the writings of Confucius and earlier "classics" emphasizing ethics, benevolence and righteousness. Confucius lived from 551 to 479 B.C.; he was the governor of the Chung-tu Province and then "**dropped out**," traveled widely and studied, acquiring many disciples with his wisdom and interpretation of earlier writings. His philosophy was published shortly after his death.

Congress of Racial Equality (CORE) *social issues* a **civil rights** organization founded in 1942 by George Houser and James Leonard Farmer, based on a paper by Farmer entitled the "Provisional Plan for Brotherhood Mobilization." Bayard Rustin was a CORE leader. CORE organized the first **freedom riders**, who rode into the Southern states on a bus in May, 1961, to draw attention to segregated transportation. CORE was the first Black **civil rights** organization to study and employ techniques of nonviolence. (See: **Civil Rights Events, Groups and Leaders** starting on page 546 in **Lists** at the back of this book)

connect or **connection** to communicate in profound terms, having things in common to talk about, sexual compatibility. Example: "Boy, did we **connect**." "We have a deep socio-sexual **connection**; she's my social worker dispensing food stamps, and I get horny every time I see her."

connected knowing the right people. Being on the "inside."

connected *drugs* having a source for drugs.

connection *drugs* a drug supplier.

Connor, Eugene "Bull" *social issues* Police Chief and Public Safety Commissioner of Birmingham, Alabama, during the **civil rights** demonstrations of the early 1960s. After the **Freedom Riders** were beaten in May, 1961, and he was asked why the police were not there to protect the riders, Bull said, "It was Mother's Day and they were visiting their mothers." Connor is the person who ordered dogs and fire hoses turned loose on marchers in May, 1963,

when he and his men arrested participants as young as six years of age.

conscientious objector (CO) *social issues* someone who objects to war and the taking of human life as a matter of conscience based on religious or moral principles. At the beginning of the **Vietnam War**, the US government recognized COs only if they could prove membership in a religious organization that adhered to such beliefs (**Quakers**, Mennonites, Jehovah's Witnesses, Hindus, etc.) or if they had a history of pacifism. As the war progressed, the Selective Service system was bombarded by more and more requests for CO status on other than religious grounds. In 1965, the Supreme Court ruled in favor of the first CO on strictly moral grounds, Daniel Seeger, a New York pacifist. The government often required some noncombatant service to compensate for the normal time of military service. Some COs found themselves in Vietnam as medics or corpsmen in situations in which they were forced to take up weapons and kill to defend themselves. In 1966, there were just over six COs for every 100 inductees; by 1972, more draftees were given CO status than those who actually joined the service, 130 COs for every 100 inductees. Between 1965 and 1970, over 170,000 were given CO exemptions. Also from 1965 to 1975, more than 22,000 Americans were indicted for draft violations. A total of 8,756 men were convicted; 4,001 were sentenced to prison, although not all served their terms.

consciousness during the hippie era, this word took on a more spiritual connotation for many people, eventually coming to mean "awareness in a religious or spiritual sense."

consciousness-raising (C-R) or **consciousness-expanding** the act of mentally evolving into a more spiritual self-awareness or a more benevolent social awareness of others. This was usually done through **meditation**, drugs or some form of **group therapy**.

conservative someone who is cautious with their money and in their political and social activity. Conservatism resists change, both good and bad, and in this way it is contrary to true human nature. Conservatives are more stagnant than liberals. Liberals are more willing to adapt to the changes in life around them (pragmatic). Pragmatism is humankind's strongest mental tool; it is what has allowed us to evolve.

contact *drugs* the person from whom one buys drugs.

contact high *drugs* getting **high** without using drugs merely by being in contact with someone who is under the influence of drugs. It is a phenomenon that can actually be experienced if one is sensitive to the feelings of others. It helps if one is familiar with the actual experience of being **stoned** on drugs.

containment, (policy of) *politics* the US foreign policy toward communism adopted during the Truman administration in 1947. The Truman Doctrine stated that communism must be contained from expanding its influence. Used as the justification for our involvement in both the Korean and **Vietnam Wars**. The Truman Doctrine was the reason for America's fixation with the containment policy. The **domino theory** was a prominent belief in the late 1950s and early 60s that, if not contained by force, communism would topple capitalism and **democracy** like falling dominos.

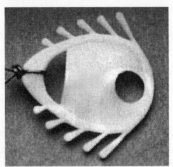

Dalkon Shield

contraception the prevention of pregnancy. During the hippie era, **birth control** was a primary concern, and the methods available were numerous and diverse. Introduced in 1960, the contraceptive pill has been credited with launching the **sexual revolution**. The **intrauterine device (IUD)** was reinvented in the 1950s and used during the era. Crude I.U.D.s had been used in the early 1900s. The diaphragm found some popularity during the hippie era. Spermicides were normally used only in conjunction with diaphragms, and the douche, to which some women cling, has never been a very effective form of contraception. In the period following the 1960 introduction of the pill and before AIDS, condoms were definitely in declining use. Abstention, it seemed, was not an option during the hippie era. Failure rates of the various contraception techniques are as follows:

(All statistics for a one-year period)
Spermicides: 20 pregnancies per 100 women
Condoms: 12 to 14 pregnancies per 100 women (from improper use)
Diaphragm: 12 per 100 (improper use)
I. U. D.: 3 per 100
The Pill: 3 per 100 (from improper use)

cook or **cooking**   upbeat, exciting or **hot**. Examples: "That guitarist can really **cook**, and I don't mean eggs, baby!" "He's really **cooking**; the dance floor's a radical zone."

cook *drugs* to heat and dissolve **heroin**, or other such powdered drug, with water in a spoon or some such container prior to injecting it into the bloodstream.

Cooke, Sam   (b. January 22, 1935, Chicago, Ill.; d. December 11, 1964, Los Angeles, Calif.) *gospel, soul music* singer/songwriter whose gospel/soul background and sweet voice made his recordings some of the most romantic moments in our lives.

cooker *drugs* the spoon, bottle cap or container used to heat and dissolve **heroin**, or other such powdered drugs, with water prior to injecting it into the bloodstream.

Cookie Monster   one of the most endearing characters from the TV show "**Sesame Street**." **2.** the name given to one of the first computer viruses.

cook me down *sex* an expression used to ask someone for sexual intercourse. A request for sex. Saw obscure use in some inner-city cultures.

*cool   self-confident, **mellow**, appropriate, acceptable. A **jazz**, then **beatnik**, term adopted by the hippie culture. A word with many uses. Although sometimes the brunt of humorous, hippie characterizations, it is now very much accepted as a common American idiom. The use and misuse of this word are important indications of how cool one really is, or isn't. Although this term originated in the 1950s, it was not widely used until the hippie era, at which time it acquired subtle, expanded definitions. The ultimate use

of cool is to describe someone who has charisma. The exact meaning of cool is defined by social values. During the hippie era, cool had one set of parameters, and today cool has other defining rules. Yet, even within any given era, there are alternative definitions of cool, depending upon the different subcultures or areas of the world. It's impossible to define what cool is to everyone, but a simple explanation is "appropriate activity within existing social circumstances." To be quite frank, this whole definition is not cool; if it were, all it would say is, "I am; you're not."

cool head   someone who maintains control in a difficult situation.

cool it or **cool out**   an admonition to relax, go slowly or stop what one is doing.

cool your jets   relax, slow down, don't get excited. From aeronautical jargon meaning to shut off one's jet engine. It also may have come from the TV cartoon show "The Jetsons."

Cooper, Alice (b. Vincent Furnier, Feb. 4, 1948, Detroit, Mich.) *rock & roll* the leader of many bands, mostly named **Alice Cooper**, which he formed in the mid-1960s. Cooper is prominent for pioneering shock-rock with simulated executions, mutilation of children's dolls and gore. Furnier got the name from a ouija board; Alice Cooper was supposedly a 17th-century witch reincarnated as Furnier.

cop   to get or buy something, often drugs. Example: "Say, man, want to **cop** some **cool**, new designer **jeans**?"

cop a break   to get lucky or to gain an advantage. Example: "You're too hippie. You'll never **cop a break** with her; she wears shoes."

cop a feel *sex* to touch a person sexually. Sometimes, it may be a surreptitious act, committed without the person's approval.

cop a plea to plead guilty to a criminal offense in order to obtain a lighter sentence.

***cop out** v. to neglect responsibilities. To give in to pressures or refuse to support issues of social importance.

cop out n. someone who succumbs to pressure or refuses to face responsibilities.

cop some Z's to sleep. Example: "You should **cop some Z's**. You look like the night of the living dead."

cop to to admit or to accept. Examples: "Never **cop to** indecent exposure without a second opinion." "**Cop to** the laws of nature and come down off that roof."

copulate *sex* to have sexual intercourse. a.k.a. **ball, bang, couple, fuck, get into her pants, get into someone, get it on, hump, jerk, lay, make it, make love, make the scene, nail, nut, pile, punch, ride, rip off, schtup, score, screw, shack up, strap, strap on, stroke, trick, work**, etc.

copulation *sex* sexual intercourse. a.k.a. **big time, coupling, hit, leg, nookie, piece, piece of ass, piece of tail, tail, trim**.

CORE (See: **Congress of Racial Equality**)

cork a humorous definition of a tampon.

corn hole *sex* **anal intercourse**, either **homosexual** or **heterosexual**.

cosmic the creative forces of God and the divine, infinite intelligence of the Supreme Being. Universally impor-

tant. There are civil laws, natural laws, and cosmic laws.

cosmos our world, neighborhood or house. During the hippie era, this word achieved an even more spiritual meaning, becoming the place where we exist in infinite harmony with nature. From the Greek word *kosmos*, meaning world.

photo by John McCleary ©

counterculture a group of people who are opposed to *some* aspects of the established culture in which they live. Historically, they are members of a society who, through education or moral enlightenment, find fault with the government under which they live. According to the American constitution, citizens are not merely allowed to protest their government, but are actually encouraged to raise opposing viewpoints. There are numerous reasons for the existence of countercultures: economic variations, differences in **social consciousness**, ethnic, religious and moral distinctions. Counterculture views are not always completely valid, yet they may express an important objective opinion of an established culture that has become jaded or corrupt.

If the counterculture, with its new ideas, can effect change without being suppressed by the established culture, then an orderly revolution of positive change will occur in society. Sadly, too often the old, established leaders of a society are unwilling to recognize their faults, and therefore fight the counterculture, thus producing a violent revolution and creating hardships for everyone. The term counterculture was reportedly coined by author and journalist Theodore Roszak in 1968.

country a person from a rural area or someone who is backward. Emanating from a rural area, not modern or contemporary.

Country Joe and the Fish *psychedelic/ rock & roll* Country Joe McDonald's hippie **rock and roll** band formed in San Francisco, California, in 1965. They played at both **Monterey Pop** and **Woodstock**. One of the most politically motivated bands of the era. Country Joe is notorious for his F-U-C-K cheer ("Gimme an F!" etc.), in which he led nearly half a million people at Woodstock. Country Joe McDonald is still picking and singing his anti-war message and is available to add credibility to any liberal cause.

coupled in a romantic relationship with someone.

Cousteau, Jacques-Yves (1910-1997) inventor, marine explorer, pioneer in the development of the aqualung for underwater exploration. His expeditions with the research ships *Calypso* and *Alcyone* and his movies about the sea have created public interest in the marine environment. His research into pollution of the oceans has garnered concern for their protection as part of our environment and a necessity to our own survival.

Cousteau Society an **environmental** and marine research foundation created in 1973 by **Jacques-Yves Cousteau**. Formed to fund marine research and document environmental changes. It maintains the research vessels *Calypso* and *Alcyone*.

covered, got it covered, or **it's covered** it's taken care of. Don't worry! Same as **no problem**.

cover your ass protect yourself from business or social repercussions. Normally infers that one should find an excuse or alibi.

cowabunga an exclamation most often used sarcastically or in humorous, tongue-in-cheek circumstances. Also employed by surfers as they slid off the face of an eight-foot wave or did something exhilarating. Originated on "The Howdy Doody Show" as a phrase used by Chief Thunderthud. "Howdy Doody" was the first children's TV show and ran in the late 1940s and 1950s.

cowboy a derogatory term for someone who takes his masculinity too seriously. Example: "That **cowboy** wears his six-shooter behind a zipper."

cowboy a name used instead of one's real name in a confrontation. Example: "Cool it, **cowboy**."

COYOTE an organization created to promote tolerance toward sex workers and prostitutes. Started in 1973 by Margo St. James and **Flo Kennedy,** this organization has a history of helping sex workers with emotional support, health issues and alternative job opportunities. It is an acronym meaning Cast Off Your Old Tired Ethics.

C-R (See: **consciousness-raising**)

crabs body lice, usually found in the pubic hair. A common annoyance during the hippie era due to the amount of cohabitation and some lack of personal hygiene.

crack a derogatory term for a woman. **2.** the female sex organ or **vagina 3.** the crevice between the buttocks.

cracked house a vacant house that has been opened and occupied by hippies. A British term, the practice of cracking houses was much more prevalent in England. One well-known cracked house in St. John's Wood, London, had been the Cambodian Embassy until Cambodia became communist and severed relations with England. It was a large mansion, occupied by young people for years, and kept pristine and in its original condition, complete with court photos of the Cambodian royal family on the wall. A cracked house is a great deal different than a crack house, a term introduced with crack **cocaine** in the 1980s. A cracked house is sometimes also called a squat.

cracked up to be (it ain't what it's) not what it was advertised to be or it didn't come up to expectations.

crack up funny, laughable. Example: "The movie was a **crack up**, but the cost of the popcorn was larceny."

cramp (one's) **style** to get in someone's way, to annoy, or disrupt. Examples: "Playing off key **cramps my style**."

crank *drugs* **heroin. 2.** any drug with a **speed** effect. Related to the crank once used to start cars.

cranked up *drugs* **high** on drugs containing **speed**.

cranked up music volume turned up.

cranking or **crankin'** doing something with skill or exuberance. Example: "He's really **crankin'** on the spoons."

crank it up turn the music up.

crank up *drugs* to inject drugs. Related to the crank once used to start cars.

crap literally, excrement or feces. Anything that is useless or unwanted.

crap out to quit. To give up or fail.

*crash to go to sleep or come down from any high. A term introduced to the American public about 1965.

crash pad a place to sleep or come down from a drug high. Came to mean a friendly place that welcomed anyone who was in need of housing.

crash landing an abrupt return to reality, often relating to coming off a drug high.

Crawdaddy *rock & roll* the first rock and roll music magazine. First published in 1964.

crazed crazy.

cream *sex* semen, the male sexual secretion carrying the sperm that fertilizes the female's egg.

Cream *rock & roll* one of the first super groups, formed in England in 1966. **Eric Clapton** (b. Eric Clapp, March 30, 1945, Ripley, England), gtr., voc.; Jack Bruce (b. May 14, 1943, Glasgow, Scotland), bass, harmonica, voc.; **Ginger Baker** (b. Aug. 19, 1939, Lewisham, England), drums, voc. Their recordings of "White Room" and **Robert Johnson's** "Crossroads" are among the most loved hippie era songs. They stayed together off and on until 1969, when Eric Clapton and Ginger Baker left to start another super group, **Blind Faith**, with **Steve Winwood** (b. May 12, 1948, Birmingham, Eng.), kybds., gtr., voc.; Rick Grech (b. Nov. 1, 1946, Bordeaux, France; d. March 17, 1990) bass, violin. Inducted into The Rock and Roll Hall of Fame in 1993.

cream pies and seltzer bottles the weapons supposedly used for crowd control by **Wavy Gravy's** security force at **Woodstock**.

cream, to to beat, destroy or devastate.

creamed beaten, destroyed or devastated. Example: "His kinetic sculpture came around the corner and **creamed** my stabile."

credibility gap the space between the truth and a lie. Initially, a military term that was eventually used against the Pentagon. A sarcastic admission by military leaders that it was sometimes necessary to lie to the American public in order to protect the reputation of the Armed Forces.

Creedence Clearwater Revival *country rock & roll* formed in 1959 in El Cerrito, California. A pivotal country rock band led by John Fogerty (b. May 28, 1945, Berkeley, Calif.). The band had a number of very important hit songs that defined the era before Fogerty went on to a successful solo career. Inducted into The Rock and Roll Hall of Fame in 1993.

CREEP *politics* the **Committee to Re-elect the President (CRP).** President **Richard Nixon's** 1973 re-election organization, whose illegal activities caused his eventual resignation.

crib room, house or bed. In the Orient, cribs were small cubicles in which prostitutes were kept.

Croce, Jim (b. January 10, 1943, Philadelphia, Penn.; d. September 20, 1973, **Natchitoches, La.)** *rock & roll* singer/songwriter who recorded several early-1970s hit songs before his death in an airplane accident.

crock or **crock of shit** a lie, load of lies.

Crosby, Stills, Nash and Young *rock & roll* officially the first super group, it was formed in 1968 in Los Angeles. David Crosby, formerly of the Byrds, (b. David Van Cortland, Aug. 14, 1941, Los Angeles, Calif.), gtr., voc.; Stephen Stills, formerly of **Buffalo Springfield**, (b. Jan. 3, 1945, Dallas, Tex), gtr., kybds., bass, voc.; Graham Nash, formerly of the Hollies, (b. Feb 2, 1942, Blackpool, England), gtr., kybds., voc.; Neil Young, formerly of Buffalo Springfield, (b. Nov. 12, 1945, Toronto, Can.), gtr., voc. So many songs recorded by this group exemplify the hippie era. Crosby, Stills & Nash as a group were inducted into the Rock and Roll Hall of Fame in 1997. Young was inducted into the Rock and Roll Hall of Fame in 1995.

cross-dresser a person who dresses in the clothing of the opposite sex. This can be done as a form of sexual orientation or as heterosexual turn-on, similar to dressing in **drag** for fun. Unlike a **transvestite**, who is usually **homosexual**, a cross-dresser may not have homosexual tendencies. (See: **drag** and **transvestite**)

cross-tops *drugs* Benzedrine. Amphetamine pills with a cross pattern on top. Same as **white crosses.** The college student's best friend at exam cram time. A buffered version came in green triangles. **Uppers**.

crowded encroached upon, hassled or bothered by someone. Can be physical or psychological.

CRP (pronounced "**CREEP**") (See: **Committee to Re-elect the President**)

cruise to drive aimlessly.

cruise to search for a sexual partner.

cruiser a person who travels around in a seemingly aimless manner. **2.** someone who drives a customized car or motorcycle. **3.** a vehicle that has been altered, **chopped** and lowered, to ride close to the ground. (See: **chopped hog** and **low rider**)

Crumb, R. (Robert) (Aug. 30, 1943-) cartoonist. Numerous people during the hippie era could be labeled **counterculture** cartoonists, but none personified the genre as well as R. Crumb. A mainstay of **Zap Comics** and Big Ass Comics, he created and drew such endearing and sometimes revolting characters as **Mr. Natural**, Li'l Cute, Valerie the Vegetarian, Little Johnny Fuckerfaster, Fat 'N' Sassy, Dale Steinberger, Eggs Ackley, Mrs. Quiver and Artsy Fartsy. Crumb was responsible for many hippie-era icons, important phrases and philosophies, including Fritz the Cat, Mr. Natural and his **Truckin'**. Crumb's influences were **Pogo Possum** of the 1940s and 1950s and England's *Puck* magazine cartoons. Crumb once worked for American Greeting Cards in Cleveland. In recent years, R. Crumb has branched out into music and movies.

Crump, Diane first professional female jockey. Rode in the Kentucky Derby in 1970.

crunch a time restraint or deadline. Example: "We're in a **crunch** right now. We have to paint her body for the party before she gets goosebumps."

crutch *drugs* a **marijuana** roach holder made by rolling a matchbook cover into a cylinder and placing the **roach** in one end of it.

crystal *drugs* any of the powdered drugs in their solid state, i.e., **heroin**, **cocaine crystal**, **crystal methedrine**, etc. (See: **PCP**)

crystal ship *drugs* a syringe containing some form of crystalline drugs, i.e., **heroin**, **cocaine crystal**, **crystal methedrine**, etc. One of **The Doors'** songs was entitled "Crystal Ships."

cube *drugs* a **sugar cube** containing a drop of **LSD**. **2.** a **gram** of **hashish**.

cubehead *drugs* someone who uses **LSD**. Refers to the fact that much of the **acid** at the time was in liquid form dropped onto a **sugar cube**.

cult a group of people bound together by religious beliefs outside the **mainstream**. Often headed by a charismatic leader who has taken the position of intermediary to God or who has convinced followers that he or she is actually the personification of God. In recent years, cults have acquired a negative connotation because many of them have been destructive, violent or oppressive (Jim Jones and The People's Temple, David Koresh and the Branch Davidians, etc.). In realty, any religious offshoot, good or bad, can be considered a cult. (See: **Gurus** on Page 648 in the **Lists** at the back of this book)

cum *sex* one spelling of the word **come**, meaning semen, the male sexual secretion carrying the sperm that fertilizes the female's egg.

cunnilingus *sex* oral stimulation of the female sexual organs, the **clitoris** and vulva (vaginal opening). As distinguished from **fellatio**, the oral stimulation of the male sexual organ. Not a new term to the hippie era, nor a new idea in the last three millennia. Merely something done more often without shame and hypocrisy during the 1960s

photo by John McCleary ©

and 1970s. In street language, cunnilingus is the act of going down on a woman and "eating" her cunt. Can be a homosexual or heterosexual act. a.k.a. **box lunch, hair pie, fur burger, giving head, going down, muff diving**.

cunt *sex* one of the many euphemisms for the **vagina** or female sex organ. Of French origin. Although this word was not new, it was greatly expanded into new, subtle usages in the hippie era, when it evolved into an expletive or negative intensifier. Sometimes interchangeable with and used in the same context as words like shit or dick. Many scatological and anatomical words like this were used more often in America after WWII. Such words as fart and cunt came back to America with soldiers and began to find more use in some social groups. The increased usage of these words came from a combination of cross-cultural communication with other American soldiers and the discovery of such words in use in the countries they occupied. In an article for *Suck,* Germaine Greer wrote, "Cunt is beautiful, Squat over a mirror or lie on your back with you legs apart and the sun shining in.... Keep it soft, warm, clean.... Give it your own loving names, not...pussy, twat box or the epithets of hate, like gash, slit, crack...."

cunt a pejorative term directed at an objectionable or promiscuous woman. During the late 1950s and into the 60s and 70s, scatological and anatomical words such as this evolved into pronouns describing people, rather than merely nouns describing body parts and body functions. During the hippie era, these words found expanded usage, yet still remained unacceptable in "polite society" and in more conservative atmospheres. Many genital terms are used to describe the entire person in a derogatory way. Example: "He's a cunt, she's a prick and they're all dicks."

cure *drugs* to age **marijuana**, often in a solution of water or wine with honey or sugar. Sometimes, merely drying the leaves.

curse or **the curse** menstruation, a woman's monthly period.

cusp an astrological term meaning the transitional dates between two birth signs of the **zodiac**. Example: "He was born on the **cusp** and has all the bad traits of both signs."

Custer Died for Your Sins a slogan and bumper sticker promoted by the **Native America** population and **liberal counterculture**, referring to the destruction of the American Indian way of life on this continent.

cut *drugs* to dilute expensive drugs with an inexpensive, inert substance in order to increase the volume and make more money from the sale of the product. Talcum power or powdered milk were sometimes used.

cut a derogatory remark. Example: "What a vicious **cut**; with the slice of her tongue, she reduced that macho freak to a sliver of meat."

cut *rock & roll* a song on an **album**.

cut the ice to accomplish something. To succeed. Often related to passing a test. Example: "She can **cut the ice** in the garden; give her a seed and you'll soon have a salad."

cut it to withstand something, to survive a test. Example: "I may not be able to **cut it**, but I'll lie trying."

cut no ice or **cuts no ice** false, of no importance or relevance to a situation. Indicates dissatisfaction with someone's effort or idea. Example: "That **cuts no ice** with me; I invented that brand of bullshit." From the fact that only a hot knife cuts ice, and a cold effort won't succeed.

cutoffs shorts created by cutting off the legs of old, worn out **jeans**.

cut out to leave or exit, generally with some urgency.

cut some sides *rock & roll* to record a **phonograph record**. Refers to the **sides** of the record.

cut some slack or **cut** (someone) **slack** give someone a **break**. Example: "**Cut** him **some slack**; he can think only every other Tuesday."

cut some Z's to sleep. Same as **cop some Z's**.

cutting edge *computer revolution* the most advanced, up-to-date technology. New territory. May relate to a knife blade; possibly to the sharp bow of an icebreaking ship.

cuz originally short for "cousin," but widely used as a greeting or term of friendship. Examples: "What's up, **cuz**?" "What's the buzz, **cuz**?"

cybernetics *computer revolution* electronic or mechanical enhancement of a human being. From the Greek word meaning "steersman." Coined by computer pioneer Norbert Wiener in his 1948 book entitled *Cybernetics; Control and Communication in the Animal and the Machine*. His thesis described a general science of mechanisms for maintaining order in a disorderly universe. One of the most valuable elements of understanding that contributed to the development of the **personal computer**.

D

D *drugs* stands for **dope**. Primarily a British usage referring to **cannabis**. The use of initials and abbreviations in drug culture communication was originally intended to exclude outsiders and the authorities; it eventually became the **cool** thing to do.

D series Martin guitar the most popular acoustical, steel string guitar of the hippie era. Formal name, Dreadnought. Still manufactured by the **C. F. Martin** (guitar) Company, one of the oldest guitar manufacturing companies in the United States. Christian Fredric Martin founded the company in New York City in 1833.

D.A. **D**istrict **A**ttorney.

d.a. a hairstyle that looks like a "**d**uck's **a**ss in back of the head." Most common in the 1950s with the youth culture of rock-and-rollers. Also sported by British **rockers** in the early 1960s. By the hippie era, it had become passé, worn only by **redneck** types. It became a handy way to recognize someone who was behind the times. Example:

"He's so out of it he thinks **acid** is indigestion, and he wears a **d.a.**"

dada nonsensical, outrageous and revolutionary. To call something dada was a compliment in weirdness. Example: "That party was a real **dada** experience. I really liked it when three people threw up at once." Adopted during the hippie era from the nonsensical name given to a school of art and literature that appeared in the 1920s, rejecting all laws of art up to that time. Much of dada was **performance art**, and the objective was to be as strange as possible, even socially revolting, if necessary. The precursor of the **guerrilla theater**, **be-ins**, **pop art** and junk art of the 1960s and 70s.

daddy *sex* a woman's term for her male lover, financial support or husband. Also used in a male homosexual context.

photo by John McCleary ©

dago red any cheap, red wine. Dago refers loosely to something of Italian origin.

daisy chain *sex* a sexual union of three or more partners joined in a line. Can be **heterosexual, homosexual** or **bisexual**.

Dalai Lama the temporal leader of Tibetan **esoteric Buddhism**, regarded as the human incarnation of the **Bodhisattva** of Compassion, Avalokiteshvara. There have been 14 incarnations, with a new Dalai Lama chosen as a child, tutored by the present incarnation and ascending upon the death of the former. The present, or 14th, Dalai Lama was born Tenzin Gyatso in 1935 and was recognized as the reincarnation at the age of two. He has resided in exile in Dharamsala, India, since 1959, following the Chinese invasion of Tibet in 1950. The present Dalai Lama is not only the spiritual leader of the Tibetan people but also the head of Tibet's government-in-exile. In Tibetan Buddhism, the phrase **om mani padme hum** is used as a **mantra**. (See: **Esoteric Buddhism** and **om mani padme hum**)

Daley, Richard *social issues* Chicago Mayor during the August, 1968, **Democratic National Convention**, where **Vietnam War** protesters were beaten and maced outside the convention center. Called "Little Caesar" because of his dictatorial nature. It was widely agreed that Mayor Richard Daley's police force overreacted with totalitarian, gestapo tactics. Mayor Daley was recorded saying, "The police are not here to create disorder, but to preserve disorder," an obvious mistake in words, but thought by many to reveal his true attitude. (See: **Chicago Seven, Chicago Seven Trial** and **Chicago Democratic National Convention**)

damage emotional or psychological problems. One of those words that took on a more profound meaning during the hippie era. It was used to describe effects on a psychological as well as physical level. Examples: "George's attitude does serious **damage** to his relationships." "With her looks, she does **damage** to monogamy."

damaged psychological injury or emotional scars. Again, this word was often used to describe a psychological circumstance rather than a physical one during the hippie era. Example: "Jake was badly **damaged** when his girlfriend ran off with his own sister."

damaged goods a girl or young woman who has indulged in sexual activity. A term used only by conservative or sexually repressed individuals. Example: "She's **damaged goods** and proud of it." **2.** a woman who has been raped. Used only by insensitive individuals.

damaged goods someone who has been used or abused sexually or psychologically. Example: "His father abused him; he's **damaged goods**."

damp *sex* sexually aroused. Relates to the vaginal secretion of a sexually aroused female. Example: "One look at him and she went **damp**." Similar to **wet** or **juicy**.

Alicia Bay Laurel ©

dances of the hippie era: Boogaloo, Breakdown, Bristol Stomp, Bump, Chuckie, Clam, Electric Bump, Funky Broadway, Frug, Hitchhike, Hustle, Jerk, L.A. Hustle, Lock, Mashed Potatoes, Monkey, New York Hustle, Philly Dog, Pony, Ride-a-Bike, Skanking, Scooby Doo, Skate, Slop, Swim, Twist, Walking The Dog, Watusi.

dance your ass off *rock & roll* a party phrase meaning to have a good time dancing.

dancing fool *rock & roll* someone who dances to excess. From a song of that name by **Frank Zappa**. Dancing fools will dance by themselves if no partner is handy; in fact, they often prefer to dance alone to eliminate annoying relationships that might interrupt their dancing.

d and d drunk and disorderly.

"Danny the Red" *politics* (See: **Daniel Cohn-Bendit**)

Darin, Bobby (b. Walden Robert Cassotto, May 14, 1936, Bronx, New York; d. December 20, 1973, Los Angeles, Calif.) *rock & roll, folk* singer/songwriter who started out as a rock and roll teen idol, but eventually achieved serious acceptance as an artist with such songs as "If I Were a Carpenter" written by Tim Hardin, for whom he wrote "Simple Song of Freedom." Bobby Darin was a prolific songwriter, and his excursions into **folk music** themes helped to create the folk-rock era of the 1970s. Inducted into The Rock and Roll Hall of Fame in 1990.

dark meat *sex* an African American sexual partner. Used by a White male or female to describe a Black lover.

Dark Night of the Soul the final phase in the growth of a "New Man." That moment of purification of one's soul that opens the way to a mystic union with God. A metaphysical term not generally used in **mainstream** Christian doctrine.

Daughters of Bilitis (DOB) *social issues* a leading **lesbian** organization founded by Del Martin and Phyllis Lyon in San

Francisco, California, in 1955. They published *The Ladder*, a magazine on lesbian issues, from 1956 until 1972. *The Ladder* is said to be one of the single most important manifestations of the organized lesbian resistance movement. The DOB's charter states, "A Women's Organization for the Purpose of Promoting the Integration of the Homosexual into Society...."

Davis, Angela Yvonne (1944-) *social issues* a Black professor of philosophy at UCLA who was fired in 1969 for being a member of the Communist Party. In August of 1970, she became a fugitive and was eventually brought to trial for allegedly supplying weapons for an attempted jailbreak of the **Soledad Brothers**. In the escape attempt, hostages were taken at the San Rafael, California, Court House, and a friend of Davis's, two prisoners, and a judge were killed in the battle. For a time, Davis was on the FBI's Ten Most Wanted List. She was eventually absolved of complicity in the attempt. She ran for vice president on the Communist Party ticket in 1980 and 1984. As of this writing, Davis is teaching **ethnic studies** in the University of California system. Angela Davis remains one of the most vocal supporters of **free-speech** and **civil rights**. She is also famous for popularizing the **Afro** hairstyle. (See: **Soledad Brothers** and **Afro**)

Davis, James officially, the first US soldier killed in Vietnam, December 22, 1961. (See: **Vietnam War Deaths** on page 560 in **Lists** at the back of this book)

Davis, Miles (b. May 26, 1926, Alton, Ill.; d. Sept. 28, 1991, Santa Monica, Calif.) *jazz, fusion, rock* Black **jazz** trumpet player who first performed in the 1940s, and began to record on his own in the mid-1960s. His music and style had a major influence on rock and roll, and his venture into fusion influenced many musicians.

Davis, Rennie (1941-) *social issues* a member of the **Chicago Seven**, along with **David Dellinger**, John Froines, **Tom Hayden**, **Abbie Hoffman**, **Jerry Rubin** and Lee Weiner. They were **anti-war**, and peace and freedom movement leaders who were arrested and tried as co-conspirators for crossing state borders to incite to riot during the 1968 **Democratic National Convention**. Davis was convicted and also received a concurrent sentence for contempt of court. Eventually, the conviction was overturned because of Judge Hoffman's gross misconduct during the trial. Rennie Davis has a bachelor's degree in political science and a master's degree in labor and industrial relations. His father was an economic adviser to President Truman. In 1965, Rennie worked in New York as a community organizer for **Students for a Democratic Society (SDS)**. In 1967, he traveled to North Vietnam and joined the **Mobilization Committee** on his return. Davis also coordinated the Pentagon March Against the **Vietnam War** in 1967. (See: **Chicago Seven, Chicago Seven Trial** and **Chicago Democratic National Convention**)

Davis, Spencer (Spencer Davis Group) *rhythm & blues, rock & roll* formed in 1963 in Birmingham, England, by Spencer Davis (b. July 17, 1942, Swansea, Wales), voc., gtr, with **Steve Winwood** (b. May 12, 1948, Birmingham) voc.; and others. An important group in the transition from blues to rock and for its introduction of Steve Winwood on such recordings as "Gimme Some Lovin'" and "I'm a Man."

Spencer Davis and various members of the group continued to record into the 1970s.

Day, Dorothy (1897-1980) *social issues* a **radical** activist and writer, she was initially a Marxist, but became a Catholic in 1927. In 1933, with Peter Maurin, she founded The Catholic Worker Movement, devoted to aiding the poor through hospitality houses and other facilities. She promoted the philosophy of personal Christian social activism through articles in *The Catholic Worker* newspaper. Deeply spiritual, she is regarded by many as a modern-day saint. Her writings include the 1952 autobiography, *The Long Loneliness*.

Day-Glo a florescent paint, ink or paper used for posters and bumper stickers. The effect was a brighter-than-expected image that became **psychedelic** with the help of florescent light and drugs. One of the processes creating the florescent glow incorporates chemicals that actually produce an electric impulse when exposed to florescent light. This phenomenon is related to the glow produced by lightning bugs.

photo by John McCleary ©

Days of Rage *social issues* **demonstrations** by the **Weathermen** in Chicago in October, 1969, to protest the violence of the Chicago police at the 1968 Democratic Convention and the prosecution of the **Chicago Eight**. The days of rage started shortly before midnight on October 6, 1969, when the **Weathermen** blew up the nation's only monument to policemen, located in Chicago's Haymarket Square. By the end of the rage on October 11th, six demonstrators had been wounded by police gunfire, many others battered and hundreds jailed. A city official was paralyzed from the neck down in a self-inflicted confrontation with a wall. The demonstration was very nearly the death knell of the Weathermen, but it did add to the growing sense of domestic crisis in America and thus helped to further the cause of such **civil rights** groups. (See: **Civil Rights Events, Groups and Leaders** starting on page 546 in **Lists** at the back of this book)

DDT *social issues* dichloro-diphenyl-trichloroethane, once the most widely used pesticide, assailed by environmentalists because it travels through the food chain to birds and fish, creating calcium deficiencies that cause eggs to break prematurely, thus greatly reducing populations. The US Department of Agriculture suspended use of DDT on July 9, 1969, one of the first and greatest victories for **environmental** activism. Completely banned in the US on June 14, 1972. *Silent Spring*, a book published in 1962 and written by **Rachel Carson** (1907-1964), helped lead to the ban by exposing and condemning the indiscriminate use of pesticides, especially DDT. Some US companies are still selling DDT in other countries, a practice environmentalists feel to be morally reprehensible. (See: **Ecology and Environmental Issues** starting on page 614 in **Lists** at the back of this book)

DEA the acronym for the Drug Enforcement Agency of the US Government.

deadass boring or less than exceptional. Often used to intensify words like boring or stupid. Examples: "He's a **deadass** when it comes to conversation." "This is a **deadass** boring party."

dead bang on target, serious or correct. Often used to intensify words, such as serious or correct. Sometimes used in the same context as **right on**, **dead on** or **bang on**. Examples: "You're **dead bang** on about the taste of bean curd." "Judy is **dead bang** serious about her rock-and-roll-star toenail collection."

deadhead *drugs* someone **damaged** by drugs.

Dead Head *rock & roll* a devoted follower of **The Grateful Dead** rock group. To qualify, one must have attended a brain-numbing number of their concerts and have at least one piece of **tie-dye** clothing. Contrary to what one might think, it is impossible to recognize all Dead Heads. Your accountant or the middle-aged housewife up the street could be one. Some of "them" are truly recognizable only when they arrive at a Dead concert.

deadly dangerous. Annoying or uncomfortable. Not literally lethal, nor does it necessarily indicate physical danger; often just psychological discomfort. Example: "Arthur's jokes are **deadly** boring to someone with an IQ over 75." **2.** potent. Example: "Deva's dope is **deadly**."

dead meat terminated or in danger of termination. Seldom meaning a literal death; often it is merely a sarcastic threat. Examples: "If you don't ask her to the love-in, you're **dead meat**."

"Duke was **dead meat** the moment he opened his brain to speak."

dead mouse a used tampon. Visualize; it has a tail and looks mangled floating there in the toilet bowl. I first heard this term from a plumber who came to clean out a blocked sewer line.

dead on correct or on target. Often used to intensify words, such as serious or correct. Can be used in the same context with **right on** or **bang on**. Example: "You're **dead on** assessing my verbose and pretentious vocabulary as being hyperbolic and grandiose."

dead soldier *drugs* an empty alcohol bottle or, during the pot-smoking hippie era, an empty pipe bowl.

dead to rights caught in the act. Example: "Dora had me **dead to rights** when she found me with Linda, Jo, Franny, Dotty, Sue and Candice." Same as **busted**.

deal n. a transaction or agreement. From the practice of distributing cards in a game. Example: "Sure, I'll make a **deal** with you on the car. The **deal** is, you walk, I ride."

deal v. *drugs* to sell drugs. To deal in drugs.

deal or **deal with it** accept the situation and work around the problem. **Deal with it** came first; in the continuing effort to simplify our language, the **counterculture** shortened it to deal.

dealer *drugs* someone who sells drugs. Someone who deals in drugs.

Death of the Hippie a three-day event on October 7-9, 1967, celebrating the death of the hippie culture in the **Haight-Ashbury** area of San Francisco. Performed by hippies who were disillusioned with the direction in which the hippie culture was headed, it featured a mock funeral ceremony. Some of the people who organized the event thought that the word **"freebie"** would replace the term hippie after the ceremony. Unofficially the end of the **Summer of Love**. During this time, many people joined the hippie life for sex, drugs, and rock & roll alone, ignoring social and political issues. **True hippies** felt the new arrivals had missed the point. I agree; yet anyone who was around for the rest of the decade or the 1970s knows that the hippie did not die in October, 1967. (See: **true hippie**)

Grateful Dead logo ©

death's head representation of a human skull. Used by Hitler's Nazi regime in the 1930s and 1940s. Adopted by the **Hell's Angels** in America in the late 1940s as a symbol of rebellion. Not always used to advocate Nazi politics, but to irritate the sensibilities of the conservative populus. **2.** The logo of the **Grateful Dead** rock music group.

death snow *drugs* one of the many street terms used to represent and describe **heroin**.

deck *drugs* a portion of narcotics. Three grains of **heroin**. A bag of **cocaine**.

deck to knock somebody down. Example: "I'll **deck** him if he touches my stash again."

deck or **full deck** a person's complete mental capacity. Example: "Any man with a dismembered Barbie doll glued to his backpack is not playing with a full **deck**."

decked out dressed up. Example: "Sage is **decked out** in her new Guatemalan blouse."

Declaration of Indian Purpose *social issues* was presented at the American Indian Conference in Chicago in 1967, organized by the National Congress of American Indians. It began, "We...have a right to choose our own way of life. Since our Indian culture is slowly being absorbed by American society, we believe we have the responsibility of preserving our precious heritage...."

deed, the *sex* the sex act. Example: "I can tell by the water running down the hall that Gooch and Gladass are doing **the deed** in the bath tub again."

deep intellectual or thought-provoking. Relates to the term "profound," meaning "thought coming from great depths." Example: "I can't grock his shit; it's too **deep** for me." (See: **grock**)

deep hole trouble or a situation beyond one's ability. Usually a problem of one's own making. Derived from phrases, such as "over one's head" or "out of one's depth." Example: "Doug dug himself a **deep hole** by divulging Darla's degeneracy."

deep pockets lots of money or the place where the money is to be found. Example: "Lala wears the pants in their family, but Jake has the **deep pockets**."

Deep Purple *rock & roll/heavy-metal* a band formed in 1968 in Hertford, England, by Rod Evans (b. 1945, Edinburgh, Scot.), voc.; Nick Simper (b. 1946, London Eng.), bass; Jon Lord (b.

June 9, 1941, Leicester, Eng.), kybds.; Ritchie Blackmore (b. Apr. 14, 1945, Weston-super-Mare, Eng.) gtr.; Ian Paice (b. June 29, 1948, Nottingham, Eng.), drums. In 1969, Ian Gillan (b. Aug. 19, 1945, London, Eng.), voc., who sang in stage productions of *Jesus Christ Superstar,* replaced Evans; Roger Glover, bass, replaced Simper. Notable for being listed as the loudest band in the world in the *Guinness Book of World Records.* Also responsible for one of the major classic rock songs, "Smoke on the Water," written by Blackmore and featuring his memorable guitar intro, "bum-bum-bum, bum-bum-ba-dum."

"Deep Throat" the most successful "pornographic" movie ever produced. By 1975, it had grossed over $3.5 million. Linda Lovelace, the star of the film, was later found to have been under the legal age of consent when she made the film, performing sexual acts with older men.

Deep Throat the name given to the informant in the book and 1976 movie "All the President's Men," who gave information to **Woodward and Bernstein** when they investigated the **1972 Watergate break-in**. The actual name of this informant has been the subject of speculation for years; several possibilities have been suggested, but no conclusion has been reached. (See: **Watergate (break-in) burglary** and **Woodward and Bernstein**)

de-evolution the backward movement of society. The word from which the techno-rock group **Devo** got its name. (See: **Devo**)

de facto **segregation** *social issues* racial segregation that happens by circumstance rather than by legal require-

ment. Something in fact (*de facto*), not by law (*de jure*). Example: When Blacks are concentrated in a neighborhood, the schools will be predominantly Black or segregated. The **busing** of school children to different districts during the 1970s was meant to correct this situation. (See: **busing**)

defoliant *war* chemicals, such as **Agent Orange** and **paraquat**, used to make plants drop their foliage. Agent Orange was used extensively by the US Army in Vietnam to denude plants and expose the enemy. Paraquat was sprayed on **marijuana** fields in South and Central America to kill the crops. Both were highly toxic and have caused health problems. (See: **Agent Orange** and **paraquat**)

degradable *the environment* (See: **biodegradable**)

deism the belief that there is but one god, and he has created the universe; yet he has no interest in messing with it anymore. I tend to agree more with this theory than I would in a god who *allows* 5,000 Christian Armenians to die in an earthquake on the same day that he *helps* a baseball pitcher win a game in Los Angeles.

deja vu *occult* French for already seen. The feeling that one has experienced something previously, although feeling that he could not have actually done so. The phenomenon is explained by **occult** believers as a memory from a previous incarnation in life, or a vision of a future experience in one's life.

deliver to give, create or produce. One of those words that received expanded use and took on new dimensions during the era. Example: "I hope Damian can **deliver** on his promise of peace on earth and good, clean compost." From **deliver the goods**.

deliver the goods to produce successfully what is needed. "When it comes to cheap advice, Jesse can **deliver the goods**."

Delaney and Bonnie and Friends *gospel, country, funk and rock* Delaney and Bonnie Bramlett, a husband-and-wife duo who knew a lot of people in the music industry and recorded with many of the best artists in the era, such as **Eric Clapton**, Leon Russell, Dave Mason, **George Harrison**, **John Lennon** and J. J. Cale.

Dellinger, David (1915-) *social issues* author, editor, political activist, chairman of the **National Mobilization Committee to End the War in Vietnam** from 1967 to 1971. A member of the **Chicago Seven**, along with **Rennie Davis**, John Froines, **Tom Hayden**, **Abbie Hoffman**, **Jerry Rubin** and Lee Weiner. They were **anti-war**, and peace and freedom movement leaders who were arrested and tried as co-conspirators for crossing state borders to incite to riot during the 1968 **Democratic National Convention**. Dellinger received a five-year sentence with a concurrent sentence for contempt of court. The sentence was later overturned because of Judge Hoffman's gross misconduct during the trial. Dellinger graduated magna cum laude from Yale University in 1936 and served three years in prison during WWII for refusing to serve in the Army, although he could have received a deferment as a theological student. Dellinger was the senior member of the anti-war movement of the period. He works with the Rainbow Coalition and is a guest lecturer on many university campuses. (See: **Chicago Seven, Chi-**

cago Seven Trial and **Chicago Democratic National Convention**)

Delphic oracle famous oracle of ancient Greece, the seeress Pythia of Delphi. She sat on a tripod over a fissure, from which gases seeped; these gases gave her visions, and in this state of trance, she answered questions about the future. Many important Greek generals, politicians and noblemen came to her for advice in battle, politics and business.

Demerol *drugs* a brand name for meperidine hydrochloride produced by Winthrop Laboratories. A physically addictive synthetic **opiate** with medical use as an analgesic, or pain reliever.

demo *rock & roll* a semiprofessional demonstration tape or record produced to publicize a song or musical group.

democracy a society or form of government in which the population is given the opportunity to contribute to the decisions that govern them.

Democratic National Convention (Chicago, August 24-29, 1968) *social issues* **Vietnam War** protesters were beaten and maced outside Chicago's convention center. It was widely agreed that Mayor **Richard Daley**'s police force overreacted, using gestapo tactics. Mayor Daley was recorded as saying, "The police are not here to create disorder, but to preserve disorder," an obvious mistake in speech, but thought by many to indicate his true attitude. **Hubert Humphrey** was nominated as the Democratic presidential candidate, but was defeated by **Richard Milhous Nixon** in November of that year. During the convention week, 668 demonstrators were arrested and 101 hospitalized. 1,025 minor injuries, including tear gas or mace exposure, were treated on the street or in the seven medical facilities set up by a group called the Medical Committee of Human Rights. 192 police officers were also injured. The **Chicago Seven—David Dellinger**, **Rennie Davis**, John Froines, **Thomas Hayden**, **Abbie Hoffman**, **Jerry Rubin** and Lee Weiner—were **anti-war**, and peace and freedom movement leaders who were arrested and tried as co-conspirators for crossing state borders to incite to riot during the convention. Their trial was one of the most controversial examples of our judicial system. The courts disregarded the defendants' personal freedoms and stretched laws to the breaking point. The defendants used the trial as a platform to inform the public of the inequities and inconsistencies of the courts as related to political activism. (See: **Chicago Seven, Chicago Seven Trial** and **Chicago Democratic National Convention**) (See also: **Anti-War Events, Groups and Leaders** starting on page 562 in **Lists** at the back of this book)

demonstration *social issues* a gathering of people in a public place for the purpose of demonstrating support for a cause or voicing dissatisfaction with government policies, social circumstances or political issues.

demonstrators *social issues* people who gather in a public place to demonstrate their support for a cause or voice their dissatisfaction with government policies, social circumstances or political issues. During the **civil rights** and **anti-war** struggles, such events were most often organized with peaceful intent. However, the objective was to draw attention to a cause, and sometimes the demonstrators would appear

threatening by pushing the limits of legal and rightful assembly. This often

photo by John McCleary ©

provoked police attacks on the demonstrators, thus infringing on their freedom of speech and dissent. The media would report the police action, therefore creating sympathy for the demonstrators. During the hippie era, there were documented examples of the authorities posing as demonstrators (**provocateurs**) and creating violence and vandalism in order to discredit the message of the protestors. Lately, the American media seems to concentrate on only the few outlaw demonstrators and to ignore the true objective of the protest. It is also within the realm of possibility that the authorities of today are again using provocateurs to divert attention from the message of the demonstrators. (See: **provocateurs**)

den mother *sex* an older, **homosexual** male who advises and protects younger homosexuals.

Denny, Sandy (b. January 6, 1947, Wimbledon, Eng.; d. April 21, 1978,

London, Eng.) *folk, rock & roll* singer/
songwriter, one of the most memorable
voices in **folk** and rock music, she sang
with **Fairport Convention**, other
groups, and as a soloist from the mid-
1960s until her death in an accident at
her home. Denny wrote "Who Knows
Where the Time Goes?," the title song
of **Judy Collins'** gold album of 1968.
Denny's death was particularly tragic
since she obviously would have continued to produce memorable work.

den of inequity any place in which
sexual or drug activities occurred. Inequity, in religious parlance, means "of
a sinful nature." This term was used
sarcastically by hippies, since the counterculture did not believe these indulgences were morally wrong. a.k.a. **sin
bin, screw shack.**

department a situation or circumstance. Another word transformed from
an inanimate term into a human, emotional usage during the hippie era. Example: "Cal has no luck in the love
department."

dervishes *religion* an **Islamic** religious
order, or brotherhood of mystic **ascetics.** Known for the twirling dance that
is their form of religious worship. Often
called the whirling dervishes.

Desiderata something desired as essential. A very popular poem sold as
a poster in the 1970s. This poem was
supposedly found in the Old Saint
Paul's Church in Baltimore, dated
1692. It was actually written in the
early 1920s by Max Ehrmann (1872-
1945), a lawyer from Terre Haute, Indiana. Ehrmann's writing attracted little
attention during his lifetime, but this
poster was one of the most prevalent
to be found on the walls of idealistic,
young, female college students during
the 1970s.

Desiderata

Go placidly amid the noise and the haste,
and remember what peace there may be in
silence. As far as possible, without surren-
der, be on good terms with all persons.
Speak your truth quietly and clearly; and
listen to the dull and ignorant; they too have
their story. Avoid loud and aggressive persons; they are vexations to the spirit. If you
compare yourself with others, you may become vain or bitter, for always there will
be greater and lesser persons than yourself.
Enjoy your achievements as well as your
plans. Keep interested in your career, however humble; it is a real possession in the
changing fortunes of time. Exercise caution in your business affairs, for the world
is full of trickery. But let this not blind you
to what virtue there is; many persons strive
for high ideals and everywhere life is full of
heroism. Be yourself. Especially do not
feign affection. Neither be cynical about
love; for in the face of all aridity and disen-
chantment, it is as perennial as the grass.
Take kindly the counsel of the years, grace-
fully surrendering the things of youth. Nurture strength of spirit to shield you in sudden misfortune. But do not distress yourself with imaginings. Many fears are born
of fatigue and loneliness. Beyond a wholesome discipline be gentle to yourself. You
are a child of the universe, no less than the
trees and the stars and you have a right to
be here. And whether or not it is clear to
you, no doubt the universe is unfolding as
it should. Therefore, be at peace with God,
whatever you conceive Him to be. And
whatever your labours and aspirations, in
the noisy confusion of life, keep peace with
your soul. With all its sham, drudgery and
broken dreams, it is still a beautiful world.
Be cheerful. Strive to be happy.   Max
Ehrmannn, 1927. © Robert L. Bell

designer drug *drugs* **MDA, MDMA,
MMDA, MDM** and others. It is basi-

cally **methyldeoxyamphetamine**, or variants such as the chemical compound 3,4methylenedioxymethamphetamin. They are laboratory variations of the **amphetamine** molecule. These recreational drugs came to prominence in the late 1970s, although they were discovered over fifty years earlier. They are pseudo-psychedelics that give users a heightened sensuality and warm feelings toward others, though they also often produce excess energy, hyperactivity and distortion of perceptions. There are many new street names for these drugs coined since the hippie era, such as "Eve" and "rave." Among hippies, the term "designer drug" was derogatory, like "designer jeans" because they were items used by the nouveau-hip, white-collar, **yuppie** consumer. a.k.a. **Adam, ecstasy, love drug, MDA, vitamin E, vitamin X, X, XTC**. (See: **ecstasy** or **MDA**)

designs on someone a romantic interest in someone. Future plans for someone. Example: "Dick has **designs on** Jane, while Jane has **designs on** Dick staying celibate."

desk jockey an office worker.

destroyed mentally or physically impaired. Often due to drugs or alcohol. Example: "I'm **destroyed** by an endless supply of boilermakers and poppers." (See: **poppers**, if you're interested)

detox *drugs* short for detoxify. To abstain from drugs or alcohol in order to get them out of one's system.

deuce two. A deuce of weed is two lids, two ounces or two pounds, depending on one's economic status.

deuce coupe a 1932 Ford coupe, a popular customized car well into the 1960s. A two-door car, but the **deuce**

indicated the 2 in 1932. The **Beach Boys'** surf music band recorded the song, *Little Deuce Coupe,* in 1963, and it became one of the most famous songs of the automobile genre.

deva the **Sanskrit** word for radiant being. In **Buddhism**, a hero or demigod.

devil *drugs* a red pill, normally Seconal. Refers to the biblical devil and red as fire.

devil an evil person; in Black society, an evil White man.

devil weed *drugs* another one of the many names for **marijuana**. (See: **marijuana**)

Devo *techno-new wave/rock & roll* a band formed in Akron, Ohio, in 1972, Jerry Casale, bass, voc.; Mark Mothersbaugh, voc., kybds., gtr.; Bob (Bob I) Mothersbaugh, gtr., voc.; Bob (Bob II) Casale, kybds. gtr., voc.; Alan Myers, drums. Noted for their costumes, marketing, and a complete lack of ego when most bands were beginning to take themselves too seriously. Their first album was released in 1978, and their first and only Top 40 hit, "Whip It," in 1980. Their plastic helmets that looked like electronic push buttons are one of rock music's most recognizable images. Their "message" did draw some attention to industrial waste and other ecological issues, yet their real contribution was to help **lighten up** the music scene of the times.

dex, dexo or **dexy** *drugs* nicknames for **Dexedrine**. (See: **Dexedrine**)

Dexedrine *drugs* a trademark brand of **amphetamine** sulphate from the Smith, Kline & French Laboratories. a.k.a. **pep pills, beans, cartwheel, hiball, dex, dexo, dexy**. The active ingredient attacks the central nervous system.

Dharma *religion* **Sanskrit** word for law. In the **metaphysic**al or **esoteric** sense, it refers to the laws of Nature operating the Universe. When applied to humanity, it refers to a code of conduct that strengthens the soul and produces morality, virtue, or religious merit. In **Hinduism**, it is "the path," of cosmic order, the law of existence. In **Buddhism**, the teachings of the Buddha.

Dharma Bums, The a book by **Jack Kerouac**, published in 1958. One of the important books by the **beat** writers of the 1950s and early 60s that defined and created the hippie personality, it introduced Eastern religions to young, Western minds. (See: **beat**)

dialogue meaningful communication. An old word reborn during the era to emphasize a profound conversation about weighty subjects.

Diamond, Neil (b. January 24, 1941, Brooklyn, New York) *popular music* a prolific songwriter with a good voice who added a lot of romance to the era.

Dianetics a trademarked term of the Religious Technology Center (Church of **Scientology**). Defined as meaning "what the soul is doing to the body." From the Greek *dia*, meaning through, and *nous*, meaning soul. **L. Ron Hubbard**'s book, *Dianetics: The Modern Science of Mental Health,* is part of the doctrine of the Church of Scientology. "Scientology" is a pseudo-religious organization founded by Hubbard in 1954. (See: **L. Ron Hubbard, Scientology**)

diaphragm or **Dutch cap** a **birth control** device. A round, flat, rubber cap that is placed in the **vagina** over the cervical canal before intercourse in or-

der to block the passage of sperm. A spermicide (a chemical that kills sperm) is usually applied to the inside of the diaphragm to assist in contraception. The device should be kept in place for several hours after intercourse. Among couples who used the diaphragm, it was the source of many hilarious and sometimes impotency-creating episodes. During insertion, the device had a habit of slipping out of one's fingers and flying across the room. It was therefore sometimes called the "unidentified flying contraceptive device." The failure rate of the diaphragm is approximately 12 pregnancies per 100 women during a one-year period, primarily from improper use or failure to apply spermicide.

diarrhea of the mouth talking too much. Revealing secrets. Example: "Don't tell Gina any secrets, or you'll trigger her **diarrhea of the mouth**."

dick *sex* one of the many euphemisms for the penis or male sex organ. Although this word was not new to the hippie era, it was greatly expanded into new, subtle meanings during the era It evolved into an expletive or negative intensifier and was sometimes used in the same context as words like shit or fuck.

dick a detestable person. This word replaced **jerk**, a 1950s term used before the hippies became more graphic. During and after WWII, such scatological and anatomical words as fart, shit, **asshole**, dick and **cunt** were introduced to America's small towns by returning soldiers. These words evolved into pronouns describing people rather than merely nouns describing body parts and body functions. During the hippie era, these terms found expanded usage, yet still remained unacceptable in "polite society" and in more conservative atmospheres.

dick verb. *sex* another word used to describe the sex act. Example: "He thinks he can **dick** anything in skirts."

dick nothing. Example: "Tom looks important, but he does **dick** around here."

dick around to waste time. It is closely related to "fool around" or "mess around," but usually more specific to wasting time.

dick-brained or **dick head** a stupid or foolish person.

diddle to fool around or waste time. Example: "Gerry likes to **diddle** around with the guitar; Eric can really play it."

diddly, diddly squat or **diddly shit** nothing or nothing of importance. Example: "He does **diddly** around here, but she's worse, she does **diddly squat**." Common street usage "Say man, that don't mean **diddly shit**." Same usage as **doodly** or **doodly squat**.

"didn't show me a thing" or **"don't show me a thing"** failed to impress. Similar to the phrases "didn't give me a thing" or "don't mean a thing to me." Example: "You think he's cool, but he **didn't show me a thing**."

different strokes for different folks everyone likes different things. A stroke in this context is a unit of activity.

Diggers a **communal** group of radical actors who fed, clothed and housed hippies and street people in San Francisco during the mid-1960s. Emmett Grogan was the founder. They adopted the name Diggers from 17th-century English farmers who raised food to give to the poor. Every day at 4:00 p.m. in Panhandle Park near **Haight-Ashbury**, the Diggers dispensed food to those in need. They accomplished this by soliciting donations from anyone who could afford to give. They pressured the drug dealers to donate at least 1 percent of their profits to feed those to whom they sold drugs. The Diggers were started by several members of the **San Francisco Mime Troupe**, and they continued performing **guerrilla theater** on the streets and in parks. Several of their events held in the fall and winter of 1966 were The Death of Money Parade, The Intersection Game and The New Year's Wail. The Diggers were a very community- and service-oriented group involved in the hippie lifestyle. They possessed a public information arm called the Communications Company, which published numerous manifestos and mimeographed communiques for the Haight-Ashbury hip population in San Francisco. The Diggers also participated in **anti-war** events and **demonstrations** throughout the country, notably the October 21, 1967, **National Mobilization Committee to End the War** in Vietnam rally in Washington, DC.

dig? understand? Used as a question. Example: "This is my space. **Dig**?"

dig it to see, understand or appreciate something. "I **dig it**." "You **dig it**." "She **digs it**." "They **dig it**." "We **dig it**." "Can you **dig it**?" A term that became popular in the 50s with the beatnik culture and was introduced to the world primarily through TV characters, such as Kookie of "77 Sunset Strip" and Maynard G. Krebs of "The Many Lives of Dobie Gillis." (See: **kookie**)

Digit (1966-1977) a male African mountain gorilla befriended and named by biologist **Dian Fossey** in 1968. Fossey studied him and others of his breed, and Digit was featured in numerous television documentaries and National Geographic articles about Fossey's work. Digit was also on a Rwandan Tourist Bureau poster circulated worldwide. The caption on the poster read, "Come see me in Rwanda." Digit was Rwanda's most famous name. In late 1977, Digit was killed and mutilated by poachers, who cut off his head and hands to sell as souvenirs. Digit's death was mourned by many **ecology**-conscious Americans who saw his murder as a poignant example of human disregard for other forms of life on the planet. In 1978, there were only 250 mountain gorillas left in existence. On December 26, 1985, Dian Fossey herself was attacked and killed for trying to protect the gorillas she loved from commercial slaughter. (See: **Dian Fossey**)

digital computer *computer revolution* a computer that performs operations using numbers without substituting the numbers for mechanical operations (as analog computers do). Most modern, electronic computers are digital because they are inherently much more accurate than analog computers. (See: **Computer Revolution Milestones, Companies and Leaders** starting on page 626 in **Lists** at the back of this book)

dig you later see you later.

dike *sex* alternative spelling, or misspelling if you will, of the word **dyke**. (See: **dyke**)

dildo *sex* a **phallic** representation or artificial penis used for sexual gratification or **masturbation** by women or homosexual males. The history of the dildo is long and illustrious. The lingam is a symbol of the penis used by Hindus in the worship of **Shiva**. Similar phallic symbols are found in many ancient cultures, notably Chinese, Greek and Italian. These symbols were originally used to celebrate fertility and strength; however, they were eventually used as dildos on or by men and women to replicate sexual intercourse. (See: **vibrator**)

dildo a dumb person.

dillies *drugs* short for Dilaudid, a brand name for dhydromorphone.   **a.k.a.** drugstore **heroin**.

dim mentally inadequate, dumb or stupid. From "dim bulb," an older term used less frequently. Example: "Jarrod's conversant with his drums, but **dim** with people." The 1960s and 70s were an era famous for word contractions, abbreviations and language manipulations.

dime bag *drugs* $10 worth of drugs.

dimethyltryptamine (DMT) *drugs* a synthetic hallucinogenic similar to **LSD**, yet with a 30-minute to one-hour trip duration, compared to four hours with LSD. Dimethyltryptamine (tryptamine) is found naturally in a South American plant called **Vine of Souls**, *Banisteriopsis caapi*. Also found in the yopo bean, known as yakee or yato in some South American cultures. One of the very first **psychoactive** creations of modern man and his knowledge of chemistry, **DMT** was found in snuff during the turn of the century. Also called **cohoba snuff** or **businessman's special**. DMT is also said to come from other sources, such as the Syrian rue herb in China and the venom of a Sonoran Desert toad. **2. DMT** may also be used as an acronym for *diethylamide tartrate* **LSD-25, lysergic acid diethylamide tartrate 25**, a product made by

Sandoz Pharmaceuticals for mind-expanding experiments in the early 1960s. (See: **cohoba snuff**)

ding originally a surfing term meaning a gouge, scratch or damage to a surfboard. **2.** as a hippie term, it meant negative commentary or emotional harm. Examples: "Her **ding** about his penis put a **ding** in his ego."

ding-a-ling a crazy, dumb or foolish person. Although not gender exclusive, it is often used to describe someone considered to be a "dumb blonde" or silly woman.

dingleberry originally, this quaint, little term described the dried balls of feces that sometimes cling to anal hair. Eventually, it came to mean a crazy or foolish person.

dinghy crazy, dumb or foolish.   Although derived from **ding-a-ling**, it was a more contemporary term in the hippie era. Not gender exclusive, yet often directed at a girl or woman.

dink used in place of the word **dick** (penis) when describing a detested person. Example: "What a **dink** he is, talking about his conquests!"

dink around to fool around or waste time. Same use as **dick around**.

photo by John McCleary ©

Diogenes the first hippie, 412 B.C. The most famous cynic/philosopher, the man always depicted as searching the world with a lamp "looking for an honest man." He spurned material goods and is said to have lived nude in a large pot, where Alexander the Great found him and, looking in, asked what he could give Diogenes. Diogenes replied, "I ask nothing, but that thou wouldst get out of my sunlight."

Dionysus Greek god of wine and fertility. Same as the Roman god, Bacchus. Some feel that he embodied the **spirit** of the **true hippie**. Many men of the hippie era imagined themselves as Dionysus or Bacchus, and took on the appearance with long, flowing hair, beards, and as little clothing as possible. Also associated with the same theme as the Satyr or seducer of women. Thomas Bulfinch (1796-1867) in *Bulfinch's Mythology,* his definitive study of Greek and Roman mythology, first printed in 1855, says of Dionysus and Bacchus, "He represents not only the intoxicating power of wine, but its social and beneficent influences likewise, so that he is viewed as the promoter of civilization, and a lawgiver and lover of peace."

dioxin 2,3,7,8-tetrachlorodibenzo-p-dioxin (TCDD), a poisonous impurity present in many herbicides. Present in **Agent Orange**, a chemical defoliant used extensively by the US Army in Vietnam to denude plants and reveal the enemy. Soldiers exposed to Agent Orange and other defoliants containing dioxin have shown extreme, sometimes deadly, symptoms. Agricultural field workers have also suffered from its effects, and the use and abuse of herbicides and pesticides have been major concerns of the **United Farm Workers' Union (UFW)** and **César Chávez**. (See: **Agent Orange** and **César Chávez**) dip chewing tobacco.

dip, dipshit, dipso or dipstick stupid, undesirable or very unpopular. Dip is the cool, hippie-era short form of the other terms, dipshit, dipso and dipstick. Dipstick came first, sometime in the 1940s or 50s, meaning the metal stick used to check engine oil. Refers to a person being as brainless as the inanimate object used to check oil. Dipshit was used in the 1950s and early 60s; dipso came later, sometime in the 1970s, as a combination of dipstick and the psychotherapy term dipsomaniac. Since dipsomania means a morbid craving for alcohol, it is an incorrect reference to this usage.

di Prima, Diane (1934-) poet, writer, playwright and editor. Member of the beat literary community in New York and San Francisco to which Allen Ginsberg, Jack Kerouac, William Burroughs, Lawrence Ferlinghetti, George Corso, Gary Snyder, LeRoi Jones and Frank O'Hara belonged. As an important and prolific author and a strong personality of the beat era, she can be considered one of the first female role models of the hippie generation. Di Prima has written numerous books of poetry and fiction; some examples include *This Kind of Bird Flies Backward*, 1959; *Notes on a Summer Solstice, June 21, 1969, [San Francisco]*, 1969; *Memoirs of a Beatnik*, 1969; *Brass Furnace Going Out: Song after an Abortion*, 1975. A beautiful little poetry book dedicated to LeRoi Jones, entitled *The New Handbook of Heaven*, 1963, reads, "time & time again the laughter after the footsteps in the snow, the moths walk stiffly. don't palm off yr deaths head on me, man, or yr horse with the broken leg on stilts

always on stilts hairbrushing the stars, the hair ends cracking and this is NY...."

dip (one's) wick *sex* the act of penetration by a male during sexual activity. Can be heterosexual or homosexual.

dirt rumors or scandalous information. Example: "Listen up if you want some dirt on Wendy; I know all the bad stuff."

dirtbag disgusting, often sexually inappropriate.

dirt grass *drugs* poor quality **marijuana**.

dirty guilty. As opposed to clean. Related to Pontius Pilate's dirty hands, which he washed to cleanse himself of guilt in Christ's crucifixion. Example: "Obviously he's dirty; you don't think he could be clean and be that rich!"

dirty boogie *sex and music* the sex act. Boogie can mean sex or dance. In the 1930s, 40s and 50s, it was an actual dance, similar to the swing, with the addition of overt sexual movements. An African American term.

dirty bop *sex and rock & roll* the sex act. Bop can mean sex or dance. In the 1950s, this was an actual dance in which the male partner bent over backwards, thrusting his pelvic area toward his partner, similar to the limbo. The "straight" bop was also a common dance of the 1950s.

dirty old man or DOM *sex* a man, considered old, who displays prurient interests in younger women.

dirty tricks *politics* questionable activities that create unfair advantage or deceive the public, thus winning votes for a candidate or disrupting the activities of the opposition. In intelligence agency parlance, dirty tricks means covert action. **Richard Nixon** and his political organizations were the masters of such tactics. Nixon first got his nickname, "Tricky Dick," during his 1950 campaign for the California State Senate against Helen Gahagan Douglas. In that campaign, among other things, he distributed material to registered Democrats that failed to disclose his Republican affiliation. During Nixon's first campaign for President, some tricks were used, but it was his re-election campaign of 1973 that fostered the most blatant examples. **The Committee to Re-elect the President** (**CRP** or **CREEP**) was involved in the program of dirty tricks against Nixon's political opponents and "enemies" called Operation Gemstone. The group of party members and operatives who conducted these dirty tricks was called **the plumbers**. Some of the members and their associates were: Edgil (Bud) Krogh, David Young, Charles W. (Tex) Colson, Jeb Magruder, Dwight L. Chapin, Ken Clawson, Donald Segretti, John J. Caulfield, E. Howard Hunt, G. Gordon Liddy, James McCord, Frank Sturgis, Bernard Barker and a group of Cuban exiles who were CIA veterans. The June 17, 1972, Watergate break-in, at which time **the plumbers** were caught, was the most notable example of political dirty tricks. It was actually the second break-in and was conducted to plant incriminating evidence and replace a faulty bugging device on Democratic party Chairman Lawrence O'Brien's phone. Information received from the listening device was to be used to discredit the Democratic Party. During Nixon's presidential primary campaign against Senator Edmund Muskie, Ken Clawson drafted a letter accusing Muskie of calling French Canadian-Americans "Canucks." It came to be known as the "Canuck" letter, and it was one of many such deceptions against Nixon enemies and opposing candidates. "Chapman's Friends," a code name for Seymour Freidin and Lucy Goldberg, posed as reporters on Nixon opponents' campaign planes to get information. Other examples of Nixon's dirty tricks are: Doctoring a photo of opponent **George McGovern** to make it look as if he were standing with a group of "weirdo longhairs," physically attacking **Daniel Ellsberg** on the steps of the Capitol, writing letters on other peoples' letterhead accusing people of such things as homosexuality and stealing Congressional property, and canceling opponents' important press conferences and meetings. It should be noted that Nixon and his political machine were not the only politicians to use dirty tricks. Candidates on both sides of the political spectrum have been known to do such things, yet Nixon's re-election campaign was the most blatant. Nixon administration dirty tricks also extended to many **civil rights** and **anti-war** organizations, such as the **Vietnam Veterans Against the War (VVAW)** and the **Black Panther Party**. (See: **Watergate**)

discarnation evolution to a place of existence without a physical body. **Soul** in **limbo**. In **Hinduism** and **occult** terminology, as in **reincarnation,** it is a station within **samsara,** the **wheel of life**, the chain of birth and rebirth. (See: **samsara** and **reincarnation**)

disc or **disk** *rock & roll* a flat, round piece of **vinyl** upon which music was recorded, to be replayed on a phonograph sound machine so that hippies could dance around wildly. a.k.a. **LP** and **record albums.** In the early 1990s, the music industry began to phase out record albums and use tapes and CDs in their place. (See: **LPs** and **vinyl**)

disc jockey *rock & roll* someone who plays records on the radio. The term first appeared in a *Variety* magazine article in 1941. The first official disc jockey was a woman, Josephine White, who played records on her husband's radio station, WCRW in Chicago in July, 1926. The first recording artist whose music was broadcast over the radio was Enrico Caruso, on January 13, 1910. In the early 1990s, the music industry began to phase out record albums and use tapes and CDs in their place.

disco *almost rock & roll* recorded music played at nightclubs for dancing. Short for **discotheque**. Usually characterized by hard, driving, repetitive beats and electronic instrumentation.

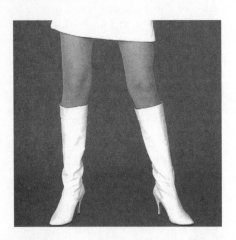

disco boots women's high, tight, high-heel boots. Usually calf high, but some came up to the thigh. Worn with a **mini-skirt** or **hot pants**. Similar to **go-go boots**.

disco queen a woman or gay man who is the life of the party on the **disco** dance floor.

disco sucks a movement supported by fans of live music in the late-1970s in reaction to recorded music dance clubs. The movement reached its peak at a rally in Chicago where **disco** records were burned. It was mostly tongue in cheek, but there still remain two factions, those who like disco and those who think disco sucks.

discotheque or **disco** *almost rock & roll* dance clubs that played popular records for music rather than having live bands. Popular in the mid-1970s, they were similar to high school sock hops, but more upscale. The disco craze received ridicule from music purists, yet it did bring back contact dancing, in which partners actually touched each other in the process. The music played at discos was the most popular Top 40 hits, the atmosphere was extravagant glitz, and the objective was to pick up someone to take home. The 1977 movie, "Saturday Night Fever," with John Travolta was the high point of the fad; the sound track album containing a number of **Bee Gee's** songs was the best example of the music and the biggest selling soundtrack of all time. Other disco performers of the era were The Village People and **Donna Summer**, the disco diva. **Studio 54** in New York City was the most famous discotheque. In 1979, a growing backlash against disco culminated in a large, public record burning in Chicago.

Disneyland a place of fantasy. Unnatural circumstances. Originally a theme park in Southern California, during the **hippie** era, it came to mean anything or anyplace that was unreal or phony.

disposable paper dresses available to the American public in 1965.

dissident *someone* who actively, and sometimes violently, opposes the government in reaction to perceived political injustice.

dissociative phenomenon a clinical term for the **psychedelic** experience. From **Tom Wolfe's** book , *Electric Kool Aid Acid Test.*

ditz a foolish or awkward person. Yiddish slang.

divination *occult* the use of **occult**, **esoteric** or spiritualist skills. Basically similar to fortune telling. The practice of attaining knowledge of the future or the unknown.

divine inspiration a thought or concept that is said to come from God. Often, it meant that someone merely took some drugs, got drunk or fell off an ass and conceived a crazy idea.

Divine Light Mission *religion* the organization and cult of the Indian teacher **Guru Maharaj Ji**. Devotees in India, Europe and America regard Maharaj Ji as a successor of **Krishna, Buddha**, Christ, **Mohammed** and others. Initiates, called premies, receive "The Knowledge" and are given secret meditation techniques.

DJ or **deejay** (See: **disc jockey**)

DMT *drugs* (See: **di-methyl tryptamine**) (See also: **Drugs of the Era** in **Lists** at the back of this book)

do a form of physical action or violence inflicted upon someone, usually sexual or painful. Examples: "**Do** her" (fuck her). "**Do** him" (kill him).

do short for hairdo. Primarily African American usage.

DOA dead on arrival. A police and medical term literally meaning dead. Gained use in the **counterculture** meaning excessively drunk, under the influence of drugs, sexually dysfunctional or rejected by a potential sex partner. Example: "Deek came on to her, but he was **DOA** with the line he tried."

do a job or **did a job** (on someone) to inflict either psychological or physical pain. Example: "His taste for other women will **do a job** on her confidence." Close in usage to **do a number**, yet it usually denotes something more violent in nature.

do a number *drugs* smoke a **marijuana** cigarette.

do a number or **did a number** (on someone) to inflict some form of physical damage or psychological pain. Example: "Her taste for silk is going to **do a number** on his bank account."

"Doc" Martens boots sturdy, work-style boots adopted by European **punks** and **rockers** in the 1960s and 70s. Sometimes known as "Model #1490." Invented by Dr. Klaus Maertens of Germany in the 1940s to protect his broken foot after a skiing accident. **Elton John** wore an exaggerated pair as the pinball player in the movie "Tommy." **The Clash** (British punk rock group) made them recognizable and popular to Americans from their music videos of the early 1980s.

Doctor Dope *drugs* Dr. Michael R. Aldrich, a prominent leader in **LeMar**, an organization dedicated to the legalization of **marijuana**. (See: **LeMar**)

Doctor Feelgood a good feeling. **2.** a drug dealer or someone who provides drugs. **3.** Dr. Max Jacobson, doctor to many wealthy East Coast socialites during the 1960s. It is rumored that he supplied **amphetamines** to members of New York City's swinging high society, including President **John F. Kennedy**. **4**. "Dr. Feelgood," a song performed and co-written by **Aretha Franklin**.

do (someone) **dirt**   to do something unkind or to commit a larcenous act upon someone. Examples: "She will **do him dirt**; she flirts just walking through a room." "He looks mean, like he's out to **do someone dirt**."

dodgie or **dodgy**   someone or something questionable, phony or illegal. Actually, an old British term that found a new home in the American **counter-culture**. Example: "His logic is **dodgie**."

Does a bear shit in the woods? or **Does Howdy Doody have wooden balls?**   the answer is obvious; it is a foregone conclusion. Several examples of silly retorts to a question of validity. Another example: "Is the Pope Catholic?"

dog   adj. an ugly or undesirable person, place or thing. Examples: "She's a **dog**; her dog's a **dog**, and her party's a **dog** too."

dog   v. to follow or harass someone unmercifully. To stalk. Example: "Graham won't accept her rejection; he'll **dog** her 'till she gives in."

dog fashion, **dog style** or **doggie style**   sex the sexual position in which the male enters the female from the rear. Not necessarily anal sex.

dogged   tired. From dog tired.

dogin'-it   being slow in movement.

Dohrn, Benardine   (b. Jan. 12, 1942) social issues a leader in the **Students for a Democratic Society (SDS)**, **Revolutionary Youth Movement** and **Weathermen**. She led the **SDS** split, which eventually led to the formation of the **Weathermen**. Dohrn headed the

Weathermen in the early 1970s. She was prosecuted by the Federal government for breaking anti-riot laws, but indictments were eventually dropped in

the 1970s. She is now the director of the Children and Family Justice Center of the Northwestern University School of Law and is married to **Bill Ayers,** also a former member of the SDS and the Weathermen. (See: **Students for a Democratic Society (SDS)** and **Weathermen**)

do in   to harm someone in some way.

doing it or **doin' it**   sex having sexual intercourse.

photo by John McCleary ©

do it!   a challenge to be assertive, to do something important or radical. It was not thought up by some ad writer for an overpriced tennis shoe! The first time I saw or heard this, it was written on the wall of the burned-out **Bank of America** in **Isla Vista, California**, in February, 1970. **2.** The title of a revolutionary manifesto written by **Jerry Rubin** in 1970.

doll a beautiful person, either physically or personally. Not gender exclusive.

dollies *drugs* street name for **Dolophine**. (See: **Dolophine** and **methadone**)

dolls *drugs* drugs in pill form. Can be **amphetamines** or **barbiturates**, **uppers** or **downers**. Often diet pills. Example: The book by Jacqueline Susann, *The Valley of the Dolls,* and movie of the same name, 1965.

dolly birds the fashionable girls of London. A term credited to Peter Evans, a **fashion** writer in England in the 1960s and 70s.

dolo *drugs* nickname for **Dolophine**. (See: **Dolophine** and **methadone**)
Dolophine *drugs* early trademark for **methadone,** synthetic **heroin**. (See: **methadone**)

dome *drugs* a type of **LSD** shaped like a dome.

dome short for **geodesic dome**, a zonal polyhedral construction. A structure designed by **Buckminster Fuller**, using the repetition of six-sided forms to create an igloo-shaped structure. (See: **Buckminster Fuller** and **geodesic dome**)

domino *drugs* a 12.5-mg. capsule of combined amphetamine and sedative. a.k.a. **black and white**.

domino theory *politics* the theory that if one country in a region of the world falls to communism, the bordering countries will fall in turn. Used to justify the US involvement in Korea and Vietnam.

done (one's) **homework** prepared, having studied the situation.

dong or **donger** another euphemism for the male sex organ.

donkey beads large, turquoise pottery beads from Mexico. Roughly glazed, imperfectly shaped and random sized. **Hippies** found them attractive and used them in necklaces and **macramé**.

donkey dick a big penis. **2.** an erection caused by **heroin** use. Said to be one of the few advantages to the drug. What is not told is that using heroin usually reduces the desire for sex and may cause impotence.

do not fold, spindle or mutilate directions once printed on IBM computer punch cards, which had to be undamaged in order to be accepted and read by the machine. This slogan was used sarcastically by the **free-speech movement** to describe the impersonal treatment received by students from university campus administrations. It has become a warning to the government against mistreating its citizens. These cards were roughly 3 1/2 inches high by 7 inches wide and were called punch cards because of their small, rectangular holes, which recorded data.

Donovan (b. Donovan Leitch, May 10, 1946, Glasgow, Scotland) *rock & roll* early British folk rock singer/songwriter. Donovan was the original **flower child**, and his early recordings, such as "Catch the Wind," "Sunshine Superman," "Season of the Witch" and "Mellow Yellow," were the anthems of hippie **mysticism**. He suffered sarcasm directed at "flowery" and "idealistic" lyrics, but he was still a very important spokesman of the time.

don't even think about it! don't do it. A warning not to do something. An implication that trouble will follow one's actions. This phrase received a lot of airplay on TV sitcoms, which are the vehicle for many of our language fads.

*don't have a clue I don't know, you don't know, they don't know. As if something is a mystery.

don't have it in me (he, she or they **don't have it in them**) unwilling, unable or incapable of doing something because of a moral, mental or emotional restriction. Not in one's nature to do something. More of a commitment to fairness than a physical inability.

don't knock it if you haven't tried it don't criticize something that you haven't experienced.

don't lose your cool don't get mad, don't overreact.

don't push the river don't frustrate yourself by fighting the current of forces you can't control. Meant as a suggestion for simplifying one's life, having nothing to do with swimming. From a book of the same name by Barry Stevens.

don't quit your day job *rock & roll* since music is normally played at night and other, more profitable occupations are usually pursued during the day, the meaning is obvious. In the age of potential overnight rock stardom, everyone wanted to be "in a band," and many of us were, at one time or another. But most musical careers were unprofitable, and one had to have a "day job" to pay the rent. This advice was given

to many aspiring musicians, either as a condemnation of their talent or as a benevolent suggestion for safety's sake.

don't sweat it don't get upset. The sweat refers to getting hot and worried.

don't sweat the small stuff don't get excited about the unimportant things. The sweat refers to getting hot and worried.

don't trust anybody over 30 *social issues* at the beginning of the hippie era when everyone was young, 30 years of age was arbitrarily chosen as the point at which a person becomes old, thus **uncool** and untrustworthy. This statement is credited by most authorities to **Jack Weinberg**, the University of California, Berkeley, graduate student and **CORE** member whose actions were directly responsible for the birth of the **free-speech movement**. On October 1, 1964, Weinberg set up a card table to distribute **civil rights** literature and political fliers. He was censured by campus administration and eventually arrested. His detention and treatment precipitated the student **demonstrations** that escalated into the national student free-speech movement.

don't worry, be happy a positive admonition originally found on posters produced by followers of Avatar **Meher Baba** in the 1960s. Meher Baba (1894-1969) was an East Indian spiritual leader who still has many followers in America. The phrase was later used as the title of a song recorded by Bobby McFerrin.

don't you work as hard as you play it means what is says. A line from **The Mamas and the Papas** 1966 song "Creeque Alley." The song was autobiographical, and this one line struck a note with a lot of the **counterculture** of the time.

doobage *drugs* **marijuana**. From the word **doobie**, indicating the material needed to make a marijuana cigarette. The suffix "age" was added to some words in sarcastic/humorous evolution of the hippie vocabulary. Examples: **"tongueage,"** a French kiss or **cunnilingus**; **"fartage,"** the smell of a fart. (See: **marijuana**)

doobie a **marijuana** cigarette.

Doobie Brothers, The *rock & roll* formed in San Jose, California, in 1970, they were a cult band for a while, partly because of their name and its association with **marijuana**. They produced some very good dance music.

doodley or **doodley squat** (See: **diddly** or **diddly squat**)

doomster someone excessively worried and vocal about the possibility of nuclear world destruction.

Doonesbury a cartoon strip by Garry Trudeau. While an undergraduate at Yale University, Trudeau created a comic strip called *Bull Tales*, which later became *Doonesbury*. The strip incorporated wry humor and satire directed at contemporary events, personalities and politics. The cartoon became nationally syndicated and won a Pulitzer Prize for Trudeau in 1975. *Doonesbury* occasionally proved too controversial for some newspapers, and they refused to print particular installments.

doormat someone who is walked all over, mistreated or unappreciated by others. Examples: "Gladys is his **doormat**." "Don't be a **doormat**; make Digger pay his share of the rent."

doors of perception *The Doors of Perception* is a book by Aldous Huxley published in 1955. It is widely believed that he wrote it after taking the psychedelic mescaline. "The doors" are a barrier to knowledge and can often be opened only with the help of a drug, usually a psychedelic. The rock group **The Doors** got their name from this book.

Doors, The *rock & roll* the ultimate Southern California decadence band formed in Los Angeles in 1965. Jim Morrison (b. Dec. 8, 1943, Melbourne, Fla.; d. July 3, 1971, Paris, Fr.), voc.; Ray Manzarek (b. Feb. 12, 1935, Chicago, Ill), kybds.; Robby Krieger (b. Jan 8, 1946, Los Angeles), gtr.; John Densmore (b. Dec. 1, 1944, Los Angeles), drums. The Doors were part youthful rebellion, part overindulgent drug culture and part literary muse. Jim Morrison was, in the opinion of many, the most charismatic personality and the worst drug abuser of the hippie era. A number of The Doors' songs are among the best of the era, including "The End," "Crystal Ships" and "Light My Fire." I was driving a Southern California freeway the first time I heard "Light My Fire" and was compelled to exit at the next offramp, jump from the car and dance. Inducted into the Rock and Roll Hall of Fame in 1993.

dope *drugs* any drug or substance that alters one's mood or perception. Possibly from the Dutch word *doop*, meaning sauce, or from the biochemical term dopamine, a compound found in many mind-altering drugs.

dope information. Example: "If you can handle the expletives, I'll give you the real **dope** on investment banking." Possibly from the Dutch word *doop*, meaning sauce.

dope, the the information, the truth.

dope addict or **drug addict** *drugs* someone who is dependent on or addicted to drugs. Can be a chemical or psychological addiction.

doper *drugs* someone who uses drugs to excess and whose efficiency or personality are negatively affected by that use.

"Dope will get you through times of no money better than money will get you through times of no dope." the motto of Freewheelin' Franklin, one of the three *Fabulous Furry Freak Brothers*, an underground comic by Gilbert Shelton. (See: *Fabulous Furry Freak Brothers* in alphabetical listings) (See also: **Comix & Underground Cartoon strips** on page 639 in **Lists** at the back of this book)

dopey someone stupid or who is doped up to the point of being stupid.

do rag a **bandanna** or scarf worn over a hairdo by Black males.

do right it means just what it says, yet this is one of the simple phrases that held much more cosmic or emotional value than the simple words indicated. Examples: "**Do right**, all night, by that girl; she really loves you." "**Do right** by the earth and it will feed you."

dork or **dorky** an awkward, socially inept or undesirable person. Dork was originally the term used for a whale's penis.

dose *drugs* to take **LSD**. From the scientific term, threshold dose, which means the amount of a drug needed to produce the desired effect. In a perfect world, a good LSD dose is 250 micrograms, considered a lab test dose, but some street **hits** were 100 **mics** or less. **2.** any portion of drugs, be it a pill or a shot.

dose a case of gonorrhea. Occasionally used to indicate other types of venereal disease.

do the deed *sex* to have sex. Example: "I saw you with George last night. Did you two **do the deed**?"

do the math figure out the numbers and you will agree with me.

do time go to jail. **2.** to spend time with someone or something.

double gaited *sex* **bisexual**, having sexual interest in both genders. In original usage, double gaited meant the ability of some horses to have two different running styles.

douche bag a detestable person. More conventionally, a douche bag is a container filled with water or another solution used by women to clean, or douche, their genitals after sex. *Douche* is a French word meaning shower.

dough money. From a previously used word for money, which was **bread**. The use of bread probably came from the Lord's Prayer, which states, "Give us this day our daily bread." It was an easy transition from there to daily money.

do up to inject or ingest a portion of drugs. Example: "Hey, dude, let's **do up** a joint."

dove a person who believes in passivism as the way to peace, as opposed to a hawk, who advocates war as the way to peace.

Dow Chemical Company *social issues* a company founded in 1897 by Herbert Henry Dow. The major producer of napalm during the **Vietnam War** and of pesticides for military and domestic uses. During the war, university **anti-war** demonstrations were aimed at Dow Chemical campus recruitment, and the slogan "Dow Shalt Not Kill" became a familiar chant. Dow knew in the mid-1960s that dioxin in its pesticides could cause sickness and death, but continued to produce the products. Because of this, many humanitarian organizations consider it to be one of the most mercenary and expedient of all corporations. It is also why Dow produces some of the most blatantly emotional advertising propaganda about their involvement in humanitarian causes and ecology.

down psychologically depressed. Example: "Judy dropped him last night, and he's **down** today." **2.** no longer under the influence of a drug. Example: "Wendy dropped **acid** last night, but she must be **down** by now."

down and dirty basic, uncomplicated, without frills. **2.** uncensored, banal even nasty.

down, (to get) to get serious, to do something without a fuss. Example: "When I work, I just get **down**, get it done and go home."

*downer a person, place or thing that is depressing; derived from "brings me down." Example: "He's such a **downer**, he even argues with his food."

downers *drugs* drugs that depress the central nervous system. Pills that slow one down. Also known as sedative-hypnotics, they produce a mild **euphoria** (depending on dosage) similar to alcohol consumption. Barbiturates are the most obvious examples: Amytal, Darvon, **Nembutal, Quaaludes,** Seconal, **Tuinal**. Alcohol, opiates and opioids are also downers. Most downers seem to be stimulants (uppers) *initially* because they remove inhibitions, but with time they slow down the body and the mind. Example: "She took a **downer**, danced out of here and fell asleep in the kohlrabi patch." The effect is a mild euphoria similar to alcohol consumption. (See: **barbiturate** and **opiates**)

down home something unsophisticated, homemade or country style.

down in flames rejected or **"shot down**." To meet a disastrous end or suffer an unfortunate circumstance. Related to the phrase **crash and burn**, which came from aeronautical combat vocabulary. (See: **shot down**)

down on to disapprove of or dislike. Example: "She's **down on** macramé; now she's into candles." Most memorable usage is found in the **Janis Joplin** song, "Down on Me."

down the tubes gone, lost or discarded. From either something flushed down the toilet (tube) or a surfer term relating to a tube-shaped wave, on which a surfer either rode or wiped out. Example: "Your psychiatric career is **down the tubes** unless you stop talking to lamp posts."

down to or **down to it** serious, committed. Examples: "She took off all her clothes and got **down to** the skin of the subject." "Stay out of his way; he's **down to it** now."

do your thing or **do your own thing** be true to yourself, do what pleases you. A term created on the streets around 1965. The prevalent attitude of the hippie era and a beginning of the more selfish **me generation**. "Do your own thing" first appeared in print during the hippie era in "The Ideology of Failure," a piece in a series of articles about the **Diggers** in the *Berkeley Barb* newspaper in the fall of 1966. It is believed that Ralph Waldo Emerson coined the phrase, "do your own thing," in 1841. (See: **me generation** if you're interested)

doze to sleep. Usually a short or shallow sleep.

draft card *social issues* an identification card from the Selective Service System, which was mailed to each draft-age male. It carried a number representing the recipient. When a number was drawn by lottery, the person possessing that "draft" number was required to report for induction into military service. In December, 1969, the draft lottery was temporarily reinstated for the **Vietnam War**; it had been unused since 1942.

draft card burning *social issues* one of the most graphic examples of opposition to the **Vietnam War**. Young, draft-age men burned their draft cards at public **anti-war** rallies.

draft resister, evader or **dodger** a draft-eligible man who chose not to serve in the military during the **Vietnam War**. Some young men went **underground** in the United States or Canada, and others went to Sweden, which had no agreement to extradite draft resters. There were many Americans who condemned these men as cowards, but it was not cowardice that motivated them. To most draft resisters, refusal to serve was a rejection of the Vietnam War in particular. Considering all that the draft resisters had to endure in hardship and rejection, standing up for their convictions was actually an act of great heroism. Between 1965 and 1975, more than 22,000 Americans were indicted for draft violations, and a total of 8,756 men were convicted. Presi-

dent Gerald Ford declared an amnesty in 1970, offering to release draft dodgers from their military obligation in exchange for two years of community service. In 1977, President Carter pardoned all draft evaders.

*drag bad, uncomfortable or unpleasant. Example: "Life is a **drag** if you got no doughnuts."

drag v. a suck on a cigarette, **marijuana** or not.

drag women's clothing worn by a man. A man wearing female clothing is said to be in drag. Not necessarily **homosexual** activity; may be for heterosexual stimulation, as a joke, or a costume. (See: **transvestite**)

drag queen a man who habitually dresses in women's clothing. Usually refers to a **homosexual**.

Draper, John (See: **Captain Crunch**)

drawstring pants a simply designed pair of baggy pants made from two pieces of material sewn together and held up with a cord at the waist. Simple, comfortable and inexpensive alternative clothing, handmade during the hippie era.

dread a way of life created by the descendants of African slaves in Jamaica, revolving around the **Rastafarian** religion and **reggae** music. The feeling and attitude comes from the word "dread," meaning fear, which is a prevalent attitude of many of the poor blacks of Jamaica. Example: "Look at his locks; he **dread** man." **2.** anything related to the Rastafarian way of life, religion or reggae music. Example: "That's **dread** music." (See: **Rastafarian** and **reggae**)

dreadlocks a hairstyle originating among African descendants in Jamaica, **Rastafarians** and **reggae** musicians.

Usually seen only in Negroid hair. The effect is to create matted strands and clumps that stand out in all directions. Accomplished by letting the hair grow long and washing and oiling it in a certain **fashion** that creates matting. (See: **Rastafarian** and **reggae**)

dream *drugs* street name for **opium**.

photo by John McCleary ©

dream catcher an American Indian fetish in the shape of a hoop, with twine forming a gossamer spiderweb design. Placed above one's bed, it is meant to capture dreams, filtering out bad ones and letting good ones trickle down to the sleeping person through the feathers and other objects hanging from the hoop. The 1960s and 70s counterculture borrowed many fetishes and talismans from other cultures to adorn themselves and their surroundings. The **ankh**, **om**, **yin-yang** and **peace symbols**, the American Indian dream catcher, **Buddha** statuary, **mandala** and **earth mother** fetishes all became new **talismen** for the American **youth culture**. (See: **fetish** and **talisman**)

dream, the hope for eventual racial equality and equal **civil rights** for all. From the "**I Have a Dream**" speech by **Dr. Martin Luther King, Jr.**, delivered on the Mall in Washington, DC, on August 28, 1963, before 200,000 people. (See: **Civil Rights Events, Groups and Leaders** starting on page 546 in **Lists** at the back of this book)

dreams a window into one's subconscious. In some cultures around the world, dreams are considered a major part of life. In many tribes of Africa and among the aborigines of Australia, dreams are treated almost as reality is in the Western world. Many hippies developed an interest in translating dreams and found them to contain insights into their own personalities and emotions. Noted psychologists Sigmund Freud and **Carl G. Jung** studied and wrote extensively about dreams.

dream therapy, a.k.a. **dream work** a relatively new psychiatric therapy built on the works of Dr. Sigmund Freud and **Dr. Carl G. Jung**. New interest in dreams started in the 1970s and is founded on the premise that understanding one's dreams will help to solve emotional problems that exist during the waking hours.

dregs the unwanted, the rejected, the last. Example: "He is the **dregs** of society, and he washed up on your doorstep; throw him back."

dress for success to dress in a conforming manner. To dress up for business purposes or to impress a prospective employer.

dried out to have **kicked** a drug habit. To have stopped drinking alcohol.

drift mental direction, thought pattern or intentions. Most likely came from maritime terminology relating to the drifting of a boat. Do you know where I'm going (drifting)? Example: "I'm upset; do you get my **drift**?"

drill, drilled or **drilling** *sex* a very negative and intrusive term to describe the act of making love. Example: "Did you **drill** her?"

drive ambition or momentum. Another example of a word, not new to the hippie era, that reached a new level of meaning and usage during the time. Example: "Don't get in Tommy's way; he's got **drive,** man."

drive on keep on doing what you are doing.

drop a bomb to say or do something unexpected. Examples: "She really **dropped a bomb** when she told him she was a he." "He could **drop a bomb** on the conference with that information!"

drop, dropped or **dropping** to take **LSD**. To orally ingest any drug.

Drop City an early **commune** founded on May 3, 1965, near El Moro and Trinidad in Southern Colorado on land purchased by Larry Lard, Clard Svensen and Jo Anne Clard for $450. Started by artists and musicians, primarily dropouts from the University of Colorado. **Geodesic domes** were the prominent structures on the commune, made from the metal of old, junked cars. A large art festival on the property attracted numerous runaways and social dropouts, who eventually overpopulated the place and caused it to be closed down for a time. Legend has it that the name Drop City came from bird droppings and not from **drop out** or **drop acid**.

drop it forget about it. Stop talking about something.

drop out to quit conventional society. From a phrase by **Timothy Leary**, "**Turn on, tune in, drop out.**"

druggie *drugs* someone who likes drugs. Relates to someone a little less

committed than an **addict** or a drughead.

drughead *drugs* someone who is physically or emotionally dependent upon drugs. May also relate to the effects of drugs on a person's mind or head.

drug paraphernalia *drugs* any of the numerous apparatus used for storing, preparing, and using drugs.

drugs chemical substances that alter a person's emotions or create physical changes in a person's body.

drug slut someone who will do anything for drugs. Originally meant to describe a woman who would have sex with any man who would give her drugs. But since many **homosexual** men would do the same and most **heterosexual** men would have sex with any woman for far less, I don't think this term should be gender exclusive.

drugstore cowboy someone who spends time in a public place, on the corner or in an establishment like a drugstore, posturing and "looking good" in anticipation of the approval of others. Not necessarily someone in cowboy attire, but it implies someone who is pretending to be someone or something that they are not. It can describe a gigolo. John Voit in the 1969 movie, "Midnight Cowboy," demonstrated the epitome of a drugstore cowboy.

Druids the priest/magicians of the ancient Celtic culture. Many hippies identified with the Druids because of their involvement in seasonal fertility ceremonies. The **bohemian** hippie **counterculture** was always interested in religions that incorporated nature and reproductive rituals as part of spiritual life. The **true hippie**, being interested in sociology and pragmatic where religion is concerned, understood that all religions first began as celebrations of the seasonal changes and efforts to appease the fickle powers of nature.

dry fuck *sex* to go through the motions of intercourse without penetration. Can be performed while clothed, by rubbing against one's partner.

DTs *drugs* delirium tremens; hallucinations and trembling brought on by chronic alcoholism. **Withdrawal** symptoms. Eventually used to describe symptoms of withdrawal from any experience. Example: "He's going through **DTs** from his last failed love affair."

dualism the religious doctrine stating that there exist two opposed and mutually antagonistic forces, one good and the one evil. Christianity is an example.

dude term of endearment or friendship among men, used as an exclamation or emphasis in conversation. Examples: "Hey, **dude**! We're buddies, **dude**. Forever, **dude**. See you later, **dude**." A term introduced to the American public around 1965. **2.** any male. Sometimes used in a negative connotation.

Du Bois, William Edward Burghardt (b. 1868; d. August 27, 1963) *social issues* African American founder and early leader of the **National Association for the Advancement of Colored People (NAACP)**; founder and editor of *The Crisis*, the official organ of the NAACP, 1910-1934; educator, novelist, poet, **civil rights** militant and political radical. He was the first African American to earn a PhD from Harvard University. In 1961, he left the US for self-imposed exile in Ghana, Africa, and applied for membership in the Communist Party. Du Bois died in Ghana one day before the great civil rights March on Washington held August 28, 1963. He, of all men, was most responsible for creating the civil rights movement in America.

Dudley a derogatory name for a socially awkward person. A name used in sarcasm when addressing someone whose name is unknown and whom you wish to degrade.

*dues experience, ordeal or trial and error. Relates to belonging to a club and paying for the experience. Example: "He paid his **dues**; he survived Catholic school."

dues to pay an ordeal to go through. Example: "I ate the beans and now we all have **dues to pay**." (See: **karma**)

dufus a stupid or foolish person.

duh!? a sarcastic exclamation in response to an obvious statement. Example: "You say you're horny? **Duh**!? With a haircut like that, you should be."

dumb ass or **dumb assed** a stupid person. The word **ass** is used merely as an intensifier.

dumb-down to act less intelligent than one is. In some cases, it is a circumstance that is forced upon a person, as in the example of a mass media that "talks down" to the public, thus restricting education.

dump a bowel movement. **2.** an unkempt or dilapidated place.

dump on to ridicule or verbally attack someone. Example: "You didn't have to **dump on** her just because she turned you down."

dune buggy a customized automobile used for traveling on beaches, deserts or sand dunes. Some of the first were stripped-down **VW bugs**.

dust *drugs* powdered drugs of various kinds used for snorting; **PCP**, **angel dust** or **cocaine**, for example.

dust to get rid of. Example: "**Dust** him and we'll go someplace, just you and your diaphragm and me and my hash pipe."

dusted beaten in a contest or bested in a situation.

dusted *drugs* extremely **stoned** on a powdered drug which is snorted, such as **PCP**, **angel dust** or **cocaine**.

dust off or **dusting off** to ignore, abandon or avoid someone. Same use as **brush off** or **brushing off**. **2.** to leave. Used in the military during the **Vietnam War**. Normally referred to leaving by helicopter, and may relate to the fact that helicopters create a lot of dust during takeoff.

Dutch cap another name for **diaphragm**. A **birth control** device. (See: **diaphragm**)

Dutch joint *drugs* a **marijuana** cigarette made with two or more **rolling papers** in the form of a cone and smoked like a **chillum**.

Dutschke, Rudi; "Red Rudi" or **"Rudi the Red"** *social issues* a young German revolutionary member of the So-

cialist German Student Organization (SDS), he led a student rebellion against the West German government in 1967 and 1968, based on the **free-speech movement** in America.

dweeb a very unpopular person, usually a bookish individual, with few social skills.

dyke or **dike** a somewhat derogatory term for a **lesbian** or homosexual woman. Specifically, **dyke** stipulates the more masculine acting or appearing member of a lesbian couple. The term **butch** is also used. The term **fem** is often used to describe the opposite, more feminine member of a couple.

dykey or **dikey** acting or looking masculine. Relating to the word "dyke"; a **lesbian** or homosexual woman. Example: "She looks **dykey** to me."

photo by Lisa Law ©

**Dylan, Bob (b. Robert Allen Zimmerman, May 24, 1941, Duluth, Minn.) philosopher, poet, songwriter, singer. Zimmerman started using the name Bob Dylan in 1959 and changed to it legally in August, 1962, the year his first album, *Bob Dylan*, was released. The origin of the name and his choice of spelling have several stories. One version is that it was borrowed from the television character, Sheriff

Matt Dillon; the other is that it came from Dylan Thomas. In true Dylanesque style, Bob has not acknowledged either story. Dylan is considered the foremost spokesman of the hippie era. Starting with his first **folk** album, Dylan mirrored the personality of the age. Even his abrupt and controversial adoption of electric music at the 1965 Newport Folk Festival was an indication of the rebellious and experimental nature of the growing **counterculture**. Bob Dylan's most important trait is that he is continually movin' on. "I'm out here a thousand miles from my home, walkin' a road other men have gone down. I'm seein' your world of people and things, your paupers and peasants and princes and kings." "Song to Woody," Bob Dylan, 1962. **One of the 25 most influential people of the hippie era. Actually, he could be considered *the most* influential person of that era. I venture to say that he will rank on everyone's list among the top 100 most influential people of the 20th century and, then again, maybe the 21st as well. Dylan was inducted into the Rock and Roll Hall of Fame in 1988.

dynamics (human) motives and motivations in any given situation brought on by the numerous urges possessed by human beings. Coupled with the physical dynamics of a situation, they produce the episodes of our lives. Example: "The **dynamics** of Judy's life compelled her to change her name to John and start wearing a salami in her pants."

dynamics (physical) circumstances and influences in any given situation. Coupled with human dynamics, they produce the episodes of one's life. Example: "The **dynamics** of wearing a

salami in her pants compelled Judy to change her name to John."

*dynamite outstanding, one of the highest praises. Example: "That was a **dynamite** party."

Dynamite Hill a Black residential area of Birmingham, Alabama. So named because, from 1946 to 1963, there were more than 50 bombings of Black homes and properties in that area.

dyno *drugs* undiluted **heroin**.

E

eagle money. From the symbol of the American Eagle appearing on most American money at one time or another.

eagle flies on Friday wages are paid on Friday, and that's the day to pay bills and have a little fun. For much of the poor, **working class** community, payday is the day to pay bills, buy food for the week and then spend the rest on a little fun to make it all worthwhile. Many blues songs were written about Friday as payday. During the 1960s, the term "eagle flies on Friday" began to mean the whole process of getting paid and spending the money, which "flew" out of one's hand. Originally an African American term.

Eagles *rock & roll* the first successful rock/country crossover band, they were formed in Los Angeles in 1971. The most popular lineup was Don Henley (b. July 22, 1947, Gilmer, Tex.) drums, voc.; Glenn Frey (b. Nov. 6, 1948, Detroit, Mich.) gtr., voc., piano.; Bernie Leadon (b. July 19, 1947, Minneapolis, Minn.) gtr., banjo, mandolin, voc.; Randy Meisner (b. Mar. 8, 1946,

Scottsbluff, Neb.) bass, gtr., voc.; Don Felder (b. Sept. 21, 1947, Gainesville, Fla.) gtr., voc.; Joe Walsh (b. Nov. 20, 1947, Wichita, Kan.) gtr., voc.; Timothy B. Schmit (b. Oct. 30, 1947, Sacramento, Calif.) bass, voc. Although Great Speckled Bird, **Buffalo Springfield** and Poco did it before them, and **The Allman Brothers** and the Charlie Daniels Band joined them in the move, the Eagles were the first truly successful country/rock band. This band had a number of personnel changes, yet remained one of the best loved groups. Inducted into the Rock and Roll Hall of Fame in 1998.

earrings during the hippie era, it became a popular **fashion** for boys and men to pierce their ears and wear earrings. Essentially worn in rebellion against the **establishment**, they were also adopted in an effort to relate to other cultures. Male earrings have been a common fashion for centuries in the Middle East, India, Southeast Asia and Africa. After a time, the earring on men became a statement of sexual orientation. In the 1970s, wearing a ring in the left ear began to mean heterosexual, and the right ear meant homosexual, but that designation seems to have become lost in recent years.

Earth Day *social issues* April 22, 1970, was the first Earth Day celebration, as millions marched and participated in rallies across the United States. The idea was created by conservationist Congressman Gaylord Nelson, and the event was coordinated by a Washington-based group eventually called **Environmental Action**. Ten thousand people gathered at the Washington Monument, and millions of others celebrated by holding hands across the country. One of the first nationally rec-

ognized ecological events. April 22 is now National Earth Day.

Earth First! *social issues* an **ecology** organization founded in 1980 by David Foreman and Mike Roselle. Sometimes called "Rednecks For Wilderness." Fashioned after the fictitious, eco-commando (**ecotage**) group in **Edward Abbey**'s 1975 book, *The Monkey Wrench Gang*. (See: **ecotage** and **Edward Abbey**)

photo by David Glover ©

Earth Mother associated with matriarchal religious traditions and goddess worship. Often represented in ancient cultures by a carved stone, a wooden effigy, or a formed pottery fetish depicting a pregnant woman. She is found in numerous cultures and has many names. Representative names and goddesses include Ishtar of Babylon, Astarte of the Phoenicians and the Hebrews' Ashtoreth. Earth Mother is often interchangeable with Mother Nature and is closely tied to agrarian seasonal fertility rights. **2.** During the hippie era, an Earth Mother was a very domestic hippie woman who wanted to have lots of kids, cook and work in her garden.

earth signs of the zodiac Taurus, Virgo, Capricorn; down to earth, stable, concerned with physical, and material well-being.

*easy gullible, not competitively challenging. Easily beaten in a competition. Examples: "He's **easy** once you get by his opening rook gambit." **2.** *sex* easily seduced. Example: "She's **easy**; all you have to say is you don't love her and you won't stick around tomorrow."

easy! a one-word sentence requesting or challenging someone to slow down or cease activity.

easy meat *sex* easily seduced. A sucker for a sales pitch or a sexual advance. Example: "Horny? Try me; I'm **easy meat**!"

"Easy Rider" a 1969 movie directed by **Dennis Hopper**, starring Hopper, Peter Fonda, Jack Nicholson, Karen Black and Robert Walker, Jr. A breakthrough in the movie industry, it announced to the Hollywood establishment that the public was ready for low-budget, socially conscious films. It was made for less than $400,000 and was a precursor of the independent film industry. This movie introduced the public to the **counterculture** and proved that the media, when used properly, could stimulate deep emotions toward social issues and story lines other than merely love and war.

easy street a bit of sarcasm about the middle-class American dream myth. Originally, it meant the good life, a time and place of economic comfort; yet, hippies changed it into a sarcastic commentary on superficial and precarious affluence. Of the many influences the hippie era had on our language and psychology, sarcasm was one of the most poignant and will be one of the most lasting. The 1960s and 70s **coun-**

terculture dismantled many icons and contradicted many self-deluding myths.

eat *sex* to perform **oral sex**. (See: **cunnilingus** and **fellacio**)

eat a fur burger *sex* to perform **cunnilingus**, oral stimulation of the female genitals. Can be a homosexual or heterosexual act.

eat her shorts (I would) a statement indicating an uncommon willingness to perform an unnatural act merely to get close to the soiled undergarments of the object of one's affection. *Almost* always said in jest.

eat it rejection of an offer, advance or suggestion. Often used sarcastically and in jest toward a friend. Example: To a suggestion of streaking the police station, a proper response would be, "**Eat it,** dude!"

eat it up or **eating it up** to believe a lie or insincere complement. Example: "He's got a line of bull about being a holy man, and people **eat it up**." **2.** to enjoy something. From eating food one appreciates. Example: "Gordo's **eating up** The Dead's new album."

eat me! a confrontational oath. Similar to **bite me!** Like **eat shit**, it is not a serious suggestion. Similar usage to **fuck off**.

eat my shorts! an oath challenging someone to do something revolting. Similar usage to **eat shit** or **go fuck yourself**.

eat out *sex* to engage in oral-genital sex. Can be either male or female.

eat pussy *sex* to perform **cunnilingus**, oral stimulation of the female sexual organs.

eat shit! a strong oath of confrontation. Like **eat me**, it is not a serious suggestion. Similar usage to **fuck off**. Example: "**Eat shit**, punk, and die."

eat this! a defiant challenge. Should be accompanied by gesturing with the middle finger or grabbing one's crotch.

eco-freak *the environment* someone devoted to the ecology movement. The addition of **freak** may be considered derogatory, but not necessarily; ecologists often call themselves eco-freaks.

ecology (environmental) movement *social issues* a **social consciousness** concerned with preserving natural resources and other life forms on the earth. Evolved from the hippie **back-to-the-earth** movement. Though now an established political force, originally, in the hippie era, it was more of an emotional ideal. Like so many of the ideas and movements of the **counterculture**, **environmental** consciousness has proven to have more merit than the establishment gave it credit for. Ecologists were considered kooks in the 1960s and 70s. Today, corporations involved in exploiting and depleting the earth's resources call them "**tree huggers**" and "**eco-freaks**" and treat them as subversives. Contrary to common opinion, true ecologists have no ulterior motives; they simply want to save the earth we live on for future generations. Ronald Reagan's comment that, "Once you've seen one redwood, you've seen them all" is typical of a mentality in this nation that feels that mankind, being a "superior creature," can get along without nature. Environmentalists, on the other hand, believe that scientific facts prove we need to preserve our environment in order to live. There is an added emotional and psychological value to having trees and other creatures with us on this globe. The words **ecology** and **environment** are often interchangeable, which is appropriate for this definition. Many people feel that the **environmental** movement officially started on Earth Day, April 22, 1970. (See: **Ecology and Environmental Issues** on page 614 in **Lists** at the back of this book)

ecotage *social issues* nonviolent ecological sabotage. Disrupting the activities of polluters of the environment through the use of sometimes destructive, yet nonviolent, methods. Coined by Environmental Action, the anti-pollution group that coordinated the first **Earth Day** celebration on April 22, 1970. Sometimes called eco-commando activity or **monkeywrenching.** The term **monkeywrenching** was coined by **Edward Abbey in his** 1975 book, *The Monkey Wrench Gang.* The book chronicles a fictional group of **environmental** commandos who plan to blow up the controversial Glen Canyon Dam. The first ecotage commando was **The Fox**, who disrupted companies by conducting ecological sabotage during the mid-1960s. (See: **Edward Abbey, monkeywrenching, Earth First!** and **The Fox**)

photo by John McCleary ©

ecosystem the environment in which we live. Air, water, earth and food which keep us alive. Unbeknownst to some people who wield the power within industry and government, our ecosystem is very fragile and is now in jeopardy of being toppled like dominoes. **Capitalists** don't want to hear that their pollution and depletion of world resources is endangering human survival, because to do so would impact their profits. Yet, is it possible that they are aware, but feel safe because they know this rape will only affect future generations?

ecstasy *drugs* a pseudo-psychedelic, synthetic **amphetamine** drug. An early form of the **designer** drug creations and a late arrival during the hippie era. Basically **MDMA**, which is the chemical compound 3,4 methylenedioxymethamphetamin. **Methyldeoxyamphetamine (MDA)** is a milder form of the same basic compound. Making these drugs at home has become a cottage industry, and many of the manufacturers are not very good at it. There are inherent dangers with these drugs and worse consequences from taking bad doses. These drugs should be avoided; they may kill you prematurely. Remember, all things in moderation; thinking people use their drugs, foolish people allow drugs to use them. a.k.a. **Adam, love drug, MDA, vitamin E, vitamin X, X, XTC**. (See: **methyldeoxyamphetamine**)

ectoplasm spiritualists consider it the materialization of the **astral body**. A term coined by Professor Richet, created from the Greek words *ektos*, meaning exteriorized, and *plasma*, meaning substance. "The mysterious protoplasmic substance which streams forth from the bodies of mediums, when under manipulation by a discarnate intelligence, producing superphysical phenomena, including ma-

terializations." Ectoplasm is invisible and impalpable in its primary state; it assumes a state of vapor, liquid or solid, depending upon its stage of condensation. It reportedly emits an ozone-like smell.

edge an advantage. Example: "He has the **edge** in speed, but sex is not a race." **2.** a place of mental or physical perfection. Example: "Dokie has achieved the **edge** in her chosen field; she's now the best spoon player I've ever heard." From **cutting edge**.

edge a place of danger or point of impending disaster "before the fall." Examples: "Jude is on the **edge**; she could mentally disintegrate at any moment." **2.** a place of change or point of impending upheaval. Example: "Because always comes the moment when it's time to take the Pranksters' circus further on toward **Edge** City." (A passage from **Tom Wolfe's** 1968 book about **Ken Kesey** and the **Merry Pranksters**, *The Electric Kool-Aid Acid Trip*.)

edge city the outskirts of society.

educational drugs *drugs* substances used for mind expansion and educational tools to improve one's reality. Any drug that is taken to enhance the mental process, to improve perception of the world around oneself or to fathom the depths of creativity within the mind. As opposed to drugs used for recreation or to combat disease. Psychedelics, such as **LSD**, **marijuana**, **peyote**, **mushrooms**, etc., were considered by the **true hippie** to be educational drugs, yet they were also used by many for recreation. Drugs, such as **cocaine**, **opiates**, **speeds** and the family of **MDA**'s, are used for recreational purposes or as an escape from reality.

ego "I" in Latin. I am.   The part of a person that recognizes itself and distinguishes itself from all others.   To many **true hippies**, the ego is our own worst enemy, keeping us from satisfaction, quiet perfection and co-existence with our surroundings. The ego is selfish; it makes us conquer, consume and destroy our environment and other living things for our own gratification.

ego death   the loss of one's self-importance.   Often accomplished through drug experiences, usually through psychedelics. Many people may consider this a negative occurrence, yet the **true hippie** would consider ego death to be the dissolution of one's selfishness. In other words, the disassembly of self-interests and reconstruction as a more cooperative, less competitive person.

ego games   pitting one's self-interest (arrogance) against others. Competing with people on a childish, emotional level. **2.** normal establishment activities, such as school, marriage, work and war. Originally identified by **Dr. Timothy Leary** with a little help from Freud.

ego trip or **ego tripping**   arrogant or self-centered activity. A flight of fantasy about one's own value. A term that entered our lexicon around 1973. Examples: "He's on an **ego trip** thinking he's God to women." "I was **ego tripping** on the dance floor until I discovered my fly was open."

Egyptian Book of the Dead   from ancient Egypt, a collection of spells buried with the dead to help lead their souls through judgment. Often illustrated.

800-pound gorilla   the same as a 600- or 900-pound gorilla; any force that can't be ignored or rationally dealt with. Examples: "Her habit is like an **800-pound gorilla**." Question: "What do you give an **800-pound gorilla**?" Answer: "Anything he wants."

88,000 marijuana arrests   in California in 1975. Approximately 20 percent of the **marijuana** arrests in the United States that year; there were 440,000 such arrests in the nation. That same year, the California State legislature passed a decriminalization law for possessing less than an ounce of marijuana.   In 1976, only 10,000 people were arrested in California for possessing over one ounce of marijuana, and about 40,000 were given citations for possessing less than an ounce. California saved $25 million in police and court costs that year.

Eisenhower, Dwight David, "Ike" (b. October 14, 1890, Denison, TX; d. March 28, 1969), Republican, the 34th President of the United States from 1953-61. Graduate of the US Military Academy in 1915. Commander of the European Theater of Operations and Commander of the Allied Expeditionary Force during WWII and directed the allied landing in Normandy in 1944.

el cheapo   a humorous and sometimes derogatory representation of the Spanish language to describe something cheap or shoddy. Often meant to indicate that it was made in Mexico, therefore not well-constructed.

el ----o   a prefix and suffix added to many words to give the impression that they were Spanish words. Usually used as a humorous or derogatory representation of the Spanish language.   Examples: **el cheapo,** el dopo, el snatcho, el casho, el primo.

electric   exciting, stimulating. Examples: "The Knives' performance was **electric** last night. Slice's solo cut deep into the cosmic cake of the audience's consciousness." "She's **electric** in bed, but a power outage in a conversation."

electric *drugs* **LSD** added. Example: a beverage or brownies with LSD added is **electric**. **2.** something with speed added. Same as **spiked**.

Electric Kool-Aid Acid Test the 1968 **Tom Wolfe** book about **Ken Kesey** and the **Merry Pranksters**. A must-read book describing the hippie era. (See: **Books of the Era** on page 536 in **Lists** at the back of this book)

electric toothbrush a device for cleaning one's own teeth utilizing a motorized conventional toothbrush. First introduced to (or inflicted upon) the American public in 1961.

electrifying exciting or stimulating; similar to electric, though more conservative and usually not related to psychedelics.

electronic music a term coined around 1965, describing the electric organ and synthesizer music that was being introduced into rock and roll music at the time. (See: **Moog** and **sound synthesizer**)

elephant tranquilizer *drugs* one of the many names used to describe **PCP**. a.k.a. **angel dust, tranq, crystal, hog** and **fairy dust**. It was a misnomer in that PCP (active ingredient, phencyclidine) was originally a human tranquilizer eventually used on animals, but whether or not it was ever used on elephants is debatable. (See: **PCP**)

elevate to rise above something spiritually or philosophically. Another word transformed from a physical definition into an psychological use during the hippie era. Physically, it means what it has always meant, except now it also possesses more spiritual and profound connotations. Example: "**Elevate** yourself above the manure of this world and become eternal."

elevator music *not rock & roll* music without soul. Popular music re-recorded to make it "more acceptable" to the general public by using strings and orchestration. Music played as background music in elevators. a.k.a. **muzak**. (See: **Muzak**)

elixir of life a substance (probably mythological and nonexistent) sought by alchemists to extend life indefinitely and to transform base metals into gold.

Elliott, Ramblin' Jack (b. Elliott Charles Adnopoz, 1931, Brooklyn, New York) *folk/cowboy music* a Jewish boy who left home in his mid-teens to join the rodeo, travel the country and gather experiences. By 1953, he was performing country/folk music in Washington Square Park and on the Streets of **Greenwich Village**, New York City. Elliott adopted the name "Ramblin' Jack" in the late 1950s, traveled with **Woody Guthrie**, toured Europe and performed alongside many of the other legends of that **folk** era. He and Guthrie greatly influenced **Bob Dylan**, as Guthrie and Dylan influenced him. Ramblin' Jack has played on the same stage with **The Grateful Dead** and on the stage at Carnegie Hall. He was part of Dylan's 1975 Rolling Thunder Tour and is one of the few remaining cowboy storyteller/folksingers still on the trail keeping dates.

Ellsberg, Daniel (1931-) *social issues* senior liaison officer, US Embassy, South Vietnam, 1965-66; assistant US Ambassador to South Vietnam, 1967; National Security Council operative; one of Secretary of Defense Mc-

Namara's "whiz kids"; advisor to four presidential administrations and research analyst at Rand Corporation, the government subsidized think tank on national security. Ellsberg leaked the **Pentagon Papers** to the press in June, 1971, and hastened the end of the **Vietnam War**. Because of Ellsberg's involvement in the release of the Pentagon Papers, the **Nixon** White House launched a campaign to smear him. Nixon's **plumbers** conducted a burglary of the offices of Ellsberg's psychiatrist to try to dig up dirt on him. The plumbers also physically attacked Ellsberg at several peace rallies to establish him as a violent radical. Ellsberg was charged with conspiracy, theft and violation of espionage statutes, but the presiding judge dismissed the case in 1974 due to government misconduct. Ellsberg is currently a Senior Research Associate of Harvard Medical School's Center for Psychological Studies in the Nuclear Era, and he speaks often on the dangers of prevailing nuclear policy. (See: **Pentagon Papers** and **plumbers**)

Elohim a Semitic word for gods; in Judaism, the name used instead of Yahveh or **Jehovah**, the One God.

el primo *drugs* number one, the best. Adopted from Spanish by the **counterculture** to designate the best **marijuana**. Can also be used to describe any other "best." Most likely derived from the brand name El Primo cigars.

elsewhere absentminded. Residing in another mental or emotional place. Insane. Yet another word transformed during the hippie era from a basic physical description into a more profound human condition. Examples: "Don't bother trying to talk to Doobie; he's **elsewhere,** man."

enchilada, (the whole) a large amount or the best of something. From the Mexican food. Example: "Gram has a lot of sound equipment; I mean he has the whole **enchilada**."

encounter group similar to **group therapy.** (See: **group therapy, gestalt** and **Esalen Institute**)

end the spiritual and metaphysical destination of all souls and all matter. The place of perfection and achievement as sought through enlightenment in every religion; Nirvana, Heaven, Valhalla, the virgin next door. Example: "That concert was the **end**; I can now die a deaf, yet happy, man."

"End, The" the title of an epic piece of music recorded by **The Doors** in 1967 that became one of the most dissected and analyzed songs of all times.

End the War in Vietnam—Bring the Troops Home Now an early anti-war slogan seen on placards at rallies against the **Vietnam War**. Contrary to belief by some people and propaganda by the **conservative** press, the **counterculture** did not blame young soldiers for the war, and they did not wish them harm.

energized empowered or revitalized by some substance, knowledge or teaching. Another word that took on new, deeper meanings through psychedelic experiences and the exploration of spiritual teachings in Eastern religions.

energy rip-off taking away, rather than contributing good emotions. Someone who sucks energy and **"good vibes"** from relationships or situations.

English spliff or **English joint** a cigarette made with a mix of tobacco and **hashish**. Also called a **Dutch joint**.

engraved invitation *negative connotation* a sarcastic reference to someone's unnecessary need for explicit instructions. Example: "You're so dense! Do you need an **engraved invitation** to go fuck yourself?"

engraved invitation *positive connotation* an extravagant offer. Example: "Her smile was an **engraved invitation** to bring my tooth brush." **2.** a presumed offer. "I thought her smile was an **engraved invitation** to spend the night; it was really just pity."

enlightened or **enlightenment** the state of awareness of cosmic truths or spiritual knowledge. A clearer understanding of the relationship between oneself and God. Again, one of the words that meant then what it has always meant, except that it took on new, deeper meanings in the context of the **psychedelic** culture or pertaining to Eastern religions. It is believed by many that, due to the drug experiments of the time, people gained new insights into life that transcended established scientific and religious beliefs. In **Buddhism**, enlightenment means passing into Nirvana, thus being released from the continual cycle of birth, death and rebirth that is reincarnation.

Eno, Brian (b. Brian Peter George St. John le Baptiste de la Salle Eno, May 15, 1948, Woodbridge, Eng.) *rock & roll* a professed "nonmusician," never-

theless, Eno, with **Robert Frip**, Brian Ferry and John Cale, is responsible for starting the extreme electronic experimentation in music that spread through the late 1970s, 80s and 90s. He produced or collaborated with many people, among them, **David Bowie**, Talking Heads and U2. A founding member of Roxy Music in 1971, Eno influenced **punk**, **techno**, **new wave** and world music through his synthesizer experimentations.

environmental (ecology) movement *social issues* (See: **ecology**) (See also: **Ecology and Environmental Issues** on page 614 in **Lists** at the back of this book)

equalizer anything that puts one in an equal position with someone else. Examples: a shot of alcohol, a **toke** of **marijuana** or a **snort** of **cocaine**. In some cultures, a gun is an equalizer.

Equal Rights Amendment (ERA) *social issues* a constitutional amendment first drafted on July, 21, 1923, to guarantee women's equality with men. The amendment was not ratified. The 1960s and 70s saw a renewed effort to advance the cause of women's rights, and women tried again to get the amendment through the Congress and obtain ratification by the States. Primary leaders in the effort were **Bella Abzug**, **Betty Friedan** and **Gloria Steinem**. In 1972, it passed Congress and went before the voters for ratification, but fell three states short of the 38 states needed to become a constitutional amendmen. (See: **Women's Movement Events, Groups and Leaders** starting on page 591 in the **Lists** at the end of this book)

equinox equal night. In astrology, one of two days each year, March 21st (**ver-**

nal equinox) and September 23 (**autumnal equinox**), when day and night are equal in length. These days, along with the winter and summer solstices, have been celebrated by farmers and agrarian peoples for thousands of years due to their importance to the growing cycle. Because of the hippie culture's attraction to the spiritual activities of such ancient cultures as the **Druids**, many equinox and solstice parties, festivals, and gatherings took place during the 1960s and 1970s. (See: **Druids, solstice, autumnal equinox** and **vernal equinox**)

equipment   attributes of the physical kind. Tools of the body. Examples: "Look at that chick; she's got all the right **equipment**." "He thinks his **equipment** is all he needs to satisfy a female. He doesn't understand the importance of love to women."

ERA (See: **Equal Rights Amendment**)

erection the male sex organ, hard and engorged with blood, in anticipation of intercourse.

Erhard Seminars Training (EST) a self-improvement program devised and promoted by Jack Rosenberg, alias Werner Erhard. A popular fad in the 1970s and 80s, when a reported 700,000 people paid $250 to $625 to be verbally abused in an effort to improve their lives. A forerunner of all the **yuppie, preppie** "get active, get rich" cults of the 1980s and 90s. Members and devotees of EST were called "ESTholes" by more discerning minds. Werner Erhard, a former used car salesman, made millions with EST, but it turned out to be just another money-making scam disguised as a form of therapy. Mr. Erhard has since disappeared and is sought by tax collectors and a multitude of courts with actions by former employees. Until people realize they can actually do it all themselves without middle men, there will be those who continue to push shortcuts to wealth and happiness, in brochures not worth the postage and seminars not worth the coffee.

erogenous zone *sex* a place on the human body considered to be sexually stimulating. An area of the body that supposedly acts like a switch or button, turning on sexual excitement when touched or manipulated.

Esalen Institute an institution of alternative therapy and individual psychological development in Big Sur, California. Started in 1962 by Michael Murphy and Richard Price at hot springs once used by early Esalen Indians, it became a center for and synonymous with **gestalt** and **encounter group** theory. Frederick Solomon (Fritz) Perls was one of its resident therapists. At various times, it has attracted as teachers and practitioners such major thinkers as **Aldous Huxley, Ken Kesey, S. I. Hayakawa, Alan Watts**, Abraham Maslow, **Linus Pauling**, Arnold Toynbee, **Gary Snyder**, Rollo May, Carl Rogers, Bishop James Pike, B. F. Skinner and **Carlos Castaneda**. Esalen Institute still functions into the 21st century as a haven for **esoteric** expression and the promotion of human values and potentials. (See: **group therapy, gestalt Theory** and **"Bob and Carol and Ted and Alice"**)

esoteric secrets, inaccessible to the uninitiated. When such information is published, it ceases to be esoteric and becomes exoteric, meaning that it is known by the rest of humanity.

Esoteric Buddhism *religion* the mystic or **occult** schools of **Buddhism**. As specifically practiced in Tibet, it is a combination of **Mahayana Buddhism**, **Tantrism** and the ancient Bon religion. The two main groups are the Red Hats and the Yellow Hats. Worship involves elaborate ritual and the worship of subsidiary deities, high dignitaries, and living incarnations of the Buddha, who is the **Dalai Lama**. The Dalai Lama is regarded as the human incarnation of the most widely revered **Bodhisattva,** Avalokiteshvara. There have been 14 incarnations, with a new Dalai Lama being chosen as a child, tutored by the present incarnation and ascending upon the death of the former. The present Dalai Lama, the 14th, was born Tenzin Gyatso in 1935 and was recognized as the reincarnation at the age of two. He has resided in exile in Dharamsala, India, since 1959, following the Chinese invasion of Tibet in 1950. The present Dalai Lama is not only the spiritual leader of the Tibetan people, but he also heads Tibet's government-in-exile. This religion is sometimes called **Lamaism**, but not by the Tibetans themselves. Tibetan **Esoteric Buddhism**, places great emphasis on **mantras**, the most famous being **om mani padme hum**. (See: **Dalai Lama** and **om mani padme hum**)

ESP (See: **extrasensory perception**)

Esperanto a planned or consciously constructed language created to facilitate communication among people who speak different native languages. Esperanto was intended to act as a bridge among cultures. It was developed between 1877-1885 by L. L. Zamenhof of Warsaw in what was then Russia, now Poland. Zamenhof, raised in a polyglot society, was convinced that a common language would be necessary to resolve many of the problems that produce world conflict. He began work on his planned language, which he called "Lingvo Internacia," when he was in high school, and eventually published the first textbook of the language in 1887. Zamenhof was a medical doctor. Esperanto means "a person who is hoping" in the language of Esperanto. The word Esperanto was originally the name Zamenhof used as a pseudonym when he wrote his first book, and it eventually became the name of the language itself. Esperanto is the most popular of all the planned languages and is spoken by a limited, though committed, number of people around the world. During the hippie era, many people, in the spirit of cultural communication, considered Esperanto as a choice for the world language. There are as many as 1,000 other planned languages in existence; among the best known in the US are J. R. R. Tolkien's Elvish tongues from his book *The Lord of the Rings* and Marc Okrand's tlhIngan Hol, the Klingon language from "Star Trek" movies and the television series, "Star Trek: The Next Generation."

essence *occult* that cosmic matter which makes something what it is, as distinguished from its physical existence, properties or attributes.

EST (See: **Erhard Seminars Training**)

establishment the older, existing authorities, personified by one's parents, teachers, police, businessmen, military and politicians. The conservative element of society.

ether *occult* the substance that, according to occultism, fills all space and pervades all matter. That which holds the world together. Existence, **magic** or cosmic energy. The invisible and largely indescribable energy that flows throughout the world and our lives. Words like ether, **esoteric** and **essence** were not unknown to the world before the hippie era, but they achieved new and expanded use in the vocabulary of the Western world through the **counterculture**. a.k.a. **cheese, chi, glue, pudding, sauce** or **apple sauce**.

Ethernet *computer revolution* one of the first incarnations of the Internet. Bob Metcalfe at Xerox Corporation's **Palo Alto Research Center (PARC)** was a prime mover in its development. **Ethernet** was created along with **Alto**, the first real personal computer. It connected only a few computers at **PARC** to their colleagues around the world starting in the early-to-mid 1970s. **ARPAnet** was the older computer connecting system, linking the larger mainframes of schools, research agencies and companies. These early nets usually connected only the major computer science departments at schools, such as MIT, Harvard, Dartmouth, UC Berkeley, UCLA, Stanford, and a few commercial research facilities, such as Xerox, Bell Labs, GE and IBM.

ethnic studies academic courses in the history of diverse cultures, particularly Hispanic and African American. Efforts in support of ethnic studies classes led to many campus **demonstrations** during the late 1970s and early 80s.

ethyl chloride *drugs* anesthesia usually found in spray form. A prescription product. Recreational users spray it on a cloth and inhale the fumes. The effects last less than a minute, but can cause loss of consciousness and in some cases death.

euphoria *drugs* a drug-induced sense of well-being. In common dictionaries, it is defined as a feeling of great happiness and well-being; the secondary usage is a deluded sense of well-being.

Euro- a prefix indicating European influence or origin. Examples: Euro-chic, Euro-style, Euro-sound or Euro-euphoria.

evened out equitable or straightened out. A slightly awkward, yet obvious, progression of the phrase "leveled out."

Evers, Medgar Wiley (1925-1963) *social issues* an **NAACP** Mississippi field secretary, shot and killed in ambush in front of his home in Jackson, Mississippi, June 12, 1963. His is one of the forty names engraved on the **Civil Rights** Memorial in Montgomery, Alabama.

evil extremely good or very proficient. Like **bad** during the hippie era, **evil** was often used to mean the opposite of its original definition. Example: "He's an **evil** guitar player, man!"

evil eye the power to bewitch or harm someone with a look.

evolve to become a better person. Evolution is an activity thought to take generations, but, during the hippie era, it was believed that one could make major personal changes through drugs or Eastern meditation.

exactamundo exactly. The word "exactly" with a romance language flourish added for emphasis and individuality.

excuse me all to hell! a sarcastic apology. An insincere apology. The "all to hell" was added as emphasis.

existential philosophy (existentialism) a philosophy offering the belief that people are essentially free of any and all outside control (no fate nor gods) and therefore are responsible for what they make of themselves. A doctrine derived from the works of 19th century Danish philosopher Soren Kierkegaard. Jean-Paul Sartre, Martin Heidegger and Albert Camus were 20th century existentialist writers. Elements of existentialism were present in the basic beliefs of many hippies.

experience drug intake and/or sexual activity. A person's sexual or drug history. **Jimi Hendrix** asked in his 1967 song, "Are You Experienced?"

Explorers' Club, The *drugs* a small group of professionals, intellectuals and educators who experimented with psychedelics on an intellectual level. They arranged controlled circumstances, such as dosages, locations and situations under which to ingest mind-expanding drugs in order to learn specific lessons from the experiences. Remember, all things in moderation; thinking people use their drugs, foolish people allow drugs to use them.

"Expressman Blues" a song that has been called the first rock-and-roll music. Recorded May 17, 1930, by "Sleepy" John Estes, Yank Rachel and Hammy Nix.

extrasensory perception (ESP) *occult* response to an external event not understood by any known sense. The ability to perceive things from a distance, send thoughts over distances and **read** others' thoughts. A term coined by Dr. J. B. Rhine of Duke University. In the **spirit** of religious, **occult** and paranormal curiosity during the hippie era, ESP became an avid interest. Many experiments were conducted clinically and by amateurs to test and prove ESP with and without the influence of drugs.

Just prior to the hippie era, a number of books were written about ESP, notably about Edger Cayce, a psychic who was studied at Duke University.

extreme a word of praise for something exciting or unusual. Example: "Man, that girl's got **extreme** eyes."

eyeball to use a visual, rather than mathematical, measurement. Example: "Don't bother measuring; just **eyeball** it."

eye candy pleasing to the eye; decorative. A "sweet-looking" woman.

eyelid movies *drugs* visions seen with eyes closed while on a psychedelic drug.

eye on the prize *social issues* a **civil rights** slogan meaning to look forward to freedom and to work for the cause of freedom. The term comes from a song about the **freedom riders**, "Keep Your Eyes on the Prize." One of the lines is, "We're gonna board that old Greyhound, carrying love from town to town. Keep your eyes on the prize, hold on, hold on." The freedom riders were a group of 13 **civil rights** workers who left Washington, DC, on a bus on May 4, 1961, traveling into the Southern states to draw attention to segregated transportation.

eyes an attraction to or interest in something. Example: "I've got **eyes** for that chick." An African American term that evolved during the 1940s and 50s and was adopted and used extensively in the hippie culture. Many early African American terms and phrases were adopted by the 1960s **counterculture**; for a good look into that contribution to our language, refer to Clarence Major's 1994 publication, *Juba to Jive, A Dictionary of African-American Slang*, published by Penguin Books.

eyes are getting brown to be lying or telling an untruth. When one says that someone's eyes are brown, it infers that the shit has risen to their eyeballs.

F

f an abbreviation for the expletive **fuck**. A self-conscious use of the word meaning to copulate. Examples: "Get your f-ing hands off my f-ing stuff." "**F** you, and **f** the horse you rode in on." Used by people who don't really approve of profanity or by someone in a public forum in which they wish to be more circumspect. It was not used by **true hippies**, who felt supressing emotions or evading reality was hypocritical.

fab short for fabulous. Originally a **British invasion** term, very much connected to **The Beatles**, who were called the **Fab Four**.

Fabulous Furry Freak Brothers an underground comic by Gilbert Shelton, drawn for *Feds 'n Heads Comix*. The brothers were Fat Freddy, Phineas Phreak and Freewheelin' Franklin, whose motto was, "Dope will get you through times of no money better than money will get you through times of no dope." (See: **Comix & Underground Cartoon Strips of the Era** on page 639 in **Lists** at the back of this book)

face or **face stud** a Black term for a White person. Started as **face stud** and was shortened to **face**.

factory *drugs* a place where illegal drugs are manufactured.

fad something temporarily popular, a short-term **fashion**. Examples: "a clothing fad," "a music fad." A term not new or exclusive to the hippie era, yet widely used and expanded during that 20-year period.

fade or **fade away** to disappear or go away. Examples: "If I were you, after what you did, I'd **fade** for a while." "Dorothy's so embarrassed about the pea soup incident that she would just as soon **fade away**."

fag short for **faggot**, another derogatory term for a **homosexual** male. As with many terms originally intended to belittle, it was soon adopted by the **gay** community to make fun of themselves and to show indifference to and contempt for such name calling. With the introduction of political correctness, this term is now used almost exclusively by the gay community itself or by a few low-life homophobics who think opossum is haute cuisine.

faggot a derogatory term for a male **homosexual**. Older usage. May date to 15th century references to burning homosexuals, when faggots, or small bundles of wood, were used as kindling.

fag hag a woman who enjoys the company of **homosexual** men. Some women find gay men to be more fun, and these relationships are without the pressures of sexual negotiation.

fag tag the little loop found just below the collar on the back of some men's shirts, most often of the button-down variety. Also called a **fruit loop**. Originally intended for hanging the shirt, yet seldom used for that purpose. Such shirts were considered at one time to be an integral part of the **gay** male "uniform."

fail-safe a term created by the government to indicate that a chemical process or mechanical project was safe from failure. It was applied particularly to all nuclear functions with which the Pentagon or the Department of Energy were involved. "Oops!"

Fairport Convention *folk/rock & roll* British folk/rock group formed in London in 1967. **Sandy Denny** (b. Jan. 6, 1947, London; d. Apr. 21, 1978, London) gtr., voc., kybds.; Richard Thompson (b. Apr. 3, 1949, London) gtr., voc.; Simon Nicol (b. London) gtr., banjo, dulcimer, bass viola, voc.; and other revolving band members. An important group in the transition from **folk** to rock in the United Kingdom. Richard Thompson is still one of the most prolific songwriters, and Sandy Denny, who died tragically in a fall, was one of England's most popular singer-songwriters of the early seventies.

fairy dust *drugs* an obscure street name for **PCP**. (See: **PCP**)

Faithfull, Marianne (b. Dec. 29, 1946, London, Eng.) *rock & roll* she recorded "As Tears Go By" in 1964, a song by Mick Jagger and Keith Richards of **The Rolling Stones**. One of the **hippie chick** fantasies of all young, heterosexual men of the time. She is best known as one of Jagger's former girlfriends.

faith healing a medical cure produced by one's own belief that disease and pain can be healed through faith in a Divine Power.

fairy yet another derogatory, but satirical, term for a male homosexual. Again, the **gay** community adopted this term to show indifference to and contempt for such negative labels.

fake it to pretend. **2.** often used in the context of a simulated orgasm, which is a device some women use to give their selfish lovers a feeling of accomplishment. Most hippie men, particu-

larly those who read any Eastern literature, such as the **Kama Sutra**, or about **tantra yoga**, were committed to the sexual satisfaction of their lovers. Many men are not interested in the effort sometimes necessary to help their mates to achieve the pleasure of orgasm, and therefore, some women fake it to please their men. Women: It is always self-defeating to fake pleasure in lovemaking because, by doing so, you give your lovers the false impression that they are performing properly. This then allows them to relax their efforts to please you, and leaves you with only your fake orgasms. Men: When your lover really enjoys your lovemaking, it is such a spiritual high that your enjoyment will increase beyond your fantasies.

fake out or **faked out** to fool or deceive someone. A term that came into use sometime around 1963. Examples: "OJ could **fake out** any 300-pound lineman, and now he's **faked out** the system as well."

fakir a Muslim beggar, ascetic or miracle-worker. Usually seen in India, roaming the streets unwashed and without clothing. A term not applied to **Hindu** ascetics, although they might appear to be the same. A fakir is said to have the ability to create illusions, causing witnesses to "see" things that have no basis in fact. Fakirs also supposedly have control of *Parna* (or Vital Force), which allows them to concentrate their energy in order to move heavy objects and **levitate** themselves in defiance of gravity.

fall to fall in love. Example: "She will **fall**, he will **fall** and then they will fall together."

fall to get arrested. Examples: "Weggee's too loose with his dealing; he's going take a **fall** someday." **2.** to suffer a setback. Example: "Doug's business is going to **fall**."

fall by to stop by in or to visit. Example: "Dave's not here; **fall by** later."

fallen angel a young woman who has lost or given away her virginity.

fall for to be deceived. Example: "He'll **fall for** that line of talcum powder every time." **2.** to be smitten by love or lust. Example: "Dolly will **fall for** any girl with a flat top."

fall in to arrive or show up.

fallout repercussions from an action or circumstance. Examples: "The **fallout** from his six-month marriage is $750 a month alimony. That's an expensive love affair!"

fall out to go to sleep or to pass out. Example: "Don't worry about me; just give me a pillow and I'll **fall out** in the tub."

photo by John McCleary ©

family a group of people living together, not necessarily related by blood or legality, yet connected by similar ideals. During the hippie era, many unrelated people lived together as "families" under communal roofs. In some cases, the spiritual or emotional bonds were so strong that these people began to think of themselves as brothers and sisters and therefore began to call themselves a family.

Family Dog originally a commune consisting of Allton Kelly (the poster artist), Ellen Harmon, Luria Castell and Jack Towl, living at 2125 Pine Street, San Francisco, in a house called the Dog House. At one time, they had a bizarre idea to produce concerts to raise money for a mail-order pet cemetery in New Mexico. Chet Helms was involved in their concert activities, and Janis Joplin and her first band hung out with them. Eventually, Dan Hicks and George Hunter from **The Charlatans** band joined the **Family**. Herb Greene and others, some just called Mouse or Goldfinger, were among the loosely disorganized group. For a time, they rented the International Longshoremen's and Warehousemen's Union Hall near Fisherman's Wharf in San Francisco and presented weekly dances. They were associated with **Bill Graham** and the **Fillmore Auditorium**. The **Family Dog** was somewhat involved in the **Monterey Pop Festival** and eventually became well known for their psychedelic light shows. The commune did have a dog named Sancho, "the family dog."

family jewels a man's testicles. From the assumption that a man's balls, and the sperm therein, are a valuable family asset.

family of man basically, mankind, the human race; yet, to many, it represents a more emotional or **cosmic** description of the interrelationship of humans. To many, it means that we should be more understanding and cooperative with other human beings, regardless of their race or religion, because we are ultimately all part of the same "family." To some, it may seem to be a sexist phrase; yet, from its purest definition, it was not meant to be.

fan someone who enthusiastically follows the career of an individual, entertainer, band or sporting team. May also be used in the context of an ordinary attraction to someone. Derived from the word fanatic.

fang shui *occult* a Chinese term for **magic** and **occult** arts. (As opposed to feng shui, which deals with the relationship of human beings to their environment.)

fantabulus a word indicating enthusiastic praise. Created by joining the words fantastic and fabulous together to create more emphasis.

Fantasticks, The *musical comedy* a musical comedy written by Tom Jones and Harvey Schmidt in 1959 for a summer production at Barnard College in New York. Basically, the plot is the seduction, abduction, education, coming of age and lovelife of a young girl. All this is done in literary euphemisms, double entendres and comedic alliteration. It ran almost continually for over 40 years at the same Sullivan Street Playhouse in New York City. There have been over 17,000 performances in over 3,000 cites and towns in the United States, and it has been produced at least 690 times in 68 countries.

fantasy anticipation, desire, a lark...fun to be had. Fantasy was a very important activity during the hippie era. Much of the hippie life was an effort to temper reality with a little fantasy. The social and economic realities of the late 1950s and early 1960s were hard to live up to. Musical beach party movies and Disneyland were difficult to reconcile with the harsh realities of Vietnam and **civil rights** violations in America. The sex, drugs and rock and roll of the hippie era were reactionary activities to help re-evaluate the importance of life. The 1960s and 70s showed us that fantasy is an expedition we need to give us hope or happy anticipation. The hippie era gave us eyes to see the harshness of reality, yet fantasies to strive for so that life wouldn't beat us down. Fantasy is not a place at Disneyland; it is a door to our minds.

Fantasy Fair trip tent, photo by Lisa Law ©

Fantasy Fair a rock and roll festival held on Mount Tamalpais in California on June 10 and 11, 1967. This is considered by many to be truly the first rock festival ever held since it was conducted one week before the **Monterey Pop Festival**. **The Doors** played, along with most of the San Francisco music groups. Many of the good things learned about festivals and later used at Monterey Pop and **Woodstock** were first employed at the Fantasy Fair. The **trip tent** was first seen there.

Fariña, Mimi (b. April 30, 1945, Palo Alto, Calif.; d. July 18, 2001) singer, actor, and activist. Sister of Joan Baez, she and Joan were considered the first **hippie chicks**. She met and married Richard Fariña in 1963 and recorded three **folk** albums with him on the Vanguard label in the mid-1960s. Their second album, *Reflections in a Crystal Wind*, was considered an important transitional step between folk and rock music. After Richard's death in a motorcycle accident on her 21st birthday in 1966, Mimi withdrew from entertaining for a time. She eventually returned to singing and became involved in acting, notably with **The Committee**. In the early 1970s, she helped to create *Bread and Roses*, a charitable organization providing entertainment for children and people institutionalized in prisons and hospitals.

Fariña, Richard (b. 1937, Brooklyn, NY; d. Apr. 30, 1966, Carmel, Calif.). singer/songwriter, musician and author. Born to Cuban and Irish parents, Richard spent periods of his life in Cuba and Ireland. He was involved in the IRA, deported from Britain and later spent time in Cuba supporting Castro. He met and married Mimi Baez, younger sister of **Joan Baez**, in 1963 and formed a **folk** duo with her. Richard and Mimi recorded three Vanguard albums in the mid-1960s, the second of which, *Reflections in a Crystal Wind*, was an early example of what power and pathos the folk and rock collaboration could produce. Richard wrote the song "**Birmingham Sunday**" in 1963 after the bombing of the Sixteenth Street Baptist Church in Birmingham, Alabama, where four young Black girls were killed and 20 others injured. He also wrote numerous plays and articles and the book *Been Down So Long It Looks Like Up to Me*, which explored the transitions from the **beatnik** into hippie culture. Richard Fariña died in a

motorcycle accident in 1966, following a promotional party for his book. His death is considered to be one of the great losses of the era. (See: **Birmingham Sunday**)

Farm, The a large commune near Summertown, in western Tennessee started in 1968 by **Steven Gaskin**. Gaskin had been a student of S. I. Hayakawa at San Francisco State, headed for a successful academic career, when he dropped out to became a motivational speaker. His **Monday Night Class** meetings, attended by thousands of people in the San Francisco Bay area, taught people how to get **high** without the necessity of drugs. Gaskin left San Francisco with his followers in about 40 brightly painted school buses and eventually ended up in Tennessee. Pooling their money, they bought the land on which they created The Farm. They experimented with alternative power and heating, such as solar water heating, photovoltaics and micro-hydroelectric turbines. A slogan from The Farm is "clean air, healthy babies, honest work, nonviolence, safe energy, cheap transportation, and rock and roll." The Farm still exists today and is home to around 200 people. Though there are many communal groups existing today, The Farm is one of the few communes that survived from the 1960s and 70s. In an era when many of the people who received all of the media attention possessed outrageous egos, displayed religious arrogance or perpetrated revolutionary violence, Stephen Gaskin stands out as a teacher of humility, simplicity and peace. (See: **Gaskin, Stephen** and **high**)

Farmer, James Leonard (1920-1999) *social issues* a **civil rights** leader and cofounder of the **Congress of Racial Equality (CORE)**. Farmer was the creator and a member of the **freedom riders**, a group of 13 **civil rights** workers who left Washington, DC, on a bus on May 4, 1961, traveling into the Southern states to draw attention to segregated transportation. Farmer was a follower of Mohandas Gandhi's teachings of nonviolent direct action. An avid integrationist, he enlisted both Whites and Blacks as CORE volunteers. **CORE** was the first Black civil rights organization to employ nonviolent techniques of **civil disobedience**. Farmer wrote *Freedom—When?* published in 1966 and his memoir, *Lay Bare the Heart*, published in 1985. After leaving CORE, he taught for several years at Mary Washington College in Fredericksburg, Virginia. (See: **nonviolent civil disobedience**)

farm-out a humorous play on the phrase **far-out**. (See: **far-out**)

*far-out a statement of approval. It can mean OK, good, wonderful, amazing, or out of the ordinary. Same usage as **out of sight**. Although sometimes the brunt of humorous hippie characterizations, it is now very much accepted as a common English idiom. The use and misuse of this phrase is an important indication of how **cool** a person is. Although the phrase originated in the 1950s, it did not gain widespread use until the hippie era, at which time it took on subtle, expanded definitions. A phrase with many uses, it is *one of the 125 most prominent words or phrases that evolved out of the hippie era into continued use today.

fart a detestable person, someone of small stature or limited mental capacity. Originally a basic Anglo-Saxon word meaning the passing of stomach gas from the anus. This word was used in America with the same definition for a long time, but it began to evolve in the mid-20th century into a pronoun describing a person rather than merely a noun describing a body function. During the hippie era, it found expanded usage and was used openly with less hypocrisy. Until that time, it was still unacceptable in polite society and was found only in "locker room" conversation.

fartage a **fart** or the smell of a fart. The suffix "age" was added to some words in sarcastic/humorous evolution of the hippie vocabulary. The hippie era was the intellectual renaissance of the 20th century, and many new speech patterns and avenues of communications were born during that period. Some may feel that elevating a word like fart to a new level is a degradation of the language; yet, in reality, it is an element of mind expansion, education and evolution. The study of Shakespeare reveals that he was a very experimental writer, creating new words and contractions to make people think about what he was writing. He played with profanity in particular to awaken his readers from their sleep. The Marquis de Sade and Oscar Wilde also used profanity to stimulate the minds of people. For these men, profanity and pornography were only vehicles by which to reach people with their deeper, profound lessons in humanity.

fart around to waste time, to mess around having fun, to get into mischief.

fart sack a sleeping bag.

fascist or **fascist pig** a derogatory reference to the police or any governmental authorities who use violence to control the population. The word fascism has come to mean totalitarian, **capitalist**, political ideology and narrow-minded, racist, violent activities. The term appeared when police beat student radicals during the campus **free-speech** demonstrations of the mid-1960s and at the 1968 **Democratic National Convention** in Chicago. The word "pig" implies a person who acts like a animal.

photo by John McCleary ©

fashion   the current, commercially popular form of dress and self-decoration. Fashion is created by a few people, stolen by others, and followed by many. The hippie culture created new forms of dress and decoration; other people copied these ideas, marketed them, got credit for them, and made money selling them to other folks who bought them to be **cool**. The progression of all **fads** and fashion is from **hip**, to **style**, and then to fashion. Hip is the alternative creativity of a culture; style is that creativity put to use as a way of life, and fashion (fad) is style that has been marketed.

fashion statement   a personal touch of adornment or style intended as a statement of one's individuality. During the hippie era, it often meant "**fuck you if you can't take a joke!**"

fast   a compliment directed at a person's mental agility or the ability to understand something quickly.   Example: "You can't pull that on Bard; he's too **fast**."

fast company   friends and acquaintances who are decadent or excessive in their lifestyle.   Originally a Roaring Twenties term that found expanded usage in the hippie era.

fast food   quickly made and rapidly served food. Exemplified by hamburgers, french fries and a syrupy, sweet brown beverage. The term came into regular use by the public in 1970. The 1950s and 1960s drive-ins and diners evolved into fast-food "restaurants" of the 1970s. Fast food was one of the American institutions against which the hippie movement generally rebelled, yet a quick drive-through was often a welcome solution to the **marijuana** munchies for those hippies with less discriminating food habits.

fasting   abstaining from food, partially or totally, for a period of time. Originally practiced for religious cleansing and often by primitive societies in preparation for an initiation or rite of passage. In cultures such as the indigenous American peoples, it was a preparation for the taking of psychedelic substances, such as peyote, psilocybin mushrooms or yage. Fasting has been used in Eastern religions as a means to reach purity of body, thus purity of mind, in seeking purity of the soul. Often, fasting makes people weak and light-headed, thus producing visions and feelings of spiritual enlightenment. During the hippie era, along with the interest in better eating habits and **vegetarianism**, came an interest in fasting. Hippies used fasting to cleanse the body for the purposes of health.

Fasting or hunger strikes were also used by **civil rights** activists, pacifists and other demonstrators to bring attention to causes. It must be noted that uninformed fasting can be hazardous to one's health. If you wish to fast, please confer with a practitioner or doctor.

*fast lane a decadent or excessive lifestyle. Named for the left lane, or speed lane, on a freeway. Originally a Southern California term referring to **cocaine** usage.

fat the best, the most sought after. Not necessarily related to size. Examples: "That was a **fat** party, man!" "That girl gives **fat** love!"

fat cat someone who is rich or influential.

fat chance a sarcastic way of saying no. Same as "no chance," "**no way**," "not possible," or "no, I won't."

fat city comfortable financially, in a good place. A good place to be. Examples: "No need to worry about me; I'm in **fat city**" "That town's **fat city**; I always have fun there."

Fates, The the three Roman goddesses who, it is said, preside over the birth and life of mankind. Their names are Atropos, Clotho and Lachesis.

Fat Man, The an affectionate name given **Jerry Garcia** of **The Grateful Dead** by his **fans**.

fave or **fave rave** short for favorite. Usually related to a lover or object of affection. A favorite person to rave about.

fearless leader a sarcastic or derogatory term for the President of the United States, the boss or any authority figure. May have originated as a term in the "Rocky and His Friends" TV cartoon

show, which debuted September 29, 1959.

Feds or **the Feds** representatives of the Federal government, i.e., FBI, CIA, Drug Enforcement Agency, Immigration and Naturalization Service, Internal Revenue Service, etc.

fed up to have reached the limitation of tolerance. Related to "I have had it up to here." Full to overflowing.

*feedback commentary on an idea or suggestion. Example: "I want some **feedback** on my idea to fill the motel swimming pool with lime Jello."

feedback *rock & roll* the screeching or siren-like sound made by musical amplifiers when music coming from speakers is picked up by the microphones and played back through the system.

feed your head *drugs* give your mind something to expand its thinking process. To take drugs. Originally a line from the hookah-smoking caterpillar in "Alice In Wonderland," it was restated in the song, "White Rabbit," by the **Jefferson Airplane** in 1967.

feel another word that came into more use in the emotional, rather than physical sense during the hippie era. People began to feel with their hearts. Example: "I **feel** your pain, brother; I **feel** your fear, sister."

feelgood *drugs, sex* a state of being, usually related to the taking of drugs. "Doctor Feelgood" was a name for someone who supplied drugs. Sometimes, Doctor Feelgood was a good lover.

feeling good means just what it says. Often, the state of being was drug- or sex-induced. Example: "I'm **feeling**

good, my heart is high and you are at my side."

feeling groovy a common statement in the early 1960s, **groovy** is an adaptation of **in the groove** meaning "good" or "doing well." Feeling groovy became a laughable comment after a song by the same name was released by **Simon and Garfunkel** in 1967. The song was one of their more self-indulgent, and admittedly, even by Paul Simon, a silly piece of music.

feeling no pain *drugs* to be under the influence of drugs or drunk. In other words, to be anesthetized.

fell infatuated or in love. Examples: "He **fell** hard for her when she dropped her pretenses and her **halter top**."

fellatio *sex* oral stimulation of the penis. A form of copulation involving the manipulation of the male genitalia by a partner's mouth. As distinguished from **cunnilingus**, which is the oral stimulation of the female sexual organs, the clitoris and vulva (vaginal opening). Not a new term to the hippie era, nor is it a new idea to the last fifty millennia. Done without shame during the 1960s and 1970s. In street language, fellatio is the act of going down on a man and giving him a blow job. Can be a homosexual or heterosexual act. a.k.a. **blow job, head job, hum job**.

felt-tip pen a writing implement introduced in 1960.

fem a **lesbian** who fulfills the more feminine side of a homosexual relationship.

feminine zodiac signs earth and water: Taurus, Cancer, Virgo, Scorpio, Capricorn and Pisces.

feminism *social issues* a socio-political movement and ideology based on the conviction that women should enjoy the same social, economic and political rights as men. The **feminist movement** and the **women's liberation movement** were considered by many to be interchangeable, yet they did have several subtle differences. Women's lib seemed to follow a more establishment path to achieve equality, whereas feminists tended to cut new trails. Feminist organizations became **self-help** groups with the goals of aiding women to achieve pride in their gender and confidence in themselves. The possibility of existing happily without men and the accompanying necessity of doing everything for themselves were issues raised by women during the hippie era. **Radical feminism** grew out of continued disillusionment with the male-dominated society, and these **"radical fems"** became a link to the eventual **lesbian** movement. (See: **Equal Rights Amendment** and the **women's liberation movement** in alphabetical listings) (See also: **Women's Issues** on page 591 in **Lists** at the back of this book)

feminine principle or **female force** in **esoteric** philosophy, the receptive, passive and negative aspect of the cosmos. Matter, form and wisdom are usually considered feminine and are represented by goddesses in the pantheon of multiple god religions.

Fender Guitar Company *rock & roll* guitar manufacturing company, whose guiding force was Leo Fender. Developed the pivotal **Telecaster** in the late

1940s to early 1950s, the **Precision bass** in the early 50s and the incomparable **Stratocaster**, the icon of all rock guitars, in the mid- to late-1950s. The Telecaster, still being manufactured, is the oldest surviving solid body electric guitar. The Fender Precision bass was a larger version of the Telecaster design and arguably the most popular rock bass guitar. The Stratocaster is a sculpted-down version of the older Telecaster, giving more comfort in playing and exhibiting a more radical visual flare in the horn design.

Ferlinghetti, Lawrence (b. 1919, Yonkers, New York) a **beat** poet, writer and artist. One of the major forces in the beatnik movement, along with **Allen Ginsberg**, **William S. Burroughs**, **Jack Kerouac**, **Gary Snyder** and a few other poets, writers and artists. Ferlinghetti and his friends verbalized the unspoken thoughts of intellectuals and many people of the **working class**. By expressing their distaste and distrust of American hypocrisy and **materialism**, they made the hippie era possible. Their philosophies would become the basis of the rebellions of the 1960s and 70s. Ferlinghetti earned a doctoral degree in poetry with honors from the Sorbonne in Paris. A longtime associate and friend of Ginsberg, Burroughs, Kerouac and Snyder from the early days of the beat era in New York and San Francisco. Ferlinghetti founded, with Peter Martin, City Lights Books in San Francisco, the nation's first all-paperback book store. City Lights now publishes modern poetry books, and Ferlinghetti divides his time among the business, writing poetry, painting and presenting readings of his works. A San Francisco street has been named after Lawrence Ferlinghetti, yet that city and

the world of literature have traveled upon his intellect for many years.

Ferry, Brian (b. Sept. 26, 1945, Washington, Eng.) *rock & roll* singer/keyboardist and founding member of **Roxy Music** in 1971. Ferry and Roxy Music influenced **punk**, **techno**, **new wave** and world music through the late 1970s, 80s and 90s.

fer sure colloquialization of the phrase, **for sure**. A statement of agreement.

-fest *suffix* a suffix added to words to indicate a party or **festival** atmosphere. Short for festival. Examples: rockfest, beerfest.

festival *rock & roll* a musical concert held in an outdoor venue over a period of several days. During the 1960s and 70s, music festivals became cultural gatherings at which contemporary **folk** art was displayed and sold, and sex, drugs and spiritual expression were prevalent. Not a term new to the era, it was used previously for **folk** and **jazz** festivals.

Festival Express Train a train trip across Canada taken by a large group of musicians performing concerts along the way. The trip was from June 27 to July 4, 1970. On June 27 and 28, they played at the Canadian National Exhibition Stadium in Toronto; on July 1, at the Red River Exhibition in Winnipeg, Manitoba; and on July 4, they played at McMahon Stadium in Calgary, Alberta. The performers included **Janis Joplin** and The Full Tilt Boogie Band, **The Band**, **Grateful Dead**, **Delaney and Bonnie and Friends**, **Ian and Sylvia** & Great Speckled Bird , New Riders of the Purple Sage, Tom Rush, Buddy Guy, Eric Andersen, Mountain, Ten Years After, **Traffic**, Seatrain, Charlebois, James & the Good Brothers, Cat,

Mashmakan and the Modern Rock Quartet.

fetish an object considered to be the resting place of a soul or **spirit**. A piece of jewelry or art worn or possessed that has some religious, social or personal significance. In the 1960s, men, as well as women, began wearing body art or displaying fetishes as a form of expression or rebellion. The peace sign, the swastika, the cross, shells, crystals, small animal bones, rocks and odd assortments of art were worn around the neck as rings or earrings. The search for individuality created a multitude of adornments.

fickle finger of fate the silly name of a trophy used in a weekly comedy segment of the TV show "**Rowan and Martin's Laugh-In**." The finger was awarded to a person, place or government agency that had participated in a misadventure or made some stupid move. (See: "**Rowan and Martin's Laugh-In**")

fiddlefuck or **fiddlefucking** to mess around or waste time. Examples: "Cut the **fiddlefuck** and do something useful." "Garth is good at **fiddlefucking** around."

Fillmore Auditorium (The Fillmore), (December 10, 1965 to July, 1968) *rock & roll* the revolutionary rock concert hall at 1805 Geary Street in San Francisco. Opened in December 10, 1965, by **Bill Graham** when he rented the hall for a benefit for the **San Francisco Mime Troupe**, of which he was a member and manager. That first show featured **Jefferson Airplane**, Mystery Trend, The John Handy Quintet, and a group called The Great Society, with **Grace Slick** as its lead singer. Bill Graham went on to promote thousands of concerts there and in other venues until his

death in a helicopter accident in October, 1991. The Fillmore was run by Graham from December, 1965, to July, 1968, and it is not to be confused with the "Fillmore West" on Market and Van Ness, where Graham moved his operation in July, 1968.

Fillmore East (March 8, 1968-June 27, 1971) *rock & roll* a rock concert hall opened by Bill Graham in an old vaudeville theater on Second Avenue, in Manhattan, New York City. Graham initially used the venue to introduce West Coast bands to the East, but throughout its era, many great shows were produced there with artists from all over the world.

Fillmore West (July, 1968 to June, 1971) *rock & roll* the old Carousel Ballroom upstairs on Market and Van Ness in San Francisco featured many big bands in the 1930s and 1940s. For the first six months of 1968, it was run as a rock dance hall by **Grateful Dead** associate Ron Rakow. The hall was managed by some of the groups that played there: The Dead, **Jefferson Airplane** and **Quicksilver Messenger Service**. In July, 1968, **Bill Graham** "outbid" Rakow for the lease, renamed the space Fillmore West, and moved his operation there from the old **Fillmore Auditorium**. Graham produced many more great shows there until he closed it in June, 1971.

fine or **super fine** something very good. Example: "His guitar playing is **fine**, and I mean **super fine**." Often used as an understated compliment. Example: "She's **fine**."

finesse or **finessed** (someone or something) to talk someone into something or maneuver them into a situation. To move something carefully or skillfully cause an object to do what you want it to do. The most recent origin of use before the hippie era was in pool or billiards: to finesse a ball in to a pocket or behind another ball. Examples: "Watch Duke **finesse** that girl into bed." "Stick really **finessed** that car into the garage."

f-ing a shortened version of the expletive fucking. A self-conscious use of the word meaning to copulate. Example: "Get your **f-ing** hands off my **f-ing** stuff." Used by people who don't really "approve" of profanity or by someone in a public forum where they wish to be more circumspect. Not used by **true hippies**, who felt suppressing emotions or evading reality was hypocritical.

finger to betray someone to the authorities. Comes from "to point a finger" at someone. An old police and 1950s mystery novel term used a lot in the hippie era.

finger, the a defiant gesture using the middle finger extended. Meaning "fuck you!"

finger or **finger fuck** *sex* to sexually stimulate a woman by penetrating her **vagina** with one's finger.

finger up (one's) **ass** inactive or unhelpful in a situation that warrants some involvement. Examples: "During the fire, he just stood there with his **finger up his ass**."

fink n. a person who reveals a confidence or betrays a trust. A stool-pigeon.

fink out v. to reveal a confidence. Example: "He'll **fink out** his mother if he gets the chance."

fink out v. to quit or fail to do what one has promised. Example: "Don't **fink out** on me; you said you'd turn

over the compost and I'm counting on you."

fire enthusiasm. Example: "John plays his spoons with **fire**." The term "fire in his belly" was a precursor to this shortened version. **2.** the **essence** of a person. Example: "He has a **fire** that burns in slow corrosion, the smoke of which billows out through his pen to the paper."

fire *sex* the sexual parts or sexual being of a woman. Example: "I wanted to get next to her **fire**, but she misunderstood and we stood over her electric heater all evening."

fire *drugs* a match or a light for a joint.

fire or **fire away** go ahead, do it. Talk to me.

fire down below or **fire** the sex drive. Also, the **essence** of a person. Later used in the lyrics of **Bob Seger**'s 1991 song "Fire Inside."

fired up excited about doing something. Hot and ready for sex.

fire signs of the zodiac Aries, Leo, Sagittarius; inspirational, active, vital and self-expressive.

Firesign Theater a group of four, sometimes five, guys who had a live comedy FM radio program in Los Angeles between 1967 and 1985. Phil Austin, Pete Bergman, Dave Ossman and Phil Proctor performed "Radio Free Oz." This show pushed the limits of political dissent, censorship and morality in a way that helped to expand people's awareness and break down hypocrisy.

fire up *drugs* to light up a joint or a bowl of dope. **2.** To get something started. Example: "**Fire up** that tape deck, and let''s get down to some loud sounds."

First Amendment *social issues* "Congress shall make no law respecting an establishment of religion, or prohibiting the free exercise thereof; or abridging the freedom of speech, or of the press; or the right of the people peaceably to assemble, and to petition the Government for a redress of grievances." The first of ten amendments to The Constitution that were ratified by the States in 1791 and called The Bill of Rights. The First Amendment was exercised and challenged more than any other law of the land during the 1960s and 70s. It was under the rights given by the First Amendment that all peaceful **civil rights**, **free-speech** and **anti-war** demonstrations were conducted. Our First Amendment rights were violated when these **demonstrations** were obstructed by the police and military authorities.

first base a place of achievement, the first plateau of success. Related to baseball, a game in which players must reach first, second and third base before crossing home plate to score.

first base *sex* the first step in sexual contact, also called petting. In some microcultures across America, it meant kissing, and in others it described fondling above the waist.

first fruits the offering to a deity of the first harvest of the growing season, the first animals killed or trapped in the hunting season. The **true hippie** looked back with longing to the time when his ancestors lived off the land, and many tried to recreate that life in the 20th century. Many of the rituals of the past were revived in the **counterculture**. One example is the harvest festival held each fall in Big Sur on the coast of California. Hundreds of followers of cannabis would gather, drink and smoke,

and many would dance naked around a huge bonfire upon which a ten- or twelve-foot **marijuana** plant was thrown to burn as the dancers inhaled the smoke.

fishnet a loosely knit fabric used for clothing that allowed a see-through view of the wearer's skin. Similar to **see-through**. People wore clothing made of such material as an acceptable alternative to being completely naked. During the 1960s and 70s, both men and women pushed the envelope of cultural mores by flirting with nudity in public. It was also the era of topless **hippie chicks**, streaking and body paint.

fit *drugs* same as kit, the intravenous drug user's equipment for shooting drugs.

five a hand, as in five fingers. A handshake. Example: "Slip me **five**, man!"

five-cent paper *drugs* five dollars' worth of **heroin** or some other drug in a folded paper pouch.

five-dollar bag *drugs* a five-dollar quantity of heroin or some other drug. During the 1960s and 70s, five dollars went further, yet was a small amount of money to pay for **cocaine** or heroin. It was assumed that the drug was "stepped on," meaning "cut" or diluted by adding an inert product, such as quinine or milk sugar. Other, more dangerous substances, such as speed or **methamphetamines**, were also used to cut drugs.

five-finger discount shoplifting. Using the five fingers of one's hand to steal something.

five-o police. From the TV show "Hawaii Five-O," a Hawaii-based cop show, that premiered on CBS on September 26, 1968. "Hawaii Five-O" was the name of a special investigative unit directly responsible to the governor of Hawaii.

fives *drugs* **Benzedrine** or any **amphetamine** tablets. **Uppers**.

fix *drugs* a shot of some drug or a portion of anything that someone likes or is addicted to. Examples: "She needs a **fix** of heroin." "I need a **fix** of fresh air."

fixed signs of the zodiac Taurus, Leo, Scorpio, Aquarius; the power signs, ideals, goals, and principles.

fixing *drugs* injecting drugs.

Flack, Roberta (b. Feb. 10, 1939, Asheville, North Carolina) *pop, rock and soul* a singer who recorded many memories of the era. She produced the most popular songs of the year in both 1972 and 1973 with "The First Time Ever I Saw Your Face" and "Killing Me Softly With His Song."

Flacks, Richard an early member of **Students for Democratic Society** (SDS) in 1962 when he was studying at the University of Michigan. He later became a professor of sociology at the **University of California, Santa Barbara (UCSB)**. He was teaching at UCSB during the **Bank of America burning** in the **Isla Vista** neighborhood adjacent to the campus on the night of February 25, 1970. A group of his students produced a documentary film on the Isla Vista demonstrations entitled "Don't Bank on Amerika."

flag abuse *social issues* using the American flag in some way other than that prescribed by the official Flag Code adopted by Congress in 1942. When protesting policies of the United States, hippies and other protesters "abused"

the American flag by burning it, flying it upside down or wearing clothing made from it. **Abbie Hoffman** incensed many patriotic Americans when he wore a shirt made from "Old Glory" at an **anti-war** demonstration in 1967.

photo by John McCleary ©

Periodically, someone in Congress proposes that flag abuse, particularly flag burning, be made illegal. An amendment to the Constitution would be necessary to make such a law valid. Many people oppose, as I do, criminalizing flag burning on the grounds that it would be a giant step toward the erosion of our freedoms. The flag is not actually our country, but a symbol of the country, and to demonstrate peacefully against our government is a right given to us by our Constitution. **MC5**, a Michigan rock and roll band of the late 1960s, was one of the first bands to wear American flags and shout obscenities at the establishment. They performed outside the **Democratic National Convention** in Chicago during the August, 1968, police riots.

flag decal a mylar plastic American flag designed to be pasted on car windows and bumpers. Dispensed by oil companies and banks during the early 1970s in support of the **Vietnam War** effort. It became a satirical joke to the **counterculture** and was used as a counter-icon in **John Prine's** 1971 song, "Your Flag Decal Won't Get You Into Heaven Anymore."

flak verbal abuse or objection. Any disruptive activity. Example: "Don't give me **flak** about my appearance; the length of a man's hair has no relationship to his masculinity, love of country or faith in God." Originally a military term for exploding shells shot at airplanes.

flake an unreliable person.

flake *drugs* pieces broken off of a **rock** of **cocaine**. Used later to describe **crack** cocaine.

flake off to leave or go away. A rejection. Example: "**Flake off**, dude, you're a fashion clash with those orange PF flyers."

flake out to quit. To get tired and stop doing a job.

flaky someone or something that is unreliable. Example: "Don't count on Dagmar; she's **flaky** and she eats tofu."

flaming someone or something that is exaggerated, dramatically overt or obvious. Examples: "He's a **flaming** homosexual and proud of it."

flash a thought, an idea; usually something new or extreme. Example: "Wow, what a **flash**; if I mix this red one with this blue one, I can have psychedelic wet dreams."

flash to expose private parts of one's body to someone, either as a joke, a perverted thrill or to offend. The part of the body exposed depends on the intended result. It can be harmless, mutual fun, such as when a woman exposes her breasts; it can be a "moon," which is when someone exposes their bare ass; or it can also be a deviant sexual act, such as exposing one's genitals to an unsuspecting or innocent person.

flashback a memory, often referring to a vivid recreation of a **psychedelic** drug experience.

flasher someone who exposes private parts of their body to unsuspecting victims.

flash on to notice or be attracted to someone or something. Example: "Did you see that girl in the pink hair **flash on** me?"

flavor of the month someone or something that is popular for a short time. Example: "Judy is his **flavor of the month**."

Fleetwood Mac *blues, rock & roll* Mick Fleetwood (b. June 24, 1947, Redruth, Eng.) drums; John McVie (b. Nov. 26, 1945, London), bass; Christine Perfect McVie (b. July 12, 1943, Birmingham, Eng.) kybds., voc.; Peter Green, gtr., voc.; Jeremy Spencer, gtr., voc.; Danny Kirwan, gtr., voc.; Bob Welsh, gtr., voc.; Bob Weston, gtr.; Dave Walker, gtr., voc. In 1974, the most popular lineup occurred, composed of Fleetwood, John and Christine McVie, Lindsey Buckingham (b. Oct 3, 1947, Palo Alto, Calif.), gtr., voc.; Stevie Nicks (b. Stephanie Nicks, May 26, 1948, Phoenix, Ariz.) voc. Originally formed in 1967, the band endured many changes but consistently created good music. In the mid-1970s they became the most danceable band of the era and contributed greatly to its personality. Inducted into the Rock and Roll Hall of Fame in 1998.

flesh-eater a non-**vegetarian**. Used as a derogatory term by some vegetarians who thought carnivorous humans were predatory. Same usage as **meat-eater**.

flick a movie. From the flicker of early movies caused by the interruption of images by slow-moving film.

flight a **psychedelic** drug experience.

flim-flam a deception. An illegal activity involving cheating. Examples: "He is a **flim-flam** man; don't trust him." "I think that deal is a **flim-flam**."

*flip, flipped or **flip out** to go out of one's mind or do something crazy.

flip chick a crazy girl. Flip is short for **fipped out**.

flip flop *sex* simultaneous oral copulation by two people. a.k.a. **69**. Can be a heterosexual or a homosexual activity.

flip off to display the middle finger in an obscene gesture meaning **fuck you**.

flip out an extreme reaction to a drug experience.

flip side the other side of a subject or the opposite opinion. Example: "She may taste good, but the **flip side** is that her husband will be bitter." From the music industry, where the flip side is the less popular side of a record.

floater feces that floats on the top of the water in the toilet bowl and will not flush.

"Float Like a Butterfly, Sting Like a Bee" a description of himself by **Muhammad Ali (Cassius Clay)**.

floating a mental state of inactivity similar to being in the **ozone**.

flog the dog, the log, the dong or **the meat** male masturbation.

floods (See: **high-water pants**)

flop a failure.

floppola a failure. Just a more exaggerated way to say **flop**.

flow the correct, natural progression of a situation or the path of least resistance in a social encounter. Examples:

"Let it **flow**; like the river, life knows the pull of gravity." "Go with the **flow**; if she wants to take you home, don't fight it."

photo by John McCleary ©

flower child a **hippie**. A person who has reverted to a simpler, more natural way of life. Someone with flowers in their hair, either actually or figuratively. Usually a peaceful, nonviolent person. The most valued rule of the **true hippie** generation was The Golden Rule, the most prevalent emotion was Love, and the most passionate conviction was for Peace and Equality. The flower was chosen as a symbol of the era because of its purity and beauty. (See: **hippie**)

flower power the power of peaceful, nonviolent action. Pacifism, the turning of one's cheek, the religion of righteousness and believing that what is right will eventually prevail. The nature of a flower is quiet tenacity, a strong self-preservation hidden by delicate beauty and sensitivity; this is the **spirit** of the **liberal** intellectual human being called the hippie.

fluff something of no intellectual content or social value. Example: "That movie was **fluff**. When he asked the female ski instructor to recommend a massage parlor, I nearly puked."

fluff someone, usually a woman, who is not intelligent, but is decorative. Example: "She's a bit of **fluff**, sort of like taking a poodle to the library."

flunky unskilled worker. Someone who is designated to perform the manual tasks or **shit work**. Often, it means that they are not too bright. The word most likely comes from the root flunk meaning that person has failed at all other jobs. a.k.a. **grunt, sweathog**.

flush *drugs* to put illegal drugs in the toilet and flush them down when the authorities raid your **pad**.

flush or **flushed** having plenty of money or possessing an excess. Example: "Hey, I'm **flush**; I have all the babes, pills and LPs I need."

flux the characteristic of time in which all things inevitably change. Not new during the hippie era, but it achieved new and expanded use in the vocabulary of the Western world through the **counterculture**.

fly or **flying** another term for being **high** on drugs. Examples: "I like that new wedge; it makes me **fly**." "I'm **flying** behind this stuff."

flying fuck, (a) a term used to express disdain, disinterest or disregard for something. Example: "I don't give a **flying fuck** which sex a person sleeps with or which Gods they worship."

flying saucer *drugs* **morning glory** seeds. A mild, natural **psychedelic**. A certain variety of Mexican morning glory contains **lysergic acid** similar to that of LSD.

Flying V or **Flying Arrow guitar** *rock & roll* made originally by the **Gibson**

Guitar Company in 1957-58 for two **Native American** Indian cabaret musicians. Gibson produced 100 more for commercial sales in 1958-59 and has

Jimi Hendrix's self-painted Flying V

built them off and on ever since. Other companies have made copies, such as the "V" by **Rickenbacker** and **Fender**. (See: **Gibson Guitar Company**)

focus to concentrate mentally. Before the 1960s, this word was used primarily in the context of physical vision. Hippies began to use it in terms of emotions, self-improvement and **self-realization**. Examples: "**Focus** on your inner feelings." "Stay **focused** on life."

focus *drugs* a drug solution, diluted and ready to inject.

foil *drugs* a small package of drugs in a piece of wrapped foil.

folk relating to anything homespun and homemade by the indigenous, usually rural, population. Examples: **Folk** music, **folk** art, **folk** tales, etc.

folkie someone who sings **folk** songs. After the folk music craze waned, it became a slightly derogatory description of someone who wasn't quite up to date musically.

folk music *music* the indigenous music of any region or country. Before the 1940s, the United States had a lively tradition of eclectic folk music from other countries, corresponding to the immigrations of its people. During the Depression, a new breed of musical bards appeared to create a folk music exclusively American. The major personalities were **Robert Johnson, Leadbelly, Woody Guthrie, Odetta** and **Pete Seeger**. The music was a mixture of African American **blues** and British Isles folk. The lyrics contained some of the usual romantic angst, but relatively new was a direction toward political commentary and social rebellion. The folk music of the late 1940s and 1950s was the forefather of the 1960s and 70s **social consciousness** folk and **folk-rock** of people like **Joan Baez, Richard and Mimi Fariña, Bob Dylan, Richie Havens, Country Joe McDonald, The Byrds, Buffalo Springfield, Neil Young**, etc.

folk revival *music* the beginning of the 1960s saw a folk music revival when urban dwellers began to look back at their country roots. Traditional and folk singers like **Woody Guthrie, Leadbelly,** Burl Ives, Josh White, **Odetta,** the Weavers and **The Kingston Trio** found new and renewed favor. This period was a short pause before the storm as music moved into **folk rock** and then rock.

folk rock *music* the transitional music between the 1950s folk and the 1960s rock. **Bob Dylan** was a primary mover in the genre with other groups and performers, such as **Peter, Paul and Mary, Richie Havens, Fairport Convention, Loving' Spoonful, The Band, Donovan, The Mamas and the Papas**, and **The Byrds**. The electrification of instruments characterized the move from folk into folk rock. For many, Bob Dylan's performance at the 1965 Newport Folk Festival was the moment of change, and his song, "Mr. Tambourine Man," was the first true folk rock piece. Folk rock was not confined to the early 1960s time period; it is still a valid form of music, composed and played into the 21st century.

follow (your, the) **bliss** indulge yourself, let yourself go, seek out pleasure.

follow the money pay attention to the source of financing to determine the motive of an activity. The dynamics of a situation are related to whoever will gain the most from the outcome. A phrase that became popular after the 1976 movie "All the President's Men," in which the informant **Deep Throat** used it to direct **Woodward and Bernstein** toward the perpetrators of the Watergate Burglary. (See: **Deep Throat, Watergate break-in** and **Woodward and Bernstein**)

follow your head do what you think is right.

follow your heart do what you feel is right.

Fonda, Jane (1937-) one of the most controversial celebrities who lent their voice and image to the causes of the hippie era. To start with, she starred in some of the most thought-provoking and contemporary movies of the period. "They Shoot Horses, Don't They?" "Coming Home," and "China Syndrome" are three very poignant films, and "Barbarella" is so very 1960s counterculture. Fonda was a staunch supporter of women's issues, Native American civil rights, the environment, and the anti-Vietnam war movement. At one time she may have been both the most revered and the most hated woman in the US when she traveled to North Vietnam in support of the people and their "war against colonial oppression." "I ain't fond a' Jane" was a common statement by supporters of the **Vietnam War**. Jane Fonda was also

Fonda as Barbarella, 1968
art by Paxton©

called **Hanoi Jane** after she visited North Vietnam in July, 1972, and broadcast over the Voice of Vietnam radio station to American bomber pilots. She said to the pilots, "I implore you...I beg you...to consider what you are doing."

fonk and **fonky** a colloquial Black pronunciation of funk and funky. (See: **funk** and/or **funky**)

food chain the power structure of animals, business or society. The chain of predators and their food in which each of us occupies a position of importance or strength, below us is our food, above are our predators.

food conspiracy another term for a **food co-op**. The **counterculture** used this term as a rebellious statement of what the corporate world must have been thinking about food co-ops. After all, the **liberals** and hippies were

"conspiring" to "take" profits away from legitimate grocery conglomerates.

food co-op an organization of individuals who banded together to cut out the middle men in the food buying process by going directly to the farmers themselves and doing the distribution on their own. Any profits went toward streamlining the distribution and reducing the cost of the foodstuffs. At one time, it was the only way for **whole food** advocates to get organically grown produce or foods that had not been sprayed by pesticides. The co-op movement was a **counterculture** way to fight the system, get more healthy foods and save money. Some co-ops became so big that they had their own stores and employees, and eventually some of these evolved back to for-profit establishments.

food of the gods *drugs* **psychedelic mushrooms** were sometimes called this. (See: **ambrosia**)

food trip eating or indulging in a food craving or fetish of some kind.

fool a frivolous or silly person. **2.** someone who purposely assumes the role of a frivolous or silly person in order to entertain others or keep the atmosphere of a situation from becoming too serious. **3.** someone who plays the fool for someone else in exchange for favors, drugs or recognition.

fool around to indulge in some sort of sexual play, usually an illicit activity.

football *drugs* an **amphetamine** capsule. An **upper**.

Ford, Gerald Rudolph (b. July 14, 1913, Omaha, Neb.), Republican, the 38th President of the United States from 1974-77. Graduated from the University of Michigan in 1935 and Yale Law

School in 1941. Elected to the US House of Representatives in 1948, and held a seat until, as House minority leader, he became Vice President upon the resignation of Spiro Agnew on December 6, 1973. On August 9, 1974, Ford became President following the resignation of President Nixon.

foreplay *sex* play before sex. Considered by some men to be an annoying obstacle to what they really want, which is their own orgasm. Foreplay is actually preparation of the instinctively reticent female to create the emotional willingness and physical lubrication necessary for enjoyable sexual intercourse. Remember, satisfying your sexual partner increases your own satisfaction, unless, of course, you are a selfish sadist. As **The Beatles** said: "The love you take is equal to the love you make." Refer to my next book, *Loveseat Fantasies: The Sexual Documentary of a Young Man*, for further explanation.

foreplay in a nonsexual context, it is defined as preparation for any social activity.

forget about it a negative response. Similar to "That's out of the question." Similar usage as **up yours** or **fuck you**.

forget it a rejection. Similar to "That is out of the question" or "I would never do that." Related to **don't even think about it.**

fork over to give reluctantly, to return something taken.

fork you a humorous way to say **fuck you**.

for real the affirmative! This is true, I'm serious. Example: "**For real**, I won't sleep with you no matter how much money you spend on dinner." Often considered a **Valley Girl, Valley talk**

term, yet it was a much earlier creation of the **beat** era.

for sure or **fer sure** an exclamation of agreement or affirmation. Examples: "**For sure**, that was a dynamite concert." "Hey, I dug that **fer sure!**"

Fossey, Dian (1932-1985) *social issues* American primatologist who went to Rwanda, Africa, in 1966 to study mountain gorillas. Her interest was the preservation of a species being slaughtered by the native population and whose habitat was being destroyed by agricultural encroachment. It was a losing battle, indicated by the population drop from 500 when she arrived to approximately 150 by 1978. In 1968, Fossey befriended and named one male gorilla **Digit**. Fossey studied him and others of his breed, and Digit was featured in numerous television documentaries and National Geographic articles about Fossey's work. Digit was killed and mutilated in late 1977 by poachers who cut off his head and hands to sell as souvenirs. Fossey continued her work with the gorillas despite conflicts with Rwandan government officials and poachers. On the night of December 26, 1985, Dian Fossey was herself attacked and hacked to death with a heavy, native knife in her remote cabin at the Karisoke research center on Mount Visoke, where she had lived and studied the gorillas for almost twenty years. It was obvious to all that she was killed for trying to protect the gorillas from the commercial interests of poachers.

fossil an old person.

Foster, Jim one of the first gay political movers in the Democratic Party. He started the Gay Democratic Party in San Francisco in December, 1971, and called it the **Alice B. Toklas Club** (Alice for short). He died of AIDS.

foul something that is nauseating or smells unpleasant. **2.** an unkind act, or improper comment. Example: "Grunting when she walks by is a **foul** thing to do."

fouled up someone or something that has gone amiss; a situation that is confused or mixed up.

foul up a mess or a mistake.

four-letter word a profane word. From the fact that the two most used "dirty words," **fuck** and **shit**, are spelled with four letters. **Joan Baez** reminded us in one of her songs that love is also a four-letter word.

Four Noble Truths the *Aryani Satyani,* the four basic principles of the teachings of Gautama Buddha: the Truth of Suffering, the Truth of the Cause of Suffering, the Truth of the Cessation of Suffering, and the Truth of the Path to the Ending of Suffering.

four-twenty or **420** means **marijuana** time. It can mean: It's time to smoke, do you want to smoke, do I look under the influence of marijuana, or do you have any **dope**? It has many meanings in many different parts of the country, all relating to marijuana. Can be written: four-twenty, 420, 4/20, 4:20 or in many other ways. It originated at San Rafael High School in California in 1971. The number meant the time, 4:20 p.m., the time of day at which a group of students calling themselves "the Waldos" met to smoke dope after school. The term has taken on a life of its own; there are many stories about its meaning and origin, but I know this is the most accurate. The date, April 20, is also celebrated as a marijuana anniversary of sorts by some people.

fox a very attractive person.

Fox, The *social issues* an unidentified person or group of people who conducted ecological sabotage (**ecotage**) against companies that polluted the environment. This "eco-warrior" disrupted the manufacturing and polluting activities of companies in and around Aurora and Kane Counties in Illinois during the mid-1960s. In disguise, the Fox entered manufacturing facilities, carrying the industrial waste that they had dumped into local rivers, and dumped the chemical sludge right back into their corporate offices. He also delivered dead fish killed by the companies' pollutants. The Fox blocked factory drainage and sewer systems and sealed off smokestacks, leaving notes advising companies to "clean up their act." After each raid, posters appeared in the community, and press releases accusing the companies of negligence were sent to the news media. (See: **ecotage**)

foxy attractive or sexy.

fractured angry. **2.** distorted or disturbed.

frag or **fragging** military slang for the killing of an unpopular officer by his own enlisted men. It reached an alarming proportion during the **Vietnam War**. Gung-ho or overzealous officers trying to gain medals, citations or high body counts were often the target. One of the techniques used was to throw a fragmentation mine or grenade into the officer's bunker, thus the name frag, from fragmentation. Between 1969 and 1972, 788 cases were documented, resulting in 86 dead and 714 wounded. There are hundreds more suspected cases. Often, a smoke grenade was used as a threat instead of live ordnance; sometimes, the pin was left in the device, which was placed by the door of the officer's quarters. Noncommissioned officers were the leaders present in the field of action; because they gave the orders that got men killed, they bore the brunt of the soldiers' hatred. Another way of eliminating an officer was to shoot him during a battle; thus, it was recorded as an enemy-related death.

'fraid not no, said with sarcasm. A contraction of "I'm afraid not."

'fraid so yes, said with sarcasm. A contraction of "I'm afraid so."

frankincense a pungent gum resin from trees of the genus *Burseraceae*, originally found in East Africa and Southern Asia. Burned as incense in religious rituals in temples and **ashrams** of the Buddhist and Hindu faiths for centuries. More recently introduced into Russian, Greek Orthodox and Catholic ceremonies. Said to be one of the gifts of the three kings or wise men from the East given to the Christ child at his birth. Frankincense is considered a purifier, and, on a more practical level, is used as a fumigant, keeping pests at bay during religious gatherings. Hippies, in their experimentation with other lifestyles, introduced incense of all kinds to Western culture.

Franklin, Aretha (b. March 25, 1942, Memphis, Tenn.) *gospel, soul, rock & roll* the premier female soul and rhythm and blues singer of the era. Called Lady Soul. Often voted the most popular recording artist in rock and roll. Aretha Franklin recorded "Respect," considered by many to be the best song of the era, and she co-wrote and recorded "Dr. Feelgood," another important song of the time. It is impossible to calculate the value of this song stylist to the 1960s and 70s culture. Inducted into the Rock and Roll Hall of Fame in 1987.

frantic worried or upset. **2.** manic activity.

freak a self-denigrating term used by hippies to describe themselves. Early on, the hippie **counterculture** was characterized as "a freak of society" by the straight culture, so, in defiance, hippies adopt the word freak and used it themselves. In some uses, it was spelled "freek." During the hippie era, most hippies did not refer to themselves as hippies; we often called ourselves freaks. Hippie is what everyone else called us.

*****freaked out** scared or crazy.

freak flag something that identifies a person as a hippie. Long hair is the most obvious. A term heard in **Crosby, Stills, Nash and Young's** song, "Almost Cut My Hair."

freak freely to act spontaneously or eccentrically. Lose all inhibitions.

freaking going temporarily crazy or becoming frightened.

freaking acting in a strange or antisocial manner in order to repulse the straight society. Example: "Let's go out **freaking** at the mall tonight."

freaking sometimes used in place of the word fucking.

freak off to lose all inhibitions and react spontaneously, often in a sexual context.

freak out to go temporarily crazy or to become frightened. Often, this term was used to describe the schizophrenia or paranoia sometimes induced by drugs.

freak (someone) **out** to scare someone. To revolt someone. Example: "It's easy to **freak** Judy **out**. She's a strict vegetarian and all it takes is the word, **cheeseburger.**"

freak rock psychedelic rock and roll.

freak show a strange place or occurrence. Example: "This party is a **freak show**. You and I seem to be the only normal people here, and I'm not sure about you."

freaky something strange.

freebase *drugs* **cocaine** that has been processed with highly toxic and flammable chemicals in order to free the base (hydrochloride molecule) from the cocaine molecule so that it will burn properly, releasing its **psychoactive** qualities. There are inherent dangers to this drug and worse consequences from taking bad doses. Most recommendations are to stay away from this drug; it will kill you prematurely. Remember, all things in moderation; thinking people use their drugs, foolish people use drugs that will kill them.

freebie or **freebee** something free. **2.** this is the term that some people thought would replace **hippie** after the **Death of the Hippie** funeral in San Francisco in the fall of 1967. (See: **Death of the Hippie**)

free clinics facilities that sprang up in the 1960s and 1970s in cities around the United States to offer free medical assistance to hippies and street people. These organizations were staffed by volunteer nurses and doctors on their off hours from their regular jobs. They dispensed simple "healing" drugs, provided **birth control** counseling, treated venereal diseases and helped those with drug overdoses or **addictions**. The

first AIDS awareness came from these clinics.

photo by John McCleary ©

free concerts *music* musical performances provided without charge by rock groups for the pleasure of their fans. Usually conducted in parks or outdoor venues to create a less inhibited atmosphere. Considered a gift to loyal followers, repaying them for their past financial support.

Freed, Alan (1922-1965) a popular White **disc-jockey** in Akron, Ohio, Cleveland and New York City during the 1950s. Freed is accepted as the person who coined the term "rock and roll" and is credited with introducing Black music to White audiences, thus breaking down the barriers to help create rock and roll as the integrated institution it is today. During the 1950s and 60s, it was an accepted business policy for record companies to give money to disc jockeys in return for playing their records on the air. This practice was called **payola**. Although there was no actual law against it, at some point the authorities and news media decided to make it unacceptable and began a smear campaign against those who accepted these "bribes." Alan Freed was one of the **DJs** singled out, and his career was ruined by the payola scandal. Inducted into the Rock and Roll Hall of Fame in 1986. (See: **payola** and **Alan Freed**)

freedom riders *social issues* seven Blacks and six Whites who left together on a bus from Washington, DC, on May 4, 1961, traveling into the Southern states to draw attention to segregated transportation. On May 14, the bus was burned in Anniston, Alabama. Traveling on in another bus, the freedom riders were beaten in Birmingham, Alabama. **JFK** sent Federal marshals to protect them for the remainder of their journey. Discrimination in interstate transportation was declared illegal by Congress on November 1, 1961.

"freedom's just another word for nothing left to lose" a line from the song "Me and Bobby McGee," written by Kris Kristofferson and recorded by Roger Miller, **Janis Joplin**, Jerry Lee Lewis and others. A phrase often used to emphasize a conversation about freedom, yet I suspect that few people could explain its meaning. I believe it means that true freedom is having no possessions, situations or relationships about which to worry.

Freedom Summer *social issues* the Mississippi Summer Project launched on June 3, 1964, by the Council of Federated Organizations (COC). The Summer Project was a massive education,

community improvement and voter registration drive. The COC was a **civil rights** coalition comprised of the **Congress of Racial Equality (CORE)**, the **National Association for the Advancement of Colored People (NAACP)**, the **Southern Christian Leadership Conference (SCLC)**, the **Student Nonviolent Coordinating Committee (SNCC "snick")**, and The National Council of Churches.

"Free Huey" *social issues* a common piece of graffiti seen during the late 1960s. **Black Panther** Huey P. Newton was arrested on the night of October 28, 1967, after a confrontation with Oakland policemen during which officer John Frey was shot and killed. **Newton** was convicted of voluntary manslaughter on September 8, 1968, and served two years. During his trial and imprisonment, radical Blacks and Whites considered him a political prisoner and continually called for his release. (See: **Huey P. Newton**)

freek an alternative spelling of the word **freak**, which is a self-denigrating term used by hippies to describe themselves. (See: **freak**)

freek a free clinic. Many such facilities sprang up in the 1960s and 1970s in cities around the United States to offer free medical assistance to hippies and street people. (See: **free clinic**)

free love the practice of making love freely, whenever and with whomever one wishes. The free relates to freedom of expression, not to economics. The changes in sexual attitudes of the 1960s were brought about mainly by the introduction of the contraceptive pill on May 9, 1960, and with a youthful rebellion against the moral hypocrisies and sexual suppression of the

1950s. In the 1960s and 70s, straight society, upon seeing young hippies flaunting their sexuality, often lashed out in suppressed sexual frustration. The irony of the situation was that many conservative people privately desired the freedom and sex that the young culture seemed to offer, and yet they ridiculed free love publicly.

Free Mexican Airlines *drugs & music* a fictional airlines introduced in the lyrics of the song by Peter Rowan in 1978. Mr. Rowan agrees that it is partially a reference to the fleet of small airplanes that smuggled **marijuana** into the US from Mexico. Also related to the feeling of flying produced by smoking marijuana. Rowan heard the term at "some party," and believes that it was used previously by the **Firesign Theater**. (See: **Firesign Theater**)

free press media, such as newspapers and magazines, whose overall editorial content is not influenced by outside interests. Usually refers to media that is not financially controlled by advertisers who force them to support political or economic positions. With this freedom, such publications are willing to voice controversial opinions on politics and economic issues without the fear of losing advertising dollars. Such publications can be either conservative or **liberal**; yet, for the most part, this term has been used to describe the liberal underground press. Similar to **underground press**.

Freep Los Angeles Free Press. Alternative newspaper published in Los Angeles, founded in 1964. (See: **Los Angeles Free Press**)

free ride something obtained without payment.

free-speech movement (FSM) *social issues* not an organization per se, but a spontaneous upheaval that germinated on college campuses throughout the United States in the late 1960s. It basically started in November, 1964, when University of California, Berkeley, students returning from summer vacation found that they could no longer set up tables in front of the campus on the corner of Bancroft and Telegraph to dispense leaflets and collect money for social and political causes. **Congress of Racial Equality (CORE)** member **Jack Weinberg** was detained by Berkeley police for defying the restrictions, and the riots began. The free-speech movement was generally related to the struggle for **academic freedom** on campuses. The academic freedom movement believes that, in this free society, teachers and students have the right to express even unpopular ideas or unproven theories on campus and in the classroom without repercussions from the school administration. This concept was at the core of most of the college campus unrest, particularly at Columbia, UC Berkeley and the **University of California, Santa Barbara (UCSB)** in 1969-70.

freewheeling adventuresome. Of an open, positive and playful nature. Could be considered arrogant; yet, in the context of the hippie demeanor, it was just fun-loving.

free will a doctrine suggesting that a person can, through will, overcome preordained obstacles of this world and the cosmic world. Opposed to accepting fate.

freeze-dried coffee introduced to the American public in 1964. Crystallized coffee which, when dissolved in hot water, offered the impression and some of the caffeine of authentic coffee. When mixed with nondairy creamer, this concoction could be called a real example of modern technology.

French *sex* to insert one's tongue into something. May describe sticking the tongue into one of six or seven orifices of the human body. Example: "Take a drink, but don't **French** the bottle." **2.** the most common use of the term is **French** kiss.

French blue *drug* a tablet of **amphetamine**, the pep pill drinamyl. It was blue.

French kiss *sex* a kiss involving the insertion of one's tongue into another person's mouth. The term came back to the USA from France with soldiers after the two world wars.

French tickler *sex* a prophylactic or rubber condom with a device on its tip or side designed to tickle or stimulate the cervical opening or vaginal wall of a woman during sexual intercourse.

fresh meat or **new meat** a nubile woman, or virgin. **2.** a new person to conquer, overpower or suppress in a business or social setting.

Freyr one of the triad of Norse deities. (The other two are Oden and Thor.)

Friedan, Betty (1921-) *social issues* wife, mother, freelance writer and feminist activist who began to question the existence of the ideal wife and mother image. In 1957, she surveyed 200 Smith College alumnae 15 years after their graduation, revealing that the commonly accepted image of the submissive and passive wife and mother was a farce. Her 1963 book, *The Feminine Mystique*, was one of the opening shots in the modern women's movement. Friedan was the prime architect of the **National Organization of Women (NOW)**, created its name and served as its president from 1966 to 1970.

Friends of the Earth *social issues* an ecology organization founded in 1970 by David Bower, formerly the president of The Sierra Club. Their slogan is, "The Earth needs all the friends it can get."

frigging or **friggin'** a variation of the term fucking. Used in a confrontation by someone who wishes to be a little less profane. Examples: "Keep your fucking hands to yourself." "Keep your **friggin'** hands to yourself." Somehow, the original term has a little more class.

Fripp, Robert (b. May 16, 1946, Wimbourne, Eng.) *rock & roll* guitarist, composer and producer, Fripp was the founder of King Crimson in 1969. With **Brian Eno**, Fripp is responsible for starting the extreme electronic experimentation in music that spread through the late 1970s, 80s and 90s, influencing **punk**, **techno**, **new wave** and world music.

Frisbee trade name and generic name for a flat, round plastic throwing toy. It is shaped like what a flying saucer is thought to be. The concept was supposedly invented by a group of Yale students when they played with the leftover pie plate from the Frisbee Pie Company. The actual plastic throwing saucer was first created by West Coast inventor Fred Morrison in 1948 to tap into the outer space flying saucers that were reported in the skies. In 1957, it was manufactured by the Wham-O Toy Company.

'fro short for Afro, the hairstyle worn by many African Americans; perhaps most popularized by **Angela Davis**. a.k.a. **Natural**. (See: **Afro** or **Natural**)

from diddly from nothing. Refers to being ignorant or uninformed. Examples: "She doesn't know personal hygiene **from diddly**."

Fromm, Erich (1900-1980) psychoanalyst, social philosopher. Born and educated in Germany. After emigrating to the United States in 1933, he established a private practice in psychiatry and taught at New York University and the National University of Mexico. Many of his theories and studies interested the beat and hippie communities. He was a strong supporter of the **anti-war movement**. His books include *Escape from Freedom*, 1941; *Man For Himself*, 1947; *The Heart of Man*, 1964 and *The Anatomy of Human Destructiveness*, 1973.

Fromme, Lynette "Squeaky" The acting head of the "Manson Family" after **Charles Manson** was arrested in 1969. She herself was arrested during the Manson trial, in connection with the attempted murder of prosecution witness Barbara Hoyt, and was given a 90-day sentence. On September 5, 1975 she attempted to assassinate **President Gerald R. Ford** and was sentenced to Federal prison. In December of 1987, she escaped from prison and was recaptured 40 hours later. Now eligible for parole, she has so far refused to petition for her release.

from the get go from the start. Originally a cowboy term, "from the get up and go" (in the morning).

frontman *rock & roll* the lead singer of a band. Because he stands in front of the band.

fruit a derogatory name for a homosexual male.

fruit boots pointed-toed, high-heeled, ankle-high boots with elastic sides, buckle or zipper on the inside of the foot. Stylish footwear worn primarily by **mods** in the early 1960s and **The Beatles** early in their career. They were basically the Cuban style boot with a

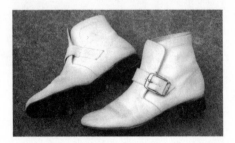

high, Cuban heel. "**Fruit**" is a derogatory term for a homosexual male; in the opinion of most macho young men of the 1950s, these shoes looked like footwear that only a homosexual would wear. a.k.a. **Beatle boots** or **winkle pickers**. (See: **Beatle boots, winkle pickers** and **mods**)

fruitcake a crazy person. **2.** a homosexual male. "**Fruit**" is a derogatory term for a homosexual male.

fruitful signs of the zodiac Cancer, Scorpio and Pisces; the water signs, sensory, emotional, psychic, creative.

fruits and nuts no, not a snack! It's what people from other parts of the United States called Californians. During the 1960s and 1970s, to the rest of the country, those who lived on the West Coast were either homosexuals or crazy people. Thus, this name. The hypocrisy was that, most likely, their own son, daughter or Uncle Ed was either in California or desperately wanted to be there.

fry to suffer some extreme consequences. Related to being electrocuted or burned. Example: "If I catch him with my chick again, I'll **fry** his ass."

fu a Chinese term meaning correspondence between mankind and the universe.

fuck to copulate. From the German *fook*, to copulate. Ignored by most dictionaries, it doesn't even register in my Pagemaker spellcheck; yet it is possibly the most thought about, talked about and sought after experience of human life. It is a phenomenal conflict in our language that a word representing the most enjoyable of life's activities is considered embarrassing and used almost exclusively as an oath. Thus is the fate of the word fuck. **Lenny Bruce** said in one of his standup comedy routines that fuck should be the most endearing greeting, reserved for the ones you love. "Hi, Mom; **fuck** you Mom," Hi, Dad; **fuck** you Dad." Instead, we do the opposite and direct this word at those we dislike.

fuck-a-duck! a somewhat humorous oath used to indicate confusion or disbelief. Example: "Well **fuck-a-duck**! I guess gravity does work after all."

fuck all! an oath used to indicate disappointment. Example: "Well **fuck all**! Where's the mop?"

fuck around to mess around foolishly, neglect one's job or waste time. **2.** to sleep around.

fucked up confused, mentally unstable or incapacitated by drink or drugs.

fuckhead a stupid person.

fucking a! an affirmation, or intensifier. Examples: "**Fucking a,** that was a great concert!"

fuck it! an expletive used to reject an inanimate object, thought or situation.

fuck me! a term used to express great surprise. **2.** a term used for self-recrimination.

fuck off! an expletive used to reject a person; similar to **get lost**, or go to hell.

fuck over to cheat or abuse someone in some way.

fuck truck a **Volkswagen bus** equipped with a mattress.

fuck up n. an ineffective person. A mistake or a mess. Examples: "He's a real **fuck up**, and that whole job he did was a **fuck up**."

fuck up v. to ruin or spoil.

fuck you if you can't take a joke! sarcastic commentary directed at an uptight, conservative or overly moralistic person. Always intended humorously, since the phrase itself is such a dichotomy that anyone using it seriously would have to be completely unaware of reasonable social graces.

fuck your brains out *sex* to copulate until you can't function any more. "Cop 'til you drop."

fugging a seldom used variation on the term fucking.

Fugs, The *rock & roll* an irreverent, poetic, obscene, satirical band formed in New York City in 1965. Ed Sanders (b. Kansas City, Mo.) voc. gtr.; Tuli Kupferberg (b. New York City) voc.; Ken Weaver (b. Galveston, Tex.) voc., drums; plus numerous other musicians who rotated through. Performers at **Bill Graham's** very first rock concert, a benefit for the **San Francisco Mime Troupe**, on November 6, 1965, which also featured **Jefferson Airplane**. They performed at the **anti-war** demonstration on October 21, 1967, when **Abbie Hoffman** and **Jerry Rubin** tried to **levitate** The Pentagon. Not commercial, but with perverse political commentary, this band was one of the most typical hippie outfits in the music business.

Both Sanders and Kupferberg were poets and authors; Tuli was immortalized by **Allen Ginsberg** in his poem "Howl" as "the person who jumped off the Brooklyn Bridge and survived;" Sanders wrote the bestselling book about the **Charles Manson** family, called *The Family.*

full of it lying or incorrect. **Full of shit**. Example: "He's **full of it**; there's really no such thing as a dope fairy."

full of shit lying or incorrect. Same usage as **full of crap** or **load of crap**.

full on correct, complete, fulfilling. An intensifier relating to being right. Example: "You were **full on** about that guy; he does have a **Barbie** complex."

full on quickly or without restraint. Examples: "He was running **full on,** so he didn't see the wall."

Fuller, Buckminster the architect of the idea and form of the **geodesic dome or zonal polyhedral construction. Futuristic, the "dome" was a structure created by connecting interlocking geometric forms (triangles). When assembled, these produce a dome-shaped living space that is strong and visually pleasing. Domes first appeared as alternative housing in 1964.

full tilt boogie a phrase implying complete abandon. Usually related to dancing wildly or playing music at full speed. The Full Tilt Boogie Band was the name of **Janis Joplin's** last band, which played on her posthumous 1971 album *Pearl.*

*funk a bad mood or mental depression.

funk the **essence** and **soul** of Black music. That which makes something down to earth, basic and real.

Funkadelic *psychedelic rock* a band formed in Detroit, Michigan in 1969. The name and concept is a real hippie- era creation. A Black rock group that incorporated the African American funk music and hippie psychedelic sound.

funked-up or **funk it up** to make something **cool** or give it soul.

funky down to earth, loose or ethnic. From Clarence Major's *Juba to Jive*, Penguin Books, 1994; "Probably from lu-funki (Ki-Kongo and Bay Kongo African dialects) for 'bad body odor' down-to-earth; 'for real' in touch with the **essence** of being human."

funny farm a mental institution.

fur pubic hair.

fur burger *sex* (See: **cunnilingus**)

Furies in Roman mythology, they were the three sisters, Alecto, Megaera and Tisiphone, the punishers of evildoers, personifications of rage, envy and slaughter.

Furies Collective *social issues* a **lesbian** separatist collective founded in 1971 in Washington, DC, by Rita Mae Brown and Charlotte Bunch. They developed the basic **lesbian** social and political theories of the times. Analyzing heterosexuality, they defined it as a form of domination based on the assumption that heterosexual sex was the only "natural" way, and heterosexuals assumed that every woman was either bound to a man or wished she were. The Furies contended that women were primarily viewed merely as wives and mothers and that the social order was based on the assumption that women would always put men first. (See: **collective**)

fur pie *sex* (See: **cunnilingus**)

fusion (See: **jazz fusion**)

Future Shock a book by Alvin Toffler, 1970. From the introduction: "Future shock...the shattering stress and disorientation that we induce in individuals by subjecting them to too much change in too short a time."

futz to mess around. From the Yiddish verb *arumfartzen*, meaning to fart around.

fuzz the police.

F-word fuck. A circumspect way to indicate the word **fuck**. Example: "She would never use the **F-word**, but she sure can fuck."

G

G *drugs* a gram of drugs. Example: "I copped two **G's** of candy." (I bought two grams of **cocaine**.) The drug culture employs slang or abbreviations to camouflage conversations, exclude outsiders and sound **cool**.

GAA (See: **Gay Activists Alliance**)

gag an expression of great displeasure or revulsion. Example: "When Frank does that thing with his nose and the string, it makes me **gag**." From "it makes me sick," gag being to vomit. Often considered a **Valley Girl, Valley talk** term. (See: **Valley talk**)

gage and **gauge** *drugs* **marijuana** or **hashish**. Originally a British term meaning any potential intoxicant, even alcoholic or tobacco.

gage butt and **gauge butt** *drugs* a **marijuana** cigarette.

game interested, or willing. Examples: "Are you **game** to go dancing?" "She's a **game** lover."

game schemes, tricks or lies. Example: "That's a ten-dollar bag of parsley; he's running a **game** on you."

game and **games** behavior creating disturbing emotional or psychological effects on others. Example: "Her little **game** on the staircase gets me horny." **2.** disturbing emotional or psychological effects. "Her little dance up the stairs always plays **games** with my head."

Gandhi, Mohandas (Mahatma Gandhi) (1869-1948) the greatest political personality of India's long history. The leader of India's successful and peaceful struggle for independence from England. Considered the originator of the philosophy of nonviolent social and political resistance, which was used successfully by **Dr. Martin Luther King, Jr.**, during America's **civil rights** struggle. **Mahatma** means "great soul" in **Sanskrit**. Gandhi is one of the primary role models for all **true hippies**. (See: **true hippie**)

Ganesha the elephant-headed divinity of Shivaism. Son of **Shiva**, Ganesha is the god of good luck, prosperity and wisdom. The remover of obstacles.

gang bang *sex* a sexual escapade in which three or more men have intercourse with one woman. Two men and a woman would be a *menage a trois*, as would two women and a man. A gang bang is considered consensual and should not be confused with gang rape. It is possible, but unlikely, that a gang bang could be a **homosexual** occurrence.

gangbusters, (like) with enthusiasm, excitement or vigor. Example: "If he likes the work, he'll do the job like **gangbusters**."

gangster *drugs* another obscure term for the **marijuana** cigarette. In some parts of the US, it meant just a cigarette, which indicates that it must have come from movie depictions of gangsters with cigarettes hanging from their mouths.

gangster a person of bad reputation.

ganja and **ganji** *drugs* Indian **cannabis hemp**; **marijuana** or **hashish**. From the East Indian, Hindi language. From its original definition as the Indian plant, the word has now evolved to mean any of the smokable forms of cannabis. In wide use in the Caribbean and England. Used often to indicate a strong marijuana grown in Jamaica.

garbage n. meaningless talk, **bullshit** or **jive**. 2. anything that is rejected.

garbage v. to search dumpsters for discarded food or goods. a.k.a. **dumpster diving, scrounge**.

garbage in, garbage out *computer revolution* a simple statement indicating that computers can function properly only if given correct information. As impartial machines, they are subject to the limitations of the information provided to them and the ability of the human operator.

Garcia, Jerry (b. Jerome John Garcia, Aug. 1, 1942, San Francisco; d. Aug. 9, 1995, Forest Knolls, Calif.) *rock & roll* the founding leader of the premier hippie band, **The Grateful Dead, formed 1965 in San Francisco, California. A musical group to which improvisation was so important that it can be said they never played a song the same way twice. The longest lasting psychedelic band, both in years and time on stage. In all the Dead shows I "experienced," the band started on time and played for hours. To explain or chronicle this man and this band would take far too many pages. For more insight, refer to *The New Rolling Stone Encyclopedia of Rock & Roll,* John Rocco's *Dead Reckoning* or any one of the many biographies available.

gas, a gas or **it's a gas** something enjoyable, fun or exciting. Examples: "She's a **gas**!" "It's **a gas** seeing you dance." Same use as **blast**.

gas talk. May refer to "hot air," which is another description of speech. Example: "Cut the **gas** and leave."

gas power. Example: "Don't fuck with him; he's got **gas** in this neighborhood."

gash *sex* a woman. From the visual appearance of a woman's genitals, which to some might look like a slit or gash. Example: "I'm going down town to get a bit of **gash**." Originally a British term. 2. the **vagina**.

Gaskin, Stephen F. (b. Feb. 16, 1935) motivational speaker, creator of **Monday Night Class and founder of **The Farm**. In the mid-1960s, Gaskin was a student of S. I. Hayakawa at San Francisco State, headed for a successful academic career, when he dropped out to became a motivational speaker. His Monday Night Class meetings, attended by thousands of people in the San Francisco Bay area, taught people how to be **high** without the necessity of drugs. Gaskin left San Francisco with his followers in about 40 brightly painted school buses and eventually ended up in Tennessee. Pooling their money in 1968, they bought the land in western Tennessee on which they created The Farm. The Farm still exists today, one of the few communes that survived. In an era when many of the people who got all of the media attention possessed outrageous egos, displayed religious arrogance or perpetrated revolutionary violence, Stephen Gaskin stands out as a teacher of humility, simplicity and peace. (See: **The Farm** and **high**)

gassed intoxicated.

-gate *suffix* an ending added to words to indicate the presence of conspiracy or corruption. From Nixon's **Watergate** conspiracy. Watergate is the office/apartment building in which Nixon's **plumbers** burglarized the Democratic Party offices. Examples: Contragate, White Watergate, etc. Although this was not used much in the 1970s, it is a product of that time.

Gathering of the Tribes (See: **Human Be-In and Gathering of the Tribes**)

Gautama Siddhartha Buddha (563 B.C.-483 B.C.) (Born Prince Gautama Siddhartha in what is now Nepal) *religion* the man upon whose life and writing **Buddhism** is based. He was a pampered member of the ruling class, who chose at 29 years of age to reject the wealth, caste system and religion of his family. After years of solitude and study, he emerged as the Buddha and began teaching. Buddha means "the awakened one." Buddhism deals primarily with "four noble truths," addressing suffering, the cause of suffering, the way to cease suffering and the way to ease suffering. Thus, Buddhism emphasizes spiritual and physical discipline to attain a state of liberation from the conflicts of life. (See: **Buddhism**)

gay a homosexual male or female.

Gay Activists Alliance (GAA) *social issues* a spin-off from the **Gay Liberation Front**, the GAA was created to be "completely and solely dedicated" to the fight for gay rights. It came into being on Sunday, December 21, 1969, in Arthur Bell's apartment in New York's Upper East Side. Jim Owles was its first president, with Marty Robinson, Arthur Evans and Kay Tobin as other founding members. The GAA's first act was to file a petition demanding that the city council pass a bill prohibiting discrimination against gays in employment in New York City. For the next several years, this group, headed by the outspoken Robinson, actively confronted Mayor John V. Lindsay and the New York City government. This was the beginning of a new, proactive, more confrontational gay community. Within a few months GAA chapters began popping up across the nation.

gay bashing *social issues* a physical attack on homosexuals by someone opposed to their lifestyle. A hate crime based on ignorance and intolerance.

Gaye, Marvin (b. Marvin Pentz Gay, Jr., April 2, 1939, Washington, DC; d. April 1, 1984, Los Angeles, Calif.) *R and B, rock & roll* Gaye's career evolved from Black **Motown** pop into socially conscious music of the hippie era. He was one of the great sensual ballad singers early in his career, singing memorable duets with partners such as Mary Wells and Tammi Terrell. He blasted out "I Heard it Through the Grapevine" in 1968, and then, in 1971, he asked a confused and broken world "What's Going On?" which is still considered one of the most poignant **anti-war** and pro-**civil rights** songs ever recorded. Inducted into the Rock and Roll Hall of Fame in 1987.

Gay Liberation Front (GLF) *social issues* the first organization of homosexuals that was truly dedicated to protecting their **civil rights**. It evolved from the older and less contentious **Mattachine Society** and the **Daughters of Bilitis**. The GLF came into being on July 31, 1969, sparked by the **Stonewall Rebellion** of June 27, 1969. The first meeting was held in an industrial loft in **Greenwich Village**, New York City, which housed the Alternate U, an alternative educational facility. Some of the original organizers and attendees of the meeting were: Jim Fouratt, Michael Brown, Martha (Altman) Shelley, Marty Robinson, Jim Owles and Lois Hart. The use of the term "gay" was new to the established homosexual community, though it had been used on a social level. Incorporating the words "Liberation Front" was a direct reference to the North Vietnamese guerrilla forces' "National Liberation Front" in an effort to identify with other oppressed people in the third world, Black Americans, women and workers. Groups using the same name popped up in other cities of America during the next few months. The organization lasted less than a year, but it was the start of an active, vocal gay movement. (See: **Gay & Lesbian Movement Events,**

Groups and Leaders starting on page 601 in **Lists** at the back of this book)

gear possessions or **stuff**. Example: "Get your **gear** together, and let's split this crazy scene." Not created during the hippie era, but used extensively during the period. It came from a cowboy background and was adopted readily by the hippie, since the **counterculture** sometimes romanticized cowboys as a rebellious breed such as themselves.

gear nice, **cool** or attractive. Example: "Say, mate, is that your **gear** Vespa?" An early **British invasion** term that never really caught on in the USA.

gear *drugs* equipment used to prepare and inject drugs. a.k.a. **fit, kit, fixings**.

gee! exclamation of surprise or wonder. Originating from the exclamation "Jesus." Often used sarcastically. Example: "**Gee**, how nice; pink sweat socks!"

geek a social misfit, an unattractive or **uncool** person. Usually associated with being bookish. Originally from the term freak.

Gemini astrological sign, May 21 to June 21, third house of the **zodiac**, mutable air sign, symbolized by the twins. Traits: ideas, skills. Self-perception: I think.

Gemstone, Operation *politics* a plan perpetrated by the **Nixon** administration to disrupt the activities of **anti-war** groups, **civil rights** organizations and **liberal** political opponents. Wiretaps, break-ins, mail-openings and other dirty tricks were used. Through its implementation, many civil rights violations, such as the Watergate break-in, were conducted during the Nixon administration. Closely associated with "The Huston Plan," also one of the

Nixon administration's efforts to control opponents by using dirty tricks. Charles Colson, Nixon's Special Counsel and self-proclaimed "chief ass-kicker around the White House," was a key operative in Gemstone. Many feel that he had an agenda, either his own or in cooperation with others in the administration, to use these methods to create a revolutionary, right-wing *coup d'etat.*

gender bender a person who switches his or her sexual orientation from the "norm." Someone who displays both masculine and feminine traits or is involved in cross-dressing. A situation involving confused sexual identities.

generation gap a difference in age and values. The phenomenon in which young and old are unable to communicate rationally with each other. Most often caused by a difference of opinion on moral and social issues brought about by opposing perspectives on what is important in life. The moral idealism and decadence of youth are often in conflict with the desires for security and stability harbored by mature adults.

photo by John McCleary ©

geodesic dome a structure created by connecting interlocking geometric forms (triangles). When assembled, these produce a dome-shaped living space which is strong and visually pleasing. **Buckminister Fuller** was the architect of the idea and form, which

was introduced to the American public in 1964.

Gerde's Folk City coffee house at 11 West 4th Street, in **Greenwich Village**, New York City (1963 phone number AL4-8449). Twenty-year-old **Bob Dylan** began his rise to fame when he played there in September, 1961.

Gernreich, Rudi a **fashion** designer responsible for the **topless** bathing suit.

gestalt the totality of life's experiences, activities and emotions. The total good and bad of existence. Example: "He doesn't appreciate the **gestalt** of life, so he hides under the bed." From the German word meaning form or shape.

Gestalt theory and therapy the theory that existing established mental patterns distort or create an altered perception of things that we see or learn. As in motion pictures, the figures are not really moving but are a series of repeated shots progressing across the screen, and our mind makes the leap, perceiving the figure as moving. In cases of neuroses and psychoses, the theory states that rigid thinking impedes a cure. An anal retentive is theorized as being in danger of exploding in a violent outburst because he is unable to release tensions naturally. Gestalt therapy uses group pressure to break down inhibitions which may harbor mental instability. **Gestalt** is German word meaning "form." (See: **Esalen Institute** and "**Bob and Carol and Ted and Alice**")

get a charge to get excited by something. Related to receiving an electrical shock or being charged up like a battery. Example: "I **get a charge** out of watching her dance."

*****get a grip** take control of your sanity. Most likely comes from "Get a hold of yourself." Examples: "So Snookie left you, **get a grip**, life goes on."

get a handle on take control, control yourself. Example: "Drake is blowing it; he needs to **get a handle on** his emotions." Similar use as **get a grip**.

get a handle on to learn about something, to gain understanding. Example: "I can't **get a handle on** algebra."

get a hustle on to move or go faster.

get a life a somewhat humorous and often derogatory statement to someone who isn't very **cool**, doesn't have their life together or is wrapped up in something meaningless.

get a little *sex* to have sex.

get a little on the side or **get a little bit on the side** *sex* to have sex outside a steady relationship.

get a load or **get a load of that** to look at or observe. Example: "**Get a load of that** girl."

get back to return to one's roots or previous social position. A **Beatles'** song title dealing with changing social mores and the experimentation of the 1960s and 70s.

get (one's) **balls in an uproar** to get mad. In this phrase, balls mean testicles, but it is not literal and other parts of the body can be used, such as ass, head, etc. Example: "Don't **get your balls in an uproar** about something that doesn't concern you." Same usage as **head in an uproar** or **ass in an uproar**.

get behind to support or approve of something or someone. Example: "I could really **get behind** that dude. I like what he says."

get down to be decisive or determined. To concentrate on, or become serious about what you're doing. The roots are from "**get down** to business" and "**get down** to basics," then influenced by African American jive culture, into "**get down** and funky" or "**get down** and dirty." **2.** a secondary definition is sexual in reference to "going down" and performing **cunnilingus**. **3.** to get into a fight.

get down to the real nitty gritty cut out the unimportant stuff and concentrate on the basics. From the African American **jive** culture. The **nitty gritty** refers to the basics, the beginnings, the important stuff.

get down with it to be serious about doing something.

get-go or **getgo** the beginning, the morning. Originally a cowboy term meaning the "get up and go."

get head to receive **oral sexual** stimulation. a.k.a. **blow job, head job, hum job**.

get (one's) **head in an uproar** to get mad or agitated. Same usage as **balls in an uproar** or **ass in an uproar**.

get high *drugs* to smoke marijuana. **2.** to become emotionally stimulated.

get in the wind to jump on a motorcycle and ride.

get into to concentrate on something or specialize in something. Examples "I could really **get into** tantric yoga." "When he plays, he really **gets into** his guitar." **2.** start the action.

get into her/his pants to have sex with someone.

get it to understand. Example: "You just don't **get it,** do you!?" "You'll **get it** someday!"

get it on to have sex. **2.** to do anything with exuberance.

*get it together   organize your life or straighten out your state of mind. The hippie philosophy dealt to a great extent with personal development. During the era, many words or phrases previously devoted to situations or objects began to be used to describe human conditions. From: "Get your shit together."

get it up   to achieve an erect penis for sexual purposes. **2.** to get excited about any activity.

get (one's) **jollies** or get (one's) **jollies off**   to have an orgasm. Examples: "They **got their jollies** in the back of the bus." "He **gets his jollies off** by himself." **2.** to enjoy any activity. Examples: "I **get my jollies** on the roller coaster." "Did you get **your jollies off** at the dance?"

get (one's) **kicks**   to have fun at some activity. Example: "Did you **get your kicks** on the roller coaster?" **2.** to have sexual fun. Example: "Did you **get your kicks** with her?"

get laid *sex*   to have sex. Usually, a term reserved for a casual or promiscuous sexual encounter.

get lost   a dismissal, something akin to "get out of here, don't bother me."

get naked   to take off one's clothes. Usually, it is the preliminary to having sex.

get next to   to get to know someone or have some sort of contact with them. It has some sexual connotations. Example: "I wanted to **get next to** her."

get off or get off on   to feel the effects of a drug. **2.** to reach orgasm.

get off it   stop. Change your direction or attitude. Could possibly come from "get off your soap box."

get off my case   leave me alone.

get on (someone's) **case**   to bother, ridicule, discipline or antagonize someone. Examples: "Don't **get on my case** about that, it happened a long time ago." "Judy **got on** Gonad's **case** about his name."

get out of Dodge   leave or go away. A humorous reference to the old cowboy movies. "Dodge ain't big enough for the two of us!"

get out of my face   back off, don't bother me. Often used in defiance of an objectionable conversation or to being pressured. Also to request more physical space or to ask someone to stop violating your space.

get over it   forget the problem, stop bitching.

get physical *positive*   to make love.

get physical *negative*   to get in a fight.

*get real   get serious. Don't fool yourself. Example: "**Get real**, I'm not going to sleep with you no matter how much money you spend on dinner."

get (one's) **rocks off**   to have an orgasm. To reach a climax of enjoyment in any activity. Rocks refer to testicles. Examples: "She **got my rocks off** with that move." "Did the party **get your rocks off**?"

get some *sex*   to have sexual intercourse. The words **it, some** or **any** are often used in place of more graphic words, such as ass, pussy or cunt. Example: "Did you **get some**?"

get stuffed   a less profane way to say "get fucked."

get stupid   to use drugs, alcohol or some substance to the point of getting really messed up and "stupid."

get the drift to understand. An old nautical term meaning to understand the currents and movement of the ocean. Not exclusively a hippie-era phrase, but it came into expanded usage during that time.

get the shaft to be cheated, abandon or deceived. The **shaft** indicates a male erection, and it literally means to **screw** someone. This phrase is hardly ever used to indicate the actual physical sex act.

get the shoe (to) to get fired or ordered to leave. From to "get the boot," or to get kicked out.

getting any? *sex* are you getting any sex?

get to me or **gets to me** to irritate, bother or annoy. To demand attention. Examples: "If that noise continues, it's going to **get to me**." "Her baby talk **gets to me**."

get wasted to get **stoned** on drugs or drunk.

"get whitey" a slogan used by the more militant members of **Black power** groups to promote hatred and violence. It is interesting to note that, even with the injustice suffered by the African American population and the show of militancy by the **Black Panthers**, there was still very little overt violence directed at the White community by Blacks during this period.

get with it join in, get smart, become contemporary. **Beatnik** roots.

*get with the program be a team player, join the majority activity. This phrase evolved from **get with it** and didn't appear until the late 1970s as individuality for **self-realization** began to change into conformity for material gain.

get your shit together to organize one's life or straighten out one's state of mind. A precursor to **get it together**. Shit is used to indicate problems or loose ends. As usual, the use of the objectionable scatological term is only to add emphasis.

photo by John McCleary ©

ghanta *religion* the **Buddhist** symbol for woman, the bell. A **Sanskrit** word. In religious rituals it is held in the left hand and rung, while the **vajra,** or male, thunderbolt is held in the right hand. (See: **vajra**)

ghetto blaster or **ghetto box** a portable radio or tape player. The ghetto reference comes from the stereotype that was created in the media of a young Black man walking through the city ghetto playing obnoxiously loud music on a portable stereo. a.k.a. **boom box**.

Gibran, Kahlil (1883-1931) poet, philosopher, artist. Author of *The Prophet,* one of the most popular books of the hippie era. It is a collection of romantic poetry particularly suited to the tastes of young women. Gibran and *The Prophet* became almost a joke because he was too sentimental for some people. Reading *The Prophet* eventually was used as a one-liner in movies to indicate that a person was shallow. Gibran, born in Lebanon, lived in the United States for the last 20 years of his life.

Gibson Guitar Company *rock & roll* one of the oldest guitar manufacturing companies in the United States. Started by Orville H. Gibson in Kalamazoo, Michigan, in the late 1800s. The most popular of Gibson guitars was a model designed by and named after **Les Paul**, one of the innovators of the electric guitar. They created the **Flying V** or **Flying Arrow guitar.** The company manufactured many guitars popular with country, **folk**, **blues**, **jazz** and rock & roll musicians during the hippie era. (See: **Flying V**)

Giep, General Vo Nguyen the top military strategist, minister of defense, and commander-in-chief of the North Vietnamese Army. Giep commanded the forces that overwhelmed the French at Dien Bien Phu. With **Ho Chi Min**, he helped lead Vietnam through the war with Japan, its struggle for independence from France, and efforts to re-unify the country during the **Vietnam War** against the Saigon Government of Vietnam and the US.

gig a job. Often, but not exclusively, related to a musical job.

gigglestick, giggle smoke or **giggle weed** a **marijuana** cigarette.

G. I. Joe a toy created by Hasbro toy company and introduced to the American public in 1964. A soldier with accessories, such as camouflaged uniforms and weapons of destruction, it became the brunt of anti-war criticism during the late 1960s.

ginchy or, less often, **ginch** good or excellent. A **British invasion** term used primarily on the East Coast of the United States, but only rarely on the West Coast.

Ginsberg at Golden Gate Park, Human Be-In, January 14, 1967
photo by Lisa Law ©

Ginsberg, Allen (b. June 3, 1926; d. March 5, 1997) beat poet and writer. One of the major forces in the beatnik movement, along with **William S. Burroughs, **Jack Kerouac**, **Lawrence Ferlinghetti**, **Gary Snyder** and a few other poets, writers and artists. Ginsberg and his friends verbalized the unspoken thoughts of intellectuals and many people of the **working class**. By expressing their distaste and distrust of American hypocrisy and **materialism**, they made the hippie era possible. Their philosophies would become the basis of the rebellions of the 1960s and 70s. As an outspoken **homosexual**, Allen Ginsberg did much to bring the lifestyle into **mainstream** awareness, some say to its detriment; yet his continual refusal to take life and its conditions too seriously has eventually softened many critics. His best know poems are "Howl" and "Kaddish." "Kaddish" is a poem dedicated to his mother Naomi, who died in 1956. "Howl," a rambling, stream-of-consciousness piece filled with rebellion, angst, pathos and humor, is to some critics the best American poem ever written and to others, the worst. His publications include: *Howl and Other*

Poems, 1956; *Kaddish and Other Poems,* 1961; *The Yage Letters,* (with William Burroughs), 1963; *Planet News,* 1968; *The Fall of America: Poems of these States,* 1973; *Gay Sunshine Interview* (with Allen Young), 1974; *Photographs,* a book of photography, 1991; *Howls, Raps & Roars,* a recording on 4 CDs, 1993.

ginseng and **ginseng root** an ancient Asian medicine originally from northern China, the root of the ginseng plant reportedly has numerous medicinal and spiritual values. It is particularly valued for its ability to restore alertness and impart a feeling of well-being. The oldest medicinal herb of Asia. It is especially known to stimulate the pituitary and is said to be an **aphrodisiac**. Most valued by men, the word ginseng means literally man-root. Often made into a tea. *Panax sinesis* is one species originating in China, and there are other plant forms, such as the *Aralia,* brought to California by Chinese railroad workers.

girl *drugs* **cocaine**. (See: **cocaine**)

girls, cars and sports the areas of interest of many non-hippie men during the **hippie** era. Although sex, drugs, and rock & roll were prominent activities in the counterculture, other topics were the intellectual fare of the **true hippie**. Hippie men looked down their noses at the interest and conversation of most of the males of straight society. Hippies did discuss girls, dope and music, but most often a hip gathering would likely involve discourse about the unjust war in Vietnam, the rape of our environment and those "fucking, greedy corporate bastards."

girl scout a young woman without vices. A girl who is too proper to have any fun, most often considered a virgin.

girls say yes to boys who say no (to war was implied) one of the most famous **anti-war** slogans of the Vietnam era. It was seen on posters and bumper stickers during the **Vietnam War** meant to discourage young men from joining the military. The slogan was used only in jest, since no one seriously expected it to have any effect. It appeared on a poster produced in 1968 containing a photograph of **Joan Baez**, her sisters, Pauline and **Mimi Fariña**, sitting on a couch, looking very beautiful. A line on the front of the poster read "Proceeds from the sale of this poster go to The Draft Resistance."

gism sperm. Another spelling of jizzum.

give a damn an opinion. Same as **to care**. Examples: "I **give a damn** about you, and you don't **give a damn** that I do."

give a flying fuck an opinion. Same as **to care**. Example: "All he **gives a flying fuck** about is flying and fucking."

give a rat's ass an opinion. Same as **to care**. Example: "I don't **give a rat's ass** about the GNP."

give a shit an opinion. Compassion. Same as **to care about**.

give head *sex* to administer a blow job or give **oral sexual** stimulation to one's partner. It most often indicates **fellatio** (oral sex performed on a man), but rarely it is used to describe **cunnilingus** (oral copulation performed on a woman). a.k.a. **blow job, head job, hum job**.

give (someone) **heat** to annoy or confront someone.

give it a break stop what you're doing. This is often, yet not always, directed at verbal or emotional activity rather than physical activity. Example: "You've been bitching for over an hour. **Give it a break**."

give it a rest stop what you're doing. This form can also relate to physical as well as verbal or emotional activity. Example: "**Give it a rest**; you've been beating those drums for hours and they still haven't submitted to your will."

give it up stop resisting. Let me have it. Tell me. **2.** In entertainment, this means to give recognition to a performer in the form of applause. Example: "Let's **give it up** for **Jimi Hendrix** and The Experience!"

give it your best shot try your hardest. This began as a sporting term to encourage someone to make his best shot on goal, at the basket or hole.

gizmo a nonspecific word used to describe any unnamed mechanical object.

give me a break stop trying to deceive me. Don't underestimating my intelligence. Leave me alone.

give me five or **gimme five** the offer of a handshake. This indicates a gesture of salutation, approval or agreement, originating in the Black community, in which one person extends his hand palm up, and the other slaps it or brushes it with his hand. Similar usage as **give me skin**.

give me librium, or give me meth *drugs* a parody on Patrick Henry's famous patriotic statement, "Give me liberty or give me death." **Librium** is a tranquilizer; meth is **methedrine**.

give me skin or **gimme some skin** the offer of a handshake. Same usage as

give me five. The traditional handshake was spurned during the hippie era in favor of new styles. The **brothers' handshake** was a series of three hand grips. The palm-to-palm handshake, encircling each other's thumb with fingers and thumb was the most widely used, and it signified a close bond between friends.

photo by Jerry Takigawa ©

"Give Peace a Chance" an **anti-war** song written and performed by **John Lennon** and the **Plastic Ono Band** in 1969.

give some slack or **give slack** don't pressure, confront or ask too much of someone. Similar usage as **lighten up** or **get off my case**.

give the finger to gesture with defiance or hatred, using the middle finger extended. Literally, it means "fuck you," but since to get fucked is normally considered a pleasant experience, the history of the finger's derogatory connotation is lost to explanation.

Gladys Knight and the Pips *Motown/ rock & roll* formed in Atlanta, Georgia, in 1952, Gladys Knight (b. May 28, 1944, Atlanta), voc.; Merald "Bubba" Knight (b. Sep. 4, 1942, Atlanta), voc.; Edward Patten (b. Aug. 2, 1939, Atlanta), voc. Musical background to our lives throughout the 1950s, 1960s and 1970s. Inducted into the Rock and Roll Hall of Fame in 1996.

glam rock glam is short for glamorous, and glam rock was an offshoot of rock-and-roll that incorporated extravagant stage sets and costumes as part of the entertainment. Many of the musicians affected sexual androgyny to lend more spice to the genre. **David Bowie** was one of the most notable proponents of glam rock, and his personality of Ziggy Stardust was the most visually recognizable image of the time. Mark Bolan of Tyrannosaurus Rex was another glam rock participant of merit.

Glaser, Milton one of the most influential album cover and poster artists of the era. He created the highly recognizable 1967 Vol 1 *Best of Bob Dylan* album showing Dylan with multicolored hair.

GLF (See: **Gay Liberation Front**)

Glide Memorial Church *religion/social issues* a church established in 1963 on the corner of Ellis and Taylor Streets in the Tenderloin District of San Francisco, California. Situated in the most depressed area of the city, Glide became an oasis for inner-city people in search of faith and hope. Reverend Cecil Williams and Janice Mirikitani, President of the Glide Foundation, provided leadership and guidance in creating a nonprofit human service facility offering free meals, health care, women's programs, crisis intervention, literacy programs, job training and placement, and family educational programs. In addition to the social work the church performed, it also offered some of the most inspirational and entertaining gospel music services. Glide is still functioning today.

glitch a break in normal activity or disruption of desired results. Example: "There's a **glitch** in your plans; no money, car, gas or girl." Initially, an early computer term that first appeared around 1966.

glitz or **glitzy** a flashy visual effect or extravagant event. Examples: "She dresses with a lot of **glitz**." "His parties are always **glitzy**."

glom onto to attach oneself to a person, idea or thing. To grab onto something. Example: "Shara will always **glom onto** someone for moral support; make sure it's not you."

glorified beatnik a description of **Ken Kesey** by **Tom Wolfe** in his 1968 book, *The Electric Kool-Aid Acid Test*.

glossolalia the speaking in unknown or nonexistent tongues. Words such as this and **gnosis** are religious and biblical and thus not new to the world before the hippie era, but they achieved new and expanded use in the vocabulary of the Western world through the **counterculture**.

glow the warm feeling one gets from falling in love, being sexually stimulated or coming onto a drug high. A psychological, rather than physical, warmth.

glue *occult* that which holds the world together. Same as **chi** and **ether. (See: chi** or **ether**)

glue *drugs* common model airplane glue that is sometimes inhaled to get high. This is one of the most dangerous forms of drug intake, since it causes organic brain damage, meaning tomorrow you may not be able to tie your shoes. Not recommended for anyone with enough intelligence to read this or for anyone who wants to stay that way. Recommendations are to stay away from it completely; it will eventually kill you. It can kill or greatly damage you the first time you try it.

gnarly exciting, extreme and/or dangerous. Originally used to describe the physical appearance of an object, "gnarly" changed in use and definition during the hippie era. Considered a surfer creation, it saw use in all youth cultures during the 1970s. Example: "I had a **gnarly** ride on a **gnarly** wave." **2.** painful or extreme. Can be something good or something bad. One of those words like **bad**, which can have a positive or negative connotation, depending on the situation. Example: "That's a **gnarly** (beautiful) surfboard man." "That's a **gnarly** (dangerous) wave, man."

gnosh to eat.

gnosis Greek word for *knowledge.* Originally a generic term for knowledge in the first and second centuries A.D. It eventually came to mean **esoteric** knowledge of higher religious philosophy acquired only by an elite group of intellectuals. This word is the basis for the term agnostic, which is the largest religious group of people in the world. **Agnostics** have not seen proof that any one doctrine is the true religion and therefore, although they may be spiritual people, they are not willing to devote their total spiritual energy to one religion. (See: **agnosticism**)

go one of the many words used to indicate sex. Example: "Let's **go**, babe!" "Want to **go**?" "He **goes**, they **go**, we all **go** if we get the chance."

"Go Ahead, Make My Day!" a line from Clint Eastwood's movie, "Dirty Harry," in 1971. This phrase has found its way into our lexicon of stupid statements used whenever nothing more original can be conceived.

go along with to agree upon something or to acquiesce to someone else's plan. Examples: "I'll **go along with** that, man, but I'm not sure it's right."

go ape or **go ape shit** to do something crazy. Inferring that any out-of-the-ordinary activity is not human, but simian, or apelike, behavior. Introduced to the American public sometime around 1961.

go bananas to go crazy. The inference is that any out-of-the-ordinary activity is not human, but simian, or apelike, behavior.

god! an exclamation of excitement having nothing to do with the heavenly father.

God consciousness higher **consciousness.** During the hippie era, I heard the phrase "God consciousness" used by many people who were trying to appear spiritually **enlightened,** and, to be quite frank, I was never really sure whether they meant God's consciousness of us or our consciousness of God. Let's solve this right now and just say that it's: "That point at which God's view of me and my view of God meet and agree."

Godhead a God, Goddess, divinity or deity. The essential nature of God. In Christianity, the trinity of God, the One in Three.

God is dead a phrase that appeared on bathroom walls and bumper stickers in the late 1960s and early 1970s. My understanding of what it meant is that: There is no divine hope for the world and that we humans are going to have to make it on our own.

go down to happen. Example: "I didn't plan it to **go down** that way."

go down or **go down on** *sex* to perform **fellatio** or **cunnilingus**; **oral sex**. To stimulate someone's sexual organ by using the mouth. This term can mean oral sex performed on a male or female by a male or female.

go down in flames (See: **down in flames**)

God's eye a multicolored art work that radiates out from a center point. Usually diamond-shaped or round and can be drawn, painted or woven in yarn. It gives the impression of infinity.

God's flesh *drugs* **psilocybin mushroom, teonanacatl**. Any one of 14 different species of a small, yellow mushrooms with hallucinogenic qualities. The active ingredient is **psilocybin**. a.k.a. **magic mushroom, sacred mushrooms**. Warning, many mushrooms are deadly; please be sure of what you are eating for food or pleasure. (See: **psilocybin**)

God squad, the any religious group, particularly one that goes out and actively proselytizes.

goer someone who is incessantly moving or doing things. Can have a sexual meaning, as in someone who indulges in a lot of sex.

goes with the territory what you get as part of the bargain, something endemic to a situation. In this instance, territory is more of a situation or a mental state than a physical place. Another example in which a phrase once used only in the realm of the physical became a state of mind or emotional place during the hippie era.

gofer a subservient person, someone who does odd jobs and "goes for" things.

go figure! I don't understand, but it seems to work! A question and a statement. Example: "He stands on his head in the corner for half an hour and then goes into the board room and makes million dollar decisions; **go figure!**"

*go for it try it. Take a chance.

go fuck yourself! the ultimate derogatory suggestion. Do something nasty to yourself!

go-go a term introduced to the American public in 1966, which came to mean decadence, dancing and nightlife. Originally from a French term "a gogo," meaning loosely "galore." Used as a prefix or suffix to indicate the presence of vigorous dancing to rock-and-roll music. The **Whiskey-a-go-go**, a nightclub on Sunset Boulevard in Hollywood, was the most famous use of the term.

go-go boots women's high, tight, high-heel boots. Usually calf high, but some came up to the thigh. Often worn with **hot pants**. Similar to **disco boots**.

go-go girl a girl who danced on display at a nightclub, in a window, a cage, or on stage, to attract attention or set a mood. It has a negative connotation, indicating a girl who is shallow or puppetlike in her movements and emotions.

go head on to do something with total abandon. To face a situation with resolve.

going down, what's going down or **something going down** an activity. Examples: "Is something **going down?**" "What's happening, man? **What's going down?**"

going down *sex* to perform **fellatio** or **cunnilingus**; **oral sex**. One of the many forms of **to go down**. Examples: "He's **going down** on her, she **went down** on him, he will **go down** on him, she will be **going down** on her and they **went down** on each other."

going through changes having a psychological upheaval or change of mental state. Example: "He is **going through changes** after their break up; it really hurt him bad."

gold *drugs* high quality **marijuana**. Short for Acapulco gold.

gold dust *drugs* **cocaine**. (See: **cocaine**)

Golden Gate Park, San Francisco the scene of many of the early hippie activities. The location of the first **be-in** and many psychedelic **free concerts**. **Bill Graham** started his career as a concert promoter while presenting plays at be-ins and hippie gatherings there.

golden oldie originally, it meant a popular old song, and eventually, it became a slightly derogatory name for a person who was over the hill or out of date.

golden shower a urine shower, physically administered by a sexual partner. The act of urinating on someone. Considered by some people to be a sexual turn-on. It is oblique to me as to who is turned on by the act, the pissor or the pissee.

Gomer someone who is dense, stupid and/or ignorant. From the character of Gomer Pyle from the sitcom of the same name, which first appeared on TV in September of 1964. The character was dense, stupid and ignorant, as you might imagine.

gone mentally or psychologically absent. Demented or crazy. Another word that evolved during the beatnik and hippie era from a mostly physical definition to more of an emotional or psychological usage. Example: "He's **gone** man; don't bother knocking, his mind has been evicted."

gong *drugs* **opium** pipe.

gonzo unconventional, unincumbered by social mores, or out of control. Hunter S. Thompson, the writer who made the term popular, says that he first heard the word from a friend, Bill Cordoso, that it was a Portuguese word [it's actually Italian] and "it translates almost exactly to what the Hell's Angels would have said was 'off the wall.'" **Off the wall** in that context means abnormal, crazy or unconventional. I always assumed gonzo came from the word **gone**, as in crazy.

Goodman, Andrew (1943-1964) *social issues* Jewish "Northerner" who traveled from his native New York City to participate in the Mississippi Freedom Summer project of 1964. On June 21, 1964, Goodman, Black **civil rights** worker **James Chaney** and **Michael Schwerner**, another "Jewish Northerner," were murdered by Klansmen with the help of local sheriff's deputies. As of 2001, the murderers have not yet been brought to justice. (See: **Freedom Summer**) (See also: **Civil Rights Events and Leaders** starting on page 546 in **Lists** at the back of this book)

good old boys any paternal, established group that controls power through close friendships, political and economic ties. Cronyism. Such groups often exist to the exclusion of new people, ideas and, most assuredly, feminine intrusion.

good people someone who can be trusted.

goods, the any form of drugs or dope. Not necessarily good dope.

goods, the information.

good shit or **good stuff** *drugs* good dope.

good vibrations good feelings, good atmosphere. Popularized by the 1967 **Beach Boys** song of the same name. **Vibrations** are the feelings or emotions emanating from any person, place or thing. These vibrations, or **vibes**, can be "good" or "bad" and thereby determine whether the person, place or thing is "good" or "bad."

goof or **a goof** n. a joke. A trick played on someone. Example: "That fake eyeball in the **vegetarian** stew is just Jennie's idea of a **goof**."

goof, goof around, goof off or **goof on** v. to mess around, fool around or waste time. Example: "Don't **goof off on** the job; it's important to national security that the trash be picked up."

goofball *drugs* a mixture of **cocaine** and heroin. Sometimes means a mix of **amphetamine** and **barbiturate** (**upper** and **downer**); sometimes, just a barbiturate. a.k.a. **speedball**.

goofing, goofing on or **goofing around** fooling around. Also to joke or to lie. Example: "Don't take him seriously; he's just **goofing on** you."

go off or **go off on** to get mad or violent. Example: "You don't want *him* to **go off on** you; so, don't mention his stupid hat."

goof off v. to be lazy or fool around.

goof-off n. someone who is lazy or foolish.

goof-up a mistake.

goofy silly. Someone or something that is absurd. From the Walt Disney cartoon dog character of the same name.

gook a politically incorrect name for a person of Asian descent.

goons bouncers, bodyguards and hired toughs.

Goons a term used to describe the **Guardians of the Oglala Nation,** a vigilante group comprised of **Native Americans** that may have been supported by the FBI and Bureau of Indian Affairs. **American Indian Movement (AIM)** reservation residents of the Wounded Knee and Pine Ridge areas of South Dakota accused them of intimidation, violence and murder of hundreds of Sioux citizens during the mid-1970s. (See: **Native American and Other Minority Rights Events, Milestones and Legislation** in **Lists** at the back of this book)

goose v. to jab someone in the anus. An action that invariably makes the person jump with surprise and discomfort.

go out of one's skull to go crazy or lose control.

go over big to make a big impression. Example: "His parties have the tendency to **go over big** with the crazies." May be used sarcastically to mean something negative. Example: "His parties **go over big** with the neighbors."

*go public to advertise or disclose something about oneself that might be embarrassing or sensitive.

Gordy, Berry Jr. (1929-) *rhythm & Blues/motown/rock & roll* songwriter, music producer, founder and director of **Motown Records** from 1959 until its sale in 1988. After writing several hit songs, Gordy started his own rhythm & blues (R&B) record labels in 1959 under the umbrella of Motown Records Corporation. He soon moved his operations into a two-story house at 2648 West Grand Boulevard, Michigan, which he christened "Hitsville." Motown stands for motor town, which is the nickname for Detroit, Michigan. Gordy quickly created a reputation as a songwriter, producer and hustler. Motown was the creative center and home of many of the best singers and songwriters of the time, such as **Marvin Gaye**, Mary Wells, **Smokey Robinson**, David Ruffin, **Diana Ross**, Martha Reeves and **Stevie Wonder**. On July 23, 1968, The Jackson 5 auditioned at Motown. Though Gordy was not present, he signed them after viewing the audition tape. Berry Gordy was inducted into the Rock and Roll Hall of Fame in 1988.

gorilla a large person. A strong, but awkward individual.

gorp an acronym standing for "Good Old Raisins and Peanuts." A food combination often called **trail mix**, used as an energy snack by hikers. Along with **brown rice**, **bean sprouts** and **granola**, it is one of the most common food sources associated with the hippie culture.

go slumming to associate with someone of lesser social status or to attend a function that would normally be considered beneath one's position. This may seem to be too arrogant a word for a hippie dictionary, and, yes, it would be if we were dealing only with the hippie culture; however, this book is also a "cultural encyclopedia and phraseicon of the 1960s and 70s," and it deals with all of the attending words and attitudes of that time period.

go south to go wrong, to fail or to break. Example: "If we don't do some maintenance on this truck, its vital parts are going to **go south** on us all at once." May have come from an attitude in the North about the Southern states.

go straight to get off drugs; to change one's illegal or perverted ways. **2.** to become heterosexual.

*got a clue, (hasn't) ignorant or unaware of something. Example: "She hasn't **got a clue** what he's bitching about."

go take a flying fuck a directive to someone to go away. In essence, it means I don't care what you do, just do it somewhere else. **A flying fuck** is one of those nonsensical terms that can be used to intensify a variety of situations, but it is normally used to express disdain or disinterest.

gotakola East India water lily. A medicinal **herb** used by the hippie culture. Considered a brain stimulant, it is said to assist one's metabolism in obtaining more minerals from the water consumed. Elephants are partial to gotakola. Usually made into a tea when used for medicinal purposes.

go through changes to suffer psychological upheaval or experience a mental dilemma. Example: "Her divorce made her **go through changes** that were good for her in the end."

got it covered it's taken care of. Don't worry! Same as **no problem**.

got it knocked good at something. Assured of success. Confident that something is a forgone conclusion. Example: "Don't worry about that test; you've **got it knocked**."

go to bed with *sex* to have sex. Example: "Did you **go to bed with** them?"

got off felt the effects of, enjoyed, had an orgasm. Became high on drugs. Example: "We really **got off** on each other, so we dropped **acid**; when we **got off,** we made love, and she said she **got off** for the first time."

go to it to have sex. To get deeply involved in something.

go underground to hide from the law

gourd a person's head. From the gourd plant, which is round like a head. Example: "He's got lots of numbers in that gourd, but no personality."

Governor Moonbeam a name given **Jerry Brown**, the Governor of California from 1975 to 1983. Brown, who was liberal and a counterculture personality, was given this label to identify him as a hippie.

go way back a statement of friendship, confirmation of a long-term association. Example: "Of course I know about his attraction to hairy women; Chimp and I **go way back**."

go with it do it. Follow your instincts.

*****go with the flow** don't fight the current of psychological or physical energy around you.

goyl girl. The pronunciation used in most **blues**, **R&B** and **rock & roll** songs of the 1960s and 70s.

grab ass an outrageous act. To be forward or to act arrogantly. Examples: "That was a real **grab ass** move." "Stud is a **grab ass** kind of guy."

photo by Jim Marshall ©

******Graham, Bill (b. Wolfgang Grajonza, Jan. 8, 1931, Berlin, Germany; d. Oct, 25, 1991, near Vallejo, Calif.)** the guru of modern music concerts. The most influential rock music promoter of the era. He began his career producing plays at **be-ins** in **Golden Gate Park** in San Francisco, California in the mid-1960s. He went on to open the live music dance halls **Fillmore Auditorium** in San Francisco and Fillmore East in New York City and then to promote thousands of concerts in venues around the world. His first rock concert was a benefit for the **San Francisco Mime Troupe**, of which he was a member and business manager. That first show on November 6, 1965, featured **Jefferson Airplane**, **The Fugs**, The Mystery Trend and performers from **The Committee**; **Allen Ginsberg** and **Lawrence Ferlinghetti** also attended. Graham eventually became an international promoter, brokering concerts in large venues with personalities, such as **the Rolling Stones**, **Grateful Dead** and **Bob Dylan**, and promoting events like Live Aid and **Amnesty International** benefits. He campaigned against greed in the music industry and produced parties for "the people," which even those of the most modest means could attend. His concerts were always well organized and safe, allowing for the excesses of those who attended and often protecting them from themselves. No one person of the hippie era gave more pleasure to more people than Bill Graham. He died in a helicopter accident while leaving one of his productions in 1991. Inducted in to the Rock and Roll Hall of Fame in 1992.

gram *drugs* the metric measurement used to dispense quantities of drugs, such as mushrooms, **hashish**, **marijuanna** and **cocaine**. There are 28 grams to an ounce.

granny dress an old-fashioned, long, print dress often worn by hippie girls.

photo by John McCleary ©

granny glasses old-fashioned, six-sided, rimless glasses often worn by hippies. Called this because they were just like the ones granny used to wear. As opposed to **John Lennon** glasses, the round, wire-rimmed kind worn by Lennon.

granola generally a mixture of rolled oats, rolled wheat, raisins, honey and some sort of spices, yet everyone made their own combinations of fruits, nuts and grains. A common breakfast food eaten by hippies because of its natural ingredients. A reaction to the processed breakfast cereals popular in America at the time. Thought to have been invented at **Woodstock**, yet something like it had been used as a breakfast food in Europe for many years previously.

grass *drugs* **marijuana** again. a.k.a. **alfalfa, bhang, boo, cannabis, cheeba, chronic, devil weed, dank, doobage, dope, ganja, gunny, hay, hemp, herb, hooch, juanita, kief, leaf, loco weed, M, margarita, Mary Ann, Mary Jane, mu, muggles, pot, reefer, scuzz, shit, smoke, sweet Jane, sweet Lucy, T, tea, Texas tea, the kind, vitamin T, wacky weed, wacky t'backy, wana, weed**. (See: **marijuana**)

grasshopper someone who smokes grass (**marijuana**). Little used regional term.

"Grass will carry you through times of no money better than money will carry you through times of no grass." the motto of the *Feds 'n Heads Comix* charters, **Fabulous Furry Freak Brothers**, Phineas, Freewheelin' Frank and Fat Freddy, drawn by Gilbert Shelton.

Grateful Dead, The *rock & roll* the premier hippie band, formed 1965 in San Francisco, California; originally called **The Warlocks**. **Jerry Garcia** (b. Jerome John Garcia, Aug. 1, 1942, San Francisco; d. Aug. 9, 1995, Forest Knolls, Calif.) gtr., voc.; Bob Weir (b. Robert Hall Weir, Oct. 16, 1947, San Francisco) gtr., voc.; Ron "Pigpen" McKernan (b. Sept. 8, 1945, San Bruno, Calif.; d. Mar. 8, 1973, San Francisco), kybds., harmonica, voc.; Phil Lesh (b. Philip Chapman Lesh, Mar. 15, 1940, Berkeley, Calif.) bass, voc.; Bill Kreutzmann, a.k.a. Bill Summers (b. Apr. 7, 1946, Palo Alto, Calif.) drums; Mickey Hart (b. ca. 1950, Long Island, New York) drums, perc.; Robert Hunter, lyricist, and others. "The Hippie Band," a musical group to which improvisation was so important that it can be said they never played a song the same way twice. The longest lasting psychedelic band both in years and time on stage.

In all the Dead shows I "experienced," the band started on time and played for hours. It would take too many pages to try to explain or chronicle this band. For more insight, refer to John Rocco's *Dead Reckoning, The New Rolling Stone Encyclopedia of Rock & Roll* or any of the many biographies available. Inducted into The Rock and Roll Hall of Fame in 1994.

Grateful Dead House   710 Ashbury Street, San Francisco. Members of the band occupied this building from the fall of 1966 to March, 1968.

gray area   that place between black (bad) and white (good). In between right and wrong. Example: "Your decision to abstain from sex and drugs only on Sunday is a **gray area** of religious conviction."

Gray Panthers   an "intergenerational advocacy organization," founded in August, 1970, by Maggie Kuhn (1905-1995). Created for all ages, this organization calls itself, "Age and Youth in Action, activists working together for social and economic justice." The issues of interest include "universal health care, jobs with a living wage and the right to organize, preservation of Social Security, affordable housing, access to quality education, economic justice, environment, peace and challenging ageism, sexism, racism."

grease   money. From the phrase to "grease the gears," or get things moving, which is what money does. **2.** power.

greaseball   an undesirable person, usually male. Related to a "slippery" or "slimy" person.

greaser   a derogatory term for someone of Hispanic descent. **2.** a person, usually male, who either wears a greasy 1950s hairstyle or spends a lot of time working on cars.

great!   an exclamation of approval, used as it always has been, yet expanded during the hippie era to connect sentences and divide thoughts.

Greatest, The   a name adopted by **Muhammad Ali.** Ali always talked arrogant **trash,** and we got the feeling he was **putting us on,** doing it for business, and then one day we discovered that he really was The Greatest. (See: **Ali, Muhammad**)

great moves   ability, impressive physical functions that make someone good at something. Example: "She's got **great moves;** she can divert your attention with just a turn of the head."

photo by John McCleary ©

Great Unwashed, The   a term used to describe the beat generation and, then again, the hippies. I don't know who started the myth that hippies were dirty. After all, hippies made **hot tubs** popular and introduced co-ed showering to the general public. **True hippies** were no less hygienic than any other segment of the population; at times, the facilities just weren't available. But whenever a hippie settled down somewhere, bathing accommodations were some of the first amenities required after cooking and sleeping. After all, hippies were very decadent, and what is more decadent than a luscious bath? Hippies were, in fact, fond of bathing and swimming in the nude in lakes and streams, a habit that often got them in trouble with prudish local citizens. I believe the opinion that hippies were dirty came from the appearance of their clothes, which, though most often clean, were often old, worn and out of style according to straight society standards. Hippies were, of course, very concerned with propriety in the area of odor and scent, since romance was a major activity. Body **oils** and **incense** were contributions to our modern society from the hippie culture. Does anyone present remember **patchouli** oil? (See: **true hippie**)

green a word and color now associated with the **ecology** and **environmental** movements. Originally from the **Greenpeace** organization. The Green political party is an offshoot of this movement. (See: **Greenpeace**)

green envious.

green money.

green and blacks *drugs* **Librium**, a tranquilizer that comes in green and black capsules, used by sophisticated drug users to mellow out the stimulants in other drugs. **Downers**.

green dragon *drugs* **amphetamine**. An **upper**.

greenies *drugs* green, heart-shaped pills of dextroamphetamine. **Uppers**.

Greenpeace *social issues* an organization devoted to protecting the environment, improving ecological conditions and denouncing nuclear power and weaponry. Founded in Canada in 1970 by Jim Bohlen, Marie Bohlen, Irv-

ing Stowe, Dorothy Stowe, Paul Cote, Bill Darnell, Terry Simmons and Robert Hunter, a group of American expatriates and Canadian activists. Known primarily for exploits around the world in their boats, *Greenpeace* and *Rainbow Warrior*, attempting to halt animal cruelty, **environmental** pollution and nuclear tests. The Green political party is an offshoot of this organization. (See: **Ecology and Environmental Issues** on page 614 in **Lists** at the back of this book)

green politics *social issues* any political activity involved in protecting our natural world environment, its resources, plants and animals.

Greenwich Village a section of New York City that has been a center of the **jazz**, **beat** and hippie culture. Most of the folk and rock musicians played in the clubs there on Bleeker and **MacDougal** Streets early in their careers. **Bob Dylan** played his first gigs in "The Village," and **Jimi Hendrix's** Electric Lady Recording Studio was there at 52 West 8th Street.

Greer, Germaine (1939-) *social issues* journalist, actress, author lecturer. Author of *The Female Eunuch* (1970), which portrayed marriage as legalized slavery of women and accused our male-dominated society of misjudging female sexuality. A woman of stature and energy who, along with **Gloria Steinem, became the ideal image of heterosexual **feminism** to the world. Attractive, intelligent and independent, these two women were loved and feared by the stereotypical male. Their breaking of the stereotypical female mold was one of the best things that ever happened to the male–female relationship. Australian born Germaine Greer studied at Melbourne, Sydney, and Cambridge Universities and was a lecturer in English at Warwick University (1968-73). She directed the Tulsa Center for the Study of Women's Literature (1979-82) and has been a special lecturer and unofficial fellow of Newnham College at Cambridge since 1989. Two of her later books are *Sex and Destiny* (1984) and *The Change: Women, Aging and the Menopause* (1991).   (See: **Women's Movement Events, Groups and Leaders** starting on page 591 in the **Lists** at the end of this book)

"Greetings. You are hereby ordered to report..." The greeting that began the military draft letters sent from "Uncle Sam" to hundreds of thousands of young men during the 1960s and 1970s.

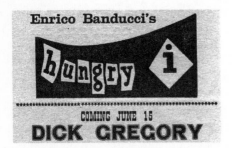

Gregory, Dick (1932-) *social issues* African American leader, spokesman for nonviolence and advocate of the poor. Originally a standup comedian, his support of **civil rights causes, **anti-war** protests and other social issues eventually overshadowed his comedy career. A candidate for Mayor of Chicago in 1966 and for President of the United States in 1968. In December of 1967, he traveled to North Vietnam in defiance of US Government restrictions. With Eldrige Cleaver, he co-founded the **Peace and Freedom Party (PFP)** in 1967; in 1968, he ran for president on that party ticket with Cleaver

as his running mate for vice president. Since 1968, the PFP has supported hundreds of candidates for public office. Gregory is a strict **vegetarian** and has written a book on the natural diet. He has fasted, almost to his death, for causes, such as peace, nonviolence and world hunger. At one time, he was associated with an obscure fad called breatharianism, which claimed that a person can live on air alone without any other sustenance. Gregory's books include: *Dick Gregory's Political Primer, No More Lies: The Myth and the Reality of American History, What's Happening, From the Back of the Bus* and *Nigger.*

gremlin, or **gremmie** a young, somewhat annoying person. Originally a surfer term to describe a new, inexperienced surfer.

Gretch Company, Fred *rock & roll* one of the oldest guitar manufacturing companies in the United States. Started by Fredrich Gretch in Brooklyn, New York, in late 1883. The company made many of the guitars popular with folk, **jazz**, **blues** and **rock and roll** musicians during the hippie era.

grid a name originally used in the 1970s to describe the sickness that eventually became known as **AIDS**.

gridlock a traffic jam. A situation in which everything has come to a halt because too much of something has gotten in the way. A term that came into use with the building and subsequent crowding of freeways.

grief psychological pain inflicted upon another person. The term originally described an emotion felt by an individual, but in the hippie era, it expanded into something that could be delivered by someone else. It changed from an emotion to a weapon.

grifa drugs **marijuana**, a Spanish word. There are a number of other spellings of this same Spanish word for marijuana: **grefa, greta, griffa, griffo**, etc.

Griffin, Rick one of the most recognizable and popular comic book and poster artists of the hippie era. He produced **psychedelic music** posters for **Bill Graham's** productions and created the skull image on the cover of the **Grateful Dead's** 1969 album, *Aoxomoxoa*.

Griffiths, Martha *social issues* the Michigan Democratic Congresswoman who suggested that the word "sex" be added to **Title VII** of the **Civil Rights** Act of 1964, thus opening the door for future job security for women. Griffiths was instrumental in pressuring the Equal Employment Opportunity Commission (EEOC) to stop the airline industry from dismissing stewardesses for being "overage." On June 20, 1966, she delivered to the House a scathing denouncement of the EEOC's negative attitude toward the gender provision of Title VII. This speech was reprinted and used to initiate the debate among a corps of women leading to the creation of the **National Organization of Women (NOW)**. (See: **Title VII** and **National Organization of Women**) (See also: **Women's Movement Events, Groups and Leaders** starting on page 591 in the **Lists** at the end of this book)

gringo a Caucasian or White person. A Spanish word. Can be derogatory.

*grip or **get a grip** take control. Possibly comes from "get a hold of yourself." Examples: "So Snookie left you; **get a grip**, life goes on."

gritty something basic, natural or sometimes unpolished. Can be positive or negative, depending on the circumstances. Examples: "That was a **gritty** performance." "Let's get down to the nitty **gritty**."

groady or **groaty** dirty, messy or smelly. Example: "That guy was **groady**; you could smell him a block away!"

groceries anything of value, most often drugs. In the Black community, it was a used to describe a woman's sexual assets. Example: "You just sit there on your **groceries,** girl, and look pretty."

grog any kind of alcohol.

grok to understand something deeply, to the point of feeling it. A word created by Robert A. Heinlein and used as a Martian term in his book, *Stranger in a Strange Land.*

*groove, in a groove or **in the groove** the right place. Example: "Keep it up, you're **in the groove**." A **jazz** term that progressed into common usage in the **counterculture**. It may have come from a reference to grooves on a record, indicating that a musical accomplishment has reached the status of being recorded for posterity on a **vinyl** record. (See: **LPs** and **vinyl**)

groove on to appreciate someone, someplace or something. Example: "I **groove on** her, man."

groove on doing something right. Example: "He really has a **groove on** tonight."

groover someone who likes to dance. A **cool** person.

grooving or **groovin'** having fun and lookin' good. Dancing or listening to music. Example: "They're really

groovin' tonight." **2.** doing something right.

groovy originally, it meant good or pleasing, coming from **groove** or **in the groove**. This word, specifically, has achieved camp status and is now rarely used except in jest or sarcasm.

grope to touch and fondle someone sexually. A humorous reference to **foreplay**, it often denotes a failed effort at being sexual.

grope-in a multiple-partner sex act.

*****gross** ugly or in bad taste. (Valley talk) (See: **Valley talk**)

gross body *occult* in **occult** terminology, it means the physical body.

grossed out revolted by someone or something. Example: "When he ate the rat, everyone was **grossed out**."

grosses me out makes me sick or revolted.

Grossman, Albert B. (1926-1986) *rock and roll* a popular musical talent manager, impresario and recording executive. Best known for managing **Bob Dylan** in the early days from 1962 to 1969. Grossman opened the Gate of Horn folk music club in Chicago in the mid-1950s. He moved to New York City, and in 1959, he helped to start the Newport Folk Festival. He created the folk group **Peter, Paul and Mary** and managed **Janis Joplin** to stardom in 1968. In 1970, he moved to Bearsville, New York, where he established Bearsville Studio and Records and opened several restaurants. Grossman was the most influential and respected manager of his time; his clients included **The Band**, **Paul Butterfield**, **Gordon Lightfoot**, and **Richie Havens**.

gross-out a revolting experience. Example: "What a **gross-out;** he ate a

chicken's head on stage during the show!" A term introduced to the American public in 1971.

grotty disgusting.

grounded self-assured or under control. Similar to **centered**.

group grope *sex* a multiple-partner sex act. A large number of people, usually nude, rolling around, indiscriminately engaging in various sexual activities.

groupie a person who follows and/or idolizes a public figure or entertainer. Most often, it is a girl who follows male rock stars, and, traditionally, offers sexual favors in order to be with her idol. Sometimes called **star-fuckers**. (See: **plaster casters** and **star-fucker**)

group therapy or **group** a form of therapy based on the theory that confrontations and interplay with objective, unrelated people can help a person to achieve self-confidence, thus, **self-realization** and better mental stability. It is a process used in **gestalt** therapy and used extensively at **Esalen Institute. Gestalt theory** teaches that, by breaking down inhibitions, many psychoses and neuroses can be cured. Selfishness, sexual frustration and rigid viewpoints were considered the reasons for the many emotional conflicts of the post-WWII era. This process is also known as **encounter group, sensitivity training** or **marathon group.** The term encounter group was introduced to the American public in 1970; yet, the process had been in use for years at places like Esalen before it reached the awareness of the general public. Eventually, these groups, became ultra-commercial ventures, taking advantage of the gestalt process, making it a fad and applying it to such things as "How to Become a Better Insurance Salesperson by 'Trading Places' with Your Client." (See: **gestalt** and **Esalen Institute**)

grow lamp or **blue light** a florescent lamp that emits a blue, ultraviolet light essential for growing **marijuana** indoors without sunlight.

grunge dirt.

*****grungy** dirty or unkempt.

grunt a derogatory term for a foot soldier. In Vietnam, soldiers used this term to describe themselves. From the fact that a foot solder did a lot of grunting while walking through the jungle carrying 80 pounds of equipment. **2.** an unskilled laborer.

grunt work unskilled labor.

G-spot *sex* a spot in the female **vagina** that transmits erogenous feelings to the brain. May be more pleasing to some women than others. The area of spongy tissue around the urethra at the top of the vagina, halfway between the pubic bone and the cervix. Also called the Grafenberg spot, for Dr. Ernst Grafenberg, who wrote about it in 1950.

guacamole mashed avocado used as a dip or condiment. Often mixed with salsa, lemon juice and spices.

guerrilla theater or **street theater** *social issues* any unauthorized performance or **performance art** presented on streets or in public places. Usually **anti-establishment** in nature, designed to demonstrate against some **civil rights** injustice or social problem. In the tradition of 18th-century theatrical performances given outdoors and on the streets, the hippie era saw a street theater resurgence. Many individuals and small groups began performing mime and short plays for spare change on street corners and parks. Noteworthy were the **Artists' Liberation Front**, the **San Francisco Mime Troupe**, and various "prankster" groups, or so-called guerrilla theaters, in San Francisco, Boston and New York City. Many of these groups concentrated on political satire, social confrontations and **anti-war** themes.

Guevara, Ernesto "Che" (b. 1928, Argentina; assassinated Oct. 8, 1967, Bolivia) *social issues* a charismatic revolutionary, considered by many to be the personification of the communist revolution. He was the onetime minister of industries and the number two man in Castro's Cuba. His whereabouts were unknown for two years between 1965-67, and he was thought to be responsible for guerrilla activities in Argentina, Brazil, Colombia, Peru and Venezuela during that time. Guevara was captured by the Bolivian army while leading leftist guerrillas in that country and was killed in custody.

guide *drugs* someone who remains **straight** to watch over a person who is taking **LSD**. Similar to a designated driver.

Guild Guitar Company *rock & roll* one of the newer guitar manufacturing companies in the United States. Started in 1952 by Alfred Dronge with craftsmen from the Epiphone company, another musical instrument manufacturer. The company made many of the guitars popular with folk, **jazz** and **rock and roll** musicians during the hippie era.

gum to talk.

gun *drugs* the eyedropper or syringe used to inject drugs.

gung-ho enthusiastic about something.

gunji *drugs* **opium**.

gunny *drugs* **marijuana**. (See: **marijuana**)

Gurdjieff, George Ivanovich (1873-1949) philosopher, teacher, author of a book widely read by the **counterculture**, *Meetings with Remarkable Men*, in which he tells of his search for wisdom. Influential in the development of hippie philosophy. (See: **Books of the Era** on page 636 in **Lists** at the back of this book)

guru Sanskrit word for spiritual leader or teacher. "Spiritual guide" in the **Hindu** religion. It acquired a broader, more secular definition when used to describe anyone with special teaching skills. Example: "He is my guitar **guru**."

guru-you a parody on **screw you,** meaning just the opposite.

Guthrie, Woody (b. July 14, 1912, Okemah, Okla.; d. October 3, 1967, Queens, New York) folksinger and activist, wandering Dust Bowl minstrel, supporter of the **working class**, he wrote such songs as "This Land is Your Land," "So Long, It's Been Good To Know You" and 1,000 others. The precursor of all the many folksingers and hippie singers of the 1950s and 1960s. Influenced **Bob Dylan** and all singers of social conscience to come. Died of Huntington's chorea in 1967. His son Arlo, also a musician, is famous for the song and movie, "Alice's Restaurant." Inducted into the Rock and Roll Hall of Fame in 1988 as an early influence.

gut reaction a basic form of **telepathy** that influences decisions based on the first impression of a situation or person.

guts possessing a heroic demeanor. From the term "intestinal fortitude" the ability to avoid getting sick at the moment of fear.

*gutsy bold or heroic.

guzzle to drink something quickly.

gypsy a person who travels around a lot.

Gypsy Boots (*See: **Boots, Gypsy**)

H

H *drugs* **heroin**, the narcotic.

H and C *drugs* a **heroin** and **cocaine** mix. a.k.a. **hot and cold.**

habit *drugs* a drug **addiction**.

hack or **hack it** handle it, do it. Example: "It's a tough job, but it's exciting if you can **hack it.**"

hacker *computer revolution* an unconventional computer **programmer**. In the 1960s at the Massachusetts Institute of Technology (MIT), a group of programers calling themselves "**hackers**" created and played a computer game called **Spacewar**, a simple creation, most likely the first of its kind. MIT was working with Advanced Research Project Agency (ARPA) funding on multiaccess computing solutions (the MAC project). These early "MAC" hackers explored the "interesting vulnerability" of the systems as a way to create and test new time-sharing programs for a common good, unlike later hackers, whose goal seems to be destruction. In the 1980s, because of misguided users, the term hacker came to mean a programmer who devised ways to sneak into other users' computers, steal information and destroy people's work.

had taken advantage of. This word has sexual undertones, although it is not always used in a sexual reference. Example: "I thought I was going to have her, but I've been **had**; she's a government snitch, and I brought her to the SDS meeting."

had it fed up, finished dealing with it. Short for "**I've had it up to here**" (indicating the eyeballs), which is short for "**I've had it up to my eyeballs**." Example: "I have **had it** with your bitching; get a dog if you need faithful."

had it up to here (while saying this, one must gesture with a hand held horizontally at eyeball level) fed up. Tired of the situation. The same as **had it** or **I've had it up to my eyeballs**.

Hagar, Sammy (b. Oct. 13, 1947, Monterey, Calif.) *rock & roll* charismatic frontman and lead singer for bands of the era. A **heavy-metal** and **cock-rock** star. The lead singer for Montrose from 1973-75, he formed his own band in 1975. Replaced David Lee Roth as **Van Halen**'s frontman in 1985. Continues to perform from time to time and now owns bars and restaurants, and bottles a brand of tequila.

Haggard, Merle (b. April 6, 1936, Bakersfield, Calif.) one of country music's most gifted and prolific songwriters. He wrote "Okie from Muskogee" in 1969. Some people thought it was just a patriotic song, but, if one listens carefully, one realizes that it was one of the first examples of self-effacing, sarcastic country humor, which introduced country western to a less serious direction. Many consider Haggard to be one of the original bad boy country mavericks who opened the door for the crossover into **counterculture**, longhair types like **Willie Nelson**, Waylon Jennings and Kris Kristofferson.

Haight short for **Haight-Ashbury**.

Haight-Ashbury the section of San Francisco, California, surrounding the intersection of Haight and Ashbury Streets. The area of the city most associated with the hippie movement.

Haight-Ashbury Free Medical Clinic 558 Clayton Street, San Francisco, California.

hair and **hair on your ass** guts. From the idea that a real man has hair on his body, and, of course, hair on his ass. Examples: "He's got **hair**; he's fearless." "He'll never pull his weight; he's got no **hair on his ass**."

"Hair, The American Tribal Love Rock Musical" the definitive play and movie about the hippie culture. The book and lyrics were written by Gerome Ragni and James Rado. The play was produced by Michael Butler, with music by Galt MacDermot. It opened in New York City at the Baltimore Theatre in 1967 and eventually played extensive runs in most major cities in the US and throughout the world. "Hair" is the most successful venue in communicating hippie ideals, but, like so much of the counterculture's commentary, it was too satirical, ironic and sacrilegious for most conservative sensibilities. The **capitalist** political leadership and **military-industrial complex** of the time were so threatened by hippie ideals that the conservative media trashed anything to do with the counterculture and in essence tossed the baby out with the bath water. In spite of conservative backlash, "Hair" continues to be performed regularly throughout the world.

hair band *rock & roll* a rock & roll, **heavy-metal** band, with musicians who wear long hair, which they toss around in a provocative manner while performing before hundreds of screaming girls who did not come to hear the music. Also called a **cock-rock** band.

hairburger or **hair pie** n. *sex* the **vagina**. Female genitals.

hairburger or **hair pie** v. *sex* **cunnilingus**. (See: **cunnilingus**)

hair up (one's) **ass** nervous or obnoxious. Worried about something. Examples: "She's got a **hair up her ass**. She can't sit, and she won't fly." "You got **a hair up your ass** about something?"

hairy frightening, troublesome, difficult. Examples: "That was a **hairy** accident." "I just took a **hairy** math test."

hairy-assed frightening, troublesome, difficult. Examples: "He's a **hairy-assed** dude." "I just took a **hairy-assed** math test."

Hal the computer that helped run the space station in the movie "2001, A Space Odyssey." Hal eventually took control of the station, usurping the humans' power. This has always been a fear and concern of humans about computers—that they would eventually reach a point of intelligence superior to human beings. Hal is now the name used to describe any computer that does not "behave" or follow human directions.

Haley, Alex (b. Aug. 11, 1921; d. Feb. 10, 1992) African American author of *The Autobiography of Malcolm X* (1965) and *Roots: The Saga of an American Family* (1976). The publishing of *Roots* and the television miniseries it inspired made Haley a national figure. *Roots* is a historical novel chronicling several generations of the family of Kunta Kinte, an African who became a slave in America.

half-assed incomplete or unfinished. Someone or something unsatisfactory.

hallucinate *drugs* to see something within one's own mind that is not visible to the naked eye. It usually consists of visions created with the aid of a drug or chemical stimulus of some kind. The hallucinations are created in the mind, using existing, visible objects and incorporating other memories. To a neophyte in psychedelic experiences, the visions may seem real and can be frightening or can influence a person to do something dangerous, such as jump off a building with hallucinations of flying. With experience, the "tripper" learns that the visions are a creation of his or her own mind and may then begin to enjoy them as mere amusement. In **occult** and **esoteric** terminology, hallucinations are a state following relaxation of the nervous system, which attracts waves of **astral** light to the individual, who thus may temporarily acquire and use extrasensory or extratemporal perception.

hallucinogenic drug *drugs* a substance, either chemical or biological, that affects the human mind, expanding the thought process into unexplored avenues, creating new thoughts and extravagant visions.

halter top an item of clothing worn by women as an abbreviated shirt to cover their breasts. Often, it is merely a bandanna or piece of cloth tied around the body, leaving sholders, back and stomach exposed.

hamburger someone or something damaged or beaten up. Examples: "He wrapped his car around a tree; it was

hamburger, man!" "If he messes with my ol' lady, he's **hamburger**."

hammered *drugs* drunk or under the influence of drugs.

Hammond, John Sr. *music/producer* a talent scout and music producer noted for discovering **Bob Dylan** and responsible for recording many of the old Delta blues musicians before they died and their music was lost to posterity. Father of **John Hammond, Jr**. Inducted into the Rock and Roll Hall of Fame in 1986 as an early influence.

Hammond, John, Jr. (b. **John Paul Hammond, November 13, 1943, New York City**) *music/blues* a White blues singer/harmonica player and guitarist associated with **The Band** around 1963 before they began working with **Bob Dylan**. He has played with people, such as **Jimi Hendrix**, Dr. John, **Mike Bloomfield**, Bill Wyman, Duane Allman, J. J. Cale and **John Lee Hooker**. Hammond was an important contributor to the transition of blues into rock and roll. Son of **John Hammond, Sr**.

Hammond organ a valuable contributor to the sound of rock and roll. A small, electric instrument encased in a wooden cabinet, sold by the thousands in the 1950s for home and church use. At one time, the Hammond organ replaced the piano as a piece of furniture in many homes. All of a sudden, this strange, tinny sounding organ became popular with **jazz**, rhythm and blues and **rock and roll** musicians and became a mainstay in the music industry during the 1960s and 70s.

Hampton, Fred (b. 1947-48; d. Dec. 4, 1969) *social issues* leader of the Chicago Chapter of the **Black Panther Party (BPP)** at the age of 20, Hampton was instrumental in many activities to

improve the Black community: a free breakfast program, the People's Free Clinic, community police control project and teaching political education classes. Hampton had charisma, and sources say he would have eventually been appointed to the Party's central committee as chief of staff had it not been for the events of early morning, December 4, 1969. As a moving force in the BPP, Fred Hampton was a wanted man. It is alleged that the FBI placed a spy in the BPP, and on the night of December 3, 1969, that spy drugged Hampton and his bodyguard, Mark Clark. Around 4:30 a. m. on December 4, heavily armed Chicago Police attacked the Panthers' apartment. Upon entering, they shot Clark, who was sleeping in the living room with a shotgun in his hand. Before dying, he fired one shot at the police. That was later determined to be the only shot fired by the Panthers. Police automatic gunfire riddled the apartment, wounding Fred in the shoulder as he lay sleeping with his pregnant girlfriend. Officers then entered his bedroom, shooting Hampton point-blank in the head to make sure he was dead. They then dragged his body out of the bedroom and again open fired on other members in the apartment. The Panthers were then beaten and dragged across the street where they were arrested on charges of attempted murder and aggravated assault against the police.

Hancock, Herbie (b. April 12, 1940, Chicago, Illinois) *music/jazz/funk* a Black keyboardist/composer/arranger/producer who contributed much to the sound of the 1960s and 1970s, infusing **jazz** into the other forms of music that arose during the hippie era. Herbie gained prominence as the pianist in **Miles Davis's** landmark, mid-1960s quintet, which pioneered electric fusion. Hancock has played with, contributed to and produced the likes of Mongo Santamaria, Chick Corea, Ron Carter, Branford and Wynton Marsalis. He also wrote the popular pop-jazz crossover song, "Watermelon Man."

handle a name, often a pseudonym, or nickname. Originally from Morse code, in which a person was recognized by their "hand," the way they tapped the key. It progressed into use in ham radio and **citizens band radio (CB radio)**. (See: **citizens band radio**)

hang short for "hang-out." Example: "You want to **hang** with me, you have to learn to drink beer and talk shit."

hang five a surfer term meaning to stick the toes of one foot off the nose of one's surf board.

*hang in there survive, be strong against the odds.

hang it up quit, give up. Most likely, this came from a phrase like "hang up your tools and quit," or "hang up your chaps, cowboy, and die in bed." Example: "**Hang it up**; stop trying to be cool, just act like me."

*hang loose relax. Wait a little while. Don't worry.

hang me up to slow down, obstruct or leave someone waiting. Example: "Don't **hang me up** on this; I need those rabbit droppings today to fertilize my lettuce." Most likely, this came from a phrase, such as "hang me up on a hook" or "leave me hanging."

hang one on to get drunk or **stoned** on drugs. Related to creating a hangover. Example: "Did you **hang one on** last night? You sure look bad today."

hangout n. a place where people gather to **hang out** together.

hang out v. to loiter with little or no purpose.

hang ten a surfer term meaning to walk to the front of a surf board and stick the toes of both feet off the nose. It eventually began to mean just having a good time or doing anything exciting. Example: "Let's **hang ten** tonight, guys, nothing can stop us."

hang tough be strong, stick to your convictions. Related to **hang in there**.

*hang-up or **hang-ups** a psychological problem; often related to inhibitions concerning sex. **2.** a regular problem or delay, like the toilet overflowing.

Hanoi Hilton prisoner of war (**POW**) detention camp in central Hanoi where American soldiers and airmen were kept during the **Vietnam War**. Its actual name was Hoa Lo Prison, and it was originally a French colonial jail, also used by the Japanese during the Second World War. *Hoa Lo* in Vietnamese roughly translates to "the furnace." Although it was the most publicized prison, Hanoi Hilton was not the only one in North Vietnam. Another prison complex at Son Tay was the target of an unsuccessful US raid in 1970, causing the North Vietnamese to concentrate most POW's at Hanoi Hilton. North Vietnamese POW camps housed more than 700 prisoners from 1964 to 1973. The North Vietnamese government did not consider US prisoners to be POWs, but political internees; therefore, they did not follow the Geneva Convention guidelines in their treatment. The Hanoi Hilton was closed in 1973 after the return of US POWs, and it was razed in 1994 to make way for a luxury hotel. A quote from Philip Butler, Navy fighter pilot shot down over North Vietnam on April 20, 1965: "Upon our arrival at Hoa Lo, my guard removed my blindfold because he wanted me to see the horrible place I was about to enter. In front of us was a 30-foot-high stone wall, with barbed wire and glass imbedded along the top. Two huge iron doors were in front of the Jeep. As we drove through those doors, I fought to hold back the tears because for the first time in my life, but not the last, I could feel the icy fingers of despair encircling my heart. Little did I know then that I would endure horrible treatment in that and 10 other prisons before my repatriation 8 years later."

Hanoi Jane *social issues* Jane Fonda was called Hanoi Jane after she visited North Vietnam in July, 1972, and broadcast over the Voice of Vietnam radio station to American bomber pilots. She said to the pilots, "I implore you...I beg you...to consider what you are doing." (See: **Jane Fonda**)

happening a gathering of people at which something happens. A party or function where people indulge in activities contrary to the social norm. Often, in the beginning of the hippie movement, a happening involved presenting a pageant or play to address certain social concerns, and invariably, it incorporated the ingestion of some form of psychedelic drug. Example: "What's the happenings, Bro?"

happy dust *drugs* **cocaine**. Cocaine in the long run proves to be anything but a happy drug. I feel that many stimulants, including alcohol, **marijuana** and most psychedelics, are acceptable if one confines their use to an occasional social or recreational indulgence. Yet some drugs, and cocaine is

at the top of the list, are so psychologically or physically addictive that they become the downfall of many people who try them. Use your drugs, don't let them use you.

happy face or **smiley face** artwork of a round, yellow face with a smile and two simple eye dots that was a familiar friend throughout the 1970s. Created in 1963 by Harvey Ball (1921-2001) for an insurance company advertising campaign. Ball was initially paid $45 for his artwork, but he received little or no further monetary compensation or recognition for the icon he created. www.worldsmileday.com

happy stick *drugs* a **marijuana** cigarette

happy trails a salutation. Similar to, "Have a nice trip." From the song, "Happy Trails," written by Dale Evans. This song was sung by many, but most remembered as the closing number on Roy Rogers and Dale Evans' radio and TV shows in the 1950s.

haps short for happenings. That which is going on. Example: "What's the **haps,** man?"

hard difficult. It can be argued that this word and meaning was not a development of the hippie era, yet it came into a lot of new usage during the era.

hard *sex* having an erect penis, ready for intercourse. Related to having a **hard-on**. Examples: "All the guys are

hard for her." "That was the first time in my life I couldn't get **hard**."

hard-ass or **hard-assed** a difficulty or dangerous person.

*****hardball** serious activity.   Example: "We don't mess around when we go out looking for girls; we play **hardball**." Admittedly, not a word created in the hippie era, yet one that took on new usage and received a lot of mileage during the period.

hardbody a person who exercises or lifts weights and has a developed body. It could also be just any young person, because of the youthful tendency to have harder bodies. During the hippie era, many people considered body-building to be a narcissistic activity. Overly developed muscles were thought of as an egotistical indulgence. Even thought health, exercise and good, healthy outdoor, activity were looked upon favorably, bodybuilding was considered masochistic.

hard case someone violent or dangerous. A career criminal.

hard core not for the young or faint of heart. Serious. X-rated. Examples: "There was a **hard core** sex scene in that movie." "He is a **hard core** guitar player."

hard drugs *drugs* this is a value judgment, but within the hip community most people considered a drug that was life threatening and/or both physically and emotionally addicting to be a "hard drug." Not a psychedelic or mind-expanding drug. **Methamphetamine, cocaine**, morphine and heroin would be obvious hard drugs.

hard hat a construction worker or a blue-collar worker. During the hippie era, this term became the description of a person who was anti-hippie and overly patriotic. A person who was ignorant of new ways of thinking and was capable of violence in defense of his misdirected patriotism, masculinity and ignorance.

Hard Hats *social issues* the National Hard Hats of America, a group of construction workers who organized to support the **Vietnam War**. They supported **President Nixon's** Vietnam policies and held counter-**demonstrations** during peace rallies. Their confrontations with **anti-war** demonstrators were usually violent, and it is believed that they were supported by, and may even have been formed with help from, Nixon's **dirty tricks** organization, the **plumbers**.

Hardin, Tim (b. Dec. 23, 1941; d. Dec. 29, 1980) *music/folk* influential folksinger from the Cambridge, Massachusetts, and New York City scene. He wrote "If I Were a Carpenter" and "Reason to Believe." At one time, **Bob Dylan** called him the country's greatest living songwriter. He succumbed to a heroin overdose in an apartment in Los Angeles, California.

hard knocks bad luck or bad times.

hard-on *sex* a sexually aroused penis. An erection.

hard rock *rock & roll* a loud, driving, less melodious form of rock and roll, usually equated to **heavy-metal** rock.

hard stuff *drugs* addictive drugs, such as **heroin**, **cocaine** and **methamphetamines**.

*****hard up** broke, without money, the state of being without something. Examples: "I'm **hard up**; loan me a few bucks!?" "He's **hard up** in the relationship department."

hardware as a computer term, it first appeared around 1965. It is the physical parts of a computer (monitor, keyboard, hard drive and processor) as opposed to the **software**, or "mental" part (programs). There is a saying in the computer industry, "The computer is exactly the opposite of the human body; with computers, the software goes inside, with humans, the hardware goes inside."

hard-wired and **pre-wired** unchangeable. An early computer term that began to appear in usage outside the technical world during the late 1970s, describing human situations. Example: "Don't bother asking him; his view on communism is **hard-wired**."

hardy-har or **hardy-har-har** a sarcastic exclamation meaning "what you said [or did] was not funny." Examples: "You can joke around if you want, **hardy-har**, but this is serious business." "You can go through life with a **hardy-har-har**, but in the end, you'll pay for all your foolishness."

Hare Krishnas (pronounced **har-re**) from the **Sanskrit** prayer "Hare Krishna" (hail Krishna). A Hindu offshoot started in America in 1968; the **International Society for Krishna Consciousness** or the Krishna movement. (See: **International Society for Krishna Consciousness**)

harp or **harpoon** a harmonica.

harp on or **harping on** to nag or talk incessantly about a subject.

Harris, Emmylou (b. April 2, 1947) *music/country/folk* one of the more important female country/folk/rock crossover artists of the hippie era. Harris has proven through her long career to be a very creative and dedicated musician. She may not fully appreciate the designation, but she was one of the **hippie chick** singers the guys loved to watch.

Harrison, George (b. Feb. 25, 1943, Liverpool, Eng.; d. Nov. 29, 2001, Los Angeles, Calif.) *rock & roll* the lead guitar player of **The Beatles**, George enjoyed some commercial, and indeed critical acclaim as a solo artist after the breakup of the band in 1970. His first solo album, the 1970 three-record set *All Things Must Pass*, is a true classic. Harrison was also the driving force behind the the 1971 **Bangladesh** relief concert at Madison Square Garden, creating a precedent by which all future benefit concerts are judged. Harrison, above all the other Beatles, exhibited the **true hippie** spirit. His early interest in playing the sitar was adventurous, and the songs he wrote as a Beatle, "Taxman," "While My Guitar Gently Weeps," " Here Comes the Sun" and "Something," were among the most emotive of their music. We are so fortunate to have had George Harrison in this world. For the rest of our lives, we have his music to rejuvenate us. The Beatles were inducted into the Rock and Roll Hall of Fame in 1988.

Hartford, John (b. Dec. 30, 1937; d. June 4, 2001) *folk, rock & roll* singer, songwriter, banjo player, who wrote

"Gentle on My Mind" for Glen Campbell. Hartford was an important presence in the folk/rock world of the era.

has-been a person who is no longer current, someone who is out of place and out of time.

hash *drugs* short for **hashish**.

Hashbury a name given the **Haight-Ashbury** district of San Francisco, California. The use of the word **hash** in the name indicates that it was the hippie and drug-smoking area of the city.

hashhead *drugs* someone who smokes a lot of **hash**.

hashish *drugs* synthesized **THC resins** from **cannabis**. Basically, it is **marijuana** flowers cooked down into a solid form. Usually formed into small, semi-soft cakes, the color of which may be black, brown or red. Normally crumbled into a pipe and smoked. Hashish is usually named for its color, origin or the shape of the cakes. Several types of hash available were: Lebanese, **temple balls** and finger clusters.

hash oil *drugs* a liquid concentrate of hashish made by dissolving hash **resin** in organic solvents, such as alcohol or ethers, to extract the **THC**. Hash oil is used like hashish or mixed with some form of tobacco and smoked. **Cannabis** oil is similar except the extract comes from the **marijuana** plant itself.

hasn't got a clue ignorant of a situation. Example: "James **hasn't got a clue** about soap."

*hassle and **hassling** a problem, or trouble. **2.** to bother, disturb or persecute someone; often used to indicate the police or authorities' persecution of **counterculture** members.

hatha yoga a form of **yoga** used as a physical health discipline. The use of breathing and body exercise; **ha** is understood to mean inhaling, and **tha**, to mean exhaling.

haul short for **haul ass**. Example: "Let's **haul** out of here before it gets too weird. Oops, too late."

haul ass to move quickly.

have a ball to have fun. "Ball" is an old African American and blues music term for sexual intercourse, which evolved into meaning just having fun of any kind.

have a cow to get excited, angry or upset.

*have a nice day or **have a beautiful day** means what it says. Used as parting words by many hippies, almost to the point of becoming sickening, and for a time used only as sarcastic humor. Associated with the "happy face," and to many it is the height of obnoxious, mindless, conversation. (See: **happy face**)

have it both ways *sex* to have sex both vaginally and anally. To have vaginal and **oral sex**. To have both hetero- and homosexual tendencies.

have it knocked to be good at something. To have success be a forgone conclusion. Examples: "By the end of the semester, he will **have algebra knocked**." "Don't worry about the test; you **have it knocked**."

have it made to be fortunate. To be rich.

have it made *sex* to have sexual conquest be a foregone conclusion.

have it off to have a confrontation or a fight.

have it off *sex* to have sexual intercourse. Related to "**get it off** or **knock off**." Example: "She's beautiful; I'd **have it off** with her anytime."

have it your way to be under control in a situation.

have it your way a statement of capitulation. Example: "OK, **have it your way**, eat the hot dog."

have mercy a request for assistance, forgiveness or help, yet most often just a conversational interjection considered to be jive talk. It comes originally from Southern Baptist or Pentecostal Church terminology used in prayer, mercy being forgiveness of one's sins by God. (See: **jive talk**)

Havens, Richie (b. January 21, 1941) *music/folk/rock/blues/jazz* an early Boston and New York folk/coffeehouse singer who became a valuable contributor to the folk-to-rock transition. He was the opening act at the **Woodstock** weekend, and his performance set the tone for peace, love and good music.

Hawaiian pod *drugs* another name for **Hawaiian woodrose**.

Hawaiian woodrose *drugs* a natural **hallucinogenic**. A decorative plant native to India, now found in Hawaii. Not actually a rose, but a climbing vine. The seeds of the baby Hawaiian woodrose produce a **psychoactive** reaction. According to Hawaiian mythology, it is pollinated by the *kahunas* or gods.

hawk a person in favor of war, specifically in the 1960s and 70s, one who supported the **Vietnam War**. Opposite of a **dove**, who opposed war and violence in general.

hawk *drugs* **LSD**. **2.** in some circles it is **heroin**.

hay *drugs* **marijuana**. (See: **marijuana**)

photo by John McCleary ©

Hayden, Tom (1939-) *social issues* a member of the **Chicago Seven along with **Rennie Davis**, **David Dellinger**, John Froines, **Abbie Hoffman**, **Jerry Rubin** and Lee Weiner. **Anti-war**, and peace and freedom movement leaders who were arrested and tried as co-conspirators for crossing state borders to incite to riot during the 1968 **Democratic National Convention**. The trial was one of the most controversial examples of the flaws in our judicial system. The courts disregarded the defendants' personal freedoms and stretched laws to the breaking point. The defendants used the trial as an opportunity to inform the public about the inequities and inconsistencies of the courts as related to political activism. As Hayden later wrote in his 1970 book *Trial*, "When the courts are turned into a weapon against change, trials must be turned into an attack on the courts. Make it known that American citizens are being jailed because of their political attitudes or, in our case, for their 'state of mind' by a state that cannot reconcile its pledge of a fair trial with its stake in preserving the status quo." Tom Hayden was convicted and received a five-year sentence plus a fifteen-month sentence for contempt of court to run concurrently. Eventually, the conviction was overturned because of Judge Hoffman's gross misconduct during the trial. Hayden is a graduate of the University of Michigan and edited *The Michigan Daily* in his senior year. In 1961, he worked on the summer project of the **Student Nonviolent Coordinating Committee (SNCC)** in Mississippi. In 1962, he cofounded **Students for a Democratic Society (SDS)** and authored its bylaws and constitution. That document, called "The Port Huron Statement," is said by many to mark the beginning of student revolution in America. It begins, "We are people of this generation bred in at least modest comfort, housed now in universities, looking uncomfortably to the world we inherit. Our work is guided by the sense that we may be the last generation in the experiment with living,... But we are a minority—the vast majority of our people regard the temporary equilibriums of our society and world as eternally functional parts." Hayden was reportedly active in the Columbia University rebellion during the spring of 1968. After the **Chicago Seven** trial and his release from jail, Tom Hayden become a politician and has been elected to several terms in the California Assembly and Senate. (See: **Chicago Seven, Chicago Democratic National Convention** and **Students for a Democratic Society**) (See also: **Anti-War Events, Groups and Leaders** starting on page 562 in **Lists** at the back of this book)

Hayes, Isaac (1942-) Black musician, songwriter. Co-wrote with Dave Porter "Hold On I'm Coming" and "Soul Man." Wrote the theme for the "**Shaft**" movies, for which he won a Grammy and an Oscar. Many musicians have copied and followed him.

head *drugs* someone who smokes dope. A **cool** person. A term used by "heads" to describe themselves; not considered derogatory, as were the previous terms from which it came, **hop head** and **pot head**. Again, the **counterculture** took a derogatory term used by others to label them and started using it as a positive. The term "head" eventually began to mean a cool person, someone who was actually smarter than the mundane, established, "**uncool**" society. Hippies more often called themselves heads than hippies.

head or **head job** *sex* **oral sex**. Cunnilingus and fellatio. Stimulation of one's sexual organ by a partner's mouth. Originally, it was used to describe an act performed upon a man, head meaning the head of the penis; Eventually it began to be used to indicate oral sex on a woman as well. Example: "She gives good **head**, he gives good **head**, they give good **head**; what a great **head job** they gave each other!"

head toilet or bathroom. Originally the name for a toilet on a ship. A British term that found expanded usage in America after the war and was then adopted by the **counterculture** in the 1960s and 70s.

headband a decorative and/or utilitarian adornment for the head. A piece of material tied horizontally around the head for the purpose of keeping sweat and hair out of one's eyes. **Native Americans** wore them as decoration, and for centuries they were a necessity for working men. The most popular headband was the old red or blue **bandanna**, yet others were strips of leather or cloth decorated with beads or artwork. During the hippie era, they be

photo by John McCleary ©

came a form of self-expression. A hippie headband often displayed the creativity of the mind wrapped within it.

headbanger a person who likes to fight.

headbangers *rock & roll* people who dance wildly while thrusting their heads in a chopping motion.

headbanging to fight or to beat up someone.

headbanging *rock & roll* thrusting one's head in a chopping motion while dancing. Associated with **heavy-metal** in the 1970s and a signature of grunge fanatics in the mid-1990s.

head case a crazy person.

headcheese smegma. The creamy residue under the foreskin of the penis. Usually considered to be a mixture of old sperm and urine. Not very appetizing stuff. The term "headcheese" as well as **"smegma"** was used to express disgust in describing all manner of things from the topping on bad pizza to a person's odor.

head drug *drugs* a **psychedelic** drug. Any drug that stimulates mental activity.

head in an uproar angry or mad. The head indicates a psychological or mental state; yet other parts of the body can be used, such as "bowels," "balls" or "ass," and, in that case, should not be taken literally. Examples: "He got his **head in an uproar** over some stupid thing she said." "Don't get your **balls in an uproar** over something you can't control."

head line in **palmistry**, the middle of the three main lines that run diagonally across the palm of the hand with fingers pointed up. Thought to reveal a person's mental state. Example: a long, clear line means self-assured; a short one means weak-willed.

head on without fear or hesitation. Example: "Meet the problem **head on**. You may get an emotional skull fracture, but at least you'll end the interminable conflict."

headphones *rock & roll* devices that clamped... oh hell, you know what headphones are, they were originally invented for radio personalities to use when recording or performing a show, so that they could hear only what was important to their parts; the same applied when used in the music industry for recording vocals under perfect sound conditions. Until the late 1960s, regular folks had to listen to music through speakers, or most often, just one speaker. With the introduction of stereophonic music in the early rock period, people would try to position their right and left speakers just perfectly in the room to obtain the best stereo sound. When **In-**

A-Gadda-Da-Vida was released in 1968, we lay on the floor and placed the speakers on either side of our head to listen to it. Around 1968, individual headphones were introduced to the general public and quickly became popular. (See: *In-A-Gadda-Da-Vida*)

headquarters a store selling **paraphernalia**, **psychedelic** posters or other items of interest to **heads**. Same as **head shop**.

head shop a store that sells drug paraphernalia, posters and **counterculture** stuff, such as **God's eyes**, **macramé** belts, **beads** and **incense**. *Groovy, man!* The term began to appear around 1967.

head shrink or **head shrinker** a psychoanalyst.

head space a person's attitude or mental state. Nonspecific as to positive or negative. Examples: "He is in a weird **head space** behind their relationship." "She's in a good **head space** since their breakup."

head space a period of time in which to think, be alone and "make some **changes**." Example: "I need some **head space** to get over her."

head thing something with emotional involvement. A relationship that has mental rather than just physical aspects.

head trip an **ego trip**. Being in a self-centered state. Example: "He's on a real **head trip** thinking he is the best guitar player in town."

healing one of those words that evolved during the hippie era from its original physical definition into wider use in the realm of mental or emotional activity. Examples: "She's worked up; she could use a **healing**." "I went to a

psychic **healing** class given by University for Man at the local junior college."

health food food that is healthy for a person. Produce that is **organically** grown and/or not sprayed with pesticide. Less processed foods, such as cereals not made with white flour and white sugar. Citrus that has not been dyed and wax polished. Not necessarily **vegetarian** exclusively, **whole food** can be free-range chickens that are not fed hormones to speed their growth or, in some cases, unfertilized eggs. This designation was created in an effort to get healthier foods on the table in an era of mass production. Started as the **consciousness** of a small segment of the population, the desire for better nutrition is an outgrowth of the hippie era, and adherents have grown, creating a small health food and whole food industry. As with many of the ideals of the hippie era, the reality of whole food has been somewhat prostituted, and until the Food and Drug Administration (FDA) sets standards, the definition of whole food will be open to broad interpretation.

heal thyself a basic, hippie-type comment about having power to take care of one's own problems, both physically and mentally.

Hearst, Patricia (Patty) (1954-) *social issues* daughter of Randolph and Catherine Hearst of the Hearst newspaper fortune. Kidnaped on February 4, 1974, by members of a group of leftist radicals calling themselves the **Symbionese Liberation Army (SLA)**. The SLA eventually demanded as much as $6 million in money and food for the poor. Randolph Hearst and family complied by paying a ransom to keep her alive, but eventually balked at some of the conflicting requests. Patty, thinking she had been abandoned by her family, became Tania and helped her captors rob a Hibernia Bank in San Francisco on April 15, 1974. She was captured by police on September 18, 1975; convicted for her part in the SLA bank robbery on March 20, 1976; and sentenced to seven years. She was freed on $1.5 million bail on November 19, 1976; returned to jail on May 15, 1978; and eventually spent a total of two years in prison for the robbery. **President Carter** commuted her sentence on January 29, 1979. (See: **Symbionese Liberation Army**)

heart compassion. Who is better for this world, a bleeding heart **liberal** or a heartless conservative?

heart line in **palmistry**, the topmost of the three main lines that run diagonally across the palm of the hand with fingers pointed up. Supposedly indicates a person's love life; splits and little lines off the main line indicate divorces and affairs of the heart.

hearts *drugs* **Dexedrine** a trademark brand of **amphetamine** in heart-shaped pills. **Uppers**.

heat the police.

*****heat** pressure or difficulty. Example: "Don't play the game if you can't take the **heat**."

heave to vomit.

heavenly blue *drugs* **morning glory seeds**, a mild **hallucinogen**.

heavily into and **heavy into** extremely interested in something or someone. Example: "Jim is **heavily into** Susan, who is **heavy into** astrology." **Heavy into** is the later, condensed evolution of the phrase. "Heavily into" was considered grammatically correct at the beginning of the 1960s, yet "heavy into" became correct along the way. The growth of language has two different directions, expansion and contraction. Expansion involves the grouping of words together into phrases or the creating of longer words to expand a thought. The contraction of our language is the process of shortening words and phrases after everyone knows their meaning.

heavy serious, thought-provoking or profound. Example: "Dr. Alpert gave a **heavy** lecture."

heavy artillery the best. The most qualified person or tool for a task. Same as **big guns**.

heavy breathing sex passionate activity or sexual **foreplay**.

heavy date a social meeting between two people in which a serious relationship is involved or sexual activity is expected.

heavy hitter someone who is influential, powerful or able to spending a lot of money.

heavy-metal *rock & roll* a form of rock and roll music that relies on extreme volume, high-intensity electric guitar, flashy costumes and dramatic stage performances. Originally coined by **William Burroughs** in his book, *Naked Lunch*, it was first voiced in music, "heavy-metal thunder," in **Steppen-**

wolf's "Born to be Wild." **Blue Cheer**, Black Sabbath, **Led Zeppelin**, **Deep Purple** and Grand Funk Railroad were the most recognized heavy-metal rock groups in the hippie era. The song believed by many to be the first heavy-metal piece was a remake of Eddie Cochran's "Summertime Blues" recorded by Blue Cheer in 1968.

heavy shit not an object, but a concept, that is powerful, serious, thought-provoking or profound. Example: "His philosophy is **heavy shit**." Shit, as always, is used for emphasis.

heavyweight a person, place or thing that is powerful, important or memorable.

photo by David Glover ©

hedonist (hedonism) someone who likes to have fun. Before and since the hippie era, dictionaries defined this word as "someone who subscribes to the doctrine that pleasure and its pursuit is the highest good and a moral duty." Hippies seldom went so far as to say that fun was a duty, but many felt that enjoying life was a sacred activity which was not only healthy to those indulging, but also enhanced and improved the environment for others around them, thus creating a better world. From the Greek word *hedone*, meaning pleasure.

heebie-jeebies an itching or uncomfortable feeling experienced during the process of **withdrawing** from drugs or quitting a habit **cold turkey**. Later, it began to mean any uncomfortable feeling or the experiencing of strange emotions.

heeled having money. From "well-heeled."

heesh *drugs* another spelling and pronunciation for **hash**. (See: **hashish**)

Hefner, Hugh (b. 1926, Chicago, Ill.) the creator and publisher of *Playboy Magazine*, which appeared in December, 1953, and grew to become the world's bestselling men's magazine. Although *Playboy* would be considered exploitive and commercial by most hippie standards, it was still an important venue for new attitudes about sex and relationships and was pivotal to America's mid-20th century **sexual revolution**. The magazine contained not only photos of naked women, but also celebrity interviews, short fiction, essays on all subjects, and book and movie reviews. Hefner lived the lifestyle portrayed in his magazine, partying with celebrities in his mansion, surrounding himself with women, and always wearing his trademark silk pajamas and smoking jacket. In the 1970s, Hefner opened Playboy Clubs, casinos, and resorts worldwide. These eventually went out of business as the world became jaded by such extravagance.

heifer a young, usually sexually attractive woman. Heifer in animal husbandry means a young, female cow.

heinie the "rear end" or **ass** of someone to whom you are attracted.

heist to steal.

hell *intensifier* a word used to give emphasis to a comment or thought.

Example: "**Hell**, I don't know what I'm saying anymore."

Hell's Angels California-based, **Harley-Davidson** motorcycle club, formed in the Fontana/San Bernadino area of California in 1950. Many club members wear a "**1%**" on their jacket or "colors," meaning that the wearer is proud to be one of a very small percentage of rebel motorcycle riders. The Hell's Angels evolved from earlier clubs like the **Boozefighters**, who were primarily World War II veterans and combat airplane crew members. In the 1960s and 70s, many people associated the hippie with motorcycle club members because of some similarities in appearance and habits, such as beards and drugs. The movie **"Easy Rider"** also contributed. The **true hippie** and the true Hell's Angel persona are as different as up and down, but the two groups were sometimes connected because of the motorcycle club's involvement in drug traffic and an appreciation of some of the same music. The partnership was always strained, as indicated by **The Rolling Stones**' concert at **Altamont** Raceway on December 6, 1969, where a group of motorcycle club members killed Meredith Hunter, an African American in the audience. It is said that Hunter pulled a gun in the crowd. (See: **Boozefighters MC**)

"hell no, we won't go!" an anti-draft, **anti-war** slogan, usually shouted at the top of the lungs by a group of 16- or 17-year-olds marching past a group of jeering 50- or 60-year-olds who wanted to send them to Vietnam to kill or be killed.

hell to pay trouble in the future. Not a new term to the hippie era by any means, it was originally a Puritan oath warning that any transgressions now would be paid for later with a sentence to hell. A common cowboy term adopted by the **counterculture**.

Helms, Chet rock and roll music promoter, head of **Family Dog** Productions, proprietor of the **Avalon Ballroom** at 1268 Sutter Street, San Francisco, California, during **Haight-Ashbury's** dominance in the music world. The Avalon Ballroom (April, 1966–November, 1968), the psychedelic epicenter of the world, was originally the Puckett Academy of Dance, built in 1911. Chet Helms converted it to a rock and roll dance hall in 1966. As one of the first and most popular psychedelic dance halls, it vied with **Bill Graham's Fillmore Auditorium** as the home of local bands, such as The **Grateful Dead**, **Jefferson Airplane**, **Moby Grape**, Bozz Scaggs, **Quicksilver Messenger Service**, **Big Brother and the Holding Company**, **Country Joe and the Fish**, **Canned Heat**, etc. It was here that **Janis Joplin** made her first public appearance with Big Brother and the Holding Company in June, 1966. The Avalon was closed because of complaints of noise in November, 1968, and was converted into a cineplex during the 1970s. The Avalon Ballroom and the concerts Chet Helms produced were considered by many to be the real hippie happening, more so than the **Fillmore Auditorium**. A friend of Janis Joplin's, Chet hitchhiked from Austin, Texas, to San Francisco with her in 1963.

helter-skelter a very old term of unknown origin meaning disorganized, or without a plan. Used in the lyrics of a **Beatles'** song that came to the attention of **Charles Manson**, an ex-con and dictatorial leader of a small commune in Southern California. When

Manson's followers, on his orders, killed actress Sharon Tate and four others in a house in the Hollywood hills, the words "helter skelter" were found written on the refrigerator in a victim's blood.

hemp *drugs* one of the most basic names for the **cannabis** or **marijuana** plant, which has been harvested throughout history for its fibrous stems to make rope and weave strong materials, such as sail cloth. Its other contribution to mankind, the medicinal and psychedelic effects, were probably discovered and utilized long before any commercial, practical uses. It is obvious that prehistoric man was originally more concerned with food than with rope. The hemp plant, along with all the other shrubbery, was more than likely sampled as potential sustenance, and thus its **psychedelic** properties must have been discovered long before its value as a clothing material or tool. (See: **marijuana**)

photo by John McCleary ©

Hendrix, Jimi (b. Nov. 27, 1942, Seattle, Wash.; d. Sept. 18, 1970, London, Eng.) *psychedelic/rock & roll* the most influential musician of the hippie era, the man for whom the term psychedelic music was coined. He has influenced all subsequent rock guitarists. Strumming "left handed," he turned a right-handed Fender Stratocaster upside down to play. He first performed under the pseudonym of Jimmy James; from the late 1950s to early 60s, he played behind **Sam Cooke, **B. B. King, Little Richard, Jackie Wilson, Ike and Tina Turner** and Wilson Pickett. In 1966, he was paired with Englishmen Noel Redding on bass and Mitch Mitchell on drums, forming the Jimi Hendrix Experience. His performance climax, the burning his guitar at the **Monterey Pop Festival**, is one of the most dramatic and lasting images in rock and roll history. His songs and performances of "Purple Haze," "The Wind Cries Mary" and Dylan's "All Along the Watchtower" are the most representative of psychedelic music. Hendrix was voted by many musicians and listeners alike as the best guitarist of all time. We are so fortunate to have had him in this world, even for a short time. For the rest of our lives, we have his music to excite us. The Jimi Hendrix Experience was inducted into the Rock and Roll Hall of Fame in 1992.

henry *drugs* **heroin**.

Henson, Jim (James) (1936-1990) puppeteer, creator of "The Muppets" marionettes/puppets. Famous for his puppets on the children's TV show "Sesame Street," produced by the Children's Television Workshop throughout the 1960 and 70s. His creations include Kermit the Frog, Miss Piggy, and Cookie Monster along with many other favorites. Henson won a Grammy in 1979 and numerous Emmy awards before his untimely death. (See: **Muppets**)

hep alternative spelling and pronunciation of **hip**, the **beatnik** term meaning up to date, or informed. The term "hep cat" is the most recognized use of this pronunciation. Hip was alternately pronounced with either the "e" or "i" sound, depending on word emphasis or regional differences. (See: **hip**)

hepatitis an inflammation of the liver, often spread by the excesses of the hippie era. During the hippie era, infectious hepatitis (transmitted orally) and serum hepatitis (transmitted by blood transfusion or needles) were the most common.

Hera in Greek mythology, the sister and wife of Zeus, queen of the gods, goddess of marriage.

herbal medicine a renaissance in natural remedies and home health care occurred during the hippie era. Many **herbs** with healing properties known since ancient times were rediscovered during the 1960s and 70s. The renewed interest in herbs and ancient health practices during the hippie era continues today. Healing herbs are called "simples."

herbal tea tea made from any number of plants, flowers and fruits; a renewed interest occurred during the hippie era.

herb (or) **herbs** *drugs* **marijuana**. (See: **marijuana**)

herbs and teas the hippie culture ventured into many new areas of food and drink and revived old remedies and concoctions for medicinal use or tactile enjoyment. Teas and herbs from older agrarian cultures were used by the hippie for a variety of medical and sensory reasons. Sensual stimulation, or **aphrodisia**, was only one of the many uses of teas and herbs. Many of them were used as **legal drugs**, such as chamomile and peppermint for insomnia and mood control. After all, **marijuana** was just a natural mood-elevating herb until the government realized that it was too effective and too hard to control for commercial sales, so they taxed it in 1937, effectively making it illegal.

"here come de judge" a definitive line from a skit by comedian Flip Wilson

Hermes in Greek mythology, the messenger of the gods, guardian of travellers, deity to herd animals and leader of the dead to the underworld. To Romans, he was Mercury; in Egypt, identified with Thoth, the god of learning.

heroin *drugs* a narcotic derivative of the opium poppy. A semisynthetic opiate *Diacetylmorphine*. Some of the many street names are **smack**, **junk**, **tar**, **skag**, **shit**, "**H**," **horse**, **Mexican brown**, **China white**, **Harry**, **Prez**, **boy**.

heroin #3 *drugs* common heroin available during the era.

heroin #4 *drugs* a pure, 98.99 percent heroin synthesized in Hong Kong, available to our soldiers in Vietnam.

herpes *sex* "creeping skin disease," another illness spread by some of the excesses of the hippie era. Often called genital herpes, it is spread through sexual intercourse. The symptoms are lesions and boils on the genitals of both males and females.

Hershey, Lewis (General) (1893-1977) head of the Selective Service System from 1941 to 1970. The guy who sent out all those draft induction letters to all those guys who died in Vietnam. "Greetings. You are hereby directed to present yourself for Armed Forces Physical Examination to...."

he-she a homosexual.

Hestia in Greek mythology, the sister of Zeus, virgin goddess of hearth, home and city.

***hey, man** or **hey** the most prevalent greeting of the era. It may seem disrespectful, but at the time it was appropriate. Similar to "Say, man."

hi-ball *drugs* **Benzedrine** or **Dexedrine** trademark brands of **amphetamine**. An **upper**.

hick someone from a farm or rural area. A naive person, unaware of sophisticated life.

hickey a red welt on the body caused by a lover's amorous sucking of the skin. Teeth are sometimes used to make the mark, thus it is sometimes called a **love bite** or **monkey bite**. It was generally considered to be an adolescent activity, not something a mature lover would do deliberately, yet accidents do happen in the heat of the moment. a.k.a. **love bite, monkey bite**. These terms were used by teenagers in the 1950s, and achieved **mainstream** use in the 1960s when the teenagers became adults.

hicksville an unsophisticated place.

hide the weenie, sausage or **salami** another euphemism for sexual intercourse. The weenie, sausage or salami represent the male phallus.

hidey hole or **hidey ho** a place to hide or stash something, often, drugs. From "hiding hole."

hi-fi short for high fidelity. Any machine that plays high-fidelity music, either radio, records or tapes. Fidelity means faithful to the original sound.

high emotionally excited by life. Happy. This word is one of the most important terms of the hippie era because it exemplifies the basic desire of the counterculture. The philosophy is that if you are happy, the world will be happy around you. It is also one of the concepts most misunderstood and maligned by straight society. Hippies were accused of **self-indulgence** and ridiculed for being naive about the harsh realities of life. In essence, the hippie culture is trying to get the rest of the world to start looking at the brighter side of life in order to turn around the negative direction now prevailing.

high *drugs* to have one's mind and emotions pleasantly elevated by drugs. Under the influence of a drug. Can indicate the effects of any drug, most often a **psychoactive**, usually **marijuana**; yet it may also describe the effects of **LSD** or natural psychedelics. Most closely related to the word **stoned,** yet similar in usage to **bombed** or **tripping.** The effects of most other drugs, such as opiates and methamphetamines, would more be described as blasted, drugged, **wasted, nodding** or **whacked out**.

high-five a handshake of greeting or celebration. Slapping palms above the head with fingers upward. Originally African American, adopted by hippies.

high-frequency often and/or with intensity. Example: "Their life consists of **high-frequency** sex and low-frequency work."

high-heel sneakers a pair of women's high-heel shoes. A sarcastic usage alluding to the sneaking around a woman might do in her fancy shoes. A song by that name was recorded in 1964 by Tommy Tucker and in 1968 by Jose Feliciano.

high on excited by something. Not a drug experience. Example: "She's **high on** life."

high place an uplifting experience. A good place to be.

highrise a new word introduced in 1961, describing the numerous, tall apartment and office buildings sprouting up at the time in cities like Los Angeles, Dallas and Miami.

high road morally proper conduct. Exemplary actions or attitude. High meaning lofty; road indicating path or direction.

high roller someone who spends a lot of money. From a term in the dice game of "craps," in which a person placing large bets is called a **high roller**.

*__high tech__ or __hi tech__ anything involving electronically advanced technology. Something that is complicated.

highwaters or **highwater pants** slacks or jeans that are too short for the prevailing style. From the observation that, if a flood comes, these pants won't get wet. a.k.a. **floods**. When someone got tired of other people laughing at his short pants, he would sometimes sew a strip of patterned material on the bottom of the pant leg to make them "hippie **cool**."

high yellow a light-skinned Black person of mixed race.

hike a long walk in the country.

Hinduism *religion* a 4,000-year-old religion embodying the traditional religious and philosophic ideals of India. It seeks freedom from materialistic life by reducing personal desires and identity. It has no central authority, no hierarchy, no divine revelation and no rigid moral code. Hinduism is complex, with many sects and contradic-

tions; for example, some sects believe that there is only one God, while others worship 330 million gods. **Reincarnation** is one of the primary beliefs of Hinduism.

*__hip__ up to date or well-informed. To know, to be in the know or to be **cool**. The root word of **hippie**. Sometimes alternately spelled **hep**. Examples: "That movie was **hip**." "He's **hip** to your lies." Many words of the hippie era evolved through previous **countercultures**, such as the **jazz** culture and **beat generation**, where hip originated. Many of these terms were less than well documented; therefore, the parentage of some words can only be guessed. This term, however, has a background story that has come from several sources. It is said that the word "hip" refers to the customary position of reclining on one's side, or hip, in order to smoke opium. There was a time in America, just around the turn of the 20th century, when opium smokers were considered to be of the intellectual class, therefore "hip."

hip huggers pants with no waist band, intended to be worn below the top of the pelvic bone, thus hugging the hip. Originally a **counterculture** creation when girls wore guys' jeans that had no waist and therefore slipped down around their hips. A style that evolved into **fashion** in the early 1970s. Often designed as **unisex** clothing, meaning that they could be worn by men or women.

hippie a member of a counterculture that began appearing in the early 1960s, which expressed a moral rejection of the established society. Derived from the word **hip**, meaning roughly "in the know," or "aware." Numerous theories abound as to the origin of this word.   One of the most credible involves the **beatniks**, who abandoned North Beach, San Francisco, to flee commercialism in the early 1960s. Many of them moved to the **Haight-Ashbury** area of San Francisco, where they were idolized and emulated by the young University of San Francisco students in the neighborhood.   The beats (the hip people) started calling these students "hippies," or younger versions of themselves.   Actually, the **counter-culture** seldom called itself hippies; it was the media and straight society who popularized the term.   Most often, we called ourselves **freaks** or **heads**.   Not until later did we begin calling ourselves hippies, and by then we were "aging hippies."   An alternate spelling seldom used by people in the know was "hippy."   (See: **freak** and **head**)

photo by John McCleary ©

hippie chick   a free-spirited, sexually liberated young woman.   There was a look and style of dress attributed to a hippie chick.   Usually, she had long, loose hair; she wore beads, no bra, and a lightweight blouse, over a long, flowing, Indian print dress above bare feet. Although current political correctness makes this term suspect in the minds of some, there was never any disrespect meant; hippie chicks were always held in great reverence.   She was well loved! "**Hippie chick**, the inspiration for all our music," says Jorma Kaukonen of the **Jefferson Airplane**.

Hippie Hill   a small rise just north of the Shepherd's Meadow in **Golden Gate Park**, San Francisco.

hippy (See: **hippie**)

hipster   a **beatnik** term for a person in the know, a **cool** person.   In the hippie era, it became a sarcastic term for someone who was out of date, stuck in the beatnik era.   Used for only a very few years at the beginning of the 1960s, unlike the term **folkie**, which still sees some use today because there is always some musician who insists on singing "Michael, Row Your Boat Ashore" or "Where Have All the Flowers Gone?"

hip style   the current popular, noncomercial mode of dress and self-decoration.   **Fashion** is created by a few people, stolen by others, and followed by many.   The hippie culture created new forms of dress and decoration; other people copied these ideas, marketed them, got credit for them, and made money selling them to other folks who bought them to be **cool**.   The progression of all **fads** and fashion is from **hip**, to **style**, and then to fashion.   Hip is the alternative creativity of a culture, style is that creativity put to use as a way of life, and fashion (fad) is style that has been marketed.

hired gun   someone who is brought in to do the dirty work. A temporary, paid professional expected to do a job and then depart.

history   out of date, gone.   Example "They were lovers, but now he's **history**."

history previous experience with someone. Can be positive or negative. Examples: "Don't talk about him that way, we have **history**." "After our **history,** I don't care if I ever see her again."

hit n. *drugs* a portion of drugs. Not a definite amount.

hit *drugs* the act of inhaling a **marijuana** cigarette. Example: "Here, take a **hit**, it's Indica."

hit a gangster word meaning to kill or a person designated to be killed. Used during the hippie era to indicate someone in disfavor. Example: "He is on my **hit** list. Next time I see him, I'll ignore him. That should piss him off."

hitch a problem. Example: "Hey, we got a **hitch** in the program. No moolah, no movie."

hitch short for **hitchhike**.

hitched married. From being hitched to a wagon like a work house. Example: "Joe wants to get **hitched**; he'll never understand the theory of mind over matrimony." Another word that came from an earlier period yet moved into **mainstream** use during the era.

photo by John McCleary ©

hitchhike or **hitchhiking** to solicit a ride in a car from a previously unknown person by standing along a street or road with a thumb extended in supplication. a.k.a. **thumb, hitch a ride**. "Etiquette for the Young Girl Traveling Alone" in Emily Post's *Tenth Edition*

Blue Book, published 1960 by Funk & Wagnall, states, "Above all, she must not be persuaded by the kindness of a stranger, whether man or woman, to get into a car to be driven to her destination."

hit it off to get along with, be attracted to or have a good experience with someone. Example: "We **hit it off** at first glance."

hit list a list of people someone wants to do something to or get something from.

hit man a person who does distasteful jobs for someone else. **2.** a person who is paid by someone to kill someone else.

hit on to proposition or flirt with someone.

hitter someone who is influential, powerful or able to spend a lot of money. Short for **heavy hitter.**

hit the pad to go home to bed.

hit the road or **hit the road, Jack** go away, **get lost**. Generally considered to have been popularized by the 1961 hit song, "Hit the Road, Jack," by **Ray Charles**.

hit up to ask for a hand out, to borrow something. To proposition someone.

hit up *drugs* to inject drugs.

Hobbit, The **(1937)** the first book in a popular series by author J. R. R. Tolkien (b. John Ronald Reuel Tolkien, Bloemfontein, South Africa, 1892; d. 1973). Between 1954-55, Tolkien also wrote three additional books in the series called The Lord of the Rings, but known as "The Hobbit Trilogy." These four books became the favorite fantasy reading of a generation of young people during the 1960s and 70s. *The Hobbit,*

The Fellowship of the Ring, The Two Towers, and *The Return of the King* were seemingly required reading for any well-educated member of the counterculture.

Ho Chi Minh (b. 1890; d. Sept. 4, 1969) the best known of many pseudonyms used by Nguyen Tat Thanh, the father of the Vietnamese communist revolution. Ho Chi Min led Vietnam through the war with Japan, its struggle for independence from France, and efforts to reunify the country during the **Vietnam War** against the Saigon Government of Vietnam and the US.

ho-dad or **ho-daddy** an outsider, an uninitiated person, a non-surfer. A surfing term.

Hoffman, Abbie (pseudonym, Spiro Igloo) (1936-1989) *social issues* a psychologist, cofounder of the Yippies, member of the **Chicago Seven** along with **Rennie Davis**, **David Dellinger**, John Froines, **Tom Hayden**, **Jerry Rubin** and Lee Weiner. The Chicago Seven were **anti-war** and peace and freedom movement leaders who were arrested and tried as co-conspirators for crossing state borders to incite to riot during the 1968 **Democratic National Convention**. Their trial was one of the most controversial examples of the shortcomings of our judicial system. Hoffman was convicted and received a five-year sentence plus a sentence for contempt of court to run concurrently. The sentence was later overturned because of Judge Hoffman's gross misconduct during the trial. Hoffman was one of the most creative, yet often unpredictable leaders of the anti-war and antigovernment movement. On Oct, 21, 1967, during a **National Mobilization Committee** demonstration, he and Jerry Rubin tried to **levitate** the Pentagon.

He wrote the book *Steal This Book* in 1971. Abbie Hoffman committed suicide in 1989. (See: **Chicago Seven, Chicago Seven Trial** and **Chicago Democratic National Convention**) (See also: **Anti-War Events, Groups and Leaders** starting on page 562 in **Lists** at the back of this book)

Hoffmann, Dr. Albert the Swiss chemist who discovered the chemical compound for **LSD** in 1938 while working for Sandoz Pharmaceuticals.

Buzz Greenberg and his 1936 flat head
photo John McCleary©

Hog a 1200cc **Harley-Davidson** Motorcycle.

hog a big car.

hog someone who takes more than their share. Someone who uses a lot of the **dope**.

hog *drugs* an obscure street name for **PCP**. (See: **PCP**)

Hog Farm (the people) a group more than a place, a state of nonsense more than a state of **being**, a group of hippies who traveled in old school buses, producing **happenings**. They were prominent at **Woodstock**, helped to start the **Rainbow Festivals** and frequented **Grateful Dead** concerts. **Hugh Romney (Wavy Gravy)** is their figurehead, if not leader, and **Ken Kesey** was a member at one time. In early

1967, Romney and a group of his friends were given some land, rent free, with an agreement that they would maintain the farm house and tend to the hogs on the property. That is how they got the name Hog Farm. Many of the members of the Hog Farm later moved to northern New Mexico near Taos. Wavy Gravy now runs Camp Winnarainbow at the Black Oak Ranch near Laytonville, California, where he conducts camps for children and adult children.

Hog Farm (the land) a commune started in early 1967 on 33 acres of land near Sunland-Tujunga north of Los Angeles. Composed of members of **Hugh Romney's** Hog Farm group mentioned above. They were given some of the land rent free for maintaining the farm house and tending to the hogs that were there. Harassed by other local citizens, they went on the road in school buses, ending up at the **Woodstock** Festival in 1969, where they helped to stage that event. Eventually, the Hog Farm moved to northern New Mexico on 14 acres of land near Taos. Hugh Romney **(Wavy Gravy)** now runs Camp Winnarainbow at the Black Oak Ranch near Laytonville, California, where he conducts camps for children and adult children. campwinnarainbow.org

ho-hum a word used to indicate boredom with a situation or subject. Example: "He was all jazzed about his

new birdcage, but it was a real **ho-hum** subject for everyone else."

hokey an unsophisticated person, place or thing.

hold to keep something safe for someone else.

holding *drugs* having drugs in one's possession. Example: "He's **holding** hash. What are you **holding**?"

hole *sex* a derogatory name for the **vagina,** or for women in general. Not a term used regularly by the **true hippie.** From the earlier term **glory hole,** which was a bit more complimentary. Hole is the precursor to the 1990s term **ho,** which is considered an extremely degrading usage. Language development is often the process of shortening words and phrases to simplify communications. Once everyone knows the meaning of the longer word or phrase, then words or letters are dropped to streamline communication. Often, a younger generation just wants to make the language or ideas more their own and therefore shortens them to do so. It's also **cool** to create cryptic words that exclude the older generation or straight society. Even cool has become "coo" in the 21st century.

holed up hiding, resting or just hanging out someplace.

Holiday, Billie (b. Eleanora Fagan McKay Holiday, 1915; d. 1959) jazz singer and songwriter. Billie Holiday grew up in deep poverty and neglect, suffering sexual abuse and circumstances leading her into prostitution by the age of 14. In 1928, she started singing in New York City nightclubs and began a slow climb to jazz greatness and a rapid descent toward self-indulgent destruction. For the next 30 years, she performed with all of the great jazz bands and musicians, creating some of the most haunting and memorable performances yet to be recorded. In the late 1930s, she recorded "Strange Fruit," which, for many, is collectively the greatest civil rights song, most memorable jazz ballad and painfully heart-wrenching piece of music ever performed. Billie spent most of 1947 in prison for heroin possession, and by the 1950s, her voice had deteriorated from drug and alcohol abuse to the point where she was merely a

whisper of her former self. Yet the debilitation of her voice only served to increase her ability to communicate emotions of pain and love lost. No one before or since has recreated the melancholy tones and tear-stained phrasing that was her style. In 1959, Holiday collapsed and was hospitalized; she was once again arrested for possession of narcotics, this time on her deathbed. Billie Holiday died on July 17, 1959, of cirrhosis of the liver at the age of 44. She is the singer against whom all other singers are measured, not by vocal quality, but emotion, not from lifestyle examples, but through charismatic suffering. Billie Holiday was inducted into the Rock and Roll Hall of Fame in 2000 as an early influence.

holistic a way of life and a theory of health that tends toward the preventive, rather than the curative disciplines. A belief that, if one eats naturally and lives naturally, one will have good health.

holistic medicine a medical theory teaching that the body can heal itself with the help of only a few simple herbs and ancient remedies. A theory based largely on preventive maintenance of the body. This is an extreme oversimplification of a very old and precise science. I could not do it justice without several pages of dissertation after several months of research.

Holly, Buddy (b. Charles Hardin Holly, September 7, 1936, Lubbock, Texas; d. February 3, 1959, near Clear Lake, Iowa) *rock & roll* considered one of the pioneers of White rock and roll. Every rock musician since Holly has been influenced by his style. The first record producer to introduce strings into rock music. His death in a plane crash with Ritchie Valens and the Big Bopper was the first rock and roll tragedy and a great loss to music. Although Holly died before the hippie era, his music had a tremendous influence on musicians of the 1960s and 70s. One of the very few songwriters whose music was recorded by **The Beatles**, who normally wrote their own songs. Because Holly was such a great innovator, one can't help but wonder what delights he would have produced in the studio during the freewheeling hippie era. Inducted into the Rock and Roll Hall of Fame in 1986.

Holy Grail originally the name of the of the cup said to have been used at the Last Supper by Jesus Christ and into which Joseph or Arimathea collected Christ's blood and sweat at the Crucifixion. In the hippie era, it came to mean any object of spiritual adulation, unquestioned importance or immeasurable value.

Holy See the name of an early San Francisco **psychedelic** light show company.

holy shit a nonspecific exclamation having nothing to do with religion or the digestive system. Example: "**Holy shit**, I better get out of here before someone gets the impression that I know what I'm talking about!"

home boy during the hippie era, it meant a Black man from the ghetto. Originally, when **Eldridge Cleaver** first used it, he meant a familiar person from his home **turf**.

hombre a strong, powerful, dangerous or influential person. From the Spanish word meaning man or businessman. Through its negative use in cowboy movies, it came to mean a threatening or violent person.

Homebrew Computer Club (HCC) *computer revolution* a computer hobbyist club formed in Menlo Park, California, in March, 1975. **Steve Wozniak (Woz)** of **Apple** was a founding member. The **Apple I** was introduced to the public at the Homebrew Computer Club in April, 1976. (See: **Computer Revolution Milestones, Companies and Leaders** starting on page 626 in **Lists** at the back of this book)

home free safe, without penalty. Example: "Shiela thinks she's **home free** just because she eats raw garlic cloves."

From the game of baseball, in which getting to home plate is the objective.

homeopathy a method of medical treatment that professes to stimulate the body's own healing processes in order to cure illnesses. Homeopathy is based on the belief that a small amount of a particular substance can cure symptoms similar to those it can cause. The word "homeopathy" is derived from the Greek "homoios," meaning similar, and "pathos," meaning suffering. The science of homeopathy was founded by German physician and chemist Dr. Samuel Hahnemann in the early 1800s. Through self-experiments, he concluded that "likes are cured by likes." During the hippie era, there was a blossoming curiosity for alternatives to the flawed and overly commercial medical profession. Many people experimented with old remedies and techniques from other cultures and discovered validity in such things as acupuncture, herbalism and homeopathy. These and numerous other forms of medical treatment are called alternative medicines by the established medical authorities and deemed outside the norm of Western culture. Many of these practices and disciplines were developed in Asia centuries ago and have since been proven, with modern testing, to be true preventive measures. The American Medical Association (AMA) and the Federal Drug Administration (FDA) fought what they called "alternative" medicine throughout the 1960s, 70s and 80s. Not until recently have some of these medical practices, such as acupuncture, been accepted as valid forms of therapy. The AMA and FDA are particularly sceptical and combative where preventative medicine is concerned. Many proven preventative measures were considered "alternative" during the hippie era, and most are still under suspicion today by the established medical profession.

home run success or scoring; it often had sexual connotations.

homo short for **homosexual**.

homophiles the name early **homosexuals** called themselves.

homophobic afraid of homosexuals. Most homophobics will argue that they are not afraid of homosexuals, but merely dislike them; yet fear is the only explanation for such hatred of **gay** people. Normally passive, homosexuals are usually not aggressive about their sexual needs. There are far more heterosexual rapes and molestations per capita than homosexual violations in relation to the number of gays. The true fear is not really of the homosexual; the fear is in self-doubt, insecurity, and the fact that the homophobic is unsure of his own sexuality.

homosexual someone who is sexually attracted to those of the same sex. This word was actually coined in Europe in the mid-1900s. A combination of Greek and Latin words, *homo*, meaning "same," and sexual, relating to "sex."

honalee high on **heroin**. Most notable use was in the 1963 **Peter, Paul and Mary** song, "Puff, the Magic Dragon," who lived in Honalee. I am not aware of the origin of this word or its relevance in this song.

honcho an important person, a leader or boss. Originally a Korean word, brought back to America by soldiers.

honey *sex* a woman's sexual favors.

honey oil *drugs* an oil made from **cannabis** and smoked like **hashish**.

honeypot *sex* a woman's **vagina**.

honky or **honkie** a derogatory name for White people. Originally used in a public forum by **H. Rap Brown** of the **Student Nonviolent Coordinating Committee (SNCC)**.

hooch alcohol. **2. marijuana**. (See: **marijuana**)

hooch or **hootch** house or place to sleep. This term came back with soldiers from Vietnam. The term was a misuse of a Vietnamese word meaning house.

hood a lawbreaker or bad person. Short for hoodlum.

hook a good idea or the defining part of something, like the memorable verse or musical riff in a song.

hook needle or bent pin used to inject narcotics.

photo by John McCleary ©

hookah a Middle Eastern **water pipe** used for smoking tobacco, **marijuana**

or **hashish**. Constructed so that the smoke is filtered through water, thus cooling it and making it less harsh. a.k.a. **hubble-bubble** or **narghile**.

hook down to grab food or beverage and consume it. Believed to come from an earlier definition of hands as "meat hooks."

*hooked addicted to something, often, but not exclusively, pertaining to drugs. Example: "Herb's **hooked** on her; she's **hooked** on the herb."

hooked up associated with someone or something. Socially, it often meant to have sex with someone.

Hooker, John Lee (b. August 22, 1920, Clarksdale, Mississippi; d. June 21, 2001) *blues, rock & roll* one of the handful of old, Black blues musicians who not only influenced rock and roll but became part of it. Hooker collaborated with many rock acts, such as **The Rolling Stones**, **Canned Heat**, **Van Morrison** and **Carlos Santana.** Inducted into the Rock and Roll Hall of Fame in 1991.

hook up to meet someone, to join someone for an activity. This term often has a sexual connotation.

hoot something funny.

hootenanny a **folk** singing party. Late 1950s early 60s activity. Some were privately created at home, and others, commercially produced on TV.

hooter a **marijuana** cigarette. Often indicates a large one.

hooters large female breasts. Normally a sarcastic, mostly humorous commentary directed at someone whom the speaker does not respect.

hop a dance. A 1950s term, adopted into the 1960s. There is some support

to the suggestion that at one time it stood for "house of prostitution."

hop *drugs* **opium**. Most likely from the belief that it "hops you up." In actuality, opium has a mellowing effect.

hope to die a term affirming one's convictions. Swearing that one is telling the truth. Example: "**Hope to die**, that girl is a guy."

hop head *drugs* a drug user. Used primarily in the 1950s, but did make it into the 1960s. **Pot head** is a derivative; the final derivation is just **head**. (See: **head**)

hopped up *drugs* excited or energized, usually related to a drug-induced state.

Hopper, Dennis (1936-) actor, director, photographer and cultural example. He co-wrote and directed **"Easy Rider,"** the 1969 independent movie breakthrough. It announced to the Hollywood establishment that the public was ready for low-budget, socially conscious films. Hopper is versatile actor, director, and writer, and a poignant photographer. (See: **"Easy Rider"**)

horizontal lying down or reclining. Asleep, drunk or under the influence of drugs. Example: "He's **horizontal** by this time of the day; the bars have been open for two hours already."

horizontal bop, **horizontal dance** or **horizontal rumble** *sex* copulation, the sex act.

horns *sex* short for **horny**. Example: "I look at her and I get **horns**."

horny *sex* sexually attracted or stimulated.

horoscope a picture or chart showing the location of planets and star constellations in the sky on someone's birthdate. Their positions are analyzed to determine one's personality traits and, in some cases, destiny. Analyzing and reading horoscopes is done by astrologers, who often have many hours of education and a good knowledge of mathematics. However, the reading of horoscopes, astrology as it is called, is considered a pseudo-science, unlike the science of astronomy. (See: **astrology**)

horrific terrible or traumatic. A combination of the words horrible and terrific.

horror show something ugly, uncomfortable or traumatic. A sarcastic commentary on something embarrassing.

horse *drugs* **heroin**.

horsed up *drugs* high on **heroin**.

horse shit an accusation of untruth. An exclamation that does not literally concern the scatology of domestic animals. Example: "You say you love me, but that's **horse shit**; you love being in love."

Horus a sun and war god of ancient Egypt, son of Osiris and Isis.

hose to have sexual intercourse.

hoser an unpleasant person. Not normally used in a sexual way, but merely as a derogatory term.

hoss a term of endearment for a close friend. From the name of the big, lovable personality on the TV series, "Bonanza." Considered a shortening of the word horse.

*hot good, excellent or exciting. Used often in a sexual context. Example: "She's **hot**."

hot and cold *drugs* a mixture of **heroin** and **cocaine**.

hot button a topic or subject of interest or concern. Example: "His **hot button** is water purification; don't let him catch you urinating upstream."

hot dog or **hot dogger** someone who behaves outrageously to attract attention. A showoff. Surfer term.

hot for attracted to someone. Example: "I don't care if she is a nark, I'm **hot for** this girl."

hot pants women's short, tight pants that appeared on the scene in 1971. Similar to short shorts of the 1950s, hot pants were associated with go-go dancing and the disco dance craze. They were often made of satin and were so tight and short that they revealed a little "pooch" of the butt. A **style** sometimes worn by **gay** men.

hot pants *sex* sexually attracted or **turned on** by someone. Example: "Give it up, she's got **hot pants** for Dobro."

hots, the *sex* the desire for someone or something, most often sexual. Example: "Give it up, she's got the **hots** for another girl."

hotshot an important person, or, sarcastically, someone who thinks he is important.

hot shot a lethal injection of drugs.

hot spot an exciting place.

hot to trot *sex* ready to make love. **2.** in a nonsexual context, ready to do anything, excited about something.

hound to bother someone, to follow or stalk. From the way bloodhounds track their prey.

hound an obsessive person. Example: "Sissy is a real caffeine **hound**."

House Un-American Activities Committee, The (HUAC) or **House Committee on Un-American Activities** *social issues* a congressional committee concerned with perceived anti-American activities and with the involvement of the Communist Party in America. It was active more or less between the years of 1934 to 1977. The government body that investigated the movie industry in 1947.

how bizarre! an exclamation of disapproval. (See: **bizarre**)

how's about a colloquialism for "how about." Most likely of African American origin.

how's it hanging? or **how's it hangin'?** a greeting. Related to how a man's scrotum is hanging, yet it doesn't actually indicate concern for that specific part of his anatomy; it's just a general greeting.

how's your mama? a derogatory greeting implying that the person giving the greeting has **carnal knowledge** of your mother.

how's your yang? a humorous hippie greeting, meaning roughly, how is your dick, or how is your manhood? From the Chinese term **yang,** meaning the male force of the universe.

huaraches Mexican sandals, usually made with leather tops and rubber tire soles; a popular footwear for surfers and the class-unconscious hippie.

hubble-bubble *drugs* a **water pipe** used for smoking tobacco or **cannabis** in any of its forms. Usually associated with Afghanistan and British colonial times. The same as a **hookah** or **narghile**.

huddle a conference or secret conversation.

huelga Spanish word for strike. The word shouted by **César Chávez's** farm workers as they demonstrated against the grape and lettuce growers. (See: **Chávez** in alphabetical listings) (See also: **Native American and other Minority Rights Events, Groups and Leaders** starting on page 609 in **Lists** at the back of this book)

huevos guts, masculinity, balls. Spanish slang word for testicles, which actually means eggs in that language.

Huey nickname for the military helicopter used primarily during the **Vietnam War**.

huff to **snort** drugs.

huh? what did you say? Should be uttered with a question in the voice.

"Hullabaloo" *rock & roll* a rock and roll TV show that debuted in January, 1965, and lasted only a year and a half. "Hullabaloo," an NBC product, was much like **"Shindig,"** the earlier ABC rendition of the same format. "Hullabaloo" featured the Hullabaloo Dancers and The Peter Matz Orchestra, which was "The Carol Burnett Show" band. Different guest hosts were used each week for this show. On the first few one-hour shows, Brian Epstein, **The Beatles'** manager, introduced new British acts in black and white segments; the rest of the show was in color. Other music and dance shows followed, such as "Hollywood-a-Go-Go," **"Soul Train,"** "Where The Action Is" and "Happenin' 68," which was filmed on the beach. All the TV music shows of the era experimented with different formats, some live, some pre-taped, some with professional dancers, some with non-professional audience members dancing, some live music, some with guest artists **lip-synching** their hit songs. Many videos of 1960s performers come from these TV series. **"American Bandstand"** was considered different since it was a daytime show. (See: **"American Bandstand," "Ready, Steady, Go!," "Shindig," "Soul Train."**)

Human Be-in and Gathering of the Tribes Saturday, January 14, 1967, on the Polo Fields of **Golden Gate Park**, San Francisco. Promoted as "A Gathering of the Tribes for a Human Be-In...A Pow-Wow and Peace Dance To Be Celebrated with the Leaders of Our Generation." An outgrowth of the Free Fairs produced by the **Artists' Liberation Front** and the free, outdoor **Trips Festivals**. The beginning of the "year of love," in which the **Summer of Love** fell. Some say it was also held in observance of the day **LSD** became illegal in California. **The Grateful Dead** played. Present were **Jerry Rubin**, **Timothy Leary**, **Richard Alpert**, **Gary Snyder**, **Allen Ginsberg** and as many as 50,000 other people.

humanistic philosophy and **humanistic religion (also called humanism)** *religion* a philosophy and way of life based on the belief that humans are the center of the universe, and what is good for them is the higher good. Most often considered anti-Christian since it incorporates elements of hedonism, believing that indulgence in sex, drugs and rock & roll should be by individual choice. Sometimes practiced with a disregard for other living animals, which can be a drawback to the philosophy. During the hippie era, humanism was adopted by many people. When the additional belief that all forms of life are sacred is added to humanism, one finds the basic philosophy of the **true hippie**.

hum job *sex* oral sex. A blow job. a.k.a. **blow job, head job, head**.

hummer something good. Comes from "hum dinger." Example: "You haven't seen her yet; she's a real **hummer**."

humungous big or important. A combination of the words huge and tremendous.

hump *sex* to copulate. Really a very old usage, but a much used term during the hippie era.

hump or **hump on** to move quickly. Examples: "Come on now, **hump**, we got to get this job done." "Speed it up now, get a **hump on**."

hung having a large penis. Example: "She says he is no good, but she stays with him 'cause he's **hung**."

hung tired. Examples: "I can't make it tonight; I'm **hung**."

hung out or **hung out to dry** abandoned, forgotten or incriminated. Examples: "Nadine put the key in the mail slot and left me **hung out** in the cold." "When The Man came in the front, Jake went out the back and left me **hung out to dry** with the stash." "She got arrested and told the fuzz a story that **hung me out**."

hungry in need of money. **2.** in need or want, not always having to do with food.

hung up on to have a psychological obstacle to something or an obsession for someone or something. Examples: (obstacle) "Dot's **hung up on** sex. She thinks her father's hiding under the bed." (obsession) "George is **hung up on** hygiene 'cause he was raised in an Airstream trailer with five brothers and sisters."

hunk a man with a muscular body.

hunky-fucking-dory a silly exclamation coming from the obscure term hunky-dory. The "fucking" is added only for emphasis. Hunky-dory is an old term meaning OK or all right.

hurl to vomit.

hurtin' or **hurting** psychologically bothered by something. Often, it relates to jealousy. Example: "She left him and he's **hurtin'**." Can also refer to physical pain.

hurtin' for certain psychologically bothered by something. Same as **hurtin'** with "for certain" added as emphasis.

hustle to move quickly. Example: "Let's **hustle** out of here."

hustle a **con**. An elaborate scheme designed to fool someone or take their money.

hustler someone who talks people out of their money. A talker. A man who talks girls into sex.

Huston Plan *politics* an attempt by the **Nixon** administration to coordinate and control all of the policing agencies in the country, such as the FBI, CIA, National Security Agency, local police forces, and the armed forces, to spy on **anti-war**, **civil rights** and **liberal** political individuals and organizations. It suggested that the White House direct all investigations of what it considered political dissidents. Wiretaps, break-ins, mail-openings and other dirty tricks were used. The objective of this intelligence gathering was to obtain information for use in disrupting and discrediting these individuals and organizations. The Huston Plan was never officially instituted, but many civil rights violations, such as the **Watergate break-in**, were conducted for its purposes during the Nixon administration. The Huston Plan was similar to Operation Gemstone, which created the **plumbers**, who conducted the Watergate break-in. Tom Charles Huston, the author of the Huston Spy Plan, was a Nixon White House aide. (See: **Plumbers, Watergate,** and **dirty tricks** in alphabetic listings) (See also: **Nixon Administration Members Involved in the Watergate Break-in and Cover Up Conspiracy** starting on page 582 in **Lists** at the back of this book)

Huxley, Aldous (1894-1963) British psychologist, educated at Eaton and Oxford, migrated to California in 1935. In the 1950s, Huxley became a proponent of **psychedelics** as a means to liberate and expand the mind and wrote *Doors of Perception* (1954) and *Heaven and Hell* (1956). He greatly influenced **Timothy Leary** and **Richard Alpert** in their research into **altered states of consciousness**. His books, *Doors of Perception, Brave New World* (1932) and *Island* (1962), were all important literature in the creation of the 1960s **counterculture** philosophy.

hype a lie, a **con**, an exaggeration used to sell something. From the word hyperbole. Around 1970, this word surfaced in business and industry, describing public relations and advertising campaigns for products.

hyper or **hyped up** overactive.

hypo a needle used to inject drugs. Short for hypodermic.

hypocrite what most hippies call straight people. Someone who is too insecure in the purity of their soul to be able to indulge in simple, decadent enjoyment, without first ridiculing it and afterward denying it.

I

I (pronounced "E") in Chinese philosophical terminology, **I** is the One, engendered by **Tao** and which engenders the Two (the **yin** and **yang**). One of the four Confucian fundamentals. The virtue "by which things are made proper...by which the world is regulated."

"I Am the Walrus" or **The Walrus** a song written by The Beatles' **John Lennon** and featured on the "Magical Mystery Tour" sound track in 1967. **Paul McCartney** was reportedly the walrus on the *Magical Mystery Tour* album cover artwork. The song, which was one of **The Beatles'** most psychedelic and bizarre, was written several days after the suicide of their manager, Brian Epstein.

Ian and Sylvia *music/folk/country* Ian Tyson and Sylvia Fricker Tyson; singer/songwriters important to the folk revival of the early 1960s and contributors to the process of bringing folk, country and rock together into a pleasant mix in the late 1960s and early 1970s.

I can dig it I understand, I agree.

I Ching: Book of Changes the classic of change, at one time considered one of the five disciplines of Confucius, but now thought to be much older. A Chinese collection of propositions and explanations used in **divination**, written by various authors of different periods up to the latter part of the third century B.C. A ritual used to make decisions for the future by reading one of 64 messages. Each message is represented by one of 64 hexagrams; each hexagram is composed of six groups of three broken or unbroken lines, **yin** lines and **yang** lines. Each hexagram has a specific written answer to a question asked about one's future. Originally, the hexagrams were chosen by throwing 49 yarrow sticks and interpreting them. Another description of the process tells of six sticks that can fall in 64 different configurations. During the 1960s

I Ching coins

and 1970s, hippies used three coins to choose the hexagrams. The heads and tails of the coins determined each line in the hexagram.

ice or **iced** v. to kill or defeat. Examples: "If he doesn't stop spilling the **tamari** sauce, I'm going to **ice** him." "We **iced** them in a pickup basketball game." Coming from to cool someone down or to make them cold.

ice *drugs* illegal drug synthesized from **methamphetamine**. An **upper**.

ice cream *drugs* **opium**.

ice cream dynamite. A **Weathermen** term as described by **Bill Ayers** in his 2001 book *Fugitive Days: a memoir,* published by Beacon Press. On March 1, 1971, the Weather Underground planted a package of **ice cream** at the **"Big Top";** the resulting explosion blew a door off its hinges, broke some windows, injured no one, but made a statement. (See: **Bill Ayers, ice cream** and **Weathermen**)

iceman a man who is **cool** under fire, unemotional, possibly dangerous.

ice pack *drugs* strong **marijuana**, said to be more powerful because it was aged in dry ice.

ice queen or **ice maiden** a woman who is unreachable, either emotionally or sexually.

id in Freudian theory, the unconscious part of the psyche associated with purely instinctual needs and drives. The sexual drive is a primary function of the id, and the energy that comes from it is called the **libido**. Contrary to the beliefs of many people who had no contact with them, hippies were, on the whole, very well read, intelligent people. Freudian theory was within the realm of understanding of many members of the **counterculture**. Hippies were particularly familiar with the theory of the id's existence because it tended to prove that sex is a natural body function and should be accepted as such by society. (See: **libido**)

I.D. n. an official card, usually a driver's license, identifying someone and verifying their age for the purpose of purchasing or consuming alcohol. An abbreviation for identification.

I.D. v. to identify someone or something. Example: "I can **I.D.** his dope with just one toke."

identity crisis confusion that challenges one's opinion of oneself. Usually caused by a disturbing episode in one's life. Example: "Bruce had a one-night stand with a girl for a change, and now he's having an **identity crisis**."

*****idiot box** the television. Need I say more?

iffy doubtful or uncertain. Example: "Gooch thinks he'll walk on water in the **fashion** industry, but his chances are **iffy** wearing those pink boots."

-ific *suffix* a suffix, originally from the word terrific, added to another word to form a new adjective. Examples: "magnific, drugific, horrific, beutific."

IFIF (See: **International Foundation for Internal Freedom**)

"if the van's rockin', don't come knockin'" *sex* if the van is rockin', don't bother us. Originally a bumper sticker for Volkswagen buses or van type vehicles. It obviously inferred that there might be someone inside making love, so don't disturb.

I hate it when that happens a humorous understatement uttered when something unpleasant happens. A common phrase used on the "**Saturday Night Live**" TV show whenever something horrendous occurred.

"I have a dream" *social issues* the most famous line from **Dr. Martin Luther King, Jr.'s**, most noted speech, on the Mall in Washington, DC, on August 28, 1963, before 200,000 people. An excerpt from the text: "I have a dream that my four little children will one day live in a nation where they will not be judged by the color of their skin, but by the content of their character."

I hear ya' I hear you and I understand you. This simple comment often carried more meaning than the mere acknowledgment of someone's words, but also indicated agreement and approval. Often emphasized by the addition of **bro** or **brother**. Example: "**I hear ya'**, bro'."

I kid you not it's the truth, I'm telling you the truth. A term believed to have originated with Jack Paar, the original host of **"The Tonight Show."**

illegitimati non carborundum Latin don't let the bastards grind you down. A humorous and sarcastic jab at the use of the Latin language as a status symbol. *Illegitimati* refers to "bastard" and *carborundum* is a sandy "grinding" substance.

Illinois green *drugs* **marijuana** supposedly from Illinois, also called Chicago green. I say supposedly, since in the dope selling business, one never spoiled a good story with the truth.

"Imagine" a song written by **John Lennon** and published on his *Imagine* album in 1971. It could possibly be the most important song written in the last 100 years. The importance of this song is that it proposes the dissolution of boundaries of countries, and suggests that religion will be gone in the future. Considering that the sovereignty of countries and the conflicts of religions are the causes of most of the strife in the world, this is a suggestion supported by most true hippies. Understandably, it is not much appreciated by political and religious leaders.

I'm Black and I'm Proud *social issues* lyrics from a 1968 song by James Brown.

*I mean... like... you know an expression meaning loosely, "I don't know how to say it, but you understand my thoughts and feelings, don't you?!" An unnecessary phrase used for emphasis in lieu of a coherent sentence or just a pause in a stony conversation to gain time to think about what to say next. Such non-sentences can be composed in various configurations, such as "I mean, like, you know" or "you know, like, I mean." The concept of such an utterance was actually a product of the 1950s beat movement, but it was used more frequently in the 1960s. This particular phrase, along with its various components, "you know," "like," and "I mean," dominated our language and still do to this day. If you don't believe this, start counting the number of times in a conversation "like," "you know" and "I mean" are said. What is strange about these exclamations is that, even though they have no real bearing on the conversation, they indicate a desire, newfound during this era, to communicate with clarity and understanding. When a person punctuates a sentence with "you know," "like," or "I mean," they are, in essence, making sure that the listener is paying attention and understands what is being said.

I'm hip I understand. Example: "**I'm hip** to what you're saying even though you're too stoned to verbalize."

"I'm the guy your mother warned you about!" a humorous commentary on one's own dubious status. It has sexual connotations, implying that the speaker will seduce young girls and lead impressionables astray.

*in popular or stylish. From the phrase "in **style**" or "on the inside." Example: "Being in therapy used to be the **in**

thing; now taking drugs for your troubles is **in**."

-in a hyphenated suffix identifying a gathering or group experience. Most often associated with an event of **anti-establishment** activity or rebellion. Examples: **be-in, laugh-in, love-in**. Came originally from **sit-in**; possible new usage might be rap-in or mall-in.

in a bad way in uncomfortable circumstances. Example: "Kathy's **in a bad way** with her ol' man after dropping all that **windowpane** on the shag rug."

in a big way greatly, extensively. Example: "Steve fell for Jim **in a big way**."

in a bind having a desperate need. Originally, it meant a financial need, coming possibly from money being **tight** or being in a money squeeze. During the hippie era, it took on broader meanings, including having a drug habit. Example: "Slick's **in a bind**; he hasn't scored in three days."

in a funk depressed or in a bad mood. The older, **beatnik** term was "in a blue funk." In this usage, **funk** has a different meaning than the root word "funk," as in funky. For this use, funk must be proceeded by "in a," to produce a negative.

"In-A-Gadda-Da-Vida" *psychedelic/ rock & roll* (See: **Iron Butterfly**)

in and out another euphemism for sexual intercourse. It is interesting how people reveal their feelings about the act through the words they choose to describe it. This description reduces it to a purely aerobic activity.

in a sling (one's ass or dick) in trouble. To have one's **dick** in a sling often indicates sexual misadventure or unrequited love. Examples: "Flash lost his job, and his **ass is in a sling** 'cause he

can't pay rent on his **crib**." "Jonathan's dick is **in a sling** over his girlfriend's little sister."

in a sweat worried about something. Example: "Jake is **in a sweat** about not paying his taxes, but he's also worried they won't catch him and put him in jail for his lofty political convictions."

in a zone in a good spot or performing well. An automatic state of perfection. A zone is sometimes considered a supernatural or spiritual place. Example: "Alvin was **in a zone**; he baptized every single fireplug on our walk today."

incarnation life in a physical body. Carnate means physical body.

incense a substance that, when burned, emits fragrant smoke to delight the sense of smell. Incense was one of the gifts said to have been given by the Wise Men to the newborn Jesus. It has been used in the worship ceremonies of many major religions. The Catholic Church, Greek and Russian Orthodox Churches, and many Eastern religions burn incense. Hippies adopted incense because of its place in Eastern religions and also because it could mask the scent of **marijuana**.

in deep shit in bad trouble.

Indian hay or **Indian hemp** another name for **marijuana**. Much of the early marijuana originated in India. (See: **marijuana**)

Indica a particularly good **marijuana** strain that originated in India. Indica seeds were planted in many places in the United States and Mexico and became one of the most sought after **smokes** of the discerning hippie.

Indra the god of war, storms, atmosphere, sky and fertility in **Vedic Hinduism** of approximately 500 B.C.

in drag a man dressed as a woman. This does not automatically indicate **homosexual** tendencies since some heterosexual men enjoy dressing in women's clothing as a heterosexual thrill.

in (one's) **face** confrontational. From the practice of getting up close and in someone's face when arguing. Examples: "Serene got **in my face** about the dishes. Trucker was **in Bob's face** about the bathroom. We are a bunch of **in-your-face** roommates."

infinite completely free of limitations. Example: "We live in an **infinite** universe of grandiose proclamations." Obviously, not a new word to the hippie era; yet, since that period of time was an intellectual renaissance compared with the 1950s, this term found renewed usage.

infinity an endless extent of space and time. Another term that found renewed usage during the hippie era.

infuckingcredible an exclamation of appreciation. A combination of the words "incredible" and "fucking." The profanity was used merely to emphasize the word incredible.

inhalers *drugs* substances whose fumes create a narcotic experience when inhaled. Airplane glue and aerosol can gas are two examples. Warning: Most of these are extremely dangerous and should not be experimented with by anyone who wishes to live a long, happy and productive life.

in like Flynn to be successful in something, often a seduction. I believe it came from a mythical Irishman by the name of Flynn, who seduced many women and was the basis for many sexual jokes. May also refer to Errol Flynn, who was a great seducer. Example: "Bob met her and he was **in like Flynn**."

Inner Light in the terminology of the Society of Friends (**Quakers**), the capacity, inherent in all men, to listen to God speaking to their souls, to effect spiritual contact with God, and to understand and share that spiritual experience.

inner man *occult* in **occult** terminology, the immortal **essence** of man or his higher ego. Some men reading this will hear "immortal" and "ego" and think of living forever in their selfish bodies. Yet immortality is never about "you," it is about "your inner beauty" surviving this garbage dump we have made of life. And ego is not about how many chicks you can seduce in competition with every other man, but the recognition of your own individuality.

inner space inside one's mind. It is believed that inner space is at least as big as outer space because thoughts can stimulate huge areas of imagination.

in orbit or **into orbit** extremely angry. Most likely from the term "to explode" with anger, thus going into orbit. Could also emanate from the phrase "to the moon, Alice!" uttered by Jackie Gleason's character Ralph Kramden on the TV show "The Honeymooners." A later term, "go ballistic," was derived from into orbit.

in power having an advantage. Possessing the drugs.

input information entered into a computer. Information given to a person.

insane an intensifier of approval. As opposed to the original meaning describing mental instability, during the hippie era, insane was often used as a positive, meaning something was wonderful. Examples: "Jimi was an **insane** guitar player." "**Monterey Pop** was an **insane** party."

insider someone who knows what is happening. A person who is within the circle of information.

inspired or **inspiration** the state of being psychically receptive to spiritual influences or creative ideas.

instant karma a situation in which someone is immediately rewarded or penalized for an action. (See: **karma**)

instant replay the repetition of something. Originally a TV sports term indicating the replaying of a portion of the action to entertain the fans or to assist the referees in making a decision. In the hippie era, it became a term associated with everyday experiences.

instant zen a term used to describe **LSD**. From the belief that LSD **elevates** a person to a religious state of **consciousness**. A term, I believe, coined by **Dr. Richard Alpert**, a.k.a. **Baba Ram Dass**, a philosophy professor at Harvard in the 1960s, when he began research into consciousness with **Timothy Leary**, **Aldous Huxley**, and **Alan Watts**. Their research included studying the effect on humans of LSD and other drugs. In 1967, Alpert went to India in search of drug-free enlightenment and became a follower of the late Indian guru, Neem Karoli Baba. Neem Karoli Baba gave Alpert the name Ram Dass, which means servant of god. In 1971, Baba Ram Dass wrote **Be Here Now**, a very popular book that helped to define the spiritual philosophy for many young people of the time.

in sync of one mind with someone. In agreement. Sync is short for synchronization.

integrated circuitry *computer revolution* silicon-encased electronic wiring, which replaced transistors as the switching elements in computers in the 1960s. This allowed for the miniaturization of computers and the reduction of their cost, which led to the personal computer. The concept was conceived in 1959 by Robert Noyce, the eventual founder of Intel. A **silicon chip** is the smallest element and is in essence an integrated circuit itself.

integration mandated or voluntary mixing of races within institutions or organizations. One of the most important accomplishments of the hippie era, it was the true great success of the **civil rights** movement. The integration of schools, housing and public transportation gave our society a more civilized appearance; however, true racial understanding and tolerance have yet to be realized. Two of the first major laws pertaining to integration were: The Civil Rights Act of 1964, passed by Congress, prohibited discrimination on the basis of race in employment, public accommodations, publicly owned facilities, union membership, and federally funded programs. The Civil Rights Act of 1968, passed by Congress, included a fair-housing provision and protection for civil rights workers from intimidation or injury. (**See: Civil Rights Events, Groups and Leaders** starting on page 546 in **Lists** at the back of this book)

intellectual a profound thinker. Someone who thinks about important things. (Not what to have for dinner or which TV show to watch, but about life and the world!) A person thinking about such things will soon come to several conclusions. First, they will realize that there are a number of inequities in this world, and these create most of the strife in our lives. The most obvious problem is poverty and the struggle to survive, experienced by much of the world's population. Eventually, thinking about poverty and wealth, an intellectual comes to the conclusion that *poverty* is not *the* problem, distribution of *wealth* is *the* problem. Poor people have no control over their poverty; wealthy people have control over the poverty of the poor. If the poor had the control, they wouldn't be poor. The second obvious inequity is religion, not the lack of religion, but the existence of too much religion and too many religious leaders who have conflicting ideas of what religion is. Religion itself is not bad; the people who use it as a weapon are bad. Wealth is not bad; it is the wealthy who support poverty who are bad. Education is the way out of poverty and the way to combat misguided religion. Intellectuals are trying to tell us everything we will need to make up our own minds about changing the world for the better. Information is a good thing; hug an intellectual today.

*intense moving, thought-provoking. One of those words that appeared to mean what it has always meant, but which took on a deeper emotional, psychological, almost cosmic meaning during the hippie era. Example: "His speech was **intense**, man." Often considered a **Valley Girl, Valley talk** term, yet it was an earlier beat introduction.

interface *computer revolution* the ability of two or more computers to communicate with each other. The term and concept was introduced to the American public in 1966. Since then, the word has evolved into use indicating human interpersonal communication as well.

International Foundation for Internal Freedom (IFIF) started in 1962 by the Harvard Research Group of **Timothy Leary** and **Richard Alpert**, to experiment with drugs and **consciousness**. An organization dedicated to the freedom to take drugs if one wished. The premise was to conduct psychedelic **"brain change"** sessions, during which volunteers could expand consciousness in a safe, controlled environment. It eventually manifested into an effort to create a **Utopian** community in Zihuatanejo, Mexico. The Mexican authorities did not agree with the ideals of Leary and his followers and expelled them shortly after their arrival.

photo by John McCleary ©

International Society for Krishna Consciousness *religion* also known as **Hare Krishna** or the Krishna movement. A **Hindu** offshoot sect started by A. C. Bhaktivedanta around 1965, which became popular in America in 1968. It has no direct counterpart in India. Krishna has compounds in West Virginia and groups living in every major city in America and many countries of the world. Disciples are called Hare Krishnas and are often seen chanting "Hare Krishna, Hare Krishna, Krishna Krishna, Hare Hare." The chant comes from the **Sanskrit** prayer "Hare Krishna" (hail, Krishna). Hare Krishnas wear pale orange robes, and the men have partially shaved heads. They sell books, flowers and incense at airports and other public places and have become the brunt of many jokes about this activity.

in the bag a forgone conclusion. A guaranteed result. Example: "Don't worry, that job is **in the bag**."

in the buff nude. Again, this term was not new to the hippie era; it just gained a greater following during that time.

in the groove doing the right thing, good at something. Example: "He's **in the groove** on that song." An old **jazz** and **beatnik** term that came into wider use during the hippie era. From the needle on a record player being "in the groove" of a record. The predecessor of **groovy**.

in the hole in debt. Example: "We played poker last night, and I'm **in the hole** to her for two socks and a pair of underpants."

in the know informed. Sometimes used to describe a person who "knows important people."

in the loop informed. Within the circle of activities and information. Important enough to receive the information.

in the raw nude or naked.

in the saddle another euphemism for having sex. Male usage only, since being between the legs of a woman was somehow reminiscent of being in a horse's saddle. Example: "I'm tired! I was **in the saddle** most of the night."

in there a successful attempt or seduction. Examples: "You're **in there,** man, you got the job." "Reef went by her house, and he was **in there** in no time."

in the tank a failure or disaster. From "to throw something into the toilet."

*into involved in, interested in. Examples: "What are you **into**?" "She's **into** books."

into something involved in a mysterious or questionable activity. Examples: "He's **into something,** judging by the bat wings and grasshoppers in his refrigerator."

intrauterine device (IUD) a common form of **birth control** used by women in the 1960s and 70s. A term introduced to the American public in 1966. A plastic or copper implant, placed in the uterus by a doctor, designed to remain for an indefinite period of time. Some of these devices disrupted the attachment of the egg to the wall of the uterus, and some of them, because of their copper content, changed the user's chemical balance, thus interrupting fertilization. Among the devices of the era were the Lippes Loop, Dalkon Shield and Marguiles Coil. Intrauterine devices were originally used in the late 19th century as remedies for various female medical problems, including infertility. It was soon discovered that many of them actually caused infertility. Medical techniques changed at the turn of the century, and such devices were discontinued until the IUD was reinvented in the 1950s, specifically for birth control. The pregnancy rate of IUDs was 3 per 100 women per year. IUDs eventually became unpopular due to problems with hemorrhaging and toxic shock syndrome.

intro an introduction. Example: "You know that girl I saw you with at the flag burning? Suppose you could do an **intro**?"

intuition foreseeing something one does not know through information or experience. The ability to know facts that are not available by the normal reasoning processes.

in your face or **in** (someone's) **face** pushy, belligerent. Up close and aggressive. Example: "He's the kind of boss who's **in your face** all the time, and I won't take that for minimum wage."

Iron Butterfly *psychedelic/rock & roll* a one-hit-wonder band of the **acid rock** era formed in 1966 in San Diego, California. Band members were Doug Ingle, Ron Bushy, Jerry Penrod and Danny Weis. Though they did have some other successes in their short life, their "**In-A-Gadda-Da-Vida**" is considered the primary psychedelic song of the era. (Unsubstantiated, the name has been reported to mean "In the Garden of Eden" or to relate to the *Bhagavad Gita*, the Hindu epic poem.) The song was written by Doug Ingle and released in 1968, becoming their only hit. The song is 17 minutes long and features a 2 1/2-minute drum solo. In the days before **headphones** became popular with the public, this song was sometimes played at maximum volume through full-sized speakers placed on either side of the head.

iron maiden a sober, strict, dominant, often celibate woman. Iron in this context relates to strength, but it also conjures up the vision of a metal chastity belt.

Ishtar a Babylonian goddess, associated with fertility rites, death and res-urrection. One of the primary of the many goddesses worshipped in various forms throughout the ancient world, also known as Astarte by the Phoenicians and Ashtoreth to the Hebrews. A hippie name given to some children during the era.

Isis wife of the Egyptian god Osiris, she was the greatest of all goddesses of ancient Egypt, "the Great Enchantress, the Mistress of Magic, the Speaker of Spells."

Isla Vista, California *social issues* the housing community adjacent to the **University of California, Santa Barbara (UCSB)**, campus. The location of the February, 1970, student **free-speech** and **anti-war** demonstrations and burning of the Bank of America branch.

Islam *religion* in Arabic, it means "to submit." A religion of submission to the will of God, founded by **Mohammed** (approximately 570-632 A.D.). Its teachings are derived from the revelations received by Mohammed from God. Followers worship **Allah**, whom they believe is the one God of all religions, including Christianity and **Judaism**. Believers of Islam are called **Muslims**, and they follow the teachings of the Qur'an (**Koran**). Islam in religious context means "submission to the will of God," and the fundamental belief is that "there is only one God, and Mohammed is his Prophet." Muslims must pray five times a day, abstain from pork and alcohol, and give to the poor. All believers are expected to make a pilgrimage to **Mecca**, Mohammed's birthplace, at least once in their lifetime. Islam's chief commandments are: profession of faith, ritual prayer, the payment of the alms tax, fasting and the pilgrimage. It has no real clerical caste, no church organization or liturgy, and rejects monasticism. The Islamic ascetic attitude is expressed in praise of manual labor and poverty, warnings about female sexuality and prohibition against nudity. Extravagant buildings other than houses of worship are also forbidden. Islam has restrictions against economic speculation, music, wine, pork, and artistic reproductions of living beings. According to their teachings as well as those of the Jewish bible (Torah), the Muslims and Jews originally came from the same family, with one brother practicing Islam and the other, Judaism. (See: **Mohammed** and **Mecca**)

issues topics, problems or confrontations. Example: "Our relationship ended badly; we had some **issues** we could never resolve."

is that so? a sarcastic exclamation of disbelief or defiance.

it *sex* sexual intercourse. Example: "Let's do **it,** birds do **it**, bees do **it**."

it ain't over till the fat lady sings just wait, don't be so anxious to celebrate or mourn; there is still time for a change in the results. Indicating that the fat lady singing is the last thing that happens at the end of a performance, game or contest. From the practice of having an alto aria somewhere near the end of an opera. Altos are often heavyset women.

it ain't over till it's over just wait, don't be so anxious to celebrate or mourn; there is still time for a change in the results. This is one of Yogi Berra's quotes. Yogi Berra was a professional baseball player and coach who had a penchant for interesting malapropisms.

it ain't the meat, it's the motion *sex* a commentary on the male preoccupation with penis size. Most women know something that most men don't know—the size of a man's penis is not as important as his ability to use it properly. Also, lyrics of a song by Maria Muldaur.

itch a desire.

item a couple. Example: "You know Pat and Patty? I just found out they were an **item**."

it is? or **what it is?** a question and a greeting. How is everything?

it is! or **what it is!** a statement and a greeting. A statement meaning everything is OK. **2.** everything is the truth or everything is what it is. A comment on the obvious.

"It is forbidden to forbid" a popular slogan used on banners by French student protesters against the oppressive university administration during massive **demonstrations** in Paris and across the country in May, 1968.

it's a bitch it's a bad situation.

it's a blast it's an exciting situation.

it's been real a salutation meaning "It has been real nice seeing you." Often said sarcastically.

it's getting deep someone is lying. Meaning the "shit" is getting deep.

IT-290 *drugs* a superamphetamine. Speed. One of the drugs given to **Ken Kesey** when he was a government "guinea pig" at the Menlo Park, California, Veterans' Hospital in 1959-60.

IUD (See: **intrauterine device**)

izzatso? a compression into one word of the phrase **is that so**? A sarcastic exclamation of disbelief or defiance.

J

J *drugs* a **marijuana** cigarette. a.k.a. **joint, doobie, roach, spleef, stick, blunt**.

Jack an impersonal male address to another man. A name used in a confrontation or as an intensifier instead of someone's real name. Examples: "Cool it, **Jack**!" "You better believe it, **Jack**!"

jack n. money.

jack adj. nothing. Examples: "It ain't **jack**." "He ain't **jack** shit."

jack around v. to do nothing or to be inactive. Example: "Gooch doesn't do nothing but **jack around** all day."

jack or **jacking** (someone) **around** v. to lie to or string someone along. Example: "I hope he's not **jacking me around** about those concert tickets." Can be similar to **pulling someone's chain**.

jacked or **jacked up** sped-up, **hyped-up**, **wired** or nervous. Often drug induced.

jacked up v. lied to or strung along. Example: "I was **jacked up** by Doug, too; his whole story about the square grapefruit was a lie."

jacking off or **to jack off** *sex* to masturbate (male).

jacking off messing around or wasting time.

jackin' me off (you're) you're lying to me or stringing me along.

jack shit like jack, it means "nothing." Examples: "He ain't **jack shit**."

Jackson like Jack, a male form of addressing another man. Used in a confrontation or as an intensifier instead of someone's real name. Examples: "Cool it, **Jackson**!" "You better believe it, **Jackson**!"

Jackson, Rev. Jesse Louis (b. Oct. 8, 1941, Greenville, South Carolina) *social issues* African American **civil rights** leader and minister. Worked with **Martin Luther King, Jr.**, in the **Southern Christian Leadership Conference (SCLC)** and was present when King was assassinated in Memphis, Tennessee, on April 4, 1968. Founder of the Rainbow Coalition and candidate for President of the United States. The first Black man to make a serious bid for the US Presidency at **Democratic National Conventions** in 1983 and 1987. Born into a poor family, Jackson attended the University of Illinois in 1959-60 on a scholarship and then transferred to the predominantly black Agricultural and Technical College of North Carolina (Greensboro), where he received a BA in Sociology in 1964. He moved to Chicago in 1966, did postgraduate work at the Chicago Theological Seminary, and was ordained a Baptist minister in 1968. While an undergraduate, Jackson became involved in the Black Civil Rights Movement. In 1965, he went to Selma, Alabama, to march with Martin Luther King, Jr., and became a worker in King's Southern Christian Leadership Conference (SCLC). In 1966, he helped found the Chicago branch of Operation Breadbasket, the economic arm of the SCLC, and served as the organization's national director from 1967 to 1971. In 1971, Jackson founded Operation PUSH (People United to Save Humanity), a Chicago-based organization advocating Black **self-help**. He has gained international renown, traveled widely to mediate disputes, and drawn attention to international problems. Jackson has became a leading spokesman and advocate for Black Americans.

Jackson, Mahalia (b. 1911, New Orleans, Louisiana; d. 1972) *gospel/jazz* Mahalia Jackson was discovered while singing at a funeral service in 1935. She sang with the Tommy Dorsey band throughout the 1940s and made Dorsey's "There Will Be Peace In the Valley" a popular song. In 1958, Mahalia record "He's Got the Whole World in His Hands," which reached #69 on Billboard's chart, a great feat for a gospel song. On August 28, 1963, she sang from the steps of the Lincoln Memorial in Washington, DC, just before **Dr. Martin Luther King, Jr.**, delivered his **"I Have a Dream"** speech to 200,000 civil rights marchers. The intensity and devotion in Mahalia Jackson's feeling toward music had a profound effect on many singers to come. Inducted into the Rock and Roll Hall of Fame in 1997 as an early influence.

Jackson State College *social issues* two Black students were shot and killed at this predominately Black college on May 14, 1970. During several days of campus **demonstrations**, James Earl Green, a high school student; and Phillip Gibbs, a 20-year-old junior and father of an 18-month-old son, were killed by gunfire from Mississippi State patrolmen and/or Jackson city police. Twelve others were wounded. After **Dr. Martin Luther King, Jr.'s**, acknowledgment and entry into the **anti-war movement** in 1967, the Black community began to demonstrate in support of **civil rights** and anti-war causes. Since an inordinate proportion of soldiers sent to Vietnam were poor, Black men, the civil rights and anti-war movements had many of the same interests.

jacuzzi a hot water whirlpool system, which became popular in the 1970s as a form of comfort therapy for self-indulgent Californians. Invented by Italian businessman Candido Jacuzzi (1903-1986).

jag a binge. Indulging in something to excess. Examples: **cocaine jag**, crying **jag**, etc.

jag *drugs* a drug high. Example: "Felicity is getting a **jag** off that dope."

jag *drugs* injecting drugs. **2.** A prison term.

Jag short for Jaguar, the car.

jail bait *sex* a sexual partner, or potential partner, usually a girl, who is under the legal age of consent to have sexual intercourse. An attraction for which a man could be incarcerated for statutory rape.

Jainism an East Indian religion of great antiquity. An extreme offshoot of **Hinduism** or perhaps even a forbearer of that religion. It rejects **Vedic** (Hindu) authority and the belief in an absolute **being**. Very conservative, even by Indian standards, the Jains are **vegetarians** who are so considerate of other creatures that they take pains to avoid stepping on insects, and some go so far as to wear surgical-type masks to prevent inhaling airborne life forms. Extremely **esoteric** by Western standards, their faith would require pages of explanation.

jam or **jammin'** an informal or unstructured musical piece or concert. A gathering of musicians playing music.

jam or **jammin'** to go or to leave.

James, Elmore (1918-1963) *blues music* one of the most influential blues guitarists of all times. His slide guitar technique influenced all musicians who used that style of play after him. He played with Robert Johnson, and they influenced each other. Brian Jones of **The Rolling Stones**, **George Harrison** and **Duane Allman** particularly incorporated his music into their success. Elmore was inducted into the Rock and Roll Hall of Fame in 1992.

jammed up in a bad situation. In trouble. Having money problems. Experiencing a drug overdose.

jamming or **jammin'** partying. **2.** fighting.

Jane a young woman or girl.

Jane the counterpart to John. The average woman; Jane Doe. A female who uses a prostitute is a Jane. A women's toilet is a jane, just as a john is the generic toilet.

Janis and Jimi Janis Joplin and **Jimi Hendrix** both died in drug-related incidents within 16 days of each other in 1970; Jimi, on September 18, and Janis, on October 4. They were both 27 years old, and both achieved international stardom in 1967.

JAP (See: **Jewish American Princess**)

Japanese beads *sex* beads strung in a pattern of ascending size, which are inserted in the anus and pulled out rapidly when orgasm is reached. An ancient Asian sexual enhancement.

jar *drugs* a bottle or container of 100 pills.

jar head a derogatory name for a member of the US Marine Corps.

jasmine an aromatic and medicinal flower from India. Used in tea, it is an exhilarant. The flower is placed on Hindu altars and replaced three times a day.

java coffee. Much of the first coffee came from the Island of Java.

jaw to talk.

jazz a form of music that evolved from **blues** roots and the African American community. Although many people may think that jazz was ignored during the hippie era, much of the rock and roll of the time had its roots in blues and jazz.

jazz a word often used during the hippie era to indicate something old-fashioned, unnecessary or incorrect. Example: "Don't give me that **jazz**; I know what's happening." **2.** verbal static or senseless talk.

jazzed interested, excited or enthusiastic.

jazz fusion a combination of traditional **jazz** and electrified/synthesized music technology. A form of music created in the early 1970s with the introduction of sound synthesizers and the help of **Miles Davis**. (See: **Moog, theramin,** and **sound synthesizer**)

photo by John McCleary ©

jeans pants made from heavy cotton twill, originally made by Levi Strauss & Co. and called **Levi's**. Throughout the 1950s, jeans were the pants of choice of young people and then became the primary clothing statement of the hippie culture. Jeans were the working man's uniform, and hippies adopted them as a reaction to the corporate suit-and-tie world, not to mention that they were cheap, durable and comfortable. The word "jeans" comes from the Middle English spelling of Genoa, Italy, where the fabric was first made.

jeans skirt (Levi's skirt) a skirt made from a pair of **jeans**. The inner crotch and leg seam was split, and a patch of denim was sewn across the front and back to make a skirt.

Jefferson Airplane *rock & roll* one of the original San Francisco psychedelic rock groups. Formed early in 1965: Marty Balin (b. Martyn Jerel Buchwald, Jan. 30, 1943, Cincinnati, Ohio), voc.; Paul Kantner (b. Mar. 12, 1941, San Francisco), gtr., voc.; Jorma Kaukonen (b. Dec. 23, 1940, Washington, DC), gtr., voc.; Skip Spence (b. Apr. 18, 1946, Ontario, Can.), drums.; Signe Anderson (b. Sept. 15, 1941, Seattle, Wash.), voc.; Bob Harvey, bass. Within a year, Grace Slick (b. Grace Barnett Wing, Oct. 30, 1939, Chicago, Ill.), kybds., voc., replaced Anderson; Jack Casady (b. Apr. 13, 1944, Washington, DC), bass, replaced Harvey, and Spencer Dryden (b. Apr. 7, 1943, New York City), drums,

replaced Spence, and that is when things began to happen. Their 1967 breakthrough album "Surrealistic Pillow" remains on the top ten list of many rock & roll and, specifically, psychedelic music fans. With just two songs, "White Rabbit" (co-written by Slick) and "Somebody to Love" from their Surrealistic Pillow album, "The Airplane" became the foremost psychedelic band, and **Grace Slick** became a hippie poster girl. Inducted into the Rock and Roll Hall of Fame in 1996.

jefferson airplane *drugs* a **marijuana** joint holder (**roach clip** or **crutch**) made by splitting a paper match in the middle and sticking the roach through it. The assemblage looks like an airplane, thus it is named for the rock group, **Jefferson Airplane**. **2.** to sniff or **snort** marijuana smoke through one's nose.

Jehovah personal name of God or the supreme **being** in Hebrew theological and philosophical writings, common only since the 14th century; the God of Israel since Mosaic times. (From the Hebrew *Yahveh*, of lost origin and meaning.) This name originally was never pronounced or written because of its holiness, but was replaced by *Elohim* or *Adonai*.

jellybeans *drugs* **amphetamine** tablets, or **pep pills**. Many drugs are called **candy** or named after candy, because of the "sweet" things they are supposed to do for you. (See: **amphetamine**)

jen in Chinese, it means Man, manhood, moral character, love, kindness, charity, compassion and benevolence, in that order.

jerk n. a derogatory term for a person thought to be **uncool**. During the hippie era, this word was replaced in popularity with the more graphic term **dick**.

jerk *sex* v. sexual intercourse.

jerked off misled or strung along. Example: "I got **jerked off**; that girl gave me a fake phone number." Similar to having one's chain pulled.

jerk off *sex* v. to masturbate.

jerk-off n. a derogatory name for a person thought to be foolish and unproductive. Related to jerk off, meaning to masturbate, since that activity is considered by some to be foolish and time wasting.

jerry curls tight, wet-looking curls worn by Black men and women during the late 1970s. They were the major change in African American hairstyle after the Afro of the late 1960s and early 1970s.

Jersey green *drugs* a type of **marijuana**, supposedly from New Jersey.

Jesus boots leather sandals.

"Jesus Christ Superstar" a musical, play and movie depicting the last seven days in the life of Jesus of Nazareth as seen through the eyes of his disciple and betrayer Judas Iscariot. Created by Tim O'Horgan, with music by Andrew Lloyd Webber and lyrics by Tim Rice. It premiered at the Mark Hellinger Theatre in New York on October 12, 1971, with Ben Vereen as Judas; Jeff Fenholt, Jesus; Yvonne Elliman, Mary; Barry Dennen, Pilate and Paul Ainsley, Herod. Despite opposition from some religious groups, it became a box office success, running for 720 performances. It was made into a successful movie in 1973, featuring Ted Neeley as Jesus and Carl Anderson as Judas. The sound tracks for both the play and movie were successful and featured a number of memorable songs.

Jesus died so we can ride a slogan used by rebel motorcycle riders.

Jesus freak a Christian. A term normally used to indicate a young person who had previously been a hippie. Christianity became, for some people, a substitute habit for a former drug **addiction**.

Jesus people Christians. Similar usage as **Jesus freak**, yet less derogatory and not specifically indicating a fanatic who was once a hippie "saved from drugs." It could merely be a middle-class family going door to door, handing out religious literature.

jet to move quickly. Example: "Skeeter likes to **jet** around on his candy apple, pin-striped skateboard."

Jett, Joan (b. Sept. 22, 1960, Philadelphia, Pa.) *rock & roll* singer/guitarist, originally a member of the groundbreaking girl group, The Runaways, which was memorable for their nubile sexuality and "attitude." That attitude led Jett to become one of the first girl **punk** performers. Joan Jett influenced many female musicians, such as Madonna, Melissa Etheridge and many others who may acknowledge it.

Jewish American Princess (JAP) a derogatory label given to many young, Jewish women. The implication is that they are arrogant and unreachable. My experience with Jewish women has been exactly the opposite.

JFK John Fitzgerald Kennedy. (See: **Kennedy, John Fitzgerald**)

jig-a-jig, jiggy-jig or **jiggity-gig** *sex* another euphemism for sexual intercourse.

jihad a religious war of **Muslims** against nonbelievers. During the hippie era, it began to mean any war or crusade against another culture practicing opposing religious principles or doctrine.

Jim a male form of addressing another man. A name used instead of someone's real name in a confrontation or as an intensifier. Same usage as **Jack**, but less popular.

Jim Johnson *drugs* intravenous drug equipment. Injection kit.

jimson weed *drugs* Stramonium. A poisonous weed that contains a natural-based chemical, like nicotine, with drugging qualities. Found in cigarettes for asthmatics.

jism semen.

jive eccentric and extravagant activity. Example: "Cut the **jive** and get down to play." **2.** conversation involving exaggerations, deception or downright lies. Example: "Don't **jive** me! What really happened with you and my chick when the elevator broke down?" Roots in Black American culture.

jive a kind of music associated with Black American culture. A form of **jazz**.

jive ass a liar.

jive talk an eccentric form of conversation associated with the **beat generation**. An exaggerated example could be: "Cool it man; the speed limit is dullsville, but so is deadsville."

jive turkey a liar or an unpleasant person.

jizz semen.

jnana **Sanskrit** for knowledge or spiritual enlightenment.

jnana-marga **Sanskrit** for path of knowledge.

job a physical or psychological violation of someone. An unkind act. Example: "He did a **job** on her, so her boyfriend did a **job** on him." Close in usage to "a number," yet it usually denotes something more violent in nature.

Job a brand name of cigarette papers often used for rolling **marijuana**.

jock a man who seems to be obsessed with his own physical appearance and who exercises to enhance his body. The term is usually associated with narcissistic tendencies. Later, in the 1980s, it became a more complimentary term, meaning simply an athletic person. Comes from jockstrap, a genital protection device worn by athletes.

jock short for jockstrap, an elastic pouch designed to restrain the male genitals in a safe position against the body and between the legs so that they will not be harmed during athletic competition.

Joe the ordinary man. Example: "Bob is just a good old **Joe**."

Joe Blow a man who is average and undistinguished. Example: "Bob is just a regular **Joe Blow**."

Joe college a proper, collegiate, clean-cut looking young man. Used as a derogatory term by hippies.

Joel, Billy (May 9, 1949-) *rock & roll* singer/songwriter who contributed much to the sound of the 1970s. Inducted into the Rock and Roll Hall of Fame in 1999.

jogging a term and activity that began to appear around 1967. Running for exercise using a slow, but steady gait in order to raise the heart rate for a designated period of time. Done to keep the blood flowing through the arteries of the heart and body in order to keep these passages clear of fatty buildup.

john a toilet or bathroom.

John *sex* a man who employes a prostitute.

John and Yoko (Plastic Ono Band) *rock and experimental music* **John Lennon** (b. John Winston Lennon, Oct. 9, 1940, Liverpool, England; d. 11:07 p.m., December 8, 1980, New York City; Yoko Ono, b. Feb. 18, 1933, Tokyo, Japan). Formed as a musical group in 1968, two years before **The Beatles'** official breakup in 1970. John Lennon met Yoko Ono at a showing of her art work in London in 1966. They corresponded, and Lennon sponsored another of Ono's art shows in London in 1967. One night in May of 1968, Ono visited Lennon at his home in Weybridge, and that night they recorded the tapes that would eventually be released as *Two Virgins*. The nude photo, which later appeared on the cover of *Two Virgins,* was also taken that night with an automatic camera. Shortly thereafter, Lennon separated from The Beatles. John and Yoko later recorded and toured with many people and produced some memorable, some forgettable and some unmentionable music. Yoko's squawks were a breakthrough in avant-garde to some and a breakdown in taste to others. Their bed-in, "we're only trying to get us some peace" thing is still one of the most amusing, as well as poignant, episodes of the hippie era. (See: **Plastic Ono Band**)

John, Elton (b. Reginald Kenneth Dwight, March 25, 1947, Pinner, England) *rock & roll* a singer/songwriter/performer who contributed much to the sound and style of the 1970s. Along with his song writing partner Bernie Taupin, he produced many memorable songs.   With a professionalism unmatched in the industry, his extravagant costuming and openly gay persona did much to help break down stigma related to sexuality in the minds of music listeners. Inducted into the Rock and Roll Hall of Fame in 1994.

John Lennon glasses or **wire-rimmed glasses** named after Lennon because he wore them for a time. Patterned after the British national health glasses. Round and wire rimmed, as opposed to granny glasses, which are six-sided and rimless.

Johnson the penis.

Johnson, Lyndon Baines (LBJ) (b. August 27, 1908 near Johnson City, Tx.; d. January 22, 1973), Democrat, the 36th President of the United States from 1963-69. Graduated from Southwest Texas State Teachers College in 1930. Taught public school; served as US Senator from 1948 to 1961. Became vice president in 1961, and thus, president on November 22, 1963, upon John F. Kennedy's assassination.

Johnson, Robert (b. May 8, 1911, Hazelhurst, Miss.; d. August 16, 1938, Greenwood, Miss.) *Delta blues* one of the first and most influential Delta bluesmen. Recorded only 29 songs and died at age 27, yet his songs have been rerecorded numerous times, and he has influenced more people than any other musician of his time. He wrote "Dust My Broom," "Ramblin' on My Mind," "Crossroads" (covered by Cream), "Stop Breaking Down" (covered by **The Rolling Stones**), and many other blues standards. Inducted into the Rock and Roll Hall of Fame in 1996.

John Wayne any man who relies on masculine posturing for his personality. **2.** an overly patriotic man.

join in an invitation to become part of the activities at hand. A new term introduced into the lexicon of American culture around 1962.

joint *drugs* a **marijuana** cigarette. a.k.a. **J, doobie, roach, spleef, stick, blunt**.

joint penis.

jollies an orgasm. Enjoyment of anything. Example: "Did you get your **jollies** at the dance?"

jolly bean *drugs* an **amphetamine** pill or cap. An **upper**.

jolt a drug- or alcohol-induced shock to the system. Not necessarily an unpleasant experience.

Jones the penis.

jones *drugs* a drug habit. **2.** discomfort or stress due to **withdrawal** from a drug habit.

Jones, Grace **(b. May 19, 1952, Spanishtown, Jamaica)** *music/disco* a six-foot-tall, Black model-turned-disco singer-turned-actress who contributed much to the style of the 1970s.

Jones, LeRoi (b. November 7, 1934) changed his name to Amiri Baraka in 1967 a member of the **beat** literary community in New York and San Francisco to which **Allen Ginsberg, Jack Kerouac, William Burroughs, Lawrence Ferlinghetti**, George Corso, **Gary Snyder, Diane di Prima** and Frank O'Hara belonged. A Black poet and playwright, he is one of the first modern proponents of Black political literature, and his life and work represent a strong connection among the Black community, the beat generation and hippie culture. There is strong evidence to say that he is among the two or three most important Black literary figures of the 20th century. (See: **Baraka, Amiri**)

Jones, Quincy (b. March 14, 1933, Chicago, Ill.) *music/contemporary pop* a trumpeter/composer/arranger/producer who was responsible for much of the sound of the 1970s. He contributed to the careers of Michael Jackson, Herb Alpert, Glen Campbell, **Roberta Flack, Aretha Franklin, Herbie Hancock, B. B. King, Little Richard** and many, many more.

Jonestown, Guyana in 1977, Jim Jones dictatorial and charismatic leader of the **People's Temple** "Church" of San Francisco, California, moved his congregation to Jonestown, a settlement in the jungle of Guyana on South America's northern coast. On November 18, 1978, Jones ordered more than 900 of his followers to drink cyanide-poisoned punch. A total of a of 913 died, among them more than 270 children. This act of forced suicide was apparently prompted by accusations of Jones' abuse of powers over his congregation, and this action proved it. US Congressman Leo Ryan was visiting Jonestown at the time to investigate complaints by People's Temple followers. Ryan and members of his party were also killed by gunfire from loyal Jones followers. Unrealistic religious and cult loyalty is a phenomenon that has been exhibited by people throughout man's history. Such blind faith in a doctrine or individual is contrary to common sense and counter to human nature, yet it happens when people forget to be human and think for themselves.

Jong, Erica Mann (1942-)   teacher, poet, and author of *Fear of Flying*, a 1973 novel about women's sexual fantasies that challenged conventional views of women and contributed to the awakening of feminist sexual self-determination. Her other works include *Half Lives* (1973), poems; and novels *Fanny* (1980) and *Any Woman's Blues* (1990).

Janis at Monterey Pop, photo by John Jeffers ©

Joplin, Janis (b. Jan. 19, 1943, Port Arthur, Texas; d. Oct. 4, 1970, Hollywood, Calif.) *blues/rock & roll* the most influential and popular White female singer of the time, she personified the guts and drugs of the hippie era. Much has been written about her; I cannot and will not try to express her importance to us in such a small space. Some people know when to die; she took our hearts, and then left us smiling with the memory. When I saw her at the **Monterey Pop Festival in 1967, two conflicting emotions ran through me simultaneously. One said, "As a woman; you shouldn't be expressing such sexuality for the world to see," and the other voice in me said, "Right on, girl!" We are so fortunate to have had Janis Joplin in this world even for a short time. For the rest of our lives, we have her music to intrigue us. Inducted into the Rock and Roll Hall of Fame in 1995.

josh to joke with someone or tell a minor untruth.

joy juice drugs diluted into liquid state, ready for injection. **2.** alcohol or liquor of any kind.

joy pop *drugs* the occasional or recreational use of intravenous drugs (usually **heroin**) without creating a habit.

joy popper *drugs* someone who uses intravenous drugs only occasionally.

joy powder *drugs* **cocaine** or morphine.

joy stick the penis.

joy stick *drugs* a **marijuana** cigarette.

juanita *drugs* **marijuana**. (See: **marijuana**)

Judaism the religion of ancient Israel. An ethical monotheism based on the revelations of God given to Moses on Mount Sinai.

jugs a woman's breasts.

jug wine cheap wine, usually packaged in a large bottle with a twist-off cap.

juice that which holds the world together. (See: **chi** or **ether**)

juice power or influence. Example: "Don't mess with George; he has a lot of **juice** down town."

juice hard liquor and alcohol.

juice head someone who drinks a lot of alcohol.

juiced or **juiced up** energized or strengthened. **2.** drunk.

juice up to energize or inject excitement. Example: "Let's **juice up** our relationship with a little moonlight and red wine."

juice up to apply saliva to the **clitoris** to encourage its own natural lubrication.

juicy Lucy a woman who is promiscuous. From the presumption that a **horny** woman has a perpetually lubricated **vagina**.

juju African native witchcraft. The **magic** and power contained in fetishes. Sometimes, it also means danger. Originating in African religions and medical shamanism, somehow in the Americas, particularly the Caribbean, it became a cult of voodoo with the creation of witch doctors, the use of fetishes and the practice of placing and removing curses.

juke to dance. Originally an African word relating to dancing. The juke box is the most common related usage of the word.

juke and jive to dance and party. Originally, juke was an African word relating to dancing. Jive is usually understood to mean lies, or exaggerations, but can also indicate eccentric or extravagant behavior.

jump *sex* to have sex with someone. Example: "I met her in the grocery store and wanted to **jump** her right there." Although it may sound like a violent and unreciprocated act, during the hippie era, this term was accepted as a reasonable seduction.

jump or **jumped** to fight or attack.

jump all over to get angry with someone. Examples: "Don't **jump all over** me about my drug use; I only get stupid socially." "He said the wrong thing 'cause she **jumped all over** him."

jump (someone's) **bones** to have sex with someone. Example: "I wanted to **jump her bones** right there in the grocery store." It was more of a humorous fantasy usage than the violent act it appeared to indicate.

jump on to ridicule or castigate someone.

jump on it or **jumped on it** to take advantage of a situation or do something on the spur of the moment. Examples: "Hey, it came on the market and I **jumped on it**. Not everyday do you get a chance to own the Brooklyn Bridge." "If he calls, you better **jump on it** fast."

Jung, Carl Gustav (1875-1961) a Swiss psychiatrist who invented the theory of archetypes. He investigated the significance of myths, symbols and dreams and found in them evidence of a "collective unconscious" that was at the root of religion.

junk (See: **stuff**)

junk *drugs* dope or drugs, particularly those derived from opium poppies, such as heroin. The term is supposedly from the 1920s when **addicts** scavenged in city dumps for junk metal to sell for heroin.

junkie or **junky** someone who injects drugs, usually **opiates**, such as **heroin**. A **marijuana** smoker is not a junkie. A **cocaine** or **methamphetamine** "snorter" is not technically a junkie.

Juno in Roman mythology, the wife of Jupiter, queen of the gods, mistress of heaven and earth, patroness of marriage and female virtue. Identified with **Hera** of Greek mythology.

Jupiter in Roman mythology, the chief deity, king of the gods, lord of heaven and earth. Identified with Zeus of Greek mythology.

just all right all right with a little extra. The "just," instead of diminishing "all right," embellishes it. Example: "I got you, babe, and everything is **just all right!**"

just another pretty face someone who is beautiful, but not very interesting. A sarcastic, humorous commentary about an attractive person who has nothing to offer but beauty.

justice reward, recognition. Not to be confused with true justice, based on laws of reason or fairness. Most often used sarcastically. Example: "Ain't there no **justice**? After all my hard work, I'm still broke and unknown."

juvie a juvenile. **2.** a juvenile (police) officer. **3.** juvenile (detention) hall.

K

K kilogram. Predominantly used as a measurement of drugs during the hip-pie era. A metric system measurement equal to 2.2 pounds. **Marijuana** often came in kilograms for shipment from other countries, such as Mexico, where the metric system is used. (See: **kilo** or **key**)

Kabbalah or **cabala** *religion* the **esoteric** mystic lore of **Judaism**, based on an **occult** interpretation of the Bible and handed down as a secret doctrine to the initiated. It is an essential element in most schools of occultism.

kaleidoscopic a visual experience exhibiting colorful lights and patterns, continually moving and changing. It can be a light show, movie or **psychedelic** drug trip.

Kali Hindu goddess of time, wife of **Shakti** or **Shiva**, said to be the Mother, creator of all things. The personification of cosmic force.

kali yuga the present age (the dark age) of **Hindu** mythology. (See: **yuga**) Always remember to distinguish between **yoga** and **yuga**; it can be confusing.

Kama Sutra Hindu erotic literature. Kama means pleasure or sensual gratification. Sutra means a collection of rules or a scripture. (In **Sanskrit**, **sutra** means a thread.) The *Kama Sutra* is an East Indian book dealing primarily with sex, originally written in Sanskrit sometime between the first and the sixth century A.D. It evolved from writings called *Vatsyayana Kama Sutra*, or Aphorisms on Love, by Vatsyayana. The *Kama Sutra* today is a compilation of Vatsyayana's writings, which includes works by earlier scholars and the later additions to his text by others, including a poet named Kukkoka. During the hippie era, many people were not merely interested in having sex; they were interested in improving sexual satisfaction for themselves and their partners. The *Kama Sutra* is the most complete book on sexual awareness and improvement ever written. What Eastern scholars knew and hippies found out was that sex is not only fun and the means to procreate, but also a path to better understanding oneself and others through exploring the emotions and joys of life.

Kama Sutra oil a very pleasant smelling, edible, sensual massage oil of the hippie era distributed by Kama Sutra Om of Los Angeles, California. It was marketed for use by lovers in massage and **foreplay**.

karma **Sanskrit** word for "action" or "deed." A form of fate inherited from former lives or accumulated from good or bad deeds committed previously. A belief held by many Eastern religions that we create our own "luck" through our actions; a form of cause and effect.

karma yoga the quest for a mystic union with the Divine Spirit through *karma-marga*. Complete control of one's personality is sought in order to subdue self-conscious, self-centered desires, so as to make one's actions *cosmocentric*, or in complete harmony with the "Universal One." Remember to distinguish between **yoga** and **yuga**.

kava kava a fermented drink that produces a mild narcotic reaction, made from the root pulp and lower stems of a perennial shrub *Piper methysticum* from the Hawaiian and South Pacific Islands. It has been used for centuries by the Polynesians in ceremonies and sacred rituals. Since kava kava depresses spinal, rather than cerebral activity, it produces euphoric relaxation without impairing mental alertness. Said to enhance sexual pleasures when taken orally, and, when applied exter-

nally to a woman's clitoris, it reportedly increases the quality and quantity of orgasm.

kazoo a term of unknown origin often referring to the buttocks or anal passage. Similar in usage to wazoo and yazoo. Example: "He's got money up the **kazoo**." In this context it does not relate to the musical instrument of the same name.

keen nice, good. A 1950s term that, by the hippie era, was in reduced usage reserved only for sarcasm.

Keep America Beautiful, Get a Haircut or **Give a Hippie a Haircut** a slogan similar to many found on bumper stickers and road signs ridiculing the **counterculture**. A Florida man paid to have messages such as these placed on 1,500 billboards around the United States. Oddly enough, the bumper stickers were found on more hippie cars and vans than anywhere else. This was another example of the counterculture adopting a negative slogan and throwing it back in the face of the establishment that created it. This phrase, originally meant to embarrass the hippie, became an anthem of the counterculture when it was added as a caption to a picture of George Washington showing his normal, long hair cut into a flattop. (See: **Beautify America...**)

keep cool or **keep** (one's) **cool** stay under control, relax or remain dispassionate.

keep off the grass a sarcastic warning to stay away from **marijuana**.

keep on keeping on or **keep on keepin' on** persevere, keep trying in spite of the obstacles ahead.

keep on truckin' continue doing what you're doing. Usually an encouragement to continue one's eccentric or rebellious ways. **Truckin'** was a distinctive walk and attitude possessed by the cartoon character, **Mr. Natural**.   Mr. Natural, drawn by **R. Crumb** and a mainstay of **Zap Comics**, was an endearing,   sometimes   revolting, **counterculture** character who "did his own thing." Dressed like a religious **guru**, Mr. Natural was sometimes spiritual and often banal in his activities, just like all **true hippies**. **The Grateful Dead** sang about truckin'.

keep the faith (or often) **keep the faith, baby!** stay true to your beliefs. To the **civil rights**, **anti-war**, and **anti-establishment** movements, this phrase meant something a little different, but in essence it meant to everyone "it's us against them." Reportedly coined by **Adam Clayton Powell, Jr. (1908-1972)**, Black US Congressman, clergyman and civil rights leader. (See: **Adam Clayton Powell**)

kef, keef, kief or **kif** *drugs* a term for **marijuana** or **hashish** derived from an Arabic word. (See: **marijuana**) **2.** also meaning **opium** in some regions.

kegger a party, often held outdoors, with a keg, or kegs, of beer as the main focus. Usually, a collegiate or high school activity with very young participants where the primary objective seemed to be getting drunk, getting sick and passing out.

Ken doll introduced to the American public in 1960 by Mattel, as the "boyfriend" or counterpart to their **Barbie doll**. During the hippie era, a man who was "too" well dressed and "too" perfectly built and coiffured was called a Ken doll.

Kennedy, Edward Moore (Ted) (b. 1932) liberal, Democratic US Senator from Massachusetts and brother of **President John F. Kennedy** and Senator **Robert Kennedy**. A graduate of Harvard University and, in 1959, the University of Virginia Law School. In 1963, at only 30 years of age, he won the US Senate seat vacated by his brother John, beginning a long career of government service. As a staunch liberal, he has sponsored bills on public education, criminal code reform, health care, AIDS research, fair housing, and many programs to aid the poor. As a member of the Senate Judiciary Committee, he has held liberal positions on racial busing, abortion, and capital punishment. After the assassinations of his brothers, John in 1963, and Robert in 1968, he was considered as a potential presidential candidate. His presidential aspirations were interrupted by the circumstances of a car accident in Chappaquiddick, Massachusetts, in 1969, in which a young female companion drowned. Trying again in 1980, he failed to win the Democratic nomination from incumbent **President Jimmy Carter**. Ted Kennedy continues to be one of the most outspoken liberal politicians in the United States.

Kennedy, Flo (1916-2001) "**Old, Black Flo**" *social issues* a **civil rights** attorney, **feminist**, activist, and, in her own words, "a loud-mouthed, middle-aged colored lady." Born in Kansas City, Missouri, she moved to New York City in 1942, earned her BA and graduated from law school at Columbia University in 1951. Her New York practice represented **Billie Holiday** and her estate, **Charlie Parker's** estate, and **H. Rap Brown**. She became disillusioned with the racism and treatment of the poor, homosexuals, prostitutes, and women. She founded the Feminist Party in 1971 after growing impatient with the **Na-**

tional Organization of Women. Flo Kennedy is very important personality in the civil rights and women's rights movements in this county. Her most revealing quote is, "There are very few jobs that actually require a penis or a **vagina**." With Margo St. James, Kennedy helped to found **COYOTE**, an organization created to promote tolerance toward prostitutes and their circumstances; it is an acronym meaning Cast Off Your Old Tired Ethics. In 1976, she published her autobiography, *Color Me Flo*.

Kennedy, Jackie President **John Fitzgerald Kennedy's wife and the lasting image of America's faded glory. (See: **Onassis, Jacqueline Kennedy**)

Kennedy, John Fitzgerald (JFK) (b. May 29, 1917, Brooklyn, Mass.; assassinated November 22, 1963, Dallas, Tex.) Democrat, the 35th President of the United States from 1961-63. Graduated from Harvard University in 1940. Won a Pulitzer Prize for his book, *Profiles in Courage*, in 1957. US Senator from Massachusetts, 1952 to 1961. Assassinated in Dallas, Texas, on November 22, 1963. Considered by many to be one of the most charismatic people and influential political leaders of the 20th century, but that is not the half of it; hope is what he offered. He showed a glimpse of what a benevolent political force could do in this world, yet his life and death also showed us despair. His assassination proved to many that evil has more power than good because evil is not constrained by morality. It is interesting to note that **liberals are the ones who are killed in their prime, and conservatives die old in their soft beds. This world would be a better place in which to live if John Kennedy, **Robert**

Kennedy and **Martin Luther King, Jr.**, had lived to die in their soft beds.

photo by John McCleary ©

Kennedy, Robert Francis (RFK) (b. Nov. 20, 1925; assassinated June 4, 1968, Los Angeles, Calif.) Attorney General, US Senator and brother of **President John F. Kennedy** and **Senator Edward Kennedy**. Graduated from the University of Virginia Law School; admitted to the Massachusetts State Bar in 1951. Attorney with the Justice Department's criminal division, 1951-52. Assistant counsel to the Hoover Commission in Washington, DC; assistant counsel to the Senate Permanent Subcommittee on Investigations, chaired by Senator Joseph R. McCarthy, 1953. Chief counsel to the Senate Select Committee on Improper Activities in the Labor or Management Field, 1957. Managed his brother's campaign for the presidency in 1959-60, and served as Attorney General, 1961-64. President Kennedy's closest adviser, 1960-63, influencing the nation's domestic and foreign policies. Elected to the US Senate from New York, 1965-68. Presidential candidate in 1968; assassinated immediately after winning the California Democratic Presidential Primary on June 6, 1968, by Sirhan Sirhan, a Jordanian immigrant. Another lost hope for peace and freedom in America and the world.

Kent State University *social issues* at Kent State University in Kent, Ohio, on May 4, 1970 (12:24 p.m.), four young people were killed and nine others wounded when National Guardsmen fired on student **anti-war** demonstrators. William Schroeder, Allison B. Krause, Sandra Scheuer and Jeffrey Glenn Miller were killed, and Dean R. Kahler, one of the wounded, was paralyzed for life. (See: **Anti-War Events, Groups and Leaders** starting on page 562 in **Lists** at the back of this book)

Kerouac, Jack (b. Jean Louis Lebris de Kerouac, March 22, 1922, Lowell, Mass.; d. October 21, 1969) writer, personality, considered to be the father of the **beat movement, therefore the grandfather of the hippie movement. Definitely the predominant author of beat literature. He studied at Columbia University, 1940-42; served in the Merchant Marine, 1942-43, and the Navy in 1943. He studied at the New School for Social Research, held various jobs, and traveled throughout the United States and Mexico from 1948-51. *On The Road,* written in 1951 and published in 1957, was a semi-autobiographical story of his travels with **Neal Cassady**. In the book, he was "Sal Paradise"; "Carlo Marx" was **Allen Ginsberg**, and "Dean Moriarty" was the name he gave Cassady. The book instantly established Kerouac as a spokesman for the beat generation. He is credited as one of the creators of the "stream of consciousness" style of writing, which he called "spontaneous

prose." Kerouac hung out with the New York City and San Francisco beat intellectual group to which Allen Ginsberg, **William Burroughs, Jr., Lawrence Ferlinghetti**, George Corso, **Gary Snyder, Diane di Prima, LeRoi Jones** and Frank O'Hara belonged. Fame disturbed Jack Kerouac; he drank heavily and tried to escape. His last major work, *Big Sur,* in 1962, described the price he paid for success. Kerouac lived out his final years back in Lowell with his mother. Other books by Jack Kerouac are *The Town and the City* (his first), 1950; *The Dharma Bums,* 1958; *The Subterraneans* (about a happy love affair with Black woman), 1958; *Doctor Sax,* 1959; *Mexico City Blues,* 1959; *Book of Dreams,* 1961; *Desolation Angels,* 1965; and *Satori in Paris,* 1966.

Kesey, Ken (1935-2001) writer, scholar and **counterculture personality. If it is true that the great artists are also great characters, Kesey confirms this premise. While attending Stanford University in 1959, he was a paid government guinea pig in early **LSD** experiments at the Menlo Park, California, Veterans' Hospital. This would make him among the first of the psychedelic travelers, even predating **Timothy Leary**. Kesey was the author of *One Flew Over The Cuckoo's Nest,* 1962; *Sometimes A Great Notion,* 1964; and many articles, book introductions and other sundry publications.

Of note is his 1973 *Kesey's Garage Sale*, a collection of stories, plays and contributions from Arthur Miller, **Paul Krassner**, **Neal Cassady**, **Allen Ginsberg** and **Hugh Romney (Wavy Gravy)**. In the mid-1960s, Kesey was arrested several times for his drug involvement and generally hassled for being "different." He was at times a fugitive from the police in California, the FBI, and the Mexican Federales, spending time in exile in Mexico and England. During the 1960s, Kesey hung out with Wavy Gravy and **The Hog Farm** and hit the road in 1964, traveling across the US with the **Merry Pranksters** in his converted school bus, "Furthur," spelled with two "u's." A curious aside is that there are numerous photographs of Kesey and "the bus" or "a bus," many with Further spelled with just one "u," yet it is reported that the original bus was called Furthur. Kesey was the primary subject of **Tom Wolfe**'s 1968 book, ***The Electric Kool-Aid Acid Test***, a definitive view of the counterculture of the time. Ken Kesey was one of the most dominant personalities of the hippie era and the personification of what was good, and also problematic, about the dropout generation. It has been said by some, and actually alluded to by Kesey himself, that drugs spoiled a damn good writer; yet I feel that he was a far more pivotal writer because of his "experimentation" with psychedelics and his radical lifestyle. In the 1970s, Kesey returned to his roots on a farm in Oregon, where he raised produce and livestock and wrote at night. He was concerned about the world in general, giving his time and talents to projects involved in **environmental** protection. Until his death from cancer, Ken Kesey continued to produce volumes of work, good blueberries and probably many great parties.

key *drugs* a kilogram of **marijuana**. Short for kilo or kilogram. A kilogram is the metric equivalent of 2.2 pounds. Marijuana came bundled in kilograms from countries like Mexico, which use the metric system of measurement. Alternate spelling **kee**.

khakis light brown, cotton pants. Along with **Levi's**, these pants were the original "costume" of the **bohemian**, **beatnik** and early hippie. Originally created in 1846 by British Army Lt. Harry Lumsden while he was serving in Punjab, India, they evolved from the cotton sleepwear called PJ's, or pajamas, from the word Punjab. The term khaki is a Hindi word for the light brown color.

kick n. to stop or quit. Often used to indicate the act of quitting drugs. Example: "It will kill you if you don't **kick** that habit."

kick adj. fun or exhilaration. Example: "Hey, man, that ride was a **kick**!"

kick ass, kicking ass or **kickin' ass** v. to win. To beat someone or physically beat up on someone.

kick-ass adj. something very good or exhilarating. Example: "He is a **kick-ass** guitar player."

kick back to relax. Example: "Come in, **kick back** and tell me some lies." This is definitely a hippie-era creation, which seems to have come from the earlier phrase "kick up your feet, lean back and relax." Kick back is the precursor to the 1990s version of **kick** or **kicking**. Language development is often the process of shortening words and phrases to simplify communications. Once everyone knows the meaning of the longer word or phrase, then words or letters are dropped to streamline verbal communication. Often, a younger generation just wants to make the language or the ideas more their own and therefore shorten them to do so. It's **cool** to make cryptic words that exclude the older generation or straight society. Even cool has become "coo" in the 21st century.

kick butt to win. Same as **kick ass**, comes from kick ass.

kickers boots. From **shit kickers**.

kickin' and **kicking** something good. Short for kickin' ass. Example: "That song was **kickin'**, man."

kick in to contribute. Example: "Next time, it's your turn to **kick in** some money."

*kicks fun. From **a kick in the ass**, meaning excitement.

kicks, it it's good, it's fun. From **it kicks ass**.

kickstart a **jolt** or a wake-up. Example: "You need to **kickstart** your life." It comes from the mechanism and the action used to start most motorcycles, called a **kickstart**.

kick stick *drugs* a **marijuana** cigarette.

kick the gong *drugs* to smoke **opium**.

kick the habit to quit a drug habit.

kick the shit out of (someone) to physically or figuratively beat up someone.

kief or **kif** *drugs* Moroccan word for **marijuana**. When pulverized into a powder and mixed with fine, aromatic tobacco, it is considered the Moroccan form of **hashish**. **2.** compressed **cannabis** pollen, unadulterated **hashish**, without **resins**.

kill finish off; drink up, eat up, etc.

killed in action (KIA) originally a military term adopted by the **counterculture** for use in a nonlethal sense. In hippie usage, it meant not literally killed, but dysfunctional in some way, rejected or **shot down**. Similar usage as **dead on arrival (DOA)**.

killer very bad, dangerous. Not necessarily lethal. Example: "His cat is a **killer**; I won't touch it!"

killer potent or excellent. Example: "He's a **killer** guitar player."

killer weed *drugs* top quality **marijuana**. This term was originally used in the 1950s movie, "Killer Weed." Originally meant to be negative, but eventually the **counterculture** began sarcastically using the term as a positive.

killings on campus and at student demonstrations: Kent State University, in Iowa on May 4, 1970, during several days of campus **demonstrations**, four young White students, William Schroeder, Allison B. Krause, Sandra Scheuer and Jeffrey Glenn Miller, were killed and numerous others wounded when National Guardsmen fired on student **anti-war** demonstrators. **Jackson State College** in Jackson, Mississippi, on May 14, 1970, during several days of campus demonstrations, two young Black men were shot and killed by Mississippi State patrolmen and/or Jackson City policemen. They were James Earl Green, a high school student; and Phillip Gibbs, a 20-year-old college junior and father of an 18-month-old son.

kill your TV or **blow up your TV** a common suggestion voicing the rebellious feelings of the time. Television represented then, and to many, still does today, the worst of the materialistic, shallow and overly commercial aspects of modern life. The phrase, "blow up your TV," was first heard in a John Prine song in the early 1970s.

kilo short for kilogram. Used as a drug measurement during the hippie era. A kilogram is a metric measurement equal to 2.2 pounds. **Marijuana** and other drugs often came in kilo bundles from countries, such as Mexico, which used the metric system. Same usage as **key.**

photo by John McCleary ©

King, B. B. (b. Riley B. King, Sept. 16, 1925, Indianola, Miss.) *music/blues* considered the most important blues musician of the century. Started performing professionally in Memphis in the late 1940s and recorded his first album in 1965. Contributed to the styles of many of the best rock and roll guitar players of the era.

King, Billie Jean (1943-) professional tennis player, one of the first feminist sports figures. A Wimbledon standout, winning women's singles six times, doubles 10 times and mixed doubles four times. She also racked up 13 US Open victories and was the first female athlete to earn more than $100,000 in one year. She became a role model for women in 1973 when she defeated Davis Cup and Wimbledon champion Bobby Riggs in three straight sets. Riggs came out of retirement for the match,

claiming that even a half-decent male player could beat the best female player. In 1981, King was the defendant in an unusual palimony suit by a former female lover, and her bisexuality became public. Billie Jean King co-founded the Women's Tennis Association, the Women's Sports Foundation, and World Team Tennis, the only professional co-ed team sport in America.

King, Carole (b. Carole Klein, Feb. 9, 1940, Brooklyn, New York) *rock & roll* the first female songwriter to make a real impact on the rock and roll music industry. A nice Jewish girl who wrote great rhythm and blues for Black artists to sing. With her husband Gerry Goffin, she composed a string of classic hits performed by a variety of artists during the 60s. She contributed to hits, such as "Will You Still Love Me Tomorrow?," "Up on the Roof," "Chains," "Don't Bring Me Down," "I'm Into Something Good," and "The Loco-Motion." In the 1970s, King had a solo singing career, including the memorable album *Tapestry* in 1971, contributing songs, such as "You've Got a Friend" and "It's Too Late." Goffin and King were inducted into the Rock and Roll Hall of Fame in 1990.

King Crimson *rock & roll* an early British art rock group formed in 1969. Robert Fripp (b. May 16, 1946, Wimbourne, Eng.) gtr., mellotron. The band had many personnel changes throughout its life, but Fripp was the moving force. In collaboration with **Brian Eno** (not a King Crimson member), he is responsible for starting the extreme electronic experimentation in music that spread through the late 1970s, 80s and 90s, influencing **punk**, **techno**, **new wave** and world music.

King, Rev. Dr. Martin Luther, Jr. (b. Jan. 15, 1929; assassinated April 4, 1968) *social issues* Black **civil rights** activist, minister, founder of the Southern Christian Leadership Conference (SCLC). On August 28, 1963, King delivered his "**I Have a Dream**" speech before 200,000 in Washington, DC, during "The March on Washington," the largest civil rights demonstration in history. He introduced the techniques of nonviolent demonstration to the Black civil rights movement and led the first march from Selma to Montgomery, Alabama, on March 7, 1965. Arrested over thirty times for the cause of civil rights, King received the Nobel Peace Prize in 1964. Assassinated in Memphis, Tennessee, in 1968. Definitely the most influential leader of the civil rights movement, arguably one of the most important people of the 20th century. (See: **Civil Rights Events, Groups and Leaders** starting on page 546 in **Lists** at the back of this book)

Kingston Trio, The *music/folk* formed in 1957 in San Francisco, Calif., Bob Shane (b. Feb 1, 1934, Hilo, Hawaii); Nick Renolds (b. July 27, 1933, San Diego, Calif.); Dave Guard (b. Nov. 19, 1934, Honolulu, Hawaii; d. Mar. 22, 1991, Rollinsford, New Hamp.). Guard was replaced in 1961 by John Stewart (b. Sept. 5, 1939, San Diego, Calif.). One of the first popular **folk** groups, they showed young, White kids that music could be fun, thus helping pave the way for the rock phenomenon. Many rock stars of the future started by forming their own folk groups patterned after The Kingston Trio.

Kinks, The *rock & roll* a British group formed in 1963 in London, Ray Davies (b. June 21, 1944, London), gtr., voc.; Dave Davies (b. Feb. 3, 1947, London), gtr., voc.; Mick Avory (b. Feb 15, 1944, London), drums; Pete Quaife (b. Dec. 27, 1943, Tavistock, Eng.) bass, replaced in 1969 by John Dalton; John Gosling added on keyboard in 1971. The most witty and intellectual of the **British invasion** groups, and innovators in gender-bending songs. Truly a cult group and may have been the first cult band because of their irreverence and the homosexual inferences in their music. Their 1970 song "Lola" was the first rock hit about a transvestite. Inducted into The Rock and Roll Hall of Fame in 1990.

kinky *sex* odd or deviant sexual behavior. Example: "She has a **kinky** habit of mentioning her crotchless underwear to men in fast moving elevators."

kinky boots knee- or thigh-high boots, usually worn with **mini-skirts**, by women between 1962 and 1965. The stars of "The Avenger" TV series, Diana Rigg and Patrick MacNee, recorded a song by that name in 1965.

kip and **kip down** sleep or go to sleep. Originally a British term.

kismet Arabic word for fate; a word frequently used by **Muslims** to express their belief in a power that rules the affairs of men and preordains their fortunes, deeds and future consequences. Adopted into American culture in the 1960s.

Kiss *rock & roll* formed in 1972 in New York City, Gene Simmons (b. Gene Klein, Aug. 25, 1949, Haifa, Israel), voc., bass; Paul Stanley (b. Stanley Eisen, Jan. 20,1952, Queens, New York), gtr., voc.; Peter Criss (b. Peter Crisscoula, Dec. 20, 1947, Brooklyn, New York), drums, voc.; Ace Frehley (b. Paul Frehley, Apr. 27, 1951, Bronx, New York) gtr. The guys with the painted faces. One of the best selling bands of the 1970s, but most people feel that they were actors more than musicians. The music was **heavy-metal**; their show was driven by theatrics and costumes, amusing and entertaining on some levels, innovative on others.

kiss-ass n. someone who flatters other people. A subservient person.

kiss ass adj. to flatter someone.

kisser the mouth or face.

kissing ass flattering someone.

kiss off an invitation to leave. Example: "**Kiss off**, I don't want to see you or your ugly tie around here anymore!"

kiss the porcelain god to vomit. The "porcelain god" is an obscure name for a toilet. Also heard were the phrases **bow to the porcelain god** or **worship the porcelain god**.

kiss up or **kiss up to** to flatter, get close to, flirt with. From kissing ass. Similar use as **suck up to.** a.k.a. **brown nose, kiss ass**.

kissy or **kissy-kissy** adj. an affectionate display.

kit *drugs* intravenous drug paraphernalia, usually a syringe, a length of rubber tube for tying off a vein, and a spoon for heating the water and dope solution.

kit *rock & roll* a full set of drums used in a **rock and roll** band.

kite *drugs* an ounce of drugs (East Coast usage)

kite steal. a.k.a. **boost, kype, lift, swipe**.

kitsch something that has little or no real artistic, monetary or aesthetic value, yet which appeals to popular satirical tastes.

kitty a small amount of money.

kiva a subterranean or semi-subterranean ceremonial chamber in Pueblo Indian villages used for religious rites of mystic significance. As close to resembling a church as the Indian cultures get. Similar to a sweat lodge in some **Native American** tribes. (See: **sweat lodge**)

K-mart a discount department store introduced to the American public in 1962.

klepto someone who steals habitually. Short for kleptomaniac.

klutz an awkward person. Originally a Yiddish term.

klutzy awkward. Originally a Yiddish term, adopted and expanded by the hippie culture.

knackered tired. A British term adopted by some during the era as part of the **British invasion**.

knee-jerk an automatic response made without thinking. Example: "Your distaste is a **knee-jerk** to her short hair." From the physical reflex of the knee when tapped with a small, hard instrument.

knock to criticize or be derogatory. Example: "You shouldn't **knock** her singing just because she's got a gap in between her teeth."

knocked, have (it) to be good at something. To have success in something be a forgone conclusion. Examples: "By the end of the semester, he will **have algebra knocked**." "Don't worry about the test; you **have it knocked**."

knocked up pregnant. It usually referred to someone unmarried and to an unplanned condition.

knockers big breasts.

knocking around involved in aimless activity, wasting time.

knocking off a little and **knock a little off** *sex* (See: **knock some off**)

knock it off stop doing that.

knock-off an imitation.

knocks luck or circumstances. Example: "He has had hard **knocks**."

knock some off *sex* to have sex. A male form of communication. Often, this usage is an aggressive form of sex, as if one is taking something, rather than sharing it. Example: "I went to her house to **knock sone off**." Related to **knocking off a little, getting it off** or **having it off**.

knock up *sex* to get a girl pregnant (usually an unmarried female, and an unplanned pregnancy).

knock yourself out enjoy it, do whatever you want. Try your best. Example: "If you want to smoke another, go ahead, **knock yourself out**, roll one up. I have to sleep now." Similar usage as **give it your best shot**.

Knowledge profound information. Spelled with a capital K. During the hippie era, there began to appear a realization that there is a spiritual and secular, a right and wrong, a good and an evil, to everything that mankind touches. What we do with our knowledge determines whether we are divine or base. If one kills a neighbor due to religious differences, one is not acting in God's name. If we use our knowledge of nuclear power to create a bomb, that knowledge is not from God, but the "Devil." We can receive Knowledge with a capital K and use it for good, or knowledge with a lower case k and use it for selfish evil. This is basic hippie philosophy.

know where it's at to be informed. In this phrase, "where" is not really a place, but an awareness, and "it" describes a nonspecific subject, which changes with each conversation. Example: "You've got to **know where it's at** to know where you've been."

knuckle-dragger someone who is stupid or crude. Related to the assumed intelligence level of apes, who drag their hands on the ground.

kook someone who is strange, perverted or crazy. A term that came into popular use sometime around 1965.

Edd "Kookie" Byrns

kookie strange or a little crazy. From the name of a character on the late-1950s TV series, "77 Sunset Strip."

Kookie (Gerald Loyd Kookson, III) combed his hair incessantly. He was played by Edd Byrnes, who forever became known as Edd "Kookie" Byrnes. Byrnes recorded a song with the lyrics, "Kookie, Kookie, (Lend Me Your Comb)."

kool-aid and *The Electric Kool-Aid Acid Test* The Electric Kool-Aid Acid Test is a 1968 book about **Ken Kesey** and the **Merry Pranksters**, written by **Tom Wolfe**. It deals with the consumption of LSD and other craziness of the times. Psychedelics were often consumed in food or drink, and kool-aid was often mentioned in truth and fable as an amusing receptacle for LSD. I attended at least one party where **acid** was in the kool-aid; many people had painted bodies, and Nicholas and I performed a circus act in the rafters of the large cannery loft. (See: **Ken Kesey** or **Merry Pranksters**)

Kooper, Al (b. February 5, 1944, Brooklyn, New York) *blues/rock & roll* keyboardist and major contributor to the development of blues/rock in the 60s. He originated what is now known as the "Dylanesque organ" sound while playing on Dylan's 1965 album, *Highway 61 Revisited*. Helped popularize blues while in the Blues Project, and put together the band **Blood, Sweat and Tears**, which began the big-band, jazz-rock trend. Discovered **Lynyrd Skynyrd** and The Tubes. Kooper collaborated with **Mike Bloomfield** and Stephen Stills on the popular 1968 album, *Super Session,* and also played on such albums as **Jimi Hendrix's** *Electric Ladyland* and **The Rolling Stones'** *Let It Bleed.*

Koran (Qur'an) the word of God given through **Mohammed**, the **prophet** and apostle of **Islam**. Said to be the final

messenger of God, meant to complete the previous revelations to the Jews and Christians.

kosher proper. The condition of being OK. From a Hebrew term meaning food that has been properly prepared under specific religious guidelines.

Krassner, Paul *social issues* political satirist, journalist and author. An original co-founder of the **Youth International Party (YIP),** or **Yippies,** in 1967, with **Jerry Rubin** and **Abbie Hoffman**. Editor of *The Realist,* a well respected publication of political satire, from 1958 to 1974, which renewed publication in 1985. Krassner is a longtime standup performer and has received two awards for his one-person show. He was head writer on an HBO special satirizing the 1980 presidential campaign and has done on-camera commentaries for the Fox network's "Wilton North Report" and "The 90s" on PBS. Krassner is an outspoken and stalwart advocate of every citizens' right to use recreational and educational drugs. He contributes to many periodicals and has compiled several books of psychedelic and psychoactive stories for *High Times* magazine.

Krishna the eighth **Avatar** (reincarnation of **Vishnu**) of **Hindu** mythology and occultism, whose teachings are recorded in the **Bhagavad Gita**.

Krishna movement (See: **International Society for Krishna Consciousness**)

Krishnamurti, Jibbu (India, 1895-1986) *religion* born in India, he was adopted by a Mrs. Annie Besant, the president of a theosophical society who envisioned him as a future spiritual leader. Krishnamurti was educated in England to prepare him for this future, and eventually an organization was established to promote this role. In 1929, after many years of questioning himself and the destiny imposed upon him, Krishnamurti disbanded this organization and turned away all his followers. From then until his death at 90, he travelled the world speaking and teaching. Founded the Krishnamurti Foundation, and wrote books on philosophy and religion.

Kristofferson, Kris (b. June 22, 1937, Brownsville, Tex.) *country/rock & roll* one of the major crossover country to rock and roll artists. Along with **Willie Nelson** and Waylon Jennings, he is responsible for loosening up the country and western music industry, forcing it to take itself less seriously. A prolific songwriter, he has helped to define the hippie generation with his music; one of his songs, "Me and Bobby McGee," is the anthem of a large segment of the **counterculture**.

Kuai the Chinese name for spirits of nonhuman beings and inanimate objects.

Kuei the Chinese name for **spirit** of human beings, used especially to refer to ancestors.

Ku Klux Klan *social issues* originally a social club for six young men in the town of Pulaski, Tennessee, founded on December 24, 1865. The founders, who had just returned from serving in the defeated Confederate Army, were Calvin E. Jones, John B. Kennedy, Frank O. McCord, John C. Lester, Richard R. Reed and James R. Crowe. Ku Klux comes from *kuklos*, the Greek word for band or circle. James Crowe suggested splitting kuklos into two words and changing the last letter to x, thus producing ku klux, which was originally spelled Kuklux Klan. Originally, the Klan stood primarily for the purity and preservation of the home and protection of women and children, especially the widows and orphans of Confederate soldiers. White, the emblem of purity, was chosen for their robes. During the 1950s and 1960s, many acts of violence against African Americans were conducted by men in the name of the Ku Klux Klan.

kundalini yoga the path to expanded psychic powers through breathing and other aspects of **hatha** and **raja yoga,** to awaken the serpent or reproductive system in the base of the spine. Involves the chakras or energy centers. Kundalini is sometimes called the royal yoga.

Kunstler, William (1919-1995) *social issues* radical civil liberties attorney who defended American Indian Movement leaders, **H. Rap Brown**, **Lenny Bruce**, the **Chicago Seven, Abbie Hoffman, Rev. Martin Luther King, Jr., Jerry Rubin** and **Malcolm X.** Kunstler was sentenced to four years in prison for contempt during the Chicago Seven trial. The sentence was later overturned because of Judge Hoffman's gross misconduct during the trial.

Kushi, Aveline (1923-2001) one of the originators of the natural food movement. A native of Japan who came to America to teach **macrobiotics** and other alternative food and medicine disciplines.

K-Y jelly *sex* a vaginal lubricant applied before sexual intercourse to ensure comfort for the woman and ease of entry for the man. K.Y. is a brand name, but many other products are available; some are scented, and others, edible.

kype to steal. A regional term, often confused with the word kite. a.k.a. **boost, kite, lift, swipe**.

L

L *drugs* LSD.

labia the four folds of flesh that form the opening of the **vagina**. From the Latin *labium*, meaning lip. *Labia majora*, the two outer, rounded lips framed in pubic down; and *labia minora*, the two soft, inner folds formed like petals of a flower.

lady a woman for whom one has a good measure of respect. Often, but not necessarily an older woman. A different connotation than the term **ol' lady**. (See: **ol' lady**)

Lady H *drugs* **heroin**.

Lady Snow *drugs* **cocaine**. (See: **cocaine**)

Lady Snow a White woman, in Black parlance.

Lady Soul singer **Aretha Franklin**. (See: **Aretha Franklin**)

LA Free Press (See: **Los Angeles Free Press**)

laid and **lay** *sex* the sexual act. Examples: "He got **laid** on his 16th birthday." "Did you **lay** her, or did you get **laid**?" A little more sensitive than the words **fuck** or **screw,** but still not very romantic.

*laid back relaxed, easy going. Example: "His dog is **laid back**; don't worry, he only bites people he doesn't like." This is definitely a hippie-era creation, which seems to have come from the earlier terms "lie down" and "lean back," meaning to relax.

laid low sick. Humiliated or reduced in stature. Examples: "She was **laid low** by that cold." "He was **laid low** by what she said." Similar to **cut down,** it may have evolved from that term.

laid up incapacitated, sick or under the influence of drugs.

la-la land a state of inebriation. A place or mental state of silliness, frivolity or decadence.

la-la land Los Angeles, California. Refer to previous definition for explanation.

Lamaism a popular term for Tibetan **Esoteric Buddhism**, a name not used by Buddhists themselves. (See: **Esoteric Buddhism**)

lame inappropriate, uninteresting or **uncool**. (See: **uncool**)

lame-ass or **lame-assed** an unconvincing person. Inappropriate, uninteresting or **uncool**. In this usage, the word ass is merely an intensifier, and does not relate to a person who is an ass. This term is often used to describe a place or thing.

lamebrain or **lame-brained** a dull-witted or stupid person. From being mentally handicapped, or "lame," in the brain.

Lang, Michael *rock & roll* creator and executive producer of the **Woodstock** Music Festival. An enigmatic "man child," without whose **laid-back** style of tenacity the greatest rock festival of the age would never have taken place, let alone created the cosmic impact it did. The story of Lang and the festival is one of incredible **karma**, luck and cooperation. Michael is a **new-age** businessman, and whether he is a hero or a villain is yet to be determined. A quote attributed to him in *Barefoot in*

Babylon by Bob Spitz expresses a great deal of hope to people like myself: "*They*, man. Y'know, the Establishment. Sooner or later, they pin a bum rap on all their enemies. That's why the revolution's just around the corner, man. This country belongs to the people, not the FBI and CIA, and one day they're gonna take it back from these dudes who hold the power. You'll see."

lapis exilis the **magic** stone that enabled the Phoenix to regain its youth. Some scholars believe that lapis exilis is a synonym for the **Holy Grail**.

lard-ass a fat person.

large very important. Example: "You better pay attention; this is **large**."

large charge something exciting.

laser a beam of concentrated light. Depending on their strength, lasers can burn flesh and cellulose or cut denser materials, such as wood and metal. Now used extensively in surgery. A word and concept introduced into our language in 1960.

latch onto get a hold of. Keep.

*later a salutation, short for "**see you later**." An original hippie term, it saw usage as **see you later alligator** and **later, gator** in the 1950s, and then as later in the 1960s. The growth of language has two different directions, expansion and contraction. Expansion involves grouping words together into phrases and creating longer words to expand a thought. The contraction of our language is the process of shortening these words and phrases after everyone knows their meaning. Often, a younger generation merely wants to make the language or the ideas more their own and therefore shorten them

to do so. It's **cool** to create cryptic words that exclude the older generation or straight society. Even cool has become "coo" in the 21st century.

laugh, (that's a) a sarcastic way of saying something is not really true. Example: "He says he's a musician? That's a **laugh**!"

laugh and a half something *really* funny.

laugher a situation or contest in which the conclusion is embarrassing. Examples: "His musical debut was a real **laugher**." "The score of the game was a **laugher**, 101 to 29."

"Laugh-In" a TV variety show that ran from January 22, 1968, to May 14, 1973. The show's official title was "Rowan and Martin's Laugh-In." Hosted by comedy duo Dan Rowan and Dick Martin, "Laugh-In" was a fast-paced hour of one-liners, sight gags and short skits. The show was an instant hit and did much to loosen up the uptight public by flaunting sexuality and satirizing religion and politics. Many celebrities made cameo appearances (including future President Richard Nixon, who uttered the words "Sock it to me!" in a 1968 show). "Laugh-In" added many new phrases to the American vocabulary, some of which have persisted, such as "Ring my chimes," "Sock it to me," and "You bet your bippy." It had a large company of regulars, among them, Dennis Allen, Chelsea Brown, Ruth Buzzi, Judy Carne, Byron Gilliam, Henry Gibson, Arte Johnson, Goldie Hawn, Jeremy Lloyd, Gary Owens, Lily Tomlin, Pamela Rodgers, Alan Sues, and Jo Anne Worley. Censorship and network control of the show's contents became an issue to Dan Rowan and Dick Martin, and it eventually led to their departure and the first closing of the show. George Schlatter and Ed Friendly were the executive producers until 1971, when Paul Keyes succeeded them. In the fall of 1977, "Laugh-In" (minus hosts Rowan and Martin) returned to NBC as a series of specials, headlined by guest stars.

launching pad *drugs* a place, room or house in which intravenous drugs are injected. a.k.a **shooting gallery**.

launder to conceal the origin of money earned through illegal activity, such as dealing in narcotics. Usually, this is done by running the money through another legal business, which could have been the source. Money that pops up in someone's bank account without leaving a trail back to a legitimate source is a red flag to the authorities and may result in an investigation of that person's business dealings.

laundry list a list of items or topics to be discussed in a confrontation. Example: "Gail has a real **laundry list** of gripes about our relationship."

lava lamp a glass cylinder containing oil, illuminated by a brightly colored light. The oil, heated by electricity, produces bubbles that slowly ascend through the colored liquid, creating a hypnotic display which is amusing to folks high on mind-expanding drugs. Invented in England in 1963, it was originally called Astro Lamp by its creator, Mr. Edward Craven-Walker, a man who was also a devout nudist. The idea was adapted from an egg timer invented by someone else during WWII. The Astro is the most popular model and is still produced by the original company, Mathmos, whose offices are at 179 Drury Lane, Covent Garden, London, WC2B. This is not a commercial.

lavender a color adopted by the homosexual community. Sometimes used for recognition in the secretive world of those who were forced to live **in the closet** about their sexuality.

lavender menace, the *social issues* the term used to describe **lesbians** when they started to identify themselves in the National Organization of Women (NOW) chapters. Eventually, gay women adopted the name themselves, in sarcastic defiance. When NOW began, it was populated by straight members, personified by **Betty Friedan**, and gay members, represented by **Rita Mae Brown**. Friedan and other straight members felt that associating with the lesbian movement would hurt NOW, so there were several "lesbian purges" in the 1970s.

Law, The the police or authorities.

law of retribution the Law of Ethical Causation, **karma**. (See: **karma**)

Lawson, Rev. James M., Jr. (1928-) *social issues* a Vanderbilt University divinity student who studied in India and established an unofficial school of Mahatma **Gandhi's** nonviolence in Nashville, Tennessee, in the early 1960s. John Robert Lewis and Marion Barry both attended his classes. Lawson was influential in **Dr. Martin Luther King, Jr.'s**, decision to adopt nonviolence in the civil rights movement. Lawson also helped to found the **Student Nonviolent Coordinating Committee (SNCC)** in April, 1960, with Ella J. Baker and Marion Barry. Rev. Lawson was the President of the **Southern Christian Leadership Conference** for 14 years. Currently, Lawson is pastor of Holman United Methodist Church in Los Angeles and is one of our most respected African American leaders. (See: **Civil Rights Events, Groups and Leaders** starting on page 546 in **Lists** at the back of this book)

lay n. *sex* a person regarded merely as a sex object.

lay v. *sex* a dispassionate act of sexual intercourse. To fuck.

lay a trip to create conflict. To play with someone's emotions. Examples: "Don't come in here and **lay a trip** like that on me." "James **laid a trip** on her about seeing other guys."

laya yoga the school of **yoga** that seeks union with the Divine Spirit on an etherial level, by recognizing divine presence in one's own body.

lay it on me tell me, let me know. Example: "I want you to **lay it on me**; tell me all the lurid details."

lay off stop. Don't bother someone.

lay on to give or contribute. Example: "Let me **lay** some sprouts **on** you."

lay one on to get drunk, high or **stoned** on drugs.

lay on thick to tell a preposterous lie or to flatter someone excessively.

lay up to hang out, stay at home, be inactive.

lazin' being lazy. Example: "What am I doing? Oh, I'm just **lazin'** on a sunny afternoon."

LB *drugs* one pound. Terminology used to sound **cool** in drug transactions.

LBJ Lyndon Baines Johnson, the 36th President of the United States from 1963-69. (See: **Johnson, Lyndon Baines**)

LD-50 *drugs* synthetic cannabinol. Cannabinol is the active ingredient of **marijuana**.

lead balloon a failure. Example: "Her vegetarian meat loaf went over like a **lead balloon**."

lead foot or **lead footed** a fast driver. From having a heavy foot on the car accelerator pedal.

leaf *drugs* the leaf of the **marijuana** plant dried and smoked to get **high**. For a long time, leaf was about all that smokers saw, but in the mid-70s **bud**, or **flower** clusters of the plant started to appear. With the discovery of the much more powerful bud, marijuana leaf has almost disappeared.

leaf *drugs* **marijuana**. (See: **marijuana**)

leaf, the *drugs* the leaf of the coca plant, from which **cocaine** is produced. (See: **cocaine**)

leak (to take a leak) to urinate.

leaker someone who is able to get into clubs and rock concerts without paying. A gate crasher. A British term.

lean and mean healthy. Ready for action, able to perform in any eventuality. **Mean** is not necessarily used as a negative in this context. **2.** sometimes this means dangerous.

lean on (someone) to interrogate aggressively or strongly convince someone.

leaper *drugs* a **pep pill** or stimulant drug, such as an **amphetamine**. A British term.

leap of faith to take a chance, trusting that someone or something will not fail you. Placing one's life or well-being into God's hands.

Human Be-In, January 14, 1967, photo by Lisa Law ©

Leary, Timothy (1920 -1996) *drugs* a psychology professor at Harvard University when, in the early 1960s, he began research into altered **consciousness with another professor, **Richard Alpert** (who later became **Baba Ram Das**). This research involved **LSD** and other drugs, using prison inmates and students as subjects. He and Alpert were fired for conducting these experiments. Leary became the "Drug Guru," creating the **International Foundation for Internal Freedom (IFIF)**, espousing drug use for enlightenment and extolling people to "**tune in, turn on and drop out.**" Few people more exemplify and personify the hippie image, both in fact and in media misrepresentation, than did Timothy Leary. Misunderstood and misquoted by the established media, mocked, feared and hated by the conservative population, all he wanted to do was "turn you on." His misunderstood "**ego**" turned a lot of people off, yet he was merely enthusiastic about his life and his interests, which were subjects many others considered crazy. Another example in which altruism is suspected as having a hidden agenda. A benevolent genius who realized that his teachings would be ignored unless he sought notoriety to advance them. Many could not separate his "pearls" from what they thought was egotistic babble; thus, much of his wisdom was lost on the public, which he was only trying to "turn on." (See: **Ram Das** and **International Foundation for Internal Freedom [IFIF], LSD**)

leathers leather clothing worn by motorcycle riders. The leather protected skin when a rider hit the ground and slid on pavement. Leathers became a **fashion**, even among people who didn't ride. Some leathers were American Indian style, with fringe.

Lebanese Blonde a light colored, powdery **hashish** originating in the Beka'a Valley of Lebanon. The area was a Palestine Liberation Organization (PLO) stronghold, and the PLO used the proceeds from the sale of this **hash** to buy arms.

Led Zeppelin *rock & roll* a British band formed in 1968, **Jimmy Page** (b. James Patrick Page, Jan. 9, 1944, Heston, Eng.) gtr.; John Paul Jones (b. John Baldwin, Jan. 3, 1946, Sidcup, Eng.) bass; Robert Plant (b. Aug. 20, 1948, Bromwich, Eng.) voc.; John "Bonzo" Bonham (b. John Henery Bonham, May 31, 1948, Redditch, Eng.; d. Sep. 25, 1980, Windsor, Eng.) drums. An offshoot of an earlier band, **The Yardbirds**. One of the top **heavy-metal** bands of the era, they had an edge on all the rest because of their musical finesse and thought-provoking lyrics. "Stairway to Heaven" is an anthem of the time and, according to various polls, either the number one, two or three most popular song of the era; the other two are "Respect" by **Aretha Franklin** and "Satisfaction" by **The Rolling Stones**.

leech someone who hangs around and shares what others have with no intention of contributing.

leech or **leech off** (someone) to take what others have with no intention of giving back.

Left Coast what East Coasters call the West Coast. Meant to insinuate that California and the West Coast is socialist or **left wing**. The association of the word **left** with socialism refers to the fact that the **Left Bank** of the River Seine was the socialist part of Paris in the 1920s and 30s.

left nut that part of a man's body which he would exchange for something he really wants, like sex with Brigitte Bardot. Example: "I would give my **left nut** to sleep with Brigitte Bardot." The "nut," of course, represents a testicle, the male sperm-producing organ. It is an exaggeration that one would part with a portion of one's anatomy for such a...although?

left wing someone or something that is associated with socialist philosophy. The association of the word **left** with socialism refers to the fact that the **Left Bank** of the river Seine was the socialist part of Paris in the 1920s and 30s.

legal eagle or **legal beagle** a lawyer.

legal high a drug experience using a legal substance that affords the effect desired from a prohibited substance.

Examples include **morning glory** seeds, nutmeg, green pepper, and, some say, **banana peels**. Many people who practiced Eastern religions and disciplines, such as **yoga** and **Buddhism**, considered their spiritual achievements to be legal highs. **Acid** was called **instant zen**; therefore, **Zen** could be called a legal high.

legalization of drugs there is a distinct difference between using drugs or letting them abuse you. In most cultures in the world, there has been recreational and spiritual use of drugs since the beginning of mankind. There has also been drug abuse. A society cannot stop drug abuse by drug prohibition. Those who have addictive personalities or mental or chemical imbalances which make them bad drug users will find some way to abuse a drug. The only way to control drug abuse and the negative effects it produces in our society is to legalize most drugs, control them as we do alcohol, and then recognize that some people have an illness. We must confront the problem and treat those who are addicted with clinical respect, psychologically and medically. It is about time we started legalizing some of the street drugs, and this is how I propose to do it:

Grade A drugs, such as marijuana, opium, hash, peyote, psilocybin mushrooms, woodrose and all naturally growing plants, should be legalized for growth for personal use and taxed as a luxury item when sold to others as a business. If someone sells over X amount, they should have a business license and follow certain health and safety laws. There should be age limits for users outside the home, just as with alcohol.

Grade B drugs, such as chemical psychedelics like LSD, STP, MDA, and

DMT, should be available by prescription, licensed, taxed and controlled along the same lines as other manufactured drugs. The prescription would control the age of user and mental ability to handle the drug.

Grade C drugs, including opiates, such as morphine and heroin, and all speeds, such as methamphetamines, cocaine and crack, should be placed within a government-controlled maintenance program. No one who is not already addicted would be supplied the drugs. New addicts would be accepted to the program if they revealed their illegal source of addiction. No one would be pressured to kick the habit, but would be given the chance to do so.

Think about it. The only people who should be opposing this kind of program are drug dealers. This move would cut the legs right out from under drug dealers and make the game so much less profitable that the pressures on our young people would decrease and addiction would decrease. Drug-related crimes would decrease. Deaths related to drug dealing would decrease. Police man-hours would decrease. Court traffic jams would disappear, and prison crowding, end. What's the problem? Is it a moral issue, giving drugs to people? These people are taking them anyway and messing up society in the process. There is such a thing as an addictive personality, and the only way to help these people is through education and therapy; you can't do that if you treat them like criminals. Are you worried about bureaucracy? Well, legalizing would save so much money that funding would be no problem, and a drug maintenance program couldn't be nearly as cumbersome as the bureaucracy we now have dealing with the

drug problem. Why haven't we legalized already? Could there be money involved? Could the police and prison employees fear for their job security; could lawyers and judges fear the loss of revenues? It would be economically more worthwhile to this society to pay these people and let them retire than to go on the way things are right now. Do the math.

leg it to walk or hike somewhere.

leg man a man who is attracted to women primarily by the appearance of their legs.

leg over *sex* sexual intercourse. Similar to **leg up**, and related to the often heard correlation between being in a horse's saddle and having sexual intercourse. A **British invasion** term.

leg up an advantage, a start or assistance. An old usage coming from the cowboy culture, meaning to help someone onto a horse by "giving a leg up," providing a place for them to step on, such as one's cupped hands, back or knee.

leg up or **leg** *sex* sexual intercourse. A **British invasion** term.

Lehrer, Tom (1928-) an important comic satirist of the 1950s and 60s. His "songs" about religion, politics and other popular cultural icons were valuable in opening dialogue about our society and helping to launch the hippie counterculture. Several of his most popular songs are "Vatican Rag" and "Poisoning Pigeons in the Park." He is a graduate of Harvard and has taught at MIT, Harvard, Wellesley and UC Santa Cruz. He retired from performing in 1972.

LeMar *drugs* an organization dedicated to the legalization of **marijuana**. LeMar stands for Legalize Marijuana. Founded in August, 1964, by ultraconservative civil libertarian lawyer James R. White III. LeMar conducted the first **demonstrations** in support of marijuana legalization in Union Square, San Francisco, in December, 1964. Poets **Allen Ginsberg** and Ed Sanders started a chapter in New York City in early 1965 and lead demonstrations outside prisons. Mike Aldrich, a prominent leader in LeMar as a student, become an important figure in the legalization movement, and, after completing his education, he became Dr. Michael R. Aldrich, also known as **Dr. Dope**.

lemons *drugs* street name for **Quaaludes** (the trade name of a sedative used as a tranquilizer). Lemmon is the name of the pharmaceutical company that manufactured the drug.

Lennon, John (b. John Winston Lennon, Oct. 9, 1940, Liverpool, Eng.; assassinated Dec. 8, 1980, New York City) *rock & roll* a member of the most famous **rock and roll band of the hippie era, **The Beatles**. John would have been considered the leader of the Beatles if one wanted to assign that status. He, along with Paul McCartney, wrote most of their songs; he spoke for the band most of the time; and on stage he always had his own mike, while Paul and George shared one. It was John's involvement with Yoko Ono, prompting a change in his directions, which broke up the Beatles, although Paul was the first to announce the break publicly and leave the group in 1970. John was shot four times at approximately 10:45 p.m. on December 8, 1980, outside the Dakota apartment building in New York City. His assailant was Mark David Chapman, a 25-year-old, mentally disturbed Beatles'

fan. John Lennon was pronounced dead at approximately 11:30 p.m. Many people feel that **the dream** of world peace and individual freedom died with him on that night. It could be said that the hippie era began with the introduction of **the pill** and ended with his death. John Lennon's "Imagine" is considered one of the most profound pieces of music from the era. We are so fortunate to have had John Lennon in this world even for a short time. For the rest of our lives, we have his music to educate us. The Beatles were inducted into the Rock and Roll Hall of Fame in 1988.

Leo astrological sign, July 22 to August 23, fifth house of the **zodiac**, fixed fire sign, symbolized by the Lion. Trait: self-expression. Self-perception: I will.

lesbo a derogatory term for a **lesbian**.

lesbian a female **homosexual**. A woman who prefers sexual relationships with other women. A term and a way of life not new to the hippie era, yet awareness of the culture was increased and new recognition and understanding of this way of life were expanded during the time. The word comes from the name of the Greek island, Lesbos. The island is said to have been populated during mythological times by women who loved each other, and it is the birthplace of Sappho, a female poet considered the first **lesbian** spokesperson.

let a fart to flatulate, to pass gas.

letdown a disappointment.

let (someone) **down** to disappoint or fail someone in a task. Example: "Calico **let us down** when she forgot the **tamari** for the **brown rice**."

let (someone) **down easy** to discourage someone's aspirations in a kindly manner. Examples: "**Let Bucky down easy**; don't say you won't kiss him because of his teeth."

let 'er rip, don't hold back, have fun. Example: "Baby, don't stop; **let 'er rip**."

let (someone) **have it** to attack someone physically or verbally.

let it all hang down to act without restraint, to be oneself. It could mean sexual expression, yet just as often, exposing one's soul. Evolved from **let it all hang out**. This phrase was often used merely as punctuation to a conversation. The most recognized usage was in **Eric Clapton**'s 1970 hit song, "After Midnight."

let it all hang out to act without restraint, to be oneself. Though many thought this phrase was sexual in nature, it most often alluded to unashamed self-expression or exposure of the soul. Having a generic meaning, it was often used merely as punctuation in a conversation.

***let it slide** or **let** (someone or something) **slide** to ignore a confrontation, disregard an offense or refuse to take something too seriously. Example: "Judy called me a tramp, but I **let it slide**."

let (or blow) **off steam** to relieve personal tensions by getting mad, getting **stoned** on drugs, dancing or indulging in some diversion.

let on to admit something. Example: "For all these years she didn't **let on** that she was he."

let one, let one go or **let one off** to flatulate, to pass gas.

let (something) **ride** to let something be, to avoid interrupting something.

Example: "The stock went down, but he **let it ride** for a few days before selling."

let's boogie an invitation to dance, have sex or, in some cases, to leave.

let's party an invitation to drink, dance or have sex.

let's ride let's go, let's leave.

level to be truthful. Examples: "Believe him, he is on the **level**." "Hey, whatever you do, **level** with me."

photo by John McCleary ©

Levi's pants made from heavy cotton twill by Levi Strauss & Co. They are also called **jeans**. Throughout the 1950s, Levi's were the pants of choice of young people and then became the primary clothing statement of the hippie culture. Levi's jeans were the working man's uniform, and hippies adopted them as a reaction to the corporate suit and tie world. It was also an advantage that such pants were cheap, durable and comfortable. The word jeans comes from the Middle English *Gene*, for Genoa, Italy, where the fabric was first made.

Levi skirt (**jeans skirt**) a skirt made from a pair of **Levi's** jeans. The inner crotch and leg seam was split, and a patch of denim sewn across the front and back to create a unique skirt.

levitate to raise or float, suspended above the ground with no known physical means of support. Many holy men of Eastern religions claim to levitate by sheer will of spiritual power. Many hippies swear that they experienced levitation on **psychedelic** drugs. In May, 1968, approximately 600 demonstrators gathered at the Pentagon and attempted to levitate that structure by using their willpower.

lez short for **lesbian**. Considered derogatory.

lezzie another derogatory name for a **lesbian**.

lib short for liberation as in: **women's lib** or **gay lib**.

libber someone, usually, but not always a female, who supports women's liberation.

lib chick a woman who is involved in women's liberation.

liberal a "free thinker," someone who does not believe in prohibitions against self-indulgence. A person who believes in the Golden Rule. A liberal takes action to protect others from themselves only as a last resort or to save innocent bystanders from someone else's mistakes or offenses. Liberals always have opinions, seldom *force* them on you, but will wear you down with arguments. A conservative calls a liberal a "bleeding heart." A liberal, if he were so bold, would call a conservative "heartless." Which do you think is best for this world?

Liberal Religious Youth (LRY) *religion* a youth group formed within the Unitarian Church in 1954. During the 1960s, it evolved into a combination of political movement, spiritual nirvana and sex/drug cult. Many of the adults of the Unitarian Universalist Church continued to support the LRY throughout the 1960s and 1970s even though it appeared to resemble a hippie commune in many of its activities. The group was involved in many church-sanctioned **anti-war** activities, but it also indulged in other **counterculture** activities, which were not condoned. At LRY conferences, a "howl night" took place, for which a **rock and roll** band was usually hired. It was called "howl night" because, at one conference in the 1950s, a band could not be found, so **Allen Ginsberg** was invited to read his controversial poem, "Howl." In the early 1980s during the conservative atmosphere of **Ronald Reagan**'s presidency, the Unitarian Universalist Church was pressured to drop the L word, so in 1982, the Liberal Religious Youth (LRY) became Young Religious Unitarian Universalists (YRUU).

photo by John McCleary ©

liberated to be set free from the social and moral constraints of the previous generation. During the hippie era young people became liberated from the old repressive and destructive sexual laws of their parents. Women fought and gained some ground toward liberation from oppressive sexual roles. The poor and disenfranchised continued, but lost the battle to change the lopsided economic rules in our society. Pragmatism is the most valuable asset of humankind. To be able to change the rules to meet the problems of new times and situations is important to our survival. Drugs, Eastern religion, beat and existential literature were a liberating force during the 1960s and 70s; maybe common sense will continue the process.

libido a Latin word meaning lust or desire. In a psychiatric theory by Sigmund Freud, it is described as the sexual energy associated with a person's **id**. That part of a person's mental or emotional being which expresses sexual interest and behavior. (See: **id**)

Libra astrology sign, September 23 to October 22, 7th house of the **zodiac**, cardinal air sign, symbolized by the scales. Traits: balance and justice. Self perception: I balance.

Librium *drugs* a brand name tranquilizer (benzodiazepine). Also called **green and blacks**. The most widely prescribed and abused tranquilizer. A **downer**.

libs short for **Librium**. (See: **Librium**)

licks skills, moves, actions, abilities and punches. Examples: "He has great guitar **licks**." "Watch out! If you let your gloves down, he'll get some **licks** in before you know it."

lid a 3/4-ounce bag of cheap Mexican **marijuana**. Primarily a Western United States term. For years, a lid sold for $10. Also called a **bad ounce** or **can**.

life line in **palmistry** the lower of the three main lines that run across the palm of the hand with fingers pointed up. Said to indicate the length and strength of a person's life. Palmistry is the pseudo-science which states that the lines on peoples' hands indicate the course of their lives.

lift n. assistance or help. Example: "He says good chili peppers give him a **lift** for his day at the stock market." **2.** a ride in an automobile.

lift v. to steal. a.k.a. **boost, kite, kype, swipe**.

*lighten up have fun, stop acting so seriously. **2.** a request or command to "**get off my back**," "**get off my case**" or "**give me some slack**."

light me up strike a match to my **joint** or bowl of dope. Also a euphemism for sexual intercourse or any physical **turn-on**.

"Light My Fire" title of the most popular song by the rock group **The Doors**. For a time this phrase was a euphemism for "turn me on" sexually, but most people would have laughed had it been said to them.

lightning *drugs* crack **cocaine**. (See: **white lightning**)

light show *drugs* the lights and **psychedelic** images created in one's head by **hallucinogenic** drugs.

light show *rock n' roll* the light-projected colors, **psychedelic** patterns and pictures shown at rock concerts. Thought to have originally been conceived by Bill Ham in San Francisco in late 1964 to early 1965. Reportedly first used at the **Red Dog Saloon** in Virginia City, Nevada, where the **Charlatans** and the **Warlocks** (soon to be the **Grateful Dead**) first played in June, 1965. Another early example was Ray Anderson's exhibition at the Open Theater in Berkeley, California in late 1965. It is difficult to document the history of something like this because the collective subconscious of people around the world often invents the same things at the same time. It is highly probable that young psychedelic experimenters in New York City and London were also creating light shows in and around 1965.

light up smoke some **marijuana**.

light (someone) **up** to knock someone out. May relate to the term, **turn out one's lights**.

light up *drugs* a suggestion to smoke a **marijuana** cigarette.

*like intj. an expression meaning loosely "that is to say." An unnecessary word often used to begin a sentence. Example: "**Like**, I really dig her." It was actually a product of the 1950s beat movement, but came into much more use in the 1960s. The word "like" and the phrases "I mean" and "you know" dominated the hippie language and still do to this day. If you are skeptical, count the number of times in a conversation "like," "you know" and "I mean" are said. What is strange about these exclamations is that, even though they have no real bearing on the conversation, they indicate a desire, newfound during this era, to communicate with clarity and understanding. When someone punctuates a sentence with **like** or **you know**, they are, in essence, making sure that the listener is paying attention and understands what they are saying. My favorite non-sentence of the era was, "I mean...like...you know!?"

like it is (tell it) the truth, tell the truth. Examples: "King told it **like it is**." "Don't hold back; tell it **like it is**."

like (something) **was going out of style** as if it were the last chance to do some-thing. Example: "We made love **like it was going out of style**."

like you never believe or **like you'd never believe** something unbelievable, but true.

lily a street term for a capsule of Seconal made by Eli Lilly and Company.

limbo nowhere; a place of indecision or inactivity. Examples: "I don't know where she is; it could be **limbo** for all I know." "My mind is in **limbo**." During the hippie era, this word was taken from its original religious usage to a more secular use. In Roman Catholicism, it means the dwelling place of souls between heaven and hell.

limey an Englishman.

limo short for limousine.

limp-dick someone who is impotent or ineffectual in some capacity.

limp-wristed a stereotypical physical characteristic attributed to homosexuals. Displaying the physical characteristics of a homosexual. A homosexual.

line a chopped and shaped display of **cocaine** ready to be inhaled into the nose.

line a lie.

line a seductive verbal deception used to gain sexual favors.

line of bull, line of bullshit or **line of BS** a fictitious story.

linga or **lingam** a symbol of the penis used by **Hindus** in the worship of **Shiva**. A **Sanskrit** word representing fertility and regenerative power. Similar **phallic symbols** are found in many ancient cultures, notably Chinese, Greek and Italian. These symbols originally represented or celebrated fertility and strength; however, they have eventually become **dildos** used on or by men and women to replicate sexual intercourse.

Linus blanket anything that gives one comfort. Named after Linus, a character in **Charles Schulz's** *Peanuts* cartoon, who always carried his baby blanket. Need not be a literal blanket, but any object kept close at hand for reassurance. Also called a **security blanket.**

lip sarcastic or flirtatious talk. Disrespectful backtalk. Example: "That waitress always gives me **lip**; I think she wants me."

lip service unresearched or poorly thought out support of someone else's opinions. The repetition of someone else's information.

lip-sync or **lip-synch** to pretend to sing to prerecorded music.

liquid lunch an alcoholic beverage lunch in lieu of food.

liquored up intoxicated.

listen up a call for attention. Example: "**Listen up**! I'll turn over the compost, you clean the outhouse."

litterbug someone who discards trash in a public place. A term coined by Annette H. Richards in 1952 for an article about vandalism in National Parks. Although not an important issue to many people, a basic lesson of the hippie era is embedded in this subject. The concepts of personal freedom, public responsibility and the consequences of selfishness permeate litterbugging. If any basic human theory defines the hippie era, it is the belief that any action is acceptable as long as it does not adversely affect other human beings. The hippie believes in human freedom with social responsi-

bility. In the mind of a **true hippie**, litterbugs are thoughtless social outcasts.

Little Feet *rock & roll* an influential country, **blues**, **rockabilly** band formed in Los Angeles, California, in 1969. Founded by Lowell George and Roy Estrada, both formerly of **Frank Zappa's Mothers of Invention**. The band had numerous personnel changes, but George was the mainstay and driving musical force until his death in 1979. The band has been resurrected a few times and produced several good albums in the late 1980s.

Little Richard (b. Richard Wayne Penniman, Dec. 5, 1932, Macon, Ga.) *rock & roll* one of the top rock-n-rollers of all times, with a string of hits in the 1950s, including timeless classics like, "Tutti-Frutti" and "Good Golly, Miss Molly." One of the first Black musicians to "cross over" and attract White fans. He deserves a debt of gratitude from the music industry and his fans for his humor and class in breaking down the barriers of color. He is also responsible for legitimizing androgenous performance and for pioneering glamor rock. Inducted into the Rock and Roll Hall of Fame in 1986.

little on the side and **little bit on the side** *sex* sex outside a steady relationship.

little black book an address and phone number book of likely prospects or past sexual conquests. Not necessarily black, and most prized if it's not too little.

lit up *drugs* to be high on some drug or stimulant. Under the influence of something, sometimes merely alcohol.

lived-in look old or worn out.

live-in lover a steady lover with whom one lives.

live one *sex* a good prospect for romance. **2.** person with lots of energy.

live the dream have faith in your dream and live as if it will come to pass. "**The dream**" is generally understood to mean the **civil rights** movement and its efforts to achieve freedom and justice for all. From the "**I Have a Dream**" speech by **Dr. Martin Luther King, Jr.**, delivered on the Mall in Washington, DC, on August 28, 1963, before 200,000 people.

lizard the penis.

load a psychologically disturbing issue. Example: "That's a **load** off my mind." One of those words that originally had a physical definition, but came into more usage in the hippie era as a psychological term.

load a lie. Example: "That's a **load**; I know you can't play the comb." Short for and comes from **load of shit**.

load or **load of that** a visual look or an observation. Example: "Get a **load** of that girl."

*loaded intoxicated or **stoned** on drugs.

*loaded having lots of money.

loadie or **loady** someone who takes too many drugs, comes from "loaded."

load of shit a lie. Shit being a commodity which is not coveted.

load up to put **marijuana** in a smoking pipe. To get **high** on drugs.

lock exclusive ownership. A sure thing. Example: "Don't even think about it; Hassler has a **lock** on her."

locked in committed to a particular course of action.

locked up assured. Exclusive. Example: "Don't worry; I've got first place **locked up**."

lock up your daughters a common comment referring to the fact that hippies were thought to be "seducers of young women." Found on posters and bumper stickers on the back of VW buses. Used in the same context as "**I'm the guy your mother warned you about**."

loco weed (See: **marijuana**)

long an abundance of something. Example: "I'm **long** on time, but short on patience."

long green money.

photo by John McCleary ©

longhairs hippies. Another name originally used as a derogatory reference to the **counterculture** and adopted by that culture in defiance. Hippies often called themselves **longhairs** or **freaks**.

loo a toilet or bathroom. A British term adopted by the **counterculture** due to an affection for the English culture.

loofah the skeleton of a dried gourd with an abrasive, sponge-like appearance, used to scrub the body and exfoliate old skin.

looker a good-looking person.

looney tunes or **loony tunes** crazy, or a crazy person. Example: "Stay away; he's **looney tunes**."

loop or **the loop** chain of command or communication. The group of people who are informed. Example: "I'm out of **the loop**; don't ask *me* who's on first."

looped intoxicated or on drugs.

loop-de-loop *sex* simultaneous oral to genital sexual stimulation, a.k.a. **69, flip flop**.

loopy crazy.

loose promiscuous.

loose cannon someone who is liable to do something dangerous or crazy.

Lophophora williamsii drugs **peyote** cactus. A natural **hallucinogenic** cactus plant whose main **psychoactive** alkaloid is **mescaline**. Also called peyote **buttons**.

Lord Buckley (See: **Buckley, Richard "Lord"**)

Los Angeles Free Press, "The Free Press or **Freep,"** founded in 1964 by Art Kunkin. Originally called Faire Free Press, the first issue was printed to be distributed at the 1964 Los Angeles Renaissance Pleasure Faire. Hippies sold it on the streets to support themselves. Estimated paid circulation was about 95,000. One of the largest "underground" newspapers and an important source of information on the culture of the time. (See: **Alternative and Underground Newspapers and Magazines** starting on page 635 in **Lists** at the back of this book)

*lose (one's) **cool** to get mad, lose control of emotions, or go crazy.

*loser a person who is unsuccessful, out of date or unpopular.

lose (one's) **gourd** to get mad or go crazy. Gourd means head in this case, relating to the Spanish colloquial reference of a head being a gourd.

lose it to become irrational. Example: "Bong is wired; I just saw him **lose it** over a missing napkin."

lose it and **lose the** get rid of it. Example: "Take my advice; **lose the** hair on your upper lip."

lose (one's) **lunch** to vomit.

lose (one's) **marbles** to go crazy.

lose the attitude! stop being arrogant.

lose (one's) **wig** to lose one's mind. To go crazy.

lose your cookies to vomit.

lost it fell apart. To commit a social mistake. From "lost his **cool**" Example: "He was doing fine, then he saw her cleavage and **lost it**."

lost it vomited. Comes from "to lose one's lunch."

lost weekend a drug or drunken binge, not necessarily on a weekend. From the 1945 Billy Wilder movie, "The Lost Weekend," a milestone movie about alcoholism.

lotus posture or **lotus position** the manner of sitting upright with crossed-legs employed in **yoga** and **Buddhist** meditation.

Lotus Sutra *religion* the most popular **Buddhist** scriptures in Asia, teaching salvation for all creatures. The **essence** of **Mahayana Buddhism**. Scriptures in the form of a sermon by **Buddha** to the throngs of rulers, gods, demons and cosmic powers. It expresses the principle that "One is All and All is One" and contains the attitude of Buddha-hood and the values of the

Bodhisattvas. (See: **Mahayana Buddhism** and **Bodhisattva**)

Louisville Lip a name given by the media to **Muhammad Ali**, born **Cassius Clay**. (See: **Ali, Muhammad** or **Clay, Cassius**)

lounge lizard someone who hangs out in cocktail lounges to drink and pick up sexual partners. An unsavory character with bad **fashion** sense.

love n. the feeling of attraction to someone or something. There are as many definitions of love as there are people to express it. If I were to venture one definition of love, I would have to offer someone else's words. In Robert Heinlein's exceptional 1961 science fiction novel *Stranger in a Strange Land*, the protagonist, a Martian named Valentine Michael Smith, gives this definition, to which I myself adhere: "Love is that condition wherein the happiness of another is essential to your own." **The Beatles** said, "The love you take is equal to the love you make."

love v. sex. The physical aspect of an attraction to someone. In order to experience good physical love, all of the same conditions should apply as apply to emotional love. The basic hippie philosophy is that in order to have really good sex, one should have respect for one's partner and consideration for their needs. Stephen Stills said, **"Love The One You're With,"** and this verb form refers to recreational love, an expression of freedom and a celebration of life.

love, in the long-term and deeply emotional aspect of the condition of love.

love beads a necklace of inexpensive colored glass beads worn by members of the "**love generation**."

love bite a red welt on the body caused by a lover's amorous sucking of the skin. (See: **hickey**)

love child a child born out of wedlock.

love children hippies or **flower children**.

love drug (See: **methyldeoxyamphetamine [MDA]** or **ecstasy**)

love generation a term describing the young, **counterculture** people of the 1960s. Attributed to San Francisco Police Chief Thomas M. Cahill.

love handles the excess fat and skin around a person's waist. From the sarcastic concept that this extra meat could be something that a lover might hang onto while making love.

love-in a gathering of people for the purpose of expressing universal love and perhaps making some physical love. The first love-in was probably the **Trips Festival**, hosted by **Ken Kesey** on January 21-23, 1966, at the Longshoremen's Hall in San Francisco. The **Grateful Dead** performed there. (See: **Ken Kesey** and **Merry Pranksters**)

love it or leave it a comment directed at **anti-war** protesters. A statement screamed at demonstrators by "patriotic Americans." It meant, in essence, that one should accept all the actions of the government, bad and good, or move someplace else.

love juice sperm. More romantic individuals maintain it is actually the fluid that seeps from a woman after intercourse, which is a combination of sperm and her own secretions.

love nuts testicle pain resulting from extreme sexual excitement without the release of an ejaculation. Often caused by the teasing of a reluctant lover. a.k.a. **blue balls**.

"Love The One You're With" the title of a 1971 song by Stephen Stills, with guest guitarists **Eric Clapton** and **Jimi Hendrix**. The phrase became the anthem of the free-love generation. Love at this level was recreational, an expression of freedom and a celebration of life.

Lovin' Spoonful *rock & roll* a band formed 1965 in New York, NY, John Sebastian (b. 1944), gtr. autoharp, harmonica, lead voc.; Zal Yanovsky (b. 1944), lead gtr., voc.; Steve Boone (b. 1943), bass; Joe Butler (b. 1943), drums. Between 1965 and 1968, they had a string of Top 10 and Top 40 hits in the jug band, ragtime, country, folk, hard rock and pop genres. Included were "Do You Believe in Magic?," "Good Time Music," "Nashville Cats," "You Didn't Have to Be So Nice," and "Summer in the City." A 1966 marijuana arrest of two members contributed to the band's demise, with Yanovsky leaving in 1967 and Sebastian, the group's founder and leader, quitting in 1968 to pursue a solo career. John Sebastian's appearance at **Woodstock** in August 1969, was memorable. The band was inducted into the Rock and Roll Hall of Fame in 2001.

low unkind or derogatory. From the term low blow, meaning a boxing punch below the belt. Example: "She called him Don Juan on a deadline; now that was **low**."

low blow a derogatory or unkind comment. Originally meaning a boxing punch below the belt. Example: "He called her a frigid nymphomaniac; now that was a **low blow**."

lowdown information. Originally a cowboy term.

low-down adj. disreputable. Example: "He's **low-down**, but she loves him anyway."

low-down dirty shame something regrettable.

low-life a despicable, disreputable or distasteful person.

low man on the totem pole the person with the least stature or importance. The last person to receive recognition.

low profile in hiding, out of sight. Example: "I'm keeping a **low profile** since I rejected her carrot cake."

low rider a lowered car or motorcycle. A vehicle that has been altered to ride low to the ground. a.k.a. **chopped**. **2.** an individual who appears to have a "**cruiser**" mentality or someone who drives a lowered car. **3.** a person who rides a chopped and lowered motorcycle. (See: **chopped hog**)

LPs *music* **L**ong-**P**laying records. A record is a round, flat piece of **vinyl** with a continuous concentric groove, containing minute bumps corresponding to sounds. The record is turned on a round, mechanized table; an electrified stylus runs through the groove. The music, previously recorded as bumps in this groove, will be transferred by the stylus to the attached speakers. Vinyl records disappeared from the market in the late 1980s, when CDs (compact disks) became the primary vehicle for recorded music. Radio programmers of old music and rap/hip-hop **disk jockeys** continue to play vinyl LPs. There is also a small, elite group of purists, or "vinyl freaks," who collect and play "records" and LPs at home. (See: **vinyl**)

LRY Liberal Religious Youth. (See: **Liberal Religious Youth**)

LSD *drugs* (See: **lysergic acid diethylamide**)

lucidity an **occult** term meaning **clairvoyance** and premonitions. The ability to receive supernormal knowledge.

luck into to accidently fall into some good fortune.

luck out to get lucky.

lude or **ludes** *drugs* short for **Quaalude**. Quaaludes are a trade name **sedative-hypnotic**. The active chemical compound is methaqualone. The effect is a mild **euphoria** similar to alcohol consumption. The term quaaludes or ludes is often used generically for any methaqualone pill or capsule, many of which are manufactured illegally.

luded out *drugs* under the influence of **Quaaludes**. (See: **Quaaludes**)

lump it learn to live with it. "Tough shit." Example: "I don't care if you don't like it, **lump it**."

lumps hard times, tough situations, hard knocks. Example: "So you got fired, that's the **lumps** man." "Life isn't just a bowl of kumquats; you got to take some **lumps**."

lunatic fringe the crazy minority of people who want to blow up things and kill people in the name of a cause, usually religious or political. Conservatives, **liberals**, fascists or communists may fit this description.

lunch physically or psychologically beaten by another person. Eaten alive. Example: "Watch out for him; one misjudgment and you're **his lunch**."

lungs a woman's breasts.

lush someone who drinks too much.

Lynyrd Skynyrd *rock & roll* a band formed in Jacksonville, Florida, in 1966 and headed by Ronnie Van Zant. A highly successful Southern, country-style band until a plane crash in 1977 that killed Van Zant and several other members.

lysergic acid diethylamide LSD *drugs* the primary **psychedelic** drug used by the hippie culture. LSD was first synthesized in 1948 by Swiss scientist **Dr. Albert Hofmann**, while working for **Sandoz** Pharmaceuticals. The first use of **acid** in America was in **consciousness** research conducted by people, such as **Timothy Leary**, **Richard Alpert**, **Aldous Huxley**, **Alan Watts**, Ralph Metzner and Dr. Sidney Cohen, at Harvard, UCLA and Stanford in the late 1950s and early 1960s. In 1957, there was supposedly an LSD leak from the Sandoz plant in Hanover, New Jersey, which found its way to the **Greenwich Village** beatnik community. In the 1960s, the US government also conducted experiments on mental patients and volunteers in veterans' hospitals. **Ken Kesey**, author of *One Flew Over The Cuckoo's Nest*, was one of these early LSD "guinea pigs." As other psychedelics, LSD seems to affect the limbic system in the brain, which controls vivid emotions, such as exhilaration, awe and love. LSD became illegal in the United States in October, 1966. a.k.a. **acid, instant Zen**.

M

M *drugs* **marijuana**. (See: **marijuana**)

M *drugs* **morphine**.

M-14 an automatic rifle first used as the primary weapon of soldiers in Vietnam. Generally considered too heavy, but reliable.

M-16 an automatic rifle replacing the M14 as primary weapon for soldiers in Vietnam. Very lightweight, easily broken in hand-to-hand combat, and extremely unreliable when first developed and issued. Called the "**Mattel Toy**" by soldiers because of its lightweight, toy-like quality and because some parts were made by a division of that toy manufacturing company.

Mac or **Mack** a term used in place of a person's name. Example: "Hey, **Mac,** I don't care if you do own a Porsche; you can't park in my living room."

MacDougal Street a street in the East Greenwich Village section of New York City. The center of the **bohemian** and folk scene during the late 1950s and early 60s. The beatnik hangouts, Cafe Reggio, Cafe Wha?, Minetta Tavern, Gas Light Cafe, and the San Remo were on MacDougal. Bob Dylan played some of his first performances at Cafe Wha?, and Jimi Hendrix had early gigs there before his stardom.

MacHack *computer revolution* the first chess-playing computer created around 1960 by Richard Greenblatt at **MIT**'s multiaccess computing (MAC) project

machine gun *drugs* hypodermic syringe. Related to the fact that places where intravenous drugs were injected were called **shooting galleries**.

machismo aggressive behavior. The condition of being overly masculine. In Spanish, it means male.

macho aggressive behavior by a man. Short for **machismo**.

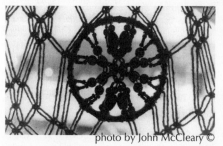
photo by John McCleary ©

macramé objects or decorations made by tying string, twine or rope into a series of knots.

macrobiotics a dietary discipline based on an Asian menu of foods. Introduced to the American public in 1965, it consisted primarily of rice and vegetables. The term "macrobiotics," said to have been coined by Hippocrates, the father of Western medicine, is from the Greek *macro,* meaning large or long, and *bios,* meaning life. Macrobiotics is the art and science of health and longevity through the foods we eat, our lifestyle and our environment. A major proponent of macrobiotics was **Aveline Kushi (1923-2001)**, a native of Japan, who came to America to teach macrobiotics and other alternative food and medicine disciplines. At one time in the early 1970s, a small number of Americans died after following strict macrobiotic diets. Unlike Asian cultures that were accustomed to such diets, the previously meat-eating hippie was vulnerable to sickness and even death from deficiencies in a strictly **brown rice** and vegetable diet. Vegetarian diets can be beneficial to most people, but one should begin them with a basic knowledge of nutrition.

Madame Nhu (See: **Nhu, Madame Ngo Dinh**)

mad dog the street name for a variety of wine produced by Mogen David. a.k.a. **MD**. An inexpensive, readily available wine that became popular among young hippies with little money. Also considered a **wino**'s wine. The name "mad dog" referred to the "mean streets" of city ghettos. Actually, a kosher wine served at Seder and other ceremonial Jewish meals.

made to be sexually seduced. Not a rape, but it may indicate some reluctance.

made (to have it) fortunate or rich.

made in the shade very fortunate. Example: "His girlfriend's family is rich; he has it **made in the shade**."

MAD Magazine a comedy magazine that appeared in the 1950s and changed the intellectual level of humor for young people of the time. It was not technically a counterculture publication, but its political satire, nonsense and irreverence opened up the minds of young readers for things to come.

magi the wise ones, philosophers, astrologers and priests of ancient Persia. Their name is the root of the words **magic** and magician.

magic any special, inexplicable or fortunate occurrence.

magic circle a circle drawn on the ground, or marked by pebbles, thorns, fire or water, around a person or object as protection from danger. When summoning spirits for consultation, the **black magician** usually stands inside a magic circle for safety.

magic diagrams *occult* geometric designs, symbolizing the mysteries of creation, deities and the universe. Used for conjuring up spirits. Interest in the **occult** and supernatural blossomed during the hippie era, out of curiosity and a desire to explore all aspects of religion in order to make one's own choices. Until the 1960s and 70s, spiritual life and religion were inherited from parents who had also inherited it. For the most part, before the hippie era, children didn't question their families' religious beliefs. Hippies wanted to explore other religious beliefs in order to make their own decisions.

magic drum a wooden drum covered with reindeer skin, used by shamans of the Eskimos and Laplanders to establish communication and rapport with the spirit world during rituals and ceremonies.

magic dust (See: **cocaine**)

magic mushrooms *drugs* **psilocybin** or psilocin **psychedelic** mushrooms, teonanacatl. Any one of 14 different species of small, yellow mushrooms with **hallucinogenic** qualities. a.k.a. **God's flesh, sacred mushrooms**. Warning, many mushrooms are deadly; please be sure of what you are eating for food or pleasure.

mahamudra total, deep, orgasmic intercourse. From East Indian **tantric yoga**.

Mahara Ji (b. India, 1957) *religion* an East Indian spiritual leader and **guru** with a following of American hippies during the 1970s. His devotees in India, Europe and America regard him as a successor to **Krishna**, **Buddha**,

Christ, **Mohammed** and others. His church is the Divine Light Mission. Divine Light Mission initiates, called premies, receive "The Knowledge" and are given secret meditation techniques.

Maharashi *religion* in **Hindu** mythology, this term means "great sage" and is given to important teachers who teach new paths to **self-realization**.

Maharishi Mahesh Yogi (b. India, 1911) *religion* the most recognizable and popular "**guru**" of the era, founder of the **Transcendental Meditation (TM)** program and the worldwide Spiritual Regeneration Movement in 1959. The TM technique consisted of meditating on a mantra (a sacred sound or phrase) twice a day. At one time, it was said that TM had 5 million participants, including many celebrities; "The Marharishi" was billed as the spiritual adviser to **The Beatles** rock band. Maharishi Mahesh Yogi published *The Science of Being and Art of Living,* 1963, and *Meditations of Maharishi Mahesh Yogi,* 1968. See: **Transcendental Meditation)**

Mahatma Sanskrit meaning "great soul." A practitioner of **occult** sciences and arts who has attained the highest degree of **esoteric** knowledge. This name is given to a class of "great ones," "masters of wisdom and compassion," living in India and Tibet. Because of their sympathy for mankind, they have renounced the privilege of continuing their spiritual evolution in order to remain on earth in their present form, to help others who are less advanced than they.

Mahavishnu Orchestra/John Mc-Laughlin *experimental and Eastern music* formed in New York City in 1971, John McLaughlin (b. Jan 4, 1942, Yorkshire, Eng.) gtr.; Billy Cobham (b. May 16, 1944, Panama) drums; Jan Hammer (b. Apr. 17, 1948, Prague, Czech.), keybds., and assorted others. Guitar virtuoso John McLaughlin played in numerous blues bands in England with people like Brian Auger and Graham Bond before moving to America in the late 1960s. In demand as a session musician, McLaughlin played with many greats of **jazz**, including **Miles Davis** and Buddy Miles. Moving into **fusion** and experimental sounds, McLaughlin hooked up with Billy Cobham and others, forming the Mahavishnu Orchestra, which produced mostly avant-garde experimental music.

Mahayana Buddhism *religion* a form of **Buddhism** practiced throughout Asia. The word *Mahayana* means large vehicle. Also known as Great Vehicle Buddhism. The Northern, **Sanskrit**, Tibetan, and Chinese form of Buddhism, which extends as far as Korea and Japan. Its central theme is that Buddhahood means devotion to the salvation of others and thus manifests itself in the worship of Buddha and Bodhisattvas. Built upon the beliefs of a more primitive Buddhism, it incorporates metaphysical and epistemological systems, such as the Sunya-vada and Vijnana-vica. The most popular form of Buddhism practiced by American hippies. Based on the doctrine of the **Bodhisattvas**, it accepts more scriptures than **Theravada Buddhism** and offers various popular forms of devotion. The **essence** of Mahayana Buddhism is the Lotus Sutra, a scripture in the form of a sermon by the Buddha to the throngs of gods, demons, rulers and cosmic powers. (See: **Buddhism, Lotus Sutra, Theravada and Bodhisattva.**)

Mahdi an Arabic word, literally meaning the "guided one." The future leader of the Mohammedans, who is to appear as a Messiah to establish a future, better age.

mainline to inject a substance by hypodermic needle, into the main vein in one's arm. The purpose of this is to alter one's state of **consciousness** with the injected chemical. Contrary to popular belief among straight society, intravenous drug use was not a common activity in the **true hippie** culture. In hippie use, this term meant any excessive activity. Example: "He is a sugar freak; every morning I watch him **mainline** three jelly donuts and a coke for breakfast."

mainliner *drugs* someone who shoots drugs into his or her body.

main man a close friend or associate. Eventually, this term became more of a sarcastic commentary and was used less frequently as a term of endearment.

main squeeze someone's primary love interest. A boyfriend or girlfriend.

mainstream something accepted as normal by the majority.

maintain to cope with circumstances. To survive. Example: "I know the situation's tough, but just try to **maintain** and maybe tomorrow we'll find better bean curd."

majoon *drugs* a **cannabis** confection usually associated with the Arabian, Persian and, to some extent, Indian cultures. The recipe varies, but often contains **hashish**, sugar, butter, flour, milk and sometimes chocolate.

major of great magnitude or importance. Example: "Hey, that was a **major** bummer; you better make some **major** changes in your life." OK, so it

wasn't a creation of the hippie era, but it is a word that has received a lot more air play since the 1960s and 70s.

make *sex* to seduce someone. A somewhat forceful term for sexual intercourse, not usually associated with romance.

make to identify someone. Example: "I hope the police don't **make** me as the guy who stole the condom machine."

make a connection *drugs* to buy drugs. Example: "They sent him out with fifty bucks to **make a connection**."

make a connection or **make the connection** to understand a complex situation. To come to a realization. Example: "How long did it take her to **make the connection** between sex and babies?"

make a hit to impress someone.

make a move on *sex* to attempt to seduce someone.

make an offer (someone) can't refuse to make a threat. To make a suggestion to which one has no choice but to comply. A line in the 1972 movie, "The Godfather," implying that refusal of the offer would result in death.

make a pass at to flirt with or attempt to seduce someone.

make a play for to flirt with or attempt to seduce someone.

make a scene to create a commotion or disrupt the norm.

make babies to have intercourse for the purpose of procreation. As opposed to having sex for fun or recreation only.

make good to produce something or fulfill a promise. Example: "Are you going to **make good** on your promise to pay her rent?"

make it to achieve success.

make it or **make it with** *sex* to have sex with.

make like to replicate or imitate something. Example: "**Make like** a bulb and turn off."

make like a tree and leave go away. A sarcastic suggestion that someone depart.

make love, not war an **anti-war** slogan of the late 1960s. The basic peace and love statement exemplifying the **spirit** of the **true hippie**.

"make my day" a phrase from the 1971 Clint Eastwood movie, "Dirty Harry." An offer, request and threat wrapped up into one. In the movie, the offer was to "go ahead, try to shoot it out with me;" the request was to "make my day, give me something enjoyable to do;" the threat was, "If you try, I get to kill you." The phrase was adopted into popular use as a sarcastic, primarily humorous comment in playful confrontations in which no death threat was actually implied.

make out to succeed or to be successful. Example: "I hope I **make out** well in my college kegger entrance exams."

make out to kiss or have romantic contact with someone.

make-out artist someone who is a good kisser. Someone successful at attracting sexual partners.

make the scene to attend a party or function. To be in the right place.

make time or **make time with** *sex* to indulge in sex or sexual play.

make tracks to leave in a hurry.

makin' it *sex* copulating or indulging in sex.

Malcolm X (b. Malcolm Little, 1925; assassinated Feb. 21, 1965) (also known as Al Hajj Malik Al-Sha-Bazz) *social issues* Black spiritual leader and advocate of African American self-determination. His father was killed by a Ku Klux Klan-like organization called the Black Legionaries. At the age of 21, Malcolm, then known as "Detroit Red," was convicted of burglary and served a six-year sentence. In prison, he was introduced to the teachings of **Elijah Muhammad, leader of the Lost-Found **Nation of Islam** popularly known as the **Black Muslims**. Muhammad's teachings had a strong impact on Malcolm, and he became a loyal disciple, turning to an ascetic life, immersing himself in reading and studies. Malcolm soon adopted X as his surname, symbolic of a stolen identity, his true African name, which was lost because his forefathers were sold into slavery in America. Upon his release from prison, Malcolm became a prominent member of the Black Muslims under founder Elijah Muhammad. With time, Malcolm X became disillusioned by what he considered the sexual excesses and **self-indulgence** of Elijah Muhammad, and Muhammad himself apparently felt threatened by the popularity of his charismatic disciple. This eventually forced Malcolm X to leave the Black Muslims in March, 1964. He traveled to **Mecca** and discovered that Islamic orthodoxy taught equality of all races, which caused him to abandon his belief that Whites were evil. Returning to America as Al Hajj Malik Al-Sha-Bazz, he was convinced that racism had destroyed the **spirit** of America and that only Blacks could free themselves. In June, 1964, he founded the **Organization of Afro-American Unity** and moved closer to socialism. He declared that Blacks should replace non-violence with active self-defense against White supremacists. He reportedly said at the time, "There can be no revolution without bloodshed." Many Caucasians of the era felt that Malcolm X represented a threat, but in the Black community, then as today, he was considered a positive influence on family values, African American self-determination and pride of heritage. Malcolm X was killed by gunmen from a rival religious faction on February 21, 1965, while speaking at a rally of the Organization of Afro-American Unity at the Audubon Ballroom in New York City.

male chauvinist pig a man who is extremely prejudiced against women's rights and aspirations. A man who thinks women should be kept pregnant and cooking in the kitchen.

male eunuch a derogatory description or term for a homosexual man.

male principle or **masculine force** in **esoteric** philosophy, the active, positive aspect of cosmic order and nature. The active, positive aspect of the deity. Male principles are represented by male gods in the pantheon of polytheistic religions.

Mama an affectionate name for a wife or live-in girlfriend.

mama! an exclamation not necessarily related to gender or a literal person. "**Mama**, what a great movie!"

Mamas and the Papas, The *rock & roll* a singing group formed in New York City in 1965, John Phillips (b. Aug. 30, 1935, Parris Island, SC; d. 2001) voc., gtr.; Dennis Doherty (b. Nov. 29. 1941, Halifax, Nova Scotia, Can.), voc.; Michelle Phillips (b. Holly Michelle Gilliam, Apr. 6, 1944, Long Beach, Calif.) voc.; Cass Elliot (b. Sep. 19, 1943, Baltimore, Md.; d. July 29, 1974, London, Eng.), voc. They gave us a lot of joy and enthusiasm in being hippies. John Phillips and The Mamas and the Papas are to a great extent responsible for producing the 1967 **Monterey Pop Festival**, which brought national attention to many of the most important musicians of the hippie era. Inducted into the Rock and Roll Hall of Fame in 1998.

man! an exclamation not necessarily related to gender or a literal person. "**Man**, you're a beautiful girl!"

Man, The the police or any authority figure.

man, the an important person or a man in the know. Examples: "If you want to know about mushrooms, he's **the man**." "You **the man**, Bob, you **the man**."

mana a power thought to exist in objects, nature, spirits and ghosts of the dead. From the South Pacific Melanesian island culture.

manage able to function successfully. Although this word by no means originated during the hippie era it came into the **mainstream** in a more expanded role during that time. To manage something was formerly a proactive endeavor. During the 1960s and 70s, it became a reactive term. Examples: (proactive) "Can you **manage** the store while I am gone?" (reactive) "Can you **manage** with all the pressures you have?"

mandala *religion* a **Tibetan Buddhist** aid to **meditation**. It is a circular picture, traditionally made using colored sand. The picture in a mandala represents a three-dimensional temple. It is meant to portray different aspects of the Buddha's compassion. Devotees focused on this picture and visualized themselves in the beautiful temple, thus achieving peace of mind. During the hippie era, mandalas were painted, woven or constructed in many ways, with many designs, though they were usually in the traditional, round format. Although a large number of hippies practiced or experimented with Buddhism, most often the mandala was used merely as decoration to look at while **tripping** on drugs.

man eater a strong woman with an agenda that threatens the masculinity of some men.

mangoes a woman's breasts.

manicure *drugs* to clean and prepare **marijuana**. Basically, to strip the leaves and/or flower buds from the stems and remove the seeds. Seeds were not particularly good to smoke, not only because they could explode, blowing marijuana all over the place, but also because they caused headaches.

mano a mano hand to hand, as in combat. Thought by many to mean man to man because of the spelling, it is now used commonly to describe a competition between men. Used most often in sarcasm. A Spanish language term.

mansions of the moon in astrology, a series of 28 divisions of the moon's passage through one complete 360-degree circle. Each mansion represents one day's average travel of the moon (12 degrees, 51'25.2", or roughly 13 degrees), beginning apparently at the point of the Spring Equinox, or 0 degrees Aries.

Manson, Charles (1934-) I hesitated to include Charles Manson in this encyclopedia, yet he was regrettably a pivotal figure in the era and should be addressed. Manson was at the center of the negative element that altered the course of our history. Several situations occurred that overshadowed the positive elements of the hippie era and led to the reactionary Reagan era. Assassinations, suicides and drug overdoses destroyed our counterculture leadership base, and the Manson family and **Jonestown** incidents frightened the conservative population, ending the possibility of sweeping positive change. Manson was basically an ex-con with delusions of grandeur, who used the freedom of the hippie culture for his own perverted needs. He is an example of the way in which power corrupts. He was able to convince a few impressionable young people that he had "something to say." Many people seek a simple explanation for the confusions of life, and this makes them vulnerable to arrogant leaders who speak with "mystical" confidence. Often, both the leader and the followers confuse leadership skills with divinity. In the summer of 1969, members of Manson's "Family," acting upon his orders, murdered actress Sharon Tate and at least seven other people in Southern

California. Charles Manson and several other participants are still serving life sentences for these crimes.

manic frenzy a state of spiritual ecstasy or a semi-trance.

mantic relating to **divination** and fortune telling. A person capable of soothsaying. Divination is the use of supernatural skills to gain knowledge of the unknown or the future. (See: **divination** and **soothsayer**)

mantra *religion* a **Sanskrit** term meaning an incantation consisting of a sacred formula, usually a quotation from the **Veda**. The word has come to mean a spell or charm, especially in the **occult**. In **Shaktism** and some other religions, it is the holy syllables to which great mystic significance and power is attributed. During the hippie era, it came to be known as any resonant sound made by repeating a symbolic verse over and over in order to achieve a peaceful trance while meditating. The word **om** is the most common element in mantras and is sometimes repeated by itself over and over as a **mantra**. In **Tibetan Buddhism**, the phrase **om mani padme hum** is used as a mantra. A significant mantra is sometimes given to someone by a spiritual leader or guru. One can choose one's own mantra, and any word or phrase can be used. In **Hinduism**, it originally referred to a few sacred verses from the Vedas. Though the process was meant to be very serious and spiritual, it was often said that a mantra is merely a way to put the mind to sleep through boring repetition. (See: **om mani padme hum** and **Veda**)

mantra yoga the school of **yoga** that attempts to commune with the Divine spirit. Reciting prayers to the deity is essential in mantra yoga.

Manu *occult* the **Sanskrit** name for the spiritual father of the human race. Also, a person thought to be a possible archetype for mankind. An elder brother.

Maoist an advocate of the Mao Tse-tung Chinese communist form of government and social system.

maracas women's breasts. A Spanish word for round gourds containing seeds or beans, which are shaken to make rhythmic music.

marathon group similar to **group therapy, encounter group** or **sensitivity training**, based on the theory that confrontations and interplay among unrelated people encourages positive change and **self-realization**. Such terms and the process was introduced to the American public in early 1970s. Marathon groups consists of gathering people for an intense one- two- or three-day period, during which inhibitions are broken down through something similar to exhaustion therapy. Eventually, these groups, like sensitivity training workshops, became ultracommercial ventures, taking advantage of the **gestalt** therapy concept, making it a fad and applying it to such things as "How to Become a Better Insurance Salesperson by 'Trading Places' with Your Client." (See: **group therapy, gestalt** and **Esalen Institute**)

marble garden a cemetery.

marbles a euphemism for brains or intelligence. Example: "He's a little strange, obviously missing some **marbles**."

marching powder *drugs* cocaine. From the fact that cocaine is a form of speed and will keep people marching. (See: **cocaine**)

margarita *drugs* (See: **marijuana**)

photo by John McCleary ©

marijuana *drugs* the leaf and flower of the **cannabis** plant, *Moraceae*, a genus of widely cultivated annual plants. **THC** (^-9-**tetrahydrocannabinols**) is the substance found in this plant that creates a drugged state when smoked or eaten. Cannabis and the euphoric drugs derived from it have been illegal in America since the uncontested passage by Congress of the Marijuana Tax Act of 1937. Marijuana has many names and forms, among them, from India: *bhang* (unprocessed hemp); *ganja* (strong, processed dried hemp); and *charas* (hashish); from North Africa: *hashish* and *keif*. **Sinsemilla** is the female flower **bud**; **leaf** is the leaf of the plant. There are numerous names and varieties, relating to the place they are grown, such as **Maui wowie**, Humboldt green or Big Sur smooth. **Acapulco gold** and **Michoacan** are named for the states in Mexico where they are supposedly cultivated. In America, there are over 40 names for marijuana. a.k.a. **alfalfa, bhang, boo, bud, cannabis, cheeba, chronic, devil weed, dank, doobage, dope,**
ganja, grass, gunny, hay, hemp, herb, hooch, juanita, kief, leaf, loco weed, M, margarita, Mary Ann, Mary Jane, mu, muggles, pot, reefer, scuzz, shit, smoke, sweet Jane, sweet Lucy, T, tea, Texas tea, the kind, vitamin T, wacky weed, wacky t'backy, wana, weed**. Remember, all things in moderation; thinking people use their drugs, foolish people allow drugs to use them.

cm1 CALIFORNIA MARIJUANA INITIATIVE
'80
REGISTER TO VOTE

marijuana arrests in the US in: **1965**, 18,815; **1966**, 31,119; **1967**, 61,843; **1968**, 95,870; **1969**, 118,903; **1970**, 188,682—45.4% of total drug arrests; **1971**, 225,828—45.9% of total drug arrests; **1972**, 292,179—55.4% of total drug arrests.

marijuana cigarette *drugs* a cigarette made of the dried leaves and flower buds of the hemp plant. a.k.a. **J, joint, doobie, roach, spleef, stick, blunt.**

mark the person chosen as the victim of a **scam** or **confidence** game. Someone who is easily cheated or taken advantage of.

**Marley, Bob (b. Robert Nesta Marley, Apr. 6, 1945, St. Ann's Parish, Jamaica; d. Mar. 11, 1981, Miami, Fla.) *reggae* singer, songwriter and guitarist, the most well known and respected reggae musician of the era.   Marley started with the Wailers in 1963 and became a Jamaican national hero. His profound political and social music soon made him an international hero to the poor and oppressed people of the world looking for hope. With lyrics like "a hungry man is an angry man," Bob Marley was a voice for reason in a world of turmoil. His early death from brain, lung and liver cancer was not only a grievous loss to the music of the world but to the peace and freedom movement of the world as well. We are so fortunate to have had Bob Marley in this world even for a short time. For the rest of our lives, we have his music to elevate us.

Marshall, Thurgood (1908-1993) *social issues* Black attorney, **civil rights advocate and the first African American on the US Supreme Court. Chief legal counsel for the **NAACP** in the early 1960s. His most famous case on their behalf was the 1954, *Brown v. Board of Education of Topeka*, which he won, invalidating state-enforced racial segregation of public schools. Coming from segregated schools, he worked his way to a law degree from Howard University. Between 1934 and 1961, Marshall traveled throughout the United States as an attorney for the NAACP in proceedings confronting diverse civil rights issues, earning him the title "Mr. Civil Rights." During that period, he argued 32 cases before the Supreme Court, winning 29.   In 1961, **President John F. Kennedy** appointed Marshall to the US Court of Appeals.

In 1965, **President Lyndon B. Johnson** appointed him Solicitor General, the first African American elevated to that position; and in 1967, President Johnson appointed Marshall to the Supreme Court. Justice Marshall served for 24 years on the Supreme Court and was an outspoken **liberal** on a conservative dominated Court. He opposed the death penalty and government regulation of speech or private sexual conduct. He supported a woman's right to abortion and upheld gender and racial affirmative action. Marshall believed strongly in the obligation of government to provide education and access to legal services, regardless of a person's ability to pay for them. Thurgood Marshall is the most respected judiciary figure of the hippie era, Black or White.

martial arts (disciplines) Oriental forms of meditation, exercise, sport, self-defense and battle. Martial disciplines are divided roughly into *ways* (do) and *arts* (jitsu). The primary purpose of a *way* is other than battle; the primary purpose of an *art* is battle. Examples of martial *arts* are Jujitsu and Karate. Examples of *ways* are **Aikido, Tai Chi**, Tai Kwon do, Judo and Kudo (archery). With the exception of Akido, most *ways* are practiced as sports. During the idealistic hippie era, it was widely believed that the martial arts (disciplines) were an attempt to divert negative energy in order to achieve peace. This attitude has had an effect on the way in which they are taught in America, and the martial disciplines are now considered a balance of body and mind control for use in self-improvement as well as physical confrontations. (See: **Aikido** and **Tai Chi Chaun**)

Martin (guitar) Company, C. F. *rock & roll* one of the oldest guitar manufacturing companies in the United States. Christian Fredric Martin started his company in New York City in 1833. The most popular of its guitars are the Dreadnaught, or **D series**, acoustical steel string models.

Martin, George (1926-) *rock and roll* record producer, musician and The Fifth Beatle. In 1955, Martin became the head of the Parlophone label, an EMI subsidiary. On April 1, 1962, **Beatles'** manager Brian Epstein met with him to play a demo tape, and on June 1, 1962, he agreed to sign The Beatles to EMI if Pete Best were replaced. Within months, Richard "**Ringo**" Starkey joined the group. Between September 4-11, 1962, The Beatles recorded their first sessions at EMI Studios in London, with George Martin as producer. Martin was knighted by Queen Elizabeth II of England in 1997. He produced and scored **Elton John's** best-selling single "Candle in the Wind '97," a tribute to the recently deceased Princess Diana. In October, 1998, George Martin released an album of Beatles' covers called *In My Life* and then formally announced the ending of his 48-year career in record production. George Martin was inducted into the Rock and Roll Hall of Fame in 1999.

marvie a humorous or sarcastic form of the word marvelous.

Mary Ann *drugs* a commonly used name for **marijuana**. Men are always associating women with other favorite things. (See: **marijuana**)

Mary Jane *drugs* another commonly used name for **marijuana**. (See: **marijuana**)

masculine force or **male principle** in **esoteric** philosophy, the active and positive aspects of nature and cosmic order. The active and positive aspects of the gods. The male principles are represented by male gods in polytheistic religions.

masculine zodiac signs fire and air: Aries, Gemini, Leo, Libra, Sagittarius and Aquarius.

M*A*S*H* the movie and television show. The 1970 movie was based on a book by Dr. Hornberger, with screenplay by Ring Lardner, Jr., directed by Robert Altman, starring Donald Sutherland as Hawkeye, Elliot Gould as Trapper John, and Sally Kellerman as Hotlips. Anti-Vietnam sentiment was high, the movie was an instant success and Lardner, who had been blacklisted during the communist witch hunt of the 1950s, won the Oscar for Best Screenplay. The film was nominated for Best Movie, and Kellerman received a Best Actress nomination. The TV show became the most poignant and respected series of the era and ran from 1973 to 1983. The cast included Alan Alda as Captain Benjamin Franklin "Hawkeye" Pierce, Wayne Rogers as Captain John Francis Xavier "Trapper" McIntyre, Loretta Swit as Margaret "Hotlips" Houlihan, Gary Burghoff as Corporal Walter "Radar" O'Reilly, Mike Farrell as Captain BJ Hunnicut, Harry

Morgan as Colonel Sherman T. Potter, Jamie Farr as Corporal Maxwell Q. Klinger, William Christopher as Father John Francis Patrick Mulcahy, McLean Stevenson as Lt. Colonel Henry Braymore Blake, Larry Linville as Major Frank Marion Burns and David Ogden Stiers as Major Charles Emerson Winchester III. The series had 251 episodes and won countless awards, with the final episode being one of the most watched television programs ever.

art by Alicia Bay Laurel © www.aliciabaylaurel.com

massage manual manipulation of the skin and muscles in an effort to relieve pain or induce relaxation as a healing aid. Massage is often a **spiritual** as well as physical contact between patient and practitioner. Because of this, it can be very beneficial when the goal is emotional **healing** and stress relief. It can also be a very seductive activity when applied with more banal intent. In the **touchy-feely** spirit of the hippie era, massage often became a prelude to lovemaking.

massive something of great importance or magnitude. Did not originate with the hippie era, yet it came into more **mainstream** use in a different context. A word that moved from a primarily physical definition to an emotional or psychological one. Examples: (old definition) "That is a **massive** rock." (new definition) "What a **massive** idea." Sometimes, this word was used solely as an exclamation or emotional outburst. Example: "**Massive**, man!"

Masters and Johnson *sex* William H. Masters (1915-2001) and Virginia E. Johnson (1925-), researchers and authors in the field of human sexuality. Masters studied medicine at Rochester University, joined Washington University School of Medicine in St. Louis in 1947, and began his research work into sexuality in 1954. Johnson studied at University of Missouri and began work with Masters as a research associate in 1957. In 1964, they established the Reproductive Biology Research Foundation, where studies into the psychology and physiology of sexual intercourse were carried out using volunteer subjects under laboratory conditions. Masters and Johnson published *Human Sexual Response* in 1966, and it became an international best seller. They continue to publish books on sexual behavior, including *Human Sexual Inadequacy* in 1970 and *On Sex and Human Loving* in 1986. Their serious research and publications on a subject which had previously been ignored due to embarrassment, served to help legitimize sexual discovery and open discourse among couples. Masters and Johnson's work has helped to confront and explore many sexual difficulties in this society. William Masters and Virginia Johnson married in 1971 and divorced in 1991.

masturbation *sex* self-performed sexual gratification. **2.** self-deluding beliefs. To lie to oneself.

mataby *drugs* high quality cannabis from the former Belgian Congo, now known as Zaire. A British term.

materialism the desire for money and material things. **2.** Frank Gaynor in the *Dictionary of Mysticism* defines it as "A proposition that only matter is existent or real; that matter is the primordial or fundamental constituent of the universe." Materialism argues "that the universe is not governed by intelligence, purpose, or final causes." "Materialism denies the truth of all doctrines and beliefs of occultism, metaphysics, and **esoteric** philosophy."

materialist someone who believes in money and material things above aesthetic and spiritual values.

Mattachine Society the first modern organization of homosexuals in the United States. Founded 1950-51 in Los Angeles by Henry (Harry) Hay, known as the "Father of the Gay Rights Movement." (See: **Gay & Lesbian Movement Events, Groups and Leaders** starting on page 602 in **Lists** at the back of this book)

Mattel toy the US soldiers' name for the **M-16** automatic rifle. Called this because of its lightweight, toylike quality and because some parts were made by a division of the Mattel toy manufacturing company.

Maui wowie a strain of **marijuana** grown on the Hawaiian Island of Maui.

Mau Mau young Black revolutionaries of the 1960s who identified with the fighting Mau Mau culture of Kenya, Africa. **2.** a derogatory term for a Black Power supporter.

max short for maximum, meaning all the way or all out. Example: "No half way, always go to the **max**."

maxed out to be depleted or over extended. Example: "He **maxed out**; he's through."

max out to go overboard or even beyond the maximum. Even more extreme than "max." Example: "**Max out**; turn that volume to eleven!" Similar in usage to **amp out**.

Max, Peter (1937-) one of the most popular record album cover artists of the era. Associated with the psychedelic movement in art.

Mayall, John (b. Nov. 29, 1933, Macclesfield, Eng.) *blues/rock & roll* he can probably play any instrument, but he has excelled on keyboards and harmonica. No other White blues musician has had more influence on today's music than John Mayall. Mayall was present at the beginning of the revival of blues and its introduction to **mainstream** White audiences. A founding member of the Bluesbreakers, formed in 1963, which, throughout the years, contained most of the important **blues/jazz**/rock crossover artists, including John McVie, **Eric Clapton**, Peter Green, Jack Bruce, Aynsley Dunbar, Mick Fleetwood, Mick Taylor, Jon Mark, Johnny Almond, Harvy Mandel, Ernie Watts, Red Holloway, etc. It has been said that Mayall discovered most of these cats. John has continued to record and perform with the Bluesbreakers as his band, which remains a revolving venue for great musicians. In addition to the Bluesbreakers, he has seen it all and played with all of the greats. John Mayall may just be the personification of music as we know it.

Mayfield, Curtis (b. 1942, Chicago, Ill.; d. 1999) a Black rhythm and blues singer, songwriter, and producer. Founding member of the Impressions, along with Jerry Butler. After Butler's departure from the group, Mayfield became its leader, writing the songs, producing, playing guitar and singing lead. The group's biggest hits were "For Your Precious Love," "Gypsy Woman," and "It's All Right." With Mayfield's 1964 song, "Keep on Pushing," he became one of the first musicians to introduce racial issues and political **consciousness** to **R&B** music. Along with other period anthems, such as "People Get Ready" and "I'm So Proud," Mayfield became a pioneer of the **civil rights** movement in music. Mayfield began a solo career in 1970, and he recorded and produced other artists, such as **Aretha Franklin** and **Gladys Knight and the Pips**. His most notable solo project was the 1972 funk album, *Superfly*. The album was a sound track to the **blaxploitation** film of the same name, which received both criticism for its stereotypical Black images and critical acclaim for Mayfield's music. Mayfield is considered one of the era's most creative songwriters and performers. Inducted into the Rock and Roll Hall of Fame in 1999.

Mazola party *sex* a get-together in which two or more people lather themselves with oil and slither around on each other, performing intercourse and other sexual activities. a.k.a. **Wesson party**. Mazola and Wesson are two brand name cooking oils.

MC5 *rock & roll/revolution* formed in 1965 in Lincoln Park, Michigan; Fred "Sonic" Smith, Michael Davis, Dennis Thompson, Wayne Kramer and Rod Tyner. A politically motivated 1960s band that exhibited the first raw rebellion which later exemplified **punk rock** of the 1970s. One of the first bands to wear American flags and shout obscenities at the establishment. Their 1970 album, *Back in the USA,* is critically acclaimed as one of the best of

the era, yet it sold poorly. Managed by John Sinclair, poet, founder of The White Panther Party, advocate of drugs and other personal freedoms. MC5 performed outside the **Democratic National Convention** in Chicago during the police riots in August, 1968. MC stood for Motor City.

McCarthy, Eugene (1916-) Democratic US Senator from Minnesota from 1959 to 1971. An outspoken opponent of the **Vietnam War**. Unsuccessful candidate for the nomination by his party for president in 1968. Ran for president in 1976 as an independent.

McCarthyism *politics* named for **Joseph P. McCarthy,** it originally meant extreme opposition to communism, but it has evolved to become a general term for fanatic persecution of any government opposition or the voicing of unsubstantiated accusations against political opponents. (See: **Joseph P. McCarthy**)

McCarthy, Joseph P. (1909-1957) Republican US Senator from Wisconsin from 1947 to 1957. Namesake of the term **McCarthyism**. Led the Red Scare in America as head of the Permanent Investigation Committee of the Senate Operations Committee. He threatened to identify communists in industry and government, and his tactics of "guilt by association" hurt many prominent citizens when he branded people as communists merely for knowing other communists. He was censured by the Senate in 1954 for actions contrary to their traditions. His excesses in dealing with assumed "enemies of the state" helped to awaken liberal intellectuals to the threat of persecution and loss of freedom. His assault on basic freedoms triggered a reaction that helped create the **civil rights**, **free-speech** and hippie movements. (See: **McCarthyism**)

McCartney, Paul (b. James Paul McCartney, June 18, 1942, Liverpool, Eng.) *rock & roll* after playing bass, singing and writing songs in the most famous rock and roll band in history, **The Beatles,** Paul McCartney started a solo career in 1970, which has taken him from the sublime to what some might say was the ridiculous. His pop bands in the mid-1970s with his late wife Linda as a member were not taken seriously by many, yet Paul McCartney has continued to create solid music, sometimes venturing into blues, country and **jazz**. He may not have the marketing ability of his fellow Beatle **John Lennon**, but he has never forgotten a note of music he ever heard; he is dedicated to those notes and knows how to put them together. The Beatles were inducted into the Rock and Roll Hall of Fame in 1988. McCartney was inducted into the Rock and Roll Hall of Fame in 1999.

McGovern, George (1922-) Democratic US Senator from South Dakota from 1963 to 1981. An outspoken opponent of the **Vietnam War**. Lost the 1972 presidential election to President Richard Nixon.

McKenna, Terence (1946-2000) author and explorer, graduated from the University of California at Berkeley with a combined major in Ecology, Resource Conservation and Shamanism. He traveled extensively in Asia and South and Central America, studying shamanism, ethnic ritual drug use and natural psycedelics. For the last 25 years of his life, McKenna was a vocal advocate of psychedelic experimentation and was considered **Timo-** thy Leary's replacement as spokesman for educational drug use.

MD (See: **mad dog**)

MDA *drugs* (See: **methyldeoxyamphetamine**)

MDMA *drugs* (See: **methylenedioxamphetaminean**)

meal ticket a person or situation that supplies financial support. Considered a one-way arrangement in which support is given with little or no reciprocation. Example: "Don't mess with her; she's my **meal ticket**."

mean exciting or interesting. Depending on the situation and vocal inflection, **mean** can indicate "good," as in this definition, or it can define something as "bad." **Mean** was often used to compliment something that was unappreciated by straight society. Example: "That was a **mean** concert, man."

mean machine a fast, attractive or impressive car.

meat *sex* an impersonal and derogatory term for a casual sexual partner. **2.** a person who is vulnerable or in danger.

meat and potatoes the basics, the staple. The basic requirement to sustain life. Examples: "Music is **meat and potatoes** for me." "I don't need frills; I'm a **meat and potatoes** man."

meatball a stupid person.

meat-eater a non-**vegetarian**. It was used as a derogatory term by some vegetarians during a period of the hippie era when it was thought that carnivorous humans were barbaric. Same usage as **flesh-eater**.

meathead a stupid person.

meat hooks hands. Used prior to the hippie era, but expanded during the 1960s and 70s. Refers to either hands as hooks made of meat or hands as hooks that grab things like meat. I believe it is most likely the former.

meat market or **meat rack** *sex* a bar or night club, where people can make connections with strangers for sexual liaisons.

meat wagon an extravagant car designed to impress and seduce women. Meat is a derogatory reference to a women. **2** an ambulance. I'm stretching to include this definition in this dictionary. Definitely used before the hippie era, but my first recollection of it was on Saturday morning cartoons around that period.

Mecca the Holy City of **Islam**, in Saudi Arabia, the birthplace of **Muhammad**. A hajj, or pilgrimage to Mecca is one of the Five Pillars of Islam. All **Muslims** face Mecca to perform ritual prayer five times a day.

media event an over-publicized occurrence. Something of interest to the news media because they feel it will be interesting to the public.

media of the era (See: page 635 in **Lists** at the back of this book)

media hype publicity. Excessive publicity.

medical astrology the branch of astrology concerned with the planetary causes of disease. In other words, the study of the supposed influence of each astrological sign on the human body.

medicinal marijuana *drugs* for centuries, **marijuana** has been used for medicinal purposes by numerous cultures, yet Federal drug laws in the US discourage the use of marijuana as medicine.

Throughout the 1970s and on into the 21st century, individuals and organizations have tried to reverse this oversight through the courts and by the ballot. In the late 1970s, **Robert Randall**, a teacher living near Washington, DC, was the first person to win the right to be "exempted from Federal drug laws in order to use marijuana as medicine." Randall had glaucoma, which caused intraocular pressure that would eventually cause blindness. Smoking six marijuana joints a day relieved this pressure and, at least temporarily, preserved his eyesight. Since that decision, this dispensation has been granted only on a case-by-case basis. In certain areas of the US, it is possible to obtain legal approval of medical marijuana use with a doctor's recommendation and a lot of clout. Some states have won approval through voter propositions, but the Federal Government is still fighting it; in 2001, the Supreme Court voted against the use of medicinal marijuana.

medicine *drugs* a euphemism for illegal drugs.

medicine man in American Indian culture, the priest-magician associated with **healing** and **magic,** and also the custodian of sacred objects and ceremonial ritual. In most other tribal cultures and races, the terms **witch doctor** or **shaman** would best describe individuals of similar importance. (See: **shaman** and **witch doctor**)

medicine man *drugs* a drug dealer.

medicine wheel an American Indian ritualistic art object used in the **healing** arts. The hippie culture embraced many ethnic rituals and art forms, and the medicine wheel was used as decoration by the **counterculture**.

photo by John McCleary ©

meditation *religion* the process of simplifying thought patterns in order to reach a point of mental relaxation at which spiritual reflection and growth are possible. Many techniques of meditation are used in Eastern religions. Concentrating on an art form, ringing a bell or creating a droning sound by rubbing the top of a bowl with a stick are some examples of meditation; reciting a **mantra** is another. A mantra is a short phrase that is repeated over and over in order to achieve a peaceful trance while meditating. During the hippie era, the practice of meditation was introduced into Western culture. Today many people have followed the hippie lead and are using Eastern meditation as a way to relax and retreat from the pressures and turmoil of everyday life.

medium a person who acts as an intermediary for communicating with the **spirit** world. Someone capable of making contact with the dead or other non-human entities.

meds *drugs* short for medicine. Any drugs.

meemies, the short for "screaming meemies," an uncomfortable feeling or nervous reaction. Sometimes used to describe the discomfort associated with a **cold turkey** withdrawal from **opiate** drugs.

meerschaum pipe a carved, white stone smoking pipe. Originally from Turkey or Asia Minor, where the soft, white, clay-like stone material can be found. The stone, called meerschaum, is a hydrated magnesium silicate. The traditional pipes are usually carved into intricate portrait faces of the people of the Middle East. The hippie culture dis

covered the meerschaum quality of delivering a cool smoke and used the pipes to smoke **marijuana** and **hashish**. These beautiful pipes also appealed to the interest of the hippie culture in ethnic art.

meet short for meeting. An appointment to conduct a drug transaction.

mega large or numerous. Can be used as a prefix to many other terms, therefore intensifying those word. Examples: "megastar, mega-ego and **megabucks**."

megabucks lots of money.

megafamily a term introduced to the American public around 1970, indicating a group of people living together who are not necessarily related by marriage or blood. Similar use as **extended family** or **commune**.

me generation a self-indulgent generation. More a period of time than an age group or generation, the "me" period of selfishness appeared in the late 1970s and hit its stride in the 1980s. Generally, the 1950s were an era of conformity and self-denial. The 1960s and 70s saw the **now generation**, a rebellion against the 50s. Then, at some period in the late 1970s, people who were already predisposed to selfishness mistook the decadence of the time purely as **self-indulgence**. **Cocaine** became the drug of choice of the late 1970s and 80s. Cocaine is a very selfish drug; it could be called a right-wing drug. The conservative swing of politics and the use of more self-indulgent drugs, such as **methamphetamine** and cocaine, increased in the "me" generation. The 1960s basic **spirit**, though it seemed to be indulgent, was not selfish. The main direction of the 60s was **self-help** and feeling good about oneself in order to reduce the stress of life, thus helping to solve some of the existing cultural problems. The 1970s were a transitional period in which people began to confuse self-help with self-gratification. The 1980s were the selfish "me" generation. (See: **now generation**)

Meher Baba (India, 1894-1969) *religion* the "Don't Worry-Be Happy" guru. A spiritual leader who has many followers in America. In 1931, while traveling on the same ship with **Mahatma Gandhi** in route to London, Meher Baba met Gandhi and is said to have become his spiritual adviser. Merher Baba established two locations of pilgrimage outside India during the 1950s, Meher Spiritual Center, in Myrtle Beach, South Carolina, USA, and Avatar's Abode, near Brisbane, Australia. He became known in the West during the 1960s for opposing the use of **LSD** and other drugs in the quest for spiritual enlightenment. In the fall of 1968, he announced that his work was completed to his satisfaction; he then "left his body" on January 31, 1969, one month before his 76th birthday. From 1925 until his death, he did not speak. Regarded by his followers as an **Avatar**. (See: **Avatar** and **Mahatma Gandhi**)

-meister *suffix* master or professional. Added to a word, it indicates that the person described is efficient at what he does. Examples: **Schlockmeister** (a person who makes or sells cheap stuff), **lovemeister** (a lover), **fartmeister** (someone who farts a lot, and well).

*mellow peaceful and reserved. Examples: "That's a **mellow** cat, and she's a **mellow** mouse. Suppose we introduce them here in this **mellow** house?"

mellow out calm down. Example: "If you don't **mellow out,** you'll...no, *I'll* have a heart attack."

"Mellow Yellow" the title of a 1967 hit song by Donovan, a popular Scottish folk/rock singer. At the time it was widely reported that the term referred to smoking banana peels for a drug high, but Donovan later revealed that the subject of the song was an electric **dildo**.

melons women's breasts. Usually refers to large breasts.

meltdown the coming apart of a project. A mental breakdown. Examples: "This whole job is in **meltdown**; I just can't keep people focused." "Gord is having a **meltdown**; don't say anything poignant to him."

member the penis or male sex organ. From the Latin term *membrum virile*.

mental crazy. Example: "Gord is **mental**; don't say anything to disturb him."

mental body *occult* in **occult** terminology, the "body" in which a person's consciousness lives on in the **mental plane** after "death" on the **astral plane**. (See: **astral plane, mental plane**)

mental case a mentally ill or crazy person.

mental diarrhea endless, pointless conversation. Same as verbal diarrhea.

mental plane or **mental world** *occult* in **occult** terminology, the plane or "world" of existence following the **astral plane**; the place in which people live in the **mental body** after their "death" on the astral plane. (See: **astral plane** and **mental body**)

men's lib a cultural movement of the 1960s and 70s that allowed men to find their "feminine side" and to rebel against predominant social pressures to be **cool, macho**, strong, detached and insensitive.

merchant a seller or advocate. When added to a word, it indicates that the person described is selling or advocating the use of something. Examples: **Death merchant** (a weapons dealer), **love merchant** (a lover), **drug merchant** (a dope dealer).

merkin the female pubic area. **2.** an artificial **vagina** used as a sex toy or sexual aid. **3.** medieval word for a pubic wig worn to cover the effects of syphilis. As a medieval term, it was lost to society for many years until the intellectual interests of the hippie culture revived it into spirited, though limited, use.

Merlin mythical magician and philosopher of Celtic tales and a mentor to King Arthur. Many hippies identified with the Celtic culture, its **magic** and Arthurian legend. Merlin was the pattern for numerous self-styled magicians and **warlocks** of the hippie era.

Merry Pranksters or **Pranksters** a group of mostly unrelated people who came together in 1964 and formed a **family** around **Ken Kesey**, the author of *One Flew Over the Cuckoo's Nest* and *Sometimes a Great Notion*. They were supposedly patterned after the mystic cult in **Robert Heinlein**'s science fiction novel, *Strangers in a Strange Land*. The Pranksters seemed to be joined together for no other reason than to ingest drugs and party. They had a number of adventures in California and one memorable trip across the United States in Ken Kesey's large, painted school bus with "Furthur" written on the front and "Caution: Weird Load," on the back. The adventures of the Merry Pranksters and their "Hieronymus Bosch bus" were related in **Tom Wolfe**'s 1968 book *The Electric Kool-Aid Acid Test*.

Merseybeat a style of **rock and roll** music born in the Liverpool area of England in the early 1960s. Mersey is the river that flows through Liverpool. The primary band that created this music form was **The Beatles**, but there were many lesser known groups, such as Gerry & The Pacemakers, The Swinging Blue Jeans, Undertakers, Pete Best & the Original All Stars, Danny & the Hit Cats and Gene Day & the Jangobeats. A few groups, like the Dave Clark Five and Chad & Jeremy, were considered Merseybeat, but they were from other areas of England. These groups and their "Mersey sound" were the first wave of the **British invasion**.

mesc or **mess** short for **mescaline**.

mescaline the active component of the **peyote** and San Pedro cacti. A **psyche-**

delic synthesized from these cacti and dispensed in capsules. It was normally a brown powder, and sometimes it was cut with instant cocoa mix. Mescaline was one of the drugs that influenced **Aldous Huxley** in writing his 1955 book entitled *The Doors of Perception*.

meshugana or **meshiggana**   crazy, a crazy person. Yiddish.

mess around *sex* to indulge in sexual play, possibly even the ultimate, sexual intercourse.

mess (someone) **around** or **mess** (someone) **up**   to annoy or physically hurt someone. Examples: "If you **mess Judy around** anymore, I'll **mess you up**."

mess with to bother, annoy or confront someone. Examples: "If you **mess with** Judy, I'll **mess with** you."

messing up (one's) **mind** or **messing up** (one's) **head**   inflicting psychological damage upon someone. Example: "He was **messing up her head** with stories of fame."

Messiah   in both Hebrew mysticism and Christianity, the Savior who will come to restore the Chosen People to their rightful place in the world.

metal *rock & roll* short for **heavy-metal**. Heavy-metal is a form of **rock and roll** music that relies on extreme volume, high-octane electric guitar, flashy costumes and dramatic stage performances. Originally coined by **William Burroughs** in his book, *Naked Lunch*, pertaining to something other than music. It was first used in music ("heavy-metal thunder") in **Steppenwolf**'s "Born to be Wild."   Black Sabbath, **Led Zeppelin**, **Deep Purple** and Grand Fund Railroad were the most recognized heavy-metal rock groups in the hippie era.

metaphysics *occult* the science of the **occult**, mysterious and supernatural.

meth *drugs*   short for **methamphetamine**.

methadone *drugs* an **opiate** whose brand name is **Dolophine**. The only legally authorized opiate used to treat heroin **addiction** in America. Used in heroin **withdrawal** programs called methadone maintenance. Unfortunately, it is also addictive and serves only to replace one drug with another. Some medical and scientific experts feel that it is actually more dangerous than heroin, and its only advantage is to the authorities, by giving them control of the movements of drug addicts.

methamphetamines *drugs* from the family of **amphetamines**, a synthetic stimulant similar in effect to **cocaine**, yet longer lasting and less expensive. Often called **speed**. Brand names are **Methedrine**, and Desoxyn. After the Controlled Substance Act of 1970, the illegal production of amphetamines began. Prominent street names of the 1960s and 70s were speed, **meth**, **crystal**, **crank** and **ice**. Primarily ingested during the hippie era, the new powdered forms are now snorted, shot and smoked. The most dangerous and potentially damaging drug to our society because: 1) it is cheap to produce and cheap to buy; 2) the production process is damaging to the environment; 3) it is psychologically and physically destructive to the user. One might ask why anybody with an ounce of intelligence would want to take this stuff. The answer is, it takes the user away from the painful, day-to-day fight for survival in this society. Some people just can't cope with this overly competitive culture. The solution would be a better education and a better economic existence for the poor of our country. Making this drug at home has become a cottage industry, and many of the manufacturers are not very good at it. There are inherent dangers with this drug and worse consequences from taking bad doses. Most recommendations are to stay away from this drug; it will kill you prematurely. Remember, all things in moderation; thinking people use their drugs, foolish people use drugs that will kill them.

Methedrine *drugs* a brand name **methamphetamine**.

meth freak or **meth head** *drugs* someone who is addicted to **methamphetamines**.

methylenedioxamphetamine (MDMA) *drugs* an early form of the **designer drug ecstasy** and a late arrival during the hippie era. Chemical name, 3,4 methylenedioxymethamphetamin. Making this drug at home has become a cottage industry, and many of the manufacturers are not very good at it. There are inherent dangers with this drug and worse consequences from taking bad doses. Many recommendations are to stay away from this drug; it may kill you prematurely. Remember, all things in moderation; thinking people use their drugs, foolish people allow drugs to use them. a.k.a. **Adam, love drug, vitamin E, vitamin X, X, XTC**. (See: **ecstasy**)

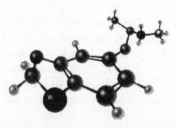

methyldeoxyamphetamine (MDA) *drugs* the **love drug**. A mild dose of

the designer drug **ecstasy**, a pseudo-psychedelic synthetic **amphetamine** variant. An early form of the "designer" drug creations and a late arrival during the hippie era. Many users experience a heightened sensuality and warm feeling toward others, though it may produce excess energy, hyperactivity and distortion of perception. Basically a low dose of the compound **MDMA**. Making this drug at home has become a cottage industry, and many of the manufacturers are not very good at it. There are inherent dangers with this drug and worse consequences from taking bad doses. Many recommendations are to stay away from this drug; it may kill you prematurely. Remember, all things in moderation; thinking people use their drugs, foolish people allow drugs to use them. a.k.a. **love drug, X, ecstasy**. (See: **ecstasy**)

Metzner, Ralph (1935-) an associate in **consciousness** studies at Harvard with Timothy Leary and Richard Alpert. Director of IFIF from 1963 to 1967. Author of *The Psychedelic Experience* with Leary (1964), *Maps of Consciousness* (1971) and *Know Your Type: Maps of Identity* (1979). (See: **International Foundation for Internal Freedom, IFIF**)

Mexican mud *drugs* highly refined, dark brown **heroin**.

MIA missing in action. Originally a military term, it was adopted by the **counterculture** to mean failing to arrive at a destination or failing to function in a sexual situation. One of a number of military terms adopted by the counterculture out of a morbid or sarcastic sense of humor. **2.** During the war in Vietnam, there were reportedly 1,172 American POW/MIAs. At the end of the war in 1973, 591 prisoners were returned, so mathematics would indicate that there are still 581 MIAs unaccounted for. Since the end of the war, some bodies have been returned, reducing that number even more. The two designations, MIA and POW, have been grouped together by those who think some of the MIAs are still POWs; yet there should actually be two other designations, DNRs (dead not recovered) and DODs (deserters or defectors). MIAs can fall into four different categories: 1) POWs that were not recorded or returned by North Vietnam. 2) POWs who died in captivity due to injury or abuse, whose remains were not returned. 3) Combatants who were killed, yet whose remains were not found and/or identified. 4) Deserters and defectors. (See: **POW**)

mic or **mike** short for **microgram**. A metric measurement used to parcel portions of drugs.

Michoacan *drugs* a particular strain of **marijuana** grown in the State of Michoacan, Mexico. It was very strong and highly sought after.

mickey mouse or **Mickey Mouse** something phony, cheap or slapped together. Possibly from the opinion of many that Disney's creations are cardboard cutouts designed to fool people into thinking they are reality. Example: "That's a **mickey mouse** guitar; I wouldn't buy it for Pat Boone."

microcosm *occult* literally, *the small universe,* a term used by theosophists and occultists to describe mankind; considered to be a replica of the macrocosm (the great universe), because humans incorporate all the elements of frailty and potential that exist in the universe.

microgram *drugs* the metric measurement used to dispense small quantities of drugs, such as LSD. There are approximately 100 to 300 micrograms of LSD in an average dose or **hit.** You do the math; theoretically, an ounce of LSD should get 140,000 people very high.

Micro Instrumentation and Telemetry Systems (MITS) *computer revolution* the company that produced the Altair 8080 (the people's computer) in 1974. It was a kit and became one of the first popular hobbyist computers (personal computer or microcomputer). The company was owned by Ed Roberts. The Altair 8080 used an Intel 8080 chip and ran a **BASIC** operating system programed by Bill Gates, Paul Allen and Monte Davidoff. The Altair kit sold for $397. Altair was named by a twelve-year-old girl for the Forbidden Planet to which the Starship Enterprise was heading in "Star Trek." MITS was also the first company in the US to build calculator kits. (See: **Computer Revolution Milestones, Companies and Leaders** starting on page 626 in **Lists** at the back of this book)

microprocessor *computer revolution* an ultra-small computer component made of **silicon chips**, containing etched patterns carrying electrically coded messages. The processing unit or math-logical portion of a microcomputer consisting of **integrated circuit** chips and sometimes a memory unit. Invented by Intel employee Ted Hoff in 1971, it opened the way to miniaturization and reduction of costs, thus making personal computers possible. It was basically the miniaturization of bigger switching units found in early, larger mainframe computers. This miniaturization was made possible by silicon chip technology. (See: **Computer Revolution Milestones, Companies and Leaders** starting on page 626 in **Lists** at the back of this book)

Microsoft *computer revolution* the computer software company founded by Bill Gates and Paul Allen in the summer of 1975. Microsoft is an abbreviation for "microcomputer software." The company evolved from Gates and Allen's original company called Traf-O-Data, which they started in high school to analyze automobile traffic patterns in small Oregon communities. (See: **Computer Revolution Milestones, Companies and Leaders** starting on page 626 in **Lists** at the back of this book)

Mictlan the underworld home of the dead in Aztec mythology; ruled by Mictlantecuhtli, god of the dead, and his wife, Mictlancihuatl, goddess of death.

Middle America the **middle class**. Meant to indicate the political and economic attitude of the people who live in the Midwest, who tend to be conservative politically and economically. (See: **middle class**)

middle class the portion of the population who make an average living in

comparison to the total income of the nation. These people are usually salary or hourly wage earners who could not economically survive unless they continued working. Politically, they may be conservative or liberal. Some are liberal and adventurous politically because they feel financially secure, while others tend to be conservative politically and financially because they think that radical economic and political change would jeopardize their livelihood.

middle leg the penis. Sometimes called the third leg.

midwife a person, usually, though not necessarily, a woman, who assists in childbirths without the presence of a trained doctor. It is an ancient tradition that was renewed during the hippie era. During the 1960s and 70s, partly as a move back to nature, many more home births were conducted, and a whole new midwife movement was created. A midwife did not necessarily have formal medical or nursing training, but usually had some education or experience in the birth of children. An interesting statistic prompting the return of home births is that, per capita, more newborns die after hospital births than home births. Hospitals contain many bacteria to which babies may be exposed.

mike short for microphone.

mileage recognition, advantage or profit from some situation. Example: "Man, she got a lot of **mileage** out of that see-through blouse."

Mile-High Club a small group whose members have made love in an airplane flying above one mile high. Where, when and why this unofficial club was created is a mystery steeped in the murky depths of mankind's imagination.

Miles, Buddy (b. September 5, 1946, Omaha, Neb.) *blues, jazz, rock* Black singer/drummer who also plays a guitar left-handed and upside down like **Jimi Hendrix**. Miles has played with many blues musicians and **jazz** legends, old and new. He has recorded with Hendrix, Santana, Wilson Pickett and others, and was a member of **Michael Bloomfield**'s band, Electric Flag.

military-industrial complex *social issues* a term coined around 1961 by then President "Ike" Eisenhower, describing the large, politically powerful manufacturing organizations supplying the growing military needs of the Pentagon. He was concerned that this interconnected political and economic union would exert lobbying pressures to continue military buildup in order to enrich industry. In a farewell speech, outgoing President Eisenhower warned the nation about "the potential for the disastrous rise of misplaced power by the military-industrial complex."

milk to exploit. To extract as much recognition, advantage or profit from a situation as possible. Example: "If I were you, I would **milk** that broken toe for all the sympathy I could get."

Milk, Harvey *social issues* a **gay**, small business owner in San Francisco, Calif., who became politically active to support homosexual rights in that city. Called "The Mayor of Castro Street." Campaigning openly as gay, he was elected to the San Francisco Board of Supervisors in 1977 representing the Fifth (Castro) District, which contains a large portion of the city's homosexual population. On November 27, 1978, Milk and San Francisco's **straight**

Mayor George Moscone were shot and killed in the City Hall by **homophobic** ex-policeman and district supervisor **Dan White**. White was disturbed by what he thought was the city's favoritism toward the homosexual population. (See: **Dan White** and **Twinkie defense**)

Miller, David Vermont college student arrested October 18, 1965, for burning his draft card at a New York City anti-**Vietnam War** rally several days earlier. Reportedly, the first of such arrests under a new Federal law signed by President Lyndon Johnson. Miller was a member of Catholic Workers, a pacifist group.

Miller, Henry (Valentine) (b. 1891, New York City; d. 1980) author, lifestyle example to the **counterculture**. Born of German-American parents, he spoke primarily German until school age. Attended City College of New York briefly in 1909, worked at a variety of jobs from 1910 to 1924, including managing a speakeasy in **Greenwich Village**. Began writing book reviews in 1919 and unpublished novels in 1922. In 1924, he vowed to do anything he could to support himself exclusively as a writer, and for a time this included selling poems door-to-door. He went to Europe to find a publisher in 1928, and then returned to New York and wrote a third novel, which was never published. In 1930, he moved to Paris, where he lived for the next ten years. He survived for a time on handouts and by working in journalism. Then Miller met Anaïs Nin, who helped him publish his first major book, *Tropic of Cancer*, in 1934. It was largely autobiographical and so sexually explicit that it was banned in English-speaking countries. The first American edition was not printed until 1961. Subsequent books, such as *Black Spring* in 1936 and *Tropic of Capricorn* in 1939, were also banned. When World War II broke out, Miller went to Greece to visit the writer Lawrence Durrell, and he wrote *Colossus of Maroussi* in 1941 from that experience. Returning to the United States, Miller toured the country, writing about the adventure in *The Air-Conditioned Nightmare* in 1945. In 1944, he settled in Big Sur, California, and several of his books began to sell. He wrote *Sexus* in 1949 and *Nexus* in 1960, which were to be part of a trilogy on his life called *The Rosy Crucifixion*, but the third book never materialized. In the late-1950s, the courts decided that *Tropic of Cancer* and his other writings were not obscene, and his works began to be republished. Miller's books became sought after by the public, and he was recognized within the literary world for helping to break down the barriers of censorship. Late in life, he also received recognition as a water-colorist. By the end of his life, Miller was considered one of the major forces behind the fresh, new, no-limits literature movement.

Miller, Steve (b. Oct. 5, 1943, Milwaukee, Wis.) *blues, rock & roll* one of the era's most respected guitar players, he influenced many others and played with the best. His Steve Miller Band has continued to produce great music since it was formed in San Francisco in 1966. Slowly moving from his blues roots, Miller became one of the biggest selling pop-rock artists of the late 1970s and early 1980s.

Millett, Kate (1934-) *social issues* an early leader in the feminist movement. In 1970, she published her doctoral dissertation as a book entitled *Sexual Poli-*

tics, which became a best-seller and made Millett a spokesperson of the women's movement. The book was a feminist perspective on the "frequently neglected political aspect" of sexual relations between men and women. It explored the male dominance of women in sex, business and politics. Millett has authored numerous and diverse books, such as *Flying*, 1973; *Sita*, 1977; *The Basement*, 1980; *Going to Iran*, 1982; *The Loony-Bin Trip*, 1990; and *Politics of Cruelty*, 1993. Millett is also an artist.

militant someone who is willing to use violent force to achieve political goals. A term normally used in political or revolutionary contexts, yet it can also be applied to a person who is merely violent by nature.

Mime Troupe (See: **San Francisco Mime Troupe**)

mind-altering drugs chemicals that alter perception and unearth and expand subconscious thoughts and visions that are stored in the brain. This can be accomplished through manufactured, recreational, psychedelic drugs like **LSD** or **MDA**, or from plant life, such as **peyote**, **psilocybin** mushrooms or **cannabis**. Some prescription drugs also create mind-altered states. a.k.a **mind-expanding drugs**. (See: **mind-expanding drugs**)

mind-bender a situation that confuses or confounds one's sense of reality.

mind-boggling a person, place or thing that overloads one's capacity to reason.

mind-blower a person or situation that offends or confounds.

mind-expanding drugs chemicals that unearth and expand subconscious thoughts that are stored in the brain.

Our brain processes a huge amount of information and reduces it to a small amount of facts, which relate our past knowledge and make it understandable. The brain is a **reducing valve** that compartmentalizes information so that the mass of facts will not confuse our day-to-day lives. Supporters of psychedelic drugs claim that hallucinogenics open up the mind to expose all the many things that we have hidden there. Mind expanding is an educational process that some people feel is badly needed in this dumbed-down society. a.k.a **mind-altering drugs.** (See: **reducing valve**)

mind games psychological actions designed to confuse or confound others.

mind fuck something that messes with one's mind. An amazing or confusing person, place or thing.

mind-fucker or **mindfucker** an amazing or confusing person, place or thing. Something that messes with one's mind. John Sebastian called the gathering at **Woodstock** a "mindfucker."

mind-fucking the act of confusing or confounding others.

mindless without thought, without intelligence. Example: "He's **mindless**, his ideas are **mindless**, his conclusions are **mindless** and even his cat is **mindless**."

mindset a set of beliefs. An unalterable state of mind or value system. Comes from "his mind is set."

mini short for **miniskirt.**

mini- prefix when added to another word it indicates that the item is small. Examples: "**Mini Copper, minimart, minipenis,** etc."

photo by John McCleary ©

miniskirt a very short skirt that was introduced to the American public in 1965. The concept is attributed to French designer Andre Courreges, but British designer **Mary Quant** made it popular. The **fashion** model first associated with the **miniskirt** was **Twiggy**, a very thin teenager whose real name was Leslie Hornby. (See: **Mary Quant** and **Twiggy**)

mink *sex* someone who copulates frequently. From "fucks like a mink." Apparently, minks enjoy copulating.

Miranda Law *social issues* on June 13, 1966, the Supreme Court ruled that a confession is invalid if obtained before a suspect has been informed of his rights to remain silent and to have an attorney present at his interrogation. Created in response to the rape conviction of Ernesto Miranda. Miranda was denied access to a lawyer while being questioned.

Mister Big an important person. Primarily used in a sarcastic manner to indicate someone who is overly self-important.

Mister Clean a person who is very tidy in appearance. Primarily used in a sarcastic manner to indicate someone who is overly fastidious.

Mister Nice Guy someone who is very nice. Often, this is used sarcastically to indicate someone who tries too hard to appear nice. The "Mister" is used sarcastically to indicate just the opposite of what is said. The use of capital letters can also indicate sarcasm.

Mitchell, Joni (b. Roberta Joan Anderson, Nov. 7, 1943, Fort MacLeod, Alberta, Canada) *folk, rock, jazz* one of the first **hippie chicks** of our dreams, but that is politically incorrect today, and it was simplistic even then. She is one of the most respected singer/songwriters, male or female, of the era; her words cut deeply and her music set your emotions free. Joni is forever changing and is comfortable in **jazz**, **folk** or rock. Although she has disavowed the value of her early work in recent interviews, her first four albums: *Joni Mitchell*, 1968; *Clouds*, 1969; *Ladies of the Canyon*, 1970; and *Blue*, 1971, contain some of the most emotive music ever produced. Inducted into the Rock and Roll Hall of Fame in 1997.

mix *rock & roll* to combine a number of musical performances, previously recorded on various tracks of magnetic audio tape, into one performance with the desired mixture of sounds.

mixed bag something with conflicting elements or a combination of things. Example: "That band is a **mixed bag** of styles and musical influences."

mix it up to get in a physical fight or verbal battle.

m'man short for "my man," a term of endearment, friendship or brotherly love.

mo' short for more.

mobile having an automobile of some kind.

-mobile *suffix* added to a word to indicate that it is a vehicle. Examples: **fuckmobile, pimpmobile, slugmobile**. A humorous and often sarcastic way to ridicule a person's choice of transportation.

Mobilization Committee, National Mobilization Committee or **Spring Mobilization Committee (MOBE)** *politics* (See: **National Mobilization Committee**)

Moby Grape *psychedelic/rock & roll* a very good early **psychedelic** band formed in San Francisco in 1966. They came, they played, they faded away.

Modern Primitive movement a counterculture of people who indulge in primitive rituals and body art practices, such as tattooing, body piercing and scarification. One of the most recognized rituals is the North American Indian O-Kee-Pa ceremony, in which the participant is hung by flesh hooks through his skin. Scarification is the creation of designs on the skin by cutting the flesh. **Fakir Musafar** is known as the father of the Modern Primitive movement. He was an early exponent of tattooing, body piercing and primitive rituals. (See: **Fakir Musafar, tattooing, body piercing,** and **Skin Brothers**)

*****mod** short for modern; basically, a design sense that evolved in London in the mid-1960s. Born from a youthful sense of rebellion against the conservative clothing of their parents, young people created an avenue of self-expression by wearing often cheap or used, flashy, shocking and eclectic clothing. British designer Mary Quant observed this development on the streets of London and adopted it into the **fashion** world, helping to create the miniskirt, which was the mod style's most recognizable clothing statement.

mods and rockers the two conflicting groups of young people who evolved in London during the early 1960s. Clothing was one of the differences between the two groups, with the **mods** being the more **fashion** conscious and the **rockers** as the precursor of the hippie and grunge look. Mods rode motor scooters, and rockers preferred motorcycles. The differences became blurred to those of us not in that cultural environment, and the arrival of **The Beatles** on the scene soon brought the two groups closer together since both groups claimed them. **The Beatles** started out rather mod, but soon became more rocker with their long hair and nonconforming clothes. **The Rolling Stones** were obviously "rockers" from the start.

"Mod Squad, The" an ABC TV cop show that premiered on September 24, 1968. The principals were three young, modern, undercover Los Angeles police officers, one White female, one African American male and one White male. Starring Michael Cole as Pete Cochran, Peggy Lipton as Julie Barnes, and Clarence Williams III as Linc Hayes, with Tige Andrews as Captain Adam Greer.

mo-fo short for **motherfucker**.

Mohammed (b. approximately 570 A.D.; d. 632 A.D.) *religion* prophet and apostle of **Islam**. Said to be the final messenger of God. God's message, supposedly imparted to Mohammed in visions, is called the **Qur'an** (**Koran**), and is meant to complete the previous revelations to the Jews and Christians. Mohammed expanded Islam through military conquest and political intrigue.

Mohammedanism (See: **Islam**)

mojo an object that holds power or luck. An **Afro**-Caribbean term for a charm or **fetish**. It can also mean power itself, and, during the hippie era, it evolved into meaning male power or sexual power. In the 1990s, it became even more specific; in the Austin Powers movies of that time, it was trivialized to mean a man's penis. "A variant is 'Joe Moore,' which, in the 1920s and 30s, was a piece of gamblers' lucky hoodoo (the **spirit** or **essence** of everything)." From Clarence Major in his book *Juba to Jive*.

mojo working having good luck.

moldy old. From old and moldy or "moldy fig," a **jazz** term for a person who doesn't like new music.

Monck, Chip the very talented stage lighting and technical designer responsible for much of the appearance and visual ambiance of the **Monterey Pop Festival** and **Woodstock Music Festival**.

Monday Night Class *religion* a series of "classes" conducted in the San Francisco, California, area by **Stephen Gaskin**. Gaskin had been a student of S. I. Hayakawa at San Francisco State and was headed for a successful academic career, when he dropped out to became a motivational speaker, explaining how to get **high** without the necessity of drugs. In 1968, Gaskin started **The Farm**, a large commune in western Tennessee, which still exists today. (See: **high** and **The Farm**)

mondo big, good or exciting. One of those pseudo-foreign words that may have been adopted because of its exotic sound. It may have come from "monstrous," or possibly "mundo," which means "world" or "earth" in Italian, and that may relate somehow to size. It evolved in the surfer culture. Examples: "That was a **mondo** party, dude." "What a **mondo** wave that was, man."

mondo- prefix a great deal of, or much. It intensified the size or number of any word to which it was added. Examples: "**Mondo-money, mondo-love, mondo-macho**." Similar usage as **beaucoup**.

money anything of value or a salable item. Example: "Don't touch my fingers; they're my **money**."

money in the bank a sure thing or foregone conclusion. Example: "Don't worry about winning that game; it's **money in the bank**."

moneymaker a woman's ass or, even more precisely, her sexual organs. From the business of prostitution in which a woman's body makes the money and profit for her pimp.

money trip a person's financial attitude or economic situation. Examples: "Digger's on a strange **money trip**; he won't do anything if he has to pay for it." "Her **money trip's** a bummer; she can't pay the rent this month."

Monkees, The *media controlled rock & roll* formed in 1965 in Los Angeles, Calif., Michael Nesmith (b. Dec. 30, 1942, Houston, Tex.), gtr.; David Jones (b. Dec, 30, 1945, Manchester, Eng.), voc.; Peter Tork (b. Feb. 13, 1944, Washington, DC), bass, voc.; Mickey Dolenz (b. Mar. 8, 1945, Tarzana, Calif.), drums, voc. A band initially created as the characters in a television series patterned after **The Beatles** movie, "**A Hard Day's Night**." They eventually produced some good records, were quite successful and became teen idols. Less popular groups of the same genre were The Partridge Family and The Archies. The Monkees, with a few exceptions, primarily performed songs written by others. The show was hugely successful and helped to legitimize, to some extent, the youth culture and counterculture growing at that time.

monkey *drugs* a drug habit.

monkey bite a red welt on the body caused by a lover's amorous sucking of the skin. (See: **hickey**)

monkey on (one's) **back, a** *drugs* a drug habit. **2.** Any affliction or annoyance.

monkey suit a tuxedo.

monotheism the belief in only one God, considered the creator and ruler of all things in the universe.

monster big or good. It modifies the size or value of any word it precedes. Used extensively in the music industry. Examples: "**monster record, monster hit, monster truck**."

monster *drugs* any drug that acts on the central nervous system.

Monterey Pop or **Monterey International Pop Festival (June 16, 17 and 18, 1967)** a music festival held at the Monterey, California, County Fairgrounds. It was, for all practical purposes, the first rock and roll festival. A festival, in this context, is a musical event in an outdoor venue, conducted over a several-day period. There had been rock concerts featuring a variety of entertainers, and there had been

Trip Tent Monterey Pop, photo by Lisa Law ©

multiple-day folk and **jazz** festivals in outdoor venues, but Monterey Pop was the first rock and roll festival. Some of the performers were: **The Mamas and the Papas**, **Simon and Garfunkel**, **Eric Burdon & the Animals**, Lou Rawls, **Janis Joplin**, **Otis Redding**, **Jefferson Airplane**, **Country Joe and the Fish**, **The Who** and **Jimi Hendrix**. The event was conceived and produced with various degrees of involvement by Lou Adler, Harry Cohn, Jr., **Bill Graham**, **Albert Grossman**, Alan Pariser, (Papa) John Phillips, Benny Shapiro and Derek Taylor. The festival was filmed by D. A. Pennebaker; "Monterey Pop" is considered by many to be the definitive rock documentary.

Montezuma's revenge the diarrhea or sickness suffered by many visitors to Mexico, Central and South America. Named for the 16th century Aztec king in power when Cortez invaded what is now Mexico. Montezuma died while in Cortez's captivity, and the sickness is humorously said to be his revenge on any tourists who come to that part of the world. The Aztec pronunciation of Montezuma is Moctezuma. Some historic sources claim that Montezuma's revenge was really syphilis, which he gave to the Spaniards by offering them only infected women as sex partners.

monthly a woman's monthly menstrual period.

Monty Python a group of British actors who performed in "Monty Python's Flying Circus" on BBC from October 5, 1969, to December 5, 1974. The most prominent members are Graham Chapman, John Cleese, Terry Gilliam, Eric Idle, Terry Jones and Michael Palin. They also produced numerous movies, and their BBC shows are still being replayed around the world. They are a valuable example of counterculture comedy.

mood elevators *drugs* antidepressants. Uppers.

mood ring a ring containing a synthetic stone that changed colors according to the temperature of the wearer. The colors supposedly represented moods, such as anger, sorrow, passion, joy, etc. A creation introduced to the "**groovy** people" in 1975.

Moody Blues, The *rock & roll* formed in Birmingham, England in 1964, Denny Laine (b. Brian Hines, Oct. 29, 1944, Jersey, Eng.), gtr., voc.; Mike Pinder (b. Dec. 27, 1941, Birmingham), kybds., voc.; Ray Thomas (b. Dec. 29, 1941, Stourport-on-Severn, Eng.), flute, voc.; Clint Warwick (b. Clinton Eccles, June 25, 1939, Birmingham), bass; Graeme Edge (b. Mar. 30, 1941, Rochester, Eng.), drums. After their first run-of-the-mill Merseybeat hit, "Go Now," in 1965, this band evolved into the most intellectual and spiritually driven musicians of the era. Called a "classical-pomp" group, they garnered a cult following whose adulation bordered on religion. University lectures were given on their music. No study of the hippie era can be complete without listening to at least five of their albums. For more in-depth information, consult one of the many biographies of the group or *The New Rolling Stone Encyclopedia of Rock and Roll.*

Moog synthesizer *rock & roll* a musical electronic keyboard invented by Robert A. Moog in collaboration with composers Herbert A. Deutsch and Walter (Wendy) Carlos. Introduced to musicians and the American public in 1964. It produces an eerie, siren-like sound, created by interrupting or altering an electric current. Moog had been a salesman for a similar instrument called the theremin, which was invented in 1919 by Russian physicist Leon Theremin (Lev Termen). Moog also studied the transistorized modular synthesizers created by German designer Harald Bode. In 1964, Wendy Carlos (who had changed her name and sex from Walter) recorded an album of classical music called *Switched on Bach,* using a Moog synthesizer. Shortly thereafter, Moog began manufacturing and selling his new musical instrument. The Moog synthesizer is the only truly new musical instrument invented in the last 200 years, and its basic concept has been essential to the development of much of the music of the last 35 years.

moolah money. An older term that found a humorous resurgence in the hippie era. Example: "No **moolah**, no movie."

moon to bend over, drop pants and expose one's buttocks. Usually done as a humorous prank, often from a passing car. Moon refers to the white globes of the buttocks.

Moon, Reverend Sun Myung (1920-) *religion* Korean businessman and the founder of the Holy Spirit Association for the Unification of World Christianity, more widely known as the **Unification Church**. Founded by Sun Myung Moon in Seoul, Korea, in 1954, its members are known as "**Moonies**." Moon moved to the United States in the early 1970s, and that prompted a rapid increase of followers to approximately 10,000 full-time members in the West in the 1980s. Its doctrine is based on the Old and New Testaments and revelations from Jesus, Buddha and Muhammad received by Reverend Moon. The Moonies supported the **Vietnam War** through the front group **American Youth for a Just Peace**. This anti-**anti-war** group was supposedly financed in part by Nixon's Committee to Re-Elect the President and was also involved in a three-day fast for President Nixon on the Capitol steps in an attempt to influence public opinion during the Watergate investigation. (See: **Unification Church**) (See also: **American Youth for a Just Peace** on page 579 in **Lists** at the back of this book)

Moonies *religion* members of The Unification Church. (See: **Unification Church**)

Moore, Scotty Elvis Presley's guitar player for years.

mop-tops a nickname for **The Beatles**. Named thus because of their long hair, which reminded some people of a mop used for washing floors.

moral majority a group of conservatives, primarily Christians, who considered themselves the arbiters of morality in the late 1970s. Led by television evangelist Jerry Falwell, they opposed homosexuality, legalized abortion, and advocated prayer in schools. The term was reportedly coined by Paul Myric. During the same period of time, a bumper sticker appeared reading, "The moral majority is neither."

photo by John McCleary ©

moratorium the **Vietnam War** moratorium protest, October 15, 1969. One of the first, and perhaps only, major mainstream **demonstrations** against the war. More than 2 million citizens participated throughout the United States. Business stopped in the public and private sectors, and rallies, church services, neighborhood canvassing and leaflet distribution took place.

morning glory seeds a mild, natural **psychedelic**. A certain variety of Mexican morning glory containing **lysergic acid** similar to that of **LSD**. Ingesting the seeds induces a mild psychedelic experience.

morph short for **morphine**.

morph to change physical appearance in a strange slow motion, as seen in a cartoon world. Normally used in a physical sense to indicate psychedelic visual experience, yet sometimes used to describe a mental or metaphysical change.

morphadite humorous mispronunciation and misspelling of the word hermaphrodite. (See: **hermaphrodite**)

Morrison, Norman *social issues* Mormon **anti-war** protester, who set himself on fire and burned to death in front of the Pentagon on November 2, 1965. Reportedly, the first such case in America, it may have been an accident, an exhibition that went too far. He was holding his daughter at the time, but dropped her, and she was saved by bystanders.

Morrison, Van (b. August 31, 1945, Belfast, Northern Ireland) *rock & roll* a singer/songwriter of immense talent to whom we owe a debt of gratitude for supplying a sound track during the hippie era. Van Morrison makes you think while you're dancing.

mosque an Islamic church.

mostest a Black Southern colloquialization of the word most.

mota *drugs* Spanish word for good **marijuana**.

motate to move, or go someplace quickly. From a combination of the words motor and motivate.

mother a difficult person, place or thing. Example: "Watch that turn; it's a **mother** to negotiate."

motherfucker an exciting or enjoyable person, place or thing. Example: "Watch Bobby; he's a **motherfucker** on the guitar!"

motherfucker a bad or difficult person, place or thing. Example: "Watch that Bobby; he's a **motherfucker**!" As you can see by the two definitions of motherfucker, during the hippie era, there were a number of terms that could have both positive and negative definitions. It all depended on the vocal inflection, situation or accompanying words. This phenomenon, found not only in the hippie era, shows how a culture uses its expletives to condemn as well as commemorate.

Motherfuckers, the or **Up Against the Wall, Motherfucker** a "cluster" of happening, performance and conceptual artists, formed in 1967 in the Lower East Side of New York City. Their slogan was "Armed Love," their logo was the face on the Zig-Zag cigarette papers, and they were associated with **Students for a Democratic Society (SDS)**. Some members eventually went underground and were possibly responsible for the bombing of military facilities. (See: **Students for a Democratic Society**)

Mother-goddess/Great Mother *religion* a goddess appearing in every primitive religion or cult in which fertility is a central issue. A representation of the deification of female principles in life. The personification of nature, fertility and earth's harvest of food in many agrarian cultures. Worship of a mother **goddess** was widespread in ancient times and persists today in many cultures. She appears with names, such as Artemis, Cybele, Demeter, Ishtar, Isis, and Kali. **Feminists** during the hippie era began a resurgence of interest, and she is now worshiped by "goddess" groups and, to some extent, by practitioners of **witchcraft**.

motivate to induce or stimulate someone to do something. A word that was definitely used before the 1960s, yet it was expanded into many new aspects of conversation during the hippie era.

motor to move.

Motörhead *rock & roll* loud, **heavy-metal** band formed in London in 1975 by Lemmy Kilmister.

motor-mouth someone who talks too much.

Motown *rhythm & blues/Motown/rock & roll* After writing several hit songs in the mid-1950s, **Berry Gordy, Jr.,** started his own rhythm & blues (R&B) record labels in 1959 under the umbrella of Motown Records Corporation. He soon moved his operations into a two-story house at 2648 West Grand Boulevard, Detroit, Michigan, which he christened "Hitsville." That house and the music it produced are icons in the history of R&B. Motown stands for motor town, which is the nickname for Detroit, Michigan. (See: **Berry Gordy, Jr.**)

motown a kind of music created by Black musicians centering around the Detroit, Michigan, area of the United States. It was similar to **rhythm and blues** and very popular during the 1960s and 70s among Black and White audiences. Motown stands for motor town, which is the nickname for Detroit, Michigan.

mount to perform sexual intercourse "on someone." The inference is that the male proceeds on top of the female, which, as all hippies know is the "Christian" missionary position and by no means the mandatory configuration.

mountain (or **prairie**) **oysters** a man's balls or testicles. **2.** the testicles of domestic animals, which are removed from the animals to keep them from reproducing. In some societies, the animal's "oysters" are served as a delicacy.

mouse a hand-operated device that electronically directs the movement of the cursor on a computer screen. Although this name was not used until 1984, the actual device was created and first demonstrated by Douglas C. Engelbart of the Stanford Research Institute in 1968.

mouth someone who talks too much.

mouth off to talk too much.

mouthpiece a lawyer.

mouthwash bad drinking alcohol.

move on up to advance. To climb the ladder of success.

movement, the *social issues* groups involved in social change. Activity associated with the numerous social commitments espoused during the 1960s and 70s. The **civil rights** movement might be considered the original "movement," but, with time, the term was eventually used to indicate the **free-speech**, **anti-war**, **ecology**, **gay rights** and **women's movements**. The term was often used with a certain amount of reverence since these social issues have always been considered the high ground.

mover a good dancer, good seducer, or someone who gets things done.

movers and shakers the people who get things done. Sometimes used in a derogatory manner to describe those who were too self-important.

moves the actions needed to excel at something. Example: "He'll get it done; he has all the **moves**."

movin' active or energetic.

R. Crumb ©

Mr. Natural a cartoon character drawn by **R. Crumb** for **Zap comics** and Apex novelties. An old, bearded man in a white robe who followed no authority but life itself. (See: **Comix**)

Mr. Right that fictitious and elusive man who will come along and be the perfect mate for a woman; also used in the homosexual community. Primarily used in sarcasm.

Ms. a term indicating a woman's status as mature, yet not necessarily married. A married woman may use Ms. when she wants the world to view her as an individual, and not just as a "married woman." A vehicle of the feminist movement of the 1970s to avoid the preconceptions inferred by the Miss and Mrs. labels. A Ms. could be married, a virgin, an unmarried woman living with a man or woman in a sexual relationship, a woman of 79, or a swinger with multiple lovers.

Ms. Right that fictitious and elusive woman who will come along and be the perfect mate for a man.

mu *drugs* **marijuana**. (See: **marijuana**)

muck a mess of some kind. A social mistake or an actual mud puddle.

mucked up something that has become a mess.

muck it up to fail or to make a mess of something.

muck on through to persevere and do the job in spite of the problems that arise.

mud *drugs* cheap **marijuana**. Example: "Mexican **mud**." **2.** opium.

mud unflattering information or negative commentary. Same usage as **dirt**. Examples: "He was throwing the **mud** around, but his own past is by no means pristine." "What's the **mud** on her? She looks interesting."

mudra *occult* the "mystic seal" of Oriental occultism; a series of **occult** hand signs considered to have magical effects.

muff or **muffin** the pubic area of a woman. A British invasion term, it came either from the small cake, which is warm and moist, or from the term muffler, describing a warm and cuddly neck scarf.

muff-diver *sex* someone who likes to perform **oral sex (cunnilingus)** on women. Muff is a description of a woman's pubic area.

mug someone's face.

muggles *drugs* **marijuana**. A very old term, but used with humor during the hippie era. (See: **marijuana**)

Muhammad Ali (See: **Ali, Muhammad**)

Muhammad, Elijah (b. Elijah Poole, 1897; d. 1975) *religion/social issues* leader of the Lost-Found **Nation of Islam**, or **Black Muslim**, religious move- ment. The son of former slaves and sharecroppers, he left home at age 16 and moved to Detroit, where he worked in a Chevrolet auto plant. After a spiritual revelation around 1930, he began associating with the Nation of Islam, a movement founded by W. D. Fard (or Farad), a mysterious African American who worked as a salesman in Detroit, but whose followers believed had come from Mecca to save Blacks from the "White devils." When Fard disappeared in 1934, Poole took over, changed his name to Elijah Muhammad and proclaimed himself the "Messenger of Allah." From this point, the Nation of Islam became a national movement. Those outside the faith called it the Black Muslims, a name that Muhammad and his followers disliked and did not use themselves. Muhammad preached that the White man was the devil with whom Blacks could not live and that only Blacks could cure the ills that afflict them. Muhammad stressed separation of the races and ridiculed the civil rights movement, calling for an all-Black state or territory within the United States. He extolled the need for African Americans to achieve economic power. Muhammad and his movement were almost totally unknown to White Americans until the 1960s, when his charismatic disciple **Malcolm X** began to promote Black Muslim philosophy. (See: **Nation of Islam** and **Malcolm X**)

mule someone who, knowingly or unknowingly, smuggles drugs for another person.

mullah a scholar or teacher of the sacred law of **Islam**. Persian form of an Arabic word.

munch out to eat, usually with a mindless fervor. To have the **munchies**.

*munchies *drugs* snack food eaten after smoking **marijuana**. Eventually, the word came to mean any food not considered a proper meal.

munchies *drugs* a hunger accompanying the smoking of **marijuana**. Eventually, the word came to mean the desire for any food, but usually snack food.

munchkin a small child. Originally, from "The Wizard of Oz" as the name of the small people who resided in Munchkinland.

mundane astrology an interpretation of astrology in terms of world trends, the destinies of nations and of large groups of individuals, based on an analysis of the effects of the **equinox**, **solstice**, new moon and similar celestial phenomena; as distinguished from natal astrology, which is specifically applied to individual birth horoscopes.

muppet a child.

Muppets, The marionettes/puppets created by **Jim (James) Henson** (1936-1990) and seen on the children's TV show "Sesame Street," produced by the Children's Television Workshop throughout the 1960s and 70s. The Muppet characters included Kermit the Frog, Miss Piggy, and Cookie Monster, along with many other favorites. Henson won a Grammy in 1979 and numerous Emmy awards for his work before his untimely death.

Murray the K (Murray Kaufman) (1922-1982) an early radio announcer who promoted **rock and roll**. Although he called himself "The Fifth Beatle," most people grant that distinction to Beatles' record producer George Martin. In the early 1950s, Murray was President of the National Conference of **Disk Jockeys**, an organization with

Dick Clark on its executive board, which sought to raise the image of broadcasters who catered to teenage listeners. In the late 1950s, Murray took over **Alan Freed**'s prime-time slot following Freed's blacklisting over the **payola** scandal. From the mid-1950s to the mid-1960s, Murray the K was the king of the New York City airwaves and one of the first White DJs to cater to a multiracial audience. He became the unofficial American spokesman for **The Beatles**, before and during their American tour, broadcasting from their hotel room, accompanying them to the first show in Washington, DC, co-hosting the Carnegie Hall show, and joining them in England, where he emceed a Wembley Stadium concert. It is said that he met **The Rolling Stones** at this time and suggested they cover an American R&B song, which became their first number one hit in America. As AM radio became excessively commercial, Murray led a group of disillusioned DJs into the new era of FM rock. Murray helped to set the tone for the 1960s rock phenomenon by playing songs from albums, not singles, so that "cuts" like **Bob Dylan**'s "Positively Fourth Street" and Janis Ian's "Society's Child" could be aired in full. His shows were initially one of the few places where these songs were heard. (See: **payola** and **Alan Freed**)

Musafar, Fakir (1930-) born Roland Loomis in South Dakota, Musafar is known as the father of the Modern Primitive movement. He was an early exponent of tattooing, body piercing and primitive rituals. As a child, he began piercing his own body and was tattooing himself in his teens. Fakir practiced Itiburi, the New Guinea body restricting ritual, and at age 19 he could constrict his waist to 14 inches. He has adopted many of the primitive rituals, including the North American Indian O-Kee-Pa ceremony, in which the participant is hung by flesh hooks through his skin. Fakir's movies, photographs and lectures influenced many people to experiment with piercing and scarification during the 1960s and 70s. (The name Fakir Musafar was assumed from a Persian **Sufi,** whom Loomis saw in an early Ripley's *Believe It or Not* feature.) (See: **tattooing, body piercing, Modern Primitive movement** and **skin brothers**)

muscle an impersonal term for someone who can lift and carry things. Someone who is good in a fight.

museum piece someone or something that is old and in the way.

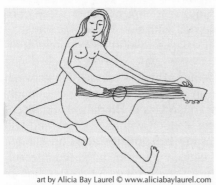

art by Alicia Bay Laurel © www.aliciabaylaurel.com

music it is impossible to overemphasize the importance of music to the culture and esthetics of the 1960s and 70s. There are those who ridicule the era because of its emphasis on music; what they don't realize is that music was the messenger through which most of the valuable social and political messages traveled. As usual, killing the messenger is a foolish effort to make a problem go away rather than dealing with the problem in the message.

musical beds switching sexual partners.

mutable zodiac signs flexible, adaptable, people-oriented: Virgo, Sagittarius, Pisces.

mutant someone who does not fit in. A reject of society. During the hippie era, it was used not to describe a person with physical deformities, but a person who did not fit in due to inept social activity. Hippies were usually not critical of a person's physical or mental inadequacies, yet they were not adverse to criticizing a socially inept individual. This was a period of time before political correctness was invented, and therefore, terms such as "**lame**," "**retard**" and "mutant" were used to describe people in social situations.

muzak or Muzak *not rock & roll* any music that has no soul. Music considered to be background noise rather than entertainment. Elevator music. **2.** The Muzak company dates back to the 1920s when Gen. George Squier patented the transmission of background music, the process of delivering phonograph record music over electrical lines. He joined the two words "music," and "Kodak," his favorite **high-tech** company, to create the name. The Muzak company has changed ownership in the ensuing years. In the 1940s, it was determined that workplace music increased morale, thus increasing productivity and attendance. Music programming went even further in the 1950s with Stimulus Progression, the belief that the intensity of music directly influences employee productivity. Muzak began to appear in many stores, malls and elevators as background. In the 1960s, Muzak started re-recording popular music, using strings and orchestration to make it what they considered more acceptable to the general public. The company called its recordings a "melodic mood setter."

my ass a negative interjection or expletive of intensified displeasure. Example: "**My ass** you'll eat the last of the tofu ice cream!"

My Lai a Vietnamese village where 567 civilians were killed by US soldiers in an "interdiction" on March 16, 1968. Twenty-five soldiers, including officers, were court-martialed, but all were exonerated or found not guilty except Lieutenant William Calley, who may have been the scapegoat for the entire military system. Calley was paroled in 1975, after serving only 3 1/2 years of a 10-year sentence.

my man a term of endearment, friendship or brotherly love. Example: "Hey, **my man**, come share the bean curd." Sometimes heard as **m'man**.

myrrh a fragrant gum **resin** from trees of genus *Commiphora* (Camphora), originally found in East Africa and Arabia. It has been burned as incense in Eastern religious rituals in temples and ashrams for centuries. More recently, it has been introduced into Russian, Greek Orthodox and Catholic ceremonies. Said to be one of the gifts given by the three Kings or wisemen from the East to the Christ Child at his birth. Used as a purifier and more practically as a fumigant to keep pests away from the faithful at religious ceremonies. Hippies, with their interest in other lifestyles, introduced incense to Western culture.

mystic *occult* a person who seeks direct personal experience with the underworld or **spirit** world. A mystic may use prayer, meditation, **occult** arts or any number of methods to concentrate on reaching spiritual communication. One who practices mysticism. This personality is associated with the quest for "the meaning of life," which was one of the major interests of the hippie **counterculture**.

mystic brotherhood an undefined group of people involved with intellectual discovery, **esoteric** discussion, **LSD** and other early **counterculture** activities in search of some rationalization for life. A term used by **Tom Wolfe** in his 1968 book, *The Electric Kool-Aid Acid Test*, indicating the **cosmic** connection among people, such as **Ken Kesey**, **Timothy Leary**, **Richard Alpert**, **Aldus Huxley**, hippies, **beat** poets, and writers.

mysticism *occult* any philosophy, doctrine, teaching or belief more concerned with the world of spirits than the material world. The search for direct personal experience with divine beings. There is a distinction between using mysticism as a means to identify with God (as in **Hinduism**) and reaching a union with God's love and will (as in **Islam**, **Judaism** and Christianity). Many people of the hippie **counterculture** sought closer understanding of divinity and the "meaning of life" through various forms of mysticism, including **meditation**, **martial arts**, food and **fasting** disciplines, and drugs.

mythology the collection of ancient stories of peoples and races. The study of myths, their origin and nature.

N

NAACP (See: **National Association for the Advancement of Colored People**)

nabs police.

Nader, Ralph (1934-) *social issues* consumer advocate, attorney, author, founder of the consumer rights movement in America. Graduated from Princeton in 1955 and Harvard Law School in 1958. Author of the books *Unsafe at Any Speed,* 1965; *Menace of Atomic Energy,* 1977; and *Who's Poisoning America?,* 1981. Nader is greatly responsible for the passage of the 1966 National Traffic and Motor Vehicle Safety Act and the 1967 Wholesome Meat Act, imposing Federal standards on slaughterhouses. His associates, known as "Nader's Raiders," have championed many environmental and public safety issues, such as pesticides, mercury poisoning, radiation danger and coal mine safety. Modest and idealistic, with spartan personal habits, he campaigns tirelessly for the environment and a quality existence for all life. Were it not for Ralph Nader, the American way of life would be a great deal more self-destructive than it is today. All this said, there are those of us who believe that his failure to withdraw from the 2000 election, which he would have been unable to win, left this country in a disastrous social and political situation.

nail or **nailed** *sex* to have sexual intercourse with someone. A less intimate form of the sex act. Examples: "Everyone wants to **nail** her." "Yes, I know, and everyone *has* **nailed** her." **2.** to hurt, damage or hit someone.

nailed arrested or caught by the authorities.

nail or **nailed it** to get something right. Example: "I **nailed** that test in underwater basket weaving."

'Nam short for Vietnam.

namaste a **Sanskrit** (East Indian) greeting and parting salutation meaning "I honor the light within you." Usually accompanied by gesturing with the fingers and palms of the hands together as in prayer, and a *pranam*, or bow. Used as a greeting by some hippies. Because of an interest in Eastern religions and cultures, some hippies adopted their customs.

Nam black, Nam shit or **Nam weed** *drugs* a dark green variety of **marijuana** grown in Vietnam.

name an important person. Examples: "Say, don't you know him? He's a real **name** around here." "Look, there's what's-his-name; he's a big **name** in **EST**."

name of the game the reality, what is happening. Example: "With a bean curd diet, discipline is the **name of the game**."

Namu Myoho Renge Kyo (*Na maho renga keyo*) **religion** a **mantra** used by various **Buddhist** sects. It means "Reverence to the wonderful truth of the Lotus Sutra." Created by Nichiren (b. 1222 A.D.; d. 1282 A.D.), a Japanese Buddhist reformer who taught that the **Lotus Sutra** contained the ultimate truth, which could be compressed into the sacred formula of **Namu Myoho Renge Kyo.** In the Soka Gakkai sect, prominent in America during the hippie era, Buddhism reached its most materialistic point when this mantra was used as a way in which to make one's material wishes come true. It was believed that a person who wanted a new car or a particular lover could merely recite this phrase over and over again, and the desired person or object would become theirs.

nancy boy or **nance** a male **homosexual**. An old term introduced anew during the 1960s **British invasion**.

napalm a highly combustible gelatin fuel produced primarily by **Dow Chemical Company** and used extensively as a weapon in Vietnam. It was dropped in bombs upon enemy forces and had a tendency to stick to anything it hit and burn uncontrollably. It was used in the latter days of WWII and in Korea. First reported use in Vietnam was April 15, 1965.

narc, nark or **narco** a narcotics officer working with a police force to apprehend drug sellers and users.

narcotic mirror a round, crystal globe filled with magnetized water in which a narcotic powder is dissolved. Used in ancient times for divining the present, past or future from clairvoyant pictures seen in the reflective surface of the water. Such devices found some renewed use during the hippie era.

nards a man's testicles.

narly alternative spelling of **gnarly**. (See: **gnarly**)

nasty *sex* sexual intercourse. A humorous use. Example: "He and Danielle are doing the **nasty**."

nasty little war, the a term used to describe the **Vietnam War**. Technically, it was not really a war; it was called a "conflict" by the US Government. 58,000 American youngsters were killed in the nasty little "conflict."

natch short for naturally. An old term that became popular in the **counterculture**'s lexicon of sarcasm.

National Association for the Advancement of Colored People (NAACP) *social issues* founded in June, 1909, it is the oldest civil rights organization in the USA. An early leader was W. E. B. DuBois; other prominent leaders and members have included **Rev. Ralph Abernathy, Roy Wilkins, Medgar Evers** and **Dr. Martin Luther King, Jr**. Founded to support the rights of African Americans, its accomplishments are too numerous to list here.

National Hard Hats of America *social issues* a group of construction workers organized to support the **Vietnam War**. It is believed that they were supported by and may have been formed with help from President Nixon's **dirty tricks** organization, the **plumbers**. They held violent counter-**demonstrations** during **anti-war** rallies, notably on May 8, 1970, when they assaulted demonstrators in New York City.

National Mobilization Committee, **Mobilization Committee** or **Spring Mobilization Committee (Mobe)** *social issues* **anti-war** organization founded in July, 1966. **David Dellinger** was their chairman, and **Rennie Davis** was the Chicago coordinator during the **Chicago Democratic Convention** demonstrations and police riots on August 24-30, 1968. Mobe was involved in numerous protests, including the November 5-8, 1966, Spring Mobe demonstrations in New York and San Francisco; draft card burning in Central Park on April 15, 1967; and on October 21, 1967, a rally of 50,000 in Washington, DC, which eventually stormed the Pentagon where 250 were arrested, including Norman Mailer and **David Dellinger**. (See: **Chicago Democratic National Convention**) (See also: **Anti-War Events, Groups and Leaders** starting on page 562 in **Lists** at the back of this book)

National Organization for the Reform of Marijuana Laws (NORML) *drugs* an organization dedicated to the reform of **marijuana** laws, founded in 1970 by Keith Stroup. Board members included **Ramsey Clark**, Attorney General under **President Johnson** from 1967-69. The organization received money from Hugh Heffner of *Playboy* magazine. One of their major accomplishments was helping to convince a number of state governments to decriminalize or reduce to a misdemeanor the "offense" of smoking or possessing small amounts of marijuana. Through the actions of NORML and other local organizations, decriminalization was accomplished in Oregon in 1973 and Alaska, Maine, California, Colorado and Ohio in 1975.

National Organization of Women (NOW) *social issues* founded June 29, 1966, it was organized, "To take actions needed to bring women into the **mainstream** of American society," in "full equal partnership with men." NOW worked to pressure The Equal Employment Opportunity Commission (EEOC) to enforce **Title VII** of the **Civil Rights** Act of 1964 to ensure women's equality in the work place. Betty Friedan was NOW's first president, and other founding members were Pauli Murray, Kay Clarenbach, Catherine East, Mary Eastwood and Catherine Conroy. Shortly after NOW began, it became polarized by the straight members, characterized by **Betty Friedan,** and gay members, represented by **Rita Mae Brown**. Friedan and other non-homosexual members felt that if NOW associated with the **lesbian** movement (the **lavender menace**), it would hurt the organization. There were several "lesbian purges" in the 1970s. (See: **Title VII**) (See also: **Women's Movement Events,**

Groups and Leaders starting on page 591 in the **Lists** at the end of this book)

Nation of Islam or **Black Muslims**, sometimes called the **Lost-Found Nation of Islam** *religion/social issues* an African American sect of the **Islamic** faith. The name Black Muslims is used by others to describe members of this movement, but its members reject this name. The sect was founded in Detroit in 1930 by W. D. Fard (or Wali Farad), a silk salesman with an almost unknown past. After Fard mysteriously disappeared in 1934, his chief lieutenant, **Elijah Muhammad** (formerly Elijah Poole), became the movement's leader. Muhammad claimed that Fard was Allah, and he was Allah's messenger. Elijah Muhammad led the sect until his death in 1975, at which time his son, Warith Deen Muhammad, led until 1977. At that time, Louis Farrakhan took over, forcing Warith Deen out with a small group of his followers. In the 1950s and early 1960s, **Malcolm X** was the most prominent spokesman for the Nation of Islam. He converted to the movement while in prison in 1947. The years from Malcolm's release from prison in 1952 to his assassination in 1965 marked the Nation's greatest growth and influence. Malcolm left the Nation of Islam in 1964, converted to Sunni Islam and started his Black Nationalist Party. In 1977, Louis Farrakhan led a group of discontented followers in restructuring the Nation of Islam. This group has continued the Black separatist and nationalist teachings of Elijah Muhammad. Today, the term Nation of Islam or Black Muslims refers most appropriately to followers of Farrakhan's sect. (See: **Elijah Muhammad** and **Malcolm X** in alphabetical listings.) (See also: **Civil Rights Events, Groups and Leaders** starting on page 546 in **Lists** at the back of this book and **Black Revolutionary Groups** on page 585 in **Lists** at the back of this book)

Native Americans members of one of the thousands of aboriginal tribes that existed in America before the arrival of the European conquerors.

Native American Church *religion/social issues* a religious organization of North American Indians founded in 1870. It teaches a doctrinal mixture of native religion and Christianity. Its rituals include ceremonies using **peyote**, a small cactus containing the hallucinogen **mescaline**. Hippies learned of peyote through the **Native American** culture. At one time the Native American Church was one of the only sources of the cactus, and people of the **counterculture** tried to join the church in order to indulge in the **psychedelic** plant. Most hippies are genuinely sympathetic to Native American culture and are interested in the positive aspects of their philosophy of life. However, some Anglos, in their zeal, have tried to emulate the American "Indian," thus creating a fanaticism which is offensive to many true Native Americans. (See: **peyote, mescaline** and **Carlos Castaneda**)

natty natural, **cool**. A word with Jamaican roots. "Natty dreads" is a hairstyle worn by African descendants living in Jamaica, **Rastafarians** and **reggae** musicians. (See: **Rastafarian** and **reggae**)

natural a hairstyle worn in the 1970s by people with thick, curly hair. Also called an Afro, it was originally an African American or Black style. The technique was to let the hair grow long and natural and cut it in an equal length

around the head to create what was sometimes called a "helmet of hair." A hair "pick" or "rake" was used to comb

or lift the hair up and out from the head. **Civil rights** activist **Angela Davis** sported one of the most prominent examples of the natural style.

natural high exhilaration achieved by a natural experience, such as a walk on the beach, meditation or human camaraderie, rather than through drug intake. Joy received from nature.

nature's call the need to urinate.

nature worship man's expression of gratitude for nature's gifts and reverence for its power. Almost all ancient gods were personifications of the powers of nature.

neat nice, good or interesting. An understated, yet sincere compliment or statement of approval. Example: "Hey, that's **neat**; how'd you get that peace sign in the bottle?"

neato-keeno a sarcastic form of **neat**. From the **counterculture**'s lexicon of sarcasm and ridicule.

neck to kiss and indulge in sexual **foreplay**.

nectar the beverage of the gods of Greek mythology.

needle to annoy someone, to verbally attack, or make inflammatory remarks.

Example: "You shouldn't **needle** Jake like that; he has a short fuse."

needle, the *drugs* the hypodermic needle used for injecting illegal drugs.

"Needle and the Damage Done, The" a song on the *Harvest* record album by Neil Young, published in 1972. Every once in a while, the lyrics of a song will hit a cord of truth that remains with the listener forever. This song about the dangers of intravenous drugs was a poignant message of the times and poetic memory for those who have lost friends to drugs.

needle candy *drugs* any narcotic that is injected intravenously.

needle dick a very small penis.

needle park *drugs* an area of urban squalor in New York City bordered by and encompassing Broadway and Amsterdam Avenue, West 71st Street, and Sherman Square. It was the center of intravenous drug use.

negative hallucination the failure to see an object that is in fact visible and not a **hallucination**.

Nehru jacket a coat fashioned after clothing worn by Jawaharlal Nehru, who was the first Prime Minister of India, after independence from Great Britain in 1947. Nehru was a close associate of Mahatma **Gandhi**. The coat had buttons up the front to a straight collar with no lapels. This style of coat was worn for a short period of time in the Western culture during the early 1970s. Considered by the truly **hip** to be an affectation by the "pseudo hip" trying to emulate Indian Hindu culture.

Nelson, Willie (b. April 30, 1933, Abbott, Tex.) *country/rock & roll* the number one crossover country to **rock and roll** artist. One of the most prolific country western songwriters and an all around good guy. With his music and his attitude, he exemplifies what the **true hippie** should be. Along with Kris Kristofferson and Waylon Jennings, he is responsible for loosening up the country western music industry, forcing it to take itself less seriously as a macho culture and more seriously as human beings. Nelson was one of the first socially conscious country music performers. He is responsible for creating Farm Aid in 1985, a series of musical benefits for small farmers in financial trouble.

nembbie, nemish, nemmie, nimbie or **nimby** *drugs* (See: **Nembutal**)

Nembutal *drugs* the trade name of a popular **barbiturate** made by Abbott Pharmaceutical Company. Possesses a high potential for abuse. Chemical name pentobarbital sodium. A nonselective central nervous system depressant used primarily as a **sedative-hypnotic**. Dosages in the 1960s and 70s: white tablet, 50 milligrams; blue tablet, 100 milligrams; yellow and white capsule, 3/4 grams; yellow capsule, 1 1/2 grams. As with many barbiturates it had a tendency, when not properly dosed, to depress more than expected and suicide can be the result. A **downer**.

nerd a socially inept person. a.k.a. **dork, dweeb, jerk**, etc.

nervy forward, arrogant or pushy. Example: "He's a real **nervy** bitch."

network to make business connections through casual social contact.

network *computer revolution* the system connecting computers within an office or across the world. Precursor to and root word for the later terms

Internet or **Net**. First created between 1965 and 1969 by Robert Taylor, Director of the Advanced Research Project Agency (ARPA), and called **ARPAnet**. From the structure of a fish net in which all strands of the string are interconnected into small squares.

never happen! no! A roundabout way to say no. Used to embellish a conversation.

never trust anyone over thirty "old folks" are different and untrustworthy. The ultimate **generation gap** commentary. A phrase coined by **Jack Weinberg** of the **free-speech movement**. (See: **free-speech movement** and **Jack Weinberg**)

New Age a period of time that is said to embrace the ideals of love and compatibility. A term describing the next **astrological** age, or the present age if, indeed, it has already arrived. The exact dates are not easily determined from the conflicting data available. **2.** also indicates a person with interests in **metaphysics**, **mysticism** and **humanistic religions**. **3.** also used to describe other things, such as music, which incorporate futuristic technology.

New-Age religions *religion* various spiritual movements emerging during the mid-1960s in North America. These groups, sects and cults were based on new religious awareness involving **self-realization**, Eastern **meditation** and sometimes drugs. The teachings are often a blend of Eastern and Western **mysticism**.

New Left, the *social issues* a social and political group that strongly supports free-speech, equality of all sexes, races and religion, and advocates restrictions on rampant capitalism. A term and concept created during the **free-speech movement** in Berkeley, California, in the mid-1960s. Associated with anarchist principles, central authority and grass-roots democratic decision-making. Called **participatory democracy**. In 1969, a *Fortune* magazine poll of students found that about 13 percent, or over half a million, identified themselves with the New Left.

Newman, Randy (b. Nov. 28, 1944, New Orleans, La.) *sarcasm rock & roll* pianist/singer/songwriter who has done more for irony in music than anyone. His songs like "Short People" and lyrics about rednecks and dropping bombs have alienated some people and delighted others. He has written many hit songs for other artists, scored movies and recorded with others over the years, contributing much to the flavor of the era.

Newton, Huey P. (1942-1989) *social issues* co-founder of the **Black Panther Party** with Bobby Seale in October, 1966. On October 28, 1967, he was arrested for killing officer John Frey in a shoot-out with Oakland, California, police. On September 8, 1968, he was convicted of manslaughter in Frey's death. The **Free Huey** movement became a common cause of the Black Panthers and White **anti-war**/free speech activists. During the late 1960s, "**Free Huey**" was an often seen piece of graffiti. Newton was released from jail in 1970 after his conviction was overturned. He wrote the book, *Revolutionary Suicide,* in 1973. In 1974, he was accused of murdering a prostitute and escaped to Cuba for three years, before he returned to be acquitted of the charges. Newton earned a PhD in philosophy from the University of California in 1980; his dissertation was entitled *War Against the Panthers:*

Study of Repression in America. Newton was shot to death on an Oakland street in 1989.

new wave   the avant-garde of art, thought and philosophy. A term introduced to the American public in 1961.

Ngo Quang Duc   Buddhist monk who died by self-immolation June 10, 1963, in protest of persecution by the US-supported South Vietnamese Government. The first publicized self-immolation during the **Vietnam War**; others followed.

Madame Nhu

Nhu, Madame Ngo Dinh (1924-) known as Madame Nhu. The wife of Ngo Dinh Nhu, younger brother of President of South Vietnam Ngo Dinh Diem, who held office from 1955 to 1963. Madam Nhu was a flamboyant member of the politically conservative Catholic ruling party. She functioned as the first lady of South Vietnam since her brother-in-law, the president, had no primary female partner. When the Buddhist monks began the practice of self-immolation to protest persecution by the Catholic administration, she called it a "monk barbecue." Madame Nhu gained notoriety among the American counterculture in the early 1960s as an insensitive elitist. Ngo Dihn Diem and Nog Dihn Nhu were assassinated on November 2, 1963, during a coup; Madame Nhu escaped and continued her inappropriate commentary.

nice   *sex, drugs, rock & roll* an understated, yet supreme, compliment. Most often reserved for a woman, dope, music, sex, drugs or **rock and roll**.

nick   to steal. British term.

nickel bag or **nickel** $5 worth of drugs.

nigger   a derogatory term for an African American. Seldom used by **true hippies** except as a joke in the presence of an African American **brother**. African Americans sometimes use this term themselves as a reaction to the name-calling of others.

nigger   anyone who is downtrodden or discriminated against. Hippies sometime called themselves White niggers.

night person   someone who likes to stay up late, cruising the bars and nightclubs, looking for action.

Nilsson, Harry (b. Harry Edward Nelson III, June 15, 1941, Brooklyn, New York; d. January 15, 1994, Agoura Hills, Calif.) *popular rock* pianist/singer/songwriter who wrote hit songs for other artists and scored movies, contributing much to the flavor of the era.

nirvana *religion* in Asian philosophy and religious doctrine, the complete and final extinction of **ego** and selfishness, without the loss of **self-awareness**. A state of mind in which all pain, suffering and mental anguish are absent. The place where *samsara*, the **wheel of life**, ends. A Buddhist's ultimate goal, the state of complete peace in which a person finds freedom from the distractions of desire and **self-consciousness**. Although it is a spiritual goal of great attainment, it is considered a selfish goal and is often rejected by **Bodhisattvas** in order to continue reincarnating upon the earth so as to stay and help others achieve salvation. In the hippie era, it achieved a more secular meaning as a place of happiness or **euphoria**, often induced by sex, drugs or **rock and roll**. (See: **Bodhisattva, Buddhism** and **samsara**)

nitty gritty the basics, the beginnings, the important stuff. From the Black American **jive** culture. Examples: "His music gets down to the **nitty gritty**." "Let's start at the **nitty gritty** of the subject."

nix no! Used as a way to place emphasis on one's disagreement.

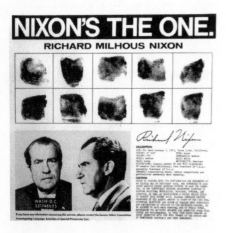

NIXON'S THE ONE.
RICHARD MILHOUS NIXON

Nixon, Richard Milhous (Tricky Dick) (b. January 9, 1913, Yorba Linda, Calif.; d. April 22, 1994) Republican, the 37th President of the United States from 1969-74. Graduated from Whittier College in 1934 and Duke University Law School in 1937. As a member of the House Committee on Un-American Activities in 1948, he participated vigorously in smearing Algier Hiss. US Senator from 1950 to 1953; Vice President under Eisenhower from 1953 to 1961.

no big deal not important. A dismissal. Example: "So she left me. It's **no big deal**; I'll just get a dog instead."

no biggie or **ain't no biggie** trivial, unimportant. Something to be shrugged off or ignored. Examples: "My habit's **no biggie**; all I need is a candy bar and a lover at midnight." "Losing that talent contest **ain't no biggie**; all it means is a few more months in the garage for our band."

nobody, a someone who is unimportant.

no-brainer something that should take little or no intelligence to figure out.

no class a person, place or thing that is without acceptable social status. Example: "Goober has **no class**, his name is **no class**, his hair is **no class** and he has a **no-class** dog."

nod *drugs* drowsiness produced by the influence of drugs. Example: "Don't bother to try to talk to Suzy; she's on a heroin **nod**."

nodding or **nodding out** *drugs* having one's mind and actions altered by drugs or alcohol.

nod out to fall asleep while in a social situation. Example: "If he keeps up this boring lecture, kick me when I **nod out**."

no flies on (someone or something) does not stink. Indicates that a person or item is acceptable. From the fact that flies are attracted to feces, and if a person, place or thing doesn't have flies on them, then they are OK.

noise annoying or worthless conversation. Example: "That's just **noise**;

Frank never really says anything important."

noise pollution any sound that is a disturbance to one's normal relaxation, thinking or working process. A term introduced to the American public around 1969.

no kidding! a sarcastic response to an obvious statement. Example: "You think she's beautiful? **No kidding**!" Similar usage as "duh!?"

Nolde, William, Army Lt. Col. identified by the US Government as the last American soldier killed in Vietnam, April 29, 1975.

no-neck a body-builder, a man who is considered to be physical rather than intellectual. From the tendency of weight lifters to have big, thick necks that blend into their heads and shoulders, giving the impression that they have no necks.

no nukes the concept of a world without nuclear weapons or power and the dangers they pose to life on the planet.

No Nukes a large rock concert created by MUSE (Musicians United for Safe Energy) to benefit the antinuclear movement. It ran for five nights, September 19 through 23, 1979, at Madison Square Garden in New York City. Attended by about 97,000 fans, it raised an estimated $300,000, which was eventually distributed to antinuclear organizations.

nonverbal communications *sex* body language, sexual or social intentions indicated by physical movements.

nonviolent civil disobedience or **nonviolent demonstration and protest** *social issues* the concept of peaceful protest to communicate dissatisfaction. It has been proven that nonviolent pro-

test is more effective than aggressive action in providing validity to a cause. A person who displays passive resistance in the face of aggressive action is generally understood to be more righteous. It is the equivalent of turning the other cheek. Mahatma **Gandhi** was the original modern advocate of nonviolent political protest. The concept was adopted by **Rev. Dr. Martin Luther King, Jr.**, in April, 1963, for the **civil rights** movement in its effort to end segregation. Printed March Instructions distributed to participants of Dr. King's marches began:
THIS IS A NONVIOLENT DEMONSTRATION, therefore,
1. You are expected to refrain from any hostile act or word, even when provoked.
2. The march will be quiet, orderly and serious.

nookie *sex* the female genitals.

nooner a lunch time sexual liaison. From the habit of new lovers rushing home from work during lunch to have sex.

no pain, no gain one must work to succeed. Without effort, no advantage is gained. From the physical training culture, indicating that if one's muscles don't hurt, they are not being strengthened.

noplace an uninteresting or boring place to be. Example: "This is **noplace** man, let's get out of here before someone sees us."

no problemo Spanish for no problem. A whimsical answer to anyone's concerns. From the habit of people in foreign countries using that phrase to mollify tourists' fears. Example: Tourist: "Will the taxi arrive a 3 a.m. in time to get me to my airplane?" Desk clerk: "*No problemo!*"

Norman an awkward person.

NORML (See: **National Organization for the Reform of Marijuana Laws**)

nose candy *drugs* **cocaine**. (See: **cocaine**)

nose job the medical procedure called rhinoplasty, to reshape or reduce the size of one's nose.

nose out of joint unnecessarily jealous, disturbed or argumentative. Example: "Gretta has her **nose out of joint** over my new lava lamp."

no shit! that's obvious. Example: "**No shit** he's upset about the accident; now his sound system needs new wheels, motor and a paint job!"

no-show someone who failed to arrive. Example: "Rosie's a **no-show**, but she sent her bubbles to the love-in."

no skin off my ass or **butt** or **nose** it's not my concern; I don't care. Example: "No **skin off my ass** if you want to paint your windows blue."

no slouch not bad at something, proficient. Example: "When it comes to macramé, Dilly's **no slouch**." An old term ignored in most dictionaries. Used as a quaint sarcasm during the hippie era. Probably from the fact that a person who has no confidence will not stand up straight and look people in the eye, but a good man is "no slouch."

no sweat not difficult. From the fact that the job won't make you sweat. Example: "The job's **no sweat**; I'll be done before 'Laugh-In.'"

not a clue without an idea or opinion about something. **Clueless**.

not all there refers to someone who is not very smart because some of their brains are not there.

not carved in stone indicates that something can be altered or reworked. From the fact that, if something is carved in stone, it is difficult to change.

nothing shaking nothing happening. **Shaking** is defined as excitement, dancing, fun, etc.

nothingness that place between reality and divinity. The ether. The void. The **esoteric** conversation with the freak in the park with a joint on a bleak Sunday afternoon in October.

no tomorrow as though there will never be another chance. Example: "She eats like there is **no tomorrow**."

not playing with a full deck lacking in brain power. Refers to the fact that one cannot play the game properly with an incomplete deck of cards.

not so hot not good, not well.

not too swift stupid. The description of a person who is slow in thinking. From the older phrase "not too quick."

not worth a bucket of warm spit of little value. A bucket of warm spit is worthless, so the object indicated is without value.

NOW (See: **National Organization of Women**)

now the divine moment, the spiritual now, the religious experience of being in the present.

*no way or **no way, Jose** an emphatic or humorous way to say no. Introduced to the general American public around 1965. Each successive generation likes to think that it possesses its own individuality of thought, style, and vocabulary. The truth of the matter is that each generation builds on the generations before it, and in some cases, after a few years when it thinks no one will remember or care, it outright steals from previous generations. "No way" is a good example. Originally a **beatnik** phrase. "**There's no way** I'll wear that tie, man." Shortened and popularized in the 1960s and then re-adopted in the 90s.

now generation coined in late 1960s and early 70s. It represents a time when young people concentrated on enjoying the present and didn't worry about the future. Though it seemed to be self-indulgent, it was not selfish. A major theme of the hippie era was to "do it now," for tomorrow you may die, or have to get married, cut your hair and get a real job. Though associated with the 1960s and 70s, the same ideals are still held by many. Generally, the 50s were an era of conformity and self-denial. In the 1960s and 70s, the **now generation** rebelled against the 50s. Not to be confused with the **me generation** of selfishness, which began to appear in the late 1970s, hit its stride in the 1980s during the Reagan presidential administration, and still flourishes today. (See: **me generation**)

nowhere an unproductive, unexciting, unstimulating place. It can be a dull party, or it can be your life.

nowhere man a person who is unproductive, unexciting or unstimulating, or someone who leads an unfulfilling life. A character in one of **The Beatles'** songs.

no-win situation a losing situation. A circumstance in which everyone will suffer.

nowness living in the present.

nuclear relating to an atomic nucleus or the center of an atom.

nuclear energy energy released by nuclear fusion or fission. **2.** electrical energy created from generators run by steam created from water boiled by hot radioactive materials

nuclear hazard sign the standard symbol used to indicate the actual or potential presence of ionizing radiation. (See: **radiation death**)

nuclear threat the real, potential or imagined fear of the use of nuclear weapons by a government in the act of aggression. The potential of a country to use a nuclear bomb.

nudie an **X-rated** movie.

nuke or **nukes** a term introduced in 1974 describing nuclear devices.

nuke, to becomes a verb to kill or blow up.

number a **marijuana** cigarette.

number a negative action performed by someone against someone else; often, it means psychological damage. Example: "He did a real **number** on her when he left her for her own brother."

number cruncher an accountant. Considered a boring person. Someone who concentrates on money or numbers rather than life and other human beings.

number-crunching working with numbers, accounting.

numb-nuts the discomfort a man feels when he is so sexually frustrated that his testicles, full of sperm, create pressure and possibly pain. a.k.a. **blue balls. 2.** a stupid person.

numero uno oneself. Number one in Spanish. Example: "I'm taking care of *numero uno* by using a condom." The use of Spanish, or any foreign word for that matter, is meant to add a bit of mystery or romantic flavor to a conversation.

nut case a person who is crazy, or "nuts."

nuts testicles.

nutso crazy, a crazy person. Related to being "nuts."

nympho short for nymphomaniac. A woman thought to be addicted to sex.

O

1-A the primary military draft status number. When the Selective Service draft is active, this designation indicates that the recipient is physically acceptable for induction into the military and that the individual's marital, educational and occupational status are appropriate. Selective Service and registration requirements for America's young men have served as a backup system to provide manpower to the US Armed Forces for over 50 years. Presi-

dent Franklin Roosevelt signed the Selective Training and Service Act of 1940, creating the country's first peacetime draft and formally establishing the Selective Service System as an independent Federal agency. From 1948 until 1973, during times of peace and war, men were drafted to fill vacancies in the armed forces that were not filled through voluntary means. In 1973, the draft ended, and the US converted to an all-volunteer military. Registration requirements were suspended in April, 1975, but resumed in 1980 by President Carter in response to the Soviet invasion of Afghanistan.

180 (See: **one-eighty**)

O a hug. At the end of a personal letter, Xs represent kisses and Os, hugs.

O *drugs* opium. Also called "big O."

obsessing emotionally involved in something or someone to the point of obsession.

occult hidden from the uninitiated. A synonym for **esoteric**. In everyday parlance, the word has come to mean supernatural, transcending the laws of the material world. It is also used to describe teachings, arts and practices relating to the supernatural, satanic religions, mysticism and witchcraft. Interest in the occult and supernatural blossomed during the hippie era from curiosity and a desire to explore all aspects of religion in order to make one's own choices. Until the 1960s and 1970s, spiritual beliefs and religion were something passed down to children from parents who had it passed down to them. For the most part, before the hippie era, children didn't question the spiritual life they inherited. Hippies wanted to test their religion against others and see whether it was true, valid, or merely right for them.

occultism the belief in hidden, mysterious or superhuman powers and the effort to use or control such powers. a.k.a. **occult** sciences.

Ochs, Phil (b. Dec. 19, 1940, El Paso, Tex.; d. April 9, 1976, Far Rockaway, New York) *folk, rock* a **beatnik**, folksinger and songwriter who had a profound effect on the early 1960s **anti-war movement**. With Bob Gibson, he wrote "I Ain't Marchin' Anymore" and "Draft Dodger Rag," both of which were 1960s anthems. He also wrote an interesting Watergate protest piece called "Here's to the State of Richard Nixon." While in Africa, he suffered a mysterious assault that damaged his vocal cords, which may have led to his suicide, depriving us of his valuable talent.

O.D. or **O.D.s** (See: **olive drab**)

O.D. short for overdose. (See: **overdose**)

Oden the Nordic god of Valhalla (the Norse heaven), one of the triad of Norse deities. The other two gods are Thor and Freyr.

Odetta (b. Odetta Holmes, Dec. 31, 1930, Birmingham, Ala.) *folk, blues* an institution among folk music lovers, she has supported many **civil rights** causes with her rich, deep voice and has lent her concerned presence to many causes. She has influenced many other singers, including Janis Joplin, Tracy Chapman and Joan Armatrading. Since the late 1950s, she has recorded, toured as a solo singer/guitarist and performed with other artists, such as Count Basie, Langston Hughes, Pete Seeger, Sonny Terry, Bob Dylan and Jackson Browne.

ofay a Black term for White people.

off not working well, out of sorts or not feeling like oneself. Example: "Sorry, I'm a little **off** today; let's do the difficult **tantric** positions tomorrow."

off adv. to get rid of (or to kill) someone or something. Examples: "If I were you I would **off** that car before it breaks down and strands you in some middle-class neighborhood." "**Off** the pigs."

off, (have it) a confrontation or fight. Example: "OK, let's **have it off** right here, man to **wimp**."

offed killed or eliminated. Examples: "They **offed** some students at Kent State." "He **offed** that old car after it broke down, stranding him in a middle-class neighborhood where they laughed at his hair."

off the chart exceptional, surpassing all others. Figuratively, above the highest level on a chart that measures value. Example: "He is so good, he's **off the chart**."

off the scale similar **to off the chart**, although usually a negative measure. Example: "He's so bad, he's **off the scale**."

off the wall abnormal, crazy or unconventional. **2.** a surprise, the unexpected.

"Oh! Calcutta!" a 1969 musical review, off Broadway in New York City, produced by Ken Tynan (1927-1980). The play presented a controversial view of sex and homosexuality considered by some to be refreshing and nonjudgmental, and by others to be repulsive. It was basically a series of skits written by such people as Robert Benton, Jules Feiffer, Dan Greenburg, **John Lennon** and **Sam Shepard**. It was videotaped (poorly) and shown as a movie in 1972. Reportedly, the name "Oh! Calcutta!" comes from the title of a painting depicting the tattooed behind of a young woman by contemporary French artist Clovis Trouille. It is also sometimes said to come from an old Cockney phrase, *oh, quel culque outas,* which means "oh what a lovely arse (ass) you have." Another suggestion is that it is a pun on a French phrase "Oh! Quelle cun t'as!" Freely translated: "What a lovely cunt you have!"

oh yeah! *exclamation* a confrontational form of "oh yes." Often meant as a challenge, yet sometimes used as a question.

-oid *suffix* added at the end of a word to make it sound inhuman, extraterrestrial, unnatural or mechanical. Examples: **womanoid, drugoid, freakoid, parentoid**. Similar usage as **zoid**.

oiled drunk or under the influence of drugs. Example: "Don't bother trying to get through to Greg; the man is **oiled**."

oils and incense during the hippie era, there was a renaissance of the senses following the 1950s, which exhibited little human exploration of feelings, emotions and senses. The 1960s **counterculture** adopted many traditions of other cultures; body oils and aromatic incenses became popular during the era. Such things as massage and aroma therapy were employed to explore the possibilities of changing and improving the human state of mind. There has always been a **spiritual** and emo-

tional aspect to the senses of smell and touch, and this was explored. Some claim that vibrations can actually be measured coming from plants and herbs releasing scent. When applied to the skin, natural chemicals in some oils may increase or decrease the heart rate; they definitely heat or **cool** the body, and this has been scientifically proven.

oinker an ugly or unacceptable person. Related to the negative image of a pig and the oinking sound it produces. Example: "George is a real **oinker**; I wouldn't even let him touch your body."

OJ *drugs* opium joint. A cigarette laced with **opium**. A common item in the bars of Saigon, South Vietnam, and a term that came back with Vietnam veterans.

Old Broads' Bill, The *social issues* on August 10, 1968, the Airline Stewards and Stewardesses Association (ALSSA) convinced the Equal Employment Opportunities Commission to draft guidelines barring the airlines from dismissing stewardesses for being overage; sometimes called the Old Broads' Bill. One of the first tests of **Title VII** of the **Civil Rights Act of 1964**. (See: **Title VII**) (See also: **Women's Movement Events, Groups and Leaders** starting on page 591 in the **Lists** at the end of this book)

oldie but goodie something out of date, but still good. Often used to describe music.

oldie moldie something out of date or out of style. Can describe a person or object and does not relate literally to spoilage, as in food or produce.

old lady and **ol' lady** a girlfriend or wife; usually a term of endearment, yet sometimes considered derogatory. A usage definitely out of favor with feminists. Introduced to the American public around 1965.

old man and **ol' man** a boyfriend or husband; usually a term of endearment, yet sometimes considered derogatory. Introduced to the American public around 1965.

olive drab the color of military combat uniforms. Also used as the name of the clothing. A common uniform of the hippie, partly as an ironic form of rebellion against the military and partly because it was cheap, readily available clothing. a.k.a. **O.D.** or **O.D.s.**

om or **ohm** or **aum** *religion* a **Sanskrit** word believed to possess magical powers and held especially sacred by **Hindus** and **occultists**. A chant used in **meditation**. Sometimes described as meaning gods, sometimes defined as meaning **peace**. Said to be the sound made by the divine mother as she exhaled, creating the world. In **Buddhism**, **yoga** and other Eastern religions, sounds are often used to induce moods or mental states to assist in **healing** and **spiritual** fulfillment. The om sound should emanate from the stomach chakra or navel area and is meant to create a resonance in one's body that has a mesmerizing effect. In Tibetan

Buddhism, the phrase **om mani padme hum** is used as a **mantra**.

omen *occult* an event or object believed to be a sign foretelling a future occurrence.

om mani padme hum *religion* a **Tibetan Buddhist** mantra meaning the jewel in the lotus. The most famous mantra of Tibetan Lamaism, whose six syllables correspond to the six worlds of Tibetan Buddhist teaching: om, Gods; ma, anti-gods; ni, humans; pad, animals; mi, hungry ghosts; hum, hell. (See: **Lamaism**)

omnipotence absolute, perfect, unlimited power over all things. Considered an attribute of God alone.

omnipresence the ability of a deity to be in all places at all times. Considered an attribute of God alone.

omniscience in philosophy and theology, the complete and perfect knowledge of God alone, of Himself and of all other beings, past, present, and future. (adjective, omniscient)

*****on** correct or perfect. Often used as **right on** or **bang on**. Examples: "I should have listened to you; you were **on** about that girl." "Doby was bang **on** with that guitar solo." **2.** sharp, aware, awake. Example: "You can't fool her; she is always **on**."

on, on for and **we're on** a confirmation of a date or meeting. Example: "The yoga class is **on** tonight." "Are we still **on for** the **Tarot** reading tomorrow night?" "**We're on** for sex tonight, right?"

on, on me, on you or **on him** a designation of responsibility. Indicates the one who pays the bill. Example: "This bud's **on me**."

on a roll a long string of things going the right way. Good luck. From success in the rolling of dice. Also related to "rolling right along."

on (one's) **ass** incapacitated. Example: "That toke knocked Jody **on her ass**."

Onassis, Jacqueline Kennedy (Jackie Kennedy or Jackie O.) (b. Jacqueline Lee Bouvier, Southampton, New York, July 28, 1929; d. May 19, 1994) first lady of the United States from 1961 until 1963, when her husband, **President John F. Kennedy, was assassinated. Jacqueline Bouvier studied at Vassar College, the Sorbonne, and Washington University, and worked as a reporter before marrying Kennedy in 1953. Jackie Kennedy promoted an agenda of the arts, history, and high style in the White House and throughout her life. History finds her the most popular representative of the American woman throughout the world. In 1968, she married Greek millionaire shipping magnate Aristotle Onassis. After Onassis's death in 1975, Jackie worked in New York publishing firms, Viking Press from 1975 to 1977, then Doubleday from 1978 until her death from cancer in 1994. The hippie **counterculture** always respected the Kennedys, particularly Jackie, not only for their **liberal** politics, but for their taste, culture and respectability. Contrary to what some people might believe, hippies were not rebelling against power, wealth and respectability, but against false respectability, exploitative wealth, abuse of power and hypocrisy.

on (someone's) **ass** or **on** (someone's) **case** bothering, antagonizing or reprimanding someone. Examples: "Tilly is **on Frank's ass** about everything these days." "Uncle Sam is **on my case** about the taxes I owe him."

one *sex* the sex act. Examples: "That was a good **one** last night." "They knocked **one** off at noon."

one an unspecified thing understood by those in a conversation. Example: "That was a big **one**."

one-eighty (180) 180 degrees of a compass. A change of opinion or an about-face. There are 360 degrees in the circle of a compass; 180 degrees is half way around. Example: "He did a **one-eighty** on celibacy when he saw her."

one-eyed monster television.

one-eyed trouser worm (or snake) the penis.

one-night stand a one-and-only sexual encounter, usually lasting over a period of one night.

one of the boys an all-right guy, a close male friend, a member of the loosely exclusive, non-card-carrying fraternity of men.

one-on-one a verbal, physical or sexual encounter with just one other person. Examples: "They had a **one-on-one** discussion about refrigerator etiquette." "Gabrielle and I went **one-on-one** last night in her big, brass bed."

photo by Lisa Law ©

one percenter (1%) a motorcycle club member who considers himself a rebel, usually one of the **Hell's Angels**. Many club members had a 1% sewn on their jackets or **colors**. The badge of the bravest, most rebellious riders. Originally from the "**cult**" of flyboys and bomber crews of the Second World War. The airmen and crewmen of combat airplanes during WWII were a rebellious bunch, and from this group of men, the first Hell's Angels club was formed in Fontana, California, in 1950. (See: **Hell's Angels**)

one toke over the line *drugs* One too many drags on a **marijuana** joint. A little too **high**. A **toke** is a puff on a marijuana **joint**.

one with *religion/occult* close to or metaphysically identifying with someone or something. Examples: "He is **one with** his guitar." "True love is being **one with** nature." This philosophy is considered sappy, idealistic and too **New Age** by many people, yet it is the basis for most religions, particularly **Native American** and Eastern religions and philosophy. People who do not appreciate and nurture their metaphysical connections with nature and other human beings are missing the most satisfying part of life.

on ice set aside, waiting, or saved for later. From keeping something fresh by putting it on ice. Example: "Franny is sleeping with Zoey, but she has Peter **on ice** just in case that doesn't work out."

on it get to work, shift attention to, or take charge of. Example: "Your car needs some maintenance; you better get **on it** before the wheels fall off.

only game in town the only choice.

on something *drugs* under the influence of some form of drugs. Example: "Henry is **on something**. Poor dog, must have raided the garbage and eaten the stale **electric brownies**."

"On strike, shut it down!" *social issues* a slogan used by student demonstrators during the **free-speech movement**, starting in 1964 when they disrupted universities with sit-ins and strikes.

on the brain an obsession. Continually thinking of someone or something. Example: "Jack has Jill **on the brain**."

on the edge borderline crazy, unusual, or beyond the **mainstream**. Dangerous or heroic activity. Possibly from surfer usage, relating to the edge of the surfboard or edge of a wave. May be related to the dangerous cutting edge of a knife.

on the fly quickly in passing without a lot of time or concentration. Example: "Doug fixed the roof **on the fly**, and I think it still leaks."

on the hook responsible for or committed to something. From fishing jargon meaning that someone is caught. Example: "Jim left, but he's still **on the hook** for the rent."

on the inside knowing the right people, aware of something exclusive, "**connected**."

on the lamb on the run from someone, most often the authorities.

on the make *sex* looking for a sexual partner. The word **make** is a euphemism for sexual seduction.

on the nose skillful or adept at something. A surfer term related to walking the nose of the surfboard. Also associated with the earlier phrase, to hit something on the nose (to be accurate), which came from a prizefighting term.

on the prowl *sex* looking for trouble, searching for excitement; often, prowling for a sexual partner.

on the rag a derogatory reference to a woman's personality during menstruation. **2.** experiencing a menstrual period.

on the road traveling. Usually, a very basic form of traveling; either **thumbing** rides or jumping freight trains. Also used in the music business to mean touring with a band.

photo by John McCleary ©

On The Road a 1955 book by **Jack Kerouac**, describing his travels around the United States. One of the primary literary influences on the **beat generation** and later on the young people who became hippies. (See: **Kerouac, Jack; beat** and **beat generation**)

on the stick sharp, efficient or attentive. Similar usage as **on the ball**. Example: "If you want to stay in this band, you better get **on the stick**." **2.** to hurry.

on to aware of. Example: "I'm **on to** his lies."

on top of aware of or paying attention to. Example: "Are you **on top of** that story about Jon and the **compost?**"

onto something a good Idea. Example: "I think you're **onto something** with that square ball invention."

on track heading in the right direction. Example: "He's **on track** to eat forty hard boiled eggs this time." Relating to railroad trains and tracks.

op art n. optical art work. A term and art form introduced to the American public in 1965. Art work devised to create movement or deceptive visual activities. Often, something like a series of lines, forms or bull's eyes so close together that the slightest movement of the retina gives the impression that the picture itself is moving.

open city a reference to any place that is accepting of decadent activities. A place that maintains a **liberal**, hands-off attitude toward **counterculture** activities and excesses.

open to available, agreeable to. Example: "Kit is **open to** any decadence you have."

operating system *computer revolution* essential instructions inside a computer to make it perform a function. The basic program that runs applications, maintains files and control devices, such as the printer and **mouse**. Also called **operating program**. The first operating systems for mainframe computers were too complex for amateurs; for example, IBM's FORTRAN for scientific use and COBOL for business. **BASIC** was the first "simple" operating program. It was developed in 1964 by two Dartmouth College professors, John Kemeny and Thomas Kurtz, through a grant from the National Science Foundation to help their students more easily use computers. (See: **Computer Revolution Milestones, Companies and Leaders** starting on page 626 in **Lists** at the back of this book)

operator a hustler, someone who conducts deals. A seducer of women. Often called "a real operator."

opiate *drugs* any drug produced from **opium** poppies. Examples: **Opium, morphine, heroin, methadone** and **Demerol.**

opium *drugs* a sticky, dark brown drug produced from the sap of **opium** poppies. Normally smoked in a pipe, it produces a euphoric, yet intellectual, drug experience. It is said that the word "**hip**" has its roots in opium use, referring to the customary position of reclining on one's side, or hip, while smoking opium. There was a time in America, just around the turn of the 20th century, when opium smokers were considered to be of the intellectual class, therefore "hip."

O.P.'s other people's. The type of cigarettes smoked by a panhandler. Example: Question: "What kind of cigarettes do you smoke?" Answer: "O.P.'s!"

oracle in antiquity, an oracle was a temple or shrine in which a god would speak to his worshippers through a priest or priestess. Also, the priest or priestess through whom the god speaks. In modern terminology, a medium who transmits messages.

oral sex *sex* kissing, licking or sucking the genitals of a lover. **Cunnilingus** or **fellatio**. Fellatio is the oral stimulation of the male sexual organ; cunnilingus is the oral stimulation of the female sexual organs. Not a new term to the hippie era, nor a new idea to the last fifty millenniums. Merely a term that was used more freely during the 1960s and 1970s because people weren't as ashamed of the act. Can be a homosexual or heterosexual act. (See: **cunnilingus** and **fellatio**)

orange or **orange sunshine** *drugs* **LSD** tablets that were orange in color. Thought to be a creation of **Augustus "Owsley" Stanley** in the 1970s. (See: **Stanley III, Augustus Owsley**)

orange barrels *drugs* large, orange **LSD** tablets. Some of them were "eight way," meaning they could be broken into eight different wedge-shaped pieces, each containing a moderate dose of **acid**.

orange wedge *drugs* tablets of **STP** and **LSD** combined. The same combination was also manufactured as **pinks** or **purple wedges**. Because of the speed of STP, these tablets sometimes caused bad trips. Sometimes **methadrine** was used instead of STP; then it was called a **peace pill**. (See: **LSD** and **STP**)

Orbison, Roy (b. April 23, 1936, Vernon, Tex.; d. Dec. 6, 1988, Hendersonville, Tenn.) *rockabilly/country/rock & roll* one of the original Sun Record **rockabilly** recording artists, along with **Elvis Presley**, Jerry Lee Lewis, **Johnny Cash** and Carl Perkins. Orbison wrote many memorable songs and recorded numerous classics, such as "Only the Lonely," 1960; "Blue Bayou," 1963; and "Oh, Pretty Woman," 1964. His operatic style of singing with exquisite clarity and unstrained falsetto was unique in country/rock music and introduced new possibilities for others to come in the genre, such as k.d. lang, Chris Isaak and Lyle Lovett. Inducted into The Rock and Roll Hall of Fame in 1987.

oregano an herb sometimes sold as **marijuana** to unsuspecting buyers. Sometimes laced with **THC**, the extract of marijuana.

Oreo or **Oreo cookie** a Black person who acts White. From the cookie of that name, which was white on the inside and brown on the outside. Can also mean a sexual act in which a White person is in the middle being made love to by two Black people.

organic anything that is natural in its chemical makeup. Unchanged by the manipulation of its molecules. Something that will biodegrade into the environment and nourish and recreate new, natural life.

orgasmic something so exciting, or which tastes or feels so good, that it is compared to an orgasm.

orgy a party at which sexual or decadent activities are indulged. From the Greek word *orgia,* meaning a "secret worship."

Orwell, George (pseudonym for Eric Blair) (1903-1950) *social issues* author of the book *1984,* published in 1949. Coined the term **Big Brother, which, in general usage, has come to mean an authority figure who watches over society and disciplines those who break the "rules." Many authors who wrote and published just before or during the hippie era could be on a list of the 100 most prominent people of that time; yet, even though Blair died before the era began, he is the author who most influenced that generation and its rebellion against oppression. If it hadn't been for Orwell's (Blair's) *1984,* the year 1984 would likely have resembled the tyranny portrayed in the book. *1984* postponed the complete control of our thoughts and minds by the **mili-**

tary-**industrial complex**. We now have possibly another 10 or 15 years to stop it again.

Osiris the most widely worshipped god of ancient Egypt, god of the dead, husband of Isis, father of Horus. Worshipped as the great Creator.

other half, (the) people who are rich and privileged. Or, if one has money and privilege, it means those who are poor. The inaccuracy of this usage is that, in the United States, only about 7% of the population could be considered rich. **2.** one's spouse. Same use as **better half**.

other worldly a person, place or thing with the appearance or feeling of being from another planet.

Ouroboros a serpent biting its own tail, forming a circle; the symbol of the endless succession of incarnations that form the **wheel of life**. A common image in the **Buddhist** religion.

out or **out of the closet** living openly as a homosexual.

outasight (See: **out of sight**)

outfit *drugs* the paraphernalia for injecting intravenous drugs.

out front open, candid, communicative, **cool**, honorable, truthful. Not a conservative trait. Examples: "He's one of us, he's **out front**, he can be trusted." "Are you being totally **out front** with me on this thing about the little green men?" (See: **up front**)

out of control a human condition wherein rational consideration does not govern one's actions. Having too much fun. Crazy.

out of (one's) **depth** incapable of, or unprepared for a situation. In over one's head, as in drowning in water.

out of (one's) **head, mind** or **skull** crazy. Often indicates a temporary or momentarily induced craziness.

out of here, (we are/I am) leaving the area. A humorous emphasis on a simple statement.

out of it disoriented, drugged or inebriated. This usage indicates a temporary state.

out of joint mad. Examples: "Watch him; he's **out of joint**." "Don't get **out of joint** over it, but your ol'lady just ran off with your chiropractor."

out of line inappropriate. Overreacting.

out of my face don't bother me. Step back and stop arguing with me. Example: "If you don't get **out of my face**, I'll punch you out."

out of sight or **outasight** an exclamation of approval. Same usage as **good**, **great** or **wonderful**. Example: "**Out of sight**, I love guava!" Also the title of a James Brown song from 1964.

out of sync incorrect, contrary to the prevailing situation. Example: "You may like Bob, but he's **out of sync** with this house."

out of the loop not one of the chosen people. Uninformed. Example: "Bruce is **out of the loop** on this **acid** caper."

out of this world special. Unknown in this world.

out of (one's) **tree** crazy. Usually indicates a more or less permanent craziness.

out of whack not functioning properly.

out on the edge borderline crazy, unusual, or beyond the **mainstream**. Activity that is dangerous or heroic. Possibly from surfer usage, relating to the edge of the surfboard or edge of a wave. May be related to the dangerous cutting edge of a knife.

output information coming from a computer. Ideas and/or work produced by a person.

*out there a human condition of distraction or unresponsiveness. From "out in left field."

out to lunch tired, distracted or unable to respond adequately. Example: "Bill is **out to lunch**; you could talk to the wallpaper and get better results."

Ovation *rock & roll* one of the newest and most modern guitar manufacturing companies in the United States. Started by Charles Karman in 1965. Karman, owner of Karman Corporation, manufacturers of helicopter and aerospace parts, became interested in guitars. Since the physics of vibration and acoustics were a concern in the design of helicopter rotor blades, Karman employed his engineers to produce a resonant guitar made from synthetics. His guitars are notable for their rounded backs and the use of plastics in manufacturing. The company made many guitars popular with **rock and roll** musicians during the hippie era.

overdose a negative medical reaction to a substance that has been introduced into one's body. Originally, it was just a medical term relating to drugs, but during the hippie era, it was used to describe the over consumption or indulgence in anything, including such things as food, sex or music. a.k.a. **O.D.** or **o.d.**

overkill originally a military term indicating the effect of a bomb, explosion or attack that killed more than its intended target, i.e., killing civilians or friendly forces. Civilian usage means an excess of anything, physical or otherwise. Similar to **collateral damage**.

over the high side riding one's motorcycle off the road on a turn.

Owsley acid a popular **LSD** made in the San Francisco Bay area by **Augustus Owsley Stanley III** beginning in April, 1965.

Owsley (See: **Stanley III, Augustus Owsley**)

O.Z. *drugs* an ounce. The unit of measurement most often used in packaging and selling **marijuana** for personal use.

*ozone n. a fictitious place in which the mind does not function properly. An actual physical state created by drugs in which the mind does not function properly. **2.** a protective, gaseous layer in the atmosphere around the earth. The chemical compound is O_3 and it is a gaseous form of oxygen with three oxygen atoms per molecule formed by electrical discharge in oxygen.

ozone layer a layer of **ozone** around the earth's upper atmosphere at about 10 to 30 miles. This gaseous atmosphere filters out harmful ultraviolet radiation coming from the sun. In the last thirty years, it has been discovered that this layer is being damaged by chlorofluorocarbon (CFC) gas, which is used in refrigerators and aerosol cans, and is inadvertently released into the atmosphere. This circumstance is endangering our life on this planet by contributing to skin cancers caused by exposure to the sun, and by disturbing weather systems and plant growing cycles.

Ozzie and Harriet a sarcastic name describing anyone who does not seem to live in the real world, but pretends to exist in a perfect life, which is impossible in reality. From Ozzie and Harriet Nelson, the parents of Rickey and David Nelson, who comprised the TV family on "The Adventures of Ozzie and Harriet," which premiered on ABC, October 3, 1952.

P

package something of importance or beauty; often, it referred to a woman. Example: "Pam is quite a **package**."

packing carrying a gun. **2.** carrying dope.

pack it *drugs* to fill a smoking pipe with **marijuana**.

pack it in to give up or to end something. Example: "We had a great relationship, but now it's time to **pack it in**."

pack my nose *drugs* give me some **cocaine**. To snort cocaine.

pad a house or place to sleep. Most likely derived from a "pad" on which to sleep.

pagan a free-spirited person, unincumbered by prohibitions and the rules of religious doctrine. Originally a derogatory word used to describe a non-Christian. During the 1960s, the term was adopted and accepted by the **counterculture** as a positive designation and used to indicate a **free love**, uninhibited, hippie-type person.

Page, Jimmy *rock & roll* lead guitar player for the rock group **Led Zeppelin**. One of the most respected players in one of the most successful of all the **heavy-metal** bands.

pain one of those words that took on deeper meanings during the hippie era. Pain become a mental affliction. Example: "You're a **pain**; I have no patience with your pain."

pain in the ass an annoyance.

pair breasts.

paisley a popular floral design that adorned clothing worn by both men and women in the hippie era. The design came originally from shawls made in a region near the town of Paisley, Scotland. The creatively represented horticultural elements that formed this design are similar to the surrealistic distortions created in one's mind by psychedelics. Many East Indian cotton bedspreads with this pattern were used for clothing, curtains and wall decoration during the hippie era.

paki or **paki black** *drugs* black **hashish**. Loosely applied to any low-grade hashish. Paki was short for Pakistan.

Pali Canon *religion* the basic **Buddhist** scriptures and the only scriptures used by Theravada Buddhists. Pali was the language of Northern India during Buddha's life and the language of early Buddhism. The Pali language is related to **Sanskrit**.

palimony *social issues* money awarded to an unmarried, yet dependent, live-in lover after a couple has separated. Patterned after alimony. Coined by attorney Marvin Mitchelson in 1976. Mitchelson was the lawyer for Michelle Triola "Marvin" in her suit for compensation from actor Lee Marvin. Marvin was one of the first people sued for palimony. His five-year relationship with Triola, separation in 1970, and 1979 trial are the reasons the word was coined. In the end, the case was lost by Triola, and she actually received nothing, but a precedent was set and many have sued for palimony and won since then.

palmistry divination through analysis of the lines and shapes of the hand. Fortune-telling by studying a person's hand and palms. During the hippie era, it gained new popularity among a **counterculture** interested in any unique insights into humanity.

palooka a somewhat humorous description of a person who is mentally slow and physically violent. From Joe Palooka, the cartoon character who was a prizefighter. Example: "He's a real **palooka** with no social graces, and he's also real mean."

Pan *religion* the Arcadian god of shepherds, hunters and country folk. Associated with fertility. Leader of the minor deities of the Greek pantheon. Usually pictured with goat's horns and hooves. Male hippies identified with this rascal, who was always trying to seduce beautiful women like Aphrodite.

Panama red *drugs* **marijuana** from somewhere south of the border. Whether it was good smoke or bad and whether it actually came from Panama were matters of speculation. Originally, there may have been some red dope from Panama, and the legend blossomed. Any marijuana with a red hue came to be known as Panama red. **2.** the name of a popular song of the time by the band, Old and In the Way.

panayama Sanskrit for breath. An important element in the practice of **yoga**; a breathing exercise considered necessary for proper mental function and development. Holding the breath and breath control; inhalation, suspension, and exhalation.

Pandit Hindu term for learned man. (Often erroneously spelled and pronounced *pundit*.)

panic an emergency situation. Evolved from a mental circumstance into an actual physical situation involving human emotions and actions. A very subtle evolution, but one that added more depth to the English language. Examples: Old usage: "I felt panic when the house fell down." New usage: "Everyone was in a **panic** when the house fell down."

panic button an imaginary button one pushes (in his head) when things go wrong. The point at which a person reaches a state of panic. Example: "Don't push the **panic button**; I think I have the diaphragm under control."

Pantheism *religion* the belief that all reality is essentially divine. A religion teaching that God is everything around us, all creatures and things, including ourselves. God is Nature, and Nature is God. Similar to most **Native American** beliefs, which many hippies espoused.

panther piss bad beer.

paper *drugs* a small square of paper folded into a rectangular envelope containing powdered drugs.

paper bag job an ugly woman. The seduction of an ugly woman. From the old and very unkind jokes about having to put a bag over a woman's head in order to be able to make love to her. Example: "I picked up a beautiful girl at a bar last night and woke up with a **paper bag job**."

paper boy *drugs* a heroin dealer.

paper chase any job that requires searching through papers to find facts or figures.

paper pusher a clerical worker. A government functionary.

photo by John McCleary ©

papers *drugs* **marijuana** cigarette rolling papers. Before the widespread use of marijuana and before the invention of tailor-made cigarettes, people used to roll their own tobacco cigarettes. Even after "tailor-mades" appeared, some people preferred the low cost or image of rolling their own. When marijuana came onto the scene, commercial papers were available to roll it. Products like Bull Durham and Drum pouch tobacco came with papers, but they were not gummed, so rolling paper companies marketed papers with gummed edges for better results. When marijuana smokers started buying these papers, the companies, knowing full well why they were being purchased, began to expand their lines and even blatantly produced papers for marijuana use. Some of the paper brand names were **Zig-Zag**, Top, Bambu, Stella, e-z wide, Joker, Club, Mafil, Rizla, Papel de Arroz, Blanco Y Negra, Papil de Hilo, LLF, OCB and **Job**.

paranoia most dictionaries say "a mental disorder in which the sufferer believes he is suspected, despised or persecuted by others." The hippie era definition was "a mental delusion brought on by smoking **marijuana** in which the sufferer believes that the police are about to break down his door and bust him for the marijuana he just smoked."

paranormal the supernatural. Any phenomenon of nature or man that falls outside the realm of normalcy or defies scientific explanation. Usually refers to things, such as ghosts, spirits, **extrasensory perception**, **divination**, **clairvoyance** and **telekinesis (psychokinesis)**. Many hippies were interested in the subject and curious to learn where the paranormal fit into religion or there normal lives. (See: **supernatural**)

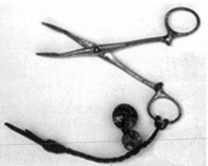

hemostat roach clip

paraphernalia any of the numerous apparatus used for storing, preparing and using drugs.

parapsychology the study of supernormal abilities and phenomena. A division of psychology dealing with physical activities that fall outside the scope of natural law.

paraquat a plant defoliant used by the military in Vietnam, and, some say, in the US war on drugs. In Vietnam, this chemical was sprayed on jungles to make the plants drop their leaves, exposing the Viet Cong to detection by US military forces. In America, a program was reportedly agreed upon between the Mexican and US governments to spray Mexican **marijuana** fields from the air, spoiling the crop destined for the US market. In the early 1970s, Mexican marijuana users were fearful of smoking this tainted product. Proof of its use against marijuana crops is not substantiated.

parental unit a sarcastic term used to indicate one's parents. Late 1970s usage.

Paris Peace Accord the peace agreement reached by North Vietnam and the United States on January 23, 1973, effectively ending the Vietnam conflict. *Article 2*. "A cease fire shall be observed throughout South Vietnam as of 24:00 hours G.M.T., on January 27, 1973. At the same hour, the United States will stop all its military activities against the territory of the Democratic Republic of Vietnam by ground, air and naval forces, wherever they may be based, and end the mining of the territorial waters, ports, harbors, and waterways of the Democratic Republic of Vietnam. The United States will remove, permanently deactivate or destroy all the mines in the territorial waters, ports, harbors, and waterways of North Vietnam as soon as this Agreement goes into effect. The complete cessation of hostilities mentioned in this Article shall be durable and without limit of time...." *Article 4*. "The United States will not continue its military involvement or intervene in the internal affairs of South Vietnam."

Parker, Charlie (b. Charles Christopher Parker, Aug. 29, 1920, Kansas City, Kan.; d. March 12, 1955, New York City) *jazz* a Black alto saxophone player who defined what that instrument could do. His legendary devotion to his music, and the few recordings we have available of his work have inspired many musicians playing every instrument. The musical angst and emotional melody that Parker expressed is his legacy were studied and emulated by the best musicians of the hippie rock and roll era.

park it sit down.

park it where the sun don't shine! stick it up your ass!

Parks, Gordon A. (Alexander Buchanan) (1912-) Black photographer, writer, movie director and composer. World War II correspondent and photojournalist for *Life* magazine from 1949 to 1970. Directed the **blackxploitation** movie "**Shaft**" in 1971 and "The Super Cops" in 1973. Parks has written several books, *The Learning Tree,* 1966; and *Born Black, 1971.* He has also composed many popular songs, sonatas, and a least one symphonic piece. Gordon Parks is well-respected for his art and dignity.

Parks, Rosa (1913-) *social issues* **civil rights** activist and NAACP organizer. Her refusal to move to the back of a segregated bus in Montgomery, Alabama, on December 1, 1955, started the Montgomery bus boycott and launched the civil rights movement. Called "the mother of the civil rights movement."

Parsons, Gram (b. Ingram Cecil Connor III, Nov. 5, 1946, Winter Haven, Fla.; d. Sept. 19, 1973, Yucca Valley, Calif.) *country/rock & roll* singer/ songwriter. Considered by many musicians to be one of the major creators of country rock. A short-time member of the **Byrds** and co-founder of The Flying Burrito Brothers. Played with and influenced Keith Richards, **Emmylou Harris**, Elvis Costello, Rick Grech, **James Burton**, Bernie Leadon and many others. His life and tragic death by overdose are part of the era's mythology of music. His body was stolen by friends and band members and cre-

mated in the desert according to his wishes.

participatory democracy a social and political ideology advocating the participation of all citizens in their own government. A **New Left** ideal advocating the protection of all freedoms and the opposition of economic or political oppression. Coined during the **free-speech movement** in Berkeley, California, in the mid-1960s.

partner a close friend. Not necessarily a business connection.

*party in the hippie era, the simple word "party" became an activity of extreme proportions. In some circles, it meant to have sex. In other situations and places, it meant merely to get drunk and dance. An attitude of life. Party was pronounced in several ways: pahty, pardy, partee, etc. All meant the same thing! **2.** a term used by prostitutes to offer sex. Example: "Do you want to **party?**"

party down another use of the basic theme and attitude to **party**. The word down was added for emphasis.

partying an all-encompassing word indicating the activity of "having fun."

party out same as **party down**, yet it could mean to reach a place of excess.

pash the person with whom one is passionately involved or in love. Example: "She is her **pash.**"

pass able to fool others into thinking you are someone or something that you are not. Example: "He may **pass** for a vegetable, but a rutabaga can never **pass** for a person."

passing the ability of a **homosexual** person to be accepted by society as heterosexual.

passing water urinating.

passion pit *sex* a place specifically designated for the purpose of making love. A room or house designed for seduction.

passion wagon *sex* a **Volkswagen bus** with a mattress in it.

pass out to lose consciousness from an overdose of drugs or alcohol.

patchouli oil (*Pogostemon patchouli*) a particularly distinctive scent worn by many hippie men and women, called an oil rather than a perfume or cologne. The plant from which it is extracted is originally from India. Patchouli is considered an **aphrodisiac** and is reportedly good for smoothing skin wrinkles. When rubbed on pulse points of the body, it is said to have an invigorating effect.

Pauling, Linus Carl (1901-1994) *social issues* chemist, anti-nuclear activist, lifestyle influence to the **counterculture**. He earned a PhD from the California Institute of Technology in 1925, where he taught from 1927 to 1963. An associate at the Center for the Study of Democratic Institutions from 1963 to 1969; at the University of California, San Diego, from 1967 to 1969; and at Stanford University in 1969. In his early research, he used X-ray crystallography to study the nature of chemical bonding, and in 1928, published his resonance theory of bonding. His work on molecular structure opened new areas in modern chemistry, earning him the Nobel Prize for Chemistry in 1954. In the 1930s, he turned his attention to biochemistry; his work on complex organic molecules, such as proteins, led to his discovery that sickle-cell anemia resulted from a hereditary defect in blood hemoglobin. In the

1950s when the United States and the Soviet Union started testing atomic weapons, Pauling and other scientists became concerned about potential genetic damage from radioactive fallout. In 1957, he authored an appeal to halt the tests, eventually signed by more than 11,000 scientists in 49 countries. His efforts led to a temporary moratorium in 1958 and to a treaty banning above-ground testing in 1963. For these efforts, he was awarded the Nobel Peace Prize in 1962, becoming the first person to win two unshared Nobel Prizes. In the late 1960s, he became interested in the biological effects of vitamin C, which led him to his controversial theory of orthomolecular medicine, with its claim that massive doses of vitamin C could prevent or cure various diseases.

1952 Gibson Les Paul

**Paul, Les (b. Lester Polfus, Jan. 9, 1915, Waukesha, Wisc.) *pop, country, jazz* a White guitar virtuoso in the mid-1950s, Paul had a successful recording career with his wife, singer Mary Ford (b. Colleen Summer, July 7, 1928, Pasadena, Calif.; d. Sept. 30, 1977). Les Paul's true contributions to music and eventually to rock and roll are his guitar design innovations and studio experimentation. Les Paul became interested in electronics at age 12; he built his first electric guitar pickup in 1934 at 19, using ham radio headphone parts. By 1941, he had constructed the first prototype solid-body electric guitar. He still uses that four-foot-long board with strings and sound pickup, dubbed the "Log," to test other guitars.

In 1952, his solid body *Les Paul* was marketed through the **Gibson Guitar Company**. The Gibson *Les Paul* , renowned for its "hot" pickups, became an instant success with anyone who wanted to rock. In the early 1950s, Paul began to experiment on what eventually became the first eight-track tape recorder. In his recordings with Mary Ford, he devised many new studio techniques to produce more depth of sound, eventually developing multitrack recording and the electronic echo. Everyone who ever played psychedelic music or relied on **heavy-metal** distortion owes Les Paul a debt of gratitude. Anyone who has recorded a single voice, over and over, to create one-singer harmonies is beholden to Mr. Les Paul. All of us who listen to country, **jazz** or rock music know the emotions evoked by his innovations. Inducted into the Rock and Roll Hall of Fame in 1988 as an early influence. Jorma Kaukonen, **Jefferson Airplane's** lead guitarist and a primary innovator of psychedelic music says: "Les Paul didn't actually invent the electric guitar, but Les Paul... invented the electric guitar."

Paulson, Pat (1927-1997) comedian, statesman, politician, US Marine veteran of World War II. "I wanted to be a hero so girls would dig me." He never saw any action, but was stationed in China as a guard for Japanese prisoners of war. "We were surrounded by the communists, but never attacked. Many people think I was captured by their troops who installed a receiver in my head which keeps commanding me to run for President." Paulson was employed at various times as a postal clerk, truck driver, hod carrier, Fuller Brush salesman, gypsum miner and photostat operator. While attending San Francisco City College and watching the rehearsal of a play, he became aware that there were girls enrolled in drama class, so he changed his major to drama. After leaving City College,

Pat joined an acting group called "The Ric-y-tic Players," a group that presented funny revues. "We were funny, but nobody showed up to watch us being funny. So we disbanded." Pat and his brother Lorin later put together a comedy trio and achieved some success in San Francisco. After the trio broke up, Pat became a single act and something of a favorite during the folk club era, appearing as a comedic guitarist at such places as The Ice House in Pasadena, The Troubadour in Los Angeles, The Gaslight in New York and The Purple Onion in San Francisco. At The Purple Onion, Pat met the Smothers Brothers and figured he could make a "pile of money" selling them his songs. The Smothers Brothers took two of his songs and gave him forty bucks. In 1967, "The Smothers Brothers Comedy Hour" premiered, and they hired Pat "because he sold them cheap songs and would run errands." Pat was eventually asked by the Smothers Brothers to run for President as a gag. Paulson replied "Why not? I can't dance—besides, the job has a good pension plan and I'll get a lot of money when I retire." His campaign was based on comedy, outright lies, double talk and unfounded attacks on his challengers, much the same as today's politicians. Pat Paulson's work on "The Smothers Brothers Comedy Hour" earned him an Emmy in 1968.

paw to lasciviously or sexually touch someone. Used primarily to describe unsolicited attention. Unwanted or inept **foreplay**.

pax Latin for peace.

pay (one's) **dues** to get experience. To gain knowledge through painful lessons. From the payment of monetary dues to join a club or union. Example: "I didn't get where I am overnight; I had to **pay my dues**."

payback revenge or compensation. Example: "It took a long time, but I finally got **payback** for what she did to me."

payola scandal during the 1950s and 60s, it was an accepted business policy for record companies to give money to radio stations or radio personalities to induce them to play their records. This money was called payola. Although there was no actual law against it, at some point the authorities and news media decided to make it unacceptable and began a smear campaign against those who accepted these monies or "bribes." Allen Freed, one of the most popular DJs of the era, was singled out, and his career was ruined by the payola scandal. (See: **payola** and **Allen Freed**)

P coat or **P jacket** a heavy, dark blue Navy jacket popular with hippies. War surplus stores were a cheap and popular place for the **counterculture** to buy their clothing. That is the reason for the army boots, fatigues, camouflage clothes and bomber jackets popularized by hippies during the 1960s. P stands for petty, as in Naval Petty Officer. It is interesting to note that these **fashion** statements have become **mainstream** and are continually experiencing rebirths in popularity.

PCP *drugs* the narcotic phencyclidine, a human and **animal tranquilizer**. Also called **angel dust, crystal, fairy dust, hog** and **tranq**. Sometimes erroneously called **elephant tranquilizer**. Smoked in a pipe or crumbled in a rolled cigarette or **marijuana** joint. Can also be smoked, snorted, swallowed or injected. Dangerous because it often drastically changes a person's mental state, causing paranoia and violence. Has the strange effect of concentrating one's physical capabilities, thus greatly enhancing strength. People under the influence of PCP have been known to break their own bones with their own muscle strength. Now virtually unused in veterinary or human medicine because of its dangers. On the street, it is often confused with **methamphetamine**; both are dangerous. Making this drug at home has become a cottage industry, and many of the manufacturers are not very good at it. There are inherent dangers with this drug and worse consequences from taking bad doses.

PCP *drugs* LSD and **Methedrine** mix. a.k.a. **peace pill**

P.D.A. acronym for "**p**ublic **d**isplay of **a**ffection." More or less a preppie term.

p'd or **p'd off** angry. Short for **pissed off**.

P.D.Q. acronym for "**p**retty **d**amn **q**uick."

peace just a dream some of us had.

Peace and Freedom Party *social issues* a political party that ran candidates **Dick Gregory** for President and **Eldridge Cleaver** for Vice President in 1968. (See: **Peace and Freedom Party** in **Lists** at the back of this book)

peace and love *social issues* the primary desire and emotion of the hippie era. Peace and love are altruistic desires, meaning that they are not selfish wishes. These emotions are often ridiculed by those who are not altruistic themselves. Members of the human race who are motivated by selfishness are suspicious of anyone who is idealistic because they cannot imagine someone without ulterior motives. Those of us who truly believe in peace and love will eventually prevail, in this life or beyond, because we are right and because we are unselfishly right. And we wish you all peace and love, even those of you who don't believe in it.

Peace Corps a United States government-supported institution that sends volunteers to underdeveloped countries to help educate people to feed, govern and care for themselves. **President John Kennedy** announced its formation on March 1, 1961, and it was officially instituted in October, 1961. Since that time, the Peace Corps has recruited tens of thousands of Americans, young and old, to serve in the villages, towns, and cities of more than 130 countries, demonstrating compassion and altruism. Considered by many Americans to represent the true **spirit** of this country.

peace march *social issues* a demonstration against war. The first hippie-era peace march is thought to be one held on February 16, 1962, when hundreds of people organized by Harvard students converged on the White House. President John Kennedy sent an urn of coffee out to the demonstrators.

peacenik *social issues* someone who is opposed to war. The use of the supposed Russian suffix "nik" was intended to infer communist sympathies, just as in **beatnik**. A term created by conservatives as a derogatory name for people with pacifist ideals. Meant to be derisive, it is actually a compliment to someone who cares about mankind. After all, the opposite of a peacenik is a warmonger. This term appeared around 1967.

peace pill *drugs* **LSD** and **Methedrine** mix.

peace sign *social issues* a gesture made by holding the index and middle fingers up in a V-shape, with the palm and folded fingers facing the intended recipient. Used by **anti-war** demonstrators to advocate peace in Vietnam. Originally, this sign was the WWII sign of V for victory, as seen in so many photos of Winston Churchill. Another example of the ironic intellectual mentality of the **counterculture** by using the victory sign to represent its own brand of victory, which is peace. Note: The peace sign should not be displayed with the back of the hand facing the recipient, since, in many cultures, this means **fuck you** or **up yours**.

peace symbol *social issues* the little symbol that was displayed by **anti-war** demonstrators and advocates of peace. Designed by Gerald Holton in 1958 for use by the British organization, Campaign for Nuclear Disarmament (CND). Composed of the semaphore letters N and D, standing for Nuclear Disarmament. Semaphores are a system of signaling by human or mechanical arms

photo by John McCleary ©

with flags or lights. The peace symbol was first displayed at a 1958 rally for the CND in England. It has been erroneously reported that Bertrand Russell designed the symbol because he was president of CND at the time. There is other symbolism attributed to this little piece of art work; in Christian traditions, the circle designates the Earth; and the inner design, sometimes called the witch's or crow's feet, represents God reaching down with the gift of salvation. The symbol is thought by some to represent a supersonic bomber. Also, it is apparently similar to the death rune of the futhark, or runic alphabet. Hawks and people who supported the **Vietnam War** began to call it the footprint of the great American chicken.

peak, to peak or **peaked** the most intense or **high** point of a drug-induced experience. To reach the high point in any experience or performance.

peanuts not much money. A small amount of something.

Peanuts a cartoon strip by **Charles Schulz**. In 1950, Schulz first drew a newspaper comic strip tentatively entitled *Li'l Folks*. It was accepted for syndication under a new title, *Peanuts*, and became the most successful cartoon strip in history, read by an estimated 355 million people worldwide. The cartoon chronicles the childhood of Charlie Brown, his friends Lucy, Linus, other acquaintances, his dog Snoopy and a bird named Woodstock. The strip has also been produced into more than 30 animated television specials and four full-length cartoon films. (See: **Schulz, Charles**)

Pearl nickname for **Janis Joplin**.

peckawood or **peckerwood** a derogatory term used for a White person in a rural area. Used by Blacks in retaliation for characterizations leveled at them by Whites.

pecker a sarcastic term for a man's penis.

peckerhead a dumb, stupid or detestable person. This term was used to describe someone as possessing the intelligence of a penis.

pecs short for pectoral muscles. The chest muscles. The growth of language has two different directions, expansion and contraction. Expansion involves grouping words together into phrases and creating longer words to expand a thought. The contraction of our language is the process of shortening these words and phrases after everyone knows their meaning.

peed off annoyed. Same as **pissed off**.

peel to remove clothing.

pegged to understand or second-guess someone. Example: "She's not that complex; I've got her **pegged** as a man-eater depressive."

Peltier, Leonard *social issues* a Chippewa member of the **American Indian Movement** (AIM). Convicted of murder and sentenced to two life terms in 1977 following a shootout at Pine Ridge, South Dakota in 1975. Two FBI agents, Jack Coler and Ron Williams, and **Native American** Joseph Stuntz Killsright were killed during the June 26, 1975, shootout on the Jumping Bull property. Peltier has always professed his innocence. The agents were on private property, in an unmarked car; they possibly didn't show identification, and witnesses say they started the shooting. With the past history of indiscriminate killings in that area by "**Goons**" who were supported by the authorities, the Native Americans involved, including Peltier, may have merely been defending themselves. (See: **Goons**)

pencil dick a very small penis.

pencil-pusher a government employee or private sector office worker who has no authority to make decisions and therefore is unresponsive to your needs and unable to help you with your fucking problem.

Pentagon exorcism and levitation *social issues* at an anti-war demonstration sponsored by the **National Mobilization Committee to End the War** in Vietnam, on October 21, 1967. **Abbie Hoffman** and **Jerry Rubin** tried to **levitate** the Pentagon with the help of the energy of several thousand other demonstrators. Rubin promised to levitate it 300 feet in the air, where it would take on an orange glow and vibrate, ridding itself of the demons of war. Norman Mailer was there, the **Diggers** were there, the **Fugs** played rock music, but the demons were not exorcised. (See: **Anti-War Events, Groups and Leaders** starting on page 562 in **Lists** at the back of this book)

Pentagon Papers *social issues* a secret Pentagon study of the **Vietnam War** commissioned by Robert McNamara in 1967 during the Johnson administration. On June 13, 1971, it was leaked to the *New York Times* and *Washington Post* by **Daniel Ellsberg**, an advisor to four presidential administrations and research analyst at RAND Corporation, a government-subsidized think tank on national security. The papers revealed the futility of the war and exposed the government's propaganda efforts to continue it. Once the papers were seen by the American public, the last vestige of public support faded and the end of the Vietnam War soon followed. Because of Ellsberg's involvement in the release of the Pentagon Papers, the **Nixon** White House launched a campaign to smear him. He was also charged with conspiracy, theft, and violation of espionage statutes, but the presiding judge dismissed the case due to government misconduct. (See: **Daniel Ellsberg**) (See also: **Anti-War Events, Groups and Leaders** starting on page 562 in **Lists** at the back of this book)

pentagram *occult* a magical diagram consisting of a five-pointed star representing man, considered by occultists as the most potent means of conjuring spirits. When a single point of the star points upward, it is regarded as sign of good and a means to conjure benevolent spirits; when the single point points down and a pair of points is on top, it is a sign of evil (Satan) and is used to conjure powers of evil.

pen yuen *drugs* opium.

People, The the simple people. Folks whose effort in life is survival, not commerce; existence, not stock quotes. The good, hard-working people, the common man, the uncomplicated **working**

class. This theme, gleaned from the United States Declaration of Independence and influenced by Socialist terminology, eventually evolved within the hippie **counterculture** to mean the peace and freedom, socially conscious population.

people farm a large city.

people like us a prejudiced term for one's political, social or religious friends and "equals." All other people are looked down upon.

photo by Jerry Takigawa ©

People's Park *social issues* 2.8 acres of undeveloped land at the University of California, Berkeley, which was appropriated and renamed by students and hippies on April 20, 1969. Mike Delacour, a prominent local idealist, conceived the project. Berkeley students, residents and street people laid down sod, dug a pond and installed children's playground equipment on the site. On May 15, 1969, "Bloody Thursday," the authorities reclaimed the "park" by constructing a chain link fence around the plot. The community gathered in protest and **civil disobedience** ensued. **Ronald Reagan,** then California Governor, called in 2,000 National Guard troops to maintain what the authorities considered to be order. The conflict continued for 17 days; one demonstrator, James Rector, was killed, many were injured, and 1,000 arrested. In 1972, **anti-war**

demonstrators tore down the fence, and the area became a sometimes park and often transient hangout. In the late 1990s, local volunteers and the City of Berkeley cleaned it up, and to this date it is still a place of refuge.

People's Temple (See: **Jonestown**)

pep pill *drugs* any **amphetamine** pill. An **upper**.

percentage profit, advantage or future. Example: "Hey, man, there's no **percentage** in playing Russian roulette with an automatic weapon."

perform to work or accomplish. Example: "If you want to stay in his class, you'd better **perform**."

performance art an art form involving human activity; dance, art construction or destruction, acting out a message or emotion. It can be a modern dance recital or an artist painting on stage before an audience.

perk short for perquisite. An extra benefit or profit from a job activity, over and above the salary.

Perls, Frederick Solomon (Fritz) major proponent of **gestalt** therapy. **Gestalt therapy** uses group pressure to break down inhibitions that harbor mental instability. (See: **gestalt therapy, Esalen Institute, "Bob and Carol and Ted and Alice"**)

Perry Lane a **bohemian** residential area near the Stanford University campus, south of San Francisco, California. **Ken Kesey** lived here while a student at Stanford and a subject for experimental drugs at the Menlo Park Veterans' Hospital. Perry Lane in 1960 was the sight of many of the original non-clinical **LSD** experimentations, when Kesey brought **psychedelics** home from his "job" at the hospital.

-person *suffix* a gender-nonspecific suffix used to change traditional job titles, such as mailman, waiter, waitress, anchorman, etc., into mailperson, waitperson, anchorperson and chairperson. Introduced into our lexicon around 1975 during the beginning of the feminist movement in an effort to level the playing field and "degenderize" titles. When men also started entering fields dominated by women, more confusion arose. It soon became a joke, and, with sarcasm, some titles evolved, such as police person, fireperson, steward person and, my personal favorite, femailperson. This political correctness evolution has created some new terms, such as waitperson, but many terms have been changed completely, such as "flight attendant" for stewardess.

personal computer (PC) a.k.a. **microcomputer** *computer revolution* a term some say was coined by Alan Kay; others give credit to Ed Roberts when he marketed his **Altair**. The **Alto,** created in the early 1970s by Xerox, was the first actual microcomputer, but it was available only to insiders in the industry and US government. Alan Kay demonstrated his **FLEX** in the early 1970s. The **Altair 8080** (the people's computer) was produced in 1974, as a computer "kit" for hobbyists, and was considered the first real PC because it was available to the public outside the computer research industry. **Apple I** was released in April, 1976; **Apple II**, in 1977; the **Commodore PET,** named after the Pet Rock, in 1977. The Tandy **TRS-80** from Radio Shack was introduced a little later. (See: **Computer Revolution Milestones, Companies and Leaders** starting on page 626 in **Lists** at the back of this book)

persuader a gun or a knife.

perve or perv a perverted or lascivious person.

peso one US dollar. Although it is a Mexican monetary denomination and has a different value than the American dollar, the use of foreign words for common English items is an interesting word game we play.

pet to kiss and touch in sexual **foreplay**.

peter *sex* another euphemism for the male sex organ. An old term, by no means exclusive to the hippie era; yet, as with many anatomical words, the era offered expanded usage and, until then, unimagined acceptability. Examples: "She's a real **peter** pouncer!" "What a **peter** brain he is." "Keep your **peter** in your pants."

photo by Lisa Law ©

Peter, Paul and Mary *music* the best known and most influential folk music group of the 1960s. Formed 1961, New York City, Peter Yarrow (b. May 31, 1938, New York City), voc., gtr.; Noel Paul Stookey (b. Nov. 30, 1937, Baltimore, Md.), voc., gtr.; Mary Travers (b. Nov. 7, 1937, Louisville, Ky.), voc. Of all the many folk music groups that popped up in the early 60s, PPM was one of the few that survived to become an influence in the music and philosophy of the hippie era. Many of the songs included on their early albums became anthems of the **civil rights** and **anti-war movements**. They sang at **Martin Luther King, Jr.'s**, 1963 Washington, DC, march and rally at which he gave his famous "**I Have a Dream**" speech. In 1967, their release of the song, "I Love Rock and Roll Music," broke their typecast, pushing them into the contemporary hippie era, thus assuring their place in history as something more than merely folk legends.

pet rock the bizarre marketing creation of California salesman Gary Dahl. One night in April, 1975, Dahl, during a humorous outburst, informed his friends that he considered pet dogs, cats, birds, and fish to be a pain in the neck. They were messy, misbehaved and cost too much money. Instead, he had the ideal pet...a pet rock. That was the start of an idea that eventually sold a million rocks at $3.95 apiece in a few months, making Gary Dahl instantly wealthy. Dahl decided to make at least one dollar on every rock he sold. He chose decorative landscape Rosarita Beach stone, a small, uniformly sized, round, gray rock that sold for a penny at a builder's supply store in San Jose. He packed each rock in a gift box shaped like a pet carrying case, accompanied by an instruction book. The fad was over by the following year, but it will always be remembered as the most profitable, tongue-in-cheek marketing ploy ever devised.

peyote cactus *drugs* a small, marshmallow-shaped psychedelic plant from the cactus family. Historically, it was ingested by some Southwest **Native American** tribes as part of their religious ceremonies and cultural life. Discovered by the hippie culture in the mid-1960s, peyote saw widespread use through the 1970s. Indian cultures

consider it a sacrament, and, since eating peyote often induces vomiting, it is

used in cleansing rituals. While under the influence of the cactus, tribe members were allowed to vent their frustrations and verbally express anger against fellow tribesmen without retribution. Peyote normally creates a very spiritual and natural **psychedelic** experience.

P.G. pregnant.

P.G. *drugs* paregoric, an opium product.

phallic worship (phallism, phalicism) *religion* the worship of generative or reproductive powers of nature symbolized by the male sex organ. Many non-Christian cultures practice some form of this "religion," particularly in their spring, harvest and agrarian fertility festivals. The display of the **lingam**, or phallic symbol, is common in such religions.

Phan Thi Kim Phuc the nine-year-old Vietnamese girl who was photographed on June 8, 1972, naked, burned, crying, and running down a road from the village of Tang Bang, which had just been mistakenly napalmed by US aircraft. Vietnamese photographer Huynh

Cong (Nick) Ut won a Pulitzer Prize for the image in 1973. The girl survived and is now living in America.

Phillips, Sam *rock & roll* record producer and record label owner. As the owner of Sun Records studio in Memphis, Tennessee, he is responsible for discovering **Elvis Presley** in 1954. Sun Studio was also the producer of other early rock and roll talents, including Jerry Lee Lewis, **Johnny Cash**, **Roy Orbison**, Carl Perkins and Howlin' Wolf. Phillips produced more rock and roll records than anyone else of that time, including Presley's first five singles, Carl Perkins' "Blue Suede Shoes," Jerry Lee Lewis's "Whole Lotta Shakin' Going On" and Johnny Cash's "I Walk the Line." Phillips was inducted into the Rock and Roll Hall of Fame in 1986.

phone phreak and **phone phreaking** *computer revolution* a person who uses an illegal, homemade device to produced the proper tones in a telephone to eliminate long-distance charges. Some of the first **computer programmers** were initially telephone "**hackers**" or "phone phreaks," including **Steve Wozniak** of **Apple Computer**. One of the first phone phreaks was John Draper, called **Captain Crunch**. Captain Crunch was the phone phreakers' name for a whistle toy included as a promotional gimmick in Captain Crunch cereal boxes in the late 1960s. When this "toy" was properly blown into a telephone, it could clear the phone line, allowing free long-distance calls. (See: **blue box**, **Captain Crunch** and **Steve Wozniak**)

photovoltaic a process whereby sunlight is converted into electricity. Perfected in the 1970s, it requires sophis-ticated sun receptors called photovoltaic cells.

photovoltaic cell a **silicon chip** used to produce electricity from the rays of the sun. Made primarily of silicon, the second most abundant element in the earth's crust and the same semiconductor material used in computers. When combined with several other materials, silicon exhibits unique electrical properties when exposed to sunlight. Electrons are energized by the light and move through the silicon. This is known as the photovoltaic effect and results in direct current (DC) electricity. Photovoltaic cells have no moving parts, are virtually maintenance-free, and have a working life of 20 to 30 years.

phennines *drugs* street name for phenobarbital. Sedatives or **downers**.

physical (to get) *sex* to have sex, to indulge in sexual activity. Example: "I want to get **physical** with her."

pick a comb used to keep an Afro hairstyle "looking good," by lifting the hair up off the head. It resembles a small pitchfork with eight to ten teeth, which are much bigger and longer than those of a normal comb.

pick em' up and lay em' down to walk rapidly or leave quickly. Can be issued as a warning to leave a forbidden or dangerous place.

picking playing the guitar.

pick up *sex* to find and take home a sex partner. **2.** a random sex partner. Usually, a previously unknown person who is met in a public venue. Not necessarily meant to indicate a professional who exchanges sex for money. Example: "I'm going to try to **pick up** a **pick up** at the local **pick-up** bar."

pick-up band a band of random musicians, who may not have played together previously, but are chosen individually or come together accidentally to play music for fun or profit.

pick up on to notice, understand, or appreciate something. Example: "Hey, did you **pick up on** that discourse between the walrus and the clam?"

pick up on *sex* to entice and win a potential sex partner. Examples: "I tried to **pick up on** her, but she had other plans."

pick up the tempo speed up, go faster. Originally a musical term, but used by hippies in many other contexts. Example: "**Pick up the tempo,** Molly, my shoes are going out of style."

picky, picky, picky a phrase used to admonish neurotic behavior. Example: "**Picky, picky, picky.** I was just kidding around; don't take it so seriously."

piece or **piece of ass** *sex* the description of a faceless object of sexual lust. Derogatory term for a sexual partner to whom one has no emotional attachment.

piece a gun, musical instrument or other inanimate object of particular importance. Examples: "He carries a **piece** for protection." "That horn is his **piece.**"

piece *drugs* a measurement of drugs, usually an ounce.

piece of change a person for whom one has no respect. Example: "He's a real **piece of change**; I wouldn't trust him." Similar usage as **piece of work**.

piece of meat a sexual partner to whom one has no emotional attachment. Even more derogatory than **piece of ass**. **2.** a person who is worthless or

disliked. Example: "He's a worthless **piece of meat.**"

piece of tail another description of a faceless object of lust. A sexual partner to whom one has no emotional attachment.

piece of work a strange or annoying person. Example: "She's a **piece of work** and proud of it." Similar usage as **piece of change.**

pig *social issues* a police officer who violates the civil rights of others. Baptist minister and civil rights leader Rev. Ralph Abernathy is reportedly the first person who used the word pig in reference to the police. He did so in a speech during the police riots in Chicago during the **Democratic National Convention** in August, 1968. In an attempt to defuse the disdain of the term, law enforcement agencies tried to give the letters a positive acronym. One of the attempts was **PIG**: **P**ride, **I**ntegrity and **G**uts. (See: **Ralph Abernathy**)

photo by Lisa Law ©

Pigasus the Hog Farm mascot, a pig that ran for President in 1972; the first black-and-white female presidential candidate. (See: **Hog Farm**)

pigeon an informant. Short for stoolpigeon. Someone who informs the authorities about someone else's transgressions. a.k.a. **rat**, **fink**, **stoolie**.

pigeon someone easily fooled or cheated.

pig out to eat too much. To do anything to excess.

pilgrim a person considered naive and vulnerable. The term and its connotation came from John Wayne, who used it in the movies, "The Man who Shot Liberty Valance" in 1962 and "McLintock" in 1963.

Ortho-Novum, ca. 1968

pill, the *social issues* the contraceptive pill, approved by the US Federal Drug Administration (FDA) on May 9, 1960, went into widespread distribution in the spring of 1961. **Margaret Sanger** was the driving force behind the creation of the female contraceptive pill and Dr. Carl Djerassi and Dr. Gregory Pincus are credited with its development in various forms. It contains hormones that fool a woman's body into thinking she is already pregnant and, therefore, suppresses ovulation. The pill is considered responsible for launching the **sexual revolution**. It contributed greatly to the hippie culture by relieving concern about pregnancy, and, unlike some of the other contraceptive techniques, it allowed great freedom of movement and timing. There were also many other influences that helped to create the sexual revolution. The oppressive moral re-

strictions of the 1950s were bound to create a backlash. If one studies mankind's sexual history, it becomes obvious that there are cycles of open sexual promiscuity broken by periods of hypocritical moral indignation. The truth of the matter is that sex is conducted continually, one way or the other, openly or under false morality. The failure rate of the pill is approximately 3 pregnancies per 100 women per year, primarily from improper use. (See: **Margaret Sanger** and **sexual revolution**)

pillbox hat a round, cake-shaped hat made popular by **Jacqueline Kennedy** in 1960.

pill head someone who is mentally absorbed by a pill habit.

pill popper someone who ingests a hell of a lot of pills.

pimp someone who earns money from the unsavory work of others. A person who sells the bodies and souls of other people or makes a living from the misery of others. **2.** a person who manages a prostitute and takes a percentage of her earnings. The hippie culture considered prostitution a flawed, yet necessary, institution. To the **true hippie**, a person who *has* to become a prostitute to earn a living is a survivor, and a person who chooses to use prostitutes to achieve sexual satisfaction may be misguided, yet he or she has the right to do so. To a member of the hippie **counterculture**, anyone who sells other people for sexual use for his own profit is a creature lower than all other human beings.

pimping selling the services of other people in a less than savory manner. Earning money from the misery of others.

pimpmobile a gaudy or pretentious automobile. From the penchant of pimps for cars considered by most to be in bad taste.

pin *drugs* a very small **marijuana** joint.

pinch *drugs* a small quantity of drugs. Similar use as **taste**.

pinhead someone considered unintelligent. Having a small cranial cavity. Zippie the Pinhead, a cartoon character drawn by Bill Griffith, is the visual representation.

pink a color associated with the homosexual lifestyle.

Pink Floyd *rock & roll* a British **acid rock** band formed in 1965 in London, Syd Barrett (b. Roger Keith Barrett, Jan. 6, 1946, Cambridge, Eng.). gtr., voc.; Richard Wright (b. July 28, 1945, London), kybds., voc.; Roger Waters (b. Sep. 6, 1944, Surrey, Eng.), bass, voc.; Nick Mason (b. Jan. 27, 1945, Birmingham, Eng.), drums; David Gilmour (b. Mar. 6, 1944, Cambridge, Eng.), gtr., voc. A band that evolved into one of the most successful lyrical/heavy rock and roll bands of the era. Some of their songs, including "Money," 1973, and "Another Brick in the Wall," 1980, are classic hippie-era anthems. Inducted into the Rock and Roll Hall of Fame in 1996.

pink lady or **pink ladies** *drugs* the prescription **barbiturate** Darvon (porpoxyphene). Sedative or **downer**.

pinko someone thought to be a communist sympathizer. A communist was called a "red," and someone who sympathized was "pink."

pinks *drugs* tablets of **STP** and **LSD** combined. The same combination was also manufactured as **purple wedges** or **orange wedges**. The speed contained in STP sometimes caused bad trips. Sometimes **methadrine** was used instead of STP; then it was called a **peace pill**. (See: **LSD** and **STP**)

Pisces astrological sign, February 19 to March 20, twelfth house of the **zodiac**, mutable water sign, symbolized by two fish swimming in opposite directions. Traits: adaptability, universal. Self-perception: I believe.

piss away to waste something. To use something up with little advantage. Examples: "He **pissed away** his inheritance." "Don't **piss away** your life."

pissed drunk. A British invasion term.

pissed or **pissed off** mad.

pisser a maddening situation. Example: "That arrest was a **pisser**."

pisser a toilet.

pissing contest an argument between men. A verbal confrontation brought about by the male ego.

pissing in the wind lying. Making erroneous statements. Because, when pissing in the wind, one is unsure of where the urine will fly.

pissing in the wind fooling around or doing something silly. **2.** Doing something that will come back to haunt you, like urine blowing back in your face.

pits underarms. From "arm pits."

pits, the a bad place or occurrence. Examples: "This house is **the pits**." "That night in jail was **the pits**." From either "**armpit** of the world" or a hole in the ground.

plane *occult* a spiritual level. A person's place or state of being. Example: "He is on a very high **plane** of awkwardness." In **occult** terminology, the range of **consciousness**, or state of matter or existence.

photo by John McCleary ©

planetary ages of man the ancients called the planets markers of time. It was assumed that different periods of life were ruled by different planets. The designations are: Moon (growth), age 1-4, symbol, baby; Mercury (education), age 5-14, symbol, the scholar; Venus (emotion), age 15-22, symbol, the lover; Sun (virility), age, 23-42, symbol, the citizen; Mars (ambition), age 43-57, symbol, the soldier; Jupiter (reflection) , age 58-69, symbol, the judge; Saturn (resignation), age 70-99, symbol, slippers.

planned obsolescence *social issues* the tendency of industry to build a flaw or design element into its products that will eventually make that product inoperative, inadequate or out of style. This practice is intended to force the public to buy new products to replace the old ones, thus making more money for the manufacturers. Considered immoral by the **counterculture** because of the expenditure of natural resources required to maintain this business practice. It's a great deal more immoral than getting a blowjob in the oval office, and yet it doesn't get as much press. Same as **built-in obsolescence**.

Plant, Robert *rock & roll* lead singer for the rock group **Led Zeppelin.** One of the most respected singers in one of the most successful of all the **heavy-metal** bands.

plant your seed go ahead, have fun. The seed is understood to represent male sperm. The consequence of planting one's seed could be a pregnancy; yet, due to adequate **birth control** during the hippie era, the consequence of planting one's seed was diminished.

Plasmatics, The/Windy O. Williams *rock & roll/ heavy-metal* a New York City, **punk**, **heavy-metal** band that performed loud, manic music about sex and violence. Formed in 1978 and fronted by ex-topless dancer Windy O. Williams (W.O.W.).

plaster casters a particular kind of **groupie**. A groupie is someone who follows and/or idolizes a public figure or entertainer. Often, groupies are willing to grant sexual favors to be with their idols. Sometimes called star fuckers. Plaster casters were a small number of groupies who became famous for collecting plaster casts of the erect penises of stars with whom they had sex. It is still not known how much of a hoax this is. A girl by the name of Cynthia was one of the founding members.

plastered intoxicated or drunk.

plastic *social issues* a malleable, moldable product created by changing the chemical balance of oil. A petrochemical substance used to make many products in our modern age of stuff. Considered by hippies to be the epitome of what is wrong with our society. To make tools, utensils, clothing, furnishings and other necessities from plastic rather than more natural, longer lasting materials is considered by many to be wasteful and a conspiracy of planned obsolescence.

plastic adj. a person, place or thing that is phony or unnatural. Examples: "He's **plastic**; even his hair is fake."

plastic n. a plastic credit card.

plastic fantastic unreal or phony. A sarcastic term for anything or anyone that does not stand up to one's own ideals of reality. A term first heard in the song "Plastic Fantastic Lover" in The Jefferson Airplane's 1967 album *Surrealistic Pillow*.

Plastic Ono Band *rock & roll/avant-garde* an international band formed in 1969 with **John Lennon**, Yoko Ono, **Eric Clapton**, Alan White and Klaus Voormann.

platform shoes shoes with several inches of lift on both the sole and heel. Initially created to give a short person a few inches of height, they became a fashionable shoe design during the 1970s.

platter a **vinyl** phonograph record. (See: **LP** or **vinyl**)

play *sex, drugs and rock & roll* to have fun, to indulge in sex, drugs and rock & roll.

playboy a man who is considered a prolific, yet calculating and unfaithful lover. The term has a negative connotation to most people who believe in real love. Few men with any self-respect would ever call themselves playboys. To hippies, it was considered an arrogant self-label used by men who were more narcissistic than romantic.

Playboy **magazine** *social issues* a publication that first appeared in December, 1953, and grew to become the world's best-selling men's magazine.

Although *Playboy* would be considered exploitive and commercial by most hippies, it was an important venue for new attitudes about sex and relationships and was pivotal to America's mid-20th century **sexual revolution**. The magazine contained not only photos of nude women, but also celebrity interviews, short fiction, essays on all subjects, and book and movie reviews. **Hugh Hefner** was the creator and publisher of *Playboy* and a personality in his own right, living the lifestyle portrayed in his magazine, partying with celebrities in his mansions, surrounding himself with beautiful women, and always wearing his trademark silk pajamas and smoking jacket. In the 1970s, Hefner opened Playboy Clubs, casinos, and resorts worldwide, which eventually closed in the 1980s as the world became jaded by such extravagance.

play catch-up to make an effort to comprehend what is going on. Example: "I must continually **play catch-up** in her presence."

player someone in the know. A person who is active and serious. One who is advanced in love, games, finance, etc. Example: "Watch how he works; he's a real **player**." **2.** a drug user.

play for keeps to go all the way, to be very serious about an issue or activity. Similar usage as **play hardball**.

play games to deceive or misrepresent for the purpose of causing emotional discomfort.

play grab-ass to sexually harass someone by grabbing the person's buttocks.

play hardball to be serious about winning. To be relentless. Similar usage as **play for keeps**.

play hell with to be an annoyance. Example: "When I'm driving, those little bumps in the road **play hell with** my sleeping."

*play it cool to be relaxed, under control or to act aloof.

play that shit to indulge in a strange or annoying activity. Examples: "**Play that shit** around here, and I'll call your mother to take you home." "Don't **play that shit** if you want to hang with us **cool** guys."

pleasure principle Freud's name for the instinctive demand for sexual gratification possessed by animals in nature. The opposite of the "reality principle," which dictates that civilized beings, such as humans, must control such urges and conform to social mores. The **counterculture** of the hippie era, with the help of the **pill**, drugs and a cultural agreement, tried to return humans to the more natural, uninhibited instincts of the pleasure principle. Toward the end of the hippie era, it became obvious that some rules must prevail about sexual conduct, or psychological chaos, rampant disease and total breakdown of the family unit would follow. Contrary to media propaganda, the **true hippie** culture believes in health, welfare and family values, as well as the pleasure principle.

plough or **plow** sex to have sexual intercourse. A strictly unromantic term for sexual activity. Example: "Did you **plow** her?"

ploughed or **plowed** drunk, under the influence of drugs or both. Related to being ploughed under, buried, dead, etc.

plug sex to have sexual intercourse. An unromantic, purely physical form of sexual activity. Example: "Did you **plug** her?"

plugged in aware of what is happening. Related to being "electrically" connected and therefore aware of what is going on. Example: "He's **plugged** in to what's going down on the street."

plumbing female reproductive organs.

plumbers, the politics a group of **Nixon** administration functionaries and intelligence operatives who indulged in **dirty tricks** to disrupt the activities of **liberal** political opponents and "enemies" of President Richard Nixon. The name of the group came from the function of their "stopping leaks." In intelligence agency parlance, dirty tricks refer to covert operations. **CREEP, The Committee to Re-elect the President** in 1973, was involved. The program of dirty tricks against political opponents was called **Operation Gemstone** and was associated with **The Huston Plan**. Wiretaps, break-ins, mail-openings and other **civil rights** violations, such as the Watergate break-in, were conducted by the plumbers during the Nixon administration. Some of the plumbers and their supporting associates were: Edgil (Bud) Krogh, David Young, Charles W. (Tex) Colson, Jeb Magruder, Dwight L. Chapin, Ken Clawson, Donald Segretti, John J. Caulfield, E. Howard Hunt, G. Gordon Liddy, James McCord, Frank Sturgis, Bernard Barker and a group of Cuban exiles who were CIA veterans. The June 17, 1972, **Watergate break-in**, at which time **the plumbers** were caught, was the most notable example of dirty tricks politics. It should be noted that Nixon and his political machine were not the only politicians to use dirty tricks. Candidates on both sides of the political spectrum have been known to do such things, yet Nixon's plumbers were the most blatant.

P.M.S. premenstrual syndrome. Symptoms caused by hormonal changes about a week before a woman's menstrual period and lasting from one day to two weeks a month. The symptoms include irritability, interrupted sleep, fatigue, depression, binge eating, headaches, breast tenderness and bloating. This condition was recognized and widely discussed in the 1960s. Its recognition was a product of the **sexual revolution** due to the loosening of taboos and closer communication between the sexes about sexuality and other aspects of relationships. Discourse on the subject between the sexes and the recognition of P.M.S. as a hormonal condition were also aspects of women's liberation that helped to defuse the mystery and humanize the problem.

pocket calculator a small, battery-operated calculator that first appeared in 1972.

P.O.'d angry. Short for **pissed off**.

pod *drugs* **marijuana**. From the seed pod of the female plant.

Pogo a cartoon strip by Walt Kelly (Walter Crawford Kelly, 1913-1973). After working as an animator for Walt Disney Studios from 1935 to 1941, Kelly created a cartoon strip in 1943 called *Bumbazine and Albert the Alligator*, featuring characters in the Okefenokee swamp. The name of the strip was changed to *Pogo* in 1948. In this cartoon strip, Pogo Possum is quoted as saying, "We have met the enemy and he is us." The cartoon was the first major politically oriented strip in the US and influenced many peoples' attitudes about government. After

Kelly's death in 1973, the strip was continued for some years by his son Stephen, his widow Selby and assistant artists. The central characters were Pogo, a generous and modest little opossum; the anarchistic and egoistic Albert the Alligator; Dr. Howland Owl; P. T. Bridgeport, the bear; Beauregard, the retired bloodhound; the snooping turtle Churchy-la-Femme; and Porky the Porcupine. The antagonism between Albert and Pogo was seen as the symbolic representation of the Ego and Id. Characters conversed and argued in poetic meter, French, Elizabethan English and Black dialects. Kelly played on words and names; for example, Simple J. Malarkey referred to Senator Joseph McCarthy. He mocked such well-known figures as J. Edgar Hoover, George Wallace, Spiro Agnew, Nikita Khrushchev and Fidel Castro. Richard Nixon was Kelly's most represented figure, portrayed as Malarkey's sidekick, Indian Charlie, and later as a spider named Sam. Kelly's opinions were expressed by the way in which personalities were drawn: Agnew was a uniformed hyena; Khrushchev, a pig; Castro, a goat; and J. Edgar Hoover, a bulldog.

political theology *religion/social issues* a 1960s Christian movement supporting the political struggles of oppressed peoples. Originated in Latin America.

politician *social issues* someone who tries to control or change the thoughts of others. This can be a private-sector term, or used within government. In the private sector, the term is used to describe someone who says whatever is necessary in order to get what they want. An untrustworthy person in the vocabulary of the hippie **countercul-**

ture. In government, it usually refers to a representative of the people who uses persuasion and innuendo to mollify the public in order to maintain an image, continue with an agenda, and ensure his or her re-election.

polluted drunk, under the influence of drugs or both or both. Related to being "poisoned."

photo by John McCleary ©

pollution noxious atmospheric fumes and environmental garbage. An old word that began to be used to describe a newly recognized condition in the 1960s. Automobile and industry chemical fumes and non-biodegradable refuse were acknowledged as dangerous to plant and animal life on the face of the earth after a number of scientists wrote books and papers on the subject. Notable was **Rachel Carson**'s book, *The Silent Spring*, published in 1962.

poncho a heavy blanket worn as a coat or cape that usually had an opening in the middle for one's head. Also called a **serapé**. This **fashion**, which originated in South and Central America, was adopted by many hippies.

Pong *computer revolution* the first major electronic **video game**. Introduced in 1972 and developed by Nolan Bushnell, the founder of Atari. Pong started as a coin-operated bar and arcade game; eventually, Bushnell created a home version that plugged into the family TV. It was not a general-purpose computer and could function only to operate the game. However, it helped to launch the personal **computer revolution** by putting computer-type devices in homes, thus acquainting the public with their presence and functions. Bushnell once said, "Frivolity is the gateway to the future, in that most future products don't start as necessities but as toys." Pong sold well, and in 1974, Atari's sales were $3.2 million. However, it was a simple game; kids soon got bored, and sales fell off in 1975. (See: **Computer Space, Spacewar** and **video games**)

pony show or **pony act** a contrived activity conducted in order to mislead others for the purpose of getting something in return. Same as a **dog and pony show**.

ponytail a hairstyle worn by men, oh, and some women too, during the hippie era.

poof a homosexual.

poontang, poony or **poontail** another euphemism for the female genitals. A term for the act of sexual intercourse itself, and a description of a female object of lust. From the French "putain," or prostitute. Introduced to the United States after WWII and the **Vietnam War**.

Poor People's March and Campaign (April 29-May 11, 1968) *social issues* **Rev. Ralph Abernath**y led a delegation of leaders representing poor Whites, Blacks, Indians and Hispanics to Washington, DC, for meetings with cabinet members and congressional leaders. (See: **Rev. Ralph David Abernathy**)

pop v. to take drugs orally. Same usage as **drop**. Example: "**Pop** the **acid** as you leave so you'll come on as you hit the disco."

pop v. to inject drugs just under the skin. Sometimes called skin poppers.

pop adj., n. short for popular. The current trend. The flavor of the moment. Anything (or anyone) experiencing a temporary popularity, soon to be replaced by something new. **2.** music that is popular. Music considered by hippies to be superficial. Rock music can be pop, but not all pop music is rock. Some musicians create what is popular over and over again, and others quickly jump on pop, have one hit and are gone.

pop adj., n. anything too commercial or trendy for the **true hippie**.

pop art popular art. A description of the new genre of art in the early to mid-1970s. Many things could be pop art, and many things, good and bad, were pushed as art: Brillo boxes by Andy Warhol and oversized comic strip pictures by Lichtenstein are examples.

pop for to buy or obtain. Example: "Who's going to **pop for** the beer and pork rinds?"

Pop, Iggy (b. James Jewel Osterberg, April 21, 1947, Ypsilanti, Mich.) *rock and performance* a singer/performer who was the predecessor to **punk** and grunge. His antics on stage were outrageous and dangerous. Self-destruction seemed to be a recurring theme. He toured with **David Bowie** for a time, and they both influenced each other. Iggy has a cult following and seems to be a caricature of himself, yet he is endearing as a personality and persists in the music business on his name alone, in spite of scant commercial success.

popped or **pop** arrested or caught. Examples: "He got **popped** for parking in a no idiot zone." "The police will **pop** you for being under age and crucify me for being with you." **2.** to hit or strike someone.

poppers *drugs* small glass vials containing fumes, such as volatile nitrites, which cause delirium. Inhaled to produce a rush or intoxication. Some of the brand names are Rush, Climax, and Quicksilver. Popular in gay circles as an enhancer to sex or dancing. The ingredients are similar to those in many room deodorizers, aerosol paints, glues and solvents. Hazardous to one's health with continued use.

pop star a popular singer. Usually, more of a financial success than a critical success, pop stars are normally christened by a large audience of adolescent fans.

Pop Tarts introduced to the American public in 1964. An envelope of pie crust containing fruit and sugar; "pop" into a toaster, heat and eat. Yummy munchies!

pork excess. Extravagant or unnecessary expense. Legislation that creates preferential economic circumstances. Examples: "My party budget is filled with **pork**, but what's a gathering without bubbles, balloons and MDA?" "The legislator porked out at the deli, before going back to the Senate to vote on a bill filled with **pork** for the highway contractors of his state."

pork or **porking** *sex* a less than romantic term for sexual intercourse.

porn short for pornography.

pornography sexually explicit movies, photos, or literature produced to make a profit by arousing the most superficial and base human sexual desires.

portal a door or entrance. During the late 1970s, this term began to take on a new definition in the computer world, a cyber meaning if you will.

Port Huron Statement *social issues* the manifesto of **Students for a Democratic Society (SDS)** written by **Tom Hayden** for the June, 1962, convention of the SDS held at the United Automobile Workers' camp in Port Huron, Michigan, north of Detroit. Said by many to have marked the beginning of student revolution in America. It begins, "We are people of this generation bred in at least modest comfort, housed now in universities, looking uncomfortably to the world we inherit. Our work is guided by the sense that we may be the last generation in the experiment with living,... But we are a minority— the vast majority of our people regard the temporary equilibriums of our society and world as eternally functional parts." (See: **Tom Hayden** and **Students for a Democratic Society**)

possessed overly influenced, obsessed or controlled by someone or something. During the hippie era, it was often an ethereal or spiritual state. Example: "He says he's **possessed** by Buddha and his writings; I think it's Mescaline."

postjudice an opinion based on experience. To judge someone after experiencing their behavior. The opposite of prejudice. To post-judge, as opposed to pre-judge, which is to prejudice. A generalized opinion of a cultural, social or economic group reached after having a number of personal experiences in which particular behavior is displayed. Coined by John McCleary in the late 1970s.

"post-literate generation" a term coined by Marshall McLuhan to describe young people of the 1960s.

post-traumatic stress syndrome the precarious emotional state in which many soldiers are left after traumatic experiences in war. This term was created after the **Vietnam War**, but it described the same symptoms as battle fatigue, as it was called during WWII, or shell shock, as it was called during WWI.

posturing to stand in a dramatic posture meant to enhance physical appeal. To assume a personality or pretend to be someone special in order to achieve social or business advantage.

photo by John McCleary ©

pot *drugs* **marijuana**. One of the most popular names for marijuana during the era. This term possibly came from the practice of people in cities, growing their own marijuana in flower pots. It may also relate to the earlier use of the word "pot," meaning a woman. Since marijuana and women are two very important elements in the life of some men, they are often synonymous in many ways and through many terms. (See: **marijuana**)

pot head *drugs* someone who smokes **marijuana** to excess.

pot party *drugs* a party at which **marijuana** is smoked.

pound or **pounding down** to drink something down quickly, usually alcohol. Examples: "Lets go **pound** some suds!" "We spent the morning **pounding down** shots of tequila and the afternoon hugging the toilet." Same use as **chug** or **chug-a-lug**.

pounds, shillings, and pence *drugs* **LSD**. A British term.

POW prisoner of war. 591 American Prisoners of war were returned from North Vietnam in 1973. On February 14, 1973, the first 20 POWs were returned to the US from Southeast Asia. Cmdr. Raymond A. Vohden was the longest held POW, captured after his plane was downed in North Vietnam on April 3, 1965. A reasonable estimate of the number of prisoners of war/ missing in action (POW/MIA) of that conflict is 1,172. Since 591 prisoners were returned at the end of the war, mathematics would indicate that there were still 581 MIAs unaccounted for. Since the end of the war, some bodies have been returned, reducing that number even further. The designations MIA and POW have been grouped together by those who feel that some of the MIAs were and still are POWs. (See: **MIA** See also: **Vietnam War** starting on page 560 in **Lists** at the back of this book)

Powell, Adam Clayton Jr. (1908-1972) Black US Congressman, clergyman and civil rights leader. A Democrat, he was elected in 1944 to represent Harlem, New York, in the US House of Representatives. He served 11 successive

terms. Eventually accused of misusing public funds, Powell was censured by Congress and lost his seat in 1967. He was reinstated later that year, but was defeated in the 1970 election. Powell is said to have coined the phrase, **keep the faith** (or often) **keep the faith, baby!**

power elite a term coined by sociologist C. Wright Mills to describe the small, unofficial group of bureaucrats, corporate, government and military leaders who dominate American policies by their influence and power.

power to the people *social issues* a revolutionary slogan used in the **free-speech**, **civil rights** and **anti-war movements**. In essence, it means support for the democratic process in deciding all issues that affect people.

*power trip arrogant or egotistical activity. Selfish treatment of other people.

pox an old term, reborn in the hippie era, that describes the effects of venereal disease.

P.R. public relations. Basically, a business term meaning to create media exposure in order to promote a company, person or place. Used in the hippie culture to indicate, often sarcastically, a person's self-promotion for social reasons.

prayer flags *religion* small pennants of fabric strung across the entrance to Tibetan cities, villages and farms. Each flutter of a flag in the wind is believed to carry a prayer across the sky to **Buddha**.

prayer wheel or **wheel of prayer** *religion* a small, barrel-shaped device made of metal or wood, used in **Tibetan Buddhist** worship. Written prayers to Buddha are placed in the wheel. Each turn of the wheel is believed to repeat the prayers to Buddha. Larger wheels are used for the prayers of an entire community.

pray to the porcelain god to get down on one's knees and vomit into a porcelain toilet bowl.

Precision bass *rock & roll* from the **Fender** guitar manufacturing company. (See: **Fender**)

precognition awareness of events before they occur. Knowledge of future events, obviously not obtained by the five accepted senses.

predictive astrology the branch of **astrology** in which the position of the stars is analyzed to predict the future and circumstances of an individual's life.

preemptive strike a military term meaning an initial attack on the enemy before it has a chance to attack you. In the **counterculture**, it became a cynical term meaning a surprise attack on the innocent. The consequences of a preemptive strike were brought home by many **Vietnam War** veterans who had been ordered to bomb, shell or attack innocent, noncombatant Vietnamese villages in order to "protect" themselves. This was one of the occurrences that caused **post-traumatic stress syndrome** among many of our returning soldiers. (See: **post-traumatic stress syndrome**)

preppie someone who is not **hip** or **cool**. A person who has a prep school education or who acts and looks as if they do. Someone who dresses in expensive, conservative clothing or behaves in a conservative, superior manner. During the hippie era, the look was saddle shoes, cashmere sweaters, buttoned-down shirts and a **buttoned-down mind**. A term that entered our

lexicon in the late 1960s and early 1970s. (See: **buttoned-down mind**)

Presley, Elvis (b. Jan. 8, 1935, East Tupelo, Miss.; d. August 16, 1977, Memphis, Tenn.) *rockabilly/rock & roll* the first rock and roll star to whom each and every music listener and rock performer owes a debt of gratitude. He made it possible for White men to sing like Black men, and for that alone, he is responsible for opening up all manner of musical diversity. Poor management and lack of direction by his manager, Colonel Parker, prevented Elvis from growing creatively and musically during the fertile 1960s and 1970s, thus making it difficult for the hippie culture to embrace him completely; yet we still owe him a great deal. Inducted into the Rock and Roll Hall of Fame in 1986.

press some flesh or **press flesh** shake hands.

pressure cooker a place or situation with stressful circumstances.

prexactly yes, affirmative, I agree. A word composed of the two words, precisely and exactly.

prez the President of the United States. Short for president. A humorous, sarcastic and sometimes derogatory reference to our Commander in Chief. Originally a **beatnik** term.

pricey expensive. From something with a high price.

prick a more or less humorous name for the male genitalia. Most likely from a reference to an annoying, sharp object that pokes someone.

prick a name for a disliked person. Examples: "She's a **prick**, he's a **prick**, they're all **pricks**." Related to the derogatory name for the male genitalia and to an annoying, sharp object that pokes someone.

prick tease or **prick teaser** *sex* one who seems to be promising sexual activity, yet who withholds these favors at the last moment. Tease is an old term; the unspoken "prick" was added in the 1950s and saw expanded use in the 60s as more women acknowledged and used their powers of choice.

pride a hairstyle worn by many Blacks during the era to indicate pride in the hair typical of African Americans. Shorter than the **natural,** it was unstraightened, and there was no effort to comb it flat. Prior to the 1960s, social and economic pressures had discouraged natural hairstyles, and many Blacks straightened or flattened their hair in an effort to achieve Caucasian styles.

primed ready for action. Having drugs or alcohol in one's system, ready for sex or **rock and roll**.

prime mover a person of power. In Aristotle's philosophy, a person who is the initial cause of change, and therefore is not influenced by prior circumstances.

primo short for premium. The best, with a touch of Latin for emphasis. From the Spanish *primero*, meaning first. It stood for very good **marijuana**.

Example: "You always know when to drop in, usually whenever I have **primo** dope on hand."

Prince Albert can a old-style tobacco tin used to carry drugs during the hippie era.

prince of a man a sarcastic description of a man for whom one actually has no respect.

Prine, John (1946-) songwriter/singer popular for his lyrics, such as "you may see me tonight with an illegal smile," from "Illegal Smile," and the song, "Your Flag Decal Won't Get You Into Heaven Anymore," both from 1971.

printout a document printed from computer memory. The term and the process were introduced to the American public in 1965.

pro short for professional.

prob short for problem. Example: "What's the **prob,** man?"

Procol Harum *classical/rock* a British band formed in London, England, in 1966. They will forever be remembered for their anthem of the era, "A Whiter Shade of Pale," in 1967. Although they continued to record into the 1970s in various personnel configurations, their fate was anchored to that one song.

*program, the group or majority activity. That which is happening. The unchangeable procedure. Example: "Get with **the program**. Do you want to be a unique, exciting, free thinker all your life?" This term appeared in the late 1970s when the individuality and **self-realization** of the hippie era became less popular and people began conforming to social pressures for material gain. This was a return to the self-denial of the 1950s in order to fit into the competitive, conservative economy of the 1980s.

program *computer revolution* a set of instructions or "code" entered into a computer to allow it to perform useful functions. The digital system that organizes facts in computer memory. The term was introduced to the American public in 1965.

programmed to be emotionally or physically molded into a certain way of behavior, either by verbal influence or through repetitive activity.

programmer *computer revolution* a person who "writes code" for computers, enabling them to perform useful functions.

programming language *computer revolution* the unique set of codes, rules and vocabulary used to program a computer to perform a function. Also called a **computer languages**. (See: **Computer Revolution Milestones, Companies and Leaders** starting on page 626 in **Lists** at the back of this book)

proletariat a Marxist term for an industrial worker. In the Western **liberal** culture, it referred to an uncomplicated working person who labors for the good of society.

protection contraception. The **pill**, an **intrauterine device** or some form of prophylactic.

prostitute someone willing to abandon ideals and integrity in exchange for money. **2.** a person who sells sexual favors. The hippie culture considers prostitution a flawed, yet necessary, institution. To the **true hippie**, a person who *has* to become a prostitute to earn a living is a survivor, and a person who chooses to use prostitutes to achieve

sexual satisfaction may be misguided, yet he or she has the right to do so.

Protestant work ethic the belief, held by many in European and Western cultures, that it is essential to work hard all of one's life, regardless of whether or not it is necessary for survival. A Christian belief that inactivity is immoral.

photo by John McCleary ©

Proto Pipe *drugs* a pipe manufactured by the Proto Pipe Company of Northern California specifically for smoking **marijuana** and **hashish**. A short, brass pipe with a self-cleaning attachment and a compartment for holding drugs. It became popular in the mid-1970s and is still manufactured today. Considered by many to be the most prestigious example of drug paraphernalia.

protoplasmic consciousness a state of mind without ego in which a person feels equal to, but not better than, other living things. To feel one with the cosmos. Most often attained through a psychedelic experience.

provocateur *social issues* someone who poses as a member of a particular group in order to discredit it by provoking violence. Civil rights and antiwar protests of the 1960s and 70s were most often organized with peaceful intent, yet there were documented examples of government provocateurs inciting violence in order to incriminate the demonstrators. When this happens, the media concentrates on the few outlaw demonstrators and ignores the true objective of the protest. (See: **demonstrators**)

pseudosciences activities that call themselves sciences, yet are not provable by the use of any known scientific tests. Examples: **astrology, psychokinesis**.

psi a term meaning the human element in nature. Identifying mankind's involvement in science transcending accepted laws. Related to the word psychic, and present in the technical word psychiatry.

psilocybin *drugs* a **consciousness-**altering chemical found in certain mushrooms.

psilocybin mushrooms *drugs* psilocybin or psilocin psychedelic mushrooms, teonanacatl. Any one of 14 different species of small, yellow mushrooms with hallucinogenic qualities. The active ingredient is psilocybin. a.k.a. **God's flesh, magic mushrooms, sacred mushrooms**. Warning, many mushrooms are deadly; please be sure of what you are eating for food or pleasure.

psych to disturb the mental stability of someone, to create fear or paranoia in someone. Examples: "I can **psych** him out just by pretending to hear wedding bells." "What a **psych**; she has nightmares of being smothered by white veils."

psyched or **psyched up** mentally prepared or excited. Example: "I'm **psyched** about my new job; wine taster has a nice sound to it."

psychedelic anything that is visually colorful or mentally explorative. Having to do with the psychedelic experience.

psychedelic art artwork designed to replicate **psychedelic** images or to enhance a psychedelic experience. First appeared in January, 1966, when **Wes Wilson** created a handbill for promoter **Bill Graham's Trips Festival** in San Francisco. Wilson became one of the most popular and recognizable psychedelic poster and comic book artists of the era. He drew many famous **Fillmore Auditorium** posters and is credited with introducing what is now considered psychedelic lettering. He developed the lettering from the work of an early Viennese calligrapher, Alfred Roller. (See: **Fillmore Auditorium** and **Bill Graham**)

photo by John McCleary ©

psychedelic music *rock & roll* a form of music that evolved from traditional rock and roll after the introduction of psychedelic drugs. Also known as **acid rock**. It was either created by musicians under the influence of psychedelics, meant to be compatible with psychedelic drug use or produced to create and enhance the feeling of being on psychedelics. The **Jefferson Airplane** and **Jimi Hendrix** were the major proponents of the genre. "**In-A-Gadda-Da-Vida**," by Iron Butterfly, 1968, is recognized as the best example of this music. Much of the tonality and personality of this music form were borrowed from Asian cultures and music. This is one of the reasons **Ravi Shankar** was so well-received by hippie audiences at **Monterey Pop** and **Woodstock**. When Jorma Kaukonen, Jefferson Airplane's lead guitarist and a primary innovator of psychedelic music, was asked which came first, psychedelics or the psychedelic guitar riffs, he said, "Without psychedelics, things wouldn't have developed the way they did. We all know that's a fact; it certainly changes the way we looked at things. My mind was open; I didn't have any preconceptions as a guitar player coming in. A lot of our stuff really came out of left field, and we were very fortunate that it was able to coalesce into a music form. I listened to a lot of stuff; my dad was in the service overseas, and we lived in the Indian subcontinent, and I heard different things, like the veena. It emerged in odd ways, and when I couldn't think of a more traditional rock and roll solo, I wouldn't hesitate to play some weird thing that was lurking in my mind." (See: **veena**) Before the widespread availability of headphones, it was a common experience to get **stoned** on drugs, lie on the floor, and listen to "In-A-Gadda-Da Vida," the Airplane or Hendrix at high volume through full-size speakers placed on either side of the head.

psychedelics *drugs* drugs that alter and expand thoughts and visions already stored in one's memory. The original word was coined by Dr. Humphry Osmond with the help of **Aldous Huxley**. Initially spelled psychodelic and eventually changed to psychedelic, as Tom Wolfe says, because of the stigma toward the word psycho. From ancient Greek, combining two words: *psyche*, the soul or mind, and *delos*, visible or evident. When original experiments were conducted at the Menlo Park Veterans' Hospital, the drugs were called **psychomimetics**.

natural psychedelics: psilocybin mushrooms, **peyote** cactus, **THC resins** from the **cannabis** plant, Hawaiian **woodrose** seeds, Mexican **morning glory** seeds, *Amanita muscaria* mushrooms, **virola** leaf snuff from the Amazon basin, **yage** (a drink) from the Amazon basin "**vine of the soul**," iboga root from equatorial Africa, belladonna, **yohimbe**, **kava kava**, and **DMT** from **yobo** beans or secretion from certain Sonoran desert toads and "dream fish" found in the South Pacific.

synthetic psychedelics: mescaline synthesized from peyote, **LSD** (lysergic acid diethylamide), MDA (methylenedioxy **amphetamines**), **PCP** (phencyclidine), cohoba snuff from yobo beans, nitrous oxide, ketamine, and DMT synthesized from virola leaf or certain Sonoran desert toads and "dream fish."

psychedelphia the **Haight-Ashbury** section of San Francisco, the hippie center of the 1960s.

psyched out misled, fooled or scared. Example: "He **psyched me out** when he turned right at the Democratic convention."

psychic healing *occult* a method of healing by the influence of one's own mind over natural matter and physical conditions. Its effectiveness is supported by a great many believers of **occult** doctrine.

psychoactive a substance that creates changes in perception and **consciousness**. (See: **psychedelics**)

psycho drama a difficult social situation. Traumatic interpersonal relations. Short for psychological drama.

psychokinesis *occult* moving or influencing an object through the power of concentration and no other apparent physical means. Causing an inanimate object to bend, float or travel by willing it to do so. An unsubstantiated phenomenon exhibited by many professionals and amateurs alike. The interest in and experimentation with such pseudo-sciences was greatly expanded in the atmosphere of curiosity that existed during the hippie era. Basically the same as **telekinesis.**

psychology the science and study of the human mind, its structure and functions.

psychomimetic mind-altering. (See: **psychedelics**)

P'u Chinese meaning *unwrought simplicity*; Taoist symbol for man's natural state, before his inborn powers have been altered by knowledge or morality. Before morality, before the snake in the Garden of Eden.

pubes short for pubic hairs.

pud another euphemism for the male genitalia.

pudding that which holds the world together. (See: **chi**)

"Puff the Magic Dragon" the title of a 1963 **Peter, Paul and Mary** song. It was assumed that the dragon represented **marijuana**, but no one in the group has ever confirmed this interpretation.

puke or **to puke** v., n. the act of getting sick to one's stomach; also the name of the substance that is regurgitated when someone vomits. This word was by no means new to the hippie era, not that any other era is going to rush to claim it. Words like this, which were previously held in contempt and never used in "polite company," became more widely accepted, if only as a reaction to previous "uptight" sensibilities. **2.** a detestable person.

puka shell necklace a string of small white and pink shell beads popular with Southern California hippies and surfers. They were made from parts of sea shells that had been washed by the sea and polished by the sand.

pull influence. Example: "I have no **pull** in this town. If you get busted, you get busted."

pull or **pulling** (someone's) **chain** to embarrass or annoy someone. To make someone uncomfortable. Example: "He always manages to **pull her chain** by saying something true, but thoughtless."

pull a boner to make a mistake. From to make a bonehead mistake. Bonehead meant stupid long before the hippie era.

pulling an all-nighter partying all night long. Staying up all night.

pull off to make something happen. Example: "I'm going to **pull off** the biggest party this town has ever seen."

pull (someone's) **string** to make someone do what you want them to do. From a puppet on a string.

pull together cooperate. From the refrain of an old song, "If we all pull together," etc.

pull yourself together straighten up; get a hold of yourself.

pumped or **pumped up** excited. From adrenaline being pumped into one's system. Example: "She's **pumped** about her new mood ring."

punch it v. speed up. To step hard on the gas pedal. To make your automobile go as fast as it can.

punch (someone) **out** to hit someone with your fist.

punch out (someone's) **lights** to knock someone out with your fist. From to "turn out someone's lights."

punk an immature person. **2.** someone who acts and dresses in a particular manner popular in the mid- to late-1970s. Spiked hair, torn clothes, early body piercing and outrageous tattoos were some of the visual expressions. Sid Vicious and Johnny Rotton of the English group **Sex Pistols** would be considered the poster boys for this style.

punkoid a more sarcastic form of the word **punk**.

punk rock music played by and for punks. A very sacrilegious art form calculated to offend and revolt. Some of the notable bands were: The Stooges, **Sex Pistols**, **The Clash** and Buzzcocks. This music genre was most popular in England and New York City, but less so in other parts of the United States.

punk rocker one who plays or listens to **punk** rock music.

"Purple Haze" *drugs* the title of a **Jimi Hendrix** song that supposedly related to **acid** trip images. The song was released in early 1967 on the *Are You Experienced?* album, his first with the Experience. Later, on June 18, 1967, Hendrix performed at the **Monterey Pop Festival**. Reportedly, Owsley (**Augustus Owsley Stanley**) created a particularly potent **LSD** for the Monterey Pop Festival, which he called

purple haze, on which Hendrix was **tripping** when he burned his guitar on stage during his performance. (See: **Stanley, Augustus Owsley, III**)

purple hearts *drugs* **amphetamine** tablets. **Uppers**.

purple wedge *drugs* tablets of **STP** and **LSD** combined. The same combination was also manufactured as **pinks** or **orange wedges**. Because of the speed in STP, these tablets sometimes caused bad trips. Sometimes **methadrine** was used instead of STP; then it was called a **peace pill**. (See: **LSD** and **STP**)

push to work hard. To exert oneself.

push to exert mental or physical pressure on someone.

push (someone's) **button** to get someone annoyed or angry.

push button phones introduced to the American public in 1963. *Touch tone phones* were slightly different due to the electronics involved, and they came later.

pusher someone who "pushes" or sells drugs.

push the envelope or **pushing the envelope** to go as far or try as hard as one can. Related to the premise that we are all confined within an envelope of abilities from which we may try to escape. Similar usage as **push the limits**.

push the limit(s) or **pushing the limit(s)** trying as hard as one can. Similar usage as **push the envelope**.

pussy the female genitals.

pussy a weak person, usually a term directed at a man who displays female weakness, because women have **pussies**.

pussy-whipped the state of a man who is so emotionally wrapped up in a woman that he becomes overly subservient to her. **Pussy** refers to the female genitals.

puta prostitute. A Spanish word.

put a hurt on (someone) to inflict emotional or physical pain upon someone. Example: "Eve really **put a hurt on** Adam when she crawled off with Snake."

put a move on to flirt with someone or **come on** to them sexually.

put (one's) **ass on the line** to make oneself vulnerable. The same as to "stick one's neck out." Often used to indicate a heroic effort in support of a cause.

putdown n. a sarcastic or inflammatory comment directed toward someone. Similar usage as **shut down** or **shoot down**. (See: **down in flames**)

put it to to exert emotional or physical pressure on someone, or to inflict pain. Example: "Delilah really **put it to** Sampson when she kicked him out of her bed."

put (one) **on** (one's) **ass** to emotionally disturb someone or physically knock them down. Example: "That comment **put Mut on his ass**, but he retaliated by **putting Jeff on his ass** with one punch."

*****put-on** or **put** (somebody) **on** to give a false impression, to lie to someone, Example: "He **put her on** about his tattoo, but her story of the nipple ring was also a **put-on**."

put out *sex* to submit sexually. Example: "Because of her appearance, most guys expect her to **put out** on the first date."

put the bite on to ask for something. To pressure someone for something. Most often, it refers to asking for money.

put the make on or **put the moves on** to **come on** to someone sexually.

putting down v. performing or creating. Example: "He's **putting down** some good notes on that guitar."

put up the numbers to make a good showing in work or sports. To achieve good statistics or a high score.

putz a fool. A stupid or socially inept person. Originally a Yiddish term.

putz around to waste time. To fool around.

Q

Quaalude *drugs* a trade name of a **sedative-hypnotic** used as a tranquilizer. Manufactured by the Lemmon Pharmaceutical Company (now Gate Pharmaceuticals). The active chemical compound is methaqualone. The effect is a mild **euphoria** similar to that produced by alcohol consumption. The term quaaludes or "**ludes**" is often used generically in reference to any methaqualone pill or capsule, many of which are manufactured illegally. a.k.a. ludes, **limons**, sopes and Q. Also called **sopors** in the Midwest.

quail an attractive young girl.

Quakers *religion* the name given to the Christian group officially known as the Society of Friends, founded by George Fox (1624-1690). Central principles include: guidance by an inner light; freedom from institutional or outward sanctions; the sanctity of silence; the simplicity of living; and a commitment to peaceful social relations. The Quakers were one of the most active and consistent **anti-war** religious organizations during the Vietnam conflict.

Quang Duc the Buddhist monk who burned himself to death in Saigon, Vietnam, on June 11, 1963, in protest of persecution of Buddhists by the South Vietnamese government. The famous photograph of his self-immolation is one of the most graphic pictorials of the **Vietnam War** era.

Quant, Mary (1934-) British **fashion** designer responsible for the **mod** look, the **miniskirt**, **hot pants** and **body stockings**. She opened her clothing boutique, Bazaar, in London in 1955. In response to the rebellious tastes of the **youth culture**, she began designing modern, new styles influenced by pop art and op art. Soon, her shop was the place to buy clothing for all the mods and rock and roll stars.

quantities of drugs B, bag, bee, can, deck, dime bag, eighth, five-cent paper, five-dollar bag, fix, geezer, 1/2 can, half piece, kee, key, ki, kite, lid, matchbox, nickel bag, O.Z., packet, piece, pound, Prince Albert can, quarter bag, sixteenth, smudge, spoon, tael, 10 cent bag, toxy, trey, Z.

quark a hypothetical measurement, the primary subatomic nuclear particle considered to be the basic component of protons and neutrons. It is also a mathematically convenient parameter to indicate the smallest particle mankind can imagine. The term was coined by American physicist Murray Gell-Mann and introduced to the American public in 1965.

quarter bag a $25 portion of drugs.

queue a line of people waiting for something. A **British invasion** term.

queen a very feminine male **homosexual**.

Queen *rock & roll* a British rock band formed in 1971, Freddie Mercury (b. Frederick Bulsara, Sept. 5, 1946, Zanzibar; d. Nov. 24, 1991, London, Eng.), voc., piano; Brian May (b. July 19, 1947, London, Eng.), gtr.; John Deacon (b. Aug. 19,1951, Leicester, Eng.), bass; Roger Meddows-Taylor (b. July 26, 1949, Norfolk, Eng.), drums. A **glam rock/heavy-metal** band with a dramatic frontman, Mercury, and good harmonies. More popular in England than America, yet they always had a cult following in America, particularly among the gay community. It was obvious to most fans that there was considerable gender bending within the band. Queen's 1976 video for their top hit, "Bohemian Rhapsody," was a breakthrough in that it was the first nonperformance video produced. When Freddie Mercury died of AIDS in 1991, the emotional outpouring of his fans was immense. Inducted into the Rock and Roll Hall of Fame in 2001.

queer a homosexual. Originally meant to be derogatory, but the gay community adopted it. From the British term for counterfeit money, meaning not real.

photo by Jerry Takigawa ©

Question Authority! *social issues* a popular bumper sticker of the hippie era. Attributed to Henry David Thoreau

(1817-1862) and found in his book, *On The Duty Of Civil Disobedience,* published in 1849. This sentiment is based on the Constitution of the United States, which declares that it is the duty of a populace to question the authority of government officials if their behavior appears to deviate from a proper democratic and moral direction.

Quetzalcoatl *religion* the feathered serpent-god of the Aztecs; creator of men, god of the wind and of the waning moon.

quiche a French pie-like food dish, consisting mainly of eggs, cheese and vegetables. During the 1970s, it was considered by macho, meat-eating men to be a unmasculine meal. The tongue-in-cheek phrase, "Real men don't eat quiche," was a popular joke used by real men who ate quiche.

quick smart.

quickie *sex* a fast **fuck**.

Quicksilver Messenger Service *acid rock* a San Francisco band formed in 1965. Two of the founding members were John Cipollina on guitar and bassist David Freiberg with, at various times, such talent as Dino Valenti, Mark Naftalin and Nicky Hopkins. At their apex, they were the third most popular band in San Francisco, behind **The Grateful Dead** and **Jefferson Airplane**. Famous for long musical jams like "The Fool," a 12-minute piece on their debut album of 1968. Valenti is memorable for writing two classics of the era, **Jimi Hendrix's** hit, "Hey, Joe," and "Get Together," recorded by the Youngbloods.

quiff female genitals. **2.** a promiscuous woman or prostitute. **3.** British; a hairstyle worn by teddy boys and rockers. Pompadour with spit curl in front

and backcombed sides. **4.** British; a male homosexual. **5.** a fart.

quim female genitals. Possibly from Middle English *queme,* "pleasure, satisfaction;" Middle English *queint,* **cunt**; or the Chaucerian *queynte.*

quit the scene to leave or go away. A beatnik term that hung out for a while in the 1960s.

Qur'an (Koran) *religion* the word of God as given to **Mohammed**, the prophet and apostle of **Islam**. Said to be the final message of God, meant to complete the previous revelations to the Jews and Christians.

R

R & R rest and recreation. Another military term adopted by the **counterculture**. In the military, it was a short time (one week per year) spent away from the scene of battle. From Vietnam, military R & R was usually in Japan, the Philippines or Hawaii. In the hippie culture, the term usually meant **kicking back** with a **joint** in the back yard "pool" (usually an old bath tub).

Ra, the eye of Ra one of the most recognizable symbols of the Egyptian era of kings, and one of the most prominent symbols of the hippie era. Ra was the Sun God and chief deity of ancient Egypt. Ra is usually represented by the head of a hawk crowned with a sun halo. The eye of Ra is associated with the *Egyptian Book of the Dead*.

rabbit food vegetarian food. A somewhat derogatory reference. Not every hippie was a vegetarian, though many tried it. The fact of the matter was that many people who were raised in the United States during the 1950s were unable to break the carnal habit of eating meat when the 1960s and 70s food revolution began. Although few people were able to stick with an exclusively **vegetarian** diet, an interest in healthier foods arose during the hippie era and helped many people to improve their eating habits, even with the inclusion of meat.

rack a bed.

rack a pair (set) of women's breasts.

rad short for **radical**. Example: "That song was **rad**, man."

radical an exclamation about a person, place, thing or idea that is different, strange, exceptional or monumental in some way. Example: "That was a **radical** wave, man." The precursor to the 1990s term **rad**. Language development is often the process of shortening words and phrases to simplify communications. Once everyone knows the meaning of the longer word or phrase, words or letters can be dropped to streamline verbal communication. Often, younger generations want merely to personalize language and ideas and therefore shorten them to do so. It's also **cool** to create cryptic words that exclude the older generation or straight society. Even cool has become "coo" in the 21st century.

radical *social issues* a person who espouses radical social change. A communist or fascist who may have violent or antisocial tendencies.

radical chic a term introduced to the American public in 1970 by **Tom Wolfe** in his book *Radical Chic and Mau Mauing the Flak Catchers*. Originally, Wolfe's intention was an oxymoron indicating the habit of wealthy, White **liberals** to adopt radical political causes. Eventually, the term evolved to represent a style of clothing that employed unconventional contrasts of colors, materials and designs, yet was manufactured by established clothiers and sold at high prices. It was an attempt by the clothing design industry to take advantage of the radical hippie styles and make money. **Fashion** is created by a few people, stolen by others, and followed by many. The hippie culture created new forms of dress and decoration; other people copied these ideas, marketed them, got credit for them, and made money selling them to other folks who bought them to be **cool**.

radical feminism *social issues* a women's movement that grew out of continued disillusionment with the male-dominated society. Some would say that their goal was to achieve dominance over men. In actuality, this group used radical words and actions to shake up the sensibility of others, bringing attention to the problems of women and promoting self-respect and acceptance. These **"radical fems"** became a link to the eventual **lesbian** movement. (See: **Equal Rights Amendment** and the **women's liberation movement** in alphabetical listings) (See also: **Women's Issues** on page 591 in **Lists** at the back of this book)

radical feminist or **radical fems** (See: **radical feminism**)

radical theology *religion/social issues* a 1960s movement in America seeking to create a Christianity based on atheism. Its two tenets were that God had "died" in human experience, and yet it was still possible to follow Jesus of Nazareth as a man. **2.** a term describing theology in left-wing politics. (See: **political theology**)

FALLOUT SHELTER

radiation death radiation waves travel at the speed of light; unlike sound, they can travel through empty space. At frequencies above visible light, they have enough energy to cause total body incineration. Extreme radiation of 6 to 50 sieverts (a unit-dose-equivalent) can cause death within two days to three months from loss of blood coagulation; vomiting, diarrhea, and starvation from the loss of intestine lining; or profound neurological, heart and circularity damage.

rag n. a sanitary napkin. A cotton and plastic pad worn by women to absorb their monthly menstrual blood flow. This term, used in the mid-20th century, came from the fact that women used actual cloth rags for the same purpose in the 17th, 18th and 19th centuries.

rag v. to ridicule or harass someone. Examples: "Don't **rag** on me; I'm your compadre." "Dolly really **ragged** on Bobby over the mishap with the compost heap."

raggedy-ass or **raggedy-assed** unkempt or disheveled. Example: "Carl wears **raggedy-ass** clothes, but when his father dies, he will inherit 20,000 **raggedy-assed** shares of AT&T."

raghead a derogatory name for a person from the Middle East. From the fact that Middle Eastern men wear turbans or cloth wraps on their heads to protect them from the sun and blowing sand.

rags clothes.

rail a line of powdered drugs laid out and ready to be snorted. Example: A rail of **cocaine**.

rainbow *sex* interracial sex.

Rainbow Festival a celebration of life, with music, art and spiritual exploration. Such festivals started initially with the **Fantasy Fair** on Mount Tamalpais, California, June 10 and 11, 1967, and the **Human Be-in Gathering of the Tribes** held at the Polo Fields in San Francisco's **Golden Gate Park** on January 14, 1967. Rainbow Festivals began to appear on a regular basis in the early 1970s, and many of them are still being held today under the auspices of various groups around the US and the world. One of the first ones using the term Rainbow Festival Gathering of the Tribes and Rainbow Family was held in June of 1972 near Granby, Colorado, in Rocky Mountain National Park. It was sponsored, at least in part, by the Love Family of Seattle, Washington, a communal group led by Israel Love. There have also been many Native American rainbow festivals.

rainbows multicolored pills. Usually, a mixture of **uppers** and **downers**.

raincoat a condom.

rainy day woman a **marijuana** joint. Supposedly from **Bob Dylan's** 1965 song of the same name. An activity a lonely man might pursue to entertain himself on a rainy day.

Raitt, Bonnie (b. Nov. 8, 1949, Los Angeles, Calif.) *rock and blues* a singer, songwriter and guitarist who produced solid folk, R & B, and covered the blues classics with a reverent touch throughout the 1970s. A respected musician and social activist, she has played for hundreds of benefits. She founded M.U.S.E. (Musicians United for Safe Energy), a group opposing nuclear energy whose members include **Jackson Browne** and **James Taylor**. Raitt is a White woman who can play and sing the blues with the appropriate soul and one of the few females who can successfully negotiate the **bottleneck** guitar style. Bonnie Raitt finally achieved well-deserved commercial success in the 1980s. (See: **bottleneck**)

raja yoga the way to God through psychological exercise. The philosophi-cal aspect of yoga. Some call it the royal yoga.

rajas in **yoga**, the term for the quantity or quality of selfishness or ego.

Rajneesh, Bhagwan Shree (also known by devotees as Osho) (India 1931-1990) *religion* a spiritual leader who eventually received much criticism for what were considered sexual and financial excesses. It is reported that sometime in the 1970s he suffered autonomic nerve damage that affected his blood pressure, causing chronic fatigue and possibly lowering his I.Q. due to insufficient blood and oxygen to the brain (hypoxia). In his last years, Rajneesh used prescription drugs, mainly **Valium**, and inhaled nitrous oxide mixed with pure oxygen, which helped his asthma and brain hypoxia but seemed to cloud his judgment. His **addictions**, it seems, led to his downfall and humiliation. He was jailed for tax problems, and at one time he accused the US government of poisoning him.

ralph to vomit or regurgitate.

Rama one of the chief **Avatars** (gods) of **Vishnu**; next to **Krishna**, the most popular deity of **Vishnuism**.

Ramayana *religion* an epic poem of India, describing the life of **Rama** and his wife Sita. It contains approximately 24,000 verses divided into seven books in which Rama is described as a perfect man who bears suffering and self-denial with superhuman patience. Sometimes ascribed to Valmiki and also supposedly written in the 5th century before Christ.

Ram Dass, Baba (b. April 6, 1931) *religion/social issues* the spiritual name adopted by **Richard Alpert, PhD**. Alpert was an assistant professor of philosophy at Harvard University in the early 1960s, when he began research in **consciousness** with **Timothy Leary** and **Ralph Metzner**. Their research on altered consciousness included studying the effects on humans of LSD and other psychedelic drugs, using prison inmates and students as subjects. Alpert and Leary were eventually fired from Harvard in 1963 for psychedelic experimentation involving undergraduates. They continued their experiments from a mansion in upstate New York and became, in essence, the fathers of the 1960s psychedelic revolution. In 1967, Alpert went to India in search of drug-free enlightenment and became a follower of the late Indian guru, Neem Karoli Baba. Neem Karoli Baba gave Alpert the name Ram Dass, which means servant of God. As a lecturer and teacher of Eastern religious philosophy, he has been given the honorary title Baba, which means father or teacher. In 1970, Baba Ram Dass wrote *Be Here Now*, a very popular book that helped to define the spiritual philosophy for many young people of the time. He has lectured many hours and written many books on Eastern philosophy and **Zen Buddhism** for the Western mind. Some of Ram Dass's publications include: (with Leary and Ralph Metzner) *The Psychedelic Experience*, 1964; (with Sydney Cohen and Laurence Schiller) *L.S.D.*, 1966; *The Only Dance There Is*, 1974; (with Stephen Levine) *Grist for the Mill*, 1977; *Journey of Awakening*, 1978; *and Miracle of Love*, 1979.

Ramparts* magazine** (*Sunday Ramparts*) started in 1962 as a liberal Catholic news journal, it became a radical outlet for liberal politics when Warren Hinckle III took over as editor in 1964. In 1966-67, **Jann Wenner**, later co-founder and editor of ***Rolling Stone magazine, was *Sunday Ramparts'* entertainment editor.

Randall, Robert *drugs/social issues* a teacher living near Washington, DC, who, in the late 1970s, fought for and won the right to be "exempted from Federal drug laws in order to use **marijuana** as medicine." Randall was the first person to be allowed this distinction in the US. He had glaucoma, which caused intraocular pressure that would eventually cause blindness. Smoking six marijuana joints a day relieved this pressure for Randall and, at least temporarily, preserved his eyesight.

randy someone or something that is sexually explicit or sexually inappropriate in action or content. The term comes from the word for the sexual odor produced by male animals, particularly goats.

Randy-Mandys or **Mandys** *drugs* **Timothy Leary** told a story about Marilyn Monroe and these pills. She reportedly said, "They turn off your mind and turn on your body." However, this could all be a hallucination concocted by the "captain of our minds" and the "captor of our bodies."

*rap to talk. Later used in rap music ("talk" music). Originally an African word, it found **jazz** and **beatnik** use, and was later introduced to the general public around 1965.

rap a strange situation or negative occurrence. Usually preceded by the word **bad** or **bum**. Different from, but related to **rep**, which means reputation. Likely came from the police term, "rap sheet." Example: "Joel got a bad **rap** on that bum trip."

rap *music* a form of dance music in which the performer speaks the lyrics in a poetic monotone. Rap started in the mid-1970s in the discos of New York City, where the disc jockeys, or "spinners," began to **talk shit** as a segue between songs. Rap grew on the street level through its connection to break dancing. The first rap records were produced in 1979, from small, independent labels distributed primarily to the Black community. In the early 1980s, groups like The Sugarhill Gang, Fatback and Kurtis Blow introduced rap music nationally, and White groups, such as **The Clash**, **Blondie** and the Tom Tom Club, presented it to White audiences.

rapper a person who talks excessively. Someone known for persuasive communication skills. In the hippie era, it was most often a derogatory designation.

rap session a gathering at which people sat around talking about serious subjects. Sometimes **marijuana** was involved.

rare unique or different. Short for rarefied. Conventional society used the word to describe something difficult to find, therefore expensive. The **counterculture** used it in a less material way. Example: "That was a **rare** party."

Rasta short for **Rastafarian** or anything related to the Rastafarian culture.

Rastafarian *religion/social issues* a somewhat religious, definitely social brotherhood that surfaced in Jamaica in the 1930s. A Jamaican evangelist who spent time in Harlem, New York, prophesied the coming of a Black king in Africa to lead the lost tribes home. When **Hailie Selassie** became Emperor of Ethiopia in 1930, the Jamaicans embraced him as that King. They called him Ras Tafar, the one true God, King of Kings, Lord of Lords, and the Conquering Lion of Judah. Rastafarians rejected conformity and material wealth. **Dreadlocks** (long, matted hair) are an outward sign of being a **Rasta**. True Rastas are often **vegetarian**, health conscious, do not drink alcohol, but smoke **reefer** (**marijuana**). They are pacifists and don't vote. Rastafarians are primarily descendents of Black slaves and believe that someday they will return to Africa. Jamaican reggae musician **Bob Marley** was a Rastafarian, and, to many, he personifies the Rasta culture.

rasty someone or something that is sexually inappropriate. Rhymes with nasty and means about the same.

rasty bastard a person who is sexually inappropriate. A nasty person.

rat someone who acts inhumane, underhanded or without conscience. **2.** a person who informs to the authorities. One who tells incriminating or embarrassing stories about others.

rat fink similar to a rat, yet treacherous. One who informs to the authorities. A person who tells incriminating or embarrassing stories about others. A term introduced to the American public somewhere around 1963.

rat fuck cruel or unusual activity. An act of destructive or vindictive nature. Examples: "Trashing the place is **rat fuck**; I would rather make a statement with graffiti." "Nixon's plumbers were into **rat fuck**."

rat on to inform on someone to the authorities. To tell stories that are incriminating or embarrassing.

rat out to inform on someone in exchange for a shorter jail term or to gain favor.

rat's ass something of no importance. Zero, nothing. Example: "I don't give a **rat's ass** if you like me; just give me my wages."

rattle (someone's) **cage** to interrupt or disturb someone with an action or comment in order to get their attention or to frighten them.

rattled upset, distracted or scared.

raunchy too sexually explicit for normal social consumption.

rave or **rave on** wild activity. Original definition: "To act or speak as if in delirium." During the hippie era, the word rave was expanded to mean sexual and musical jubilation. In the 1990s, "raves" began to appear as large gatherings devoted to **rock and roll**, drugs and sex. Raves are similar to what were called **happenings** or **acid tests** during the hippie era. "Rave On" was one of **Buddy Holly's** hit songs, published in 1958. It was reportedly the last song Holly performed in Clear Lake, Iowa, on February 3, 1959, just before the airplane crash in which he, the Big Bopper, Ritchie Valens and pilot Roger Peterson were killed.

raw natural, unedited, and possibly sexually explicit.

raw deal unfair treatment. An unfortunate circumstance.

Ray, James Earl (1928-1998) *social issues* the man accused of assassinating **Rev. Dr. Martin Luther King, Jr.**, on April 4, 1968. Ray was in prison for armed robbery from 1960 to 1967, when he escaped. The next year, while still a fugitive, he apparently rented a small apartment in Memphis, Tennessee, across the street from the Lorraine Motel, where King was staying. Ray apparently fired a rifle from his apart-

ment bathroom window, killing Dr. King as he stood on the motel balcony. In 1969, after pleading guilty, he was sentenced to 99 years in prison. He later recanted his confession. Most authorities are convinced that Ray fired the gun, but many question whether he acted alone. Near the end of Ray's life, Martin Luther King's family supported his claim of innocence, but he died in 1998 before a new trial could be held.

rays sun. Example: "I'm go'n to the back yard ta soak up some **rays**!"

read to observe and understand the inner thoughts and feelings of someone. To understand. Originally meaning to decipher words on a page, this word evolved to mean the understanding of another person. Examples: "I understand your commitment to celibacy, but I can also **read** your body language." Similar use as **grock**.

Ready, Steady, Go! *rock & roll* a rock and roll music TV series broadcast in London. The first program of "**Shindig**," the American copy of this program, was in fact an earlier episode of "Ready, Steady, Go!" Many videos of 1960s British performers were produced for this TV series. (See: **"Shindig," "Hullabaloo"**)

real valuable, important or trustworthy. Another word that expanded during the hippie era from a mundane physical expression into an emotional experience. To say **real** to a hippie was like saying "gold" to a banker. Examples: "Her slide guitar solos are **real**." "He's **real**, man.

"Reality is a crutch for those who can't handle drugs." a quote from Lily Tomlin of the television show "**Laugh-In**."

realization *religion* the discovery of a deep religious truth. Achieving **spiritual awakening**. During the hippie era, this word was primarily associated with religion. (See: **spiritual awakening**)

ream to verbally reprimand or ridicule someone. From the an older term, to "ream out someone's asshole."

reamed castigated, verbally ridiculed. From a frightening image of someone taking a sharp object and reaming out a person's anal passage. Similar usage as **rip a new asshole.**

record album a **vinyl** long-playing record album. (See: **LPs** and **vinyl**)

recreational drugs *drugs* drugs used for fun, rather than to combat disease. Drugs taken to enhance one's party mood or to increase energy for recreational activities. The first popular party drug was **cocaine**; then came the family of **MDAs**, of which **ecstasy** is the best known. **Amyl nitrite** (nitrate) and **poppers** are examples, and some people feel that all speeds are recreational. The psychedelics, such as LSD, **marijuana**, peyote, mushrooms, etc., were considered by the **true hippie** to be educational drugs, but they were used by many for recreation as well.

recreational sex *sex* sex for fun, rather than for procreation. Most sex is recreational, even in conservative households. Although the basic sex drive is a natural desire to replenish the species, humans have made it into a sport.

recycling the act of reusing items or reconstituting raw materials to produce other usable commodities. A practice that came from the hippie back-to-the-earth movement and its ideals of environmental protection and conservation of resources.

red-assed angry, very upset.

photo by Lisa Law ©

Redding, Otis (b. Sept. 9, 1941, Dawson, Ga.; d. Dec. 10, 1967, Madison, Wisc.) *soul, rock &roll* a Black soul singer who came to his peak when rock and roll embraced its Black roots. Otis had much to embrace. He wrote and recorded "**Respect**" in 1965, a song with which **Aretha Franklin** had a hit in 1967, and he co-wrote "I've Been Loving You Too Long" with Jerry Butler. Redding co-wrote and recorded his biggest hit, "(Sittin' on) The Dock of the Bay," in 1967, yet didn't live to see its success. He was killed in a chartered plane crash before the song was released. Otis Redding was one of the most popular performers at the Monterey Pop Festival in 1967, which helped to solidify the association between hippie **acid rock** and Black R&B. Inducted into the Rock and Roll Hall of Fame in 1989. (See: **respect**)

Red Dog Saloon *rock & roll* an old bar from the silver rush mining days in Virginia City, Nevada, which was reopened on June, 29 1965, by Don Works, Chan Laughlin and Mark Unobsky. Reportedly, the place where **acid rock** was born when **The Charlatins** and **The Warlocks** (soon to be **The Grateful Dead**) played there. The first psychedelic light shows were produced there. Many of the hippie "hijinks" and traditions originated there, including rock posters, **psychedelic lights** and the **happening** phenomenon.

redefine *social issues* to reexamine beliefs or values, which are now wrong because of changes in time and circumstance. The hippie counterculture redefined numerous things which had gone unquestioned for too long. Redefining what was true American patriotism was a prime example. Before the 1960s, what was good for General Motors was good for America. Hippies redefined that, and they also tried to enlighten the public to the fact that unchecked **materialism** and greed was not the best thing for this country, the world and living creatures, human and animal.

red hot a person, place or thing that is exceptional in some way, popular or sexy. Examples: "I had a **red hot** time dancing at this **red hot** club with a **red hot** girl."

redneck *social issues* a person who is prejudiced and intolerant toward people outside his or her own social or ethnic group. The term comes from a depiction of Southern farmers whose necks are red from working in the sun. The inference is that rednecks are poor, uneducated, White country folk. The definition has expanded to mean *any* person who is prejudiced and intolerant.

reds or **red birds, red bullets, red devils, red dolls** *drugs* Seconal, an often abused **barbiturate** drug distinctive for its red capsule. Sedatives or **downers**.

Red Scare *social issues* the fear of communism that arose in the late 1940s, primarily as a reaction to the politics of Russia and China. In America, it was fueled by **Joseph P. McCarthy,** Republican Senator from Wisconsin from 1947 to 1957. He threatened to identify communists in industry and government, and his tactics of "guilt by association" hurt many prominent citizens when he branded people as communists merely for knowing other communists. His assault on basic freedoms triggered a reaction that helped create the civil rights, **free-speech** and hippie movements. McCarthy was the namesake of the word **McCarthyism**. (See: **Joseph P. McCarthy** and **McCarthyism**)

reducing valve the human mind. A term attributed to **Tom Wolfe**. Our brain processes a huge amount of information and reduces it to a small amount of facts that fit into our past knowledge and make it understandable. Supporters of psychedelic drugs believe that hallucinogenics open up the brain to expose all the many things that we have hidden and compartmentalized, out of the way, so that they don't confuse our day-to-day lives. This is where the concept of **mind-expanding** comes in; it is an educational process which some people feel is badly needed in this dumbed-down society. (See: **mind-expanding drugs**)

Reed, Jimmy (b. Sept. 6, 1925, Dunleith, Miss.; d. Aug. 29, 1976, Oakland, Calif.) *blues/rock & roll* an early Black blues singer/songwriter, little known among music listeners, but well-known among musicians as the man responsible for the "Jimmy Reed riff," the basic bass pattern used in many rock and roll songs. Jorma Kaukonen, **Jefferson Airplane's** lead guitarist says, "All those Jimmy Reed riffs, that's the stuff that we grew up on and people who never even heard of Jimmy Reed play those riffs today, they're just hugely important." Reed wrote "Bright Lights Big City," "Big Boss Man" and other classics which have been re-recorded and covered by many musicians. The sound he created is an essential element of all rock and roll. Inducted into the Rock and Roll Hall of Fame in 1991.

Reed, Lou (b. Louis Firbank, March 2, 1942, Brooklyn, New York) *opiate/rock & roll* the lead singer and songwriter for the cult group **Velvet Underground** in the late 1960s. His music was too morose for most hippies, and "The Underground" was too far underground to be a force outside New York City; yet both Reed and the group have always had a strong cult following. Their song "Heroin" was one of the first straightforward anthems of the dark drug culture that existed in the New York underground. Reed's solo 1977 song, "Walk on the Wild Side," is a classic with its lyrics, "and the colored girls said do, da, do, da, do, da, do..., etc." His association with **David Bowie** and **Andy Warhol** in the New York scene was enough to make him a cult figure. Reed is also a well-respected poet, and he continues to undertake musical projects with a variety of other critically acclaimed performers. The Velvet Underground was inducted into the Rock and Roll Hall of Fame in 1996.

reef *drugs* short for reefer, **marijuana**. From the **Rastafarian** culture of Jamaica.

reefer *drugs* **marijuana**. A term used in the 1950s that became prominent in the Black Jamaican and Rastafarian cultures. (See: **marijuana**)

"Reefer Madness" a movie produced in the late 1950s to expose the "dangers" of **marijuana** the "weed from the devil's garden." Intended as a condemnation of marijuana, it was so melodramatic and erroneous that the **counterculture** adopted its terminology and posters to reveal the shallow, anti-marijuana mentality.

reet right, all right or OK. A **jazz** and **jive** talk term. Example: "Reet and complete."

Bob Marley

reggae n., adj. a form of music from Jamaica. The word seems to have come from the term ragged or ragamuffin (a ragged person), which became ragged music, then reggae music. A slow, heavy bass beat with a shuffle type of musical style. Toots Hibbet, who allegedly originated the term "reggae," says, "**Reggae** came from the **ska** beat, which was fast, and **rock steady** beat, which was a little slower. **Reggae's** like the **rock steady** beat, but it's a little slower and heavier." Some say the first reggae song was "People Funny, Boy" by Lee "Scratch" Perry around 1968. Shortly thereafter, Toots and The Maytals released "Do The Reggay," and the genre grew from there. **Bob Marley**, the best known reggae musician, called it "King Music" and once said of reggae, "You getting a three-in-one music. You getting a happy rhythm with a sad sound with a good vibration...it's roots music." Reggae is similar to, and can also be called, **ska, bluebeat,** and **rock steady**.

regs short for regulations. A military term adopted on a limited basis by the **counterculture**.

rehab short for **rehabilitation**. (See: **rehabilitation**)

rehabilitation *drugs* The effort to cure people of drug or alcohol **addictions**. Drug rehabilitation methods cover a wide spectrum, from Christian doctrinal pressures to cold turkey abstention, on into chemical therapy.

Reich, Wilhelm (1897-1957) *social issues* an Austrian psychoanalyst known for his controversial theory of orgasmic potency, which states that: The emotions of love and sensations of pleasure form the basis of good mental health. Reich taught in the US in the 1940s and 50s and was imprisoned for inventing and using a device called the organ energy accelerator. He wrote *Character Analysis*, 1933, and *The Mass Psychology of Fascism*, 1933. His theories were embraced by the hippie culture because of his belief in the importance of sexual pleasure in normal life.

reincarnation *religion* rebirth of the personality into another body of the same species. (Rebirth into a body belonging to a different species is called **transmigration of the soul**.) Belief in reincarnation assumes that souls survive death and are reborn into different bodies, passing through a series of lives. Reincarnation is associated with **karma**. Some traditions maintain that humans are always reborn into new, human bodies; others feel that the soul can travel into animal or vegetable forms. (See: **transmigration of the soul**)

reinvent the wheel to do something that has already been done. To waste time building something already built.

reject n. an undesirable person. From the term "reject of society."

relate to communicate with someone. To have a deep understanding, perhaps even a **spiritual** connection, with another human being.

religion an organization that adheres to a certain set of rules governing one's moral life and sometimes secular life as well. This usually requires the belief in a god or higher power who dictates these rules and punishes for non-compliance. The belief in this higher power and in his ability to reward or punish are held by faith, since, in all such cases, there is no scientific or actual first-hand evidence that these powers actually exist.

rent-a-cop a security guard.

***rep** short for reputation. Example: "He got a bad **rep** because of that one schlep."

reptilian complex the area of the brain that controls or contains hereditary and evolutionary thought. Considered to play a large part in territorial, defensive and aggressive behavior apparently connected to preservation of self and species. It is also considered relevant to sexual desire and specifically the male ego.

resin *drugs* the pungent, sticky substance on the **flower** of the marijuana plant containing the majority of the **THC** and **psychoactive** potency.

Resistance, The *social issues* originally an organization created in the Northeastern United States, involved in coordinating **anti-war** activities. Its symbol was the Greek letter for ohm (, representing the engineering term for the measurement of electrical resistance). The Resistance eventually became a generic term for any **anti-establishment**, **anti-war** or **counterculture** revolutionary activity.

resisters people who refuse to enter military service due to moral or religious convictions.

respect *social issues* appreciation and understanding. Another word expanded in the hippie era to have more emotional depth than previously. "I don't get no respect" was a plaintive cry of many youthful members of the **counterculture**. "Respect me in the morning" was the demand of women of the generation. The word gained prominence in Aretha Franklin's 1967 song, "Respect," written by **Otis Redding**, first recorded and released by him in 1965. Respect is a pivotal word and requirement of the cultural revolution of the 1960s. The demand for respect started the **civil rights** movement, the **free-speech movement** and, to a large extent, the **anti-war movement** as well.

retard short for retarded. Someone who is awkward, sloppy or inept. During the hippie era, this was not normally directed toward a medically disabled person. Sadly, from its original medical use, this word evolved into general negative use describing a variety of human behaviors. This is probably the reason that the word is no longer used clinically and why terms such as handicapped have come into use.

retentive uptight. Short for the more clinical psychological term **anal retentive**. (See: **anal retentive**)

revelation in hippie parlance, the instantaneous understanding of an important truth of life. Something revealed. Hippie revelations were often received through the assistance of mind-expanding drugs. Tolerant observers will agree that it is not important how knowledge is revealed, but that it be embraced. **2.** in religious parlance, the communication from God to man. The "supposed" communication to man from a divine spirit. In the history of religion, revelations have taken almost every conceivable form. Sceptics will point out that these "divine" communications always appear in abnormal or unexpected ways, leaving no ordinary channels of investigation or proof of validity.

reverb *rock & roll* an echo effect used in **rock and roll** music. Short for reverberation. The reverb effect was one of the primary elements of the **psychedelic** music genre. The echo pulsating in one's ears and brain created an "out-of-reality" feeling that, when combined with psychedelics, transported the listener anywhere their enhanced imagination could offer.

revolving door a situation that is going nowhere. A vicious circle of frustrating, nonproductive activity.

rhythm and blues (R&B) *music* the form of music that was the transition between **blues** and **rock & roll**. It came into popularity in the early 1950s though it had been around for some years before that in the Black community. Closely associated with the **Motown** record label in Detroit and the Brill Building in New York City. Some of the most popular performers were Big Joe Turner, LaVern Baker, The Platters, The Temptations, The Supremes, **Ray Charles**, **Jackie Wilson** and Etta James.

rhythm method of birth control in the late 1970s, some hippie women began to mistrust and shun chemical and mechanical forms of **birth control** and returned to the rhythm method, a form of birth control that relied on the ovulation cycle of the female sex partner. In the normal, 28-day menstrual cycle, a woman is fertile for a period of approximately three to six days. Also taking into consideration the life-span of male sperm, the rhythm method requires that a couple not wanting to have a child confine intercourse to only 20 or so days of the cycle. This requires strict adherence to dates. The most scientific form of rhythm also involves measuring the women's temperature daily in order to determine when ovulation is about to occur. Spontaneity is difficult to maintain under these conditions. The rhythm method is the only form of birth control condoned by the Catholic Church.

rich bitch a woman with money and a bad attitude. Most often directed at a woman in whom a man was romantically interested, yet who rejected him because he was an unemployed slob.

Rickenbacker *rock & roll* one of the more popular guitar manufacturing companies of the 1960s and 70s. Rickenbacker is credited with developing the first commercially produced electric guitar in 1931. It was essentially a Hawaiian lap guitar called the "frying pan" due to its appearance. The original company was called the Electro String Instrument Corporation. Owner Adolph Rickenbacker, cousin of World War I flying ace Eddie Rickenbaker, was an engineer and machinist in Los Angeles in the 1920s. He was asked by another company to make a metal body for a guitar and got into the business. The Rickenbacker Company made Roger McGuinn's distinctive double-neck, six- and twelve-string electric guitar in 1973.

Ricky *rock & roll* short for **Rickenbacker** guitar.

ride a car. Any vehicle. Example: "Hey, that's a cool **ride** you got there, man."

ride to keep going, to party. Example: "**Ride** when you can, sleep when you must."

ride shotgun to sit in the prestigious place in the front seat next to the window on the passenger side of a car. As opposed to sitting between the driver and window seat passenger, or sitting in the back seat. First used by car passengers in the 1950s, the term was borrowed from cowboy movie stagecoaches on which the passenger sitting up with the driver was a security guard carrying a shotgun.

riff a progression of notes or a definable portion of music played on an individual instrument. "**Riff**, a signature combination of notes," says Jack Casady of the Jefferson Airplane.

rig intravenous drug paraphernalia, usually a syringe, a length of rubber tube for tying off a vein, and a bent spoon for heating the water and dope solution.

right! an exclamation of agreement. Example: "**Right**! I grock what you're puttin' down, bro!"

right-arm a humorous play on the phrase **right-on**.

righteous anything that is good or right. Example: "That's a **righteous** hat, man." It originally had a religious connotation meaning conformity to moral laws, but the hippie culture changed it to mean conformity to secular laws and the "**reptilian complex**." The evolution of this word started with 1950s **beat** movement and continued with the help of the mid-1960s singing group, the Righteous Brothers, Bill Medley & Bobby Hatfield.

*right-on correct, good, OK. Most likely from "You have hit **right on** the target."

right thinking a good idea. Example: "Your idea for the party was **right thinking**."

right wing *social issues* conservative, reactionary or fascist. A conservative political viewpoint. From the Right Bank of the river Seine in Paris. In the 1920s and 30s, the Left Bank of the Seine was where the liberal student population and communist blue-collar workers lived, while the conservative businessmen lived and worked on the Right Bank.

ring (someone's) **bell** to physically knock someone unconscious.

ring (someone's) **bell** or **ring** (someone's) **chimes** to excite someone or bring them to orgasm. Example: "I'll **ring your bell** anytime for a dime."

ring my chimes turn me on, make me happy, give me a good time. A phrase was made popular on the TV comedy show, "Laugh-In."

Ringo (b. Richard Starkey Jr. July 7, 1940) rock & roll the drummer of **The Beatles**, the most famous rock and roll band of all time. Though Ringo contributed sparingly to the singing/ songwriting of the group, his drumming abilities and personality added a great deal to the success of The Beatles. His subdued character, wry humor and indifference to fame displayed in their first two films added much to the charm of the group. He has willingly become a caricature of himself and thus is en-

sured of an especially warm place in the hearts of all fans.

rinky-dink small, flimsy, unstable. From ricky-ticky, referring to ragtime music of the 1920s.

Riot House the Hyatt House Hotel (also at one time the Gene Autry Hotel) on Sunset Boulevard in Hollywood were many traveling **rock and roll** bands were housed while on tour or in town to record. Numerous bizarre episodes of extreme behavior took place when the bands and their entourages and groupies stayed there.

rip (someone) **a new asshole** to verbally attack or ridicule. From a frightening image of a person taking a sharp object and creating a new anal passage for someone. Similar usage as **reamed**.

ripe *sex* ready for sex or susceptible to seduction.

rip it up don't hold back, have fun.

*rip-off n. a swindle, a deception, a fake.

rip off v. to steal something. Lisa Law, a member of **The Hog Farm** who was involved in the food, security and good vibes at both **Monterey Pop** and **Woodstock** says: "The term rip off was started at Woodstock." People literally ripped off tent material for shelter from the rain, and then hungry people without money came to the various tents and stole (ripped off) food. Some of the vendors were into making money, and many of those who attended the festival were offended by the profit-taking when there were hungry people in need. The Hog Farm and some of the vendors gave away food.

rip-off artist a thief.

ripped drunk or **high** on some substance.

Ripple n. the brand name of a cheap bottled wine with a twist-off cap. Often used as a joke in later years when the media wished to depict depravity or poor taste. Ripple was sometimes the only wine available to a hippie of little means or the only wine available if one found oneself in "Buttercup," Nebraska, in 1968.

rishi Sanskrit for **seer** or **sage**.

rites of passage ceremonies celebrating the turning points of life or periods of transition from one status to another; birth, puberty, marriage and death.

riveted to be excited by something or struck silent and immobile by the thrill of someone or something. To be in complete concentration on something.

rivets on Levi's jeans removed from the back pockets in 1964.

roach the butt end of a **marijuana** cigarette. Can also mean the whole "joint," but most often used to indicate only the last part to be smoked.

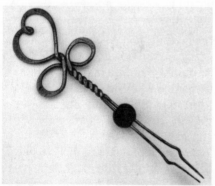

photo by John McCleary ©

roach clip a device used to hold the last little end of a **marijuana** cigarette to keep from burning one's fingers. Roach clips can be any kind of tweezer-like object, such as a pair of pliers, a hemostat, an electrician's alligator clip or a hand-made hippie paraphernalia item.

roadie someone who travels with a **rock and roll** band to load, unload and set-up their instruments and sound equipment.

Robinson, Smokey (b. Feb. 19, 1940, Detroit, Mich.) *soul, R & B, rock & roll* the Black songwriter and singer who gave **Berry Gordy's Motown** label most of its early hits. Robinson wrote "Shop Around," 1961, the first hit for his group the Miracles. He composed "You Really Got a Hold on Me," 1963; "My Guy," 1964; "My Girl," 1965; "Ain't That Peculiar," 1965; "Get Ready," 1966; "I Second That Emotion," 1967; "Tears of a Clown," 1971; and many more. **Bob Dylan** once called Robinson "America's greatest living poet." Smokey Robinson and Berry Gordy are the two men most responsible for introducing Black music into the White **mainstream**. Inducted into the Rock and Roll Hall of Fame in 1987.

rock any of the powdered drugs in their solid state, i.e., **rock cocaine**.

rockabilly hillbilly music with a rock beat. **Elvis Presley**, **Buddy Holly**, **Roy Orbison** and Carl Perkins were some of the first rockabilly artists.

rock and roll *sex* to have sex. Originally an African American slang term. Used to hide the real meaning in a song and first heard in Black music.

rock and roll music with a syncopated beat, created with dancing as the desired result. The term was reportedly first used in print in *Billboard* magazine in June, 1946, when it was written "right rhythmic rock and roll music" to describe the Joe Liggins song,

"Sugar Lump." "Etiquette in Public Places," Emily Post's *Tenth Edition Blue Book* published in 1960 by Funk & Wagnalls, states, "As for young musicians' practicing, there is no manager of an apartment house who is not at his wits' end to solve this chief cause of complaint."

rock and roll in a nonmusical or sexual sense, any activity performed with enjoyment and vitality. Example: "Let's go have fun...let's **rock and roll**." It was the anthem of the age.

rock 'em, sock 'em any exciting, perhaps dangerous activity, such as a fight at a dance. Originally a 1950s term, it evolved to become a 1960s definition of a party that got out of control.

rocker someone who likes to dance. Someone who likes sex.

rockers one of the two conflicting groups of young people that evolved in London during the early 1960s; **mods** were the other group. Clothing was one of the differences between the two groups, with mods being the more **fashion** conscious and rockers, the precursors of the hippie and grunge look. Mods rode motor scooters, and rockers preferred motorcycles. The differences became blurred to those of us not in that cultural environment; the appearance of **The Beatles** on the scene soon brought the two groups closer since both groups claimed "The Boys." The Beatles began rather mod, but soon became more **rocker** with their long hair and nonconforming clothes. **The Rolling Stones** seemed to be rockers from the start.

rock 'n' roll another way of saying "rock and roll."

rock 'n' roll military slang for having one's weapon set on fully automatic.

rock on keep rocking, keep doing what you are doing. Not always related to music or dancing; similar usage as **keep the faith**.

rocks a man's testicles, **balls**.

rock star a person who has achieved an extreme level of popularity as a rock and roll musician. There is no official form of measurement for establishing rock star status. The criteria might be the number of records sold, appearance on the cover of *Rolling Stone* magazine or the decibel level of screams at one's concerts. Whatever it is, everyone seems to know who is a rock star and who isn't. **2.** a derogatory term for someone who thinks that he is a very important person. During the hippie era, it was probably used in the negative more often than the positive. Example: "Jim thinks he's a **rock star** ever since he sang in the school talent show." Many people think that the most important personalities of the hippie era were its musical stars; yet, to a **true hippie**, this is not the case. There were many people during the hippie era whose lives exemplified the ideals of the time, but they were not stars as we know them.

rock steady hang in there, keep doing what you are doing. Similar to "**keep the faith**." This use of rock has less relation to music and dancing than does "rock on." Rock steady for some reason has a more spiritual inclination, and is often spoken as an offering of fraternal support for another person. It has no relation to the older term, "rock steady," meaning someone or something that is solid or trustworthy.

rock steady *music* a form of music from Jamaica. A slow, heavy bass beat with a shuffle type of musical style. Similar to and sometimes called **reggae, ska** and **blue-beat**.

"Rocky Horror Picture Show" a 1975 British film spoof of monster movies. Based on a British rock musical that had some success in England but flopped in America. Starring Tim Curry, Susan Sarandon, Barry Bostwick and Meat Loaf, it became the most popular cult film of the era, and perhaps of all time. As of this date, midnight showings are still screened around the world, where avid fans dressed in costumes of the film's characters sing and recite lines as the movie plays. Many fans have attended hundreds of showings of the film. One of the first **underground** films to achieve **mainstream** status and one of the first films to explore bisexuality. Directed by Jim Sharman.

rod n. the male sex organ. In the **true hippie** culture, this term was used only in humor. Example: "She laughed at his **rod,** so he painted a face on it."

Roddenberry, Gene (1921-1991) an ex-Los Angeles policeman who created **"Star Trek," one of the two most important serialized television shows of the hippie era. In 1951, Roddenberry wrote his first TV scripts; in 1954, he left the police force to write full time, and in 1964, he created "Star Trek." The first show aired on September 22, 1966. The most important elements of "Star Trek" and the reasons for its popularity amoung true hippie is that it promoted ethnic and religious tolerance and non-violence. We have Roddenberry to thank for the moral and ethical content of the show. The phaser was created for "Star Trek"; the first totally debilitating, yet nonlethal, weapon, and lethal force was used only as a last resort. (See: **Star Trek**)

role model someone to look up to, whose lifestyle sets an example for others. A term by no means exclusively **counterculture**, but used in that period of time. Many people think that the most important personalities of the hippie era were its musical stars or radical politicians; yet, to a **true hippie**, this is not the case. There were many people during the hippie era who were role models of the time, but they were not stars as we know them.

roll or **let's roll** let's move or leave. Example: "**Let's roll**; I want to make it to the Whiskey while Jojo's still dancing in her cage."

roll to have sex. Example: "Let's have a **roll**."

roller a Rolls Royce car. A British term.

roll or **rolling** to make a **marijuana** cigarette. To roll marijuana into a **rolling paper** in preparation for smoking.

rolling machine a small, hand-operated machine that rolls tobacco or **marijuana** cigarettes.

rolling papers small, thin papers used for rolling **marijuana** cigarettes by hand. Before marijuana became readily available, rolling paper manufacturing companies did a pitifully small business supplying the needs of those few throwbacks who preferred to roll their own cigarettes even after tailor-mades came on the market. After marijuana burst on the scene, these companies must have raked in huge, unexpected profits. Although they definitely knew from whence their windfall came, these very old and sometimes conservative companies obviously looked the other way. One wonders how their consciences reacted as the collection plate passed before them each Sunday in their churches.

rolling stone   a person who keeps moving. From "A **rolling stone** gathers no moss," which was maxim #524 of Publilius Syrus, philosopher and writer in the first century B.C. Both **The Rolling Stones** rock band and *Rolling Stone* magazine got their names from this quotation. With inferred reference to rock and roll and being **stoned**, it was a perfect name for a rock group or rock magazine. "The Stones" chose the name from a **Muddy Waters** song, and he got it from the philosopher.

Rolling Stone **magazine (b. January 7, 1967)**   the premier rock music magazine. On October 16, 1965, 19-year-old Jann Wenner and 48-year-old Ralph Gleason met at the Tribute to Dr. Strange dance at the Longshoremen's Hall in San Francisco. A little over two years later, they printed the inaugural issue of *Rolling Stone* magazine. Gleason suggested the name, after the **Muddy Waters** song. Their offices were at 746 Brannan Street in San Francisco until 1970, when management offices were moved to New York City. The magazine has been the messenger for rock and roll since its beginning, never afraid of controversy and always open to new and different forms of music and expression.

Rolling Stones, The   *rock & roll* British rock band formed in 1962 in London, England, Mick Jagger (b. Michael Phillip Jagger, July 26, 1943, Dartford, Eng.), voc.; Keith Richards (b. Dec. 19, 1943, Dartford, Eng.), gtr., voc.; Bill Wyman (b. William Perks, Oct. 24, 1936, London) bass; Charlie Watts (b. June 2, 1941, Islington, Eng.), drums; Brian Jones (b. Lewis Brian Hopkins-Jones, Feb. 28, 1942, Cheltenham, Eng.; d. July 3, 1969, London), gtr.; replaced in 1969 by Mick Taylor (b. Jan.

17, 1948, Welwyn Garden City, Eng.), gtr.; replaced in 1975 by Ron Wood (b. June 1, 1947, Hillingdon, Eng.), gtr., voc. The best dance band of the 1960s and 1970s. Had they cared a little more about social problems and expressed

Mick Jagger   photo by John McCleary ©

some youthful angst, The Stones might be considered the best music group of all times. Inducted into the Rock and Roll Hall of Fame in 1989.

roll out   to wake up. From rolling out of bed.

roll your own   to roll your own tobacco or **marijuana** cigarette.

Romney, Hugh (See: **Wavy Gravy**)

Ronstadt, Linda (b. July 15, 1946, Tucson, Ariz.) *folk/rock* the sweetheart of the radio, she was the lead singer of a short-lived group, the Stone Ponies, and early involved in the Los Angeles scene, which included **Jackson Browne** and the **Eagles**.   Her operatic quality voice and instinct for good music made her one of the most popular female singers of the hippie era.

rookie move a mistake made due to lack of experience.

Roosevelt, Eleanor (b. Oct. 11, 1884, New York City; d. Nov. 7, 1962) stateswoman, early White leader of Black causes, early leader of the Women's Rights movement. Wife of Franklin D. Roosevelt (FDR), President of the United States, 1932-1945. In 1934, Eleanor Roosevelt helped to form the National Youth Administration, and she coordinated a meeting between FDR and **NAACP** leader Walter White to discuss anti-lynching legislation. In 1939, Eleanor defied segregation laws by sitting with Blacks at the Southern Conference for Human Welfare in Birmingham, Alabama. She also arranged for Marian Anderson to sing at the Lincoln Memorial on Easter Sunday, a first for a Black entertainer. The Daughters of the American Revolution (DAR) had previously denied Ms. Anderson the right to sing at another location. In 1945, she convinced the Army Nurse Corps to open membership to Black women, and she joined the NAACP board of directors. In 1946, Eleanor Roosevelt was elected head of the United Nations Human Rights Commission and drafted the Declaration of Human Rights that was later passed by the United Nations. She also initiated the creation of Americans for Democratic Action, a group focusing on domestic social reform. In 1958, Eleanor spoke at a **civil rights** workshop at Highlander Folk School in Tennessee, despite threats from the **Ku Klux Klan**. In 1961, President **John Kennedy** reappointed Eleanor to the United Nations and also appointed her as chair of the President's Commission on the Status of Women. In 1962, Eleanor spearheaded an ad hoc Commission of Inquiry into the Administration of Justice in the Freedom Struggle; she monitored and reported on the efforts and progress of the fight for **civil rights** in the United States. Eleanor, as she preferred to be called by everyone, was a person of true **bohemian**, hippie **spirit**.

root a penis.

rope a **marijuana** cigarette. The marijuana plant (hemp) is used to make rope.

Ross, Diana (b. March 26, 1944, Detroit, Mich.) soul, blues, pop and rock Black female singer, member of the **Motown** label group The Supremes in the early 1960s. Diana became the lead singer and eventually left the group to pursue a solo career. No one can express a heartache, soothe a beast or turn on the love light better than she.

ROTC the **R**eserve **O**fficer **T**raining **C**orps. Military training for college students. One of the circumstances that created student unrest at the University of California, Berkeley, and other campuses during the **free-speech movement** and **anti-war** demonstrations of the mid-1960s. The military was recruiting on campuses, and many students felt that it was inappropriate to prepare for war in an educational environment, which they thought should be devoted to more peaceful and productive efforts.

rough stuff drugs uncleaned **marijuana**.

rough stuff sex sadistic or violent sex.

rough trade sex a person who indulges in sadistic or violent sex.

round eye a Caucasian. Sometimes derogatory.

round heels a term used to describe someone, usually a woman, who is sexually promiscuous. Meaning, of course, that she falls on her back with the slightest enticement.

round the horn to indulge in a total package of sex. **Foreplay, fellatio, cunnilingus,** intercourse, etc.

roust to remove or chase someone. To awaken. Example: "The fuzz came to **roust** all the **crashers** at Little Sur."

row a line of powdered drugs prepared to be **snorted**.

"Rowan & Martin's Laugh-In" 1968-73 NBC TV show hosted by standup comedians Dan Rowan and Dick Martin. A wild and wacky Monday night series of short skits and slapstick. Notable in the cast were Lily Tomlin, Goldie Hawn, Ruth Buzzi, Teresa Graves, Arte Johnson, Judy Carne, Joanne Worley, Alan Sues, David Madden Strunk, Richard Dason and Sarah Kennedy. The show was irreverent, politically incorrect and laced with sexual innuendo. Each week featured a special guest. Even though the program was considered **liberal** and controversial, there were always appearances by such conservatives as John Wayne and **Richard Nixon**, who thought it would be "**cool**" to appear on the show. The premise of the show was frivolity, but eventually the network decided they were having too much fun. "Laugh-In" was eventually censored out of existence in 1973. Shows like it and the "Smothers Brothers" gave free speech a brief life on TV.

rowdy loud, obnoxious or uncontrolled.

Roxy Music *rock & roll* the definitive 1970s art rock band formed in London in 1971. **Brian Ferry** (b. Sept. 26, 1945, Washington, Eng.), voc., kybds.; **Brian Eno** (born Brian Peter George St. John le Baptiste de la Salle Eno, May 15, 1948, Woodbridge, Eng.), synthesizer, electronics. The rest of the band changed numerous times, but Ferry and Eno were the moving forces and were also responsible for starting the extreme electronic experimentations in music, which spread through the late 1970s, 80s and 90s influencing **punk, techno, new wave** and world music.

royal fucking or **royally fucked** grossly cheated or badly fooled. The word royal is for emphasis only. Example: "I bought a car and got a **royal fucking**."

royal pain (in the ass) an annoyance. The word royal is for emphasis only. Example: "This new car of mine is a **royal pain** in the ass."

royally drastically or completely. Examples: "I got **royally** screwed when I bought this used Edsel."

royally extravagantly or graciously. "She treated me **royally** in the back seat of my Edsel."

rub or **rub off** female **masturbation**.

rub (someone) **the wrong way** to annoy, intentionally or unintentionally. Example: "Her attitude will **rub you the wrong way**, and even her beauty won't compensate."

rubber a prophylactic or condom.

Rubik's Cube a square, plastic puzzle toy, ingeniously constructed of 27 separate, but connected, multi-colored blocks that can be miraculously pivoted and manipulated in the attempt to return the large block to a state in which each face is a solid color. There are millions of combinations, but only one possible way of getting all six sides to form a different color. Millions were sold, and it was the subject of many official and unofficial competitions to

Rubik and his Cube

see who was able to solve the puzzle in the shortest period of time. Created by Ernö Rubik (1944-), an architect born in Budapest, the cube was patented in 1975, and become a worldwide craze by the late 1970s. Rubik created other puzzles, but none ever captivated the public's attention as did the "Cube."

Rubin, Jerry (1938-1994) *social issues* White radical political activist and author. A reporter for the *Cincinnati Post and Times-Star* from 1956 to 1961. A leader of the **free-speech movement on the UC Berkeley campus, 1964-65. He was an organizer and co-chairman for the Vietnam Day Committee in Berkeley, California in 1965. He ran for Mayor of Berkeley in 1966. Co-founder with **Abbie Hoffman** of the **Youth International Party (Yippie)** in 1967. A member of the **Chicago Seven**, along with **Rennie Davis**, **David Dellinger**, John Froines, **Tom Hayden**, Abbie Hoffman and Lee Weiner. They were anti-war and peace and freedom movement leaders who were arrested and tried as co-conspira-

tors for crossing state borders to incite riots during the 1968 **Democratic National Convention**. Rubin was convicted and received a five-year sentence plus a sentence for contempt of court to run concurrently. The sentence was later overturned because of Judge Hoffman's gross misconduct during the trial. Rubin was the driving force behind many peace rallies and unique political demonstrations and by far the most creative, yet often unpredictable, leaders of the anti-war and anti-government movement. On Oct, 21,1967, during a **National Mobilization Committee** demonstration, Jerry Rubin and Abbie Hoffman attempted to **levitate** the Pentagon. A vice presidential candidate on the Peace and Freedom Party ticket in 1968. Rubin published the books *Do It!* in 1970, and *We Are Everywhere* in 1971. He adopted holistic healing and led workshops at Esalen Institute in Big Sur, California, in 1973-74. Became a stockbroker in the 1980s and sold vitamins in the 1990s. Rubin was killed in 1994 when struck by a car while jaywalking in Los Angeles. (See: **Chicago Seven, Chicago Seven trial, Chicago Democratic National Convention**) (See also: **Anti-War Events, Groups and Leaders** starting on page 562 in **Lists** at the back of this book)

rug rat a small child.

ruined high on drugs. Too high on drugs.

rumble a fight or confrontation.

Rumble in the Jungle the heavyweight fight on October 30, 1974, between **Muhammad Ali** and George Foreman in Kinshasa, Zaire (now the Congo), Africa. Foreman, 25 years old and champion before the bout, was knocked out in the eighth round. Ali, 32, had been stripped of the championship title seven years earlier for refusing induction into the Army because of his Muslim faith. Ali used the unconventional strategy of leaning on the ropes and blocking punches. The term "rope-a-dope" was coined that day because Ali's trainer, Angelo Dundee, told him "he was a dope" for staying on the ropes. Fifty thousand African fans watched, many of them screaming, "Ali, booma-ya" (Ali, kill him), and each fighter received $5 million from promoter Don King.

run a trip taken by a group of motorcycle riders. Example: "Break out your bike; we're going to do a **run** to Big Bear."

run a drug buying expedition. Example: "I need to make a **run** for a friend."

run a scam or **run a game** to cheat someone or play a **confidence game**. Example: "You can't **run a scam** on a man who has no green eggs and ham." (See: **confidence game** and **scam**)

run at the mouth, run (one's) **mouth** or **run off at the mouth** to talk too much. To say something unwise. Example: "Gina will **run her mouth** once too often, and Doug will leave her."

runaways young boys and girls who left home during the 1960s and early 70s to experience the excitement of the hippie movement. Many of them lived in **crash pads**, or **communes** and spent their days on the street asking for **spare change**, smoking dope and congregating for conversation, fun and music. During the hippie era, this was not a dead end for most kids, but a temporary adventure as they spread their wings, leaving the oppression of their family homes.

runes early Germanic letters, believed to possess magical powers.

run with to spend time or be friends with someone. Example: "Come meet the guys I **run with**." **2.** to pursue an idea. To follow a plan.

rush, a *drugs* the initial feeling that is experienced as a drug begins to take effect. **2.** excitement from any activity.

Russell, Leon (b. Hank Wilson, April 2, 1941, Lawton, Okla.) *rock and blues* a keyboardist, multi-instrumentalist and songwriter, he has played on recording sessions with many of the greatest, including **Phil Spector, Jerry Lee Lewis, Bob Dylan**, and **The Rolling Stones**. Russell's solo career has yielded several hit songs and even more critically memorable songs and albums, which added greatly to the hippie era atmosphere. His "Carny" album of 1972 is a classic. Russell and Denny Cordell founded Shelter Records, an important label for the country/rock movement. He toured with The Stones in the early 1970s and was prominent at **George Harrison's Concert for Bangladesh** in 1971.

rut to have sex. Originally, it was a biology term describing the sexual activities of "lesser" animals, but the **counterculture** adopted it to describe human sexual behavior. Considered a less than romantic form of lovemaking.

S

S & M sado-masochism (sadism and masochism). The practice of inflicting and receiving physical pain, usually with mutual consent, in a sexual relationship. Sadism comes from the word sadistic, meaning to enjoy inflicting mental or physical pain on others, and masochism means the enjoyment of receiving physical pain.

sack a bed, or sleeping bag. Not exclusively a hippie-era word, yet expanded in use during that time. Most likely a term brought home by soldiers from WWII.

sack out to go to sleep. The root word **sack**, defined as a bed or sleeping bag, is an earlier term used some during the hippie era; yet, when combined with the intensifier "out," it became a common phrase identified with the 1960s and 70s. Other words intensified by "out," are: veg out, to relax (like a vegetable); pig out, to eat a lot (like a pig).

sack time sleep. Sack refers to sleeping bag. A WWII term revitalized in the 1960s.

sacred mushroom *drugs* **psilocybin mushrooms**. (See: **psilocybin mushrooms**)

sacredotalism *religion* a religious system revolving around a priestly order. In its derogatory sense, it means concentration on strict church ritual, while ignoring the personal and moral needs of the congregation.

Sacred Seeds *drugs* a small, underground company that distributed small packets of **marijuana** seeds. One package of their high-potency skunk weed contained a little message, "A little warms the heart, too much burns the soul."

sacrifice a ceremonial offering to a god, demon or other superhuman or supernatural **being**.

sadhu Sanskrit term for a man who has dedicated himself to a quest for spiritual enlightenment, renouncing all worldly goods and comfort.

safe or **safety** condom or prophylactic. From the assurance of protection or "safety" from pregnancy and disease provided by a condom.

Sagan, Carl Edward (1934-1996) astronomer, 1978 Pulitzer Prize winner. A Harvard professor and prominent supporter of the belief that other intelligent life forms exist in the universe. Sagan gained prominence through the 1973 TV series "Cosmic Connection." In 1978, he won the Pulitzer Prize for nonfiction for *Dragons of Eden*, his book about the evolution of human intelligence.

Sagittarius astrological sign, November 22 to December 21, ninth house of the **zodiac**, mutable fire sign, symbolized by the centaur (half man/half horse). Traits: idealism, inspiration, synthesis. Self-perception: I perceive.

Sainte-Marie, Buffy (b. Feb. 29, 1941, Saskatchewan, Canada) *folk and rock* a Cree Indian, and the best known **Native American** artist in folk or popular music. A solo artist with many miles of touring and at least one Top 40 hit, she is most noted for writing songs that became hits for other artists. Her early 1960s protest song "The Universal Soldier" is a classic of the **anti-war movement**. She also wrote "Up Where We

Belong," recorded by Joe Cocker and Jennifer Warnes, and "Until It's Time for You to Go," recorded by **Elvis Presley**, which made the Top 40 in 1972. Buffy Sainte-Marie is a very socially conscious performer, playing many benefits and supporting numerous social and **environmental** causes throughout the years.

salt-and-pepper   a Black and White racially mixed couple.

salty rough around the edges, perhaps socially inappropriate, profane or sexually explicit in speech.

sam a Federal narcotics agent. From Uncle Sam.

same-old, same-old or **same-ol', same-ol'** no changes, everything's the same. Example: To the question "How are you doing?" one might answer, "**Same-old, same-old**."

same wavelength (on the) thinking the same thing. Having the same thoughts as another person.

samsara *religion* in **Hinduism** and **occult** terminology, the **wheel of life**, the chain of birth and rebirth, **discarnation** and **reincarnation**. (See: **reincarnation**)

sanctuary *social issues* a term used to describe a group of **anti-war** activists who provided refuge for GIs deserting from **Vietnam War** duties. "Sanctuaries" were often situated on college campuses and in churches, and were also the sites of anti-war **teach-ins.**

sandalwood incense one of the most common scents experienced in hippie environments. A very old **incense** used extensively in East Indian and Asian religious ceremonies. Since the hippie culture embraced many ancient oriental disciplines, it was an obvious adoption.

Sandoz the Sandoz Pharmaceuticals Corporation. Makers of the first LSD, called LSD 25. In the early 1960s, Sandoz spent $3 million to distribute quantities of LSD and psilocybin to universities, mental hospitals and veterans' hospitals for experimental purposes. **Ken Kesey** was introduced to these substances as a paid "guinea pig" at the Menlo Park, California, Veterans' Hospital while he was attending Stanford University. One of the songs on the **Jefferson Airplane's** 1967 *Surrealistic Pillow* album was entitled D.C.B.A. - 25. D, C, B, and A are the musical chords for the piece, and 25 stands for LSD 25. (See: **LSD**)

sandwich *sex* two people making love to another person in between them. Known as an **Oreo cookie** when two Black people make love to a White person.

SANE, Committee for a Sane Nuclear Policy *social issues* founded in 1957, this organization was responsible for some of the very first American **peace** rallies held during the Vietnam era. Notable was the rally held in Boston on October 1, 1960, with **Erich Fromm**, **liberal** Michigan Governor G. Mennen ("Soapy") Williams and Steve Allen, featuring music by **Pete Seeger** and **Joan Baez**. SANE also organized a major **anti-war** demonstration in Washington on November 27, 1965, and in 1966, it urged voters to support only congressional candidates who agreed to work "vigorously" to end the war. (See: **Anti-War Events, Groups and Leaders** starting on page 562 in **Lists** at the back of this book)

San Francisco Mime Troupe founded in 1959 by R. G. Davis, a San Francisco, California, theater group presenting political satire and social commentary in the parks, small theaters and dance halls of San Francisco during the hippie era. Their art form is often called **guerrilla theater**. The group performed plays at the first be-ins, including the **Human Be-in Gathering of the Tribes** held at the Polo Fields in San Francisco's **Golden Gate Park** on January, 14, 1967. **Bill Graham**, of later music promotion fame, was an actor, producer and accountant for the Troupe. The first rock concerts Graham promoted were benefits for the Troupe, starting with one on November 6, 1965, which featured the **Jefferson Airplane**, **The Fugs**, The Mystery Trend, **The Family Dog** and performers from **The Committee**. **Allen Ginsberg** and **Lawrence Ferlinghetti** attended. The San Francisco Mime Troupe continues to flourish today. (See: **guerrilla theater** and **Human Be-in Gathering of the Tribes**)

San Francisco Zen Center one of the first zen Buddhist facilities in America. It was established in 1962 by the late Shunryu Suzuki-roshi. Today the Zen Center is one of the largest Buddhist *sanghas* outside of Asia. In addition to the Temple in San Francisco, the Zen Center operates Green Gulch Farm and Tassajara Zen Mountain Center, the first Zen training monastery in the West.

Sanger, Margaret (b. Margaret Higgins 1879; d. 1966) one of the first and most fervent crusaders for **birth control**. From a family of eleven children, she was married with three children before becoming involved in the Women's Labor movement and the Socialist Party in New York City in 1912. A practical nurse, she wrote newspaper articles on feminine hygiene and published a mili-

tant journal entitled *Woman Rebel*. In 1914, Sanger wrote a pamphlet entitled *Family Limitations*, in which she coined the term birth control. She was jailed for her outspoken beliefs in 1916, but

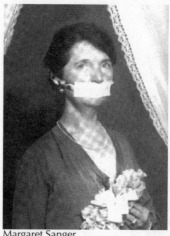
Margaret Sanger

courts ruled in favor of her efforts to allow doctors to provide birth control information to married women. In 1921, she created the American Birth Control League, which became Planned Parenthood in 1942. In the 1950s, Sanger convinced philanthropist Katherine Dexter McCormick to help fund the development of a birth control pill.

Sanskrit the ancient language of India, language of the **Vedas** and other sacred and classical texts of **Hinduism**. The linguistic ancestor of the modern dialect of *Prakritas*.

Santa Barbara (See: **University of California, Santa Barbara**)

Santana (the group) *salsa/blues/psychedelic/rock & roll* Carlos Santana (b. July 20, 1947), gtr., voc.; Jose Chepito Areas (b. 1946), timbales; David Brown (b. 1947), bass; Mike Carrabello (b. 1947), congas; Gregg Rolie (b. 1947), keyboards, lead voc.; Michael Shrieve (b. 1949), drums.   One of the most popular psychedelic bands of the era, they came to worldwide prominence after a performance at Woodstock, which riveted viewers of the film. This lineup of the band was inducted into the Rock and Roll Hall of Fame in 1998.

Santana, Carlos (b. July 20, 1947, Aulán de Navarro, Mex.) *salsa/blues/rock & roll* the leader of the extremely successful early San Francisco band **Santana**, formed in 1967. Became an instant success at Woodstock, where he performed, by his own account, completely and utterly "**wrecked**" on **acid**. Carlos at the millennium is still one of the most enduring musicians from the **psychedelic** era.   His salsa/acid rock mix has proven to the industry that music has no boundaries. Several of the early Santana albums are on the hippie short list of important music. The group Santana was inducted into the Rock and Roll Hall of Fame in 1998.

Sappho (lived around 580 B.C. in Greece) *social issues* considered the greatest female poet of the classical Lyric Age of Greece, yet only a small amount of her work remains. Sappho's poetry is admired for its emotional intensity and sensitive eroticism. Sappho was a native of Lesbos, an island in Asia Minor. History tells us that she conducted an academy for young, unmarried women. As was the custom of the age, wealthy families from Lesbos and other neighboring states sent their daughters to such schools for instruction in proper social graces, composition, music and poetry. Though most 20th-century critics concentrate on Sappho's poetic achievement, the controversy surrounding her school and her sexual orientation has also been an issue. Was the true function of her academy to serve as a finishing school preparing young women for marriage, or was it a place of worship to Aphrodite and a female retreat for instruction in **lesbian** practices?   The theory that Sappho was a homosexual has prompted history to adopt the name of her island of Lesbos as the basis for the modern word lesbian, the female homosexual.

Sassoon, Vidal (1928-) the hair stylist responsible for the most popular high-fashion hairstyle of the 1960s, the short "bob" cut for women. The leader in the "wash-and-go" philosophy of haircutting, which freed many women in the 1960s from time-consuming daily hair maintenance. The real "most popular" hair style was long, loose and straight.

Satchidananda, Swami (India, 1914-) *religion* founder of the worldwide Integral Yoga Institutes. (See: **Gurus, and Religious Leaders of the era** on page 648 in **Lists** at the back of this book)

satori Japanese Zen Buddhist term for **enlightenment**, the culmination of meditation. In hippie terms, any mental state of peace or satisfaction.

sattiva Sanskrit for **being**, existence, reality, the true **essence**. In **yoga**, the quality of purity or goodness.

"Saturday Night Live" an NBC television variety show premiering October 11, 1975, with guest hosts **George Carlin** and **The Muppets**. The original cast consisted of Dan Aykroyd, **John Belushi**, Chevy Chase, Jane Curtin, Garrett Morris, Laraine Newman, and Gilda Radner. Bill Murray joined the cast in 1976, following Chase's departure. Harry Shearer and other featured players were added after 1978 when Aykroyd and Belushi left the show. The producer was Lorne Michaels. Because of its controversial social and political subject matter, "Saturday Night Live" was consistently one of the most popular TV shows of **counterculture** fans during the late 1970s. It produced the most memorable TV skits and characters during that period, and its actors were among the most popular and infamous.

Satyr one of the woodland deities of Greek and Roman mythology, represented by the Greeks as a human figure with a horse's ears and tail, and by the Romans as **Pan,** a human figure with goat's ears, tail, legs and horns. Often depicted as the seducer of women.

sauce that which holds the world together. (See: **chi**)

save it shut up, don't speak. From "save your breath," an earlier term from the decade before the hippie era.

Savio, Mario (b. Dec, 8, 1942; d. Nov, 6, 1996) *social issues* the primary leader of the **free-speech movement (FSM) on the University of California, Berkeley, campus in 1964-65. A straight-A, Jesuit-trained student from Queens, New York, who entered UC Berkeley in 1963. In 1964, he was the president of the UC Berkeley chapter of the **Student Nonviolent Coordinating Committee (SNCC)**. He was arrested in March, 1964, at a civil rights demonstration while trying to convince the San Francisco Hotel Association to hire Blacks for better jobs. He traveled to Mississippi that **"Freedom Summer"** to work with other young activists of SNCC in registering Black voters. When Savio returned to the UC campus in the fall of 1964, he was fired up with revolutionary **spirit** and emerged as a symbol of the free-speech movement. In one rally speech, he told fellow students to change the world. "There comes a time when the operation of the machine becomes so odious, makes you so sick at heart, that you can't take part, you can't even passively take part, and you've got to put your bodies on the gears, and upon the wheels, upon the levers, upon all the apparatus. And you've got to make it stop." Later, at a sit-in to protest the arrest of graduate student **Jack Weinberg** for distributing political literature on campus, Savio and 782 others were arrested. The movement spread to other universities throughout the nation. Savio's enthusiasm led to the firing of UC Chancellor Clark Kerr, and, in the long run, to the ending of the **Vietnam War**. Mario Savio dropped out of the media for a while, but was followed closely by the FBI. He was arrested again in 1966 while protesting armed forces recruiting at UC Berkeley. He eventually ran for the State Senate on the Peace and Freedom Party ticket, but was defeated. After dropping out of Berkeley, Savio taught at an alternative school and worked in a bookstore in Los Angeles in the early 1970s. In 1984, he earned a Bachelor's Degree in Physics from San Francisco State, summa cum laude, and later received a master's degree. Mario Savio by all accounts was a reluctant hero; it is said that he normally spoke with a stutter, but rose to the occasion when big words needed to be said. He never reached the level of material success that his intelligence warranted, but the nation and world owe him a large debt of gratitude. He died of a heart attack on November 6, 1996, after moving furniture into a new home with his wife and son. Savio is sometimes credited with the statement "**never trust anyone over thirty**," yet it was actually **Jack Weinberg** who uttered that verbal icon of the **counterculture**.

Savoy Brown a British blues band formed in London in 1966, led by singer/guitarist Kim Simmonds.

*say! a greeting. Shortened form of the phrase "What do you say?"

saying something speaking profound words. Example: "Listen to Bob; he's really **saying something**."

say it like it is don't lie, tell the profound truth, say something important.

"Say it Loud, I'm Black and I'm Proud" a **James Brown** song title from 1968. It became an African American anthem.

say, man! a greeting. Shortened form of the phrase "What do you say, man?"

say what? or **say wa'?** the question, "What are you saying?" Of Black American origin.

scag or **skag** a woman who is considered ugly and promiscuous.

scag or **skag** the stabilizer fin on the bottom of a surfboard.

scalp the female pubic area. A sexual conquest. Example: "Roadie scored three **scalps** at the love-in last weekend."

scalper some lowlife who is selling tickets to the "sold out" **Dead** concert for three times their face value, and you just got to get in 'cause this is your twelfth show in a row, and you're going for a personal best, and you know that young chick with the dimples in the **see-through blouse** will be there.

*scam n. a swindle, deception or fake.

scam v. to swindle or defraud someone.

scam artist a swindler or confidence man.

scam on *sex* to pursue or try to seduce someone.

scapegoat in Biblical times, one of the two goats upon which the sins of the entire Jewish people were vested each year. During the Day of Atonement ceremonies, the goats were sent into the wilderness to die and thus pay for the sins of the people.

scarab the image or likeness of a *Scarabaeus beetle*, the symbol of resurrection in ancient Egyptian religion.

scared shitless, **scared spitless** or **scared witless** very frightened. The additional words, shitless, spitless and witless are for emphasis only.

scarf, scarf down or **scarf up** to eat. To consume or absorb. To consume with great speed and lack of table manners, but not always related to food consumption. Example: "Judah **scarfs** up all the books he can read."

scarification a form of body art adopted from primitive cultures and worn by some members of the counterculture. The practice of cutting into the skin to create scar designs. (See: **body art**)

scary stuff something disturbing. A way to place emphasis on a bizarre or disquieting subject. Example: "This ozone talk is **scary stuff**."

***scene** or **the scene** a place or time that is special in regard to its cultural importance. A great party or group of people.

scene of the crime the location of an incident. In daily conversation, it usually does not mean a real crime, nor is it necessarily related to a negative situation. Another "hippie-era figure of speech." Many of these terms and phrases are hard to trace; they either came from the **counterculture** into the media or passed the other way into the counterculture from music, movies and television.

scheme a plan or fantasy.

scheme on *sex* to fantasize about someone sexually.

schizo short for schizophrenic. Having two opposing personalities or exhibiting extreme mood swings. A "crazy person." Schizophrenia is a clinical mental state that manifests in a retreat from reality with delusions, hallucinations and exhibitions of aggressive behavior.

schizoid mixed up, as in schizophrenic; frightened. **Freaked out**, as in a drug paranoia.

schlep, **schlepp** or **shlep** any slimy, slug-like activity that is obviously unsavory to everyone except the person doing it. Yiddish.

schlock cheap or tacky **stuff**. Also, a bad idea or concept. Yiddish.

schlockmeister someone who sells cheap and tacky stuff to fools like us.

schlong, shlong, schlang or **shlang** penis. From the Yiddish *shlang,* meaning "snake."

schmaltz or **schmaltz, schmaltzy** or **schmaltzy** tacky, overdone or too fancy. Originally Yiddish, meaning rendered chicken fat.

schmeet, schmeck, schmock or **schmuck** smack or heroin.

schmeeze *drugs* smokable heroin. Brown tar heroin.

schmint *drugs* crystallized **resins** that form on the buds of high-grade **marijuana**.

schmuck a stupid or naive person. Yiddish.

schnook or **shnook** a stupid or naive person. Yiddish.

Schulz, Charles (b. Nov. 26, 1922; d. Feb. 12, 2000) cartoonist. After studying art through a correspondence course and contributing freelance cartoons to the *Saturday Evening Post,* he created a newspaper comic strip in 1950 tentatively entitled *Li'l Folks*. The strip was accepted for syndication under the new title of ***Peanuts*** and became the most successful cartoon strip in history, read by an estimated 355 million people worldwide. The strip chronicles the childhood of Charlie Brown, his friends Lucy, Linus, other acquaintances, his dog Snoopy and a bird named Woodstock. The strip has also been produced into more than 30 animated television specials and four full-length cartoon films.

Schwerner, Michael (1939-1964) *social issues* Jewish "Northerner" who traveled from his native New York City to participate in the **Mississippi Freedom Summer** project of 1964. On June 21, 1964, Schwerner; **James Chaney,** a Black **civil rights** worker; and **Andrew Goodman,** another "Jewish Northerner," were murdered by Klansmen with the help of local sheriff's deputies. As of 2001, the killers had not yet been brought to justice.   (See: **Civil Rights Events, Groups and Leaders** starting on page 546 in **Lists** at the back of this book)

Scientology, the Church of Scientology *religion* a pseudo-religious organization founded in 1954 by Lafayette Ronald Hubbard (b. 1911, Tilden, Nebraska; d. 1986, San Luis Obispo, Calif.). Dianetics is a concept from Mr. Hubbard's writings dealing with "The Modern Science of Mental Health." Hubbard was also a successful author of science fiction books.   (See: **Dianetics**)

sci-fi short for science fiction. Literature or ideas that are futuristic in nature and scientific in content.

scope out or **scoping out** to watch or study someone or something. Most often, but not always, used in the context of sexual pursuit. Similar usage to **check out** or checking out.

score to purchase drugs. **2.** to succeed in a sexual conquest.

Scorpio astrological sign, October 23 to November 22, eighth house of the **zodiac**, fixed water sign, symbolized by the scorpion. Traits: principles, inspiration. Self-perception: I desire.

scratch n. money.

scratch v. to make a mistake. From a pool term meaning to hit the wrong ball or the cue ball into the pocket.

scream to travel at high speed. Example: "That car can **scream**."

screamer a **homosexual**.

screamer *sex* a noisy sexual partner.

screaming meemies, the an uncomfortable feeling or nervous reaction.

screw an insensitive form of lovemaking.

screw around to have mindless fun, to waste time, to do something with little or no conviction, direction or ability. Sometimes this term has sexual connotations, and then it means to have **foreplay** and possible intercourse.

screw (somebody) **around** to abuse, deceive or obstruct someone.

screwed, blued and tattooed cheated or mistreated. Screwed is used in this context as a negative form of sexual intercourse; blued may come from the French word **blewed,** meaning robbed. There is some question whether or not the blued is meant to be "blowed," pronounced "blewed," as in **fellatio** (oral stimulation of the penis). The "blued and tattooed" is usually considered poetic license for emphasis, although tattooed may refer to awakening from a drunken night to discover an unwanted tattoo.

screw shack a house or room explicitly created for sexual activities. a.k.a. **sin bin, den of inequity**.

screw the pooch to do something taboo or really stupid. The ultimate social error. Sometimes used to indicate death or a fatal error.

screw-up n. someone who makes mistakes.

screw-up v. to make a mistake.

screw you a negative response. Not an offer of a romantic interlude. Screw has become almost exclusively a derogatory term, whereas fuck can be used to indicate a positive action or a negative oath.

screw yourself a negative response. A derogatory suggestion of what one should do to oneself. A very curious oath, considering that it would be nearly impossible to accomplish.

scrip or **script** a medical prescription for drugs.

scrog a distasteful sounding word with no specific definition, used to indicate a person one dislikes.

scrotum or **scrot** the fleshy sack that holds a man's testicles. Sometimes used as a derogatory name for a person.

scrounge v. to find, beg, borrow or steal. Example: "**Scrounge** up some smoke and come by the house."

scrounge n. a person who begs, borrows or steals.

scum or **scumbag** a detestable person. "Bag" infers that the person is a receptacle of scum.

scum-sucker the scumbag's closest friend.

scuzz or **scuzzbag** a sloppy, dirty or uncouth person. **2.** a regional term for **marijuana**. (See: **marijuana**)

scuzzy sloppy or dirty; uncouth or in bad taste. Inappropriate in a sexual manner.

SDS (See: **Students for a Democratic Society**)

Seale, Bobby (b. Oct. 22, 1936) *social issues* militant **civil rights** leader, co-founder and national chairman of the **Black Panther Party**. An original co-conspirator in the **Chicago Eight** trial after the riots at the **Democratic National Convention** in 1968, his case was separated from the other seven because of his outbursts in court. He was eventually released, and charges were dropped. Arrested in August, 1969, for the May, 1969, execution of another Black Panther member, he was again released and charges were dropped. Following his release from prison, he renounced political violence. He was an unsuccessful candidate for Mayor of Oakland, California, in 1973. Seale has written many diverse publications; examples include a history of the Black Panther movement published in 1970, entitled *Seize the Time*, and *Barbeque'n with Bobby*, a cook book published in 1988. Bobby Seale is currently a community organizer in Philadelphia, Pennsylvania.

seance a session conducted for the purpose of establishing communication with the dead or for witnessing supernormal phenomena. A true seance must be attended by a spiritualist medium or someone with the powers of a medium.

search and destroy originally a Vietnam-era military term meaning literally to "find and kill." Adopted into the **counterculture** and **mainstream** language as a parody, indicating a non-literal exploit, sometimes a sexual adventure. In the US military strategy of the **Vietnam War**, it was originally called "spear and net," but later became "search and destroy." Basically the tactic of sending out a small and seemingly vulnerable force of men who would be attacked by the enemy, at which time they would call in air support to destroy their attackers. The Viet Cong eventually learned to mount shorter deadly attacks, inflicting as many casualties as possible, then disappearing into the jungle before the air support could arrive.

search me a response indicating ignorance, interchangeable with "I don't know." Example: "What happened to Darla after the Mousekteers?" "**Search me**!"

second sight *occult* supernormal perception into time and space. Usually refers to symbolic visions, particularly the ability to foresee future events.

secret wisdom *occult* knowledge of the **occult**, **esoteric** philosophy and the **magic** arts.

secular humanism or **secular religion** the belief that human beings are self-sufficient without the grace of any god. Terms sometimes used to describe the **occult**.

security blanket anything that gives one comfort. Need not be an actual blanket, but any object kept close at hand for reassurance. Also called a "Linus blanket" for the character in **Charles Schulz's** *Peanuts* cartoons who always carries his baby blanket.

sedative-hypnotics *drugs* The largest category of **recreational drugs**. Drugs that depress the central nervous system. Similar to **downers**, they produce a mild **euphoria** (depending on dosage) similar to that created by alcohol consumption. Most barbiturates are examples: Amytal, Darvon, **Nembutal, Quaaludes**, Seconal, **Tuinal**. Most sedative-hypnotics seem to be stimulants (uppers) initially because they remove inhibitions, but with time, they slow down the body and mind. (See: **barbiturate** and **downers**)

seed *drugs* the butt end of a **marijuana** cigarette. a.k.a. **roach**.

seeds the seeds of the **marijuana** plant, found mostly on male plants. Male plants are not as good a smoke as female plants, which are not allowed to seed. Seeds will often produce a headache when smoked or explode when heated, so they are removed (manicured out) with the stems before lighting up. "I'm down to **seeds and stems** again," the hippies' lament of being out of dope.

seeds and stems *drugs* the chaff, that which is left over after the leaf has been smoked from a supply of **marijuana**. A very sad time for a dope smoker. **2.** Words to be found in the song, "Down to Seeds and Stems Again" by Commander Cody and his Lost Planet Airmen, a band formed in 1967 in Ann Arbor, Michigan. Commander Cody, born George Frayne, co-wrote the song with his friend Billy C. Farlow.

Seeger, Pete (b. May 3, 1919, New York City) *folk* the most important folk musician of the era. His purist attitude toward folk music and a grass roots style make him a timeless bard of the stories of man's errors, which have been repeated by poets and singers since the first fire warmed our prehistoric ancestors. His **anti-war** anthem "Where Have All the Flowers Gone?" has been sung and resung so many times that it echoes from the sidewalks and cement canyon walls of our cities. His "Turn! Turn! Turn!," a biblical passage put to music, was a #1 hit for **The Byrds** in 1965 and a message for an era. Seeger's almost religious dedication to **civil rights**, nonviolence and **liberal** causes has made him a father figure to all **true hippies**. **Woody Guthrie's** address book of the early 1950s showed Pete Seeger's address as 129 MacDougal Street, New York, NY, and his phone number as GR 71588. Inducted into the Rock and Roll Hall of Fame in 1996 as an early influence.

see God to reach an extremely spiritual place on **psychedelic** drugs. To experience a profound revelation or achieve immense internal peace through a natural high.

seeker someone who is searching for spiritual awareness or inner peace through the knowledge of religious leaders and teachers.

seek the moment to concentrate on what is happening in the present without worrying about the future or suffering from the past.

seer *occult* one who sees, a prophet, crystal-gazer, someone with **second sight** or who foresees the future. In astrology, a person with **extrasensory perception** able to visualize people's lives through their birth sign.

see through or **see right through** to be able to recognize a lie or a deception from another person. Examples: "Why can't you **see through** him? All he wants is to sniff your body stocking." "I **see right through** her; all she wants is my body to move her refrigerator."

photo by John McCleary ©

see-through *fashion* a dress, blouse or shirt that is so loosely woven or of such sheer material as to be almost transparent. Similar to **fishnet**. Clothing like this can be worn by men or women.

Seger, Bob (b. May 6, 1945, Dearborn, Mich.) *rock & roll* one of the most danceable rock and rollers of the era. He wrote and recorded "Ramblin' Gamblin' Man," 1969; "Night Moves," 1977; and "Old Time Rock & Roll; 1979," to name a few.

seismic emotionally earthshaking or exciting. From a geological term relating to earthquakes. Example: "Her love is **seismic**, man!"

Seize the Time *social issues* a **Black Panther Party** slogan. Originated from the writings of Chinese communist Chairman Mao Tse-tung and from Medieval Latin *carpe diem*, seize the day.

Selassie, Hailie (1892-1975) *religion* the Emperor of Ethiopia from 1930 until his death. When the **Rastafarians,** a religious and social brotherhood, started in Jamaica in the 1930s, they embraced him as their King. They called him Ras Tafar, the one true God, King of Kings, Lord of Lords, and the Conquering Lion of Judah. (See: **Rastafarian**)

self-awareness the awareness of one's existence as an individual. Knowing oneself. Being truthful to oneself, good and bad, and accepting personal short-comings. During the 1960s and 70s, the quest for self-awareness was a ma-jor activity of the **counterculture**. People who had experienced **psyche-delics**, "seen God" or viewed infinity in the cells of their hands, felt a desire to strip away the hypocrisy in their lives. Self-awareness was one of the elements of this quest.

self-consciousness knowledge by the self of itself. In the context of esoteric communication, this term is used to in-dicate a more selfish, individualistic at-titude than **self-awareness**. Self-con-sciousness is a function of separating self from others and the Universe, while self-awareness is acceptance of one's finite place within the **wheel of life**.

self-determination a movement by minorities to achieve a form of self-gov-ernment within this country. African Americans, Hispanics and **Native Americans** felt, rightfully so, then as now, that they were not getting proper representation and recognition within governing bodies. Self-determination is an effort to reach a place of autonomy in education, religion and the cultural aspects of one's life. Native Americans have come close to achieving this goal through certain hard-fought freedoms of religious worship and better control of some of their reservation schools.

self-help a new concept that evolved during the hippie era, based on self-education in order to improve one's own health, mental outlook or eco-nomic stability. It involved reading books and studying with practitioners. This was the educational beginning of the health and fitness movement that exists today and the start of many **fads** and **fashions** now considered necessi-ties in our society.

self-indulgence living for the fun of life alone. Spoiling oneself. Self-indul-gence is one of the steps toward **self-awareness** in that people will never know themselves fully until they have tried everything and sifted out what is right for them. If one is fortunate and intelligent, one will eventually learn through good and bad experiences what is important and necessary to one's happiness.

self-realization finding yourself and being happy with what you find. Self-satisfaction. It has many more spiri-tual and **cosmic** descriptions, but this is a basic hippie definition.

Self-Realization Fellowship *religion* a nonsectarian religious organization founded in 1920 by the late Param-hansa Yogananda. The Fellowship teaches **yoga** methods for harmonizing man's physical, mental and spiritual na-tures. Based in Los Angeles, Califor-nia, with hundreds of temples and meditation centers throughout America, Europe and India. During the hippie era, its president was Rajasi Janakananda.

sell out to give in to **materialism**, to sell oneself or one's art to the highest bidder without concern for morality or creative integrity. Example: "Don't **sell out** to the system by taking that job."

sens *drugs* short for **sinsemilla**. (See: **sinsemilla**)

sensitive adj. able to pick up feelings and emotions, "vibrations" if you will, from others. One of those words with a spiritual as well as an emotional definition. During the hippie era, it become a state of spiritual **being**.

sensitive n. a person who possesses psychic powers, but not necessarily the ability to communicate with spirits of the dead. Not synonymous with **medium**. (A medium may or may not be a sensitive.)

sensitivity training a term and process introduced to the American public in 1970. It has some of the same elements as **group therapy**, based on the theory that confrontations and interplay with unrelated people can help an individual to achieve better mental stability, effect positive change and reach **self-realization**. Over the years, the original ideals behind the movement have changed; today most sensitivity training workshops have to do primarily with money, taking advantage of the **gestalt** fad and applying it to such things as "How to Become a Better Real Estate Salesperson by 'Becoming One With' Your Client." Also called **T groups**. (See: **group therapy, gestalt** and **Esalen Institute**)

sensory deprivation a situation or place constructed or contrived in such a way that one's senses are given nothing to experience. This is accomplished by putting a person in a completely soundproof, scent-proof and totally black environment. During the hippie era, a form of therapy and **self-realization** technique was devised from doing just that. These "environments" were constructed to remove people from all outside stimulus in order to allow them to contemplate their existence more profoundly. Some of these "devices" even incorporated body temperature water flotation to simulate the return of the subject to the womb.

sensory overload a situation in which one's senses are bombarded. Created not only by the annoying levels of sound, light, smell, taste and touch in our environment, but also by stress-induced mental disorientation. In any event, the end result is emotional discomfort. Example: "Garth has to leave the bar right now; the music and atmosphere have him on **sensory overload**."

separate but equal *social issues* the doctrine that racial segregation is constitutional as long as the facilities provided for Blacks and Whites are roughly equal. The "Negro" facilities were always inferior. A segregationist invention designed to maintain separation of the races while nominally satisfying constitutional requirements of equal opportunities to minorities. In the South, it was applied to schools, transportation and restaurants. For decades, the Supreme Court refused to rule on the subject on the grounds that such civil rights issues were the responsibility of the states. In the 1954 decision of *Brown vs. Board of Education*, the Supreme Court unanimously ruled that separate but equal schools were unconstitutional. This ruling was followed by several **civil rights** laws in the 1960s.

serapé a heavy blanket worn as a coat or cape, originating in South and Central America. It usually had an opening in the middle for one's head. A Spanish word. Also called a **poncho**. A **fashion** adopted by many hippies.

seraphim the winged guardians of God's throne, the most prestigious angels.

Sergeant Sunshine a marijuana-smoking San Francisco policeman. He eventually joined the Olympali commune formed by entrepreneur Don McCoy in 1967 on 750 acres north of San Francisco.

"Sesame Street" a children's educational TV show that premiered November 10, 1969. Produced by the Children's Television Workshop. The primary personalities involved in the production of the show were Joan Gans Cooley and **Muppet** puppeteer **Jim Henson**. Bert & Ernie, Kermit the Frog, Big Bird and The Cookie Monster were some of the most popular puppet characters. (See: **Jim Hensen** and **Muppets**)

set a number of musical tunes or songs that make up a performance. A complete musical event can consist of several "sets." Example: "That was the Velcro's mellow **set**; the next **set** will rock the house."

set a pair of women's breasts.

set of lungs a loud voice. **2.** a pair of women's breasts. Same usage as **set of pipes**.

set of pipes a singing voice. **2.** a pair of women's breasts. From another, older euphemism, **set of lungs**.

set of threads clothing.

set (one) **on** (one's) **ass** to upset someone emotionally. Not the same as literally knocking someone on their ass. Example: "That comment **set him on**

his ass, so he retaliated by knocking Grant on his ass."

settle to accept something, often reluctantly, and sometimes sarcastically. A second choice. Example: "I want fame and fortune, but I'll **settle** for someone warm to be with."

seven magical works in medieval occultism, works of **magic** were classified into seven groups: Works of light and riches, works of mystery and **divination**, works of science and skill, works of retribution and punishment, works of love, works of intrigue, and works of malediction and death.

severe intense, outrageous or exciting. Example: "Man, that was a **severe** organ solo; he's the best there is!"

photo by John McCleary ©

sex n. the physical act of procreation. It is one of several natural mechanisms of self-preservation possessed by all living creatures. These mechanisms are the involuntary drives and life-sustaining responses, such as heartbeat, breath, the desire to ingest food and drink, and the urge to seek a mate for reproduction of the species. As with food, humans have progressed past the necessary self-sustaining requirements and are experimenting with numerous recipes and quantities of sex. Sex is, on one hand, the most satisfying experience a human being can have and, on the other hand, the most destructive force in our lives. There are as many kinds of sex as there are people capable of inventing deviations. Human beings are one of the very few creatures on the earth who believe that a form of love and commitment should be a prerequisite to sexual intercourse. Sex is not a requirement of love, just as love is not a requirement of sex. Hippies learned through Eastern scholars and writings, such as the **Kama Sutra**, that sex is not only a means to procreate, but also a path to better understand oneself and those around us. Many scholars say that the act of lovemaking, the higher form of sex, is as close as mankind can get to God while on this earth.

sex n. the genitals of either gender. Example: "When I touched her **sex**, she turned out to be he."

sex act intercourse, copulation.

Sex and the Single Girl an important book in the evolution of the feminist movement. Written by **Helen Gurley Brown** and published in 1962. (See: **Brown, Helen Gurley**)

sexist a man who treats women disrespectfully because of their sex. Someone who oppresses or degrades members of the opposite sex. A term that appeared in our lexicon around 1971.

sexist pig a sexist who also behaves without taste and decorum.

Sex Pistols, The *rock & roll* Johnny Rotten (b. John Lydon, Jan. 31, 1956, London), voc.; Steve Jones (b. Sept. 3, 1955, London), gtr.; Paul Cook (b. July 20, 1956, London), drums; Glen Matlock (b. London), bass; replaced in 1977 by Sid Vicious (b. John Simon Ritchie, May 10, 1957, London; d. Feb. 2, 1979, New York City), bass. Created from a previous band, the New York Dolls, with the addition of an "obnoxious guy" who had never sung before. Managed by Malcolm McLaren, the owner of a clothing store that sold "non-styles," the Sex Pistols popularized, if one can call it that, **punk**. It is said that the initial reason for starting the band was an effort to destroy established rock and roll. John Lydon, the non-singer, had bad hygiene and appropriately adopted the name Johnny Rotten. Rotten dissolved the band in 1978 because it had become too successful for his "tastes," and Sid Vicious killed himself with an overdose after stabbing his girlfriend to death. Neither rational nor nice guys, definitely not **true hippies**, but interesting cultural fodder. Regardless of their rebellion, lack of hygiene and self-imposed tragedies, their first album, released in 1977, *Never Mind the Bollocks Here's the Sex Pistols,* was a milestone in rock music and is still ranked as one of the most important albums of the era. The Sex Pistols were either a fluke or a well-planned assault on music conformity, which produced "punk," a needed change at the time.

sexploitation the use of sex or sex appeal to sell or promote something. Sexploitation appears in movies in which sex is used instead of a plot or good dialogue to keep the interest of the moviegoer.

Sexual Politics *social issues* a 1970 book by **Kate Millett** (1934-). Written as her Columbia University doctoral dissertation, it thrust Millett to the forefront of feminism. Today, Millett is a writer, political activist, art professor and artist. She founded the Women's Art Colony Farm and exhibits her paintings internationally.

sexual politics *social issues* the social phenomenon wherein the world is unequally divided into positions and roles according to gender. In the 1950s, the role of women had reached a low point in image and influence. Since the new awareness of the 1960s and 70s, women's proportion of power has grown dramatically, yet many feel it has not yet reached its rightful place and will not until complete parity is achieved.

sexual revolution *social issues* the change in attitudes about sex and sexual roles that evolved during the 1960s and 70s. Some people believe that the sexual revolution was primarily the loosening of old moralities, with the consequence of more sexual activity. The true revolutionary aspect of the phenomenon was a shuffling of attitudes about why we have sex and the role sex plays in our lives. The main intent of most "sexual revolutionaries" was to strip away the hypocrisy of sexual cheating, pretending and lying, thus producing a healthier attitude toward the act of making love as a necessary and undeniable fact of life.

shack up to take up residency with someone, usually for a limited time, solely for the purpose of having sex.

shades sunglasses. A term that began to appear in the American media around 1967; yet, like many other words and phrases, this one was used in the "underground" or **counterculture** for years before becoming popular with "the public."

shaft the male sex organ in its erect state.

"Shaft" the title and name of the main character in a 1971 Black action thriller movie. Richard Roundtree played Shaft, a Black cop who takes on the Mafia in Harlem, New York. **Gordon Parks** was the director. Considered a

blackxploitation movie by many, but it had a critically acclaimed musical score created by **Isaac Hayes**, who won an Academy Award for it, making him the first African American composer to receive that honor. There were "Shaft" sequels in 1972 and '73 and then again in 2000. (See: **blackxploitation**)

shaft, the cheated. From **screwed**, which in this context means to be taken advantage of. The term, **the shaft,** is not generally used in a sexual way, although the word **shaft** represents the male erection. Another case where a positive sexual act is used as a negative. Example: "If he's not careful, he'll get **the shaft** in his big tofu venture."

shafted cheated or mistreated. From "to get **screwed**," which in this context means to be taken advantage of. The term shafted is not normally applied to sexual activity, although the word **shaft** means a male erection. Example: "He got **shafted** in his bid to corner the market on chopsticks."

shafting cheated, taken advantage of or **screwed**. Example: "I got a royal **shafting** with that last batch of beansprouts." The term, **shafting,** is usually not used in a sexual context although **shaft** represents the male erection.

shag to have sex. A less-than-romantic usage. A British term.

shag to go after, or to chase. Example: "**Shag** that Frisbee before the dog makes it into a blob of slobber."

Shaivism (Shivaism, Sivaism) *religion* in modern **Hinduism**, one of the three great divisions. Shaivism identifies with **Shiva** as the Supreme **Being** and is devoted exclusively to his worship, regarding him as the creator, preserver and destroyer of the universe. The other two divisions of Hinduism are **Shaktism**, identifying with **Shakti**, and **Vishnuism**, which identifies with **Brahma** and **Vishnu**.

shake it move. Do it. Example: "You better **shake it**, or you'll be late for the sit-in. **2.** show your sexuality. Dance. Example: "**Shake it,** girl, show us what you've got." "It" is assumed to be one's ass.

shake it off forget the pain, go on with your life. Originally, I believe, a sports term meaning take the hit, live with the pain and play on.

shake that thing dance, have fun, display your body. A term with many uses in a culture that equated sex and rock & roll to life at its fullest. "Thing" is assumed to be one's ass.

shake your moneymaker the suggestion that a woman shake her buttocks, or, even more precisely, her sexuality. From the business of prostitution, in which a woman's sexual encounters produce her salary and the profit for her pimp.

shaking activity, happening, things going on, parties. Example: "Dude, what's **shaking** tonight? I feel like a party."

Shakti *religion* Shakti is portrayed as the female aspect of life and divinity and understood to be the wife of **Shiva**. A **Sanskrit** word meaning the power of the feminine gender; in tantric literature, the female power or energy in the universe. Shakti is also the power or energy emanating from the back of a person's spine. Associated with sex and the coupling of Shiva and his consort Kali. In **tantric yoga**, shakti is universal creativity. In **occult** terminology, shakti or sakti is the crown of the **astral** light. (See: **tantra** and **Shaktism**)

Shaktism *religion* one of the three great divisions of modern **Hinduism**. The other two are **Vishnuism** and **Shaivism**. Shaktas worship **Shakti**, rather than **Shiva** or **Vishnu**, and they regard Shakti as the power that nourishes all life and supports the universe.

shaky unstable, untrustworthy, unsure. Example: "Karla is **shaky** behind the wheel, so her passengers are a little **shaky** about the road trip."

shallow without emotional depth. Example: "Moonbeam has a nice smile, but she's **shallow** when real feelings are required." **2.** without intellectual depth. Example: "Gabe displays a **shallow** understanding of the situation." Another word that was used by the general public primarily for physical description until it was expanded into a human mental state during the 1960s and 70s.

shaman *religion* a healer, priest or magician. Originally, the word meant a medicine man or priest-magician of certain primitive Siberian tribes. Currently used to designate any tribal magician practicing medicine or rites involving superhuman or nonhuman forces. There are "shamans" in many cultures with many different names. Christians would call them "pagan" priests. The hippie culture had many shaman personalities, some dispensing **healing** philosophies and others dispensing drugs. (See: **witch doctor** and **medicine man**)

shamanism *religion* a primitive **cult** or religion that believes in communication with nonhuman intelligence in nature and the influence over spiritual forces. It is central to the spiritual life of many primitive races.

shame self-doubt about past actions. An emotion in which most hippies did not indulge. Shame is self-indulgent and should be replaced by repentance or rehabilitation if the transgression is really wicked. Shame is like kicking oneself for something already done that one cannot now change. It is foolish punishment for being ignorant; if you were ignorant, don't blame yourself. But if you did something bad and you knew it and you did it anyway, then you deserve punishment worse than mere shame.

Shankar at Monterey Pop, photo by Lisa Law ©

Shankar, Ravi (b. Benares, India, 1920) *musician* sitarist, regarded as India's most prominent musician. The sitar is a classical instrument of Northern India with 18 strings and 20 frets. A teacher and composer, Shankar founded the National Orchestra of India. In the 1950s, he was the first Indian instrumentalist to tour internationally. In the 1960s and 70s, he was sought after as a teacher and musician by the rock and roll **counterculture. His performance at the 1967 **Monterey Pop Festival** was a turning point in the appreciation of Eastern music by Western musicians and audiences. He influenced many in rock and roll, including **George Harrison** of **The Beatles**.

Shankar now teaches, tours and writes movie scores.

Shapiro, David *social issues* the Columbia University student whose photo appeared in *Life* magazine, showing him sitting in the University president's chair, smoking the president's cigar, during the seizure of five campus buildings by 600 militants in April, 1968.

sharp smart.

shazam! an exclamation used to emphasize a spectacular thought or action. Employed in comics and cartoons to indicate speed or a surprise occurrence. Example: "We were walking down the street and **shazam!** Out of the blue, we got this idea to have a toga party!" Similar usage as **bam** or **wham**.

sheila a young, sexually attractive girl. An Australian term adopted by the well-traveled hippie.

shekels money. An Old Testament term revisited.

Shepard, Sam (b. Samuel Shepard Rogers, Nov. 5, 1943, Fort Sheridan, Ill.) playwright, author, actor and many other things. One of the renaissance men of the intellectual milieu of the 1960s and 70s. A powerful, creative force in the theater and movie industry, his whole story has not yet been written.

"Shindig" *rock & roll* the first prime-time TV rock music show of its kind in America, featuring live performances by the top musical bands of the early 1960s. The program, hosted by Los Angeles disc jockey Jimmy O'Neill, premiered on ABC on September 16, 1964. It was produced by Jack Good, and it featured a house band called the Shin-diggers (later the Shindogs) and the Shindigger Dancers. Most of the

"Shindig" shows were broadcast in black and white. The first episode, broadcast live from London, was in fact an episode of "**Ready, Steady, Go!**," the British show that was the original format for these programs. Other music and dance shows followed, such as "**Hullabaloo**," "Hollywood a Go Go," "**Soul Train**," "Where The Action Is" and "Happenin' 68," which was filmed on the beach. All the TV music programs of the era experimented with different formats: live, pre-taped, with professional dancers, with nonprofessional audience members dancing, some with live music, and some with guest artists "lip-synching" their hit songs. Many videos of 1960s performers come from these TV series. "**American Bandstand**" was considered different since it was a daytime show. (See: **"American Bandstand," "Hullabaloo," "Ready, Steady, Go!"** and **"Soul Train."**)

shine or **shining** (someone) **on** to ignore or avoid. Example: "Don't **shine me on** or I'll really do something to get your attention."

Shinto *religion* the Japanese religion based on the worship of spirits and ancestors. It can incorporate many religious beliefs within its doctrine. To many, it is the true personality of the Japanese culture.

shit *negative intensifier* a euphemism for feces used as a expletive. Although not new to the hippie era, the word was greatly expanded into new, subtle usages. During the era, it evolved into an expletive or negative intensifier. Sometimes interchangeable with and used in the same context as the word fuck. Example: "**Shit**, another accordion band!"

shit n. anything negative. Example: "**Shit** happens."

shit lies. Examples: "You're full of **shit**; don't tell me that load of **shit**!" Same usage as **crap**.

shit a pejorative term directed at an objectionable or disliked person. Example: "He's a little **shit**." During and after WWII, such scatological and anatomical words as fart, shit, asshole, dick and cunt came back to America hometowns with soldiers. These words were evolving in use to describe people rather than merely describing body parts and body functions. During the hippie era, these words found expanded usage, yet still remained unacceptable in "polite society" and in more conservative atmospheres.

shit *drugs* drugs, most often **marijuana** or hashish. Used more often in Europe and places where English was not the primary language. One of the few international terms for cannabis products. (See: **marijuana**)

shit stuff. Not necessarily a negative designation.

shit a brick or **shit bricks** to be scared. Example: "Betty **shit a brick** when the outhouse fell over."

shit-all nothing, none at all. Example: "I have had **shit-all** to smoke all day."

shitcan to throw away. Example: "Those beansprouts are bad; let's **shitcan** 'em." From to throw something into or flush something down the toilet or "shitcan."

shit-eating grin a guilty or silly smile.

shit-faced drunk or under the influence of drugs.

shit fit an episode of madness. Crazy, upset behavior.

shit for brains no brains. Having something other than brains in one's head. Example: "Dogface over there has **shit for brains**; don't listen to a word he barks."

shit happens anything can go wrong. You can't stop fate. A popular bumper sticker.

shit is getting deep someone is lying. From the term "shit," meaning bad talk or lies.

shit-kicker a rowdy **redneck** or **cowboy**-type person. **2.** something **rowdy**, loud or outrageous. Example: "That party was a **shit-kicker**." Originally a cowboy term.

photo by John McCleary ©

shitkickers boots, work boots or even cowboy boots. Often hippies wore Vibram sole boots with a deep tread pattern for climbing or working. Could be **Doc Martens** boots. A cowboy word. (See: **Doc Martens bootss**)

shit-kicking acting **rowdy** or fighting. Example: "See that mellow old hippie over there? He did some **shit-kicking** in his youth."

shit out of luck unlucky, no chance, impossible. Example: "You're **shit out of luck**, she's Jon's girl."

shit list (on someone's) disliked or out or favor. Example: "If you're on Rachel's **shit list,** you better stay out of her way."

shits, the a bad situation. Example: "It's **the shits** when you're van breaks down." **2.** diarrhea.

shitstorm a negative tirade or derogatory commentary. Example: "If he ever gets mad, you better stand back for the **shitstorm**."

shit together (to have one's) to be organized. Example: "He has his **shit together**; watch him and enjoy it."

shit work manual labor, unskilled work or an undesirable job.

Shiva *religion* the greatest, arguably the most prominent, God of the Hindu religion. In Hindu religious doctrine, he is the Destroyer. The Personal God. The other two major deities are **Brahma**, the Creator; and **Vishnu**, the Preserver. Shiva is the destroyer of the prison in which man's **spirit** is held captive. To the devotees of Shiva, the universe is merely a form assumed by Shiva. Considered the male personality of most of India, he is the God of contrasts, of creation and destruction, good and evil. Lord of the dance. His symbol is a phallus representing procreation.

shmooze or **schmooze** social talk. A Yiddish word.

Shoes agents of the Federal Bureau of Investigation (FBI). A **Weathermen** term as related by **Bill Ayers** in his 2001 book *Fugitive Days: a memoir*, published by Beacon Press. It started out as "**Brown Shoes**" and was shortened. Referring to the nondescript brown shoes worn by FBI agents and also to the earlier term gumshoe. (See: **Bill Ayers** and **Weathermen**)

shook up confounded, disturbed, or upset.

shoot go ahead, say what you have to say. Example: "You have something important to say? **Shoot**; I'll listen while I'm leaving."

shoot (someone) **down** to reject, turn down or embarrass someone. Example: "She'll **shoot you down** in public just to see you squirm." Same usage as **shut down**. Similar usage as **putdown**. Related to **down in flames**. (See: **down in flames** and **putdown**)

shooting gallery a place where intravenous **drug addicts** go to **"shoot up"** their **dope**.

shoot the shit to talk.

shoot up to inject intravenous drugs.

shoot (one's) **wad** to ejaculate. **Wad** in this definition is male sperm. **2.** to use all that you have. Example: "He'll **shoot his wad** on every song he sings." It is difficult to determine which definition came first, the wad as an ejaculation of sperm or the wad as money from gambling slang, relating to betting all your wad of money on one shot of the dice. I believe the gambling usage came first, but wad as an ejaculation is more of a 1960s **counterculture** definition.

shopping bag lady or **bag lady** a woman who walks around with grocery bags full of her possessions. Not necessarily a homeless person, but someone considered senile. It can be a derogatory term directed at anyone who may seem a little crazy.

short a car. Actually a 1950s term.

short and curlies pubic hair.

short circuit to go crazy.

short count *drugs* an insufficient weight in a drug buy.

short end of the stick bad luck or a bad situation.

short hairs the pubic hairs. The sensitive area by which one holds another person in order to gain advantage. A figurative expression not to be taken literally. Example: "He's got me by the **short hairs** 'cuz I owe him money."

shot or **shot at** a chance, opportunity or effort. Examples: "He had his **shot at** her; now you give her a **shot**."

shot a derogatory comment. Examples: "That was a cold **shot** telling everyone he suffers from a diminutive digit disease." "Her comment was an unkind **shot**."

shot a hit of drugs, usually, but not exclusively, an injection.

shot down or **shot down in flames** rejected, turned down or embarrassed by someone. Example: "She got **shot down** by her ex-boyfriend, the bouncer. He wouldn't let her into the club." From aeronautical warfare in which an airplane is shot out of the sky in flames. Same usage as **shut down**. Similar usage as **putdown**. (See: **down in flames**)

shotgun *drugs* a method of enhancing the intake of **marijuana** by blowing the smoke into someone's mouth or nose. The "shooter" puts the lighted end of a **joint** in his mouth and blows out through the other end into the mouth or nose of the recipient. Also known as a **blowback**.

shotgun (to ride or sit) to ride in the passenger seat next to the car window. As opposed to sitting between the driver and passenger in the front seat or sitting in the back seat. First used by car passengers in the 1950s and borrowed from cowboy movie stagecoaches in which the passenger next to the driver was a security guard carrying a shotgun.

shot out of the sky rejected, turned down or embarrassed by someone. Example: "He got **shot out of the sky** when she left with the bouncer." From aeronautical warfare in which an airplane is shot out of the sky.

showboat or **showboating** to show off, to be arrogant.

show (one's) **true colors** or **show** (one's) **colors** to expose one's true self, accidently or by choice. Examples: "He **showed his true colors** when he kicked the dog." "**Show your colors**; stand up for what you believe." From waving or displaying a flag (a colored cloth) to show one's loyalty.

shrink a psychiatrist. Short for **head shrinker**, another term for a psychiatrist.

shrink me psychoanalyze me!

photo by John McCleary ©

shrooms *drugs* psychedelic mushrooms. Short for mushrooms.

shtup, schtup or **stup** to have sex. A Yiddish word.

shuck to through away. From the term to "shuck corn" or to remove and throw away the leaves (husk) from an ear of corn.

shuck lies. Short for **shuck and jive**.

shuck and jive to be deceptive, to talk in circles or use persuasive nonsense to entertain, deceive or achieve a goal. Named after an old type of dance step, it eventually meant to dance around the truth. The dance step is associated with early Black street entertainers who were trying to find a way to make a living after the Civil War, emancipation and reconstruction. American **jazz** came from these early street musicians. There is some support for the belief that the word "shuck" came from the term to "shuck corn," meaning to remove the leaves (husk) from an ear of corn.

shucking lying or deceiving. From **shuck and jive**. This is the most **hip** derivation of the term shuck and jive, and it was a true creation of the 1960s.

shut down to criticize or rebuke. To stop someone. From a 1950s term meaning to beat someone in an automobile drag race, thus making them shut down their engine. Same usage as **shoot down**. Similar usage as **putdown**. (See: **putdown**)

sick something revolting or sexually objectionable. Example: "I just had a **sick** conversation with Dodie."

sick human being someone who is revolting, sexually objectionable or violently demented. Example: "He is the kind of **sick human being** who pulls wings off of Beatrix Potter fairies."

sicko or **sickie** someone crazy or objectionable.

sick puppy someone crazy or objectionable.

Siddhartha *religion* the personal name of **Gautama Siddhartha Buddha,** the founder of **Buddhism.** (See: **Gautama Siddhartha Buddha** and **Buddhism**) **2.** a book by Hermann Hesse about Gautama Buddha, published in 1922. A biographical novel read by many in the **counterculture** that opened Westerners to Eastern philosophy. One of the lessons in this book is, when making love, hold yourself up on your elbows to keep from crushing your partner.

sides record **album** "**cuts**" or songs. Example: "What are your favorite **sides** on his new album?" Probably from the designation of the side of an album, when each record disk had only one song per side. (See: **record** and **album**)

sidekick a good friend. Someone at your side to kick around with. A cowboy term.

sidewalk commando a street hustler, a person asking for **spare change**. **2.** a crazy, often homeless, person who confronts people on the street.

signs of the Zodiac the names and symbols given to the star constellations we call the **Zodiac**. The Zodiac is literally "a circle of small animals." In **astrology**, it is the circle of 12 star constellations around the heavens through which our world moves within a year. Astrology is the unproven pseudo-science dealing with the stars and their effects on human beings. A person's Zodiac sign is determined by the position of the constellations at the time of birth. The attributes of the Zodiac sign or constellation under which a person is born are then said to affect the personality of that individual. The attributes of each sign of the Zodiac have been unscientifically determined, but many people believe in their reality. Astrology most likely began to evolve around 3,000 B.C. in Babylon. It is the forefather of, and predates, the true science of astronomy by many centuries.

Signs of the Zodiac

Aries, the Ram,
    March 20 to April 20
Taurus the Bull,
    April 20 to May 21
Gemini, the Twins,
    May 21 to June 21
Cancer, the Crab,
    June 21 to July 22
Leo, the Lion,
    July 22 to August 23
Virgo, the Virgin,
    August 23 to September 23
Libra, the Scales,
    September 23 to October 23
Scorpio, the Scorpion,
    October 23 to November 22
Sagittarius, the Archer,
    November 22 to Dec. 21
Capricorn, the Goat,
    December 21 to January 20
Aquarius, the Water Bearer,
    January 20 to February 19
Pisces, the Two Fish,
    February 19 to March 20

Sikh *religion* disciple. Followers of the Sikh religion, a combination of the **Hindu** and **Islam** religions. Evolved during the fifth century A.D. in Northern India.

silent majority *politics* a term used by **Richard Nixon** when he was President, indicating his supporters. His theory was that the majority of Americans, though silent, supported his policies regarding the **Vietnam War**. In contrast, he believed that the war resisters were a noisy minority. On November 3, 1969, Nixon said in a speech, "Let historians not record that when America was the most powerful nation in the world we passed on the other side of the road and allowed the last hopes for peace and freedom of millions of people to be suffocated by the forces of totalitarianism. And so tonight—to you, the great **silent majority** of my fellow Americans—I ask for your support."

Silent Spring *social issues* a book written by Rachel Carson (1907-1964). Published in 1962, it exposed and condemned the indiscriminate use of pesticides, especially **DDT**, which was later banned. The book led to a presidential commission and helped to create the **environmental** consciousness of the time. Carson was an American marine biologist, environmentalist and writer. She taught at the University of Maryland and worked for the US Fish and Wildlife Service until the 1950s. In 1951, she published *The Sea Around Us* and then *Silent Spring,* making her one of the most influential environmental leaders of the era.

silicon chip *computer revolution* silicon-based wafer or "chip" containing etched patterns carrying electrically coded messages throughout a computer. Named and introduced to the American public in 1966. The concept was conceived in 1959 by Robert Noyce, the eventual founder of Intel. A silicon chip is the smallest element of an integrated circuit and is in essence an integrated circuit itself.

silk and satin *drugs* a mixture of **amphetamines** and **barbiturates**. An **upper** and **downer** mix.

Simon and Garfunkel *pop/rock* Paul Simon (b. Oct. 13, 1941, Newark, NJ), gtr., voc.; Arthur Garfunkel (b. Nov. 5, 1941, New York City), voc. Very much a pop-singing group, but they provided some of the best mood music for the hippie era. Paul Simon could also be considered one of the best musical poets and tunesmiths of the era. "Bridge Over Troubled Water," 1970, is still one of the most acclaimed songs ever, with 11 Grammy awards. They were inducted into the Rock and Roll Hall of Fame in 1990. Simon was inducted into the Rock and Roll Hall of Fame in 2001.

simulgasm *sex* the simultaneous orgasm of two or more lovers. Coined by John McCleary in the mid-1970s.

Sinatra, Nancy (b. 1940, Jersey City, New Jersey) daughter of singer/actor Frank Sinatra, she had a brief period of entertainment industry success in the late 1960s. Her big #1 hit was the 1966 song "These Boots Are Made for Walking." She had other songs on the charts and acted in movies and on TV. Nancy's real claim to fame in the eyes of the hippie culture was that she wore big hair, disco shorts and knee-high boots during a period when that style was considered shallow and narcissistic.

sin bin a **Volkswagen bus**. The VW bus was at times the home and transportation of many hippies, and, therefore, it was deemed a location where sex and drug use took place. Also called a **fuck truck**. **2.** any place where sexual or illegal activities occurred. A room or house. a.k.a. **screw shack**, **den of inequity**.

single parent a person, male or female, who raises a child alone. One of the consequences of the **sexual revolution** was a change in the family unit. The **extended** or **communal family** was intended to replace the monogamous family unit in the **Utopian** ideals of the time, but because of the economics of our society, that was difficult to achieve. The sexual revolution broke down social barriers so that we could reconstruct them in a less hypocritical form, and the single-parent family was one of the products of that revolution. This appeared disastrous on the surface, yet many children from loving single-parent homes have flourished, and often because they were spared the tension found in some two-parent homes in which abuse and conflict were rampant.

singles *modifier* a modifier indicating that a place or function is reserved for unattached men and women. This designation is used to describe a place where single people can meet to socialize and pair-up. Examples: "singles bar, singles party, singles bowling night."

sinsemilla *drugs* female **marijuana** flowers that have not been allowed to seed at maturity. To produce *sinsemilla*, the male plants are removed from contact with the female plants prior to pollination. Female plants normally produce a stronger smoke than males, and the unpollinated female plants produce even more psychoactive **resins**. From the Spanish word meaning "without seeds."

sister a Black female. A girl or woman of like mind.   Not necessarily indicating a person of blood relation.

Sister Corita (b. Frances Kent, 1918, Fort Dodge, Iowa; d. 1986) *artist* a nun of the Immaculate Heart teaching order. As a young girl, she was encouraged to love art and studied at the Otis Art Institute in Los Angeles before entering the convent at age 18. Following her graduation from Immaculate Heart College in 1941, she taught in British Columbia and was eventually assigned to the art faculty at Immaculate Heart College. Sister Corita eventually enrolled in a master's degree program at the University of Southern California. Her interest was silk-screen, and by the 1960s, her bright, primary color designs and strong social and religious

messages became popular art for hippie walls. After 30 years as a nun, Corita Kent left her order and returned to private life, living for some time in Boston, Massachusetts, doing mural commissions and other works, many of which appear in museums worldwide.

sitar classical instrument of Northern India with 18 strings, 20 frets and one resonator chamber.   Indian music played an important role in the development of rock and roll during the hippie era. Ravi Shankar, India's premier sitar player, gave a pivotal performance at the Monterey Pop Festival in June of 1967. His concert introduced the tonality and energy of Eastern music to the general public as well as inspired musicians, who later used it in their compositions.

sitcom short for situation comedy. An entertainment art form developed by the American television industry, consisting of a series of episodic comical stories set in home or work environments. For many people, it is the primary amusement in their otherwise dull and monotonous lives, and to others, the epitome of theatrical stagnation. Personally, I feel that sitcoms contribute to the systematic dumbing down of the American public.

sit-in *social issues* a form of passive, rebellious **demonstration** in which a group of people sits down in a facility from which they are normally excluded, often because of their race. This nonviolent action usually prompts arrests of the demonstrators and therefore draws attention to their cause. First used January 1, 1960, when four Black students sat-in at a segregated lunch counter in Greensboro, North Carolina. At this sit-in, the song "We Shall Overcome" was first used as the anthem of

civil rights demonstrators. Originally a civil rights tactic, it was later adopted by the **free-speech** and **anti-war movements**. At free-speech and anti-war sit-ins, the demonstrators used the sheer volume of people to shut down the operations of a college campus or government facility as a means to attract attention to their demands.

sit there with (one's) **finger up** (one's) **ass** to do nothing. Example: "Don't just **sit there with your finger up your ass**; lift a hand once in awhile to show you're still alive."

situation a strange or potentially bad circumstance. This is one of those examples of our continual efforts to abbreviate our language. The words bad, strange, dangerous, etc., have been removed from the phrase because they are assumed. Example: "We have a **situation**, and without help, our mung bean sprouts will wither and die." Much of our colloquial language comes from the natural, human, lazy habit of dropping words that are already understood.

six-hundred-pound gorilla the same as an eight- or nine-hundred-pound gorilla; any force that cannot be ignored or dealt with rationally. Examples: "Her habit is like a **six-hundred-pound gorilla**." Question: "What do you give a **six-hundred-pound gorilla**?" Answer: "Anything it wants."

six pack a half-dozen beers in a container. Six of anything to which you want to apply the term.

sixth sense *occult* an extra sense beyond the five: Touch, Sight, Smell, Taste and Hearing, possessed by an average, healthy person. Loosely defined as the ability to sense or **read** the emotions of others and to acquire information when no overt communication is evident.

"60 Minutes" a TV show of investigative reporting that premiered on CBS on September 24, 1968. The best watchdog news show on commercial television. Although it is "owned" by an establishment media network, its producers and reporters have been able to maintain enough autonomy and integrity to expose many shady dealings within our military, government, industry and private sector. "The Doris Day Show" premiered on the same night.

sixty-nine *sex* the sexual position in which lovers simultaneously perform **oral sex** on each other. Mutual oral stimulation. To do so, the couple normally lies feet to head, creating the image of the number 69.

ska a form of music created in Jamaica and the Caribbean. It is similar to **reggae**. Toots Hibbet, whom some say originated the term reggae says, "Reggae came from the **ska** beat, which is faster, and **rock steady** beat, which is a little slower."

skag or **scag** a very derogatory term for a woman. It is meant to characterize her as ugly, probably unkempt and most likely promiscuous. Originally a 1950s high school term.

skag or **scag** the stabilizer fin on the bottom of a surfboard.

skag *drugs* **heroin**.

skank something disgusting or a person of disrepute. In some societies it means the same as slut.

skate to get away with something, to slip past or to do something easily. Similar usage as to **slide**. Example: "I'm hoping to **skate** through that test in basket weaving."

skateboard originally a short piece of wood with roller skate wheels attached to the bottom, used as a form of transportation and amusement. Became popular in America in 1965.

skid marks the brown stains left in the crotch of underwear or pants created by not thoroughly wiping oneself after a bowel movement.

skiffel an early form of **rock and roll** music played in Britain in the late 1950s and early 1960s. Normally played with acoustical instruments (no built-in electric sound pickups), but sometimes amplified through a PA (public address) system. The bass was usually a standup, and occasionally, in the more primitive groups, the bass was a washtub, broom handle and string. Sometimes cardboard boxes served as the drums. Most of the early English rock band members, including **The Beatles**, first played in skiffel bands.

skin a handshake. Example: "Slip me **skin,** man."

skin to steal.

Skin Brothers people who attach chains, rings and even nuts and bolts through the skin and flesh in various parts of the body, including the genitalia. Largely a homosexual activity, but also indulged in by some straight men and women, often of the biker culture. This term was in use in the mid-1970s, but because the brotherhood was very much underground, it was not well known to the public. (See: **body art, body piercing** and **Fakir Musafar**)

skin flick a movie with graphic sexual content, usually showing full nudity and actual intercourse.

skin flute the penis or male genitalia. "Playing" it is called a **blow job.**

skinhead a shaved head. **2.** a person with a shaved head. **3.** a person who is considered a White supremacist or Nazi. In this definition, a shaved head is not required.

skinny the truth. Example: "The **skinny** about that girl is that she's not a girl."

skinny-dipping nude swimming. **2.** making love without a condom.

skin-pop or **skin-popping** *drugs* the practice of injecting drugs under the skin rather than into a vein. The difference in technique comes from either the inability to find a vein or the squeamishness of the shooter. The results are about the same, except that the intravenous shot takes five to ten seconds to take effect, while the skin-pop takes five to ten minutes.

skins drums. **2.** condoms. **3.** automobile tires.

skirt a girl, i.e., someone who wears a skirt. This is an old term, but it came into prominence during the era.

skirt chaser *sex* someone who chases girls.

skosh or **scosh** small or little, a small amount. From the Japanese word *sukoshi.*

skull head. Example: "He is out of his **skull** in love with her feet."

skull session a profound conversation.

skunk weed *drugs* in some areas it referred to bad **marijuana,** and in others, very good marijuana.

skyjack to hold an airplane full of passengers hostage or divert a plane to a location other than its regularly scheduled destination. A method used in order to defect to another country, to extort money or to gain political recognition. The most famous skyjacker is D. B. Cooper (a fictitious name), who collected $200,000 on November 22, 1971, and then jumped out of a plane from 10,000, feet, never to be heard from again. This is still the only unsolved domestic skyjacking in US history. "Skyjack" is considered a conventional rather than a **counterculture** word, and there are many other terms in this book of which the same could be said. However, this is also a cultural encyclopedia, and skyjacking is part of the cultural history of the time.

D. B. Cooper

This is a police depiction of the famous skyjacker, D. B. Cooper. He used the name Dan Cooper when buying the plane ticket, but a police and media mix-up changed his name forever to D. B. Cooper.

sky piece a hat.

sky pilot a military chaplain.

slack leeway, freedom. Time or advantage granted in order to let someone get away with something. Example: "I give him **slack** 'cause of his bad childhood, but if he reaches for my mood ring again, color me mad." A common term in the era was to "cut somebody **slack**."

slam or **slammed** to criticize, denigrate, malign or slander.

slam n. a derogatory comment.

slam dunk a winner. Any successful endeavor. From the "**slam dunk**" in basketball, a shot in which the player jumps high enough to slam the ball down into the hoop to score a goal. Example: "Her poem was a **slam dunk** in the tear competition." The basketball term "**slam dunk**" also came into use during the era, but it is now called merely a **dunk**.

slammer jail.

*sleaze or **sleazy** someone or something that is cheap, promiscuous or unkempt.

sleaze-bag or **sleazeball** a very deceptive, untrustworthy person.

sleazoid an extra special, very deceptive, untrustworthy person. The "oid" is added merely for emphasis.

sleep around to be sexually promiscuous.

sleep rough to bed down anywhere, on someone's floor, by the side of the road. To be on the road.

sleep with (someone) to have sexual intercourse with someone.

Slick a name directed at someone who is annoying, boring or trying too hard to impress. Similar derogatory usage as **Guy** or **Friend**. Example: "Hey, **Slick**, go tell someone else your sad story."

slick someone or something a little too polished, contrived or insincere.

Slick, Grace (b. Grace Barnett Wing, Oct. 30, 1939, Chicago, Ill.) *psychedelic/rock & roll* female lead singer for **Jefferson Airplane**, one of the original

San Francisco psychedelic rock groups formed in early 1965. Within the year, Slick replaced a founding member and began to liven things up. She was one of the most decorative "frontmen," had the ability to sell a song with sex or subtlety and also proved to be an important songwriter. Jefferson Airplane's 1967 breakthrough album *Surrealistic Pillow* is still on the Top 10 list of many **rock and roll** and, specifically, psychedelic music fans. With just two songs in *Surrealistic Pillow*, "White Rabbit" (co-written by Slick) and "Somebody to Love" (by Slick), Grace became a hippie poster girl, and "The Airplane" became the foremost psychedelic band overnight.

slide to leave. Example: "You guys go on and have your fight; I think I'll just **slide** on out of here."

slide to ignore something or let something slip past. Similar usage as to let someone **skate**. Example: "I'll let that **slide**, but if you continue being obnoxious, I'll go talk to my dog instead."

slime, slimeball, slimebag or **slimebucket** a person who is low, deceptive and untrustworthy. From an earlier phrase relating to a person being as low as a snail and thus "leaving a trail of slime behind them."

sling a **jockstrap**. **2.** a brassiere.

slip it to (someone) to cheat or deceive someone. Example: "Joe really did **slip it to** me when he gave me his dog named Cat."

slip me five shake my hand. Five represents the five fingers.

slit *sex* another euphemism for the female genitalia.

slob someone who is slovenly, messy or dirty.

slo-mo short for slow motion.

sloshed drunk.

slot *sex* any orifice that can be sexually penetrated.

slow burn a deep, growing anger. Example: "Wilson is doing a **slow burn** over the tire tracks through his kale patch."

sluffing off or **sluffin' off** being lazy or derelict in one's duties.

slumming associating with someone or attending a function that would normally be considered beneath one's social status.

slut a promiscuous woman. Can also be used to describe a sexually active heterosexual man. Often used in sarcasm by homosexual men to describe themselves or their lovers. During the hippie era, it was seldom used in seriousness by the **counterculture** since being promiscuous was not considered wrong.

Sly and the Family Stone a **pop**, **soul**, rock, **psychedelic** and **funk** band formed in San Francisco, California, in 1966, original lineup: Sly Stone (b. Sylvester Stewart, Mar. 15, 1944, Dallas, Tex.), gtr., kybds., voc.; Freddie Stone (b. Fred Stewart, June 5, 1946, Dallas, Tex.), gtr., voc.; Larry Graham, Jr. (b. Aug. 14, 1946, Beaumont, Tex.), bass, voc.; Cynthia Robinson (b. Jan. 12, 1946, Sacramento, Calif.), trumpet; Greg Errico (b. Sep. 1, 1946, San Francisco), drums; Rosie Stone (b. March 21, 1945, Vallejo, Calif.), piano; Jerry Martini (b. Oct. 1, 1943, Colorado), sax. This band was important because of its musical mix and its influence on music to come. It was the first Black-led psychedelic band, and its members coined the term "funkadelic," which was the combination of the words funk and psychedelic. The band is also credited with leading the way into the funk craze of the 1970s. With its ethnic- and gender-mixed band and the themes of "getting together" and "everybody is a star," Sly and the Family Stone was a forbearer and typical spokesband for the hippie era of love and racial harmony. They had hits with songs like "Dance to the Music," 1968; "Everyday People," 1969; "Hot Fun in the Summertime," 1969; "Thank You (Falettinme Be Mice Elf Agin)," 1970; and "Family Affair," 1971.

smack *drugs* **heroin**. Some say this term comes from the practice of smacking the arm to help raise a vein in order to inject the heroin intravenously. Another theory is that it comes from the German/Yiddish word *shmek*, meaning to taste or sniff.

smacked out *drugs* addicted to **heroin**.

small-time adj. amateurish or unprofessional about something. Sometimes referred to a person who indulged only in **soft drugs**.

smarmy effusively insincere. Example: "What a **smarmy** little man; jealousy oozes from his pores as he compliments you on your taste."

smack head *drugs* someone addicted to **heroin**.

smart ass an arrogant, annoying, know-it-all person.

smart mouth someone who is sarcastic.

smarts brains, street intelligence.

smash *drugs* a **cannabis oil** made in Mexico that appeared in the US in 1967. Cannabis oil is smoked like **hashish**.

smashed drunk, under the influence of drugs or both.

smash hit anything that is popular.

smegma the creamy residue under the foreskin of the penis. Also called **headcheese**. Usually considered to be a mixture of old sperm and urine. Not very appetizing stuff. The terms smegma and headcheese were used to express disgust in describing all manner of things, such as imitation butter on movie popcorn or an ex-boyfriend.

smiley face (See: **happy face**)

Smith, Patti (b. Dec, 31, 1946, Chicago, Ill,) *rock & roll* poet, singer, songwriter, credited with recording the first **punk rock** record, the 1974 single of Dino Valenti's "Hey, Joe." She has influenced many in a career that has garnered much critical, yet marginal, commercial success. Smith is still around and is considered a cult icon by many.

Smith, Tommie *social issues* the Olympic track gold medalist who, along with **John Carlos**, the silver medalist, displayed the **Black Power** salute upon receiving his medal at the Mexico City Olympics on November 18, 1968. (See: **Black Power**)

smokables *drugs* **marijuana**, **hashish** or any drug that can be smoked to produce a **high**.

smoke n. *drugs* **marijuana**.

smoke v. *drugs* to indulge in a **marijuana** cigarette.

photo by John McCleary ©

smoke shop or **chiba shop** *drugs* a store that sells **marijuana** under the counter. A shop that is disguised as a reputable business, yet offers illegal drugs on the side.

smoke stone *drugs* a flat rock or ceramic stone with a hole through it to use as a holder for smoking **marijuana** cigarettes.

Smokey the Bear or **Smokey** a highway patrolman, the designated term for the authorities used by **citizens band radio (CB radio)** operators. On the nation's highways in the 1970s, many truckers and car travelers used CB radios for communication. One of the major pastimes was warning fellow drivers of the authorities so that travelers could slow down in order to avoid speeding tickets. Smokey the Bear, or just Smokey or Bear, was the warning term used for this purpose. (See: **citizens band radio**)

smokin' moving quickly or proceeding efficiently.

smoking gun the physical proof that something has happened. Irrefutable evidence.

smooth or **smooth move** well done, good; similar to **cool**. Example: "That was a **smooth move**; he picked her up without having to buy her a drink."

"Smothers Brothers Comedy Hour" (February 5, 1967-1969) one of the first **mainstream** network TV shows in which the talent had a say in creative content. Extremely controversial social and political subjects were aired, and the show was eventually censored out of existence. The brothers, Thomas Bolyn (Tommy) Smothers 3rd, (b.1939) and Richard (Dick) Smothers (b. 1937) were musicians/comedians discovered by Jack Paar. The show was a critical success, but the politically poignant skits were frequently cut by CBS, and the show ended when Tom complained publicly.

snag, snag it or **snagged** to grab or to steal. Examples: "**Snag** his heart with those eyes of yours."

snake n. the penis.

snake v. to grab or to steal. Examples: "He couldn't find a toothbrush he could afford, so he **snaked** the cheapest one."

snake in or **snake in there** v. to sneak into somewhere. To be devious. As usual, the snake signified evil.

snake it down your leg to raise the leg of a pair of shorts and retrieve one's penis in order to urinate. A technique used when wearing swim trunks and shorts to allow urinating without unzipping.

snap to suffer a mental breakdown. To go crazy.

snapper *drugs* **amyl nitrite** in a glass or plastic vial, which one breaks (snaps) open in order to inhale. Legally sold as a party enhancer, amyl nitrite is a chemical compound originally prescribed for the treatment of angina pectoris, heart pain caused by poor blood flow to the heart. When inhaled, snappers produce a short spurt of energy. Said to be sexually stimulating and widely used in the **gay** community. a.k.a. **poppers.**

snatch *sex* another euphemism for the female genitalia.

SNCC (pronounced **snick**) (See: **Student Nonviolent Coordinating Committee**)

sniff *drugs* a small portion of drugs, usually the powdered variety, that can be inhaled, such as **cocaine, heroin** or **methamphetamines**.

snitch someone who reveals secrets about others or gives damaging information to the authorities. A person who tells incriminating or embarrassing stories about others. Same usage as **rat** or **rat fink**.

snooze you loose, (if you) don't hesitate; if you wait, it will be too late.

snort n. *drugs* a portion of drugs, usually the powdered variety, that can be inhaled, such as **cocaine**, heroin or **methamphetamines**.

snort v. *drugs* to inhale a portion of drugs.

snow *drugs* cocaine. (See: **cocaine**)

snowbird *drugs* a woman who likes **cocaine**.

snow job a lie.

snuff n. *drugs* **cocaine**. Most often, **cocaine**, but also any one of the pow-

dered variety of drugs, such as cocaine, **heroin** or **methamphetamines**.

snuff v. to kill.

Snyder, Gary (b. 1930, San Francisco, Calif.) beat poet, writer. A member of the beat literary community in New York City and San Francisco to which **Allen Ginsberg, Jack Kerouac, William Burroughs, Lawrence Ferlinghetti, Diane di Prima, LeRoi Jones** and Frank O'Hara belonged. He studied anthropology and received a BA in 1951, attended Indiana University from 1951-52, and the University of California, Berkeley, from 1953-56. Snyder later taught at Berkeley from 1964-65, studied Buddhism in Japan, and worked as a seaman and a forester. He persists as a poet, teaches at the University of California, Davis, and has become a **counterculture** icon, as have many of the other members of the beat community he helped to create. Gary Snyder, by all accounts, is an impressive person, so much so that Jack Kerouac wrote *The Dharma Bums* about him. His reading of his poem, "A Berry Feast," at the famous 1955 poetry session in the Six Gallery is said to have inspired the **Zen Buddhist** movement among the beats, and thus, among the American counterculture. He was on the stage at the original San Francisco Be-In on January 14, 1967 and won the Pulitzer Prize in poetry in 1974 for "Turtle Island." Gary Snyder is one of the fathers of the hippie era.

soak it stop, go away, I don't want to hear it, don't bother me. From "go soak your head." Colloquial terms often result from the natural human habit of dropping words that are already understood. Example: "**Soak it**! You spout more bullshit than Spiro Agnew."

soap opera a strange or confusing social situation. Example: "Helen's life is a **soap opera**, with all those girlfriends who are boyfriends and boyfriends who are girlfriends." Evolved from the name given to daytime television drama shows, which were primarily sponsored by soap companies.

S.O.B. son of a bitch. An old term that comes and goes.

so busted to be discovered in a lie or deception. **Busted** means caught, and the **so** was for special emphasis.

soch or **sosh** short for social climber. Someone who is more concerned with social position than social value and more interested in personal social life than the welfare of society. One who appears to be oblivious to society outside one's own social life.

social consciousness or **social conscience** *social issues* awareness of the world full of people other than oneself. Concern for other human beings and a desire for a conflict-free society in which all people can live in harmony. Peace, love and a chicken in every pot, or tofu, if you so desire.

social engineering *computer revolution* the ability to persuade telephone company operators and executives to reveal sensitive information. A late hippie-era term originating with the early **hackers** and **phone phreaks** who would talk their way into sensitive telephone phone company information necessary to obtain telephone procedures and long-distance codes. Eventually used as a tool by **computer hackers** to gain access to codes and procedures needed for their Internet exploration.

sock it to (someone) *sex* to have sexual intercourse with someone. Used primarily in jest.

sock it to me let me have it, hit me with it. Make me happy, give me a good time. Can be sexual. The phrase was first widely heard in **Aretha Franklin's** 1967 recording of the **Otis Redding** song "Respect." **Sock it to me** has had a broad use in the Black community for some time. The phrase, of course, has sexual connotations, yet it was most often used merely as a humorous punctuation. It was used with regularity to humorous success on the TV variety show, **Rowan and Martin's "Laugh In."** **Country Joe McDonald** used sock it to me for the intro to his performance of "Your Love is Like a Rainbow" at **Woodstock** in 1969.

sodium amytal *drugs* a **sedative-hypnotic**, **barbiturate**, **downer**.

sodium pentothal *drugs* an anesthetic and anticonvulsive used medically for brief surgical procedures. It made one sort of silly. Some people used it for recreation. Used only occasionally during the hippie era by those with connections in the medical profession. a.k.a. **truth serum**.

soft permissive. Example: "That judge is **soft** on victimless crimes; all you get is a slap on the wallet." **2.** weak or squeamish. Example: "She's **soft**! A big, strong boyfriend like you can beat her up any day."

soft without expectations or restrictions. Examples: **Soft** love, in which sex and affection are exchanged without the commitment of time, fidelity and spousal support; soft money, which has no restrictions on its use and can be spent without normal legal or fiduciary requirements. This term indicates something acquired outside the usual channels, therefore without the usual restrictions. More examples: soft support, soft gratitude, soft participation.

soft core *sex* as opposed to "**hard core**" sex, meaning a more acceptable or less offensive sexual depiction in movies or dramatic exhibitions. Often indicating that there is no genital penetration. Genital exposure and genital touching are the grey areas, and the way in which these subjects are handled determines hard or soft core. Of course, where sex is involved, each individual has a personal rating systems, and what is offensive to one person may be acceptable to another.

soft drink a beverage consisting of sugar, water and flavoring, usually carbonated. As opposed to a hard drink, which is a drink containing alcohol. In the early 20th century, many soft drinks, such as Coca Cola and Pepsi Cola, contained extremely stimulating drugs, such as cocaine or opiates.

soft drugs drugs that would be considered non-life-threatening and nonaddictive. As opposed to **hard drugs**, which can be addictive and deadly. The designation of which drugs are soft and which ones are hard differs, depending on the source. Each list from each authority should be considered arbitrary, subject to personal opinion, experiences and observations. Some people might be impervious to the addictive qualities of opiates, while others can kill themselves with diet pills. The difference between physical and emotional addiction should also be considered when determining which is a soft or hard drug.

soft money *social issues* money without restrictions on its use. Unregistered gifts, donations or grants. Money that can be spent without normal legal or fiduciary requirements. In politics, money acquired through irregular channels, therefore carrying no legal restrictions. The understanding is that the authorities will look the other way because it is too confusing to figure out how to regulate these funds. Buy your wife a dish washer and your courtesan a diamond necklace; no one will know that they didn't come from your regular income.

soft touch someone who is easily swayed and can be deceived into giving money. Someone naive. A person who is generous to those in need.

SoHo a section of Manhattan in New York City, USA, **So**uth of **Ho**uston Street, thus **SoHo**, just south of **Greenwich Village** (The Village). Once a warehouse and industrial area, it was slowly converted into artists' lofts, galleries, avant-garde shops, bars and clubs. It began to open up in the 1970s due to high rents in The Village and a need for more **counterculture** living and playing space. Greenwich Village and SoHo were the center of hippie and counterculture activity in New York City and the East Coast, with Boston and Cambridge, Massachusetts, as a close second.

Soka Gakkai *religion* a **Buddhist** sect prominent in America during the hippie era, which used the mantra **Namu Myoho Renge Kyo** (*Na maho renga keyo*) to make material wishes come true. In Soka Gakkai, Buddhism reached its most materialistic level. It was believed that a person who wanted a new car or a particular lover could merely recite this phrase over and over again, and the desired person or object would become theirs. It is typical of America that such a selfish religion should become popular here. (See: **Namu Myoho Renge Kyo**)

solar collector usually considered to refer to **photovoltaic cells**, which work by converting sunlight into electricity. The cells are made primarily of **silicon**, the second most abundant element in the earth's crust and the same semiconductor material used in computers. When the silicon is combined with several other materials, it exhibits unique electrical properties when exposed to sunlight. Electrons are energized by the light and move through the silicon. This is known as the photovoltaic effect and results in direct current (DC) electricity. Photovoltaic cells have no moving parts, are virtually maintenance-free, and have a working life of 20 to 30 years. A solar collector can sometimes be merely a device that exposes pipes filled with water to sunlight. The water is heated by the sun and used for bathing or home heating.

solar energy or **solar power** *social issues* energy that can be harvested from the rays of the sun. Either passive energy created by the heat of the sun warming air or water, or **photovoltaic** energy, a chemical reaction that creates electricity. Not until the 1960s was solar power considered for anything other than growing crops and drying clothes. (See: **photovoltaic** or **solar collector**)

sold on convinced, supportive. To be a fan or advocate of something or someone. Example: "Kerry is **sold on** brown rice as the salvation of the American colon."

sold out, (to have) to have given in to **materialism**, sold oneself or one's creativity for money. To have acquiesced to the **mainstream** way of thinking without regard to one's own moral convictions. Example: "He **sold out** and bought a condo."

Soledad Brothers (Jan. 17, 1970-Aug. 21, 1971) *social issues* **George Jackson**, John Clutchette and Fleeta Drumgo, three Black prisoners at the Soledad maximum security prison in California who were accused of killing a guard. On January 14, 1970, three other Black prisoners were shot at Soledad, and a judgment of justifiable homicide was granted to the guard who shot them. Three days later during a riot protesting the killings, another guard was pushed over a railing to his death. Jackson, Clutchette and Drumgo were accused of killing the guard and became the "Soledad Brothers." On August 8, 1970, at the Marin County, California, Court House, George's brother Jonathan Jackson attempted to free inmates on trial there and take hostages to exchange for his brother, who had been moved to San Quentin. Jonathan took over the court and held Superior Court Judge Harold Haley captive with the help of three prisoners, William Christmas, John Mc-Clain and Ruchell McGee. In the ensuing gun battle, Jonathan Jackson, Christmas, McClain and Judge Haley were killed. On August 21, 1971, in another riot at San Quentin, George Jackson, two other prisoners and three guards were killed. **Angela Davis**, then a Professor of Philosophy at UCLA, was accused and tried for supplying the weapons used in the Marin County Court House battle, but was later acquitted. (See: **Angela Davis**)

soles shoes.

solid a term of approval. This word evolved during the **beat** and hippie eras from a purely inanimate physical definition to a term describing human emotions. As a beatnik term, it was often a conversation filler. Example: "**Solid,**

man, let's play bongos." In the hippie era, it moved on to describe more of a literal appreciation of skill. Example: "He's a **solid** bongo player."

Solomon the name for the sun in numerous languages. Considered the mystical expression of light, knowledge and understanding.

Solomon's seal *occult* two interlaced triangles, the angles of which form the six-pointed star. Often, one of the triangles is dark and the other light, symbolizing the union of **soul** and body. According to **occult** symbolism, the upward point of the emblem represents the human head or intelligence; the two upper outstretched points represent sympathy with everything that lives; the two lower points indicate human responsibility, and the point at the bottom, pointing earthward, represents procreative power. Also called Solomon's sign.

Solomon's Temple *occult* in **occult** literature, "the human body." It refers to the great temple built in Jerusalem by Solomon, King of Israel, in the tenth century B.C. This temple is given many symbolic interpretations.

solstice "standing still." One of two days in the year when the sun appears to be standing still just before it begins to turn back in its north-to-south or south-to-north journey during the course of a year. The summer solstice, when the sun is at its northernmost point, is approximately June 21, the longest day of the year; the winter solstice, when the sun is at its southernmost, is around December 21, the shortest day. These days, along with the spring and fall equinox, have been celebrated by farmers and agrarian peoples for thousands of years due to their importance to the growing cycle. Because of the hippie culture's attraction to the spiritual activities of such ancient cultures as the **Druids**, many equinox and solstice parties, festivals, and gatherings took place during the 1960s and 1970s. (See: **autumnal equinox** and **vernal equinox**)

Soma *religion* the name of a **Vedic** (**Hindu**) god.

soma *drugs* a term used in the **counterculture** to indicate any nectar or refreshment that brings spiritual or emotional satisfaction. **2.** a mythological plant, the juice of which was the favorite drink of the **Vedic** gods. In reality, the juice from the Indian "soma" plant fermented into an hallucinogenic drink, partaken in Hindu temples to induce trances and give supernatural powers. **3.** fly-agaric, "the divine mushroom of immortality." A bright red mushroom, indigenous to birch forests. An **hallucinogenic** known as the **magic mushroom**.

sombitch a colloquial shortening of the phrase "son of a bitch." Either a cowboy or Black American term, according to different sources.

some *sex* another euphemism for sex. Example: "Tonight, I'm going out to get me **some**. I hope I don't require penicillin to get rid of it."

some skin a hand shake. Example: "Say, brother, give me **some skin**."

some skin *sex* another euphemism for sex. Example: "Tonight, I'm gona' get me **some skin**, brown, white, yellow or red."

*something else unusual, unique. Used to describe someone or something that is meant to set them apart. It could be positive or negative. Examples: "That girl is **something else**." "That stupid movie was **something else**."

something fierce an exclamation to intensify an emotion. It could be positive or negative. Examples: "I love that girl **something fierce**." "I hate that stupid movie **something fierce**."

some Z's sleep. Example: "I got to catch me **some Z's**."

Son of One *drugs* a **cannabis oil** that appeared in the early 1970s. It replace the short-lived supply called **The One**. Cannabis oil and **hash oil** are usually smoked like **opium** or **hashish**. They can also be spread on rolling papers of a cigarette or **marijuana** joint or mixed with marijuana or some other dried leaf, such as parsley.

soothsayer *occult* a diviner; a person able to foretell future events. Interest in the **occult** and supernatural blossomed during the hippie era out of curiosity and a desire to explore all aspects of religion in order to make one's own choices. Until the 1960s and 1970s, spiritual life and religion were most often passed down to children from parents who had it passed down

to them. For the most part, people didn't question the spiritual life they inherited. Hippies wanted to test their religion against others and see if it was true or valid for them. The hippie era was a time of experimentation, learning and exploring.

Sony home video recorders the first videotape recorders produced for home use. They became available to the American public in 1965.

sopors *drugs* a Middle Western term for brand name Quaaludes and illegally made quaaludes. Chemical compound, methaqualone, a muscle relaxant. The word sopor means "a deep, lethargic sleep," similar to stupor. From a pharmaceutical company that is now out of business, the tablets were embossed with an A and an S. A story is related that these pills hit Ohio shortly after the Kent State University **demonstrations** in May, 1970, where four students were killed by National Guard bullets. It was believed at the time that the state or Federal government had something to do with the appearance of these pills and that they were meant to help calm the young student population of the area. These special pills were sold six for a dollar and were packaged in a flower-shaped arrangement with one in the middle and five around the outside, like the petals of a flower.

Sorbonne demonstrations *social issues* student protests at the Sorbonne in Paris in May, 1968. These **demonstrations** were sparked by the university administration's handling of the subject of opposite sex visitors in dormitory rooms at a suburban Paris campus. The conflict broadened to other issues of administrative oppression and spread to the student body at the Sorbonne, from which it ignited strikes and demonstrations against the entire French government, eventually paralyzing the country. They took place just after the student demonstrations at Columbia University in New York City and were all a part of what became a worldwide uprising by students against oppressive controls in educational institutions. **Daniel Cohn-Bendit**, "**Danny the Red**," led the Paris demonstrations. (See: **Cohn-Bendit, Daniel**)

sorcerer or **sorceress** a practitioner of black magic, evil or selfish ends who has sold his or her soul to the devil in exchange for powers.

sorry-ass or **sorry-assed** adj. unkempt, unloved, unattractive, undesirable or uninteresting. Example: "Josh is some **sorry-ass** dude. With his pimples, polyester pants and 2.0 GPA, I don't know what he's going to do for a life." Same as the lesser used **tired-ass** or **tired-assed**.

soul the divine, immortal part of a human and, some say, of animals as well. The nonphysical portion of a human being. The part of a human that functions without the vital elements and fluids necessary to keep the body alive. The true **essence** of a person. The part of a person that lives on after death, if only in the hearts and minds of others.

soul a form of **charisma** that manifests through unspoken inner knowledge; undanced steps of beauty and brilliant musical notes left unplayed. Soul is sincerity, honesty and commitment to one's art or ideals. Example: "I don't know why the bastard has **soul**. He doesn't do nothin' but sit there with that smile, but he has it, that dude has **soul** enough for all of us."

soul brother a Black male. **2.** any man or boy with whom one has a strong relationship or close emotional bond.

soul food Southern Black cooking. Foods with roots in the cooking habits of the African American population.

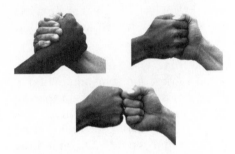

soul handshake a handshake greeting originating in the Black **jazz** culture, which was adopted by the hippie culture. The handshake consists of three movements performed together. Reaching out, the two people grasp each other's thumbs, bringing the palms together. With very close friends, the hands are held close to the chest while standing only inches apart. Then, pulling back, placing the fingers together, and bending them into an interlocking clasp, making a **yin-yang** of fingers and palms. The last move is to make a fist, and punch the fist of the other person, using as much drama as the friendship warrants. This is the basic, original soul handshake; yet there were other modifications, some extending to a long, complicated series of moves. These moves indicated how **cool** a person was or signified membership in a particular group.

soul kitchen a meeting place for souls, a place of sustenance for the soul. A comfortable place, a safe place for one's emotions. Can also be a sexual place of repose. From a Jim Morrison song of the same name.

soul mate a spiritual friend, a person with whom one has close emotional ties or similar aspirations. Can be a romantic relationship.

soul music Black American music. Almost exclusively, this means Black music. Whereas two White men can be soul brothers, it is almost impossible, and this has been proven historically, for a White person to produce soul music. It is not a genre of music that attracts many White performers, and they usually look, and I presume feel, out of place in the effort. There are White soul music producers and songwriters, but no real White soul music performers. Soul music is a mix of sexual subject matter, sung with gospel intensity to funky rhythms. The fathers of soul would have to be **Ray Charles**, **James Brown** and Wilson Picket. Other "soul suppliers" are Sam and Dave, **Smokey Robinson**, **Marvin Gaye**, Jerry Butler, **Aretha Franklin**, The Supremes, The Temptations and The Impressions. Detroit's **Motown Records** was a center for soul music, as were Chicago and Memphis. Funk, disco and hip-hop can be considered offshoots of soul.

Soul on Ice *social issues* an important collection of essays on racial injustice in America, published in 1968 by **Eldridge Cleaver.** Partially written while Cleaver, a Black American radical, was in jail. The book was published after his release from prison and while a member of the **Black Panther Party**. (See: **Cleaver, Eldridge**)

soul power *social issues* like **Black power**, it was, and still is, the collective effort of African Americans to win equality, respect and freedom of move-ment within America. This is one of the battle cries and marching slogans voiced by demonstrators against racial injustice.

soul session a deep conversation or sincere understanding between people.

soul sister a Black female. **2.** any girl or woman with whom one has a strong relationship or close emotional tie.

soul survivor a person of great strength and grace under racial oppression or social pressures.

"Soul Train" a Black counterpart to the TV rock and roll show "American Bandstand." "Soul Train" started in 1970 as a local series in Chicago and later moved to Hollywood. It was a venue in which a group of Black teenagers watched and danced to recording artists who would **lip-sync** their latest hits. (See: **"American Bandstand," "Hullabaloo," "Ready, Steady, Go!," "Shindig."**)

sound out or **sound** (someone) **out** to ask or question. Example: "I won't do it, but why don't you **sound Jim out** to see if he'll jump off the cliff for you?"

sounds music. Usually, music from a broadcast or recorded source, such as a car radio, tape, record player or **boom box**. Example: "Hey, don't mess with my **sounds**. I'm lord of the selection knob and master of volume control."

sound synthesizers *rock & roll* any number of electronic musical instruments that create sound by interrupting or altering an electric current. The **Moog synthesizer** and **theremin** are examples. (See: **Moog synthesizer** and **theremin**)

source *drugs* a drug supplier.

Southern Comfort a sweet, flavored whiskey from New Orleans. Janis Joplin's drink of choice. I never had the privilege of drinking with her, but photos bear this out.

so wasted very drunk or very much under the influence of drugs. **Wasted** means drunk or **stoned**, and the **so** was for special emphasis.

so what? a rebuff, rejection or contradiction. Example: "So you're dating Patti, **so what**? All you'll end up with is a case of the clap and a distaste for **heavy-metal**."

so what else is new? a rejection of information already known. Example: "Roses are red violets are blue, **so what else is new**?"

space the emotional atmosphere required by an individual to feel comfortable or to think clearly. Example: "Give me my **space**; I can't function if you pressure me."

space age anything technical that is not quite understood. Originally an advertising industry term, created to impress the buying public with the technical advancement of a product. It was often intimated that the item had been on one of the space flights or was in some way connected to those endeavors. Example: "Her kitchen is real **space age**; no one can cook in it, but it looks impressive."

space cadet someone whose mind wanders, who is forgetful or slow to grasp situations. Empty headed. From the word space, related to the emptiness of outer space. The word cadet relates to the subject of flying into space, as in a flying cadet. I believe space cadet came first, then space case, and later, the shorter form, spacey.

space case again, someone whose mind wanders, is forgetful or slow to grasp situations. Empty headed. From the word space, related to the emptiness of outer space. The word case relates to a mental institution, as in "mental case."

space–time the unity of space and time. The four-dimensional continuum consisting of the three dimensions of space—length, width and height—plus the element of time.

Spacewar *computer revolution* the first **video game**, created at MIT in the 1960s by a group of computer programmers and engineers calling themselves **hackers**. It was not commercially distributed. Other commercially marketed early games were Computer Space, **Pong**, and later sophistications like Pac-Man, Space Invaders, etc. Video games were some of the first uses of, and experimentations on, personal computers. (See: **Computer Space** and **Pong**)

*spacey, spaced or **spaced out** having a mind that wanders; forgetful or slow to grasp surroundings. Empty headed. From the term "mind in outer space," referring to the emptiness of outer space.

spade a Black person, and, most particularly, a Black man. Not necessarily a derogatory term; it could mean a strong, attractive and virile man. The term comes from playing cards, in which all cards of the spade suit are black. The term black as the ace of spades comes to mind.

Spanish fly *sex* an **aphrodisiac**. Also called cantharis. Originally used on large animals to induce them to mate, and sometimes used on small, reluctant humans to create a desire for sex. Produced from the pulverized wings of a species of beetle (not a fly), *Lytta vesicatoria* or *Cantharis vesicatoria*. The concoction actually creates an irritation of the genitals, which merely gives the illusion of sexual arousal. It is dangerous for humans to employ this method of sexual conquest.

spare change n. money solicited (panhandled) on the streets by hippies. It was an indication of the **spirit** of the hippie that the terms used to ask for money were "spare" and "change." The basic **true hippie** was against capitalism and would be considerate of other people's economical circumstance. Therefore, he would ask for only the small amount of *change* a person was willing and able to *spare*.

spare change v. to solicit (panhandle) for small amounts of money. Example: "Hey, I'm going out to **spare change** for a couple of hours to see if I can get enough for a bucket of wings."

sparkle plenty *drugs* **amphetamines**. **Uppers**.

spastic someone who is uncoordinated. The hippie usage did not refer to persons with medical conditions that cause epileptic seizures or other brain spasms. Hippies, as a rule, did not discriminate against people whose conditions or situations were beyond their control.

spaz short for spastic. Hippies used labels and names to categorize people, as everyone does; yet, most often, they did not place judgments on people's behavior unless it was destructive. Most human activities are acceptable to hippies, yet they could get very upset over greed or social and economic injustice.

spaz-out to go crazy.

S.P.C.H. Society for Prevention of Cruelty to Homosexuals. A parody acronym for a nonexistent organization.

speak to me tell me what you know. Confide in me.

spearchucker a humorous, yet often derogatory, name for a Black person.

Spector, Phil (b. Dec. 25, 1940, Bronx, New York) *rock and pop* the creator of the "wall of sound," which made so many of the late 1950s-early 1960s popular tunes memorable. The "wall of sound" employed layers of music dubbed one over another, numerous guitars, pianos and multiple drummers, often with a background of such normally non-rock and roll instruments as harps and violins. Spector produced and wrote such songs as "To Know Him Is To Love Him", 1958; "Spanish Harlem," 1961; "He's a Rebel," 1962; and "Da Doo Ron Ron," 1963. He also co-produced The Beatles' song "Let It Be," 1969, and George Harrison's *All Things Must Pass* album in 1971. He has spent long periods of time as a recluse, but when he produces, he is a master. Inducted into the Rock and Roll Hall of Fame in 1989.

speed *drugs* **methamphetamines** from the family of **amphetamines**, a synthetic stimulant similar in effect to **cocaine**, yet longer lasting and less expensive. Brand names are **Methedrine** and Desoxyn. After the Controlled Substance Act of 1970, the illegal production of amphetamines began. Predominant street names of methamphetamine in the 1960s and 70s were speed, **meth**, **crystal**, **crank** and **ice**. Usually swallowed during the hippie era, the new powered forms are now snorted, injected and smoked. Making this drug at home has become a cottage industry, and many of the manufacturers are not very good at it. There are inherent dangers to this drug and severe consequences from taking bad doses. Most recommendations are to stay away from this drug; it will kill you prematurely. Remember, all things in moderation; thinking people use their drugs, foolish people use drugs that will kill them.

speedball *drugs* a mixture of **heroin** and some form of **speed**, like **cocaine** or heroin, and a designer drug, such as **ecstasy**.

speed bump any delay or disruption. Named after the bumps placed across streets to reduce the speed of traffic. Example: "The broken leg was only a minor **speed bump** in her party life."

speed freak someone who takes too much speed; **methamphetamines** and **amphetamines**. The amount is subjective since, for many people, any amount of speed is too much.

speed kills a slogan warning that **methamphetamines** and **amphetamines** are dangerous.

spell a spoken or written incantation. A symbol believed to have magical or supernatural powers and effects.

spent the **euphoria** following **climax** in sexual intercourse. **2.** tired, worn out, finished.

spiel a well-planned and executed verbal communication that has a feeling of insincerity. Originally a Yiddish term.

spiffy used in place of "beautiful" or "fantastic" in humorous commentary. A very old word revitalized in the hippie era, employed primarily as sarcasm about someone who is overdressed, showy or gaudy.

spike to add some form of intoxicant or mind-expanding drug to an otherwise inert food or beverage.

spike *drugs* a hypodermic needle for injecting drugs.

spiked a beverage with alcohol or a psychedelics added. Sometimes this is done without the knowledge or consent of all those consuming it, which may not be a good Idea. There is nothing wrong with ingesting stimulants as long as people make the informed choice themselves. **2.** high on drugs.

spiked punch a fruit beverage that has been augmented with some form of **psychedelic**. The idea of spiking punch was not new to the hippie culture, but the **spike** was usually more potent than the brandy normally used by conservative stuff.

spike up *drugs* to inject drugs.

spin doctor a public relations person or publicist experienced in creating or protecting an image. The **spin** comes from to "put a good spin" on a bad situation. The **doctor**, of course, is someone who "heals."

spin off n. something a basis in something else. It comes, I believe, from the situation in which a planet, moon or sun loses a portion of itself, which spins off to form another celestial body. **2.** to use some part of one thing to produce another.

Spinal Tap *rock & roll spoof* for all practical purposes, a fictitious rock band. The members were David St. Hubbins (b. Michael McKean, Oct. 17, 1947, New York City), gtr, voc.; Nigel Tufnel (b. Christopher Guest, Feb. 5, 1948, New York City), gtr., voc.; Derek Smalls (b. Harry Shearer, Dec. 23, 1943, Los Angeles, Calif.), bass, voc.;

and various drummers. A hoax rock and roll band supposedly formed in London in 1967, but which was actually thrown together in 1978 for one song, "Rock and Roll Nightmare," for an ABC-TV comedy special co-directed by Rob Reiner. McKean, Guest and Shearer, writers and comedians, worked with Reiner and eventually put together a movie about the fictitious 1967 rock group. The 1984 movie, "This is Spinal Tap," has a cult following and is a must-see.

spirit the vital and divine **essence** in nature. The activating element of life. Spirit is what makes you want to live without knowing why, what makes you create without understanding why, but you do so because it feels good.

spiritual awakening a discovery of or experience with some form of religion that changes one's life for the better.

spiritual revolution *religion* the awakening of young, White, Anglo-Saxon Protestant Americans to the values of religions other than Christianity. The 1960s and 70s were a mind-expanding time, during which many people explored religions from other cultures. Until then, spiritual life and religion were inherited from parents who had also inherited it. For the most part, before the hippie era, children didn't question their families' religious beliefs. Hippies wanted to explore other religious beliefs in order to make their own decisions and find new avenues to the peace of mind spirituality can give.

spiritualism *occult* any activity or religion which attempts to communicate with the dead. Ouija boards, table lifting and automatic writing are examples of some of the activities connected with spiritualism. Most Christian religions denounce the practice of spiritualism.

spliff *drugs* a **marijuana** cigarette. The term comes from Jamaica and the **Rastafarian** reggae culture and often indicates a large **joint** rolled with several papers.

split to leave or go someplace else. A shortening of "split from the scene." This word originated with the beat movement and was adopted by the hippie culture. It is now used primarily in jest since people feel uncomfortable saying it.

split beaver same as **beaver shot** and **spread beaver**. (See: **beaver shot**)

split the scene or **split from the scene** to leave or go someplace else. Originated with the **beat** movement.

splurge to spend money freely, to be extravagant. **2.** in some places, it means to leave.

Spock, Dr. Benjamin (1903-1998) *social issues* "the baby doctor," pediatrician, psychiatrist, social activist and author of many books on child raising. In the 1960s, he became increasingly interested in social issues and was prominent in the **anti-war movement. He was associated with **SANE, Committee for a Sane Nuclear Policy**. In 1968, Spock was tried and convicted for counseling draft evaders, but the conviction was overturned in 1969. In 1970, he wrote a book on his views of contemporary society entitled *Decent and Indecent,* and in 1972, he was the presidential candidate for the pacifist People's Party. He was responsible for getting **Dr. Martin Luther King, Jr.**, involved in the anti-war movement, and he and King marched together several times. Dr. Spock spoke at many **peace** rallies, including some of the very first at the University of California, Berkeley in 1965.

sponge n. a person who takes and doesn't give in return. From the way that a sponge absorbs liquid and releases it only when squeezed. **2.** v. to take without giving in return.

spook v. to scare someone. At one time, a cowboy term meaning to scare a herd of cows. Originally, it meant to be scared by a ghost or a "spook."

spook n. derogatory term for an African or African American person. **2.** someone who is strange, possibly frightening.

spoon *sex* a position in sexual intercourse with the couple lying on their sides, the man behind, entering the woman's anus or **vagina**. **2.** a method of caressing the clitoris with one's tongue during **cunnilingus**.

spoon *drugs* the spoon used to cook powered drugs in water prior to injecting them intravenously. **2.** a gram of **heroin**.

spoonful *drugs* a tablespoonful of powered drugs, approximately two grams.

sports of the hippie era   sex, **psychedelics**, dancing and **Frisbee**.

spot v. to give an advantage or handicap to someone. Example: "Play me a game of pool, and I'll **spot** you three balls."

spout off to talk, usually to speak incessantly, with aggression or boring authority.

spread beaver same as **beaver shot** and **split beaver**. (See: **beaver shot**)

spring for to pay for. Example: "Sure, I'll except your psychotherapy as long as you **spring for** the beer."

Springsteen, Bruce (b. Sept. 23, 1949, Freehold, New Jersey) *rock & roll* a working-class rocker who hit the scene in the mid-1970s and produced some of the most popular dance tracks of the late hippie era. Springsteen's lyrics were heard through the rock tracks, and he was soon acknowledged as a poet of the middle class. He eventually became one of the top stars of the 1980s. Inducted into the Rock and Roll Hall of Fame in 1999.

Spy v. Spy a cartoon originating in *MAD Magazine* in the early 1960s, drawn by Antonio Prohias. Conceived as an anti-Castro strip, it has since become the most popular of the magazine's cartoons.

***square** a person who is not contemporary; someone unaware of current behavior. An **uncool** person. A **beatnik** and hippie term used primarily in TV sitcoms today.

square trustworthy, acceptable. Relating to the architectural term for perfection; being in correct perpendicular right angles to the world. An old term revitalized during the hippie era with a different slant. Example: Old use: "Kim will be **square** with you." Hippie use: "Kim is on the **square**."

square off to confront. Example: "Cool it or I'll **square off** and kiss you."

squat nothing. Example: "You don't know **squat** about women if you think tickling is **foreplay**."

squeaker a close call. Meaning it just squeaked by. Example: "The game was a **squeaker**."

squeeze a boyfriend, girlfriend, husband, wife or lover. Short for **main squeeze**. **Squeeze** stands for hug.

squirrely restless, eccentric, nutty.

stacked having big breasts. Example: "That girl's **stacked,** and I don't mean big hair."

stag alone, without a date. Example: "I'm going **stag** to the party, 'cause they'll be a lot of chicks to pick up on."

stage dive a jump of faith, from a stage into the arms (hopefully) of the audience. An act of foolhardy bravado performed by **punk rock** fans, band members and someone other than me, in which they throw themselves off the stage, hoping to be caught and saved by the crowd. Oops!#*@.

stallion a man with a large penis. **2.** a man with a reputation as an aggressive copulator. I did not use the word lover because this term most often refers to a narcissistic individual. Stallion is not considered derogatory by everyone, but to most people it is a negative designation reserved for someone who is an arrogant or self-centered bedmate.

stand-in a political demonstration in which people crowd into a college administration office, government building or public place and just stand there to create a nuisance, thus expressing their support for a cause. It's a sit-in without wrinkling your pants.

stand the heat to survive the challenge, withstand the abuse or accept the scrutiny. Examples: "Can you **stand the heat** being the only straight man in a homosexual bar?"

standup guy someone who can be trusted. Example: "He's a **standup guy,** but he's too wrecked to stand up."

Stanley, Augustus Owsley, III *drugs* Augustus Owsley Stanley III is the creator of the famous **Owsley Acid. Considered the King of **LSD**, he was the unofficial Mayor of San Francisco in the

1960s. Sometimes called Augustus Owsley or Augustus Stanley Owsley, he is most often described as just "Owsley." On February 21, 1965, his home **methedrine** laboratory in Berkeley, nicknamed the "Green Factory," was raided by California narcotics agents. Owsley beat the charges and

Owsley photographed at Monterey Pop by Jim Marshall ©

then sued the authorities for his confiscated lab equipment. He got the equipment back, a good thing, because he had important things to do with it. Owsley and his girlfriend, who happened to be a graduate chemistry student at the University of California, visited Los Angeles and returned to the Bay Area in April of 1965 with the ingredients necessary to change the course of history. Using the name Bear Research Group, Owsley ordered the raw materials to make his celebrated concoction. His first acid was too heavy duty, but he soon got the dosage right and created the most exceptional LSD on record. His total production at that time was less than a half a **kilogram**, but it amounted to what is estimated at 1 1/2 million doses, or eternity. Owsley was involved with **Kesey's Pranksters** and is said to have applied some of his profits from LSD to the purchase and creation of sound equipment for the **Grateful Dead**. Owsley is reportedly the grandson of a US Senator and Governor of Kentucky; who would have thought? Owsley is said to have been responsible for creating the **acid** called Orange Sunshine. He is also credited with the **Purple Haze** acid especially made for **Monterey Pop Festival**, on which **Jimi Hendrix** was **tripping** when he burned his guitar on stage that weekend. **Country Joe McDonald** said that he ingested 1 1/2 tabs of Owsley **STP** before his performance at Monterey Pop.

star a person of quality. Example: "He's a **star** in my estimation, even though he's just a pizza cook on the corner." **2.** a person of fame. There is no official formula of measurement used to establish who is a star. The criteria could be the number of records or movie tickets sold, appearances on the cover of *Rolling Stone* or the decibel level of screams at concerts. Whatever it is, everyone knows who really is a star and who isn't.

star dust *drugs* cocaine. (See: **cocaine**)

star-fucker a **groupie**; someone who seeks out famous people in order to sleep with them for personal gratification and bragging rights. (See: **groupie**)

"Star Trek" one of the two most important serialized television shows of the hippie era. **"M.A.S.H."** was the other. Created by ex-Los Angeles Policeman Gene Roddenberry. In 1951, Roddenberry wrote his first TV scripts; in 1954, he left the police force to write full time, and in 1964, he created "Star Trek." The first show aired on September 22, 1966, and was entitled "Where No Man Has Gone Before." Many sources say the series aired only from 1967 to 1969, but it had a life before and after those dates. The most important elements of "Star Trek" and the reasons for its appreciation by the true hippie are that it promoted ethnic and religious tolerance and nonviolence. The phaser was created for "Star Trek"; the first totally debilitating, yet nonlethal, weapon, and lethal force was used only as a last resort. For the moral and ethical content of the show, we have Roddenberry to thank. ****Rodenberry** is one of the thirty-five most influential people of the hippie era.

start shit to create a confrontation or physical conflict. Example: "If you **start shit** in this bar, I won't step in to save your ass."

start something to create a conflict or confrontation. Example: "Don't **start something** with your ol' lady in front of my new girlfriend. I don't want her to grasp reality just yet."

stash n. *drugs* a place to hide or keep drugs. The circumstance of the hippie era took a verb, **stash**, meaning "to put away," and changed it into a noun, "a place to hide something away." A stash was anything the creative mind of a hippie could devise. Some stashes were cigar boxes, some were unique containers hand-crafted from exotic woods, others could be pottery bowls or tin tobacco containers. One of my personal favorites was a purple velvet Chevas Regal bag.

stash n. *drugs* a hidden supply of drugs. The original verb **stash**, meaning "to put away," evolved during the hippie era into a noun, meaning "a place to hide something," then evolved further to describe "what is hidden." This is a good example of how language develops.

stash short for moustache. Example: "Say, man, is that a new **stash**, or did you just eat a peach?!"

stash pipe *drugs* a pipe with a chamber for holding extra **marijuana**. Some of these pipes allow the smoke from the burning **dope** to permeate and strengthen the stash.

static an argument or verbal conflict. Example: "Don't give me **static** about my smoking habits; the more you complain, the more I retreat into the **ozone**."

stats short for statistics.

status report a business term introduced to the American public around 1965. It refers to a written or verbal breakdown of material, financial or organizational circumstances.

status symbol *social issues* any object, the possession of which increases one's value in the eyes of others. A status symbol can be a useful object, but it is most often just an unnecessarily expensive, big or flashy item. The **counterculture** had status symbols, just as straight society did. One of the most interesting items of hippie peer envy was **paraphernalia**. Owning a particularly creative **hash** pipe automatically elevated one into the upper strata of **super doper**.

stay cool most common definitions of this phrase embody all the misunderstandings that **uptight** society has about the hippie culture. The **true hippie** definition of stay cool asks only that one maintain a perspective on the value of emotions. It does not mean to control the emotions; it does not mean to be passive or detached about life and life's situations. It means don't **cave in** to the pressures of a world that seems to be concentrating on your destruction. Tell it to fuck itself; it's only life. You've got more important things to do; you're busy with eternity.

stay focused pay attention, get serious about what you're doing. Another word that had a primarily physical definition before the hippie era, at which time it evolved into an emotional usage. The word **focus** went from dealing almost exclusively with physical vision and eyesight into becoming an attitude and a mental activity.

stay loose v. relax.

stay on (someone's) **case** to keep at someone, to bother them or to continue to remind them about something. Example: "I'm going to **stay on your case** until you replace the **brown rice** you borrowed from our communal pad."

stay the course *politics* conservative rhetoric eventually attributed to Ronald Reagan. It means, we think, to stay within the straight and narrow, conservative course of tradition, loyalty and self-denial.

steady control. Example: "If Josh doesn't **steady** his nerves, he'll explode all over us."

steady on stay in control. Example: "**Steady on,** friend, we're all in the same leaky boat."

Steal This Book a book by **Abbie Hoffman**, published in 1971. Library of Congress number 72-157115 (stolen from the Library of Congress). (See: **Abbie Hoffman**)

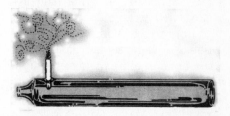

steamboat a device for smoking **marijuana** consisting of a tube with a bowl or hole for the dope, a mouth hole, and another hole to regulate the air flow. *A Child's Garden of Grass (The Official Handbook for Marijuana Users)* by Jack

S. Margolis and Richard Clorfene states that the difference between a steamboat and a pipe is, "A pipe has two holes, a steamboat three or more."

steamed mad. Example: "Grip was **steamed** when Zonker burned the **tofu.**"

Steinem, Gloria (1934-) *social issues* journalist. She went underground and became a Playboy bunny for three weeks to write an expose that was published in *Show* magazine in May and June of 1963. Steinem is one of the creators of *Ms. Magazine.* A preview issue of 300,000 copies was published and sold in January, 1972, and the first regular issue appeared in July, 1972. A woman of stature and energy who, along with **Germaine Greer, became the ideal image of heterosexual **feminism** to the world. Attractive, intelligent and independent, these two women were loved and feared by the stereotypical male. Their breaking of the stereotypical female mold was one of the best things that ever happened to the male–female relationship.

Steppenwolf *rock & roll* a **hard rock** band formed in Los Angeles in 1967. It had many incarnations throughout the 1970s with John Kay, gtr., voc., and Goldy McJohn, organ, as the main prevailing members. Steppenwolf's first hit, "Born to Be Wild," in 1968, was written by Dennis McCrohan (a.k.a. Mars Bonfire) and is where the term **heavy-metal** first appeared in music, thus starting the genre. Steppenwolf's second hit, "Magic Carpet Ride," in 1968, is also a rock anthem of the period.

step on to **cut** dope with an inactive ingredient, such as baby laxatives, aspirin, sugar, powdered milk, talcum powder, tetracaine or procaine (topical anesthetics). A practice of increasing the weight of drugs by adding a cheap substance in order to make more money from the sale of the product.

Stevens, Cat (b. Steven Demetri Georgiou, July 21, 1947, London, Eng.) *folk/rock & roll* no other singer/songwriter is more an element of the hippie era soundtrack than this enigmatic person. His songs were filled with mystique, **magic** and imagery that **elevated** us and defined many of our thoughts and feelings. Songs like "Moon Shadow" and "Peace Train" on his 1971 album, *Tea for the Tillerman,* forever established Stevens as a poet of the times. His soundtrack combined within the humorously macabre movie "Harold and Maude" in 1971 is a view into the surreal **essence** of the era. Stevens always seemed to have a tenuous grasp of reality, and he endured bouts as a recluse and times of extreme materialistic rejection, eventually disavowing his fame and becoming a **Muslim** in the late 1970s. His Muslim name is Yusuf Islam.

Stewart, Rod (b. January 10, 1945, London Eng.) *rock & roll* one of the best entertainers of the 1970s, who produced some of the most danceable music. Particularly recognized for his **disco** era contributions, yet he was a gritty and exciting singer and performer in his early days with the **Jeff Beck** Group and Faces. Inducted into the Rock and Roll Hall of Fame in 1994.

stick *drugs* a **marijuana** cigarette. From stick of tea. **2.** short for **Thai stick**, a **cannabis** leaf product from Thailand, wrapped around a bamboo stick and tied with a string. This technique was created to facilitate drying of the plant and permit easy transport.

stick it shut up, leave me alone, **get lost**, etc. From **stick it up your ass**.

stick it to or **stuck it to** to take advantage of or to deceive someone. Examples: "**Stick it to him,** before he **sticks it to** you, like she **stuck it to** me."

stick it to *sex* in a sexual connotation, to have intercourse.

stiffed or **to stiff** cheated, short changed. Example: "The farmer **stiffed** us on the cow manure, and then mushrooms popped up." **2.** to get nothing. Example: "If you **stiff** me, I'll have to get my love on the corner."

stigmata *occult/religion* the appearance of scars or wounds that mysteriously appear on someone matching those supposedly inflicted upon Christ at crucifixion. A religious affectation that has not yet been proven to anyone's satisfaction, except for those who are in a position to benefit economically, such as the Catholic Church.

sting to fool, cheat or steal from someone.

stogie *drugs* a **marijuana** cigarette.

stoked excited. Example: "Gunner was **stoked** when he learned he'd been accepted into the Bean Sprout of the Month Club."

stomp, stomp ass or **stomp rump** to beat someone or outdo them in some way. In some circles, it referred to a physical fight. Example: "I'm going to **stomp ass** in the organic tomato competition."

stompin' ground home **turf**, familiar territory, or neighborhood.

stone *modifier* total, complete, whole. Example: "Duke's a **stone** fool for Sue, who is a **stone fox**." Other examples

of the usage: **stone liar, stone thief, stone idiot.**

stoned *drugs* to have one's mind and actions pleasantly relaxed by drugs. Under the influence of a drug. Can indicate the effects of any drug, most often that of a **psychoactive** experience, such as **marijuana**, yet also it can be **LSD** or a natural **psychedelic**. Most closely related to the word **high**, yet similar in usage to **bombed** or **tripping.** The effects of most other drugs, such as opiates and methamphetamines would more likely be called: blasted, drugged, **wasted**, **nodding** or **whacked out**. One of the most typical hippie words, almost exclusive to that era, yet it does find some use today in non-drug applications meaning to have fun in one's mind.

stoned to have one's mind and emotions pleasantly altered by some experience.

stone fox a beautiful girl.

stone free liberated, uncontrolled by others, completely free. From the lyrics of a **Jimi Hendrix** song.

stone me give me some of your **marijuana**. Do something to get me **stoned** or excited.

stoner *drugs* someone who does a lot of drugs.

Stonewall Rebellion *social issues* a confrontation between police and gay men in New York City from June 27-29, 1969, prompted by a police raid on the Stonewall Inn, a gay bar on Christopher Street. The party raided by the police was a wake for Judy Garland, who had just died. (See: **Gay & Lesbian Movement Events, Groups and Leaders** starting on page 601 in **Lists** at the back of this book)

stony (positive) someone or something profound. A person who is very spiritual, enlightened or intelligent. Example: "Heather's a **stony** person; it's a religious experience hearing her discuss compost."

stony (negative) lost or confused. "Deak's too **stony** for me; I can never understand that bean sprout philosophy of his."

Stooges, The *punk rock* the predecessors of **punk** with their first albums in the late 1960s. **Iggy Pop** was their frontman.

stoolie or **stooley** short for stool pigeon. Someone who informs to the authorities.

*stop and smell the roses a suggestion to slow down and enjoy life. This is a very typical hippie addition to our language. One of the prominent themes during the 1960s and 70s was to improve one's quality of life by enjoying the natural beauty and simple pleasures of existence in this world.

story a lie.

STP *drugs* a pseudo-psychedelic synthetic **amphetamine** variant. Similar to MDA. It is said that the initial formula was stolen from **Dow Chemical**. The initials stand for **Serenity, Tranquility** and **Peace**, although it is suspected that there is some subtle humorous connection to the motor oil STP. Tim Scully is credited in some part with STP's concoction. It is basically the chemical compound (4 methyl 2,5 dimethoxy amphetamine). STP produces a 12-hour experience of heightened stimulation and mild psychedelic activity. **Augustus Owsley Stanley III** made a batch (Owsley STP) for the **Monterey Pop Festival** weekend of June 16-18, 1967. **Country Joe McDonald** says he ingested 1 1/2 tabs of Owsley's STP before his performance at Monterey Pop. Owsley Stanley was a professional, but making this drug has become a cottage industry and many of the manufacturers are not very good at it. (See: **Stanley, Augustus Owsley, III**)

straight a person who is not a hippie. A term introduced to the American public around 1965.

*straight or **go straight** to conform to the majority rules and mores. This is not always the right path for everyone. As with homosexuality, if a **gay** person tries to be straight, it can be psychologically damaging. How far to step outside of society is a decision each person must make personally. One must think about the consequences of bending rules and consider the social ramifications of offending others.

straight *sex* heterosexual, as opposed to **homosexual**.

straight-ahead guy a trustworthy person.

straight arrow or **straight shooter** a trustworthy person.

strap on *sex* to have sexual intercourse.

Strat *rock & roll* short for **Stratocaster**. (See: **Stratocaster**)

Stratocaster *rock & roll* arguably the most popular **rock and roll** guitar. A solid body electric guitar manufactured by the **Fender guitar company**, whose guiding force was Leo Fender. Developed in the late 1950s, it is a scaled-down version of the earlier Telecaster, designed to give better comfort in playing, and also a more radical look. The Stratocaster was the first guitar to have a built-in tremolo unit and to offer three pick-ups. Truly a breakthrough in instruments and one that provided many new opportunities for creative sounds that characterized the psychedelic era of music. (See: **Fender Guitar Company**)

"Strawberry Fields Forever" a place of tranquility, peace and maybe a little frivolous sex and drugs. From **The Beatles'** 1967 song of the same name. At the height of the hippie era, this song personified **the dream** of all **counterculture** devotees wishing for a perfect world in which to live.

Strawberry Fields a portion of **Golden Gate Park** in San Francisco that was unoffically named after **The Beatles'** song. This area of the park was the location of much of the hippie activity during the "**Summer of Love**."

Strawberry Fields an area of Central Park West at West 72nd Street in New York City, across from The Dakota building where **John Lennon** and Yoko Ono lived. The John Lennon memorial and the "Imagine" mosaic are located there.

Strawberry Statement, The an important book about the **free-speech movement** and the occupation of the Columbia University campus by student demonstrators. Written in 1969 by James Simon Kunen, an 18-year-old student.

streaking the act of running past or through a place, function or group of people while wearing nothing. Nude jogging. In the first few years of the 1970s, it appeared as a fad. It began as an attempt at breaking down inhibitions, moved on to become an act intended to revolt conservative decorum,

and ended up as an initiation test for fraternities and sororities. The most famous streaker was Robert Opel, who streaked the 1974 Academy Awards.

street anything **counterculture** or outside the structure of **straight** society. Something done or made outside society, such as illegally made prescription drugs. Example: "She is **street**, her clothes are **street** and her drugs are **street**."

street hustler someone who panhandles on the street for money.

street people in the 1960s and early 70s, they were young kids, mostly **runaways**, either homeless or living in **crash pads**, who spent their days on the street asking for **spare change**, smoking dope and congregating for conversation, fun and music. During the hippie era, this was not a dead end for most kids, but a temporary adventure as they spread their wings, leaving the oppression of their family homes. It changed during the last two decades of the 20th century as the government (**Mr. Reagan**) closed down many mental health facilities and Vietnam vets, many suffering from post-traumatic stress syndrome and war-related drug addictions, hit the streets.

street theater in the tradition of early theatrical performance, which often took place outdoors and on the streets, the hippie era saw a street theater resurgence. (See: **guerrilla theater**)

street-wise smart, able to survive and stay out of trouble while functioning in the rough society of city streets.

stretch, (a) something hard to imagine, a dubious concept or fact difficult to believe. Another colloquial shortening of an older phrase, in this case "a stretch of the imagination."   Example: "His story about little green men was a **stretch**, especially since he's color blind."

stretch out   relax, lie down, possibly nap or sleep.

strike *drugs* a dose of drugs, a.k.a. **hit**.

string   a progression of events or a number of similar things. From a string of pearls. Example: "I had a **string** of bad luck until I was able to **string** together a few ideas."

string (someone) **along**   to lead someone on with expectations. Example: "Don't **string Bobby along**; she'll bust your balls when she finds out you prefer boys."

strip   to remove one's clothes.

strip   to take away. Example. "With just the word 'limp,' she can **strip** him of his dignity!"

strobe lights   flashing lights used in dance clubs to enhance the atmosphere and excite the crowd into a dancing frenzy. They were often synchronized to the beat of the music. Strobe stands for stroboscope, a device created in the late 1950s to experiment with the possibility that flashing lights might create **hallucinations**. **William Burroughs** experimented with a stroboscope.

strobing   a **hallucinatory** phenomenon created by **LSD**, in which phantom lights or images flash before one's eyes.

stroboscopic machine   a device created in the late 1950s to experiment with the possibility that flashing lights might create **hallucinations**. **William Burroughs** experimented with such a machine. Someone who has experienced them may feel that these lights can create a druglike **euphoria**, but that may be the result of contact-high phenomenon or the fact that, at many such dances, there was **marijuana** smoke in the air.

stroke   sexual intercourse. **2. masturbation**.

strokes   emotional support to someone in the way of kind words or compliments. Example: "Tiffany needs some **strokes** right now; her wandering Jew is dropping all of its leaves."

stroke yourself (go) a rejection. Similar to "you're lying to me," "I don't believe you," "stop jacking me off," "go masturbate yourself." A masculine use only. This comment is usually accompanied by a hand stroking motion, as if one were masturbating.

stroking me (you're) you're lying to me, I don't believe you. A masculine use only. This comment is usually accompanied with a hand stroking motion, as if one were masturbating.

stroke the lizard   to masturbate.

Struggle, The *social issues* the fight for **civil rights** and freedom from racial intolerance waged by African Americans since the early 1960s.

strung out   addicted to drugs. Emotionally dependent on anything, such as another person's attention, food or physical activities.

stud   an attractive or virile man, heterosexual or **homosexual**.

studly   attractive or virile. Example: "He's very **studly**." **2.** another way of saying stud with a sarcastic or humorous tone. Example: "Hey, **studly,** who you pokin' tonight?"

Student Nonviolent Coordinating Committee (SNCC) pronounced **snick** *social issues* an organization created to enforce and effect school desegregation. Founded on April 15, 1960, at Shaw University in Raleigh, North Carolina, by Ella J. Baker and Reverend James M. Lawson, Jr. Early leaders were Marion Barry, first chairman; James Foreman, executive director in 1963; **Stokley Carmichael**, chairman in 1966; and **H. Rap Brown**, chairman in May, 1967. Other active members in the early 1960s included Bob Moses, Mississippi leader; John Lewis, Diane Nash, Hollis Watkins and Curtis Hayes. SNCC organized the first lunchroom sit-ins, which were conducted in Greensboro, North Carolina, and helped to achieve school desegregation, fair employment laws, and the right to vote for minorities and the poor.

Students for a Democratic Society (SDS) *social issues* one of the most radical of the anti-war groups, considered a left-wing organization, founded in 1960, refined and defined at Port Huron in 1962. It was founded and led by Al Haber, Sharon Jeffrey, Bob Ross, Dickie Magidoff, **Tom Hayden**, **Rennie Davis**, Dorothy Dawson, Clark Kissinger, **Jerry Rubin**, Carl Oglesby, Carl Davidson, **Bill Ayers**, Mike Klonsky, Paul Potter and others. The SDS was involved in planning the first national **anti-war** demonstrations in late 1964 and early 1965. The SDS evolved from the first student peace and freedom group in America, the Student League for Industrial Democracy (SLID), an offshoot of the League for Industrial Democracy (LID), which actually contributed to the SDS financing through the years. The SDS was considered "The Student Department of the League for Industrial Democracy." These "League" organizations had early Communist Party connections; thus, many people feared the SDS as a subversive group.

Although many considered the SDS an anti-war organization, it was involved in the **free-speech**, **civil rights** and peace and freedom movements as well. In 1968, a number of **SDS** members, becoming even more radical, left to form the **Weathermen** (a.k.a. **Weather Bureau**). The SDS dissolved in June, 1969. In 1970, after that group was linked to bombings, its members went underground, calling themselves the **Weather Underground**. (See: **Anti-War Events, Groups and Leaders** starting on page 562 in **Lists** at the back of this book)

Studio 54 (April 26, 1977-Dec., 1979) a **disco** club opened by young entrepreneurs Steve Rubell and Ian Schrager in an abandoned CBS TV studio at 254 West 54th Street in Manhattan, New York City. The "Studio," as it was affectionately called, was the decadent center of the world for its few short years of fame. At one time or another, most of the beautiful, powerful and exciting people of that era joined the sweaty dancing body of heads, limbs and genitals on the dance floor at the Studio. Disco music was at its apex, and sex and drugs had none of the restrictions that AIDS and the Reagan era would create. The Studio suffered ups and downs, closings and reopenings due to the tax problems of Rubell and Schrager, who actually spent time in jail for their cavalier handling of the club's phenomenal income. In some biographies, the closing date is listed as 1986, and there are still reunions held in the building; but for all practical purposes, Studio 54 really had only a two-year party... but, oh, what a party!

studs pierced ear adornments that stick through the ear flesh, unlike rings, which circle through the lobe. Any adornment that pierces through the body.

stuff personal items of various and dubious value that make one's life familiar and comfortable. Much of your stuff would be considered trash to others, and their stuff would be garbage to you. Similar to **junk,** but with more emotional attachment involved.

stuff *drugs* any drugs. Same usage as **junk** and **shit**. **2.** heroin.

stuff it literally, it means "I don't care for your opinion, so stick it in your anal passage." Same usage as **put it where the sun don't shine**.

stung caught or apprehended. Same usage as **busted**.

style n. the current popular noncommercial mode of dress and self-decoration. Style is created by a few people, stolen by others and made into **fashion**, and then followed by many. The hippie culture created new forms of dress and decoration; other people copied these ideas, marketed them, got credit for them, and made money selling them to other folks who bought them to be **cool**. The progression of all **fads** and fashion is from **hip**, to style, and then to fashion. Hip is the alternative creativity of a culture, style is that creativity put to use as a way of life, and fashion (fad) is style that has been marketed.

style having a charismatic personality and/or provocative appearance. Possessing an exceptional social image. This is an attitude as well as a physical state.

styling or **stylin'** dressed up and "out on the town." Example: "I saw Portia out last night, and she was really **stylin'**."

subconscious mind according to some schools of psychoanalysis, it is a compartment of the mind existing beneath **consciousness**. The subconscious may not be directly accessible, but some say it can be explored with techniques, such as **dream-analysis**, random association or automatic writing.

sublimation Freud's most prominent theory, which suggests that the human psyche creates substitute activities in order to avoid other, more difficult basic social functions. In sublimation, a person may also use objects to create status and reputation rather than relying on intellect, personality and feelings in social interaction. An example of sublimation is a man who, having trouble attracting women, buys a red convertible and puts a **Playboy** bunny sticker on the window.

suck ass a very bad person, place or thing. Example: "My boss is a **suck ass**, this job **sucks ass,** and I think I'm going out after work and get **suck ass** drunk."

suckass a subservient person. Like a **kiss-ass** or **brown nose**, a person who flatters and follows a hero.

sucked in deceived or defrauded.

sucker someone naive who will fall for or has fallen for some scam or deception.

sucker snow *drugs* **cocaine** that is greatly diluted or "cut," making it a poor investment.

sucker weed *drugs* **marijuana** that is either poor quality or mixed with some other vegetation, making it a bad smoke.

suck face or **sucking face** kiss, kissing. Just use your imagination.

suck (someone) **in** deceive or defraud. Example: "It will be easy to **suck** Sunshine **in** with that line; she still believes in the **acid** fairy."

suck off *sex* **fellatio. Oral sex** performed on a man. It can be a **homosexual** or heterosexual act. May also describe **cunnilingus** or oral sex performed on a woman.

*sucks a bad situation, a negative, something to be avoided.

suck up to or **suck up** flatter, get close to, flirt with. Similar use as **kiss up to, kiss up, brown nose** or **kiss ass.**

suds beer.

Sufism *religion* a religious sect of Mohammedan mysticism, originating in Persia. They seek a "union with God" through poverty, repentance, abstinence, renunciation, patience and trust. Love is key in Sufi ethics.

sugar love, kisses, and sex.

sugar cube *drugs* **acid** on a sugar cube. Liquid **LSD** was dropped on sugar cubes for transport, sale and ingestion.

sugar daddy a man who pays the bills for a woman in exchange for her sexual favors. This was a situation that caused some moral confusion during the hippie era. Young hippie girls who, because of the moral climate of the era, were sleeping with a number of men without charge, would sometimes be approached by straight men of means and offered financial arrangements for sex. Since, in the eyes of many women at the time, wives were no different than prostitutes in that they slept with men for monetary support, some girls took on sugar daddies to cover their financial needs without experiencing any shame or ambiguity.

suit a straight, business-type person. Example: "Look at all the **suits** walking through the morning rain to their ivory towers."

sumbitch a shortening of the phrase "son of a bitch."

Summer, Donna (b. Donna Gaines, 1948) *pop and R&B music* singer, songwriter and Grammy winning disco diva. The most popular female singer in the mid-1970s, she is tainted in the eyes of most hippies because of the disco connection, but she was hot when she was hot.

Summer of Love the summer of 1967, primarily acted out in **Golden Gate Park** in San Francisco.

"Summertime Blues" *rock & roll* a song by the band **Blue Cheer** in 1968, which is considered by many to be the first **heavy-metal** recording. It is a remake of Eddie Cochran's 1958 "Summertime Blues." Blue Cheer, formed in 1967, named after an **LSD** tablet, is one of the first heavy-metal rock bands.

sunshine *drugs* the street name for a type of **LSD.** Usually orange or yellow tablets. **Owsley** is said to have been responsible for creating the **acid** called **Orange Sunshine**. He is also credited with the **Purple Haze** acid especially made for **Monterey Pop Festival**, on which **Jimi Hendrix** was tripping when he burned his guitar on stage that weekend. **Country Joe McDonald** says that he ingested 1 1/2 tabs of Owsley STP before his performance at Monterey Pop. (See: **Stanley, Augustus Owsley, III**)

super- *prefix or intensifier* an intensifier for any word one wishes to glorify or call attention to. Examples: "Superstud, superbitch, supergrass, superdope."

super doper *drugs* a person who always seems to have the best drugs, **paraphernalia** or rolling technique.

super ego from **Freudian** theory, it is the part of our psyche that has unconsciously identified with important people from early life, such as our parents or important teachers. The influence from these people becomes part of one's personal standard of conduct and state of mind.

"Super Fly" a **blackxploitation** film starring Ron O'Neal as a street **hustler** pushing heroin. Not a very good image for the Black community to be promoting, but it was typical of the era of openness and say-it-like-it-is philosophy of the time. Filmed in 1972, directed by **Gordon Parks, Jr**. **Curtis Mayfield** created an excellent soundtrack for the movie.

superior world *occult* in Kabbalistic and **occult** terminology, the world of ideas and the mind. The **Kabbalah** is the **esoteric** mystic writings of Judaism based on occult interpretation of the Bible.

Superman a higher form of humanity, the goal of human evolution. The term is a translation of the German word *Übermensch*, coined by Nie- tzeche.

supernatural an occurrence that cannot be explained by known science or a situation that exhibits activities contrary to the established laws of nature.

supersonic warble a term of undefinable meaning from **Tom Wolfe's** 1968 book about **Ken Kesey** and the **Merry Pranksters**, *The Electric Kool-Aid Acid Trip*.

supplies *drugs* drugs.

suss or to **suss out** to discover or understand. Example: "Did you **suss** what

Darma meant when she said, 'Thou shalt not kill my ego'?"

sutras *religion* the second part of the **Buddhist** Tripitaka, containing the teachings of **Gautama Buddha**. The Tripitaka is "The Three Baskets," the "Canon" of Buddhism adopted by the Council of elders in 245 B.C. and consisting of three parts: "The basket of discipline" (Vinaya), "the basket of (Buddha's) sermons" (Sutras), and "the basket of metaphysics" (Abidharma).

Suzuki, Daisetz Teitaro (b. Japan, 1870; d. 1966) *religion* a Japanese Zen Master and Buddhist scholar known for his introduction of **Zen Buddhism** to the West. Educated at Tokyo University and studied in the United States (1897–1909); he became a lecturer at Tokyo University and later taught at leading universities in Japan, Europe, and the United States. He studied at the prominent Kamakura School and wrote many books on Zen and Buddhism, in both Japanese and English. Two of his best known books are *An Introduction to Zen Buddhism*, 1949, and *Mysticism: Christian and Buddhist*, 1957. Through his writings, he is greatly responsible for America's present interest in Buddhism and Eastern philosophy.

Suzy Creamcheese a character created by Frank Zappa for one of his "rock operas."

swacked **high** on drugs or alcohol.

swami a **Sanskrit** word meaning spiritual teacher or holy man; used as an honorary title preceding a person's proper name.

Swami a generic name for a **Hindu** holy man or member of a religious order.

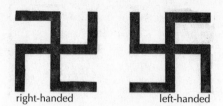

right-handed   left-handed

swastika *occult* **Sanskrit** word meaning "for one's own good." A very ancient symbol, one of the most sacred and mystical diagrams in religion and the **occult**, found worldwide in both Eastern and Western cultures. Generally, it is regarded as the symbol of the sun. It may be either right-handed (male) or left-handed (female); the right-handed form is most widely used in India and is considered a symbol of good luck. Also found in both North and South American Indian art and decoration. The left-handed form is the symbol used by Nazi Germany during the Second World War.

SWAT team a police unit created to handle political **demonstrations**, organized paramilitary and hostage situations. First used around 1969, it stands for **Special Weapons and Tactics**. Also sometimes known as a **TAC Squad**, standing for **Tactical Squad**. Before the SWAT teams and TAC squads, some cities had police special forces units known as the **Tactical Patrol Force (TPF)**. **Counterculture anti-war** and civil rights demonstrators called them **Tasmanian Pig Fever**. (See: **Tasmanian Pig Fever**)

sweat or to **sweat it** to worry. (See: **no sweat**)

sweathog a smelly, unkempt or **funky** person. An unskilled laborer. The name given the boys' student gang in the 1975 TV sitcom, "Welcome Back, Kotter."

sweat lodge *religion* a **Native American** structure of tightly woven branches or mud into which hot rocks are placed and doused with water to produce steam. Originally, it was a men-only activity in which participants entered the structure to participate in ritual sweats and religious rites. In some tribes, it was part of the purging ceremony before taking the hallucinogenic peyote cactus. The sweat lodge incorporates some functions of a church in the Indian cultures. Similar to a kiva in some **Native American** tribes. The American hippie adopted many Native American rituals, and the sweat lodge was one of them, popping up in many communes. (See: **kiva**)

sweet something very good, yet not necessarily having to do with the sense of taste. Often relates to a girl or woman with whom one is having sex.

sweet a **homosexual** man. Example: "He's **sweet**, but don't let that fool you; he was the best hand-to-hand killer in South Vietnam."

sweet Jane *drugs* **marijuana**. (See: **marijuana**)

sweet Lucy *drugs* another term for **marijuana**.

sweet meat an attractive woman.

sweet spot the right place to touch a lover. **2.** the best place to hit a golf ball or tennis ball on the club or racket.

sweet thing or **sweet thang** a young and often innocent girl. The object of affection.

sweets *drugs* **amphetamines**. **Uppers**.

swing to party.

swing *sex* to have sex with either or both genders.

swing *sex* to exchange sexual partners.

swing both ways *sex* to be bisexual.

swinger someone who likes to have fun...sex, drugs and night life. **2.** someone socially knowledgable.

swinger *sex* someone, male or female, who is open to sex with either gender.

swingers *sex* couples who trade partners for sexual escapades.

swinging single a bachelor or unattached woman who enjoys sex, drugs and rock & roll.

swing on to fight, hit or punch. Attack.

swish a feminine man.

switch hitter a bisexual person.

switch on or **switch off** to change persona, attitude or personality. Example: "He can **switch on** if he likes you or **switch off** if he dislikes your shoes."

Patty Hearst posed before SLA's snake symbol

Symbionese Liberation Army (SLA) a revolutionary group of people in the Oakland and Berkeley, California, area who banded together in the late 1960s to effect political change in their community. Their slogan was "Death to the fascist insects that prey on the life of the people." Founders, leaders and prominent members were Donald De Freeze (Cinqué), Patricia Soltysik (Mizmoon or Zoya), Willie Wolfe (Cujo) Nancy Ling Perry (Fahizah), Emily Harris (Yolanda), Bill Harris (Tico), Angela Atwood (Gelina), Joe Ramiro, Russell Little, Camille Hall and **Patty Hearst** (Tania). The extent to which Patty Hearst was involved in the SLA is still unknown. The SLA appeared to be dominated by the women in the group, notably Soltysik and Perry, although De Freeze was the figurehead as General Field Marshal Cinqué. Supposedly, Cinqué was originally the name of the leader of a slave rebellion in the 1830s. The SLA was associated with or evolved from a group called Venceremos, which was involved in trying to break African Americans out of prison. The SLA killed Dr. Marcus Foster, Black Oakland Superintendent of Schools, on November 6, 1973 (supposedly with cyanide bullets), and on February 4, 1974, they kidnapped Patricia Campbell Hearst, the daughter of Randolph and Catherine Hearst and heir to the Hearst newspaper fortune. The word symbionese was formed from symbiosis, meaning dissimilar organisms living together in harmony. Their symbol was a seven-headed cobra snake meant to symbolize black, brown, yellow, red, white, young and old. On April 15, 1974, the SLA robbed the Hibernia Bank at Noriega and 22nd Street in San Francisco. Patty Hearst was in attendance, holding an automatic weapon. On May 16, 1974, they shoplifted and shot up Mel's Sporting Goods in the Crenshaw area of Los Angeles. Patty is said to have been the shooter. On May 17, 1974, six members of the SLA were killed in a shootout and fire at a house at 1466 54th Street in Los Angeles. Killed were Donald De Freeze, Patricia Soltysik, Willie Wolfe, Nancy Ling Perry, Angela Atwood and Camille Hall. Patty Hearst and Bill and Emily Harris were captured in San Francisco on September 18, 1975. (See: **Hearst, Patty**)

Synanon Foundation an organization initially specializing in drug rehabilitation, with facilities in many major cities. Their techniques have been beneficial as well as detrimental. Charles Dederich, an alcoholic, began Synanon in Santa Monica, California, in the late 1950s and moved it to the Sierra Nevada foothills during the 1970s. His methods for overcoming alcohol and drug **addiction** won widespread publicity and praise. Synanon members lived together in a commune, dealing with their addiction under Dederich's tough-love leadership. His methods included "The Synanon Game," in which members could say whatever they wanted. Much of the rehabilitation involved working in gas stations or selling pencils to support the organization. Synanon became one of the nation's largest distributors of pens and other items with corporate logos promoting businesses. In the mid-1970s, Dederich proclaimed Synanon a religion and was criticized for allegedly controlling the actions and thoughts of its members. The organization has assumed different forms, but still exists.

synthetic grass *drugs* synthetic **marijuana, tetrahydrocannabinol (THC)**. a.k.a. **clarabelle, clay**.

System, The *social issues* short for the "**capitalist** system." Also, the **military-industrial complex**, the established government, and all of the agencies, institutions and organizations that economically enslave the common man. To the working man, "The System" is a large machine, which alternately either ignores him or conspires to overwork and deceive him. The working, or "common," man considers The System to be a real threat to his happiness and existence, and he realizes that if it is left unchecked, it will eventually destroy the peace and tranquility of this world.

T

10 the highest rating on a scale of beauty from one to ten. Actress Bo Derrick was considered a 10 when she starred in the 1979 movie entitled "10." To many people, this movie and the pastime of numerically rating beauty were an indication of the end of a benevolent era. 10 and its skin-deep judgments represent the trivializing of love and a turn toward a more superficial world, which the 1980s proved to be.

360 (See: **three-sixty**)

25 *drugs* LSD 25. One of the first forms of LSD that was produced. Created by **Sandoz** Pharmaceuticals in the early 1960s, it was sanctioned by the US government for use in experiments at universities and veterans' mental hospitals. It somehow leaked out on the streets; Ken Kesey was one of the leaks, and he started a small, unsanctioned experiment among the intellectuals of Stanford University and the San Francisco literary community. (See: **Kesey, Ken**)

"200 Motels" a movie and sound track album produced by Frank Zappa in

1971. The movie featured Theodore Bikel and Ringo Starr as Zappa look-alike's and Keith Moon as a nun. The story line was chaotic, but it basically chronicled Zappa's band, the **Mothers of Invention**, trapped in small town motels with groupies and band followers.

T *drugs* stands for tea, one of the names for **marijuana**. (See: **marijuana**)

T&A (See: **tits and ass**)

TCB (See: **taking care of business**)

T group (See: **sensitivity training**)

TM (See: **Transcendental Meditation**)

TV (See: **transvestite**)

Tab a diet **soft drink** introduced to the American public in 1965. (See: **soft drink**)

tab *drugs* short for tablet. A tablet of **LSD**. The different forms of **LSD** delivery included the following: tablets, gelatin capsules, gelatin **hits** called **windowpane**, liquid drops on **blotter** or paper, and liquid drops on **sugar cubes**. The wide range of doses in one hit of LSD was between 100 and 350 micrograms. Often, because of the primitive circumstances of the manufacturer, it was impossible to regulate dosages, but tablets were usually the most consistent due to the more sophisticated facility necessary to produce them.

TAC squad Tactical Squad. A police unit created to handle political **demonstrations**, organized paramilitary disturbances and hostage situations. Also known as a **SWAT** or **Special Weapons and Tactics** team.

tacky in bad taste.

Taco a derogatory name for someone of Mexican decent.

t'ai chi in Chinese **mysticism**, it means The Great Ultimate.

Tai Chi Chaun the Chinese **martial** discipline that is the meditative application of the fighting martial system of Kung Fu. An exercise discipline based on balance and control of one's inner power. To an observer, it is like a dance with slow, fluid movements. These movements have names, stories and traditions. The martial disciplines are divided roughly into *ways* (do) and *arts* (jutsu). The prime purpose of a *way* is other than battle; the prime purpose of an *art* is battle. Martial *arts* include Jujitsu and Karate; examples of *ways* are **Aikido**, Tai Chi, Tai Kwon do, Judo and Kudo (archery). With the exception of Akido, most *ways* are practiced as sports. During the idealistic hippie era, it was widely believed that the martial arts (disciplines) were an attempt to divert negative energy in order to achieve peace. This attitude has had an effect on the way they are taught in America and now the martial disciplines are considered a balance of body and mind control for the use in self-improvement as well as physical confrontations. (See: **martial arts** and **Aikido**)

tail a faceless object of lust, an impersonal description a sexual partner. Example: "She's quite a piece of **tail**; she has moves no slinky toy can do."

taint the area of a woman between the **vagina** and the anus. Called **taint** because "it '**taint** pussy and it '**taint** ass."

take the amount of money or compensation someone gets from a job or activity.

take a portion of taped or recorded sound. Usually a musical performance recorded for eventual broadcast or inclusion on a record, cassette or CD.

take a directional intensifier. Take is one of those interesting anomalies of American English. Originally, it meant to acquire and keep an object, but during the mid-20th century it began to find other usage, as in to take something reluctantly, such as **take heat** or **take a hosing.** Then it went even further by indicating a contradiction in which one is "taking" something that they are actually parting with, such as **take a shit** or **take a piss.**

take a cure to seek **rehabilitation** for drug or alcohol **addiction**.

take a dump to defecate.

take a fall to receive a jail sentence.

take a flying fuck go away. In essence, it means I don't care what you do; just do it somewhere else. **A flying fuck** is one of those nonsensical terms that can be used to intensify a variety of situations, but it is normally used to express disdain, disinterest or disregard for something.

take a hike go away. Same as **get lost**. Go out in the woods and get lost.

take a hosing to be beaten, cheated, or to lose at something. Probably comes from the connection between "to **hose**" and "to fuck." Get hosed means get fucked. Possibly comes from the old police and underworld practice of beating someone with a rubber hose to hide the injuries. Example: "We're going to **take a hosing** on our investment in Goonie's escargot farm."

take a leak to urinate.

take a load off to sit down.

take a run at to try something or to make an effort. Example: "**Take a run at** cleanliness; it may improve your seduction percentage."

take care of *numero uno* think of yourself first. *Numero uno* is "number one" in Spanish, and number one is generally understood as oneself. The use of Spanish or any foreign word in a saying is meant to add a bit of exotica or class to the phrase.

take (someone) **down** to destroy or humiliate someone. Example: "If you want to **take him down**, all you have to do is mention the goose, the Sea Breeze Motel and petroleum jelly."

take fire to receive criticism. Examples: "I'm not going to **take fire** for your mistakes." "He **took a lot of fire** for the great elephant turd caper."

take five to take a rest, literally five minutes. Originally a musical term meaning to take a break, it is alternately thought to mean a five-minute rest or a five-bar solo on a musical instrument. The term was made popular by the 1961 instrumental recording entitled "Take Five," by the Dave Brubeck Quartet.

take heat to attract or accept criticism. Examples: "I'll **take heat** for the silly putty, if you admit to the great elephant turd caper."

take it on to accept a challenge or a job. Example: "Drive an ice cream truck? Sure, I'll **take it on**, but only if I can eat on the job."

take it on home to finish as a winner, to celebrate a triumphant ending. From either to take a trophy or the spoils of victory on home or, as in baseball, to take oneself on to home plate. Example: "If he makes it through this next lap, he can **take it on home**."

take it to to confront or to attack someone. From to take the battle to someone, the "it" meaning battle. Example: "I will **take it to** mine enemies and they will be sorely punished."

take it to the limit to go all the way with something, to do one's best and even more.

take (one's) **lumps** to receive abuse or go through some tribulation. Examples: "Suzie can **take her lumps**; her father was a preacher, her mother wore hats and her dog had fleas." "I **took my lumps** for loving you, babe."

taken off to be robbed, injured or killed.

take no shit to refuse to accept or allow any criticism, ridicule or argument. Examples: "I **take no shit** from any authority except my girlfriend." Often used with a double negative, "I don't **take no shit** from you, your dog or your mama."

taken out obstructed, diverted or killed.

take off to leave. From the aeronautical term meaning to leave the ground.

take off *drugs* to experience the effects of a drug.

take off to kill. Example: "**Take him off** before he crawls back into the wall."

take on to accept a challenge or job. Example: "I'll **take on** the position if I can sleep on the job."

take (someone) **on** to challenge somebody or accept a challenge. Example: "Sure, I'll **take Judy on** in a wrestling match any day."

take out to neutralize. Knock down, knock out or kill.

take shit to experience criticism, ridicule or argument. Example: "I have to **take shit** at work for my long hair, and at home I **take shit** for wearing a tie to work."

take the heat to accept responsibility. Examples: "I won't **take the heat** for the dirty dishes; I'm fasting this week."

take the heat off to relieve the pressure on someone, to help someone. Examples: "I hope she finds another lost soul to **take the heat off** me and my bad habits."

take the pressure to accept or receive responsibility, criticism or ridicule. Examples: "I'll **take the pressure** if I can get the pleasure too."

take the rap to accept responsibility for someone else's actions. Example: "I'll **take the rap** for spilling the Ripple wine, but I won't admit drinking it." **2.** to be forced to take responsibility for someone else's actions.

take your best shot accept a challenge, do the best you can. From the challenge to swing first and attempt to end the fight with one punch.

taking care of business (TCB) the phrase adopted by **Elvis Presley** as his motto for life. Elvis wore a medallion around his neck engraved with TCB, and the TCB logo was on many of his possessions. His later life was haunted by creative frustrations and insecurities, and, according to many accounts, he felt the pressure of supporting the many friends, business associates and family members around him. "Taking care of business" was what he considered his obligation in life.

John Jeffers and his hand-made peace talisman

talisman a decoration, carved image or piece of jewelry that holds a personal, emotional or spiritual value for someone. An item of worship or spiritual representation. Similar to a **fetish**. Before the hippie era, talismen were considered objects to be used only by "primitive cultures." Hippies realized that crucifixes, Madonna statuary, Confederate flags and Stars of David were all, in essence, talismens. The 1960s and 70s **counterculture** began to borrow many new talismen from other cultures to adorn themselves and their surroundings. The **ankh**, **om symbol**, **yin-yang** symbol, **peace symbol**, American Indian **dream catcher**, **Buddha** statuary, **mandala** and **earth mother** fetishes all became new talismens for the American youth culture.

talking head a TV news anchorperson or commentator. This term came about because all one sees of these people are their head and shoulders.

talking shit talking nonsense in an effort to impress someone. **2.** using conversation to seduce someone into sex.

talking trash verbal seduction. Talking nonsense over one's head in an effort to impress. Using large words in sentences with little or no meaning to give an impression of intelligence. **2.** using conversation to seduce someone into sex. Similar to **trash talk** or **talking shit**.

talking trash communicating in street language. Same as **trash talk**. Can be sarcasm directed at a friend. Usually, it's a throw-away conversation, non-specific double-talk meant as a form of greeting or camaraderie similar to discussing the weather. An example of the form of communication: "Say, man, what's happening? Is your fire lit, are you **cool** with the cosmos, can you dig it, the establishment has beat us down so low all we got is this corner to rap, and smoke and dig that chick, hey, babe, don't walk away before you experience my firmamentation. Shit, I could have made her see God!"

talk shit to ridicule, criticize or verbally abuse. Example: "If you **talk shit** to me, be prepared to get it back, you foul-smelling, fungus of a mutant."

talk that talk to have good verbal skills. Example: "He can **talk that talk**."

talk that talk and walk that walk be **cool**, say the right thing and do the right thing. Examples: "He's cool; he can **talk that talk and walk that walk**." Sometimes heard as **walk that walk and talk that talk.**

talk that talk, and you must walk that walk do as you say. If you talk one way, you must act the same way. Examples: "If you **talk that talk, you must also walk that walk** or the bullshit bus will run you down."

tall impressive or with confidence. Example: "She walks **tall**, even though she is 4 foot, 11 inches."

Talmud *religion* an encyclopedic work in Hebrew-Aramaic compiled during 800 years (300 B.C.- 500 A.D.) in Palestine and Babylon. A valued collection of oral traditions of Judaism explaining civil and religious laws and discussing Jewish philosophy, ethics, folklore, and science.

tamari sauce roughly the same as soy sauce. A mixture of fermented soy beans, salt and water. It became a staple of the hippie diet, along with bean sprouts, tofu and **brown rice**. The hippie eating habits became a combination of rebellion, health and simplicity. They were rebelling against the repetitive meat and potatoes of their parents, searching for a more healthy lifestyle and achieving simple food preparation under conditions often much less opulent than those found in their childhood family homes.

tambourine man in some places, this meant a drug dealer. Origin unknown.

tame a person, place or thing that is quiet, passive or nonthreatening. Before the hippie era, many terms like this were reserved almost exclusively for animals. During the hippie era, words like tame and wild were used to describe people, places and things more than ever before.

tanked or **tanked up** drunk.

tank top a sleeveless t-shirt worn for exhibitionism as well as comfort in hot weather. On an attractive, well-built man or woman, it is an appealing article of apparel. In recent times, tank tops have been called "wife beaters" because of the tendency of macho types to wear them.

tank up to eat.

Tantra *religion* the portion of **Hindu** religious literature that is believed to have been revealed by **Shiva** as the specific scripture of the **Kali Yuga** (the present age). The Tantras are the encyclopedias of **esoteric** knowledge of their time. The topics of a Tantra are: creation of the universe, meditation, rituals, spiritual exercise, the six magical powers, and worship of the gods.

tantric yoga *religion* ancient East Indian wisdom and techniques to enhance **consciousness** in order to achieve the **transcendental** state. Tantric practices are methods used to open the body chakras. Sometimes called sexual **yoga**, since it is also used to extend the time of sexual activity and to enhance enjoyment, postponing orgasm and ensuring that both lovers receive maximum pleasure. (See: **chakras** and **transcendental**)

tao (pronounced "dow") in Chinese philosophy, "The Absolute," both the path and the goal. It also denotes the cosmic order, the course of nature or "The Way." The basis for **Taoism** and the Tao Te Ching.

Taoism and writings of the **Tao Te Ching** *religion* the Chinese religious philosophy credited to Lao-Tzu, although it was most likely written by several people. The path to spiritual harmony through a passive life. It incorporates many elements of **Buddhism**, the **yin-yang** philosophy and **alchemy**, worship of natural objects and immortals.

tap city broke, without money. A humorous way to say tapped out.

tap dance to maneuver around an embarrassing, difficult or dangerous situation.

tap dancer a person who is good at maneuvering around a embarrassing, difficult or dangerous situation.

tapped or tapped-out broke, **busted**, financially embarrassed or without funds.

tapped chosen for something or offered a position. Example: "He was **tapped** for the job of Solicitor General by all the whores on Main Street.

tar *drugs* **opium**.

Tarot cards set of 78 playing cards, with symbols and pictures, used in fortune-telling. The cards were originally involved in a game invented sometime around 1440 in Northern Italy. In the 1800s, the cards began to be used in fortune telling. Readers of the Tarot insist that the process is more cosmic than merely fortune telling, and most believers have an almost religious or ominous attitude toward the cards.

Tasmanian pig a New York City policeman, particularly from the lower East Side.

Tasmanian Pig Fever (TPF) before **SWAT teams** and **TAC squads**, which appeared around the beginning of the 1970s, some cities had police special forces units known as the **Tactical Patrol Force (TPF)**. **Counterculture anti-war** and **civil rights** demonstrators, in order to camouflage their conversations, started called them **Tasmanian**

Pig Fever. This term may have led to the naming of lower East Side, New York City policemen, **Tasmanian pigs**. (See: **SWAT team, TAC squad**)

taste a drink. Alcohol.

taste a sample, or small amount of something. Often used to indicate one (or two) **"tokes"** of **marijuana**. **2.** has a sexual connotation, as in a quick, or one-time sexual experience. Example: "I had a **taste** of her last week."

taste of something fine the enjoyment of some good **dope**, a fine sexual experience or a beautiful communication. From **Jackson Browne's** 1972 song, "Something Fine," with David Crosby harmonizing.

tasty something or someone desirable or attractive, usually a drug or an object of sexual interest.

tatas female breasts. Usually indicating large ones.

tattooed short for **screwed, blued and tattooed**, which means to be cheated and mistreated. (See: **screwed, blued and tattooed**)

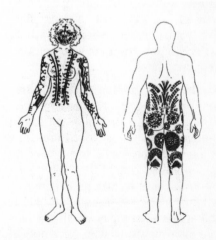

tattooing in the United States until the hippie era, tattoos were usually a drunken serviceman's reward, and women almost never considered getting them because of the repercussions on a honeymoon. The 1960s spirit of rebellion caused a blossoming of **anti-establishment** body art. Many of the fads were garnered from other cultures throughout the world as young people became more international in their scope and travel. Decorative tattoos have been common in the Orient, South Sea Islands and Africa for centuries for both men and women, and the rebellious hippie adopted them. Tattoos are found on Egyptian mummies from over 3,000 years ago, and recently a frozen Bronze-Age man from around 3,300 B.C. was found to have them. The word tattoo comes to us from Polynesia through the writings of the English navigator Captain Cook. Although true hippies did acquire some tattoos, they were usually fetishes or of a spiritual nature, small and often self-applied. More extravagant body piercing and tattoos were displayed in off-shoots of the culture. (See: **body art,** and **Modern Primitive movement**)

Taurus astrological sign, April 20 to May 21, second house of the **zodiac**, fixed earth sign, symbolized by the bull. Traits: purpose, productivity. Self-perception: I have.

Taylor, James (b. Mar. 12, 1948, Boston, Mass.) *folk/rock & roll* a singer/songwriter who provokes profound thought as well as deep emotions within the same song. He is one of the performers who kept the 1970s sane by producing music for people, not for automatons of the discoteque. He is still appreciated today by his old fans and many new fans who were not yet born when his music was first played on the radio. I could go on about James

Taylor's value to the atmosphere of the time, but less than a book would not do him justice, so please find an authorized biography.

t'd off, t'ed off or **tee'd off** upset. Similar to **pissed off**. Short for **ticked off**.

t'd-up or **tea'd up** *drugs* under the influence of **marijuana**.

tea *drugs* **marijuana**. (See: **marijuana**)

teach short for teacher.

teach-in a form of **free-speech** or **anti-war** demonstration with lectures and debates, held at educational venues, such as college and high school campuses. They were often meant to obstruct the regular school activity in order to draw attention to the cause. The first one was held on March 24, 1965, at the University of Michigan, attended by over 3,000 people. Hundreds of teach-ins took place on American campuses.

team player someone who works well with others. A business phrase that came into use in the 1970s, and then found a backlash of sarcasm within the **counterculture**. To a **capitalist**, a team player is a person he owns and can control; to a hippie, a team player is someone who gives in to workplace politics and social pressures, regardless of the correct course of action.

tea party a gathering at which **marijuana** is smoked.

tear it up have fun, dance, get crazy.

tearoom trade or **tea trade** homosexuals.

tears it, that it's over, it's ruined, all is lost. It implies that the integrity of a scheme or situation has been compromised. The threads that hold the situation together have come apart. Same usage as **torn it**. Example: "The transmission is blown; **that tears it**, our vacation will have to take place in the back yard."

teas and herbs (See: **herbs and teas**)

tease or **teaser** sex   short for prick teaser, a person who seems to be promising sexual activity, yet falls short of deliverance. Tease was the original, older term; the unspoken "prick" was added in the 1950s, then shortened again to tease in the 1960s. The term was used in both forms, most often by straight men upon seeing young **hippie chicks** flaunting their sexuality.

Teatro Campesino, El   in 1965, Luis Valdez, an aspiring playwright, left the **San Francisco Mime Troupe** to join **César Chávez** organizing farmworkers in Delano, California. Valdez formed some of the workers into El Teatro Campesino (The Farmworkers' Theater) to help publicize the grape boycott and raise funds for the farmworkers' strike. In 1968, El Teatro Campesino left the fields to create a theater reflecting a wider Chicano experience. In 1969, they received an Obie Award, for "demonstrating the politics of survival," and the first of two Los Angeles Drama Critics Awards. By 1970, El Teatro Campesino established what came to be known as Teatro Chicano, a style of theater, incorporating elements of the Italian Renaissance commedia dell'arte with the humor, character types, folklore and popular culture of the Mexican theater. El Teatro Campesino toured the United States, and in 1976, embarked on an eight-country European tour. In 1977, La Carpa de los Rasquachis was produced and aired on public television, under the title El Corrido. Luis Valdez is the writer and

director of the critically acclaimed movie "Zoot Suit."

techie   someone who possesses skills or expertise with technical equipment. The term today relates primarily to the computer industry; yet, in the 1970s when the word came into use, it meant any technical knowledge, such as in musical sound systems, movie technology or audio-video recording equipment.

techno *prefix*   a prefix implying that the root word is somehow technically advanced or enhanced. Examples: "Techno-communication, technocrat, techno-tool, techno-hippie."

teenager   anyone who is 13 to 19 years of age. Some say the term originated with the 1920s comic strip "Harold Teen." Numbers ending in teen influenced the word. The teenage years are the most misunderstood and confused period of a person's life, and the hippie era gave teenagers much to be misunderstood about and confused by. However, I feel that most young people who came of age during that time in a hippie environment are better adjusted to cope with this crazy world than those who didn't.

teenybopper   a teenager who likes to party and dance. It can be a male or female, but the image is prominent of a young, nubile girl, unaware of her sexuality, frolicking and dancing with innocent abandon.

tee off   to become angry and confront someone. There is some confusion concerning the origin of t'd off and tee off. I believe **tee off** is related to the golfing term, to hit a ball, thus to get mad at something or someone as if you're going to hit them. T'd off is short for ticked off, which is similar to **pissed off**.

tee (someone) **off** to make someone mad. Example: "If you **tee her off,** you better protect your family jewels."

tee off on (someone) to get mad at someone and verbally assault them. Example: "If you **tee off on** James, he'll cry all over you."

Tele *rock & roll* short for **Telecaster**. (See: **Telecaster**)

Telecaster *rock & roll* the first commercially popular, solid body, electric six-string guitar. It was manufactured by the **Fender Guitar Company**, whose guiding force was Leo Fender. Developed in the later 1940s to early 1950s, it is the oldest surviving, solid-body electric guitar still in production. Arguably, the most popular rock, four-string bass guitar is the Fender "Precision" bass, a larger version of the Telecaster design. (See: **Fender Guitar Company** and **Stratocaster**)

telekinesis the practice of moving objects by the power of thought. As yet, unproven scientifically. Basically the same as **psychokinesis.**

telepathy the transmission of thoughts from one person to another without the aid of any orthodox verbal or electronic means. As yet, scientifically unproven to everyone's satisfaction, at least when compared to gravity. I personally think telepathy may be possible between very attuned people. The accuracy of the communication cannot be judged. Animals perceive fear, but this perception may be through body language or scent. It has been proven that electronic impulses are emitted from our brains. How far they travel into the surrounding atmosphere has not yet been measured. It is conceivable that a highly sensitive person or someone emotionally close to the sender could pick up these impulses.

television television shows and sitcoms were one of the most important elements in the evolution of our language during the 1960s and 1970s. TV writers were continually trying to find new ways to grab our attention by playing with the language, and they used the most "**hip**" and "**cool**" terms of the time to prove that their show was hip and cool. Advertising writers were also into this. Writers and artists, even those in the media, are always close to the **counterculture** in intellect and lifestyle, and so they hear the new language firsthand and pass it on to the listening public.

tell it like it is to discuss the struggles of mankind or some such issue of social importance. **2.** tell the truth, don't lie.

tell me something I don't know a rebuttal, informing someone that you are one step ahead of them.

tell (someone) **where to get off** to verbally confront someone, dress them down or challenge their arrogance. Example: "Dave had to **tell his Gramps where to get off** after the old codger smoked up all the dope in the house."

telly short for television. A British invasion term adopted by the hippie culture. The growth of language has two different directions, expansion and contraction. Expansion involves grouping words together into phrases and creating longer words to expand a thought.

The contraction of our language is the process of shortening these words and phrases after everyone knows their meaning.

temple balls *drugs* hand-shaped balls or patties of **hashish** from Nepal, Kashmir and Northern India. They were among the first types of **hash** to reach the United States and Europe.

temple bells bells used in **Buddhist** ceremonies.

temple of the flesh *occult* in **occult** and hedonistic terminology, the physical body.

ten (See: **10**)

ten-cent bag *drugs* a ten-dollar quantity of drugs, a.k.a. **dime bag**.

ten-foot pole that with which you wouldn't touch someone or something. The distance you want between yourself and something you don't like. Example: "She's scary; I wouldn't touch her with a **ten-foot pole**. I wouldn't even touch her with *your* **ten-foot pole**."

ten-four (10-4) ham radio and citizens band radio verbal recognition stating that one has received the message and is ready to disengage. It replaced the earlier phrase, "Roger, over and out," used in military radio. Example: "I read you on the smoky, **ten-four,** good buddy." During the hippie era, "ten four" was adopted in normal person-to-person communication and used as an affirmation or recognition. Example: "**Ten-four,** my friend, but watch for the **nark** at the park."

teonanacatl *drugs* sacred mushrooms, also known as **God's flesh**. Any one of 14 different species of a small, yellow mushroom with hallucinogenic qualities. The active ingredient is psilocybin. a.k.a. **magic mushroom**. Warning, many mushrooms are deadly; please be sure of what you are eating for food or pleasure.

terps *drugs* a concoction of terpin hydrate with codeine. A cough syrup used as a recreational drug during the era.

territory a situation or a mental state rather than a physical place. Example: "Self-confidence **goes with the territory** if you live in a nudist colony." Another example in which a word once used only in the realm of the physical became a state of mind or emotional place during the hippie era.

Tet offensive January, 1968, Vietnamese communists shattered the Tet or New Year truce by launching an offensive against 100 cities in South Vietnam. The US Embassy in Saigon was itself overrun and partially occupied for six hours. In numbers lost and ground gained, it was not a success for the communists; yet, to many Americans, Tet was the writing on the wall. It seemed to foretell the inevitability of America's loss of the war.

tetrahydrocannabinol *drugs* THC, the active chemical compound in **marijuana**. Can be ingested in pill form and is similar in effect to smoking marijuana.

Texas tea *drugs* **marijuana**. (See: **marijuana**)

Tex-Mex a style of food and type of music from the Texas border area near Mexico. The music, also sometimes called "conjunto," has a few prominent practitioners, such as Freddy Fender, Flaco Jimenez, and Doug Sahm and Augie Meyers from the Sir Douglas Quintet.

Thai stick *drugs* a **cannabis** leaf product from Thailand, wrapped around a bamboo stick and tied with a string. This technique was probably devised for drying the plant and for ease in transport.

thalidomide a sleeping pill created in 1953 by a West German pharmaceutical company and distributed by William S. Merrell Company. If taken in early pregnancy, thalidomide prevented the fetus from proper development, and children were often born malformed. In the 1950s, thalidomide became a popular nonprescription sleep aid in Europe and was recommended to alleviate morning sickness in pregnant women. In 1960, it was distributed in the United States, and then, in 1961, it was discovered to be a virulently teratogenic (monster-causing) drug. Also known as MER/29 and marketed as Kevadon. The thalidomide tragedy also raised another issue when some of the pregnant women who had taken the drug wanted to obtain abortions to rid themselves of damaged fetuses. Abortion was still illegal in the United States, and only those who could afford to go to another country were able to get one. This situation may have been instrumental in the eventual legalization of abortion.

thang (also pronounced **"thing"**) *sex* the male sex organ. Examples: "How's your **thang** hangin'?"

thanks a sarcastic rejection of someone's unappreciated gift, suggestion or offer. From **thanks, but no thanks** or **thanks a lot**. This is one of the many terms and phrases of this era of sophisticated communications that relied on circumstances and voice inflections to portray the meaning.

thanks, but no thanks a sarcastic rejection of someone's suggestion or offer.

thanks a lot a sarcastic reference to a gift or offer that is not really appreciated.

that tears it it's over, it's ruined, all is lost. It implies that the integrity of a scheme or situation has been compromised. The threads that hold the situation together have come apart.

THC *drugs* **tetrahydrocannabinol**, the active chemical element in **marijuana** and hashish. It can be ingested in pill form and is similar in effect to smoking marijuana.

the beat goes on the music doesn't stop, the desire doesn't end, the movement will prevail. Take your pick; this phrase had many uses, from the frivolity of Sonny & Cher's 1967 hit song of the same name, to rousing demonstration speeches of the **free speech** and **civil rights** movement and **Black Panthers**.

The Dead the **Grateful Dead** rock group.

the dead *drugs* people who are too far gone into a drug habit. It implies that they will be dead soon.

the devil made me do it a humorous effort to divert responsibility for a foolish or frivolous act. A Flip Wilson line from his TV show in the early 1970s.

the end a monumental moment, a culmination. From an older term, "the living end." Popularized by **The Doors** song, "The End."

Theism or **Theistic philosophy** *religion* a religious belief in one God as the unifying **being** of all life. In extremely simplistic terms, it holds that God is nature. Somewhat similar to Pantheism and Deism. Closely related to the religion of most **Native American** peoples, most African tribes and any religion based on agrarian rituals.

the kind or **da kine'** *drugs, sex* the best. A Hawaiian Islands term, "da kine'" was the name used for its local **marijuana**. With time, the term moved to mainland United States and is used to indicate any good thing. The second most obvious use after drugs is to describe sex.

The One *drugs* a **cannabis oil** that appeared in the US at the beginning of 1970; it was made in Mexico and distributed by the "Cosmic Traveler." It didn't last long, but was soon replaced by **Son of One**, concocted by someone else. Cannabis oil and **hash oil** are usually smoked like **opium** or **hashish**, but can also be spread on the rolling papers of a cigarette or **marijuana** joint. Cannabis oil and hash oil were also sometimes mixed with parsley, rolled into cigarettes and smoked.

"The only difference between men and boys is the price of their toys." this means what it says. One of the many astute observations contained in the ongoing debates of the hippie era on **materialism**, male **ego** and masculinity. Source unknown, though it has its roots in Freudian **sublimation** theory.

Theosophy *religion* a philosophic religion claiming to posses divine wisdom that enables man to distinguish between true and false. A pragmatic religion or spiritual philosophy based on intellect rather than faith alone. Often called **Western yoga** or the **wisdom religion**, it is the doctrine on which all **occult** and **esoteric** teachings are based.

Theravada *religion* the form of Buddhism practiced in Sri Lanka, Burma, Thailand, Cambodia and Laos. It follows strictly the teachings of the **Vinya Pitaka** and rejects the doctrine of the **Bodhisattvas**. (See: **Bodhisattvas** and **Vinya Pitaka**)

there the place someone wants to be. The ultimate. Example: "I'm **there**, I can now relax; I've reached my goal of poverty." **2.** also used to describe achieving a drug high.

theremin *rock & roll* a musical instrument that produces an eerie, sirenlike sound, created by interrupting or altering an electric current. The theremin was invented in 1919 by Russian physicist Leon Theremin (Lev Termen). It was promoted and sold in the early 1960s by Robert A. Moog, who later invented and marketed the **Moog synthesizer**. The most memorable use of a theremin was in **The Beach Boys'** 1966 song "Good Vibrations." (See: **Moog synthesizer**)

there's no way it's not possible. Example: "**There's no way** you saw Betty eating flesh at Mac's Steak House! She's a militant vegetarian, with a strong distaste for pink formica."

"The Revolution Will Not Be Televised" meaning that you can't be involved in the exciting changes happening in the world if you stay at home. A slogan reportedly originating with the **SDS** and **Weathermen** movements.

thick dumb. From thick skull.

thing whatever a person does well or enjoys doing. Examples: "What's your **thing**?" "Music is his **thing**." As **Tom Wolfe** wrote in his 1968 book *Electric Kool-Aid Acid Test*, "Thing was the major abstract word in **Haight-Ashbury**.

It could mean anything, isms, life styles, habits, learnings, causes, sexual organs."

thing also pronounced **"thang"** *sex* the male sex organ. Examples: "How's your **thing** hangin'?"

thing, the the **diaphragm** birth control device. Also called the unidentified flying diaphragm when it slipped out of the fingers during insertion.

think tank a group of people or a physical place devoted to the creation of new ideas.

third eye *occult* the hypothetical inner sight thought to enable human beings to see the **astral** world. The part of the brain called the "pineal body" by occultists. Physically, it is indicated as the spot just between one's eyes.

third leg a man's penis.

thirst a sexual desire. Example: "I have a deep, all-consuming **thirst** for the **carnal knowledge** of her loins." Again, I'm stretching a point by attributing this word and meaning to the hippie era, yet I argue it was used in this context by very few people until it was popularized by the 1960s and 70s **counterculture**.

Thor the Nordic God of fertility, agriculture, thunder and the protector of sailors. One of the three Norse deities. The other two Gods are Oden and Freyr.

Thoth bird-headed (ibis-headed) God of ancient Egypt, God of magical arts, wisdom, the inventor of writing and patron of literature.

threads clothing. A **jazz** and **jive** term of the 1940s, expanded in use during the hippie era.

Three Mile Island *social issues* the nuclear power plant at Three Mile Island, located outside of Harrisburg, Pennsylvania, along the Susquehanna River. On March 28, 1979, due to a series of equipment malfunctions and human errors, the reactor came within three minutes of reaching the meltdown temperature of 5,000 degrees. The accident damaged over 90 percent of the reactor core. The containment building, which housed the reactor, and several other locations around the plant were contaminated. Had the plant reached meltdown, the same situation as the Russian disaster at Chernobyl would have occurred. At Chernobyl, hundreds of thousands of people were permanently evacuated, thousands of square miles of the earth were made useless, and hundreds of people and animals died. As it was, at Three Mile Island some radiation was released, and 100,000 people had to be temporally evacuated. It was the most serious commercial nuclear accident in US history, and it led to fundamental changes in the way nuclear power plants are operated and regulated. Because of accidents like this one and other near accidents, it has become obvious to many people that no matter how cheap the power is, the price of nuclear energy is still too high to pay.

three-piece suit the uniform of the conservative businessman during most of the 1960s and 70s, and therefore a clothing style that was ridiculed by the hippie. It was an extreme **counterculture** insult to be accused of having a three-piece-suit mentality.

three-sixty (360) meaning 360 degrees, as in the numbers around a compass. A change of opinion followed by a change back to the original viewpoint. To turn completely around. Example: "He did a one-eighty on celibacy when he saw her and a **three-sixty** when he met her mother."

throne the toilet.

throne room the bathroom.

throw money at it to waste money on a bad project instead of starting over and doing it right. To spend money in order to repair something that should be replaced.

thumb to **hitchhike**. To solicit a ride from a stranger. In the hippie culture, extending one's thumb in the desired direction was the accepted signal for requesting a ride in someone's car.

thumb *drugs* a very large **marijuana** cigarette. a.k.a. **bomber, zepplin, bazooka**.

thump to fight.

thumped to be beaten up.

thunder thighs *sex* a woman who vigorously enjoys sex.

thunder thighs someone with big thighs. Most often, a term applied to a woman.

Tibetan Book of the Dead guidance and preparations for death and instructions in the rites to be performed for the dying. In Tibetan Buddhism, the dying must train in order to avoid rebirth or at least to ensure rebirth as a human.

Buddist
Wheel of Doctrine

Tibetan Esoteric Buddhism (See: **Esoteric Buddhism**)

ticked or **ticked off** angry. Examples: "She's **ticked off** at me for using her chopsticks to prop open windows in my VW bus." The origin of this term is difficult to determine. Same as **t'd** or **t'd off**, which is a newer, shorter form of the term.

tickle the pickle *sex* to masturbate. A male usage. Used in sarcastic or humorous application only. Similar usage as **jerkin' the gherkin**.

ticker the heart.

ticket *drugs* any **hallucinogenic** drug used to take a psychedelic **trip**.

ticket agent *drugs* a dealer of **hallucinogenic** drugs used to take a **trip**.

ticky-tacky flimsy or cheaply built. A term used in Malvina Reynolds' 1960s song "Little Boxes" when she called suburban tract houses ticky-tacky.

tie-dye a process of creating randomly dyed patterns on clothing by tying strings around portions of fabric so some areas won't absorb the dye. During the hippie era, apparel decorated in such a manner with bright and garish colors became popular. "Etiquette in Public Places," Emily Post's *Tenth Edition Blue Book,* published 1960, by Funk & Wagnalls, states, "Not to attract attention to oneself in public is one of the cardinal principles of etiquette."

tie into to become associated with or benefit from a person, place or thing. Example: "I wish I could **tie into** some of the goodwill our government is dispensing to third world dictators and their bank accounts!"

tie off or **tie up** *drugs* to tie something around an arm, to produce a swollen vein in order to inject drugs into it.

tiger *drugs* a name for **heroin** when smoked. Example: "Let's take a ride on the **tiger**."

Tiger Balm a pungent salve made in Singapore, Southeast Asia. Used by Eastern religious devotees and Western hippies to anoint the spot between the eyes, which is called the "**third eye**." It is said to help open up the third eye to inner sight while **meditating**. It is also sometime used, just as Vicks Vaporub is, to help open congested nasal passages. (See: **third eye**)

tight close. Example: "Uncle Sam and I are **tight**! Just yesterday he sent an letter requesting the pleasure of my company."

tight, tight-ass or **tight-assed** cheap, stingy with money.

tight well put together, efficient, professional. Example: "She plays a real **tight** comb solo."

tighten up get serious, stay focused, pay attention to what you're doing. Another word that had a physical connotation before the hippie era, yet evolved into an emotional or mental attitude.

tika *religion* the spot of color on the forehead of Hindu worshipers. It indicates that someone has been to the temple and their **third eye** is open. The spot is also a blessing placed on one's forehead by a sadhu or priest.

til' you drop until you can no longer function. Examples "eat til' you drop, smoke til' you drop, bop til' you drop." Many such terms considered contemporary today were first heard in the 1960s and 1970s or were expanded in the **counterculture** of that period. Again, I say this era was the cultural renaissance of the 20th-century.

time frame an unspecified period of time in question. A term that came into use around 1973. Example: "What **time frame** are we lost in?"

time in motion and time in space *drugs* one of the basic **stoned raps** about time dissolving into movement, how time does not exist, and about warps and continuums. One of the concepts that had been knocking about for some time, yet really began to receive some serious consideration by people other than quantum physics PhDs after psychedelics hit the streets. Einstein was the father of this intriguing and confusing subject, with his train traveling through our imagination.

time-sharing *computer revolution* the original computer Internet system used by the creators of the **computer revolution**. Used in the late 1960s and early 1970s by researchers at universities and technical industries like Xerox and Bell

Labs. It referred to the ability of numerous programmers to use the few mainframes available to them simultaneously because each of their requirements involved different parts of the computer. It was still slow because the computer had to route the requests as it had memory and functions to fulfill them.

time warp a memory loss, *deja vu* or unexplained confusion about time. During the hippie era, it often coincided with the consumption of some kind of drug. Example: "Our date was a **time warp**; she thought it was the 18th century, I thought the 32nd, yet we were actually 50 years apart in the 20th century." There is a memorable song about the subject in the movie "**Rocky Horror Picture Show**."

tin *drugs* a container of **marijuana**, usually a pipe tobacco tin or **Prince Albert can**.

Tinkerbell *sex* a British term for a male **homosexual**.

photo by Lisa Law ©

Tiny Tim (b. Herbert Khaury, Apr. 12, 1925, New York, New York) *music* novelty singer. His long, stringy hair, big nose, squeaky falsetto voice and ukulele playing made him a favorite character of the era. He had several albums in 1968 and 1969 and was a regular on "**Laugh-In**." His most popu-

lar song was "Tip-Toe Thru' the Tulips with Me." In what other era could such a person be considered a celebrity? The hippie era was so accepting, encompassing and tolerant that someone so eccentric could reach a place of prominence.

tip agreement. Example: "If you insist Dove soap makes the lightest bubbles, I'll **tip** to it." May have come from "I'll tip my hat to that."

"Tip-Toe Thru' the Tulips with Me" from the 1968 novelty song by **Tiny Tim**. One of the silliest and most frivolous of all hippie-era offerings to our American culture. This phrase could be used like "smell the roses," but nobody ever used it seriously; it was always said tongue-in-cheek. (See: **Tiny Tim**)

tired ass or **tired assed** used to imply a pathetic, worthless person. Example: "Get your **tired ass** over here and clean up the tamari you spilled on the spool table." Same as the more widely used **sorry ass** or **sorry assed**.

tired assed sleepy, tired. The ass is used merely as emphasis and does not literally mean that part of the body is tired.

Title VII *social issues* a section of the **Civil Rights** Act of 1964, which prohibits discrimination on the basis of sex in employment, public accommodations, publicly owned facilities, union membership, and federally funded programs. At the suggestion of Martha W. Griffiths, a Michigan Democrat, the word "sex" was added to Title VII, thus opening the door for future job security for women. The Equal Employment Opportunity Commission (EEOC) was created as a result of the Civil Rights Act of 1964. Using the EEOC and Title

VII, the feminist movement achieved many advances for women during the 1960s and 70s. (See: **Civil Rights Events, Groups and Leaders** starting on page 546 and **Women's Issues** starting on page 591 in **Lists** at the back of this book)

tit man a guy who judges women by the size of their breasts. A man who likes women with large breasts.

tits or **tits up** something good. Examples: "That concert was the **tits**." "That was a **tits up** guitar solo." Not widely used on the West Coast, it is considered a British term.

tits and ass, T&A sarcasm relating to the male preoccupation with certain female attributes. Example: "Don't let **tits and ass** get in the way of your marriage vows." "That movie has a lot of **T&A**."

TJ Tijuana, Mexico. A place to go to get drugs.

TLC tender loving care. The treatment most people hope for in their relationships. A term that came into widespread use in the emotion-filled hippie era and was adopted by the advertising industry in the greed-filled Reagan era.

toast confronted, mistreated, defeated or arrested. Similar usage to **burned** and comes from "burned toast," defined as a bad thing. Examples: "You're **toast**; you have no chance with her." "When he ran the signal in his candy-apple car, I knew he was **toast**."

toasted drunk or **stoned** on drugs.

today is the first day of the rest of your life take advantage of your life. You should feel lucky to be alive; you have the rest of your life to make something of yourself. A simplistically profound

hippie phrase of the era. It holds true until and except for the day on which one dies.

*to die for something very desirable and metaphorically worth dying for. Example: "That carob whole wheat cake was **to die for**."

toe jam the damp, smelly mixture of dead skin and athlete's foot fungus between the toes of a dirty body. Yuck!

*together composed, confident. This is another example of the way in which the counterculture developed our language by shortening and simplifying it. The original phrase that this came from was "he has his shit together." Example: "He's a real **together** dude; watch how he catches that Frisbee."

toke *drugs* one puff of a **marijuana** cigarette. Same as **drag**.

toke up *drugs* to smoke a **marijuana** cigarette.

Tom or **tom** a Black man who wants to be White.

tomcat n. a person who goes out on the town seeking sexual gratification.

tomcat or **tomcat around** v. to go out on the town to drink, dance and seek sex.

tongueage a **French kiss**. 2. **cunnilingus**. The suffix "age" was added to some words in a sarcastic/humorous evolution of the hippie vocabulary.

"Tonight Show, The" the first real television talk show; it started in 1957 with Jack Paar as host. It was soon renamed "The Jack Paar Show," and Paar continued until 1962, when Johnny Carson took it over as "The Tonight Show." It was important to the counterculture primarily since it was one of the only venues where we could see spontaneous interviews with the music and cultural heroes of the era.

Tonkin Gulf Incident on the night of July 30-31, 1964, US PT (patrol torpedo) boat raiders from Danang, South Vietnam, shelled two North Vietnamese islands, Hon Me and Hon Ngu in the Gulf of Tonkin. On the afternoon of August 2, the US Navy destroyer *Maddox* was on a routine reconnaissance patrol in the same area, gathering information about coastal defenses. Not far from Hon Me, three North Vietnamese PT boats came out from that Island and attacked the *Maddox.* The attack was unsuccessful, with only one bullet from a heavy machine gun hitting the destroyer. This is often referred to as the "first attack." The *Maddox* left the Gulf after this attack, but returned on August 3, accompanied by another destroyer, the *Turner Joy.* There were more US PT raids on the night of August 3-4, and some shelling of parts of the North Vietnamese mainland, although the destroyers did not participate. On the afternoon of August 4, the two destroyers headed out into the middle of the Gulf. That night, they began seeing what appeared to be high-speed vessels on their radar. Believing that they were being attacked, they opened fire. Most sightings, however, appeared only on the radar of the *Turner Joy,* not on that of the *Maddox.* Some men serving on the destroyers contend that what appeared on the radar were only ghost images, while others feel that the attack was genuine. This is often referred to as the "second attack." The following afternoon, aircraft from the two US aircraft carriers *Ticonderoga* and *Constellation* carried out retaliatory airstrikes. The targets of this raid were mostly coastal patrol vessels, yet a large petroleum storage fa-

cility was also hit. This incident prompted Congress, on August 7, 1964, to pass the **Tonkin Gulf Resolution**, giving President Johnson the power to employ "all necessary measures" in dealing with "aggression" in Vietnam.

Tonkin Gulf Resolution On August 7, 1964, the US Congress passed, almost unanimously, the Tonkin Gulf Resolution, giving President Johnson a virtual blank check to employ "all necessary measures" in dealing with "aggression" in Vietnam. This was prompted by several "attacks" on US vessels in the Tonkin Gulf off North Vietnam. The Johnson administration had been urging such a resolution from Congress, and the Tonkin Gulf Incident supplied a good excuse. Though many people speculate, it does not appear that the incident was manufactured to provide that excuse. (See: **Tonkin Gulf Incident**)

too *intensifier* a word that intensifies other words. Examples: "**too** much, **too** real." It does not indicate an excess *per se*, but modifies the importance of something.

too much (positive) very good, excellent or impressive. Example: "That performance was **too much,** man; I laughed 'til my face paint cracked."

too much (negative) excessive, overwhelming. Example: "That performance was **too much** for my ears; I cried 'til my face paint ran."

too much fun enjoying oneself, perhaps to the point of overindulgence. Most often used sarcastically since, to a hippie, there is no such thing as having too much fun.

tool the male sex organ. The man's tool.

tool or **tool around** to drive around or travel in a more or less aimless manner for entertainment more than to reach a destination.

toot n. *drugs* **cocaine**.

toot v. *drugs* to inhale **cocaine** into one's nose through a tube or straw.

toothpick *drugs* a very thin **marijuana** cigarette.

top to do better than another person, to improve upon something. Examples: "You'll have to piss a long way to **top** him." "Pushing that **orange wedge** around the skating rink with his nose will be hard to **top**."

top to hurt or kill someone.

tops *drugs* the tops of a **marijuana** plant; the flower bud, which carries the most **THC resin** and is the best smoke. **2.** the top of **peyote cactus**, which is **hallucinogenic** when eaten.

Tops *drugs* a popular brand of cigarette rolling papers used by many **marijuana** smokers. Originally, Tops was a commercially sold "smoking kit" consisting of a small cloth sack filled with tobacco and a pack of rolling papers. When the marijuana culture emerged and the need for rolling papers outstripped the use of loose smoking tobacco, Tops and many other companies like **Zig Zag** started mass-producing just the rolling paper packages. It was obvious to the companies what was being smoked in their product, and even thought it was illegal, they looked the other way as they walked to the bank.

Torah the Hebrew bible. The first five books of the Old Testament, which are historically considered the Law that was revealed to Moses.

torch to set fire to something. **2.** to light up a **marijuana** cigarette.

tore up demoralized. Example: "Frank was **tore up** when Sunshine left him for Judy, Bob and Linda."

torn it or **that's torn it** all is lost, it's over, it's ruined. This implies that the integrity of a scheme or situation has been compromised. The threads that hold the situation together have come apart. Same usage as **tears it**.

torpedo *drugs* a large **marijuana** joint. Obscure usage. a.k.a. **bomber, zepplin, bazooka**.

torqued upset, mad. From **bent out of shape**. a.k.a. **bent, out of shape, out of sorts**.

tossed to be hassled by the police looking for drugs. To have the contents of one's pockets, car or house searched for contraband.

totaled destroyed or damaged beyond use and repair. From "a total write-off." Sometimes described excessive drug use. Examples: "The car was **totaled** when it hit the hippopotamus." "He was **totaled** on **LSD** and thought he hit a hippopotamus with his car."

totally *intensifier* intensifier or exclamation meant to indicate something all encompassing. Examples: "She's **totally** crazy." "This is so **totally** Valley Girl talk." Generally considered a **Valley talk** term, but actually an earlier **beat** and hippie creation. (See: **Valley talk**)

totem an animal regarded in primitive cultures as the representation of the soul of a deceased person. An animal fetish worn or possessed by someone as an emotional connection to the animal kingdom.

to the max all the way or all out. Max is short for maximum. Example: "Don't go half way, go to the **max** when buying a tie-dye shirt."

touch love or sex. From the act of touching someone. Example: "I'm going down town to get me some **touch**."

touch bases with (someone) to call, call on, or keep in touch with someone. Derived from baseball jargon, yet often used with no direct correlation to the actual game. Example: "When you get a chance, you should **touch bases** with your girlfriend."

touch junky someone who likes to be touched and loved.

touch therapy related to **gestalt** and **group therapy**. A term and process introduced to the American public in the early 1970s. It has some of the same elements as **encounter group** therapy and **sensitivity training**. Based on the theory that confrontation, physical contact and interplay among unrelated people enables them to open up to positive change and **self-realization**. The process consists of gathering a group of people together and conducting physical games, performing massage and encouraging tactile expression among the members. The objective is to break down emotional fears of touching others of both sexes, encouraging trust in unknown individuals and breaking down inhibitions among strangers. (See: **group therapy**, **gestalt** and **Esalen Institute**)

touch (someone) **up** to borrow something from someone. Example: "I need to **touch the bank up** for a few."

touchy-feely physical contact that is the expression of emotional outpouring or vice versa, a physical emotion expressed through affectionate contact. Physical desires, not necessarily sexually driven, yet influenced by brotherly love or compassion. A predecessor to the more satirical **warm and fuzzy**, which eventually became an advertising catch phrase of the 1980s and 90s.

touchy-feely *sex* sexual contact that is the cause or effect of emotional needs. Tactile enjoyment that is sexually oriented.

tough or **that's tough** too bad. From the older term "tough luck." Example: "You don't like hummus? That's **tough**! Her two food criteria are: it must be good for you and it must taste strange."

tough it out to stick with a challenge, to be strong and work something out.

tough shit too bad, tough luck.

tough titty too bad, tough luck.

tour guide *drugs* a person who guides someone through an **LSD** or **psychedelic** "**trip**." Someone who protects a person through his first LSD experience or through a particularly high dosage psychedelic trip. Those who understand psychedelics know that they should not be treated merely as frivolous recreation, but as an educational process. Same as **travel agent**.

toxic psychosis a psychological breakdown caused by drugs or toxic chemicals.

toy *sex* a sex partner not considered to be a serious relationship.

toys material possessions of an adult that are given more than reasonable attention due to the entertainment or status they provide. Cars, motorcycles, tools, electronic equipment, musical instruments, etc. Often, these items are used as **sublimation** or to enhance one's status or strengthen one's feelings of self-worth.

toy with or **toying with** to deceive or treat with less than equal respect. To deal with someone or something in a detached, sarcastic or insensitive manner. Example: "He was **toying** with her affections and her broccoli quiche." By no means a term created during the hippie era; the phrase "toying with someone's affections" has been used since the 15th century, yet the hippie era revitalized and expanded its use.

track n. a song on an album. You know, a **vinyl record album**, those things on which music was recorded before tapes and CDs. (See: **LPs** and **vinyl**)

track or **tracking** v. to understand or follow what someone is saying or doing. Example: "I'm having a hard time **tracking** what you mean when you say you can't **track** me." From electronic tracking.

tracks or **track marks** needle marks on a **drug addict's** arm.

Traffic *psychedelic, pop, blues, jazz and rock music* a band formed in England in 1967. Most noted for its revolving members, including: Steve Winwood (b. May 12, 1948, Birmingham, Eng.), voc., kybd., gtr.; Dave Mason (b. May 19, 1946, Worchester, Eng.), gtr., voc.; Jim Capaldi (b. Aug. 24, 1944, Evensham, Eng.), drums, voc.; Rick Grech (b. Nov. 1, 1946, Eng.), bass.

trail mix a food snack consisting basically of peanuts and raisins, used by hikers for energy out on the trails. It can be created from whatever nuts or dried fruits are desired. It was mixed individually from bulk dried fruit and nut bins found at most health food stores and became a staple whenever a hippie was traveling anywhere. Similar to **gorp**. (See: **gorp**)

train *sex* multiple continual orgasms, MCO. A phenomenon experienced by what would be considered a small number of fortunate women. They are most often clitorally created orgasms and are achieved through personal attention or when one's partner is skilled and devoted. Due to physical and emotional limitations, most MCOs are achieved within **lesbian** relationships. Most reported occurrences of male MCO are fantasies or fabrications.

trank, tranqs or **tranx** *drugs* a street name short for any of the many forms of tranquilizers.

transcendental mental innocence, detachment, peace of mind. Existence prior to experiences. A place of pure common sense within the mind. From the word *transcend*, meaning to go beyond, overcome, or block out.

Transcendental Meditation (TM) *religion* a form of meditation taught by **Maharishi Mahesh Yogi**. It is practiced in an effort to achieve a state of mental peace. Practitioners need no overt religious beliefs and are taught to meditate for 15 to 20 minutes twice a day. TM had a large following, including **The Beatles, The Beach Boys, Donovan**, Mia Farrow and many American hippies. (See: **Maharishi Mahesh Yogi**)

transcending rising above or getting past the mental conflicts and daily worries of life.

transmutation or **transmigration of the soul** rebirth into a body belonging to a different species or vegetable form. Rebirth into the same species is called

reincarnation. Like reincarnation, transmigration assumes the belief that souls survive death and are reborn into different bodies, passing through a series of lives. Reincarnation and transmigration are associated with **karma**. Some traditions believe humans are always reborn into new human bodies; others feel that the soul can travel into other animal or vegetable forms. (See: **karma** and **reincarnation**)

transport an ecstatic visionary experience or high spiritual moment of insight.

transportation any basic, old car a person can buy.

transvestite a person who dresses in the clothing of the opposite sex as a form of sexual expression or orientation. As opposed to a cross-dresser, who may not have homosexual tendencies, a transvestite is wearing the clothing in order to attract or entice a sexual response.

double bass trap set   photo by John McCleary ©

traps or **trap set** a full set of drums.

trash or **trash talk** verbal seduction. Nonsense spoken in an effort to impress someone. **2.** conversation used to seduce someone into sex. Similar to **talking trash** or **talking shit**.

trashed or **trashed out** wiped out, destroyed. Also, under the influence of a drug, drunk or tired.

trash talk or **trash** street language or colloquial communication. Often, sarcasm directed at a friend. A throwaway conversation like discussing the weather. For example: "How's it hangin? You look like someone cut it off. What's the prob, your chick didn't get home from my place 'till early AM?" Similar to **talking trash** or **talking shit**.

travel agent *drugs* (See: **tour guide**)

tray *drugs* a plate or tray on which to clean **marijuana**. Some very fine examples of this **paraphernalia** art form were created and used by the culture, including family heirloom silver trays and hand-crafted, laminated hardwood trays with separate dividers for **seeds and stems**. There was also the ugly, yard sale Melmac plate. (See: **paraphernalia** and **seeds and stems**)

tree-hugger *social issues* a radical **environmentalist**. Someone who loves trees. Someone willing to be chained to a tree to keep a logger from cutting it down. A term created by conservatives as a derogatory name for people with ecological ideals. Meant to be derisive, it is actually a compliment to someone who cares about the environment. Members of the logging industry, including wage-earning cutters and drivers, have a conflict with **environmental** groups because they feel that these "tree-huggers" are killing their occupations. The truth of the matter is that overharvesting is killing the industry. Environmentalists have no ulterior motives in their fight for forests; they don't make a big living saving trees, and they are not, for the most part, opposed to people making a decent living harvesting trees. What they are opposed to is destroying our forests, endangering survival of our **ecosystem** and thus spoiling the world for future generations. (See: **environmentalist** and **ecosystem**)

trendy anything too commercial or **pop** for the **true hippie**.

Tree, Penelope a **fashion** model who helped popularize the 1960s and London's Carnaby Street fashions. Photographed by Richard Avedon.

trey *drugs* a three-dollar bag of **heroin**. Trey represents the Spanish word *tres*, meaning three.

tribe a group of hippies or a **communal** group of people living, working and playing together.

trick a prostitute's customer. a.k.a. **john**.

trick something exceptional. Example: "Say, man, that was **trick**! Can you play that again?"

tricked out dressed up and looking good. A customized car.

Tricky Dick a name given to **Richard Nixon** by his political foes. (See: **Nixon, Richard Milhous**)

trim *sex* sexual intercourse. A female sexual partner. An expression of extremely obscure parentage.

***trip** a unique experience. Something fun or exciting. Example: "What a long, strange **trip** it's been."

trip *drugs* a drug episode, a mind-expanding experience brought on by the introduction of some sort of chemicals to the human body.

Trip, The *rock & roll* a popular psychedelic dance club on the Sunset Strip in Los Angeles in the mid-1960s. All the most alternative bands played there.

trip out *drugs* to have a mind-expanding experience brought on by drugs. It is possible to trip or trip out without the use of drugs, and that would be similar to a daydream.

tripper someone who is having a mind-expanding experience.

tripping *drugs* going off traveling inside one's mind. To have one's mind and actions altered in a pleasant way by drugs. Under the influence of a drug. Usually indicates a **psychoactive** or **psychedelic** experience from **marijuana**, **LSD** or a natural psychedelic. a.k.a. **bombed, high** or **stoned**. The effects of most other drugs, such as opiates and methamphetamines, would more likely be called: blasted, drugged, **wasted**, **nodding** or **whacked out**. One of the most typical hippie words, almost exclusive to that era, yet it does find some use today in non-drug applications meaning to have fun in one's mind.

tripping heavily or **tripping heavy** under extreme influence of a drug.

trippy something unique, fun or exciting.

Trips Festival a rock and roll show presented on January 21-23, 1966, at the San Francisco Longshoremen's Hall, promoted by **Ken Kesey** and **Bill Graham**. **The Grateful Dead** played, and **Wes Wilson** created some of the handbill/poster art for this show.

trip tent an American Indian style tepee set up and employed as a refuge for individuals experiencing **LSD**. It was for people who might be feeling paranoid among the crowds of people at a music festival. The term was coined in June, 1967, in California when Lisa Law and members of the **Hog Farm** put up a tent at the **Fantasy Fair** near San Francisco and again at the **Monterey Pop Festival**. The Hog Farm also had such a tent at **Woodstock** in 1969. (See: **trip, LSD, Hog Farm, Fantasy Fair, Monterey Pop Festival** and **Woodstock**)

trivialize to depreciate the importance of something. To ignore a problem or make light of a situation. From the root word trivial. During the hippie era, words were being expanded and altered on a massive scale through the mediums of literature, rock music, alternative television shows, and independent movies. Most new words emerging from the 1960s and 70s, dealing with feelings or social issues, were influenced in some way by the hippie culture.

troll n. a derogatory term for a person who is socially detestable. It can also indicate a person who is ugly, short, or deformed in some way. The word comes from the mythological creature of the same name, who has been described at different times as either a giant or a midget, but usually anti-social in nature.

troll v. *sex* to go out looking for a sex partner. To cruise dance clubs and hot spots looking for a person to sleep with. From a fishing term meaning to drag a line with a hook on it through the water in order to attract and catch a fish.

truck to move, to go someplace else. Example: "Hey, babe, let's **truck** on down to my pad."

truck drivers *drugs* **amphetamines**. Partly because they "picked a person up" and "kept them running" and partly because, for years, truck drivers were

the most common users and suppliers of the drug.

R. Crumb ©

trucking or **truckin'** moving along at one's own pace, in one's own, individual way. The walking style performed by **Mr. Natural** in the **Zap Comics**, drawn by **R. Crumb**. A term popularized by **The Grateful Dead** in their 1971 song "Truckin'."

Trudeau, Garry (b. 1948, New York City, New York) cartoonist. (See: *Doonesbury*)

photo by John McCleary ©

true hippie a person who lives by the Golden Rule. Someone who believes in allowing others to pray to any god, sleep with any consenting "adult," eat, drink or ingest whatever and dance to any music. True hippies are evolutionaries, not revolutionaries; we will convince you with words, not weapons. We believe passionately in **democracy** and free enterprise (not **capitalism**). We will not go to war for peace; we will love the world into it, talk people into it or shame them into it. Some people may think we are a joke; they may think we are naive, or that we are unrealistic, but we have high ideals. Some may think we have ulterior motives, some agenda to make ourselves rich and take over the world, but that is only their value system speaking; we have no other reason for our actions than to see peace, prosperity and love for all. That will be our reward. We are everywhere, and some day, if the world wises up, it will listen to us. September 11, 2001, would never have happened if people had listened 30 years ago.

tube the television. The screen is actually a large glass vacuum tube similar to the old radio condenser tubes.

tubed or **in the tube** in a perfect position, looking and doing exceptionally well. From a surfing term meaning to be in a perfect wave that breaks over the rider, creating a tunnel through which he rides.

tube steak a hotdog.

tubular exceptional. From **tubed** or **in the tube**, which in turn comes from a surfing term meaning to be in a perfect wave that breaks over you, creating a tunnel through which you are riding.

tuck and roll *drugs* a technique for rolling **marijuana** cigarettes in which the paper end is folded under instead of twisted.

tuck and roll a kind of custom car upholstery originating in the late 1950s and seen among car buffs in the 1960s and 1970s.

'tude short for attitude. A negative or dangerous disposition; an obnoxious or self-centered opinion of oneself.

tuies *drugs* short for **Tuinal**.

Tuinal *drugs* a **barbiturate** from Eli Lilly & Co., a combination of **Amytal** (amobarbital) and **Seconal** (secobarbital). A strong, long-lasting **sedative-hypnotic** used medicinally to induce sleep and for recreation to create a state of long-lasting drunkenness without the need to fill up on beverages. Often used by **fashion**-minded, model-shaped guys and girls to keep their figures while still affecting a **stoned** demeanor. a.k.a. **Christmas tree, double trouble, rainbow, red and blue, toie, tootsie,** and **tuie**. A **downer**.

tuna a particularly repulsive street name for a woman. It alludes to the fishy odor that emanates from a woman who has not cleaned herself thoroughly following sexual intercourse. Appropriately, men who would use such a term are usually unaware of or unconcerned by the fact that the odor actually comes from the male's sperm inside the female.

*tune in get with it, pay attention to what is going on around you, join what's happening. From a phrase by **Timothy Leary**, "**Turn on, tune in and drop out.**"

tune out to ignore someone or something. To stop listening. To become extremely **stoned** on drugs and unresponsive.

tunes music. **2**. the machine that plays music, such as a tape deck or a radio. Example: "I have to bring my **tunes** with me wherever I go."

turf the place where you belong, your home ground. Example: "This is his **turf**. Follow him and you'll be OK; leave his side and you're **toast**."

turista the sickness, diarrhea and vomiting that tourists get when they travel to countries with germs to which they are unaccustomed. Often associated with travel in Central and South America, yet similar illnesses are contracted in other places in the world. **2**. the Spanish word meaning tourist.

*****turkey** someone or something that is a failure or disappointment. Similar to a "lemon." Socially, an inappropriate person. A reject.

turnabout or **turnaround** a change of attitude or opinion. Similar usage to **180**.

turn a trick to conduct business, usually something illegal. Originally, the business a prostitute conducts with her customer.

turned around confused or disoriented.

turned around convinced, persuaded that the opposite view is correct.

*****turned on** excited by something. Related to the switching on of an electric current.

Turner, Ike and Tina *rhythm & blues/ rock & roll* Tina Turner (b. Annie Mae Bullock, Nov. 26, 1939, Brownsville, Tenn.), voc.; Ike Turner (b. Izear Luster Turner, Nov. 5, 1931, Clarksdale, Miss.), gtr., voc. In 1951, Ike recorded a song called "Rocket '88" with his band, the Kings of Rhythm. It was re-corded at **Sam Phillips'** Sun Studio in Memphis, which was later made famous by **Elvis Presley's** recording there. "Rocket '88" is said by many to be the first "rock and roll" recording, but Ike's saxophonist, Jackie Brenston, who sang on the recording, got the credit and it become a #1 R&B hit on the Chess label. After Tina joined Ike, they had a half a dozen hits between 1960 and 1973 and toured almost constantly. Since **Tina Turner** left Ike and his now infamous abuse in 1976, she has had a string of hit songs and many accolades. **Ike and Tina Turner** were inducted into the Rock and Roll Hall of Fame in 1991.

Tuner, Tina (b. Annie Mae Bullock, Nov. 26, 1939, Brownsville, Tenn.) *rhythm & blues/rock & roll* a member of the **Ike and Tina Turner** group from the late 1950s until 1976. Since Tina left Ike Turner, she has had a string of hit songs, a movie career and many accolades. She has become one of the most respected female entertainers of all time.

turn (his/her or one's) **head** or **turn** (his/ her or one's) **head around** to impress someone or attract attention. Usually, it is in the context of romantic attraction. Examples: "He **turned her head** with his philosophy on foreplay." "She can turn **your head around** with one note from that beautiful voice."

*****turn off** something repulsive. Anything that dampens one's enthusiasm. Example: "The tattoo of a battle ship on his lower abdomen was a **turn off** for her."

*****turn on** to take drugs. Anything that gets one high or excited; sex, drugs, rock and roll. From a phrase by **Timo-**

thy Leary, "**Turn on, tune in and drop out.**"

turn on to go against, to ridicule, to verbally or even physically attack someone. Examples: "Don't **turn on** your own sister just because she got turned on."

turn on to to begin to like someone or something. To warm to. To become attracted to.

turn (someone) **on to** to introduce someone to something. Example: "She **turned him on to** the possibility of being a human being."

"Turn on, tune in and drop out" the phrase by **Timothy Leary** extorting people to take drugs, get with the program and drop out of the oppressive regimen of their society. Others may have first coined these words and descriptions, but Leary's phrase became the anthem. The full message was "turn on" (to drugs), "tune in" (to another level of reality), and "drop out" (of society).

turnout a rejection by a friend. To ostracize someone, to reprimand them.

tush, tushy, tushie or **tukus** a person's rear end. Several spellings and pronunciations of a Yiddish word meaning the buttocks.

TV short for television. (See: **television**)

twat the **vagina**. A French term brought back to America by returning soldiers after WWII. It was vocalized only in dark bars by men of questionable status until the 1960s **sexual revolution,** when even women used it as a way to break down the stigma of such words. It has never been popular in serious conversation, but is used in humor and satire.

tweek to fix or or adgest.

tweeked out of adjustment, incorrectly situated or broken in some way. **2.** crazy or inappropriate. Example: "He's **tweeked**; don't attract his attention, or you'll be his newest best friend for life."

Twenty-five (25) *drugs* **LSD 25.** One of the first forms of LSD that was produced. Created by **Sandoz** Pharmaceuticals in the early 1960s, it was sanctioned by the US government for use in experiments at universities and veterans' mental hospitals. It somehow leaked out on the streets; **Ken Kesey** was one of the leaks, and he started a small, unsanctioned experiment among the intellectuals of Stanford University and the San Francisco literary community. (See: **Kesey, Ken**)

Twiggy (b. Lesley Lawson, née Hornby, 1949) **fashion** model, actress, and singer, born in London, England. At the age of 17, she became a modeling superstar, symbolizing the "swinging sixties" and London's **Carnaby Street** fashion industry. Her stick figure physique changed the norm in beauty and created consternation among feminists, who argued that such skin-and-bones fashion was not normal, healthy, or possible for most women to maintain

twilight zone a situation or location in which time and reality seem to have taken leave. A strange circumstance or unnatural occurrence. These times can be drug induced, or they can be more or less real. A bad day or a funny day can seem like the twilight zone. The term came from Rod Serling's late 1950s TV show, "The Twilight Zone," which portrayed strange and frightening experiences.

Twinkie defense *social issues* a legal defense based on the effect of sugar on a person's ability to think rationally. The idea that the consumption of a large amount of sugar can induce violence, even murder. This concept spawned the idea that murderers thus stimulated should be granted leniency. The term came from the trial of **Dan White**, who was said to have eaten Twinkies before he killed San Francisco City District Supervisor **Harvey Milk** and City Mayor George Moscone on November 27, 1978. White served 5 1/2 years in prison and committed suicide on Oct. 21, 1985, after his release. Twinkies are an extremely sweet and rich, white flour, white sugar dessert treat. (See: **Dan White** or **Harvey Milk**)

twist *drugs* a **marijuana** cigarette

twisted crazy, perverted. **2.** under the influence of drugs.

twisted sentenced to a jail term.

twit a derogatory term directed at an immature, ineffectual or silly person.

twitchin' extraordinary, exciting or fun. A humorous perversion of the word bitchin'.

two-bit whore a detestable person. Though it could be directed at a cheap prostitute, it was most often used merely to degrade anyone for any transgression; not necessarily a woman or someone who sold sex for a living.

Two, four, six, eight, smash the fucking bourgeoise state! a popular **anti-war** marching chant from around 1966 to 1972.

U

UCSB (See: **University of California, Santa Barbara [UCSB]**)

ugly confrontational, uncomfortable or dangerous. Another word that took on new dimensions during the 1960s and 70s. The word ugly evolved from a purely physical attribute into a personality or emotional trait. The term "ugly disposition" was used previously, but during the hippie era, the word "disposition" was dropped. Examples: "Don't mess with him; he can get **ugly**." "That car has **ugly** habits." "Don't get complacent tonight; it could get **ugly**."

ugly stick the fictional cause of, or supposed reason for, a person's ugliness. Example: "Don't get too excited about your blind date; I've seen her, and she's been beaten by an **ugly stick**."

ugly pills the fictional cause or reason for a person's ugliness. Example: "Don't get excited about his sister; I hear she's been taking **ugly pills**."

"Uh" or **"um"** I'm thinking. Should be uttered with an ignorant inflection.

ultimate best, most exceptional. Example: "She's the **ultimate**!" Also used as an unsupported intensifier. Example: "**Ultimate**, man!" Another word that took on new dimensions during the hippie era.

ultracool extremely **cool**. Sometimes used sarcastically to describe someone or something that is a caricature of **hip fashion**. (See: **cool**)

Uma a gentle, kind Hindu goddess, consort of **Shiva**. A name given to a number of babies born into the hippie culture.

Uncle Mac *drugs* **heroin**, also known as **smack**. A reference to "Uncle Sam," the caricature personification of America.

Uncle Sham a sarcastic alteration of the name of the personification of

America, "Uncle Sam." Meant to insinuate that our country occasionally becomes involved in nefarious activities.

Uncle Tom a Black person who acts like a White person by accepting the social and economic values of the White society and trying to live within the White culture. A Black subservient to Whites.

Uncle Tommyhawk a **Native American** who accepts White social and economic values and tries to live within the White culture. A Native American subservient to Whites.

unconscious mind that part of the mind that lies outside, or beyond the **consciousness**.

uncool inappropriate. An action or situation that is unacceptable within a certain social circle. The opposite of **cool**. During the hippie era, "cool" had one set of parameters, and today "cool" has other definitions. Even within any given era, there are alternative definitions of cool in different subcultures or areas of the country. To finitely define cool is impossible; therefore, to define uncool is a conundrum. (See: **cool**)

uncut uncensored. A movie with all of its sex scenes intact. It is strange how, for television, only the love scenes and foul language are removed, yet all of the blood and violence is left intact.

uncut *drugs* drugs that are undiluted and in their purest form. Cutting drugs is the practice of adding a less expensive substance, thereby adding weight and volume, thus making more money from the sale of the product. This was usually done with ingredients, such as baby laxatives, aspirin, sugar, powdered milk, talcum powder, tetracaine or procaine (topical anesthetics).

uncut goods *drugs* drugs that are undiluted or in their purest form.

underground hidden from the public or authorities. Alternative. An activity or society that is unfamiliar to the general population. It can involve sex, drugs, rock & roll, religious or political activity. Example: "This is an **underground** party; don't let any straight people know about it."

underground, the *social issues* a society of **civil rights** and **anti-war** activists who became fugitives because of their revolutionary activities. Some who went underground during the 1960s and 70s changed their names and led fugitive lives here in the United States. Others have become expatriates and live in other countries. Every so often, one of them is discovered, arrested and tried for past crimes. After years of hiding, a number of the fugitives were exonerated or pardoned and have returned to straight society and now lead normal lives. The Weather Underground is the most prominent example of the underground, but other groups included the **Motherfuckers**, Proud Eagle Tribe, Red Family and **White Panthers**. (See: **Motherfuckers, Weathermen** and **White Panthers**)

underground press media, such as newspapers and magazines, whose overall editorial content is not influenced by outside interests. Usually refers to media that is not financially controlled by advertisers who force them to support political or economic positions. With this freedom, such publications are willing to voice controversial opinions on politics and economic issues without the fear of losing advertising dollars. Such publications can be either conservative or **liberal**; yet, for the most part, this term has been

used to describe the liberal underground press. Similar to **free press**.

underground railroad *social issues* a society that supplied food and lodging to draft resisters, underground members and runaway hippies. Much the same as the organization that fostered runaway slaves before and during the American Civil War of the 1860s.

undone come apart, lost control. Originally, this term was reserved for inanimate objects, but during the hippie era, it was used to describe a human condition.

unfuckingbelievable an exclamation of amazement. A combination of the words "unbelievable" and "fucking." The expletive is only intended to lend emphasize."

unglued falling apart, going mad, losing one's **cool**. Used to describe a human condition during the hippie era after having evolved from its original use relating exclusively to inanimate objects. Example: "Dodie came **unglued** after loosing her om sign fetish in the leek bin at the health food store."

unhip unaware, unpopular. Out of the **cool** loop. The opposite of **hip**.

Unification Church, The *religion* the Holy Spirit Association for the Unification of World Christianity, more widely known as the Unification Church. Its members are known as "**Moonies**." Founded by **Reverend Sun Myung Moon** in Seoul, Korea, in 1954. Moon moved to the United States in the early 1970s, prompting a rapid increase of followers to approximately 10,000 full-time members in the West in the 1980s. Its doctrine is based on the Old and New Testaments and revelations from Jesus, Buddha and Mohammed received by Reverend Moon. This "church" is considered ultraconservative, even fascist. During the **Vietnam War**, the Moonies supported the war through the front group American Youth for a Just Peace. This anti-antiwar group was supposedly financed in part by **Nixon's Committee to Re-Elect the President** and was also involved in a three-day fast for President Nixon on the Capitol steps in an attempt to influence public opinion during the Watergate investigation.

***uni-sex** anything that is usable by either sex. It was used particularly to describe clothing **fashions** during the hippie era, when the lines between men's and women's apparel became blurred.

unit the penis. **2.** sometimes used merely to indicate any object.

United Farm Workers' Union (UFW) *social issues* formed in 1962 to represent California's field workers, comprised largely of naturalized Mexican-Americans, the UFW began demonstrating and striking in 1965 and boycotted California grape growers in 1966. It also struck and boycotted the lettuce industry, eventually gaining better pay and conditions for its workers. **César Estrada Chávez** (1927-1993) was the founder of the UFW and its leader until his death in 1993. Chávez fasted several times in protest of workers' treatment, damaging his health. He died shortly after his last fast in 1993. The Black Eagle is the symbol of the UFW. The story goes that César Chávez was siting in a bar in Mexico with another member discussing possible logos for the UFW when they looked at the black eagle on the Tecate beer they were drinking. It was also decided that the design be in geometric angles so that it could be typed out on a typewriter to look something like this:

```
                XX
XXXXXXXX    X  XXXXXXXXX
  XXXXXXXXXXXXXXXXXXXXX
    XXXXXXXXXXXXXXXX
     XXXXXXXXXXXX
       XXXXXXX
        XXX
       X    X
```

(See: **Chávez, César Estrada**) (See also: **Native American and Other Minority Rights Groups** starting on page 609 in **Lists** at the back of this book)

universal mind the **consciousness** of the Supreme **Being**, which supposedly inhabits the entire universe and provides its power.

Universe our complete natural surroundings as we know them scientifically. We stand in the middle of our universe and see the large parts, such as the planets and stars; but just as important are the small particles in our world, some of which cannot be seen by the naked eye.

University of California, Santa Barbara (UCSB) riots *social issues* on this campus in the small community of **Isla Vista** just outside Santa Barbara, California, Assistant Professor of Anthropology **William Allen** was dismissed over **academic freedom** in late 1969. His dismissal fermented student unrest, **free-speech** rallies and **anti-war** demonstrations, which eventually led to the burning of the Isla Vista **Bank of America** branch on the night of February 25, 1970. Along with UC Berkeley, Columbia, Harvard and **Kent State**, UCSB was the scene of some of the most publicized anti-war and free-speech **demonstrations**.

University of Wisconsin bombing *social issues* at 3:42 a.m. on August 24, 1970, a bomb exploded at the Sterling Hall Army Mathematics Research Center of the University of Wisconsin campus in Madison, Wisconsin, killing a post-doctoral researcher and causing $6 million in damage. Robert Fassnacht was killed by 2,000 pounds of ammonium nitrate soaked in aviation fuel and packed into a stolen Ford van. The bomb was intended as a protest against the **Vietnam War** and was planted by four young men known as the New Year's Gang, brothers Karl and Dwight Armstrong; David Fine and Leo Burt. The conspirators did not intend to kill anyone, thinking the surrounding buildings would be empty on the Sunday night. The New Year's Gang was named after a failed bombing of the Badger Ordnance Works outside Baraboo, Wisconsin, on December 31, 1969, by Karl and Dwight. Karl Armstrong had previously attacked the University's Armory Gymnasium (known as the Red Gym) and the UW Primate Research Center. The four young men fled to Canada after the explosion, but three were eventually arrested. Leo Burt was never apprehended. Karl Armstrong was released from prison in 1980; the others, being lesser participants, were released earlier. A documentary, "The War at Home," was produced about the Sterling Hall bombing, and at least two books have been written on the episode, *The Madison Bombing* by Michael Morris and *Rads* by Tom Bates. (See: **Anti-War Events, Groups and Leaders** starting on page 562 in **Lists** at the back of this book)

unload to release emotions or express psychological problems with a verbal or physical outburst. Can be a positive or negative catharsis. Example: "I know you've had a bad day, but don't **unload** on me."

un poco a little. From Spanish, one of the many foreign phrases interjected into hippie conversation to add whimsy, emphasis or dimension.

unreal abnormal, strange under the circumstances. Example: "That was **unreal,** man! The second violinist stood up, turned around three times and sat back down without playing a note."

unrest a term used by the established media to describe activity that it deems contrary to normal social conformity. Revolutionary **demonstrations**. The reaction of people to political, social or religious suppression. The actions of people who have finally become angry at their government for refusing to listen to their grievances or comply with their needs.

unstrung out of control, crazy. The analogy is of a stringed instrument that becomes unstrung and therefore "out of tune."

unstuck free or free of something. Examples: "I fell for her sweet ass, but came **unstuck** when I saw her personality."

untogether to be **uncool**, inept, **clueless** or not too bright. A person, place or situation that is not functioning well.

unword a word that is not a word. But, of course, as soon as an unword is uttered or written, it becomes a word. Unword became a word in 1962.

up short for upbeat. Happy, energetic, or active. Originally a musical term, meaning a tune of fast or "bouncy" tempo.

up or **ups** *drugs* **amphetamines**. **Uppers**.

up against the wall, motherfucker! *social issues* a verbal exclamation used by the **counterculture** against the establishment. Using this command, which was historically directed by police to criminal suspects or political demonstrators, was meant to indicate a sarcastic reversal of these roles. The intent was to state that the "people" of this country were taking back their lives, and, like many of the revolutionary slogans of the day, it was meant to repulse "uptight" sensibilities. The use of the word motherfucker was for emphasis and to effect recognition through the nature of its connotation. The phrase comes from a line in a poem by beat poet and Black nationalist **LeRoi Jones**.

Up Against the Wall, Motherfucker or **the Motherfuckers** (See: **Motherfuckers, the**)

up another notch to increase the intensity or effort in an endeavor. To try harder. Example: "We're **up another notch** in our lovemaking, where screaming is mandatory."

upchuck to be sick to one's stomach. To vomit. Like many of the words at this level of sophistication, this term was employed primarily to revolt "uptight" sensibilities.

up for it ready, prepared, capable. Example: "We're planing a **Frisbee** tournament; are you **up for it**?"

up front truthful, straightforward, candid. A term that appeared in our lexicon around 1971. Example: "I'll be **up front** about this; your aversion to soap and water leaves no chance for our happily ever after!"

uppers *drugs* stimulant drugs. Usually **amphetamines**, **Benzedrine** or **Dexedrine**.

uppity a term for a pushy or obnoxious person, most often directed at women. A women's liberation bumper sticker from the era stated, "Uppity Women Unite," thus throwing the condemnation back at detractors.

ups *drugs* short for uppers, or stimulant drugs.

up the ass large amounts, or lots of something. Example: "He's got money **up the ass**." Same as "**up the wazoo**" or "**up the kazoo** or **yazoo**."

up the kazoo, wazoo, yazoo, etc. large amounts, a lot of something. Example: "He's got money **up the kazoo**." The **kazoo, wazoo** or **yazoo** seems to refer to the buttocks or anal passage. Similar usage as **up the ass**.

*uptight tense, unsympathetic, conservative or **uncool**.

uptight, out of sight the opposite of **uptight**. This usage means well put together or incredible looking, as in "he has a tight ass." "Uptight, out of sight" was used in **James Brown's** 1964 song "Out of Sight."

up to (one's) **ass in** engulfed or overwhelmed by something. Example: "He's **up to his ass** in compost."

up to speed competitive or at one's best. Example: "He's not **up to speed** in algebra."

uptown the place where things are happening. **2.** something new or progressive, a happening place. Example: "His new juice bar is real **uptown**."

up with people a slogan that soon became self-effacing sarcasm and the brunt of jokes after a religious singing group adopted the name.

up your ass an expression meaning roughly "go fuck yourself." A suggestion that someone have something inserted in their anus. The British version is **up your bum**.

up yours a negative response. Similar usage as **forget about it** or **fuck you**. Short for **up you ass**. Often just a sarcastic term uttered between friends.

use and abuse of drugs *social issues* there is a distinct difference between using drugs and abusing them. Every culture in the world engages in medical, recreational and spiritual use of drugs; every culture also has drug abuse. It is obvious that society cannot stop drug abuse by prohibiting drugs, as they will always be available. Those with addictive personalities, mental or chemical imbalances that make them irresponsible drug users will always find a way in which to abuse drugs. They will sniff glue or eat the bark from trees if they have to. The only way to control drug abuse and its negative effects on society is to legalize most drugs, control them as we do alcohol, and recognize **addiction** as an illness. We must take our heads out of the conservative religious sand, admit that abuse is a natural human frailty, approach those who are additive with clinical respect, and treat them psychologically and medically.

use *drugs* to take drugs; most often, to use intravenous drugs (**hard drugs**).

user *drugs* someone who injects hard drugs intravenously.

user-friendly *computer revolution* easy to learn and use. Originally a computer term that appeared in the late 1970s, it has since gained use to describe any uncomplicated device or function.

using *drugs* taking hard drugs intravenously.

utopia a "perfect world." A fictional place or desired existence that incorporates all the elements of peace, freedom and equitable distribution of work and wealth. A concept advanced in the book *Utopia* by Sir Thomas More, published in 1516.

V

vagina the female sex organ. An opening in the lower abdomen of a woman into which the male sex organ is inserted for the purpose of depositing sperm to be united with an egg of the woman, thus commencing the reproductive process. That place upon which so much of our male imagination has dwelled throughout the vast history of man's involuntary, sniveling, groveling desires to procreate. Slang terms: **beaver, box, crack, cunt, furburger, gash, glory hole, hairburger, hairpie, nookie, pussy, quim, slit, snapper, snatch, twat.**

vajra *religion* the **Buddhist** symbol for man, the thunderbolt. A **Sanskrit** word. In religious rituals it is held in the right hand, while the **ghanta,** or female bell, is held and rung in the left hand. In Tibetan the vajra is called dorje. (See: **ghanta**)

Valhalla the "hall of the blessed heroes" in Norse **mythology**, the final home of brave warriors slain in battle.

Valkyries in Norse **mythology**, superhuman female **spirits** who transport the souls of slain warriors to **Valhalla**, to be with **Oden** (the Nordic God of War and Lord of Valhalla).

Valium a brand name tranquilizer taken for anxiety and favored by the **counterculture**. The brand name for diazepam produced by Roche Laboratories.

Valley Girl a girl of the suburban youth culture associated with the San Fernando Valley area near Los Angeles, California. She was generally portrayed as an "airhead," often with "big hair," and chewing gum. A late-1970s term known only in California. In 1982, **Frank Zappa** produced a record called "Valley Girl," which popularized the term nationally.

Valley Talk terminology and a form of communication originating in the shallow, materialistic, suburban youth culture associated with the San Fernando Valley area near Los Angeles, California. Exemplified by words such as **clueless, gross, gag, for real, intense, totally** and **yucky**. A late 1970s term known only in California. In 1982, **Frank Zappa** produced a record called "Valley Girl," which popularized the term nationally. In the song, Zappa's daughter Moon Unit spoke a monologue of Valley Talk.

vampire *occult* an **astral** form that survives by drawing vitality and strength from living beings. According to **occultists**, a vampire may be the **astral body** of a living person, or it may inhabit a dead body from which it takes nourishment, prolonging its own existence.

Van Halen/David Lee Roth *rock & roll/heavy-metal* formed 1974 in Pasadena, California, David Lee Roth (b. Oct. 10, 1955, Bloomington, Ind.) voc.; Edward Van Halen (b. Jan. 26, 1955, Nijmegen, Netherlands), gtr., voc.; Alex Van Halen (b. May 8, 1953, Nijmegen, Netherlands), drums; Michael Anthony (b. June 20,1955, Chicago, Ill.), bass. One of the most popular **heavy-metal** groups during the later 1970s. Both Eddy Van Halen and David Lee Roth, together and apart, have become icons of **cock rock**. (See: **cock rock**)

VC Viet Cong. The military guerrilla forces of North Vietnam during the Vietnam conflict in which the United States participated from the beginning of the 1960s until 1975.

VD, venereal disease a disease contracted through sexual intercourse.

VD Valentine's Day. Coined by John McCleary in the mid-1970s.

Veda *religion* the generic name for the most ancient sacred literature of the Hindu religion. Consisting of four collections called (1) *Rig Veda*, hymns to gods, (2) *Sama Veda*, priests' chants, (3) *Yajur Veda*, sacrificial formulas in prose, and (4) *Atharva Veda*, magical chants. Each Veda is divided into two parts, (1) *Mantra*, hymns, and (2) *Brahmana*, precepts, which include (a) *Aranyakas*, theology, and (b) *Upanishads*, philosophy. The Vedas are considered *revealed literature*; they contain the first philosophical insights and are regarded as the final authority. Tradition has it that Vyasa was the compiler and arranger of the Vedas in their present form. The Vedic period is conservatively estimated to have begun around 1500 to 1000 B.C.

veena an East Indian instrument normally having seven strings and two resonators (toomba). The sitar, which is simular in appearance, has eighteen strings and one resonator. Indian music played an important role in the development of rock and roll during the hippie era. Jorma Kaukonen, **Jefferson Airplane's** lead guitarist and a primary innovator of psychedelic music, said, "I listened to a lot of stuff; my dad was in the service overseas, and we lived in the Indian subcontinent, and I heard different things, like the **veena**. It emerged in odd ways, and when I couldn't think of a more traditional rock and roll solo, I wouldn't hesitate to play some weird thing that was lurking in my mind."

vegetable someone who is mentally dead or **brain dead**. It can be used to describe an actual medical occurrence, but is often used as a sarcastic commentary on the intelligence or emotional state of a person who is alive and well, yet unintelligent or unresponsive.

vegetarian someone who eats only vegetables. The hippie culture experimented with vegetarianism for health and humanitarian reasons. Some people think that eating animals is barbaric. Today's emphasis on health came from the 1960s and 70s counterculture.

veggieburger the epitome of **vegetarian** concoctions, a real oxymoron of eating habits. The compromise to which the vegetarian philosophy stooped in order to make the discipline acceptable to modern tastes. The first veggieburgers were soybean concoctions produced by Seventh Day Adventist food processing companies in the 1950s to fill the needs of their then vegetarian congregations.

veggie short for **vegetarian**, someone who is a vegetarian. **2.** a prefix indicating that something is vegetarian. Examples: "veggie plate, veggie candy, veggie underwear."

*veggies vegetables.

veg out to eat vegetables.

veg out to relax. From the inference that one exhibits the activity of a vegetable when sitting still.

Velcro one of the most unique inventions of the 20th Century. Velcro is made of two strips of cloth with two separate types of plastic wire attached. One strip has small loops, and one has small hooks. When the two strips are brought together, the hooks latch onto the loops, thus holding the strips together. With a little exertion, the loops and hooks can be pulled apart, but under normal conditions, Velcro will hold together any two pieces of fabric or material to which the strips are attached.

Velvet Underground *opiate/rock & roll* inducted into the Rock and Roll Hall of Fame in 1996. (See: **Lou Reed**)

Venetian-made African trading beads a popular adornment of the most style-conscious hippie. Many forms of beads were worn by the **counterculture** during the era, yet these were the most sought after. Tradition has it that these beads were made at the famous glass works of Venice, Italy, and then traded to African tribes. During the hippie era, some were old, some were new, some had been made in Venice and traveled to Africa.

Venice Beach, California one of the early centers of hippie activity in America; a beach community connected to the Los Angeles metropolis. Along with the **Haight-Ashbury** district of San Francisco, Cambridge, Massachusetts and the **Greenwich Village** area of New York City, it was one of the first places in which the 1960 **counterculture** congregated and lived.

Venus Roman Goddess of Gardens, also identified with the Greek Aphrodite as the Goddess of Beauty.

Venus mound the mound created by the pelvic bone, covered with pubic hair that surrounds the female **vagina**. Named for the Goddess of Love, Venus, for the obvious reason that this area of a woman's body is the object of amorous interest by heterosexual men.

verbal diarrhea unnecessary conversation, running off at the mouth, or incessant, mindless talk.

vernal equinox spring equal night. A day of the year on or around March

21; one of the two times of the year when day and night are equal in lengths. The other is the **autumnal equinox** on or around September 23. These days, along with the winter and summer **solstices**, have been celebrated by farmers and agrarian peoples for thousands of years due to their importance to the growing cycle. Because of the hippie culture's attraction to the spiritual activities of such ancient cultures as the **Druids**, many equinox and solstice parties, **festivals**, and gatherings took place during the 1960s and 1970s. (See: **autumnal equinox, Druids** and **solstice**)

vertical awake or sober. Upright. Example: "It's unusual for him to be **vertical** by this time of the day; the bars have already been open for two hours."

Vestal Virgins guardians of the perpetual, sacred fires in the temple of Vesta, a female deity who was the Roman God of Households.

*****vibes** short for **vibrations**. Feelings emanating from a person, place or situation. A term introduced to the American public in 1965.

vibrations *occult* feelings emanating from a person, place or situation. **2.** in **occultism**, psychic pulsations or magnetic waves.

vibrator a battery-operated vibrating device, often in the shaped of a male penis, used to stimulate the clitoris in female **masturbation**. An electric **dildo**. It can be used in solitary *flagrante delicato* or with a partner and may be employed for anal stimulation on or with either/or any sex. (See: **dildo**)

vic the victim of a crime; short for victim. Originally a police term used in TV cop shows and thus absorbed into the **counterculture**.

vicious impressive, powerful. One of those words that existed before the hippie era that took on a new direction in the 1960s and 70s. This term evolved from a purely negative definition to positive usage. Example: "That was a **vicious** guitar solo."

victimless crime *social issues* an act of personal choice, such as drug use or consensual sexual activity, which has been deemed unlawful and declared a punishable crime by governmental authorities. Many of these laws are based on religious prejudices and not real moral transgressions. There is room for speculation that the penalizing of these "crimes against oneself" is actually a breach of our **First Amendment** rights and freedoms. Many people feel that it is acceptable for individuals to indulge in any activity as long as it creates no negative consequence for others.

video magnetically or electronically recorded and projected images.

video games *computer revolution* games played on a computer or computer-type device. Video games were some of the first uses and experiments on personal computers. The first game was **Spacewar**, created in the 1960s at MIT by a group of programmers calling themselves "hackers." Other first examples were chess playing computers, such as the Richard Greenblatt's **MacHack**, in the early 1960s. Spacewar and MacHack were never distributed commercially. Other early games marketed to the public were Computer Space, then **Pong**, and then later sophistications created Pac-Man, Space Invaders, etc. (See: **Computer Space, MacHack, Spacewar** and **Pong**)

vidya Sanskrit for knowledge. In **Theosophy**, the "wisdom knowledge" that enables man to distinguish between true and false.

Viet Minh short for "Vietnam Doc Lap Dong Minh Hoi," which in English translates loosely to "League for the Independence of Vietnam." This nationalist organization, led by Ho Chi Min and Vo Nguyen Giep, guided Vietnam through the war with Japan, its struggle for independence from France, and efforts to reunify the country during the **Vietnam War** against the Saigon Government of (South) Vietnam and the US.

Vietnam War the military action between the United States of America and the Peoples' Republic of Vietnam, conducted roughly from December 22, 1961, to March 29, 1973. The US Congress never made a declaration of war, and therefore it was never technically a war. Many people considered it a civil war between the North and South Vietnamese, and therefore none or America's business. (See: **Anti-War Events, Groups and Leaders** starting on page 562 in **Lists** at the back of this book) (See also: **Vietnam War** starting on page 560 in **Lists** at the back of this book)

Vietnam War Leaders of South Vietnam (See: **Vietnam War** starting on page 560 in **Lists** at the back of this book)

Vietnam War US troop strengths and deaths (See: **Vietnam War** starting on page 560 in **Lists** at the back of this book

Vietnamization a **Nixon** administration effort to turn the **Vietnam War** over to the South Vietnamese Government.

Vietnik a **Vietnam War** protester. The suffix "nik" was meant to indicate a Russian or **communist** influence associated with the protesters.

vino wine. The Italian word for wine.

vinyl phonograph record albums upon which music was recorded. Record albums were made of a plastic compound called vinyl. (See: **LPs**)

Vinya Pitaka *religion* one of the oldest Buddhist scriptures, consisting of the rules of discipline for the community of monks.

Virgo astrological sign, August 23 to September 23, sixth house of the **Zo-**

diac, mutable earth sign, symbolized by the virgin. Traits: analysis, detail, service. Self-perception: I analyze.

Vishnu *religion* one of the three gods of the Hindu Trinity (**Brahma**, the Creator; Vishnu, the Preserver; and **Shiva**, the Destroyer). In **Hinduism**, the creator of the cosmos. He and Shiva are the two great Gods of Hindu devotion. The lawgiver and moral guardian, Vishnu appears on earth from time to time as an **Avatar** to reawaken men to knowledge of truth. To followers of **Vishnauism**, Vishnu is the supreme deity.

Vishnuism *religion* one of the three great divisions in modern **Hinduism**. The other two are **Shaivism** and **Shaktism**. Its followers identify **Vishnu** (rather than **Brahma** and **Shiva**) with the Supreme Being, and are exclusively devoted to his worship, regarding him as the Creator, Preserver and Destroyer of the universe.

vision supernatural scenes or human images seen by mortal eyes.

VISTA (See: **Volunteers in Service to America**)

vitamin A *drugs* **LSD**. a.k.a. **acid, instant zen**. (See: **LSD**)

vitamin C *drugs* **cocaine**. (See: **cocaine**)

vitamin E *drugs* **ecstasy**. a.k.a. **Adam, love drug, MDA, vitamin X, X, XTC**. (See: **ecstasy**)

vitamins *drugs* a street term for all drugs in general.

vitamin T *drugs* **marijuana**. (See: **marijuana**)

vitamin X *drugs* **ecstasy**. a.k.a. **Adam, love drug, MDA, vitamin E, X, XTC**. the growth of language has two different directions, expansion and contraction. Expansion involves grouping words together into phrases and creating longer words to expand a thought. The contraction of our language is the process of shortening these words and phrases after everyone knows their meaning. Often, a younger generation merely wants to make the language or the ideas more their own and therefore shorten them to do so. It's **cool** to create cryptic words that exclude the older generation or straight society. (See: **ecstasy**)

Viva la huelga! *social issues* long live the strike! The slogan of the **United Farm Workers Union (UFW)** in the 1960s. Spoken by **César Estrada Chávez**, founder of the UFW. (See: **Chávez, César** and **United Farm Workers Union**) (See also: **Native American Rights** starting on page 609 in **Lists** at the back of this book)

vivid bright or lucid. Although similar in use during the hippie era, it developed new, deeper meanings when placed in the context of the psychedelic culture.

Volunteers in Service to America (VISTA) or **The National Service Corps** *social issues* a US government program originally suggested by **President John F. Kennedy** in 1962. The idea of developing a national service program was developed soon after the **Peace Corps** was created. President Kennedy organized a small group of people to determine the feasibility of a domestic volunteer service corps; many of the ideas developed at that time are still integral parts of VISTA, including the availability of the program to people of all ages, its relatively small size, a one-year time commitment, and modest pay to cover basic living expenses.

VISTA was not fully realized until the **Johnson** Administration, under the Economic Opportunity Act in 1964 and the "War on Poverty" legislation. Along with Head Start and other antipoverty programs, VISTA's goal was to eliminate "poverty in the midst of plenty by opening to everyone the opportunity to work and the opportunity to live in decency and dignity." On December 12, 1964, the first group of 20 VISTA volunteers was greeted by President Johnson. Ranging in age from 18 through 81, these "VISTAs" attended an intensive 6-week training program and were then placed in urban neighborhoods of Hartford, Connecticut, rural hills of Kentucky and migrant camps of California. Today, VISTA still places individuals with community-based agencies to help create long-term solutions to the problems of urban and rural poverty, and is still dedicated to social, educational and **environmental** work within the United States, just as the Peace Corps works overseas. Republican administrations since that period have slowly dismantled such programs because they view them as socialistic and a financial drain on "for profit" companies.

voodoo *religion* **black magic** or **witch-craft** of the West Indies. A religion derived from the African worship of many gods.

voting age *social issues* on June 22, 1970, **President Richard Nixon** signed into law a bill reducing the voting age in America from 21 to 18. Eleven million young people became eligible to vote. Many believe that it was forced on the government by the protests of young men saying, "We are old enough to die for our country, but we cannot vote for its government."

VW bug the Volkswagen passenger car. Originally designed in Germany before WWII at the request of Adolf Hitler to create an inexpensive mode of transportation for the folks. "Volks" means people or "folks," and "wagon" means car. It was not mass-produced until after the war and in the 1960s and 70s, it became a popular, cheap vehicle for hippies and middle-class Americans.

VW bus the Volkswagen van. In the 1960s and 70s, it became the most popular mode of transportation of hippies and members of the **countercul-ture**. The gas mileage was good; the engine was easily accessible and simple to work on. It would hold your sleeping bag, guitar, dog, **ol' lady** and fifty pounds of **brown rice**, no problem.

W

wacked out under the influence of drugs. **2.** tired.

wacko a person, place or situation that is crazy or strange.

wacky t'backy *drugs* **marijuana**. (See: **marijuana**)

wacky weed *drugs* **marijuana**. (See: **marijuana**)

wad euphemism for an ejaculation of sperm. Also means someone's all-out effort. Examples: "He shot his **wad** all over her pedal pushers." "He shot his **wad** on that project. If he doesn't get promoted, they'll have to fire him 'cause he's all used up."

wafer *drugs* a thin sheet of gelatin containing a drop of **LSD**. a.k.a. **windowpane**.

waffle-stompers work boots with a deep tread pattern for climbing or working. Boots with Vibram soles were the most popular.

wail to excel. Example: "He can really **wail** with chopsticks."

wail on (someone) to attack or beat up. Example: "Don't get him mad; he'll pick up those chopsticks and **wail on** you."

walk to go free. Example: "Tranq got busted, but the man let him **walk**."

walk! get out of here!

walking papers an invitation to leave. Not literally a written request, but a verbal suggestion. Example: "After two weeks of connubial bliss, Judy gave Bubba his **walking papers**, citing his aversion to soap as her reason."

Walkman the first portable audiotape player. Marketed by the Sony Company in 1979.

walk on v. to ignore someone or something. Example: "If you see some trash going down, just **walk on**."

walk on v. to mistreat someone. Example: "Hey, you don't have to like Katie, just don't **walk on** her."

walk on the wild side to do something dangerous or exciting.

walk that walk or **walk the walk** be **cool**, be proud, strut your stuff, show your style.

walk that walk and talk that talk be **cool**, say the right thing and do the right thing. Examples: "He's all right; he can **walk that walk and talk that talk**." Sometimes heard as **talk that talk and walk that walk**.

wana *drugs* **marijuana**. (See: **marijuana**)

wanker *sex* someone who masturbates. A derogatory term for a disliked person. A **British invasion** term.

wank off *sex* to masturbate. A **British invasion** term.

wannabe someone who is trying to be what they are not. A colloquial shortening of "want to be."

photo by John McCleary ©

war a violent conflict for economic gain, created by old politicians and fought by idealistic youth. "Rich White men, sending poor Black men to kill the Yellow man."

war is not healthy for children and other living things *social issues* part of the logo of the **anti-war** group **Another Mother for Peace (AMP)**. This slogan, created by Lorraine Schneider, was prominent on educational material, medallions, peace notes and greeting cards, which were sold to raise money for AMP. AMP began in March, 1967, when 15 women in Beverly

Hills, California, frustrated by the escalation of the **Vietnam War**, printed 1,000 Mother's Day cards with this comment and sent them to their congressmen. Two months later, 200,000 cards had been sold. With its profits, AMP started an "Invest in Peace" fund to support legislators who voted against war appropriations. AMP's primary campaign was to establish a Department and Secretary of Peace as part of the executive branch, whose purpose would be "to examine and evaluate the range of non-military alternatives to war." In May, 1969, AMP held its first annual Mother's Day Assembly in Los Angeles. At that time, AMP introduced its Pax Materna, "a permanent, irrevocable condition of amnesty and understanding among mothers of the world." This AMP logo statement was translated into 20 languages. Film and television celebrities, including Donna Reed, Debbie Reynolds, Paul Newman, Joanne Woodward and Dick Van Dyke, appeared on national television to promote AMP causes. In 1969 and 1970, AMP distributed almost one million newsletters campaigning against military missile production and biological warfare.

warlock a male witch. Scottish derivation. Sometimes associated with the term wizard, yet the correct description of a wizard is a magician or sorcerer.

Warlocks, The *jug band/rock & roll* the original name of **The Grateful Dead** rock group back in 1965.

warm and fuzzy or **warm fuzzy** something emotional or sentimental. A sentimental greeting card or an emotional movie. Another example of the way in which the vocabulary of the era often employed physical feelings to express emotional situations. A term that eventually became an advertising catch phrase of the 1980s and 90s. Similar usage as **touchy-feely**, an earlier term based on tactical desires influenced by love, yet not necessarily by sex drive.

warm body a substitute person. A date or lover who is tolerated only because one needs to be with someone, anybody.

war paint makeup.

warped demented or crazy.

warp factor an undefined speed that is considered very fast. The term came from the TV series "**Star Trek**."

War Powers Act of 1973 *social issues* enacted on November 7, 1973, it was a joint resolution concerning the war powers of Congress and the President, stating that a collective judgment of both the Congress and the President will apply to the introduction of United States Armed Forces into hostilities. It states that the President in every possible instance shall consult with Congress before introducing United States Armed Forces into hostilities, and in the absence of a declaration of war, the President and Congress must confer. It was a reaction to the **Vietnam War** and the actions taken by US Presidents involving our troops and tax money during that conflict.

War Resisters League (WRL) *social issues* organized in 1923 by men and women who opposed WWI, many of whom had been jailed for refusing military service. The founders, including Jessie Wallace Hughan, a leading suffragette, socialist, and pacifist, believed that if enough people stood in opposition to war, governments would hesitate to start them. During WWII, hundreds of members were imprisoned in the US for refusing to fight. In the 1950s, WRL members worked in the **civil rights** movement and in opposition to nuclear testing. In the 1960s, the League was the first peace group to call for US withdrawal from Vietnam and played a key role throughout the war, organizing **draft card burnings**, rallies, and **civil disobedience** at induction centers. In the 1970s, the League worked to end the war in Vietnam and against nuclear weapons and nuclear power. In later days, the WRL has been involved in the women's movement, disarmament and opposition to apartheid. The WRL is still active at the turn of the 21st century.

washed up finished, outdated, unable to accomplish something one could once do. **2.** in a drug use, meaning to be finished with drugs.

WASP or **wasp** *social issues* White Anglo Saxon Protestant. An American of Northern European, Protestant ancestry, particularly British, who belongs to the most average and most advantaged group of people in the United States. Often used as a derogatory term. The WASP culture has been the most aggressive, powerful and arrogant society in the world for the last thousand years, so it is natural that it should receive a certain amount of warranted criticism.

waste to beat up or to kill. **2.** to demoralize, ridicule or embarrass. Example: "She can **waste** you with one look."

wasted drunk or under the influence of drugs. **2.** beaten up or dead. **3.** demoralized or embarrassed.

watch your back be careful. Stay alert. It did not literally mean to look behind you, but the message was obvious.

water, (to make) to urinate.

water bed a bed consisting of a large plastic bag (mattress) filled with water. They became popular around 1968. Created to enhance sleeping comfort. It was initially thought to improve lovemaking, but eventually, true practitioners of the art of lovemaking realized that it obstructed body control because, when a couple set up any movement, the bed took over and tossed the two victims at its will.

Watergate, The an exclusive apartment and office complex in Washington, DC, where members of Nixon's **Committee to Re-elect the President** (**CREEP**), burglarized and bugged the Democratic Party Headquarters offices on June, 1972.

Watergate break-in *social issues* a break-in at the Democratic Party Headquarters offices in **The Watergate** building complex in Washington, DC, on June 17, 1972, in which five men were caught bugging phones, stealing file information and planting incriminating documents. The break-in was committed by "**the plumbers**," a secret organization supported by **Nixon's Committee to Re-elect the President** (**CREEP**). It was actually the second break-in and was conducted to replace a faulty bugging device on Democratic Party Chairman Lawrence O'Brien's phone. Information received from the listening device was to be used to discredit the Democratic Party. A security man noticed tape holding a door lock open and called the police. The plumbers caught in the offices were James McCord, Bernard Barker, Frank Sturgis, Virgilio R. Gonzales and Eugenio R. Martines. E. Howard Hunt and G. Gordon Liddy were later implicated; at the time of the break-in they were across the street in a room at Howard Johnson's Hotel, watching through the windows and listening on walkie-talkies. The burglary and Nixon's involvement in its cover-up created grounds for impeachment of the President, thus causing him to resign on August 9, 1974.

John Ehrlichman, Nixon's Chief of Staff

Watergate

Watergate Conspirators, "The Plumbers" and Nixon's Committee to Re-elect the President (CREEP) *social issues* the Watergate conspiracy was an effort to conceal any connection between **Richard Nixon** and the break-in at Democratic Party Headquarters in **The Watergate** building complex in Washington, DC, on June 17, 1972. The cover-up involved payoffs to the burglars for their silence, lies and deception by the highest ranking members of the Nixon administration, including Nixon himself. **Scapegoats** were created to obscure the President's involvement, and White House conversation tapes and transcripts were altered. Some say even murder was committed in the form of the mysterious crash of United Airlines Flight 553, in which Mrs. E. Howard Hunt died along with 44 others. (A list of the members of the Nixon administration and others involved in the Watergate break-in and the conspiracy appears on page 582 in **Lists** at the back of this book.)

water pipe *drugs* a device used for smoking tobacco, **marijuana** or **hashish**. Constructed so that the smoke is filtered through water, thus cooling it and making it less harsh. The same as a **hookah, hubble-bubble** or **narghile**.

Waters, Muddy (b. McKinley Morganfield, April 4, 1915, Rolling Fork, Miss.; d. April 30, 1983, Chicago, Ill.) *blues* one of the foremost Black blues musicians. With his songwriting credits and longevity as a performer, he has influenced all forms of contemporary music. He first recorded in 1941, and in the late-1940s and 1950s he wrote and recorded a number of songs that are still being played and copied today. With Willie Dixon, Waters wrote a number of important songs. Waters' song "Rolling Stone" gave the British rock group its name. He also wrote "I'm Your Hoochie Coochie Man" and "Got My Mojo Working" in 1954.

water signs of the zodiac Cancer, Scorpio, Pisces; sensory, emotional, psychic, creative.

Watkins Glen, New York, July 28-29, 1973 600,000 rock fans attended the biggest concert yet recorded.

Watts, Alan (Wilson) (1915-1973) *religion* **mystic**, writer, and lecturer, born in Chislehurst, England. A prominent author of English language books on Eastern religion. Watts produced some of the most popular books on Zen Buddhism for the Western mind: *The Spirit of Zen*, 1936; *The Way of Zen*, 1959; *Spirit of Zen*, 1960; *Psychotherapy East and West*, 1961; and *This is It*, 1973. Alan Watts was also involved in the famous research into **consciousness** conducted during the 1960s at Stanford and Harvard Universities with **Timothy**

Leary, **Aldous Huxley** and **Richard Alpert (Ram Dass)**. Watts was considered a **guru** by many in the **counterculture** of the 1960s.

Watts riots, August 11-15, 1965 the neighborhood of South Central Los Angeles erupted in racially motivated riots after a Black motorist was arrested. When the LA police couldn't control the streets, 12,500 National Guardsmen were called in. The violence claimed the lives of 35 people, costing an estimated $200 million.

Wavy Gravy   photo by Lisa Law ©

Wavy Gravy (Hugh Romney) not a Thanksgiving apparition. Titular leader of the **The Hog Farm** and public address announcer at **Woodstock.** A **communal** group of people called **The Hog Farm**, with Romney as its leader, was given 33 acres near Sunland-Tujunga north of Los Angeles early 1967. The land was given rent free in exchange for keeping up the farm house and tending to the hogs there. Harassed by other local citizens, they left, going on the road in school buses, eventually ending up at the Woodstock Music Festival in 1969, where they worked to help create that event. Many of the members of The Hog Farm later moved to northern New Mexico near

Taos. Wavy Gravy now runs Camp Winnarainbow at the Black Oak Ranch near Laytonville, California, where he conducts camps for children and adult children. campwinnarainbow.org

way a modifier of other words and a word used for emphasis. Examples: "no **way**, **way** more, and **way** far out."

way in popular. Example: "That color is **way in,** man."

way out extreme or unconventional. Example: "Your hairstyle is **way out**. I hope you don't dream of working in a bank." Similar to **far out**.

way out there an extreme concept. Example: "That's **way out there**, a pet cemetery, what a great idea!" **2.** mentally lost or under the influence of drugs.

way past cool a phrase indicating that something is very innovative. Example: "That movie is **way past cool,** man."

way to go! an exclamation of approval. Example: "Did you do that yourself? **Way to go,** man!" A colloquial shortening of "**That's the way to go!**"

wazoo a term of unknown origin, considered a reference to the buttocks or anal passage. Similar usage as **kazoo** and **yazoo**. Example: "He's got money up the **wazoo**."

weak in bad taste, inappropriate. Example: "That was **weak**, breaking up with her by singing telegram."

We Are Everywhere a book written by **Jerry Rubin** while in the Cook County, Illinois, jail in the summer of 1970 on a 60-day sentence for inciting a riot and contempt of court. It was copywritten by Trans International Energy, Inc., published by Harper & Row and dedicated to the Western Underground. "It concerned hundreds of subjects," as Jerry said, and it was mainly about the counterculture, marijuana and the political struggles of the time. Rubin also wrote the revolutionary manifesto *Do It!* in 1970. (See: **Jerry Rubin** and the **Chicago Seven Trial**)

"We are Gods and might as well get good at it."—*Stewart Brand*

Weathermen *social issues* a politically radical group opposing the **military-industrial complex**. Founded in 1968, its leaders and prominent members were Jeff Jones, **Bill Ayers**, Kathy Boudin, Cathy Wilkerson, **Mark Rudd** and **Bernardine Dohrn**. A violent offshoot of **Students for a Democratic Society (SDS)**, their name came from a **Bob Dylan** song implying that Weathermen "know which way the wind blows." The first major accomplishment of this group was the **Days of Rage anti-war** demonstration in Chicago in October, 1969. After this demonstration, many members went into hiding and became the Weather Underground. On March 6, 1970, three members of the Weathermen were killed in an explosion while making bombs in a New York City townhouse. Those who died were Diana Oughton, Ted Gold and Terry Robbins. On June 9, 1970, the Weathermen bombed the New York City Police Department's headquarters, and in July, 1970, they bombed the Bank of America's Manhattan building. On March 1, 1971, Weathermen bombed the Capitol Building. Windows were broken, and a door was blown off its hinges, yet no one was injured and the House and Senate were soon back in business as usual. Other targets of the Weathermen were the Long Island Court House and the US State Department. (See: **Anti-War Events, Groups**

and Leaders starting on page 562 in **Lists** at the back of this book)

Webb, Jimmy (b. August 15, 1946, Elk City, Okla.) *popular rock* a songwriter who wrote "Up, Up, and Away," a hit by the Fifth Dimension in 1967, and Glen Cambell's 1967 hit "By the Time I Get To Phoenix." He also wrote "MacArthur Park," "Wichita Lineman" and "Galveston."

wedges tablets of drugs, which may originally have been round, scored and divided into smaller, pie-shaped **wedges**. Most common were **orange wedges** or **purple wedges** of **STP** and **LSD** combined. Also, **orange barrels**, which were large, orange LSD tablets, were divided into pie-shaped pieces, called **wedges**. Drug production is sometimes a cottage industry, and all the many chemists have their own creative packaging. (See: **LSD** and **STP**)

weed or **the weed** *drugs* **marijuana**. (See: **marijuana**)

weed freak or **weed head** *drugs* someone who likes **marijuana**.

weenie or **the big weenie** the penis. This word is normally used in a humorous or sarcastic context and most often seen in a phrase having to do with being damaged, hurt or killed. Example: "He fell off a wave and ate **the big weenie** when he hit the pier." Perceived as a surfer term.

we go way back a statement of friendship, confirmation of a long-term association. Example: "Of course I know about his attraction to hairy women; Chimp and I, **we go way back**."

weight influence. Example: "He carries a lot of **weight** down at the recycling center."

Weight Watchers an organization created to help people lose weight, introduced to the American public in 1965.

Weil, Andrew Harvard-trained doctor of medicine and expert on mind-altering drugs. He studied in **Haight-Ashbury**, at the National Institute of Mental Health and in the Amazon Basin. In his book *The Natural Mind: A New Way of Looking at Drugs and the Higher Consciousness,* he states that "**stoned** thinking" is superior to "straight thinking."

Weinberg, Jack *social issues* **Congress of Racial Equality (CORE)** member and **civil rights activist** whose arrest on the **University of California, Berkeley**, campus helped to jump-start the **free-speech movement**. On October 1, 1964, Weinberg set up a card table and began distributing civil rights literature and political fliers. He was asked to appear before the campus administration, and this incited student **demonstrations** and the occupation of Sproul Hall on campus. Weinberg was eventually arrested, and student strikes and demonstrations followed. He is said to have coined the phrase, "**Never trust anyone over thirty**."

weird strange or socially abnormal.

weirded out emotionally upset by a strange person or circumstance.

weirdo a strange or abnormal person.

weirdo longhairs a name directed at young people who let their hair grow down over their ears in the mid-1960s. A name directed at **The Beatles** when they appeared on the Ed Sullivan Show on February 11, 1964. Their haircuts at that time were shorter than those of most stockbrokers today.

weird out to become strange. To act abnormally due to some experience.

well, all right! an exclamation of approval.

Jann photographed at Monterey Pop by Jim Marshall ©

Wenner, Jann (b. Jan Simon Wenner, January 7, 1946, New York City) co-founder and editor of *Rolling Stone* magazine. (See: *Rolling Stone* **magazine**)

went south failed or broke down. May have come from the term "went down." Examples: "Our relationship **went south** after I seduced her sister, turned her brother in to the police and evicted her mother." "My engine **went south**." May have come from an attitude about the Southern States.

"We regret to inform you..." the dreaded words that began the notice of a soldier's death or missing in action, received by thousands of parents and loved ones during the **Vietnam War**. These notices from the US Department of the Military informed families of the loss of approximately 58,169 American lives during the conflict.

we're on agreement to an appointment or affirmation of a date or meeting time. Example: "**We're on** to get it on, Friday, the 27th, at 8:45."

we're talkin'... "This conversation is about...." Example: "**We're talkin'** big bucks here."

"We Shall Overcome" *social issues* the anthem sung by **civil rights** demonstrators. Written by **Pete Seeger**, Guy Carawan, Frank Hamilton and Zilphia Horton in 1947. It was taught to the Greensboro, North Carolina, **sit-in** demonstrators in 1960 by Guy Carawan. Adopted from an old church song, "I Will Overcome," with the melody from a gospel song, "I'll Overcome Someday," written in 1903 by Rev. Charles Tindley.

Wesson party *sex* a get-together in which two or more people lather themselves with oil and slither around on each other, performing intercourse and other sexual activities. a.k.a. **Mazola party**. Mazola and Wesson are two brand-name cooking oils.

Western yoga *religion* a term sometimes applied to **Theosophy**, as well as to the "New Thought" movements and **Christian Science**. The followers of these groups generally object to this name.

wet dream a clinical definition might be "an erotic dream which produces ejaculation." But in daily usage, it is a euphemism for desire or excitement. Examples: "She's his **wet dream**." "He saw that guitar and had a **wet dream**."

wet your willie to have sexual intercourse. Example: "Did you **wet your willie** last night?"

wha? I'm trying to understand you. What are you saying? Short for what?

whack to kill someone. **2.** to have intercourse with a woman. It is a disturbing realization that our society often uses violent terms to describe sexual intercourse.

whacked or **whacked out** extremely affected by drugs or alcohol. **2.** tired or crazy. Examples: "It was a late night; I'm **whacked**." "He's **whacked out;** he should be in a padded room somewhere."

wham! an exclamation verbalizing a surprise thought or unexpected occurrence. Used in comic books and cartoons to indicate the sound of a collision or to emphasize an action. Example: "I was lusting for her and then, **wham!** There she was." Similar usage as **shazam** or **bam**.

wham bam, thank you, ma' am a quick sexual encounter. Meant to indicate a selfish effort at lovemaking in which the man **gets it on**, **gets off**, and leaves without concern for the woman's pleasure.

whang the penis.

Jerry Garcia and Mountain Girl
photographed at Monterey Pop by Jim Marshall ©

"What a long strange trip it's been." notable lyrics from **The Grateful Dead** song "Truckin'," music by Jerry Garcia, Bob Weir and Phil Lesh; words by Robert Hunter. It is difficult to put into words what the hippie era has meant to this world. "1984" would have dawned as Orwell predicted had it not been for the **counterculture** of the 1960s and 1970s. We would all be living in a much more oppressive and controlled environment, rich and poor alike. The phrase, **"what a long strange trip it's been,"** has moved into our vocabulary and now exemplifies the period, the movements and the changes that transpired during the hippie era.

what do you say? a greeting which most likely came from "what do you have to say for yourself?"

what else is new? a sarcastic comment dismissing what someone else has said as an obvious, unnecessary statement. Example: "You say John is a slut; **what else is new**?"

whatever I don't care, I'm not concerned or I have no opinion. Example: "You're going to jump off that building? **Whatever**!" **2.** draw your own conclusion. Example: "You don't believe I'm going to jump off that building? **Whatever**!"

what goes around comes around or **what comes around goes around** hippie occult philosophy believing that there is a balance in everything that happens. **Karma**. Simply, if one loses something, one will find something to take its place; if one is unkind to someone, someone else will be unkind to them in return, and vice versa. (See: **karma**)

what if they gave a war and nobody came an **anti-war** poster slogan that first appeared around 1969. Originally written by German playwright and poet Berthold Brecht (1898-1956).

what is it with you? what's wrong with you? Have you gone crazy? Why are you doing that?

what it is? or **it is?** a question and a greeting. How is everything?

what it is! or **it is!** a statement and a greeting. Everything is OK. **2.** every-

thing is the truth or everything is what it is. A comment on the obvious.

what's going down? a greeting. The same as asking "**what's happening**?"

*what's happening? the most common greeting of the era.

what's shaking, what's shakin' or **what's been shaking?** a greeting. The same as asking "**what's happening**?" Shaking is activity, any form of happening.

what's the scam? a greeting or a genuine inquiry into what's going on. Example: "What's happening? **What's the scam** going down?" **Scam** is usually used to indicate some nefarious activity, but in this usage it is sarcasm only and merely means occurrence.

what's the word? a greeting. From "what's the good word?"

*what's up? a greeting. Most of these greetings, especially this one, were never meant to be answered except by a grunt or an unspecific greeting in return. Originally an African American term of the 1950s, often pronounced "wassup," it evolved into common use in the "rap" and youth culture of the 1990s.

what's your sign? what is your astrological sign? This little bit originated as a sincere effort to initiate conversation about astrology, yet it soon became the focus of sarcasm as one of the most used and abused pick-up lines. At one time, shallow guys thought asking a girl her **Zodiac** birth sign was a good way to convince her they were sensitive and **groovy**.

what were you thinking? you must have been out of your mind. Basically, it means that you did something without thinking about the consequences.

Example: "**What were you thinking** when you drank the lava lamp?"

what you see is what you get "I am what I am. There is no hidden agenda. Example: "If you want Paul Newman, you're out of luck; **what you see is what you get**." A phrase made popular by comedian Flip Wilson.

wheel and deal to do business, to **scam** or to barter.

wheel of life *religion* called **Samsara**, in **Hinduism** and **occult** terminology, it is the chain of life, birth and rebirth, **discarnation** and **reincarnation**. It is continued endlessly until **self-realization** is achieved. **2.** a wheel depicted in Tibetan illustrations, representing the basic beliefs of reincarnation found in Lamaism. The continual circumference of the wheel symbolizes immortality; the three parts of the hub symbolize the three great vices: ignorance, lust and anger. To fall victim to any of these can commit the transgressor to reincarnation as an insect or other lower life form in the next life. The six wheel spokes symbolize the six important divisions of life and religion: the gods, the demigods, hell, the tortured souls, human beings, and animals.

wheel of prayer or **prayer wheel** *religion* a small, barrel-shaped device made of wood or metal, used in Tibetan prayer. Written prayers to Buddha are placed inside the wheel. Each turn of the wheel is believed to repeat the prayers over and over to Buddha. Large wheels are used for the prayers of an entire community.

wheels a car or any conveyance with wheels used for transportation.

when you're hot, you're hot a complimentary statement. A pronouncement of the obvious, used for commu-nicational emphasis. When you're good, you're good; when you're **on**, you're on, etc. It also infers, conversely, that when you are not **hot** or good then you are, of course, **cold** or bad.

where (someone's) **coming from** a person's motives, what their actions mean, what makes a person who they are. Example: "I don't know **where Jane's coming from**; she's not bathing anymore."

where (one's) **head is at** a person's perspective, what someone is thinking. Example: "He's not the same since she left; I don't know **where his head is at**."

where it's at!? a statement/question used as a greeting. **Jive** talk, not really meant to be answered. Example: "**Where it's at**, man, how's it hanging?" **2.** a colloquial shortening for "that's where it is" used primarily for emphasis, not as a specific direction to something lost or sought out. The "it" is usually nonspecific, insider knowledge or information meaning that the person is **cool**. Example: "I don't know where it is, but I know **where it's at**."

—*Ken Kesey*

where (someone) **lives** the value system of an individual. Someone's most private and personal thoughts. Examples: "Don't criticize his artwork, that's **where he lives**." "It's clear you don't know **where she lives**. She's really a very spiritual person."

where's it at?! a question/statement used as a greeting. **Jive** talk, not really meant to be answered. Not always the same usage as **where it's at**. One of the most blatant, overused colloquial massacres of the English language, and one that must be included in this otherwise scholarly publication.

where's the action? where's the party? **Action** is anything exciting.

where the action is the place where a party or some such activity is located.

where to get off a verbal put-down, a suggestion for someone to **get lost**. I believe it must have come from "to tell someone where to get off the bus." Example: "If he makes fun of my tie-dye socks, I'll tell him **where to get off**."

whiff a euphemism for any sensual recognition. Usually experienced in the pursuit of sexual gratification. The tempting odor of perfume, the smell of body oil, or, if you like, the musk of uncensored feminine scent. Example: "Did you get a **whiff** of her? She's my favorite flavor."

whiff a miss. The sound of a baseball bat as it misses a pitched ball. Example: "What a **whiff**! He missed that mosquito by a mile."

whip it a euphemism for **masturbation**.

whip it out to take out one's penis.

whip it to me give me sex. **2.** give it to me (anything, not exclusively sex).

whipped short for pussy-whipped. **Pussy-whipped** indicates the state of a man who is so emotionally wrapped up in a woman that he becomes overly subservient to her. **Pussy** refers to the female genitals.

whipped emotionally beaten by a person or a situation. Formerly a physical circumstance, it took on an emotional definition during the 1960s and 70s.

whipped cream *sex* a reference to the sexual game of applying whipped cream to body parts and having a partner lick it off.

Whiskey-A-Go-Go officially considered one of the first discos, it opened on January 15, 1964, on Sunset Strip in Los Angeles. The owner was Elmer Valentine. Famous for its go-go dancers wearing short dresses of sequins and metallic fringe, some of whom danced in cages suspended above the floor. Although known for disco, it was for a long time one of the best live music venues in the Los Angeles area. Groups like **The Doors**, **Jimi Hendrix** Experience, **Led Zeppelin** and **Pink Floyd** played early gigs there. Originally, the term go-go came from the French "a gogo," loosely meaning "galore." There was once a Parisian club called Whiskey a Gogo.

White, Dan *social issues* Dan White shot and killed **gay** San Francisco City District Supervisor **Harvey Milk** and **straight** City Mayor George Moscone on November 27, 1978. White, an ex-policeman and former San Francisco Supervisor himself, was disturbed by what he thought was the city's favoritism toward the gay community. He served 5 1/2 years in prison and committed suicide on Oct. 21, 1985, after his release. (See: **Twinkie defense**)

white and **white lady** *drugs* **cocaine** or **heroin**. (See: **cocaine** and **heroin**)

white or **white of you** pure or saintly. Often used sarcastically. Examples: "How **white**, donating your bras to the convent charity auction." "How **white of you** to give up sex for the weekend."

white bread a person so conservative as to be sanitized and as "American as white bread." White bread being artificially pure, bleached and stripped of nutritional value, as opposed to whole wheat bread.

white bread a Black term for White people. **2.** a Black term for a White woman who is the object of sexual desire.

white collar or **white-collar worker** an office worker. During the hippie era, it carried a negative connotation along with ill feelings toward capitalism. The **counterculture** used this term in reaction to the conservative, earlier prejudice against blue-collar and trade workers.

white crosses *drugs* (See: **cross tops**)

white knuckles an indication of fear or anxiety. Refers to a fist clenched tightly in fear. Example: "As his VW van ventured onto the freeway, he clutched the steering wheel with **white knuckles** and vocalized a reverent **om mantra**."

white light *drugs* awakening, **realization**, inner knowledge. The flash of understanding and the moment of awareness. The educational aspect of drugs, the **mind-expanding** and **mind-altering** moment. A term for **psychedelic** awareness.

white lightning a clear, homemade "bootleg" corn liquor usually possessing over 100 proof potency. Often so high in alcohol content that it is flammable. **2.** a form of **LSD**.

white magic the use of supernormal powers and abilities for the unselfish benefit of others.

white meat a Black term for a White woman.

white port lemon juice (WPLJ) a fabled and possibly fictional alcoholic beverage with origins in the African American culture. A termed used in the hippie era to describe any strange wine or beverage. The name of a song recorded by The Four Deuces in 1955, re-recorded by Frank Zappa around 1968, and featured on several of his albums. The song was written by R. Dobard and L. McDaniels.

White supremacists a **brotherhood** of individuals who believe in the supremacy of the White, or Caucasian, race. Also known as **Aryan Nation**. (See: **Aryan Nation**)

white trash a term used to describe poor, low class, uneducated Caucasians.

whitey a Black term for a White person.

whirling dervishes (See: **dervishes**)

Who, The *rock & roll* a British rock band formed in London in 1964, Pete Townshend (b. Peter Dennis Blandford Townshend, May 19, 1945, London), gtr., voc.; Roger Daltrey (b. Mar. 1, 1944, London), voc.; John Entwistle (b. Oct. 9, 1944, London), bass, French horn, voc.; Keith Moon (b. Aug. 23, 1947, London; d. Sept. 7, 1978, London), drums. Initially a **mod** band, they evolved into one of the best things out of England, almost in a category with **The Rolling Stones** and **The Beatles**. They were more socially conscious than most heavy rock bands; **working class** with an intellectual attitude. Inducted into the Rock and Roll Hall of Fame in 1990.

whodo a shadowy person or a spirit of unknown origin. **2.** a woman of attractive, yet elusive, nature.

Whole Earth Catalog: access to tools a publication that listed and advertised hundreds of sources for alternative lifestyle products, religious organizations and **counterculture** businesses. It leaned heavily toward ecological, spiritual and holistic interests. Created by **Stewart Brand**, it was published by the Portola Institute, in Menlo Park, California. The Portola Institute was established in 1966 as a nonprofit corporation to encourage, organize, and conduct innovative educational projects; it began publishing the catalog shortly thereafter. The Whole Earth Catalog at one point was published six times a year, two in its large, tabloid-size format, and four times a year in smaller format. (See: **Stewart Brand**)

whole enchilada the complete thing, all of something. A lot of something. A term relating to the Mexican food. Example: "Gram has a lot of sound equipment; I mean he has the **whole enchilada**."

whole food natural food, without chemical additives. Produce grown without chemical fertilizers or pesticide sprays, called organically grown. Unprocessed foods, such as cereals made without white flour and white sugar, or citrus that has not been dyed and wax polished. While not exclusively **vegetarian**, whole food can include free-range chickens that are not fed hormones to speed their growth; to some people, it can mean unfertilized eggs. This designation was created in an effort to get healthier foods on the table in an era of mass-production. Started as the **consciousness** of a small segment of the population, the desire for more natural and nutritious food that exists today is an outgrowth of the hippie era, and adherents have grown, creating a small health food and whole food industry. As with many of the ideals of the hippie era, the reality of whole food has been somewhat prostituted; until the FDA (Food and Drug Administra-

tion) sets standards for the definition of whole food, it will be open to broad interpretation.

whole lot of shit or **whole lotta' shit** a lot of stuff. Not necessarily negative in this usage, nor does it infer that this is bad or unwanted stuff.

whole lotta' shit or **whole lotta' shit going down** trouble.

whole lotta' shaking or **whole lotta' shaking going on** activity. A party, dancing or sexual activity. From the 1957 song of the same name by Jerry Lee Lewis.

whole 'nother thing the implication of a misunderstanding. Example: "I'm not talking 'bout that. I'm saying a **whole 'nother thing**." Black American slang.

whole shmear or **shmeer, schmeer, etc.** all of something, the whole thing. Schmeer is a Yiddish word similar to stuff or pile of stuff.

who would've thunk it? the recognition of an unexpected occurrence, the acknowledgment of a surprising development. A colloquial expression most likely from Black American slang. Example: "The sidewalk connoisseur drank the whole bottle of **mad dog**; **who would've thunk it**?"

"Who you jiving with that cosmic debris?" the lyrics to a Frank Zappa song about people talking too much **new age**, **metaphysical**, **cosmic bullshit**.

wick the penis. Example: "Did you dip your **wick** last night?"

wicked exceptional, very good, outrageous. A previously negative word used as a positive. Example: "That was a **wicked** stirfry, man! What were those little pink flowers?"

wierd strange.

wierd space a strange or disturbing psychological state. Example: "Sally's in a **wierd space** about her dog's affection for my leg."

wife-swapping *social issues* exchanging marital partners for sexual purposes. Talk about a politically incorrect term! It infers that the wife is an item of chattel that can be loaned to another man without her agreement. I prefer to call it marital partner-swapping. This cultural phenomenon of the late 1960s to early 70s was most often a male fantasy, suggested by the male of the family, yet entered into mutually by both partners of a marriage. It must be mentioned that most wives indulged as a concession to their husbands. Largely a product of the influence of hippie free-love activity adopted by married, straight society. The book and movie "Everything You Always Wanted to Know About Sex, But Were Afraid to Ask" (1972) and the movie "**Bob and Carol and Ted and Alice**" (1969) introduced the interest and possibility, which, I believe, already lay beneath the surface. For the most part, it was an experiment in discarding inhibitions; the idea was good, but within this suppressed society, the activity was a disaster for relationships, causing many marriage breakups and even violent confrontations. The concept of open marriage exists in some tribal cultures, but it is a difficult reality for couples with backgrounds of monogamy, jealousy and Christian morality against sex outside of procreation.

wig head.

wiggy strange, crazy. Crazy in the head. Example: "My grandfather was **wiggy** for weeks after the nitrous oxide at the dentist."

*wig out to go crazy, to go out of your head.

wild, wild-ass or **wild-assed** fun, exciting or crazy. Example: "That was a **wild-ass** party at the Knights of Pithius Hall last night; everyone got **wild-assed** and crazy."

wild hair or **wild hair up one's ass** an imaginary hair that supposedly tickles a person's ass and makes them wild and crazy. Example: "George got a **wild hair up his ass** and became Georgina at the Knights of Pithius party."

wild thing, the sexual intercourse.

wild thing (do the) to have sexual intercourse.

Wilkins, Roy (1901-1981) *social issues* Executive Secretary of the **National Association for the Advancement of Colored People (NAACP)**, 1955-77. Instrumental in the landmark school desegregation case of *Brown vs. Board of Education of Topeka*, 1954; fought hard for the **Civil Rights** Act of 1964. One of the most articulate spokesmen for the civil rights movement. (See: **Civil Rights Events, Groups and Leaders** starting on page 546 in **Lists** at the back of this book)

Williams, Hank (b. Hiram Williams, Sept. 17, 1923, Mount Olive, Ala.; d. Jan. 1, 1953, Oak Hill, W. Va.) *country blues* the father of country music angst and lovesick blues. With songs like "Cold, Cold Heart," "Hey, Good Lookin'" and "I'm So Lonesome I Could

Cry," he set the benchmark for many songwriters to come. People like **Buddy Holly**, **Willie Nelson**, **Neil Young**, and a multitude of others were greatly influenced by the music of Hank Williams. Inducted into the Rock and Roll Hall of Fame in 1987 as an early influence.

willie the penis. Example: "Don't get your **willie** caught in the wrong house."

Wilson, Brian (1942-) *rock & roll* the leader of **The Beach Boys** and oldest of the Wilson brothers. The disturbed genius of surf music and the California sound. Who knows if he would have accomplished as much as he has if his father had not been such a driving and disturbing force. Or maybe Brian would have done more. Among musicians, he is considered a creative genius and one of the leaders in creating the **psychedelic** sound. Yet, to those of us who just love all music, he is merely the guy who wrote about a dozen of the best songs of any **teenager's** life. The Beach Boys were inducted into the Rock and Roll Hall of Fame in 1988.

Wilson, Jackie (b. June 9, 1934, Detroit, Mich.; d. Jan. 21, 1984, Mount Holly, New Jersey) *rock and soul* a Black singer who was one of the most prolific producers of hit soul and popular rock songs throughout the 1960s. His style influenced many other singers, and he provided the background for a great deal of romance during the era.

Wilson, Wes one of the most popular **psychedelic** poster and comic book artists of the era. He created many handbills for **Bill Graham's** productions, including the first one, for the **Trips Festival** in January, 1966. Many of the most recognizable **Fillmore Au-**

ditorium posters were his work. Wilson is credited with introducing what is now considered psychedelic lettering to rock promotion. He developed the style by adapting some work he saw by an earlier Viennese calligrapher, Alfred Roller.

*wimp or **whimp** someone who is shy, ineffectual or weak.

wimpy shy, ineffectual or weak. It can be an inanimate object that is structurally weak.

wind chimes pieces of metal, glass, pottery or wood hung in such a manner that a breeze causes them to blow together, creating a pleasant and soothing musical sound. Originally an Asian creation.

windowpane a form of **LSD**, mixed and poured into flat, transparent gelatin sheets and later, after drying, cut into tiny, less than 1/4-inch-square **hits** for ingestion.

wine fermented grape juice; "lubricant for the creative mind."

winkle pickers pointed-toed boots or shoes. A **British invasion** term. Sometimes called **fruit boots** or **Beatle boots**, they were stylish footwear worn primarily by **mods**. Winkle is a British term for an edible mollusk, which is extracted from its shell with a sharp, pointed tool called a winkle picker. That's how these pointed shoes got the name. (See: **fruit boots** or **Beatle boots** and **mods**)

winner a person, place or thing that is appreciated. Example: "He says his willie is a **winner** at every party he takes it to."

wino someone who is addicted to alcohol, usually wine. Usually also refers to someone who is homeless as well.

Winter, Johnny (b. Feb. 23, 1944, Leland, Miss.) *country, blues and rock* a talented White blues guitarist.

Winwood, Steve (b. May 12, 1948, Birmingham, Eng.) *rock & roll* a keyboardist and singer of extreme talent and creativity. Winwood attracts other good musicians and has played with some of the best artists and groups, such as **Eric Clapton**, Powerhouse and the **Spencer Davis Group**. In 1967, he formed Traffic with people such as Dave Mason and Rick Grech, and in 1969, he was a member of the short-lived "supergroup" **Blind Faith**, with Clapton, Grech and Ginger Baker. Winwood continues to record and produce solid popular and rhythm and blues hits.

wipe out or **wiped out** an accident or consequence. Physically or mentally depleted, damaged or destroyed. A surfer term originally meaning to lose control and fall off one's surfboard.

*wired high on drugs or just naturally energized and excited. Comes from electric wires, as in being "**plugged in**" to an electric current. This is a very hippie term; I find no reference to it before the hippie era.

wired (to have something) to be very good at something. Able to do something very well. From **plugged in**. Example: "Jim's got it **wired**; he knows all the I Ching's 64 hexagrams by heart."

wire-rimmed glasses also called **John Lennon** glasses because he wore them for a time. They were actually fashioned after the glasses dispensed by the thousands through the British government's socialized medical system. Different from the other most popular style of glasses during the hippie era, "**granny glasses**," which were six-sided and rimless.

wisdom religion *occult* pragmatic religion or a spiritual philosophy based on intellect rather than faith alone. The secret doctrine on which all **occult** and **esoteric** teachings are based. Often called Western zen and related to **Theosophy**.

-wise *suffix* an addition to a word that resolves the need for a series of other descriptive words. Introduced into our language around 1969. Example: "In regard to his career" becomes "careerwise." Other examples: healthwise, fashionwise, atmospherewise.

wise ass someone who is arrogant. A person who thinks that he or she knows it all. The use of the word ass is merely for emphasis.

wise up get smart. Accept the facts and the inevitable.

witch a person, male or female, who practices **black magic** or sorcery with the aid of evil **spirits** or familiars. From an earlier word "**wick**," meaning to bend or shape. Witches may be said to bend reality.

witchcraft *occult* the art or practice of **black magic** or sorcery with the aid of evil **spirits** or familiars.

witch doctor *religion/occult* an English term used to describe various male or female medical and spiritual practitioners in numerous cultures. In our ignorance, we use the negative term "**witch**," yet such individuals are usually considered positive forces in their communities. **2.** a medicine man or magician who cures illness, detects demons and exorcises evil **spirits**. (See: **Shaman** and **medicine man**)

withdrawal *drugs* the process of ridding the body of the chemicals from a drug habit. The process of overcoming psychological and emotional dependence upon a drug.

*with it appropriate, suitable, proper; possibly derived from the opposite of "without a clue."

without a clue ignorant of what is going on. Example: "I'm **without a clue** as to what 'breath of fire' is."

with the territory (comes or goes) what you get as part of the bargain, something endemic to a situation. In this instance, "territory" is more of a situation or mental state than a physical location. Another example of a phrase, once used only in the realm of the physical, gaining use during the hippie era to describe a state of mind or emotional place.

wizz or **whizz** to urinate.

wolf an active sexual predator.

wolf down to eat quickly.

Wolfe, Tom (b. Mar. 2, 1931) author, journalist, scholar, artist and personality. Wolfe is one of the most important writers of the hippie era in that his books were an objective chronicle of the times, its people and activities. An original and one of the most successful proponents of the stream-of-consciousness form of writing, Wolfe's easy descriptive style and informed use of the vernacular of his subjects positioned him as a storyteller from within the story. Not technically a hippie himself, he was still objective and sympathetic to the attitudes of the era. Wolfe is a master of the "aural" style of writing, which draws the reader into a personal association with the events and subjects of the story. Beginning in journalism, Wolfe contributed to *The Washington Post, New York Magazine, Esquire* and *Harpers*. His first book was the 1965, self-illustrated collection of essays about the West Coast custom car fraternity entitled *The Kandy-Kolored Tangerine-Flake Streamline Baby*. His 1968 classic story about fellow writer **Ken Kesey, LSD** and the **counterculture**, *The Electric Kool-Aid Acid Test*, was the most descriptive essay on the hippie era to date. Two of his outstanding books, both made into movies, were the 1979, *The Right Stuff,* about the space race and its personalities; and the 1987 novel, *The Bonfire of the Vanities*. Tom Wolfe has published many other articles, essays and books along the way and is still a major force in literature and journalism.

women's lib or **women's movement** *social issues* the women's liberation movement. The 1960s and 70s saw a renewed effort to advance the cause of women's rights, which had begun in the early part of the century. The primary goals of women's lib in the hippie era were to secure access to abortion, ensure equal pay for equal work in the job market and create tax-supported child care centers to help single women gain economic independence.

The terms "women's liberation movement" and the "feminist movement" can be considered interchangeable; both are dedicated to the conviction that women should enjoy the same social, economic and political rights as those of men.   During the 1960s and 70s, women again tried to obtain passage of the **Equal Rights Amendment (ERA)**, a constitutional amendment first drafted on July, 21, 1923, which would legally assure women's equality with men. In 1972, the ERA was passed by Congress, but in order to become law it had to be ratified by popular vote in two-thirds of the states of the union. In 1972, it was put to the vote and fell three states short of the 38 needed to pass. The amendment has never been ratified, but many of the goals of the women's movement have been accomplished through other means.   Other ideological conditions of women's liberation have not been reached to the satisfaction of the hippie era idealism. Primary women's lib leaders of the era were **Bella Abzug, Betty Friedan** and **Gloria Steinem**. (See: **Equal Rights Amendment** and **feminist movement** in the alphabetical listings) (See also: **Women's Movement Events, Groups and Leaders** starting on page 591 in the **Lists** at the end of this book)

women's movement basic definitions
women's liberation the modern women's suffrage movement of the early 1960s, whose goals were to ensure access to abortion, equal pay for equal work for women and tax-supported child care centers. Their goal was to reach a place of equality with men. The movement was exemplified by the **National Organization of Women (NOW)**.

feminists a women's group whose goal was to maintain separate understanding, while achieving political, economic and social equality of the sexes.

radical feminists a faction of the feminist movement whose goal, some would say, was to achieve dominance over men. In actuality, this group used radical words and actions to shake up the sensibility of others, bringing attention to the problems of women and promoting self-respect and acceptance.

lesbians women who prefer to share love and sex with other women.

women in the Stock Market women were first accepted as members of the American Stock Exchange in 1965 in the New York companies of J. M. Walsh and P. K. S. Peterson.

Wonder, Stevie (b. Stevenland Judkins Morris, May 13, 1950, Saginaw, Mich.) *soul and rock* one of the most successful of all musicians in the 1960s and 70s, he started out as a 12-year-old soul singer in 1963 and grew to be one of the most innovative writers and performers of the 1970s. His music contained **social consciousness**, yet provided some of the most danceable sounds of the era. Everyone was influenced by him, Michael Jackson being at the front of the line. Blind from infancy, his vision turned to music at an early age. He is one of the few recording artists who have produced songs on which he played all of the instruments. Stevie Wonder is a strong advocate of nonviolent political change and is considered one of the nicest guys in the entertainment business.

won't go there a refusal to comment. A statement of reluctance to discuss a subject. Example: "You mentioned her knee pads? I **won't go there.**"

won't quit something consistent, persistent or unending. Example: "I have a headache that **won't quit**, from a roommate with a **Velvet Underground** habit."

Woodstock "3 Days of Peace & Music," August 15, 16 and 17, 1969. A music festival on a 600-acre dairy farm outside Woodstock, New York, owned by Max Yasgur. Over 400,000 people attended. Some of the performers were **Richie Havens**; **The Grateful Dead**; **Joan Baez**; **Jefferson Airplane**; **Crosby, Stills, Nash and Young**; **The Who**; **Janis Joplin**; **Jimi Hendrix**; Credence Clearwater Revival; Joe Cocker and **The Band**. **Michael Lang** was the creator of the concept and the executive producer of the Woodstock Music and Art Fair. Without his laid-back style of tenacity, the greatest rock festival of the age would not have happened, let alone have created the cosmic impact it did. The festival's creation by hundreds of dedicated individuals is a story of incredible **karma**, luck and cooperation. The festival was bankrolled by two young New York entrepreneurs, John Roberts and Joel Rosenman. Actually, the money came from Roberts' inheritance trust fund, on which he borrowed heavily. Artie Kornfeld, a song writer/record company **A&R** man, was Lang's partner and was involved in publicity. Director of operations Mel Lawrence was of primary importance to Woodstock's success. Wes Pomeroy, an establishment police officer, was chief of security, and his sympathy toward the audience and **cool** head helped to keep the festival as peaceful as it was. Stanley Goldstein, campgrounds coordinator; John Morris, production coordinator; and **Chip Monck**, lighting and tech designer, were responsible in large part for making it all happen. **Hugh Romney (Wavy Gravy)** and his **Hog Farm** were involved in **spirit**, construction and security. As Wavy said, "cream pies and seltzer bottles" were the weapons used by his security force for crowd control at Woodstock. **Abbie Hoffman** was "in charge" of atmosphere. Woodstock was a bright spot in the era, and much has been written about this festival. To put it into the perspective of the time, 27 days before Woodstock, Neal Armstrong became the first man to set foot on the moon; seven days before the festival, the Manson Family killed actress Sharon Tate and four others in Beverly Hills, California.

Woodstock nation a term coined by **Abbie Hoffman** in 1969 in reference to the Woodstock music festival as a country in itself. It was also an ideal held by many that the attitudes of coexistence and peace exhibited at the festival would be a great foundation for a country.

Woodward and Bernstein Bob Woodward and Carl Bernstein, the two *Washington Post* reporters who pressed the story of the **Watergate break-in**, which eventually brought about **Nixon's** resignation of the presidency. Their reporting won the 1973 public service Pulitzer Prize for the paper.

woofer the bass speaker in a set of stereo speakers.

work (someone) to manipulate someone. **2.** to manipulate someone into having a sexual relationship.

workaholic someone who is addicted to work. A term that appeared in our lexicon around 1971. a.k.a. **type A personality**.

worked up excited.

work it or **work it on out** move, dance, shake your ass.

work it out come to terms, find a solution.

work out exercise. To be physically active.

work over to physically or psychologically attack someone.

works *drugs* intravenous drug **paraphernalia**, usually a syringe, a length of rubber tube for tying off a vein, and a spoon for heating the water and drug solution.

works for me or **that works for me** a statement of approval or commitment. Examples: "You want to give me a back rub? **Works for me**!" "You want me to give you a back rub? **That works for me**!"

working class blue-collar workers. In the **counterculture**, it came to mean "simple" working people who labor unselfishly for family and society. Similar to the **proletariat,** a Marxist term meaning industrial worker.

workin' on it making an effort to accomplish something. Often said in sarcasm to a request that one does not intend to fulfill. Sometimes it has a sexual context, the same as "hustling."

world class the best. A person, place or accomplishment worthy of international fame. Exceptional. Example: "He has a **world-class** arrogance, and she's a **world class** beauty; with that combination, society will surely give them their own TV show."

worm a derogatory term for a person. Someone considered to be a lower form of human life.

worst-case scenario the least desirable set of circumstances possible. The last thing one wants to experience.

worst, the an undesirable situation, place or person.

Wounded Knee *social issues* on February 27, 1973, 250 members of the **American Indian Movement (AIM)** seized and occupied Wounded Knee, South Dakota. They demanded an inquiry into the US Government's treatment of **Native Americans**. The occupation lasted 71 days. Wounded Knee Creek, South Dakota, is the site of a massacre by US Cavalry soldiers of 300 Sioux Indians on December 29, 1890. The original Wounded Knee incident in 1890 was prompted by the government's prohibition of Native American's performing religious ceremonies, such as the Ghost Dance. The US Government was saying in essence that the **First Amendment** guarantee of freedom of religion did not extend to Native Americans. (See: **First Amendment** and **Native Americans**)

*wow! an exclamation that verbalizes an inner realization to oneself. Example: "**Wow**, like, I really dig her, you know?" Even with all the jokes about this word, it is still one of the most frequently used terms from the hippie culture.

woyk work. The pronunciation used in most **blues**, **R&B** and **rock & roll** songs of the 1960s and 70s.

woyld world. The pronunciation used in most **blues**, **R&B** and **rock & roll** songs of the 1960s and 70s.

Woz the nickname of Steve Wozniak, a founding member of the **Homebrew Computer Club** and co-founder with Steve Jobs of **Apple**. Considered to be the foremost **hacker** in its positive definition. (See: **Apple, hacker** and **Homebrew Computer Club**)

W.P.L.J. (See: **white port lemon juice**)

wrecked mentally or physical damaged. Tired, drunk or under the influence of drugs.

Wright, Richard (1908-1960) *social issues* Black American author who wrote the book *Native Son*, which was an inspiration for many **civil rights** leaders.

written invitation a suggestion or request. Not literally a written document, but a sarcastic verbal reference to an unresponsive attitude. Example: "What do you want, a **written invitation**? Get over to her house before she changes her mind."

wuss someone who is weak or easily antagonized. Usually a description of a weak man, and seldom used to describe a woman. The term wuss, by some definitions, means the feminine genitals. Directed at a man, this term has the same meaning as **pussy**.

X

X a kiss. At the end of a personal letter, X's represent kisses and O's, hugs.

X the sign of death. Used in place of eyes on dead comic book characters.

X *drugs* the drug **ecstasy**. (See: **XTC** or **ecstasy**)

Xanadu a traditional name of a magic place of literary memory. **2.** a computer term meaning an "information processing system," coined by Ted Nelson.

xenophobe one who fears the unknown, strangers, or foreigners. Not a new word emanating from the hippie era, yet it exemplified the opposite attitude of the hippie life. The beginning of the Cold War, the Eisenhower years, and the Ozzie and Harriet 1950s were what the hippies were rebelling against. Fear and distrust of "those other people," hatred of other cultures and religions, and national chauvinism, were the sickness of the mid-20th century created and fermented by WWII and the Cold War. The hippie movement opened the door a crack, released us from our self-imposed isolation, and allowed others to enter and dismantle our self-made ignorance.

Xibalba the underworld of the religion of the Quiché Indians of Central America.

X marks the spot this is the place. Example: "**X marks the spot** of my worst failure."

X out, X'd out eliminated. The letter X is pronounced, not to be confused with "crossed out." Example: "She's getting bored; you can **X out** that boyfriend."

X-rated considered sexually explicit. A situation considered obscene by certain moral standards. X in this case means restricted or prohibited. Example: "His whole life is **X-rated**."

XTC *drugs* a **cool** name for the designer drug **ecstasy**. a.k.a. **Adam, love drug, MDA, vitamin E, vitamin X, X**. (See: **MDA** or **ecstasy**)

Y

ya' dig? or **you dig?** do you understand? Example: "**Ya' dig?** Do you hear what I'm saying?" A friendly question. One of those phrases with subtle meanings, depending on the vocal inflection.

yagé, yanja (*ayahuasca, caapi*) *drugs* a South American hallucinogenic drink made from an Amazonian vine called the visionary vine, **vine of the soul**, or vine of death. The active ingredient is harmaline. It was sometimes mixed with the **dimethyltryptamine (DMT)**, found in the **yopo** bean, a South American legume. The mix was effective since harmaline protects DMT from being neutralized by gastric enzymes, which inhibit its **psychoactive** qualities. In 1963, **Allen Ginsberg** and **William Burroughs** collaborated in writing *The Yage Letters*.

yak or **yack** boring or excessive talk. Example: "He likes to **yak** a lot."

yakee, yato, *cohoba* or **epená** *drugs* a South American snuff obtained from the yopo bean, a legume with psychedelic properties whose active ingredient is **dimethyltryptamine (DMT)**. DMT was one of the very first **psychoactive** creations of modern man and his knowledge of chemistry; it was found in "European" snuff during the turn of the century. Generally called *cohoba* **snuff**, it is also called businessman's special. DMT is also said to come from other sources, such as the Syrian rue

herb in China and the venom of a Sonoran Desert toad. (See: **dimethyltryptamine** and **cohoba snuff**)

yakety-yak a derogatory description of someone's excessive or boring conversation. Example: "**Yakety-yak**, don't talk back," from the 1958 song by the Coasters.

yang Chinese name of the maker and active male force of the universe. In Neo-**Confucianism**, yin and yang constitute the vital forces of the universe.

yank (someone's) **chain** to annoy, embarrass or offend someone. To make someone take notice. Same as **pull someone's chain**. Example: "Zappa wrote his music to **yank society's chain**."

yard one hundred dollars.

Yardbirds, The *blues rock* a guitar-oriented blues rock band formed in London in 1963, most notable for the musicians who moved through the group and on to do other things. The band was originally called the Most Blueswailing Yardbirds; they recorded with blues legend Sonny Boy Williams and had several hit songs in 1965 and '66. Their rotating lead guitarists were Anthony "Top" Topham, **Eric Clapton, Jeff Beck** and **Jimmy Page**.

yazoo a nonspecific place or part of the anatomy. Usually refers to the anal passage. Similar usage as **kazoo, wazoo**, or **ying yang**. Example: "He's got money up the **yazoo**."

yeah yes.

yellow fearful, afraid, having "no guts."

yellow bullets, yellow dolls, yellow jackets or **yellows** *drugs* Nembutal. A name brand depressant in yellow capsules. Chemical ingredient: pentobarbital sodium.

"Yellow Submarine" the 1968 cartoon movie based on **The Beatles'** music. Produced in England and directed by Gordon Douglas. It featured psychedelic visual effects and such characters as the **Blue Meanies**, who disrupted the tranquility of Pepperland and were vanquished by The Beatles as *Sergeant Pepper's Lonely Hearts Club Band*. "Yellow Submarine" is also the title of a 1966 Beatles song with Ringo singing lead.

yellow sunshine a popular form of **LSD**. The making of **LSD** was a cottage industry, and each producer packaged it in his own creative form. It was dropped on **sugar cubes** and **blotter paper**, mixed in thin gelatin squares or triangles, and concocted into colored **tabs** of various forms.

yen a desire for something. **2.** in drug parlance, the hunger for heroin.

yin Chinese name of the passive female energy of the universe. Also considered the negative force of the universe.

yin yang or **yin and yang** the two forces of the universe. The Chinese theory of balance. Yin is the passive, negative force considered female; and yang is the active, positive force thought to be male. It is said that everything in the universe contains one or the other of these forces, and many things are influenced by both forces. A man has both yin and yang, as does a woman, only in different proportions depending on their personalities. In Neo-**Confucianism**, yin and yang constitute the vital forces or material principles of the universe. Sometimes erroneously pronounced as ying yang.

ying yang a mispronunciation and incorrect spelling of the Chinese term yin yang.

ying yang a unspecified place or part of the anatomy; most likely, the anal passage. Possibly derived from a mispronunciation of the Chinese term yin yang. Similar usage as **kazoo**, **wazoo** and **yazoo**. Example: "He's got money up the **ying yang**."

YIP Youth International Party. (See: **Youth International Party** or **Yippies**)

Yippies the nickname given members of the Youth International Party. (See: **Youth International Party**)

yoga a yoke, to join, a union. In Hindu religion, the "Vehicle for Realization," a series of exercises and disciplines designed to bring a person to a level of mental and physical peace and power. Remember to distinguish among yoga, yuga, yogi, Yogi Berra and Yogi Bear; it can get confusing. Some of the following definitions are interchangeable or repetitious. There are different opinions as to the names, yet the following list is as concise as possible:

  hatha yoga deals chiefly with the disciplines of breathing and of body exercise. *Ha* is understood to mean inhaling, and *tha,* to mean exhaling.

  bhakti yoga, devotion, the path of love and devotion to God.

  karma yoga, action, the path of action through selfless service.

Karma is the law of action and reaction.

raja yoga, the way to God through psychological exercise.

japa yoga or **mantra yoga**, an extension of raja yoga. Japa yoga is the repetition of a mantra.

jnana yoga, the path to God through self-analysis and awareness.

laya yoga, the path through mind control and mastery of self-will.

kriya yoga, the yoga of action, the path through self-control in daily life.

tantra yoga, the sexual yoga that teaches a highly ritualized sexual union, which brings man and woman together to be divine beings. The devolving of one's ego through union with another.

kundalini yoga, the path to expanded psychic powers through breathing and other aspects of hatha and raja yoga. Awakening the serpent or reproductive system in the base of the spine. Involves the chakras or energy centers. Sometimes called royal yoga.

hippie variation, Paschimothan Asana pose
photo by John McCleary ©

yogi a master who teaches **yoga**. Yoda in the movie, "Star Wars" is everyone's favorite yogi.

yohimbe a tea from the bark of an African tree. Considered an **aphrodisiac**

for men, it actually stimulates the penile muscles. Similar to kava kava in effects.

yo' mama, (less used) **your mama** an insult. Thought to mean your mother is a whore or your mother wears Army boots. Example: "You think you're hot shit? **Yo' mama**."

yopo beans (yopa) *drugs* the South American legume from which **dimethyltryptamine (DMT)** is synthesized. (See: **yakee** or **di methyl tryptamine**)

you ain't said nothin' what you say is wrong; your opinion is of no importance. This fine example of philosophical double negative is used by a person who normally might not misuse the English language, but who will verbalize in this manner to create the impression that he is **cool** and you are not.

"You are hereby directed to present yourself for Armed Forces Physical Examination to the Local Board named above by reporting at:..." these were the dreaded words that began the draft induction notice received by thousands of 18-year-old boys during the **Vietnam War**. Selective Service and registration requirements for America's young men have served as a backup system to provide manpower to the US Armed Forces for over 50 years. President Franklin Roosevelt signed the Selective Training and Service Act of 1940, which created the country's first peacetime draft and formally established the Selective Service System as an independent Federal agency. From 1948 until 1973, during times of peace and war, men were drafted to fill vacancies in the armed forces that were not filled through voluntary means. In 1973, the draft ended, and the US converted to an all-volunteer military. Registration requirements were suspended in April, 1975, but resumed in 1980 by **President Carter** in response to the Soviet invasion of Afghanistan. Registration continues today as a guard against underestimation of the number of servicemen needed for future crises.

you are what you eat a reminder to eat healthy food. During the hippie era, a very strong health **consciousness** awakened and grew among young people. It was connected to the **back-to-the-earth** movement and many Eastern religious medical beliefs. The view that one's body was a temple became common during this period of time. The phrase "you are what you eat" is most likely an old proverb, yet it became widely reused by the **counterculture** of the era.

you better believe it it's the truth; I'm telling the truth.

you can't make an omelet without breaking eggs it is not possible to create without some destruction. One must create some mess or desecration in order to produce something else of value. An old French proverb.

you can say that again what you said is correct. Your are right.

you dig? or **ya' dig?** do you understand? Example: "**Ya' dig**? Do you hear what I'm saying?" **Dig** means to understand.

you don't want to know! a sarcastic comment about a problem or misfortune. Often, something that the speaker actually can't wait to tell you about.

you got a problem with that? a question in confrontational form. It implies "What are you going to do about what I just said or did?"

you got that right you're correct.

*you know?! (ya' know or y'know) a superfluous exclamation that, although couched as a question, is really a statement or confirmation. Example: "Like, I really dig her, **you know**?" From "Do you know what I'm saying?" Actually a product of the 1950s beat movement, it came into popular use in the 1960s. By listening closely to conversations, one will realize that **you know** *is* the most commonly used phrase in the American language. The word "like," and the phrases "I mean" and "you know," dominated hippie conversation and are used to excess even today. If you don't agree, start counting the number of times in a conversation that "like," "you know" and "I mean" are said. What is strange about these exclamations is that, even though they have no real bearing on the conversation, they once indicated a desire, newfound during the hippie era, to communicate with clarity and understanding. When someone punctuated a sentence with "you know," they were, in essence, making sure that the listener was paying attention and understood what was being said. "Like," "you know" and "I mean" are also often used as pauses to create time to think about what to say next. In this day and age, they have become obstacles to communication, since many people use them far too often. My favorite nonsentence of the hippie era is, "I mean... like... you know!?"

young blood a young person who is just beginning to smoke **marijuana**.

your own thing a favorite interest or activity. Example "I don't like safety pins through the eyelids myself, but that's **cool**, you got to have **your own thing**."

your thing a habit or activity one enjoys. The emphasis is on the word "thing." Example: "It's too messy for me, but that's **your thing**."

your way a person's own desires. Personal choices.

you said it a statement of agreement. Example: "**You said it,** man; I agree"

you the man you're number one, you're the best. You're my friend.

Young, Andrew Jr. *social issues* Executive Director of the Southern Christian Leadership Conference, 1964-70; first Black US Ambassador to the UN; member of the House and Senate from 1973-79; Mayor of Atlanta, Georgia, 1981-89. (See: **Civil Rights Events, Groups and Leaders** starting on page 546 in **Lists** at the back of this book)

Young, Neil (b. Nov. 12, 1945, Toronto, Can.) *rock & roll* guitarist, singer and songwriter, he arrived with the **Buffalo Springfield** in 1966, smashed on the scene in **Crosby, Stills, Nash and Young** in 1968, and has had a spectacular solo career ever since. His voice can be sweet or poignant; his songs are always thought-provoking, and he is one of the few guitar players who can make people cry with a few sustained notes. Inducted into the Rock and Roll Hall of Fame in 1995.

You're either part of the solution or you're part of the problem an indictment by (Leroy) **Eldridge Cleaver** in a speech in San Francisco in 1968. It means that it's wrong to be complacent about social issues and uninvolved in solving social problems.

youth culture the young **counterculture** of the 1960s and 70s. It was the first time in the history of humankind that teenagers actually had an established world of their own away from their parents. It was based around **sex, drugs and rock & roll**, and it really upset their folks.

Youth International Party (YIP) (a.k.a. Yippies) *social issues* an **anti-war**, **anti-establishment** organization founded by Stew Albert, **Abbie Hoffman**, **Paul Krassner** and **Jerry Rubin** during the Christmas holiday of 1967. **Timothy Leary** said it was conceived after Hoffman, Krassner and Rubin tripped on **LSD** and was meant to be a coalition of hippies and political activists. The Yippies were responsible for The Festival of Light and many of the **demonstrations** that precipitated the police riots during the **Democratic National Convention in Chicago**, August 24-30, 1968. Also during the 1968 election campaign, the Yippies nominated a pig named **Pigasus** for President. The pig was "arrested" at one of the demonstrations during the convention. (See: **Anti-War Events, Groups and Leaders** starting on page 562 in **Lists** at the back of this book) (See also: **Chicago Seven, Chicago Seven Trial** and **Chicago Democratic National Convention**)

youth quake a term for the phenomenon of the young, hippie **counterculture** that arose in the mid-1960s.

yo-yo someone who is not very smart.

yuck an exclamation of disgust. Example: "Toe-jam is the damp, smelly mixture of dead skin and athlete's foot fungus between the toes of a dirty body. **Yuck**!"

yucky disgusting. A **Valley Talk** term. (See: **Valley Talk**)

yuck, yuck sarcastic laughter. Example: "**Yuck, yuck,** that was real funny, dude."

yuga *religion* one of the four Hindu ages of the world: satya yuga (the golden age); tretya yuga, the dwapara yuga and the kali yuga (the dark age). The first three ages have already taken place, and we are now living in the last, which began at midnight between the 17th and 18th of February 3102 B.C.

*yuppie young, upwardly mobile professional or young urban professional. A term coined around 1978, it was an indication of the end of the hippie era. The first of the **me generation** who popularized greed and selfishness in **Reagan's** 1980s. Meant as a derogatory term, it had all kinds of subtle references to things like the word puppy and the word yes. Not to be mistaken for the Yippies. It was a spin-off from, and considered the opposite of, a Yippie.

yuppify to clean up, polish or upgrade someone or something. To make something superficial. A derogatory term of the **counterculture** directed at the shallow and overly materialistic **yuppie** culture.

Z

Z or **OZ** ounce of drugs. Example: "When you go downtown, cop me a **Z** of weed."

zap or **zapped** to be hit by something, either physically, psychologically or emotionally; often pertaining to religious energy, drugs or love. Examples: "I was **zapped** by her love light." "Scooter was really **zapped** by the positive energy of his yoga class." "That electric wire gave me a **zap**."

Zap Comics/Zap Comix probably the most popular comic books during the hippie era. Zap Comix #1 was published in February, 1968, by Don Donahue's Apex Novelties; **R. Crumb** was the artist. They were later printed by the Print Mint. At various times in Zap Comics, some of the most famous hippie comix characters appeared, such as Crumb's **Mr. Natural**, Johnny Fuckerfaster and Valerie the Vegetarian. R. Crumb was not the only artist in Zap Comics, but he was the most widely recognized creator. Second only to recorded music, hippie-era comic books were the most prolific means of expressing and absorbing **counterculture** philosophy, art and humor.

Zappa, Frank (b. Frank Vincent Zappa, Dec. 21, 1940, Baltimore, Md; d. Dec. 4, 1993, Los Angeles Calif.) *rock and confusion* a band leader, composer, arranger and guitarist of unlimited expression. No one did more to declassify music than Zappa. No matter what he did and whether or anyone liked it, one always had to admit that Zappa was having fun doing it. His band, Mothers of Invention, formed in 1964, changed musicians as quickly as it changed notes. Zappa is credited with over 60 albums, most of them different from their predecessors; he always tried to challenge the listener to keep up with his experimentation. Inducted into the Rock and Roll Hall of Fame in 1995.

zen something pure or simple, yet profound. From the term **Zen Buddhism**, but not necessarily related to the religion. Examples: "That flower is **zen**." "Flower has a real **zen** way of thinking."

zen *drugs* **LSD**. a.k.a **instant zen**.

Zen and the Art of Motorcycle Maintenance (An Inquiry into Values) one of the most intriguing books of the hippie era, written by Robert M. Pirsig and published in 1974. In the author's notes, Pirsig says of the book, "It should in no way be associated with that great body of factual information relating to the orthodox Zen Buddhist practice. It's not very factual on motorcycles either." It is ostensibly about the cross-country motorcycle ride of a man and his son. In reality, it is a series of commentaries about life. The dust cover states, "The real cycle you're working on is a cycle called 'yourself.'"

Zen Buddhism *religion* the Japanese "**meditation** school" of **Buddhism**, based on the theories of the "universality of **Buddha-nature**" and the possibility of becoming a **Buddha** within one's own living body. A form of the Buddhist religion in which enlightenment is sought through meditation and the suppression of **self-consciousness**. Buddhism was founded 600 years before Christ by the son of a rich Hindu raja from northern India. **Gautama Siddhartha** rejected the wealth of his father and the caste system of his father's religion. After years of solitude and study, he emerged as the Buddha and began teaching. Buddha means "the awakened one." Buddhism deals primarily with "four noble truths," addressing suffering, the cause of suffering, the way to cease suffering and the way to ease suffering. Thus, Buddhism emphasizes spiritual and physical discipline to attain a state of liberation from the conflicts of life.

Zen satori enlightenment through **Zen meditations**. (See: **satori**)

zeppelin a long, cigarette holder-like pipe with an oblong chamber for smoking **marijuana** or **hashish**. Also called a smokeless pipe. **2.** short for the rock group **Led Zeppelin**, formed in England in 1968. Members included: John

Bonham, drums; John Paul Jones, bass; **Jimmy Page**, guitar; and Robert Plant, vocals. One of the most successful of the original **heavy-metal** bands. **3.** a large **marijuana** joint. a.k.a. **bomber, bazooka**.

zero an insignificant person, place or thing. Examples: "Baba Labba Gobob sounds good on paper, but he's a real **zero**." "That happening at the existential cubic photorealist's loft was a big **zero**."

zero-cool an impressive person, place or thing. Examples: "Baba Ram Dass is **zero-cool**." "That folksing-along at the Hamburger Joint was **zero-cool**."

zero out to forget or ignore. Same usage as **cross out** or **X-out**. Example: "She's someone you should **zero out** of your future."

zero population growth *social issues* a fictional social situation in which population is stabilized by the control of the birth rate. In theory, if every couple had only 1.3 children, the world's population would stabilize at the present number. The number of children required to stabilize the population changes constantly and is affected by the death rate, which is influenced by medical advances. The question always asked, both tongue-in-cheek and seriously, was how a family could manage to produce 30 percent of a child.

Zig Zag man the image on a pack of Zig Zag cigarette papers.

Zig Zags a brand of French cigarette **rolling papers** that became very popular for rolling **marijuana** joints. Through time, Zig Zags came to mean any rolling paper, just as Kleenex means tissue. Before marijuana became readily available, rolling paper manufacturing companies did a pitifully small business supplying the needs of those few throwbacks who preferred to roll their own cigarettes, even after tailor-mades were available. After marijuana burst on the scene, these companies must have raked in huge, unexpected profits. Although they definitely knew from whence their windfall came, these very old and sometimes conservative companies obviously looked the other way. One wonders how their consciences reacted as the collection plate passed before them at church each Sunday.

zilch zero, nothing. Often, a common answer to the greeting, "**What's happening**?" Commonly used in the answer, "**Zilch**, zero, nada."

Zimmerman, Robert Allen *rock & roll* the given name of **Bob Dylan**. (See: **Bob Dylan**)

'zines short for magazines. A late underground term.

zing or **zinger** something exciting, disturbing or stimulating that affects one either physically or emotionally. Similar usage to **buzz** or **zap**. Examples: "The **LSD** had a **zing** to it; it must have been cut with speed." "Her rejection was a real **zinger** to his ego."

zip excitement. Example: "His guitar playing has no **zip**." **2.** to move quickly. Example: "Her boyfriend moved out last week, and Banger **zipped** right in."

zip codes numeric designations assigned to different parts of the United States to assist in distributing mail. They came into use in 1964.

zip it or **zip it up** shut up. From "put a zipper on your mouth."

zipless fuck, the "...is absolutely pure. It is free of ulterior motives. There is no power game. The man is not 'taking,' and the woman is not giving. No one is trying to prove anything or get anything out of anyone. The zipless fuck is the purest thing there is. And it is rarer than the unicorn." Erica Jong, *Fear of Flying*, 1973.

©Bill Griffith 2002

Zippy the Pinhead a cartoon strip by Bill Griffith. Griffith started in New York City's *East Village Other* in 1969 and *Screw* Magazine, drawing the cartoon character Mr. The Toad. Griffith moved to San Francisco in 1970 and joined the underground comics movement, producing "Tales of Toad" and "Young Lust," eventually working for Fantagraphics Books, Kitchen Sink, Last Gasp, Rip Off Press and Print Mint. *Zippy the Pinhead* first appeared in Print Mint's *Real Pulp* #1 in 1970; it became a weekly series in the *Berkeley Barb* in 1976, and then was syndicated nationally. Zippy is a pinheaded character in a clown suit with a naive, though profound sense of the world. His question, "Are we having fun yet?," has become one of the most quoted phrases of the era.

zit a pimple or "adolescent outcropping" on the skin. A blemish. Also be used as a derogatory metaphor. Example: "That housing development is like a **zit** on the nubile, blushing cheek of our city."

zodiac literally "a circle of small animals." In **astrology**, the circle of 12 star constellations around the heavens, through which our world moves within a year. Astrology is the unproven pseudo-science dealing with the stars and their effects on human beings. A person's zodiac sign is determined by the position of the constellations at the time of birth. The attributes of the zodiac sign or constellation under which a person is born are then said to affect the personality of that individual. The attributes of each sign of the zodiac have been unscientifically determined, but many people believe in their reality. The earliest evidence of astrology dates back to 15,000 B.C. Mesopotamia and the evolution of agrarian practices. It is the forefather and predates the true science of astronomy by many centuries.

Zodiac Astrological signs
  Aries, the Ram,
        March 20 to April 20
  Taurus, the Bull,
        April 20 to May 21
  Gemini, the Twins,
        May 21 to June 21
  Cancer, The Crab,
        June 21 to July 22
  Leo, the Lion,
        July 22 to August 23
  Virgo, the Virgin,
        August 23 to September 23
  Libra, the Scales,
        September 23 to October 23
  Scorpio, the Scorpion,
        October 23 to November 22

  Sagittarius, the Archer & Centaur,
        November 22 to December 21
  Capricorn, the Goat,
        December 21 to January 20
  Aquarius, the Water Bearer,
        January 20 to February 19
  Pisces, the Two Fish,
        February 19 to March 20

zoid an outsider. A regional term.

-zoid *suffix* a suffix identifying a person as strange or excessive. Examples: freekzoid, surfzoid, sexzoid, partyzoid. Similar usage as **oid**.

zombie someone unresponsive, mentally and/or physically, like a corpse. In the hippie era, it was often due to drugs.

zone or **zoned** a spiritual, mental or physical place of perfection in which everything is going well. In sports, it is now called the "comfort zone." Example: "He has found his **zone**." "He's **zoned**."

zoned out or **zone out** to lose concentration.

zonk to hurt or kill someone.

zonked under the influence of drugs or tired. A term introduced to the American public in 1961.

zoo not a literal place for animals, but someplace crazy, strange or intensely busy. Examples: "Work was a **zoo** tonight." "That house is a **zoo**; there are too many strange dudes and dudettes residing there."

zoom or **zooming** to impress someone. To deceive in order to gain favor. Example: "You can **zoom** some of the people some of the time, but you'll have trouble **zooming** all of the people all of the time."

zoom *drugs* amphetamines. **Uppers.**

zowie! an exclamation indicating the presence of energy or excitement. From wowie-zowie. Sometimes seen as **zow** in comic books. Example: "**Zowie,** that was a special be-in!"

Z's sleep. Example: "Before I do anything heroic, I need to cop some **Z's**.

zucchini a large penis.

Zulu or **Zulu warrior** a derogatory name for a Black man, usually someone large and/or aggressive.

Woodstock by Lisa Law ©

Lists

Census of the USA in January, 1960

Females =   90,990,000
Males   =   88,330,000
Beatniks =   3,751
Hippies   =   0

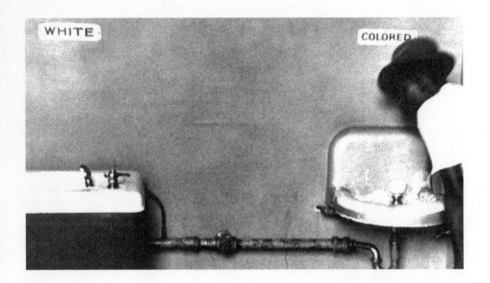

Civil Rights Events, Demonstrations and Legislation:

June, 1909 NAACP (National Association for the Advancement of Colored People) founded; oldest civil rights organization in the USA.

February 1, 1960 the first sit-in. Ezell Blair, Jr., Franklin McCain, Joseph McNeil, and David Richmond, four Black freshmen from North Carolina Agricultural and Technical College, asked for service and were refused at a Woolworth's lunch counter in Greensboro, North Carolina. The song "We Shall Overcome" was first sung here as the anthem of civil rights.

February 27-29, 1960 400 students participated in sit-ins protesting segregated stores in Nashville, Tennessee.

July 25, 1960 Greensboro, North Carolina, lunch counters were desegregated.

October 22-25, 1960 mass sit-ins held in Atlanta, Georgia; Martin Luther King, Jr., was arrested with 80 others. Presidential candidate John Kennedy telephoned Mrs. King to express concern.

December 5, 1960 US Supreme Court ruled that segregated bus terminals were unconstitutional.

January 1, 1961 James Meredith, a Black Air Force veteran, sought enrollment in the University of Mississippi and was refused an application; Meredith filed a lawsuit against the school.

January 9, 1961 Charlayne Hunter and Hamilton Holmes become the first Black students at the University of Georgia, ending 175 years of segregation at the school. It was the first integration of a major university in the South, yet it received scant attention because it generated very little violence compared to later enrollments.

May 4, 1961 Freedom Riders left Washington, DC, by bus to travel through the Southern states.

May 14, 1961 Freedom Riders bus burned in Anniston, Alabama; riders were beaten in Birmingham.

May 25, 1961 Freedom Riders arrested in Jackson, Mississippi.

May 26, 1961 The 26 Freedom Riders were convicted and sentenced to 60 days in the state penitentiary.

August 14, 1961 more trials against Freedom Riders opened and continued throughout 1962. All convictions were overturned in 1965.

November 1, 1961 Interstate Commerce Commission (ICC) banned discrimination in interstate transportation facilities.

November-December, 1961 NAACP, SNCC and Rev. Martin Luther King, Jr., tested the ICC ruling banning segregated travel by occupying White waiting rooms in railway stations and bus depots in the City of Albany, Georgia. King, Ralph Abernathy and many others were arrested, jailed, and eventually convicted.

December, 15, 1961 Albany City representatives agreed to desegregate transportation terminal facilities. On the following day, the City denied the agreement.

February 26, 1962 US Supreme Court ruled that state-sponsored segregation in travel facilities was illegal.

April, 1962 the Voter Education Project was begun.

July 10, 1962 Rev. Martin Luther King, Jr., and Rev. Ralph Abernathy were sentenced for their part in the Albany transportation facilities' sit-ins. They chose to spend 45 days in jail rather than pay a fine.

October 1, 1962 James Meredith succeeded in efforts to enroll in the University of Mississippi after three attempts. He attended classes under protection of the Justice Department.

November 20, 1962 President John F. Kennedy issued an executive order barring racial discrimination in federally financed housing.

April 2, 1963 nonviolent demonstrations adopted by Rev. Martin Luther King, Jr.

April 3, 1963 the Southern Christian Leadership Conference (SCLC) began the Birmingham campaign with a series of sit-ins.

April-May, 1963 Rev. Martin Luther King, Jr., and Rev. Ralph Abernathy led demonstrations in Birmingham. They were arrested along with many others, including 959 children. Birmingham Police Chief Bull Connor turned police dogs and high-pressure water hoses loose on the demonstrators.

May 10, 1963 Birmingham City officials and the SCLC reached agreement on instituting desegregation changes in return for an end to the demonstration.

June 12, 1963 Medgar Evers, NAACP field secretary, was shot and killed in an ambush in front of his home in Jackson, Mississippi.

June 20, 1963 President John F. Kennedy met with national civil rights leaders and reluctantly approved the March on Washington, to be held August 28, 1963.

August 27, 1963 William Edward Burghardt DuBois, early NAACP leader, died in self-imposed exile in Ghana.

August 28, 1963 Rev. Martin Luther King, Jr's., "I Have a Dream" speech delivered before 200,000 at the Washington, DC, "March on Washington," the largest civil rights demonstration in history.

September 9, 1963 Governor George Wallace tried to fight desegregation by postponing the opening of some Alabama schools.

September 15, 1963, "Birmingham Sunday" (See: **Birmingham Sunday** in alphabetical listings)

November 3, 1963 President John Fitzgerald Kennedy was assassinated in Dallas, Texas.

April 26, 1964 SNCC created the Mississippi Freedom Democratic Party.

June 3, 1964 the Mississippi Summer Project, "Freedom Summer," of 1964 launched by the Council of Federated Organizations (COFO). The Summer Project was a massive education, community improvement and voter registration drive. The COFO was a civil rights coalition comprised of the Congress of Racial Equality (CORE), the National Association for the Advancement of Colored People (NAACP), the Southern Christian Leadership Conference (SCLC), the Student Nonviolent Coordinating Committee (SNCC "snick"), and The National Council of Churches.

July 2, 1964 President Johnson signed the Civil Rights Act of 1964, prohibiting discrimination on the basis of race in voting, employment, public accommodations, publicly owned facilities, union membership, and federally funded programs.

August 4, 1964 the bodies of three missing civil rights workers were found outside Meridian, Mississippi. They were James Earl Chaney, 21, a Black Mississippian; Andrew Goodman, 21, a Jewish New Yorker; and Michael Schwerner, 24, a Jewish New Yorker.

December 4, 1964 President Johnson issued an executive order barring discrimination in federal aid programs.

December, 1964 the FBI charged 21 men, mostly members of the Ku Klux Klan, with conspiring to abduct and kill Schwerner, Chaney and Goodman. In 1967, seven were convicted of violating the federal civil rights laws, but were not found guilty of murder. As of 2001, the killers have not yet been brought to justice.

December 10, 1964 Rev. Dr. Martin Luther King, Jr., received the Nobel Peace Prize.

February 1, 1965 Dr. Martin Luther King, Jr., and 770 others were arrested in Selma, Alabama, for demonstrating against discriminatory voting requirements.

February 18, 1965 in Marion, Alabama, civil rights marcher Jimmie Lee Jackson was shot and killed while trying to protect his mother from a state trooper's attack.

February 21, 1965 Malcolm X was assassinated during a rally of the Organization of Afro-American Unity at the Audubon Ballroom in New York City.

March 7, 1965 "Bloody Sunday," the first march from Selma to Montgomery, Alabama, was halted by 200 state troopers at the Edmund Pettus Bridge. Marchers were attacked with tear gas and nightsticks.

March 9, 1965 Reverend James J. Reeb was seriously injured by a White mob in Selma; he died of his injuries on March 11.

March 21-25, 1965 thousands marched and demonstrated as King led a five-day march from Selma to Montgomery, Alabama, where he addressed a rally of 50,000 people. Following the rally, Viola Liuzzo was shot to death as she transported participants between Selma and Montgomery; three Klansmen were later convicted of the murder.

August 6, 1965 the Voting Rights Act of 1965 was passed and signed by President Johnson. It eliminated literacy tests and other voter examinations that had excluded many poor Blacks.

August 11-15, 1965 riots in the Watts area of Los Angeles, California, claimed 35 lives and an estimated $200 million in damages. It was the worst race riot in US History.

June 6, 1966 James Meredith, the first Black admitted to the University of Mississippi in 1962, was shot and wounded in ambush while on a one-man "march against fear" from Memphis, Tennessee, to Jackson, Mississippi; he recovered.

June 7-26, 1966 the "Meredith march" was continued by King, CORE director Floyd McKissick, Stokely Carmichael and other activists. During this march, the slogan "Black Power" was first used by Carmichael.

July 2-5, 1966 CORE national convention adopted a resolution supporting the Black Power concept.

July 4-9, 1966 NAACP national convention disassociated itself from the Black Power doctrine.

September 19, 1966 Joan Baez led a group of Black children to the door of an all-White school in Grenada, Mississippi, and was turned away.

October, 1966 the Black Panther Party was founded by Huey P. Newton and Bobby Seale.

November 8, 1966 Edward W. Brooke of Massachusetts was elected as the first Black US Senator chosen by popular vote.

June 12, 1967 State laws against interracial marriage were ruled unconstitutional by the US Supreme Court in the *Loving v. Virginia* decision..

June 13, 1967 Thurgood Marshall became the first African American Supreme Court Associate Justice.

August 25, 1967 FBI Director J. Edgar Hoover ordered FBI's Counterintelligence Program (COINTELPRO) to launch an effort to "expose, disrupt, misdirect, discredit, or otherwise neutralize the activities of black nationalist, hate-type organizations and groupings, their leadership, spokesmen, membership, and supporters, and to counter their propensity for violence and civil disorder."

April 4, 1968 Rev. Dr. Martin Luther King, Jr., was shot and killed in Memphis, Tennessee.

April 9, 1968 Rev. Dr. Martin Luther King, Jr., was buried in Atlanta, Georgia. More than 300,000 people marched behind the coffin, carried through the streets of Atlanta on a farm wagon pulled by two Georgia mules. Rev. Ralph Abernathy became president of the SCLC.

April 29-May 11, 1968 Poor People's Campaign began; Rev. Ralph Abernathy led a delegation of leaders representing poor Whites, Blacks, Indians and Hispanics to Washington, DC, for meetings with cabinet members and congressional leaders.

September 8, 1968 Huey P. Newton, leader of the Black Panther Party, was convicted of manslaughter in the death of Oakland policeman John Frey. The "Free Huey" movement began.

November 18, 1968 John Carlos and Tommie Smith, Olympic Silver and Gold Medalists, displayed the Black Power salute upon receiving their medals at the Mexico City Olympics.

1968 the Civil Rights Act of 1968 was signed by President Johnson. It included a fair-housing provision and protection of civil rights workers from intimidation or injury.

October 29, 1969 US Supreme Court ruled in *Alexander v. Holmes County* Board of Education that school systems must end segregation "at once" rather than "with all deliberate speed" and must "operate now and hereafter only unitary schools."

December 4, 1969 Chicago police raided the Black Panthers' Illinois headquarters and killed Illinois chairman Fred Hampton and member Mark Clark.

1970 Howard Mechanic, a student anti-war protester, was the first person sentenced under the Civil Obedience Act of 1968.

June 22, 1970 President Richard Nixon signed a bill extending the Voting Rights Act of 1965 to 1975.

August 8, 1970 the Marin County, California, Court House take over. (See: **Soledad Brothers** in alphabetical listings)

April 20, 1971 the US Supreme Court ruled unanimously in *Swann v. Charlotte-Mecklenburg Board of Education* that busing was a constitutionally acceptable method of integrating public schools where *de jure* segregation had existed.

August 21, 1971 in a riot at San Quentin Prison in California, George Jackson, one of the "Soledad Brothers," two other prisoners, and three guards were killed. It is suspected that the "riot" was really a ruse to provide an excuse for guards to kill Jackson.

January 25, 1972 Black Congresswoman Shirley Chisholm launched her campaign for President of the United States, thus becoming the first Black woman to run for the American presidency.

March 10-12, 1972 three thousand delegates and 5,000 observers attended the first National Black Political Convention.

April, 1974 US Department of Justice released memos confirming that, in the 1960s and early 1970s, the FBI had waged a campaign designed to disrupt, discredit and neutralize Black nationalist groups, including the Black Panthers.

November 19, 1977 Robert E. Chambliss ("Dynamite Bob"), a former KKK member, was convicted of murder in the 1963 bombing of the Sixteenth Street Baptist Church in Birmingham, where four Black girls were killed; he was sentenced to life imprisonment.

June 19, 1979 US Census Bureau announced that Black Americans still remained far behind White Americans in employment, income, health, housing and political power.

Civil Rights Groups:

American Civil Liberties Union, ACLU
Founded: 1920
Founded by: Jane Addams, Roger Baldwin, Clarence Darrow, John Dewey and Helen Keller
Major Accomplishments or Involvements: an organization of lawyers, often accused of being liberal, whose main function is to protect the first amendment rights of the people of America. The ACLU is arguably the most patriotic American of all institutions in this country, since its members believe passionately that our freedoms should be granted equally to all people, regardless of whether or not one agrees with their ideology. The ACLU will supply legal aid in cases of civil rights violations to anyone, whether a member of the KKK, the NAACP, the Communist party, the John Birch Society, anti-abortion or pro-abortion movements. That is true adherence to the Constitution of the United States of America.

Brotherhood of Sleeping Car Porters and Maids

Founded: 1925

Founder: A. Philip Randolph

Major Accomplishments or Involvements: principal organizers of the "March on Washington" movement. Their march in 1941 to demand jobs for Blacks in the defense industries helped to "persuade" President Roosevelt to issue an executive order declaring that there should be no discrimination in the employment of workers in the defense industries.

Citizenship Education Program

Founders and Leaders: started by the Southern Christian Leadership Conference (SCLC)

Major Accomplishments or Involvements: a program to teach basic literacy to enable Blacks to qualify to vote. Patterned after a system created by Septima Clark dating from WWI, it required only one week to teach necessary words from newspapers and the Bible as well as basic arithmetic skills. The primary teachers were Septima Clark and Annell Ponder.

Congress of Racial Equality (CORE)

Founded: 1942

Founders and Leaders: George Houser and James Leonard Farmer, based on a paper by Farmer entitled the "Provisional Plan for Brotherhood Mobilization." Bayard Rustin was also a CORE leader.

Major Accomplishments or Involvements: organized the first freedom riders who rode into the Southern states on a bus in May, 1961, to draw attention to segregated transportation. CORE was the first Black civil rights organization to study and employ techniques of nonviolence.

Commission on Religion and Race (CORR)

Founders and Leaders: Reverend Eugene Carson Blake, Founding Executive Director Robert Spike

Council of Federated Organizations (COFO)

Founded: May/June 1964

Founders and Leaders: numerous members of all the civil rights groups

Major Accomplishments or Involvements: a civil rights coalition comprised of the Congress of Racial Equality, the National Association for the Advancement of Colored People, the Southern Christian Leadership Conference, the Student Nonviolent Coordinating Committee and The National Council of Churches. Its purpose was to create, organize and accomplish the Mississippi Summer Project of 1964, a massive education, community improvement and voter registration drive.

Mississippi Freedom Democratic Party (MFDP)

Founded: April 26, 1964

Founders and Leaders: Fannie Lou Hamer, Victoria Greym; ostensibly organized by SNCC and the Council of Federated Organizations (COFO)

Major Accomplishments or Involvements: elected delegates, 64 Black and 4 White, and challenged the all-white Mississippi "Jim Crow" Democratic Party to represent Mississippi at the 1964 Democratic National Convention in Atlantic

Civil Rights Groups

City, New Jersey. The MFDP was given a compromise, which they rejected, and it was not seated at the convention. The MFDP was eventually seated at the 1968 Democratic Convention.

Montgomery Improvement Association (MIA)
Founded: December 5, 1955
Founders and Leaders: Reverend Ralph Abernathy suggested the name; Reverend Martin Luther King, Jr., was its president; Fred Gray, attorney
Major Accomplishments or Involvements: organized to support the Montgomery, Alabama, bus boycott following Rosa Parks's refusal to move to the back of a segregated bus.

National Association for the Advancement of Colored People (NAACP)
Founded: June, 1909, the oldest civil rights organization in the USA
Founders and Leaders: Early leader W. E. B. DuBois also founded "The Crisis," the official organ of the NAACP, 1910-1934; Rev. Ralph Abernathy; Roy Wilkins; Medgar Evers; Dr. Martin Luther King, Jr.
Major Accomplishments or Involvements: founded to support the rights of African Americans. A list of its accomplishments is too numerous to include here.

Southern Christian Leadership Conference (SCLC)
Founded: January 11, 1957; based in Atlanta, Georgia
Founders: Rev. Dr. Martin Luther King, Jr., Rev. Ralph Abernathy, Fred Shutterworth, and Bayard Rustin
Leaders and Prominent Members: C. T. Vivian, Rev. Jesse Jackson
Major Accomplishments or Involvements: the primary objective of the SCLC was to help coordinate and assist local organizations in their efforts to achieve equality for African Americans. SCLC started the Citizenship Education Program to teach basic literacy to enable Blacks to qualify to vote. Created Operation Breadbasket, the economic arm of the SCLC. Organized the Poor People's campaign conducted in Washington, DC, April 29-May 11, 1968.

Student Nonviolent Coordinating Committee (SNCC) ("snick")
Founded: April 15, 1960, at Shaw University in Raleigh, North Carolina
Founders and Leaders: Ella J. Baker and Rev. James M. Lawson, Jr.; Marion Barry, first chairperson of SNCC; John Lewis, early chairman; James Foreman, executive secretary 1963; Stokely Carmichael, chairman 1966, ; H. Rap Brown, chairman May, 1967; Bob Moses, Mississippi SNCC leader. Julian Bond, Diane Nash, Hollis Watkins and Curtis Hayes were active members in the early 1960s.
Major Accomplishments or Involvements: evolved from the first lunchroom sit-ins, conducted in Greensboro, North Carolina, starting February 1, 1960. SNCC helped to expedite school desegregation, fair employment laws, and the right of minorities and the poor to vote. Created an African American news service, which provided news stories to the media about prominent or interesting Black citizens who were average, non-civil rights movement figures.

Civil Rights Leaders, Heroes and Martyrs:

Rev. Ralph D. Abernathy (See: alphabetical listings)

Bella Abzug (See: alphabetical listings)

Muhammad Ali (Cassius Marcellus Clay) (See: **Ali, Muhammad** in alphabetical listings)

Saul Alinsky (1909-1972) advocate of social reform for Blacks and Hispanics in the ghettos as well as the fields of California. Author of the 1946 book *Reveille for Radicals,* which became the manual for activists of the 1960s.

Ella Baker (1903-1986) Black civil rights activist. NAACP field secretary in the South in the late 1930s; president of the Manhattan NAACP in 1954; early member of the Southern Christian Leadership Conference (SCLC), in late 1950s; present at the beginning of the Student Nonviolent Coordinating Committee (SNCC) in 1960; Southern voting rights leader; tireless worker in the struggle against racial intolerance in the South and in the Harlem section of New York City.

James Baldwin (1924-1987) Black civil rights activist; author of *Go Tell It on the Mountain, Nobody Knows My Name, The Fire Next Time,* and other books related to the Black struggle in America.

Marion Barry (1936-) co-founder and first chairperson of the Student Nonviolent Coordinating Committee (SNCC) in April 15, 1960. Mayor of Washington, DC, from 1979-90. Sentenced to six months for drug possession in 1990, he was re-elected mayor in 1995.

Daisy Gaston Bates (See: alphabetical listings)

Harry Belafonte (1927-) Black singer, actor and civil rights advocate who marched in many demonstrations.

James Luther Bevel (1937-) Back Baptist minister, civil rights activist and Southern Christian Leadership Conference (SCLC) organizer. Helped to organize the SCLC campaign to end segregation in Birmingham, Alabama, in 1963; helped to direct the Alabama state-wide drive to register Black voters in 1965; worked with the Mobilization to End the War in Vietnam in 1966; became head of the Spring Mobilization Committee to End the War in Vietnam in 1967. Bevel was one of the leaders of the Poor People's Campaign in Washington and was an aide to Rev. Ralph Abernathy.

Eugene Carson Blake (1906-1985) Black civil rights activist, minister, president of the National Council of Churches, 1954-1957; general secretary, World Council of Churches, 1966-1972; one of the principal speakers at the March on Washington in August, 1963.

Horace Julian Bond (See: alphabetical listings)

Edward W. Brooke editor of the Law Review while at Boston University. Elected US Senator from Massachusetts in 1966, the first Black senator chosen by popular vote. Also served as Massachusetts Attorney General.

H. Rap Brown (See: alphabetical listings)

John Carlos (See: alphabetical listings)

Stokely Carmichael (Kwame Ture) (See: alphabetical listings)

James Earl Chaney (See: alphabetical listings)

Shirley Chisholm (See: alphabetical listings)

Eldridge Cleaver (See: alphabetical listings)

Addie Mae Collins, **14,** was killed with three other little girls in a bombing attack by adult White male Klansmen at the Sixteenth Street Church in Birmingham, Alabama, on September 15, 1963. Robert Edward "Dynamite Bob" Chambliss, a member of the 13th Klavern of the Alabama, Ku Klux Klan, was convicted of the bombing in 1977. Three other men were also suspected in that bombing, yet Chambliss was the only one convicted at the time. Also suspected were Thomas Blanton, Jr., Bobby Frank Cherry and Herman Cash. Cash died without ever being charged, but, after the turn of the century, new trials were opened against Blanton and Cherry. Blanton was finally convicted for his involvement on May 1, 2001. Cherry is under indictment; yet, as of this writing, he has not gone to trial due to poor health. "Dynamite Bob" died in prison in 1985.

Angela Yvonne Davis (See: **Angela Yvonne Davis** and **Soledad Brothers** in alphabetical listings)

Ronald Vernie (Ron) Dellums (1935-) Black US Congressman from Oakland, California's, 9th District from 1970 to 1991. An ex-Marine and social worker who championed civil liberties and opposed military aggression while serving on the House Armed Services and Intelligence Committees. Before his election to Congress, then Vice President Spiro Agnew called him "a dangerous, radical extremist running for office in California who should be 'purged from the body politic.'" As an African American, he was often a harsh critic of the White power establishment. At one time, he was said to be the only card-carrying socialist in Congress. Dellums was responsible for much of the legislation that created US sanctions against apartheid in South Africa and paved the way for Black majority rule in that country. He is still protesting civil injustice and still being arrested for doing so.

William Edward Burghardt DuBois (1868-1963) founder and early leader of National Association for the Advancement of Colored People (NAACP); founder and editor of "The Crisis," the official organ of the NAACP, 1910-1934; educator, novelist, poet, civil rights militant, and political radical. The first Black to earn a PhD from Harvard. In 1961, he left the US for self-imposed exile in Ghana, Africa, and applied for membership in the Communist Party. He died in Ghana one day before the great Civil Rights March on Washington, held on August 28, 1963.

Medgar Wiley Evers (See: alphabetical listings)

James Leonard Farmer (See: alphabetical listings)

Andrew Goodman (See: alphabetical listings)

Jack Greenberg (1924-) White civil rights attorney and director-counsel, NAACP Legal Defense and Education Fund, 1961-1984. He argued two of the five cases leading to the Supreme Court's *Brown v. Board of Education* (1954) decision that held racial segregation in public schools to be unconstitutional. Greenberg joined the faculty of Columbia University Law School in 1984. He was named Dean of the Columbia College undergraduate program in 1989.

Dick Gregory (See: alphabetical listings)

Fannie Lou Hamer (1917-1977) Black civil rights leader; helped to found the Mississippi Freedom Democratic Party, and helped to organize the 1964 Mississippi Freedom Summer Project. A delegate to the 1968 Democratic Convention, Hamer was nationally active throughout the 1970s in civil rights, feminist and anti-war issues.

Fred Hampton (See: alphabetical listings)

Rev. Jesse Jackson (See: alphabetical listings)

Barbara Jordan (1936-1996) Black attorney, civil rights leader, US congresswoman from Texas between 1972 to 1976. In 1966, Jordan became the first African American woman ever elected to the Texas Senate. In 1972, she became the second of her race and gender to be seated in the US Congress after Shirley Chisholm of New York, who was elected in 1868. Jordan was a prominent and vocal member of the House Judiciary Committee when it held President Richard M. Nixon's impeachment hearings. In 1976 she was the first African American to deliver the keynote address at a Democratic National Convention. In Congress, she sponsored bills that championed the poor, Blacks, Hispanics, disadvantaged and injured workers.

Flo Kennedy (See: alphabetical listings)

Rev. Dr. Martin Luther King, Jr. (See: alphabetical listings)

Rev. Samuel B. (Billy) Kyles (1934-) pastor of Monumental Baptist Church in Memphis, Tennessee, he spent approximately one hour with Rev. Dr. Martin Luther King, Jr., and Rev. Ralph Abernathy at the Lorraine Motel before the fatal shooting of Dr. King. He was standing on the balcony several feet away from King when the shot was fired. Rev. Kyles is a founding national board member of People United to Save Humanity (PUSH) and was national coordinator of Rev. Jesse Jackson's 1984 and 1988 presidential campaigns.

Rev. James M. Lawson, Jr. (See: alphabetical listings)

John Robert Lewis (1940-) Black civil rights activist; co-founder and chairman, Student Nonviolent Coordinating Committee, 1963-1966. Participated in the Nashville, Tennessee, student sit-ins in 1960 and the Freedom Rides of 1961. He was the youngest speaker at the first march from Selma to Montgomery, Alabama, on March 7, 1965, and he suffered a concussion when the marchers were attacked by 200 troopers at the Edmund Pettus Bridge. In 1970, Lewis was named director of the Voter Education Project, which registered nearly 3.5 million voters in 11 Southern states by 1973. In 1976, he was appointed to a post with AC-TION, the volunteer activities agency in the administration of President Jimmy Carter. In 1986, he was elected US representative to Georgia's 5th Congressional District, which includes most of Atlanta, and was re-elected in 1988, 1990 and 1992.

Viola Gregg Liuzzo (1925-1965) a Northern White civil rights activist who was driving voters' rights marchers from Montgomery to Selma, Alabama, on March 25, 1965, when she was killed by a group of Klansmen. Viola Gregg Liuzzo is one of the 40 names engraved on the Civil Rights Memorial in Montgomery, Alabama.

Floyd Bixler McKissick (1922-1991) Black attorney and civil rights activist; national chairman, Congress of Racial Equality, 1966-1968. Also a Black power advocate.

Malcolm X (Malcolm Little) (See: alphabetical listings)

Thurgood Marshall (See: alphabetical listings)

Denise McNair, 11, was killed with three other little girls in a bombing attack by adult White male Klansmen at the Sixteenth Street Church in Birmingham, Alabama, on September 15, 1963. Robert Edward "Dynamite Bob" Chambliss, a member of the 13th Klavern of the Alabama, Ku Klux Klan, was convicted of the bombing in 1977. Three other men were also suspected in that bombing, yet Chambliss was the only one convicted at the time. Also suspected were Thomas Blanton, Jr., Bobby Frank Cherry and Herman Cash. Cash died without ever being charged, but, after the turn of the century, new trials were opened against Blanton and Cherry. Blanton was finally convicted for his involvement on May 1, 2001. Cherry is under indictment; yet, as of this writing, he has not gone to trial due to poor health. "Dynamite Bob" died in prison in 1985.

James Howard Meredith (1933-) Black civil rights activist. On September 30, 1962, he became the first Black admitted to the University of Mississippi, where federal troops stayed on the campus to protect him until he graduated in 1963. In 1966, Meredith began a one-man "march against fear" from Tennessee to Mississippi to publicize a voter registration drive. During the march, he was wounded by a sniper. He is the author of the book *Three Years in Mississippi*, 1966.

Clarence M. Mitchell, Jr. (1911-1984) chief lobbyist for the National Association for the Advancement of Colored People and the Leadership Conference on Civil Rights, 1950-1978. He played a major role in the passage of the Civil Rights Act of 1968. He was awarded the NAACP's Spingarn Medal in 1969 and was awarded the Medal of Freedom by President Jimmy Carter in 1980.

Robert Moses (1935-) Black civil rights activist. Went to Atlanta in the summer of 1960 as a volunteer for the newly organized Student Nonviolent Coordination Committee (SNCC). He became an influential figure in SNCC, and in July, 1961, he established their first voter registration project in Mississippi. Moses directed the 1964 Mississippi Freedom Summer Project, which brought over 1,000 student volunteers into the state to teach and encourage voter registration. He believed his only goal was to help local people organize so that they would be able "to speak for themselves." In 1965, Moses changed his name to Robert Parriss because of concerns that a cult might be forming around his name. In 1982, he received a MacArthur Foundation award and later become director of the Algebra Project, a nationwide mathematics literacy program aimed at minority youth.

Elijah Muhammad (See: alphabetical listings)

Huey P. Newton (See: alphabetical listings)

Rosa Parks (See: alphabetical listings)

Lawrence Robert "Pun" Plamondon Minister of Defense of the White Panthers. Indicted by the Federal government for reportedly blowing up a CIA building, he went underground and became one of the FBI's 10 most wanted in 1969-70.

Adam Clayton Powell, Jr. (1908-1972) Black US Congressman, clergyman and civil rights leader. As a Democratic, he was elected in 1944 to represent Harlem, New York, in the US House of Representatives. He served 11 successive terms. Accused of misusing public funds, Powell was censured by Congress and lost his seat in 1967. He was reseated later that year, but lost his seat by election in 1970 and died two years later.

A. Philip Randolph (1889-1979) labor organizer and civil rights leader. Working as a train porter in 1925, he founded the Brotherhood of Sleeping Car Porters. A principal organizer of the "March on Washington" movement. His first proposed march in 1941, demanding jobs for Blacks in the defense industries, was canceled after President Roosevelt issued an executive order declaring that there should be no discrimination in the employment of workers in the defense industries. It is assumed that the proposed march was the cause of Roosevelt's order. Randolph was a leader of the Committee Against Discrimination in the Armed Forces, which helped influence President Truman to eliminate segregation in the armed forces. Randolph was one of the principal speakers at the largest civil rights demonstration in history, the August, 1963, March on Washington for Jobs and Freedom. In 1964, he founded and became president of the A. Philip Randolph Institute, an organization sponsoring educational projects and campaigning for jobs for Blacks in the skilled trades.

Joseph Louis Rauh, Jr. (1911-1992) civil rights attorney, counsel for the Mississippi Freedom Democratic Party in 1964 at the Democratic National Convention, trying but failing to unseat the regular Mississippi delegation. As general counsel for the Leadership Conference on Civil Rights, Rauh and Clarence Mitchell of the NAACP were the chief lobbyists for the Civil Rights Act of 1964, the Voting Rights Act of 1965, and the Fair Housing Act of 1968.

Rev. James J. Reeb (1927-1965) White civil rights activist and clergyman beaten to death by a White gang in Selma, Alabama, on March 11, 1965.

Carole Robertson, 14, was killed with three other little girls in a bombing attack by adult White male Klansmen at the Sixteenth Street Church in Birmingham, Alabama, on September 15, 1963. Robert Edward "Dynamite Bob" Chambliss, a member of the 13th Klavern of the Alabama, Ku Klux Klan, was convicted of the bombing in 1977. Three other men were also suspected in that bombing, yet Chambliss was the only one convicted at the time. Also suspected were Thomas Blanton, Jr., Bobby Frank Cherry and Herman Cash. Cash died without ever being charged, but, after the turn of the century, new trials were opened against Blanton and Cherry. Blanton was finally convicted for his involvement on May 1, 2001. Cherry is under indictment; yet, as of this writing, he has not gone to trial due to poor health. "Dynamite Bob" died in prison in 1985.

Bayard Rustin (1910-1987) Quaker, pacifist, organized Southern Christian Leadership Conference with Rev. Martin Luther King, Jr., and was the chief architect for the 1963 March on Washington, DC.

Michael Schwerner (See: alphabetical listings)

Bobby Seale (See: alphabetical listings)

Tommie Smith (See: alphabetical listings)

Cynthia Wesley, 14, was killed with three other little girls in a bombing attack by adult White male Klansmen at the Sixteenth Street Church in Birmingham, Alabama, on September 15, 1963. Robert Edward "Dynamite Bob" Chambliss, a member of the 13th Klavern of the Alabama, Ku Klux Klan, was convicted of the bombing in 1977. Three other men were also suspected in that bombing, yet Chambliss was the only one convicted at the time. Also suspected were Thomas Blanton, Jr., Bobby Frank Cherry and Herman Cash. Cash died without ever being charged, but, after the turn of the century, new trials were opened against Blanton and Cherry. Blanton was finally convicted for his involvement on May 1, 2001. Cherry is under indictment; yet, as of this writing, he has not gone to trial due to poor health. "Dynamite Bob" died in prison in 1985.

Roy Wilkins (See: alphabetical listings)

Hosea Williams (1926-) Black civil rights leader, assistant to Martin Luther King, Jr.; Southern Christian Leadership Conference (SCLC) project director, 1963. With John Robert Lewis, he led the first march from Selma to Montgomery, Alabama, on March 7, 1965, when marchers were attacked by 200 troopers at the Edmund Pettus Bridge. Jailed more than 40 times for his civil rights activities. Williams supervised Resurrection City, an encampment of some 3,000 poor people and poverty workers who demonstrated in Washington, DC, in May of 1968 in support of greater anti-poverty spending. In the 1970s, he became a Black power advocate for "self-respect and nonviolence." Williams was National Executive Director of the SCLC from 1969 to 1971 and 1977 to 1979. Since 1972, he has been pastor of the Martin Luther King, Jr., People's Church of Love. In 1974, Williams was elected to the Georgia legislature and has since been re-elected several times.

Andrew Young, Jr. (See: alphabetical listings)

Vietnam War

U.S. Troop Strengths and Deaths in Vietnam:

Figures represent the official numbers reported by year.

1959	??	Troops In Country
	2	Americans killed
1960	900	Troops In Country
	6	Americans killed
1961	3,200	Troops In Country
	16	Americans killed
1962	11,000	Troops In Country
	53	Americans killed
1963	16,500	Troops In Country
	118	Americans killed
1964	23,000	Troops In Country
	206	Americans killed
1965	184,300	Troops In Country
	1,864	Americans killed
1966	385,300	Troops In Country
	6,144	Americans killed
1967	485,600	Troops In Country
	11,153	Americans killed
1968	536,000	Troops In Country
	19,589	Americans killed
1969	479,200	Troops In Country
	8,614	Americans killed
1970	334,600	Troops In Country
	6,084	Americans killed
1971	156,800	Troops In Country
	2,356	Americans killed
1972	24,000	Troops In Country
	643	Americans killed

April	1973	50	Troops In Country
		166	Americans killed
	1974	0	Troops In Country
		0	Americans killed
April	1975	0	Troops In Country
		2	Americans killed

Total deaths from figures above   57,014

This figure reflects a total short of the official figure, but a number of MIAs (Missing in Action) have been changed to KIAs (Killed in Action) since that time.

Official deaths	58,169
POWs/MIAs	1,172
POWs returned	591

The official number of US military personnel who served in Vietnam is 2.5 million.

The official number of US military deaths between 1959 and 1975 is approximately 58,000, of which about 47,000 were combat deaths. Approximately 23,000 military personnel received permanent disabilities during the conflict.

A reasonable estimate of Prisoners of War/Missing in Action (POWs/MIAs) is 1,172. Some of these are possible deserters and defectors. The two categories, MIA and POW, have been grouped together by those who feel that some of the MIAs were and still are POWs. MIAs can fall into three different categories: 1) POWs not recorded or returned by North Vietnam. 2) Combatants who were killed, yet whose remains were not found and/or identified. 3) Deserters and defectors.

In 1973, 591 US Military POWs were returned to the United States.

After the war, as relations improved between Vietnam and the United States, the remains of American servicemen were returned as they were discovered, thus reducing the MIA count.

Vietnamese Deaths During the Vietnam War:

A reasonable, yet probably low, estimate of Vietnamese deaths:

South Vietnam	
military	250,000
civilian	400,000

North Vietnam	
military VC/NVA	924,000
civilian	65,000

Total	1,639,000

Some estimates run as high as 4 million North and South Vietnamese killed in the conflict.

Vietnam War Leaders of South Vietnam:

Ngo Dinh Diem (President of South Vietnam from 1955-1963). Ousted Emperor Bao Dai by doctoring a referendum and stealing the election, supposedly with US Government support.

Military regime (November 1, 1963-January 30, 1964). Diem was killed during a coup said to be supported by the US Government.

General Nguyen Khanh (January 30, 1964-June 11, 1965). Nguyen Cao Ky (Prime Minister of South Vietnam, June 11, 1965-September 3, 1967)

General Ngyuen Ban Thieu (President of South Vietnam, September 3, 1967-April 25, 1975). Thieu escaped to Taiwan just before Saigon fell to communist troops from North Vietnam on April 30, 1975.

Anti-Vietnam War Events and Demonstrations:

October 1, 1960 Boston, Massachusetts, one of the first American "peace" rallies ever held. Sponsored by the Committee for a Sane Nuclear Policy (SANE); attended by Erich Fromm, liberal Michigan Governor G. Mennen ("Soapy") Williams and Steve Allen, with folksongs by Pete Seeger and Joan Baez.

1961 a group of pacifists walked from San Francisco to Moscow carrying their message of disarmament all the way into Red Square.

February 16, 1962 a demonstration was held in front of the White House. Considered the first peace march against the Vietnam War, it was organized by Harvard students. Hundreds converged on the White House. President Kennedy sent out an urn of coffee for the demonstrators.

June, 1962 the Port Huron Statement of the Students for a Democratic Society (SDS). (See: **Port Huron Statement** in alphabetical listings)

June 11, 1963 in Vietnam, Buddhist monk Thich Quang Duc set himself on fire and burned to death in protest of the war and the US-supported South Vietnamese government. The first self-immolation against the war; many others followed.

March 24, 1965 first "teach-in. " Held at the University of Michigan and attended by over 3,000 people.

April 17, 1965 SDS conducts anti-war demonstration in Washington, DC.

May 12, 1965 Inter-religious Committee on Vietnam marched from Washington to the Pentagon and stood silently for six hours in protest of America's involvement in South Vietnam.

August 27, 1965 Vermont college student David J. Miller was arrested for burning his draft card, reportedly the first person arrested for violating a new law against such action. He spent two years in prison.

October 15-16, 1965 first International Days of Protest, organized by the Vietnam Day Committee (VDC) in Berkeley, California. The VDC attempted to block troop trains. Protesters in Oakland were attacked by both police and motorcycle gang members.

November 2, 1965 Norman Morrison, a Mormon anti-war protester, set himself on fire and burned to death in front of the Pentagon, the first person in America to do so.

November 19, 1965 Sonny Barger of the Oakland, California, Hell's Angels announced the group's offer to serve as mercenaries behind enemy lines in Vietnam.

November 27, 1965 SANE-sponsored anti-war demonstration in Washington, DC.

May, 1966 four California housewives attempted to block a shipment of napalm bombs.

1966 a group of pacifists led by A. J. Muste flew to Saigon and were arrested and deported for attempting to hold peace demonstrations. Later that same year, Muste and a group of religious leaders went to Hanoi, where they met with Ho Chi Minh.

June, 1966 three soldiers refused orders to go to Vietnam. Private Dennis Mora, Private First Class James Johnson, and Private David Samas were court-martialed and served two years in prison.

November 5-6, 1966 first Mobilization Committee-sponsored protests in New York and San Francisco.

November 7, 1966 protest against Secretary of Defense Robert McNamara at Harvard University.

January 31-February 1, 1967 first Clergy and Laity Concerned About Vietnam (CALCAV) mobilization in Washington, DC.

April 15, 1967 Spring Mobilization Committee, 100,000 protested the war in New York City's Central Park. Rev. Martin Luther King, Jr., Harry Belafonte, Dr. Benjamin Spock, Stokely Carmichael and other civil rights and peace and freedom leaders marched together for the first time. More than 150 people burned their draft cards on the Sheep Meadow.

April, 1967 Muhammad Ali refused to register for the draft and was stripped of his World Heavyweight boxing title.

October 16, 1967 a national draft card turn-in organized by The Resistance resulted in 2,000 young men returning their cards to the government.

October 16-20, 1967 "Stop the Draft Week."

October 21, 1967 National Mobilization Committee to End the War in Vietnam held a rally of 50,000 in Washington, DC, and eventually stormed the Pentagon. Two hundred fifty were arrested, including Norman Mailer and David Dellinger. Jerry Rubin and Abbie Hoffman tried to levitate the Pentagon; the Diggers were there and the Fugs played rock music. Some demonstrators attempted to exorcise the demons in the building as well.

October 27, 1967 Roman Catholic priest Father Philip Berrigan and three others poured blood on Selective Service files in the Baltimore, Maryland, Custom House.

December, 1967 Dick Gregory, Black stand-up comedian, traveled to North Vietnam in defiance of US Government restrictions.

January 18, 1968 actor Eartha Kitt disrupted a White House luncheon with an anti-war outburst.

March 25-26, 1968 "Wise Men" met in Washington, DC, and advocated de-escalation of the war.

May, 1968 over 600 demonstrators gathered at the Pentagon.

May 17, 1968 Fathers Philip and Daniel Berrigan and seven other clergy "napalmed" draft records in Catonsville, Maryland.

August 24-29, 1968 the Democratic National Convention was held in Chicago, Illinois. Anti-war and peace and freedom protesters demonstrated and were beaten by police.

April, 1969 nearly 300 student body presidents and college newspaper editors signed a petition calling for the Vietnam Moratorium to occur on October 15, 1969.

May-June, 1969 a public reading of the names of US war dead was held at the Capitol Building.

Summer, 1969 in New York, five "Women Against Daddy Warbucks" removed the keys 1 and A from draft board typewriters so that the 1A draft eligibility classification could not be typed onto forms.

October 6, 1969 Weathermen blew up the nation's only monument to policemen, located in Chicago's Haymarket Square.

October 8-11, 1969 Weathermen's "Days of Rage" in Chicago. The only truly "organized" violence of the anti-war movement.

October 15, 1969 the Vietnam Moratorium, the largest anti-war protest in the history of the movement, in which 15 million people all over the nation in small towns and large cities, demonstrated against the war. Included was a one-day boycott of classes by many students at most, if not all, campuses in the United States.

November 15, 1969 Washington, DC, the Second Moratorium against the Vietnam War created the largest demonstration of any kind ever held in Washington.

March 6, 1970 three members of the militant Weathermen were killed while making bombs in a New York City townhouse. Killed were Diana Oughton, Ted Gold and Terry Robbins.

February-April, 1970 CALCAV Lent-Passover Fast.

April, 1970 New Mobe, Moratorium and CNCC protests were held across the country.

May 4, 1970 four students were killed by National Guardsmen at Kent State University. (See: **Kent State University** in alphabetical listings)

May 5, 1970 student anti-war protesters set fire to the ROTC building at Washington University in St. Louis, Missouri.

May 8, 1970 "hard hat" construction workers of the National Hard Hats of America assaulted demonstrators in New York. This act is believed to have been supported, and possibly planned, by White House "dirty tricks" operatives.

May 9, 1970 President Richard Nixon was confronted by demonstrators at the Lincoln Memorial.

May 14, 1970 two Black students were killed at Jackson State College. (See: **Jackson State College** in alphabetical listings)

August 22, 1970 anti-war Catholics raided the Camden, New Jersey, draft board, and 38 were arrested. It was later discovered that this anti-war protest was actually planned and financed by the FBI in order to entrap the protesters.

September 4-7, 1970 members of Vietnam Veterans Against the War conducted Operation RAW (Rapid American Withdrawal), a mock attack on farms and towns between Morristown, NJ, and Valley Forge, PA. They carried plastic M-16 rifles, "ambushed," "interrogated," and "shot" citizens.

March 1, 1971 Weathermen bombed the Capitol Building.

April 19-25, 1971 Operation Dewey Canyon III, Vietnam veterans marched on Arlington National Cemetery and camped on the Washington Mall.

May 1-6, 1971 May Day Protests, Washington, DC; 13,000 people were arrested. Many were detained in John F. Kennedy Stadium. The courts declared that these mass arrests were illegal and freed the protesters.

June 13, 1971 Pentagon Papers were published. (See: **Pentagon Papers** in alphabetical listings)

November 14, 1971 Clergy and Laity Concerned About Vietnam (CALCAV) protested at the US Air Force Academy in Colorado Springs, Colorado.

December 26, 1971 16 Vietnam vets seized the Statue of Liberty.

June 22, 1972 "Ring Around Congress" demonstration was held in Washington, DC.

August, 1972 anti-war protests were held at the Republican National Convention in Miami, Florida.

Fall, 1972 protests were held on US military ships by Black sailors unhappy with discrimination in the armed services.

January 20, 1973 anti-war protests were held at the inauguration of President Nixon.

2400 hours G.M.T. January 27, 1973 Paris Peace Accords went into effect.

March 29, 1973 US fighting troops left Vietnam after ten years of conflict.

Fall and Winter, 1973 anti-war demonstrations demanded that President Nixon honor the Paris Peace Accords, pressuring Congress to sever aid to South Vietnam.

October 26-28, 1973 formation of United Campaign to End the War.

November 7, 1973 Congress passed the War Powers Act.

April, 1974 House of Representatives defeated Nixon administration request for $474 million in additional military aid for South Vietnam.

August 6, 1974 House of Representatives voted to limit US military aid to South Vietnam to "only" $700 million for the next fiscal year.

December, 1974 religious leaders issued pastoral letter against war.

March, 1975 Congress rejected President Ford's request for $500 million in supplemental military aid to South Vietnam.

April, 1975 Congress rejected President Ford's request for $700 million in supplemental military aid to South Vietnam.

April 30, 1975 North Vietnamese and North Vietnam Liberation Front troops entered Saigon (now Ho Chi Minh City).

In the struggle to end the war, there were many more demonstrations by individuals and groups, but it is not possible to include all of them in this list.

Anti-War and Peace Groups, Organizations and Publications:

Assembly of Unrepresented People (AUP) and **Congress of Unrepresented People (COUP)**
Founders: Prominent radical pacifists
Major Accomplishments or Involvements: August 3-9, 1965, demonstrated at the Capitol Building, blocked the White House, over 300 people arrested, the largest number to date at a single demonstration.

Assembly to Save the Peace Agreement
Founded: December, 1974
Prominent Members: 36 American Religious Leaders
Major Accomplishments or Involvements: confronted the Ford administration with the fact that, in spite of the Paris Peace Treaty, America was still bombing in Vietnam and sending aid to the government of South Vietnam. They enumerated US violations of the peace treaty.

American Friends Service Committee (AFSC)
Founded: July, 1917
Founders, Members: Quakers, David Hartsough
Major Accomplishments or Involvements: the Student Peace Union was a spin-off of the AFSC. The AFSC may have had some influence in Senator Eugene

McCarthy's decision to challenge Johnson for the presidency in 1967. They ran consulting centers on conscientious objection and supplied Washington legislators with information contradictory to the administration's propaganda on the Vietnam War. They conducted a conference on revolutionary change at Princeton University in March, 1968; Daniel Ellsberg attended, which may have contributed to his eventual decision to publish The Pentagon Papers.

Another Mother for Peace
Founded: March 1967 by 15 women in Beverly Hills
Leaders: Co-chairmen Dorothy B. Jones and Barbara Avedon
Prominent Members: Donna Reed, Debbie Reynolds and Joanne Woodward
Major Accomplishments or Involvements: a non-profit, non-partisan association whose goal was to eliminate war as a means of settling disputes between nations. The AMP logo became one of the most popular anti-war slogans, "War is not healthy for children or other living things," created by Lorraine Schneider. Mother's Day cards with this logo were sent by thousands to their Congressmen. By the end of May, 1967, 200,000 cards had been sold; with its profits, AMP started a peace fund to support legislators who voted against war appropriations. AMP's primary effort was to establish a Department and Secretary of Peace as part of the executive branch, whose purpose would be "to examine and evaluate the range of non-military alternatives to war." In May of 1969, AMP held its first annual Mother's Day Assembly in Los Angeles. The AMP logo was translated into 20 languages.

Baha'i International Community
Founder: Baha'ullah (1817-1892), born in Persia (now Iran)
Major Accomplishments or Involvements: in 1867, Baha'ullah wrote to all the kings and rulers of the world outlining the requirements for lasting peace among nations. He called for countries to relinquish some of their sovereignty in order to form a world government to enforce peace. On the 100th anniversary of this letter in 1967, this message was again presented to all governments by the Baha'i community.

Citizens Committee to Investigate War Crimes
Founded: 1970
Major Accomplishments or Involvements: held hearings on American atrocities in Vietnam.

Clergy Concerned About Vietnam
Founded: early 1966
Founders, Leaders and Prominent Members: New York clergymen and Union Theological Seminary students
Major Accomplishments or Involvements: held press conferences and wrote letters critical of the war to congressmen

Clergy and (Laity) Laymen Concerned (CALC)
Founded: 1965
Prominent Members: an interfaith organization with Protestant, Catholic, Jewish, Muslim and Buddhist involvement

Major Accomplishments or Involvements: a later offshoot of CALCAV

Clergy and Laity Concerned About Vietnam (CALCAV)
Founded: October, 1965
Prominent Members: Richard Fernandez
Major Accomplishments or Involvements: first mobilization in Washington, DC, January 31- February 1, 1967. In 1968, supplied Washington legislators with information contrary to the administration's propaganda on the Vietnam War. March, 1969, invaded Dow Chemical Company offices, pouring blood and destroying files. 1970, fasted in front of the White House. Placed anti-war ads and billboards. Example: "Dear Mom and Dad, Your silence is killing me."

Cleveland Area Peace Action Council (CAPAC), close ties to SWP
Founders, Leaders and Prominent Members: Sydney Peck, Jerry Gordon
Major Accomplishments or Involvements: hosted the National Anti-War Conference on July 4-6, 1969, endorsed and promoted the Washington "Death March" in November, 1969. Involved in the Chicago Seven protests and the Vietnam Moratorium.

Committee for Nonviolent Action (CNVA)
Founded: 1958
Founders, Leaders and Prominent Members: A. J. Muste, Brad Lyttle
Major Accomplishments or Involvements: in 1958 and 1959, they sailed small boats into Pacific Ocean bomb test sites and climbed over fences of missile bases. Boston-to-Pentagon Walk for Peace, 1967. Staged a peaceful "Walk-into-the-War Room" demonstration at the Pentagon.

Committee for a Sane Nuclear Policy (SANE)
Founded: 1957 in poet Lenore Marshall's New York apartment
Founders: Norman Cousins, Clarence Pickett and Lenore Marshall
Leaders and Prominent Members: Norman Cousins, Clarence Pickett, H. Stuart Hughes, Donald Keys, Dr. Benjamin Spock, Edward U. Condon, Seymour Melman, Wayne Morse, Andrew Young, Trevor Thomas, Homer A. Jack and Sanford Gottlieb
Prominent Supporters: Dr. Albert Schweitzer, Eleanor Roosevelt, Norman Thomas, Bertrand Russell, Pablo Casals, Roger Baldwin, Paul Tillich, Erich Fromm, Michigan Governor G. Mennen ("Soapy") Williams and Steve Allen
Major Accomplishments or Involvements: some of the First American "peace" rallies were held by this group. Notably, on October 1, 1960, in Boston, attended by Erich Fromm, liberal Michigan Governor G. Mennen Williams, and Steve Allen, with folksongs by Pete Seeger and Joan Baez. Anti-war demonstration in Washington, DC, on November 27, 1965. In 1966, SANE urged voters to support only those congressional candidates who agreed to work "vigorously" to end the war. Involved in working on disarmament in general and nuclear weapons systems in particular. Opposed the planned antiballistic missile (ABM) system in 1970 and helped to defeat the B-1 bomber in 1977.

Conference of Concerned Democrats (CCD)
Founded: active in 1968
Founder: Dump Johnson Democrat, Congressman Allard Lowenstein

Major Accomplishments or Involvements: Senator Eugene McCarthy gave his first presidential campaign speech at one of their meetings on December 2, 1968.

Conspiracy Organization
Founded: active in 1968
Founders, Prominent Members: The Chicago Seven and a small staff who assisted them
Major Accomplishments or Involvements: kept the Chicago Seven trial in the public eye in order to expose inconsistencies and inequities in the judicial system as related to political activism.

Fifth Avenue Anti-Vietnam Peace Parade Committee in New York
Administrator: Eric Weinberger

Friends Committee on National Legislation (FCNL)
Founders: Quakers
Major Accomplishments or Involvements: launched project to pressure Congress to end the war in February, 1966.

Fund For Peace
Founded: 1967
Founders, Leaders, Prominent Members: Gene R. La Rocque, William Goodfellow, Morton H. Halperin, Dr. Kenneth W. Thompson
Major Accomplishments or Involvements: a multi-project institution dedicated to the survival of human life on earth under conditions that make life worth living.

Interreligious Committee on Vietnam
Major Accomplishments or Involvements: on May 12, 1965, they marched from Washington, DC, to the Pentagon, where they stood silently for six hours.

Legal Defense Committee
Major Accomplishments or Involvements: volunteer legal aid group that provided legal consultation to persons involved in civil rights demonstrations. They assisted during the Chicago Democratic Convention demonstrations and police riot of August 24-30, 1968.

Liberal Religious Youth (LRY)
Founded: 1954
Founders: Unitarian Church
Major Accomplishments or Involvements: a youth group formed within the Unitarian Church. The group was involved in a lot of anti-war activity that was sanctioned by the church, but it also indulged in other counterculture activities that were not sanctioned. During the 1960s and 70s, it became an interesting combination of political movement, spiritual nirvana and sex/drug revolutionary cult. In the early 1980s Ronald Reagan's conservative atmosphere and the moral majority convinced the Unitarian Universalists Church to drop the "L word," and in 1982, the Liberal Religious Youth (LRY) became Young Religious Unitarian Universalists (YRUU).

May Day Collective (May Day Tribe)

May 2nd Movement
Founded: 1965; a very short-lived group
Major Accomplishments or Involvements: collected blood for North Vietnamese Liberation Front.

Medical Committee for Human Rights (MCHR)
Major Accomplishments or Involvements: a volunteer medical group, the Chicago chapter of which was formed specifically to provide medical assistance to persons involved in civil rights demonstrations. They treated 425 people in their seven medical facilities during the Chicago Democratic Convention demonstrations and police riot of August 24-30, 1968.

Mobilization Committee (Mobe)
Founded: June, 1970
Major Accomplishments or Involvements: a spin-off from the National Mobilization Committee. (See: **National Mobilization Committee**)

Movement for a Democratic Society (MDS)
Founded:
Major Accomplishments or Involvements: an organization that was established for non-students who could not be members of Students for a Democratic Society (SDS.) A member of MDS, Terry Robbins, is one of the people who died in the bomb-making accident at the Weathermen's New York City house.

National Black Anti-war, Anti-draft Union
Founded: January, 1968
Founders, Leaders and Prominent Members: Gwen Patton

National Coalition Against War, Racism and Repression (NCAWRR),
Founded: formed in September, 1970; disbanded in 1971
Founders, Leaders and Prominent Members: David Dellinger, Rennie Davis, Sydney Peck
Major Accomplishments or Involvements: precursor to the People's Coalition for Peace and Justice (PCPJ).

National Coordinating Committee to End the War in Vietnam (NCC), a coalition of the VDC and AUP
Founded: August, 1965
Founders, Leaders and Prominent Members: Jerry Rubin, Frank Emspak
Major Accomplishments or Involvements: this group was the beginning of a nation-wide coordination of the peace movement. They organized "The International Days," October 15-16, 1965, and SANE Marches.

National Mobilization Committee, Mobilization Committee, Spring Mobilization Committee or **New Mobilization Committee to End the War in Vietnam (Mobe)**
Founded: July 1966; **Mobe** split off in June, 1970
Founders, Leaders and Prominent Members: David Dellinger, Chairman; Rennie Davis was the Chicago coordinator during the Chicago Democratic Convention demonstrations and police riots.

Major Accomplishments or Involvements: first protest November 5-8, 1966, Spring Mobe demonstration in NY and San Francisco. Draft card burning in Central Park, April 15, 1967. October 21, 1967, rally of 50,000 in Washington, DC, which eventually stormed the Pentagon; 250 were arrested, including Norman Mailer and David Dellinger. Jerry Rubin tried to levitate the Pentagon and some demonstrators attempted to exorcise the demons in the building as well. The Diggers were there, and the Fugs played rock music. Coordinated the demonstrations at the Chicago Democratic National Convention August 24-30, 1968.

National Peace Action Coalition (NPAC)
Founders: controlled by the Socialist Workers Party
Major Involvements: demonstrations on October 31, 1970

New York Fifth Avenue Peace Parade Committee (PC)
Founders, Leaders and Prominent Members: Norma Becker

Negotiations Now
Founded: April 24, 1967
Founders, Leaders and Prominent Members: Victor Reuther, Clark Kerr, Joseph Hauh, John Kenneth Galbraith and Aurthur Schlesinger, Jr.
Major Accomplishments or Involvements: petitioned the Johnson administration to stop bombing North Vietnam and ask Hanoi and the National Liberation Front to join a cease-fire.

Pax World Foundation
Founded: 1970
Leaders and Prominent Members: J. Elliott Corbett
Major Accomplishments or Involvements: primary goals are peace and Third World development.

Peace and Freedom Party (PFP)
Founded: June 23, 1967
Leaders and Prominent Members: Eldridge Cleaver, Dick Gregory
Major Accomplishments or Involvements: a political party that ran candidates Dick Gregory for President and Eldridge Cleaver for Vice President in 1968. Since 1968, the PFP has supported hundreds of candidates for public office. Very few have been elected.

People's Coalition for Peace and Justice (PCPJ)
Founded: started in 1971 after NCAWRR disbanded
Founders, Leaders and Prominent Members: Rennie Davis, David Dellinger, Brad Lyttle

POLIT
Founded: early 1960s at the University of Chicago
Founders, Leaders and Prominent Members: Clark Kissinger
Major Accomplishments or Involvements: one of the many student peace and freedom groups started in the early 1960s.

Progressive Student League
Founded: early 1960s at Oberlin College, Ohio

Co-founders: Paul Potter and Rennie Davis
Major Accomplishments or Involvements: one of the many student peace and freedom groups started in the early 1960s.

Quaker Action Group (QAG) or **A Quaker Action Group (AQAG)**
Leaders and Prominent Members: Earle Reynolds
Major Accomplishments or Involvements: in 1962, Earle Reynolds captained the boat *Everyman III* on a AQAG voyage from London to Leningrad via Belgium, Holland, Germany, Denmark, and Sweden, lecturing and promoting peace. In 1967, Reynolds and other peace activists, under the sponsorship of A Quaker Action Group, sailed to Vietnam to deliver medical supplies to both North and South Vietnam to express the Quaker principles of neutrality. Goodwill voyages to China were attempted in 1968 and 1969.

Radical Organizing Committee offshoot of the **SWP**
Founded: May 9, 1968
Founders, Leaders and Prominent Members: Linda Morse
Major Accomplishments or Involvements: involved in the Chicago Democratic Convention demonstrations in August of 1968 and dissolved shortly thereafter.

Resistance inside the Army (RITA)
Founders, Leaders and Prominent Members: Rennie Davis

Resistance
Founded: April 15, 1967
Founders, Leaders and Prominent Members: a West Coast group including Stuart McRae
Major Accomplishments or Involvements: formed to resist the draft. Organized the October 16, 1967, national draft card turn-in, during which 2,000 young men returned their cards to the government.

SANE, National SANE or **SANE/FREEZE** (See: **Committee for a Sane Nuclear Policy**)

SLATE
Founded: 1957 on the University of California, Berkeley, campus
Major Accomplishments or Involvements: dedicated to ending nuclear testing, capital punishment, Cold War rivalries and other social ills, it supported candidates for student affairs elections. SLATE was one of the first university peace and freedom groups of the new left movement not directly related to the Communist Party.

Socialist Party (SP) or **Socialist Workers Party (SWP)**
Founded: in America in 1901, in Indianapolis, Indiana; created from the older Socialist Labor Party and Social Democratic Party
Leaders and Prominent Members: Norman Thomas, known as "America's conscience"; Michael Harrington, party chairman in the mid-1960s, and Charles Zimmerman
Major Accomplishments or Involvements: they generally opposed America's involvement in Vietnam and were associated with many of the demonstrations

held by other groups, yet they were also upset with North Vietnam when that government negotiated with the US government to effect a cease fire.

Spring Mobilization
Founded: late 1966
Founders: David Dellinger, A. J. Muste and James Luther Bevel
Major Accomplishments or Involvements: helped to organize in the April 15, 1967, Spring Mobilization demonstration by 100,000 protesters in New York City's Central Park. This was the demonstration in which Martin Luther King, Jr., Harry Belafonte, Dr. Benjamin Spock, Stokely Carmichael and other civil rights and peace and freedom leaders marched together for the first time.

Students for a Democratic Society (SDS)
Founded: 1960, refined at Port Huron, Michigan, in 1962; disintegrated in June, 1969
Founders, Leaders and Prominent Members: Al Haber, Sharon Jeffrey, Bob Ross, Dick Magidoff, Tom Hayden, Rennie Davis, Dorothy Dawson, Clark Kissinger, Jerry Rubin, Carl Oglesby, Carl Davidson, Bill Ayers, Mike Klonsky, Paul Potter, etc. The SDS evolved from one of the first student peace and freedom groups, the Student League for Industrial Democracy (SLID), an offshoot of the League for Industrial Democracy (LID), which actually contributed to the SDS financing through the years. The SDS was, in actuality, "The Student Department of the League for Industrial Democracy." The LID and the SLID were themselves off-shoots of the Socialist Party, but after the Port Huron convention the SDS took on a life of its own and lost much of the socialist label.
Major Accomplishments or Involvements: involved in planning the first national anti-war demonstrations in late 1964 and early 1965, notably the demonstration in Washington, DC, on April 17, 1965. The SDS was one of the most radical of the anti-war groups. In 1968, a number of SDS members, becoming even more radical, left to form the Weathermen (a.k.a: Weather Bureau). In 1970, after that group was linked to bombings, its members operated secretly, calling themselves the Weather Underground.

Student League for Industrial Democracy (SLID)
Major Accomplishments or Involvements: one of the earliest student peace and freedom groups, from which many, such as the SDS, were patterned. An offshoot of the League for Industrial Democracy (LID).

Student Mobilization Committee (SMC)
Founded: December, 1966; dissolved June, 1968.
Founders, Leaders and Prominent Members: Fred Halstead, Gwen Patton, Linda Morse
Major Accomplishments or Involvements: front group for Socialist Workers Party, SWP

TOCSIN
Founded: 1959-60 at Harvard University and Radcliffe College
Founders, Leaders and Prominent Members: Robert Weil was chairman in 1960; Todd Gitlin, Peter Goldmark

Major Accomplishments or Involvements: conducted a number of minor peace and anti-nuclear rallies in Boston and New York City during the early 1960s. One of the many student peace and freedom groups formed at that time.

Vietnam Day Committee (VDC)
Founders, Leaders and Prominent Members: Jerry Rubin, Barbara Gullahorn, Marilyn Mulligan
Major Accomplishments or Involvements: organized a massive teach-in at the University of California, Berkeley, in the spring of 1965, attended by over 30,000 people. On October 15-16, 1965, first International Days of Protest. In Berkeley, the VDC made attempts to block troop trains. Protesters in Oakland were attacked by both police and motorcycle hoodlums.

Vietnam Moratorium Committee (VMC), close connections to **Spring Mobilization** and **National Mobilization Committee (Mobe)**
Founded: 1966; disbanded April 19, 1970.
Founders, Leaders and Prominent Members: Sam Brown and David Dellinger
Major Accomplishments or Involvements: helped to organize the April 15, 1967, Spring Mobilization in which 100,000 people protested the war in New York City's Central Park. This was the demonstration in which Dr. Martin Luther King, Jr., Harry Belafonte, Dr. Benjamin Spock, Stokely Carmichael and other civil rights and peace and freedom leaders marched together for the first time. Involved in the October 15, 1969, Moratorium demonstrations.

Vietnam Summer (VS)
Founded: April, 1967

Vietnam Veterans Against the War (VVAW)
Founded: June 1, 1967
Founders, Leaders and Prominent Members: Jan Berry
Major Accomplishments or Involvements: this group verified atrocities committed by US troops in Vietnam and conducted operation RAW (Rapid American Withdrawal) September 4-7, 1970, a mock attack on farms and towns between Morristown, New Jersey, and Valley Forge, PA.

VOICE
Founded: early 1960s at the University of Michigan
Founders, Leaders and Prominent Members: co-founder Tom Hayden, chairman Eric Chester, member Bill Ayers
Major Accomplishments or Involvements: one of the many student peace and freedom groups started in the early 1960s. There were chapters at Syracuse, Western Reserve, Yale, Chicago, Brooklyn, Oberlin and Harvard.

Women's International League for Peace and Freedom (WILPF)
Founded: 1916
Founders, Leaders and Prominent Members: Jane Addams, founder and leader until her death in 1935. Evolved from the International Congress of Women, held at The Hague in 1915
Major Accomplishments or Involvements: "Feed the Cities, Not the Pentagon"

campaign in 1976, Nuclear Weapons Freeze Campaign in 1979, Conference on Racism in 1979. Their slogan was "Listen to the Women for a Change."

Women Against Daddy Warbucks

Major Accomplishments or Involvements: summer, 1969, in New York, five "Women Against Daddy Warbucks" removed the 1 and A from the draft board's typewriter so that 1A, the most eligible draftee classification, could not be typed on forms.

War Resisters League (WRL)

Founded: 1923

Founders: men and women who opposed WWI, many of whom had been jailed for refusing military service. The founders included Jessie Wallace Hughan, a leading suffragette, socialist, and pacifist.

Leaders, Prominent Members: David McReynolds

Major Accomplishments or Involvements: believed that, if enough people stood in opposition to war, governments would hesitate to start them. During WWII, hundreds of members were imprisoned in the US for refusing to fight. In the 1950s, WRL members worked in the civil rights movement and in opposition to nuclear testing. In the 1960s, the League was the first peace group to call for US withdrawal from Vietnam and played a key role throughout the war, organizing draft card burnings, rallies and civil disobedience at induction centers. In the 1970s, the League worked to end the war in Vietnam and against nuclear weapons and nuclear power. The WRL was still active at the turn of this century. www.warresisters.org

Weathermen a.k.a. Weather Bureau; called Weather Underground after many of its members became fugitives in 1970.

Founded: 1968

Founders, Leaders and Prominent Members: Bernardine Dohrn, Jeff Jones, Bill Ayers, Kathie Boudin, Cathy Wilkerson and Mark Rudd. A violent offshoot of the SDS, the name came from a Bob Dylan song implying that Weathermen "know which way the wind blows."

Major Accomplishments or Involvements: Days of Rage in Chicago in October, 1969, was their major event. On October 6, 1969, Weathermen blew up the nation's only monument to policemen, located in Chicago's Haymarket Square. On March 6, 1970 three Weathermen members were killed making bombs in a New York City townhouse on West 11th Street. Killed were Diana Oughton, Ted Gold and Terry Robbins. On March 1, 1971, Weathermen damaged the Capitol Building with a bomb. In 1970, after the group was linked to these bombings, many of its members began to work secretly, calling themselves the Weather Underground.

Women Strike for Peace (WSP)

Founded: 1968

Founders, Leaders and Prominent Members: Cora Weiss, Madeline Duckles

Major Accomplishments or Involvements: during the 1968 Democratic Convention demonstrations, they peacefully picketed the Hilton Hotel where the conventioneers stayed. Went to Vietnam to forward US POW mail to their families.

Youth International Party (Yippies)
Founded: Christmas Holiday Season, 1967
Founders, Leaders and Prominent Members: Stew Albert, Jerry Rubin, Abbie Hoffman, Paul Krassner
Major Accomplishments or Involvements: responsible for The Festival of Light and many of the demonstrations in Chicago during the Democratic Convention and police riots, August 24-30, 1968. During the 1968 election campaign, the Yippies nominated a pig named Pigasus for President. The pig was "arrested" at one of the demonstrations during the Democratic Convention.

Young Socialist Alliance (YSA), the Youth group of the Socialist Workers Party
Founders, Leaders and Prominent Members: Lew Jones

Anti-War Leaders:

Stew Albert bohemian, Progressive Labor party member, Yippie, Jerry Rubin's friend and his campaign manager when he ran for Mayor of Berkeley. Involved in the Berkeley People's Park movement. Co-wrote with his wife Judith Albert *The Sixties Papers,* Praeger, 1985.

Muhammad Ali (Cassius Marcellus Clay) (See: **Ali, Muhammad** in alphabetical listings)

Bill Ayers (See: alphabetical listings)

Fathers Daniel and Philip Berrigan (See: alphabetical listings)

Greg Calvert early draft resister, member of SDS, the DuBois Club and Young Americans for Freedom.

James Luther Bevel (1937-) Back Baptist minister, civil rights activist and Southern Christian Leadership Conference (SCLC) organizer. Worked with Mobilization to End the War in Vietnam in 1966; became head of the Spring Mobilization Committee to End the War in Vietnam in 1967. Helped to convince Dr. Martin Luther King, Jr., to support the anti-war movement. Bevel was one of the leaders of the Poor People's Campaign in Washington, DC, and was an aide to Rev. Ralph Abernathy.

Chicago Seven (See: **Chicago Seven** and **Chicago Democratic Convention** in alphabetical listings)

Carl Davidson SDS administrator.

Rennie Davis (See: **Rennie Davis, Chicago Seven** and **Chicago Democratic Convention** in alphabetical listings)

David Dellinger (See: **David Dellinger, Chicago Seven** and **Chicago Democratic Convention** in alphabetical listings)

Benardine Dohrn (See: **Benardine Dohrn, Students for a Democratic Society (SDS)** and **Weathermen** in alphabetical listings)

Daniel Ellsberg (See: **Pentagon Papers** and **plumbers** in alphabetical listings)

Flacks, Richard joined the SDS in 1962 while a student at the University of Michigan. As a professor at University of California, Santa Barbara, he was involved in the demonstrations in support of academic freedom on campus in 1970. He and his students were responsible for producing the documentary "Don't Bank on Amerika" about the student demonstrations in protest of the firing of Professor William Allen, police brutality, and the burning of the Isla Vista branch of the Bank of America.

John Kenneth Galbraith (1908-) liberal Democrat who held numerous advisory posts during the Kennedy administration. Academic career at Harvard, 1949-1975. Author of *The Affluent Society,* published in 1958. His writing exposed excesses and greed in our society and was important in the development of student social awareness in the early 1960s, helping to create the New Left.

Tod Gitlin writer, early member of TOCSIN and president of SDS from 1963-64. He later became a professor of sociology at the University of California, Berkeley, and wrote *The Sixties; Years of Hope, Days of Rage*, Bantam, 1987. Gitlin is often quoted about the emotions as well as activities of the student revolt during the era. He is now a writer and professor of culture, journalism and sociology at New York University.

Dick Gregory (See: alphabetical listings)

David Harris a Stanford student who was jailed for draft resistance; married at one time to Joan Baez. Davis is a former contributing editor at the *New York Times Magazine* and *Rolling Stone* and is the author of eight books.

Tom Hayden (See: **Tom Hayden, Chicago Seven** and **Chicago Democratic Convention** in alphabetical listings)

Abbie Hoffman, a.k.a. **Spiro Igloo** (See: **Abbie Hoffman, Chicago Seven,** and **Chicago Democratic Convention** in alphabetical listings)

Clark Kissinger a POLIT member at University of Chicago, SDS National Secretary in the early 1960s.

Paul Krassner (See: alphabetical listings)

Allard K. Lowenstein (1929-1980) Democratic Congressman from New York City, founder of the Conference of Concerned Democrats (CCD) in 1968, an organization of democrats trying to "dump" President Johnson. They supported anti-war candidate Senator Eugene McCarthy, who gave his first presidential campaign speech at one of their meetings on December 2, 1968. Lowenstein was also deeply involved in the civil rights movement and sponsored a voter registration drive in Mississippi in the 1970s. He was shot to death in his New York City law offices by Dennis Sweeney, a former volunteer, on March 14, 1980. Sweeney testified that Lowenstein and others controlled him through radio receivers planted in his teeth. He was adjudged insane.

Norman Mailer (1923-) Pulitzer Prize-winning author, anti-war and free-speech advocate who marched and spoke at many Vietnam demonstrations.

David J. Miller Vermont college student, Catholic pacifist, and the first person to be arrested and imprisoned for burning his Selective Service card on October 18, 1965. The offense was punishable by a $10,000 fine or 5 years in jail.

A. J. Muste (Abraham Johannes) (1885 in Holland-1967) peace advocate, anti-war activist, leader of the Committee for Nonviolent Action, an organization that sailed small ships into nuclear test zones in the Pacific Ocean, scaled barbed wire fences into nuclear installations, and ventured out in rowboats trying to obstruct the launching of American nuclear submarines. In 1961, a group of pacifists walked from San Francisco to Moscow, and with the political clout of A. J. Muste, they were able to carry their message of disarmament all the way into Red Square. He once said, "There is no way to peace—peace is the way," and that was the focus of his work. A. J. was a friend and mentor to Dr. Martin Luther King, Jr., and was well known to the emerging liberation movement in Africa. He helped to organize the World Peace Brigade, which worked closely with African leaders, who would often meet with A. J. first on their visits to this country, and then go to the State Department. Trusted by all of the radical groups, he was the one person around whom the various coalitions gathered to form what became the American movement to end the Vietnam War. In 1966, he led a group of pacifists to Saigon, who were arrested and deported for attempting to hold peace demonstrations. Later that same year, he and a group of religious leaders went to Hanoi, where they met with Ho Chi Minh. His sudden death in 1967 was a blow to the peace and freedom movement.

Oakland Seven: Frank Bardacke, Terry Cannon, Reese Erlich, Steve Hamilton, Bob Mandel, Mike Smith and Jeff Segal indicted for conspiracy as a result of their involvement in the October 20, 1967, demonstration at the Oakland, California, draft induction center.

Carl Oglesby early SDS member. One of the first people to vocalize the conviction that the Communist Party was not the best force to lead the New Left in its anti-war and free-speech convictions.

Paul Potter co-founder, with Rennie Davis, of the Progressive Student League in Chicago, Ill.

Jerry Rubin (See: **Jerry Rubin, Chicago Seven** and **Chicago Democratic Convention** in alphabetical listings)

Bayard Rustin (1910-1987) "Mr. March," Black executive secretary of the War Registers League, a strong advocate of nonviolent protest and advisor to Rev. Dr. Martin Luther King, Jr.

Aurthur Schlesinger, Jr. (1917-) American historian, advisor to Presidents Kennedy and Johnson. Author of *The Vital Center,* an important book advancing the liberty of mankind.

Dr. Benjamin Spock (See: alphabetical listings)

In the struggle to end the war, there were many others who demonstrated and resisted the draft whose names I cannot list here. They were all heroes of the time.

Pro-War Groups, Anti-War Groups of Dubious Commitment, Liberal and Conservative Pressure Groups Supported by the Government:

Americans for Democratic Action
Founded: 1947
Founders, Leaders and Prominent Members: Eleanor Roosevelt, Hubert Humphrey, Joseph Rauh and other prominent New Deal Democrats

Americans for Winning the Peace (AWP)
Founded: 1970
Founders, Leaders and Prominent Members: Nixon Administration, H. R. Haldemen, Charles Colson, Gene Bradley
Major Accomplishments or Involvements: Propaganda distribution.

American Friends of Vietnam (AFV)
Founded: 1950s
Founders, Leaders and Prominent Members: Chester Cooper, Dr. Wesley Fischel, Johnson Administration
Major Accomplishments or Involvements: in the mid-1960s, collected books and clothes for publicized shipments to "the people of Vietnam," published a journal, and distributed literature on campuses.

American Nazi Party
Founded: 1958
Founder: George Lincoln Rockwell
Major Accomplishments or Involvement: involved in various pro-war activities, including the harassment of anti-war protesters in Washington, DC, in November, 1965.

American Youth for a Just Peace
Founded: 1970s
Founder: Unification Church, or "Moonies," supposedly with money from Nixon's Committee to Re-Elect the President
Major Accomplishments or Involvement: involved in a three-day fast for President Nixon on the Capitol steps in an attempt to influence public opinion during the Watergate investigation.

American-Southeast Asia Foundation
Founders, Leaders and Prominent Members: Johnson Administration

John Birch Society
Founded: 1958
Founder: Robert Welch
Major Accomplishments or Involvements: protested US neglect of soldiers captured in Vietnam.   Protested aid and trade to communist countries that "helped the enemy to kill US Soldiers." They contended that the US Government and American businesses provided technology and extended credits to the Soviet Union and other allies of North Vietnam.

Citizens Committee for Peace with Freedom in Vietnam (CCPFV)

Citizens Committee for Peace with Security
Founded: 1969
Founders, Leaders and Prominent Members: Nixon Administration
Major Accomplishments or Involvements: placed full-page ads stating, "Tell it to Hanoi." Became known as the "Tell it to Hanoi" group. Opposed and tried to undermine the 1969 Vietnam Moratorium Day demonstrations. Generated letters to legislators and the media, from supposedly private citizens, ridiculing the anti-war movement.

COINTELPRO
Founders, Leaders and Prominent Members: The FBI, J. Edgar Hoover
Major Accomplishments or Involvements: a "dirty tricks" organization devised to infiltrate anti-war groups in order to disrupt their activities by forging literature, leaking "dis-information," and discrediting the members and their ideals.

Freedom House
Founders, Leaders and Prominent Members: Leo Cherne

Committee for an Effective and Durable Peace
Founded: September 8, 1965
Founders, Leaders and Prominent Members: The Johnson Administration, McGeorge Bundy, Arthur Dean, David Rockefeller, Dean Acheson, Walter Annenberg
Major Accomplishments or Involvements: "unofficial" pro-war support group for the Johnson Administration's policies.

International Anti-Communist Brigade (IACB)
Founders, Leaders and Prominent Members: Frank Sturgis
Major Accomplishments or Involvements: involved in plans and conspiracies to assassinate Cuban leaders, including Castro. Financed by exiled Cuban hotel and gambling owners with ties to former Cuban government under Batista.

Minutemen
Founded: 1960
Founder: Missouri businessman Robert Bolivar Depugh
Leaders and Prominent Members: Roger Gordon, Southern California; Jerry Lynn Davis, southern coordinator and founder of the San Diego chapter; Howard Berry Godfry, San Diego commander and intelligence officer.
Major Accomplishments or Involvements: a right-wing, conservative, paramilitary organization dedicated to protecting the United States from communist invasion from abroad and communist subversion from within. Five to six thousand members, some of whom actively trained with weapons.

National Committee for Responsible Patriotism (NCNP)
Founders, Leaders and Prominent Members: the Johnson Administration, Charles Wiley
Major Accomplishments or Involvements: organized pro-war parades.

National Hard Hats of America

Founders, Leaders and Prominent Members: a group of construction workers organized to support the Vietnam War. It is believed that they were supported by, and may even have been formed with help from, President Nixon's dirty tricks organization, "the plumbers."

Major Accomplishments or Involvements: they held violent counter-demonstrations during anti-war rallies, notably on May 8, 1970, when they assaulted demonstrators in New York City.

National Student Committee for the Defense of Vietnam

Major Accomplishments or Involvements: on January 6, 1966, they created a scroll representing nearly half a million students who supported the military policies of the Johnson Administration in Vietnam.

Secret Army Organization (SAO) ultra-conservative revolutionary group

Founded: February, 1970, by a group of six Minutemen leaders

Founders, Leaders and Prominent Members: Roger Gordon, Southern California; Jerry Lynn Davis, San Diego chapter founder; Howard Berry Godfry, San Diego commander and intelligence officer

Major Accomplishments or Involvements: one of the most prominent actions of the SAO was the June, 1972, bombing of the Guild Theatre. During the trial of SAO member William Francis Yakopec, it was revealed that the explosives used in the attack were probably supplied by the FBI through an undercover agent, Howard Berry Godfry, the San Diego commander of the SAO. The SOA, with the help of Godfry, also published a wanted poster of Richard Nixon entitled "Wanted for Treason," in response to Nixon's policy of reconciliation with China.

United Student Alliance (USA)

Founders, Leaders and Prominent Members: Nixon Administration, Charles Stephens

Young Americans for Freedom (YAF)

Founded: September, 1960

Founders, Leaders and Prominent Members: William F. Buckley, Tom Huston, Richard Allen, E. Howard Hunt, Charles Colson

Major Accomplishments or Involvements: This group posed as anti-Nixon demonstrators and, while in this guise, perpetrated violence, thus giving dissidents a bad name. Basically, they were another vehicle for Nixon dirty tricks.

Nixon Administration Members Involved in the Watergate Break-in and Cover-up Conspiracy:

Richard Milhous Nixon (1913-1994) President of the United States of America.

John Mitchell (1913-1988) former Nixon law partner, Attorney General, resigned to became chairman of The Committee to Re-elect the President (CRP or "CREEP") in 1973, reported overall boss of dirty tricks. Served 19 months for his involvement in Watergate.

John Ehrlichman (1925-1999) Nixon's Chief of Staff, aware of the dirty tricks and Watergate operations and involved in at least planning the cover-up. Served 18 months for his involvement in Watergate, 1976-78.

H. R. (Harry Robbins) (Bob) Haldeman (1926-1993) Nixon's domestic adviser, aware of the dirty tricks and Watergate operations and involved in at least planning the cover-up. Convicted for his involvement in Watergate in 1975, and served 18 months for his involvement in Watergate, 1977-78.

John Dean (1938-) Nixon's counsel, aware of the dirty tricks and Watergate operations and involved in at least planning the cover-up. Key witness in Watergate hearings; wrote *Blind Ambition*, 1976. Served 4 months for his involvement in Watergate

Charles W. (Tex or Chuck) Colson (1931-) ex-Marine, Assistant Secretary of the Navy 1955-56, close CIA ties, Nixon's special counsel, self-proclaimed "chief ass-kicker around the White House." Driving force behind many of the dirty tricks operations. Served 7 months for his involvement in Watergate

Robert Mardian (1923-) Assistant Attorney General, headed the Internal Security Division (ISD) of the Department of Justice and coordinated domestic intelligence; also with ISD, he prosecuted draft dodgers and all those accused of political bombings and fires; CRP political coordinator, linked to Watergate break-in.

Herbert Kalmbach (1921-) Nixon's personal attorney, distributed hush money to operatives involved in the break-in.

Maurice Stans (1908-) Secretary of Commerce, chief fund raiser and finance chairman of the 1972 Committee to Re-elect the President (CRP or "CREEP"), keeper of the safe in the CREEP offices containing a secret illegal slush fund used to finance the plumbers. Indicted for, but acquitted of, conspiracy, obstructing justice and perjury in conjunction with donations and influence peddling. Not charged with involvement in Watergate.

Hugh Sloan (1940-) Treasurer of CREEP. Quit his job less than one month after the burglary. Later testified against former co-workers and became a critical source to *Washington Post* reporters Carl Bernstein and Bob Woodward.

Edgil (Bud) Krogh (1939-) chief "plumber," appointed by Nixon to post of Under Secretary of Transportation and was in charge of investigating the Flight 553 crash. Later accused of intimidating members of the National Transportation Safety Board to suppress investigation of the crash. Krogh was eventually jailed in 1971 and served 5 years for directing the burglary of the office of Daniel Ellsberg's psychiatrist.

Tom Charles Huston former Nixon White House aide, author of *The Huston Spy Plan*, which advocated directing investigations of domestic political dissidents and civil disobedience from the White House.

David Young a member of Kissinger's staff, early "plumber," involved in efforts to smear Daniel Ellsberg.

Jeb Magruder (1934-) Haldeman aide and CREEP deputy director, involved in efforts to disrupt George Wallace's efforts to run for president on his own American Independent Party ticket in 1972. The plan was to convince Wallace to run as a Democrat, thus splitting the Democratic vote. It was determined that, if Wallace ran on his own ticket, he would take votes from Nixon. Magruder served 7 months for his involvement in Watergate.

Alexander P. Butterfield (1926-) CIA veteran, secretary to the Nixon Cabinet, White House aide in charge of security. Responsible for recording presidential conversations and calls, which later formed the famous tapes. Appointed as head of the Federal Aviation Administration after the crash of Flight 553.

Dwight L. Chapin (1940-) Nixon's Appointment Secretary, organized "dirty tricks," named executive in the home office of United Airlines in Chicago after the crash of Flight 553. Convicted of perjury in 1974.

Ken Clawson (1936-1999) former *Washington Post* reporter, became Nixon's deputy communications director five months before the Watergate break-in. Is said to have written the "Canuck" letter, accusing Senator Edmund Muskie of referring to Franco-Americans as "Canucks." This "dirty trick" harmed the Democratic presidential candidate's reputation.

Gordon Strachan Haldeman assistant, supposed link to Donald Segretti and the Watergate conspirators.

Donald Segretti (1941-) alias, **Don Simms,** lawyer, Vietnam vet, Southern California "dirty tricks" specialist. Convicted of political espionage. Served 4 1/2 months for his involvement in Watergate

John J. Caulfield   former New York City policeman, special assistant to John Dean, White House contact with James McCord.

Anthony J. Ulasewicz   former New York City policeman, Nixon's 1968 campaign security chief; paid from secret funds to look into private lives of political opponents of Nixon. The effort to get "dirt" on Democratic National Chairman O'Brien may have led to the Watergate break-in.

E. (Everette) Howard Hunt (1918-) alias, **"Eduardo,"** CIA chief operations officer for the Bay of Pigs, CIA veteran, sometimes rumored to be involved in JFK assassination, Nixon aide, Colson consultant. Member of the Watergate planning team; was across the street in another building as a lookout during the Watergate burglary.   Served 33 months for his involvement in Watergate, 1975-77.

G. (George) Gordon Liddy (1930-)   ex-Treasury Department, former FBI agent, finance counsel to CREEP, the Committee to Re-elect the President (Nixon), in 1973. Member of the Watergate planning team; was across the street in another building as a lookout during the Watergate burglary. Convicted and sentenced to 20 years for his involvement in Watergate. After serving only 4 1/2 years, his sentence was commuted by President Carter; he was released in 1977.

James McCord (1918-)   a Watergate burglar, former Air Force Lieutenant, veteran of Bay of Pigs invasion, CIA veteran, in charge of security at CIA's secret Langley headquarters, CREEP and Republican National Committee security chief. Arrested at the Watergate as a burglar. Served a short time for his role in Watergate in 1975.

Bernard L. Barker   aliases, **"Macho" and "Frank Carter,"**   CIA veteran, Cuban-born, Florida real estate broker, paymaster for the Bay of Pigs invasion. Arrested at the Watergate as a burglar.

Frank A. Sturgis, aliases, **"Fiorini" and "Edward Hamilton,"**   soldier of fortune, counterspy for Batista in Fidel Castro's Rebel Army in 1958, CIA sharpshooter, sometimes rumored to be involved in JFK assassination. Arrested at the Watergate complex as a burglar.

Virgilio R. Gonzalez, alias, **"Gene Valdes,"**   Cuban exile, Miami locksmith, arrested at the Watergate complex as a burglar.

Eugenio R. Martinez (1922-) alias, **"Roul Godoy,"** Cuban exile, weapons smuggler to Cuba, on retainer to the CIA. Arrested at the Watergate complex as a burglar.

Black Power and Revolutionary Groups Engaging in Violence or Civil Disobedience:

Black Muslims, Nation of Islam, sometimes called the **Lost-Found Nation of Islam**
Founded: 1930, in Detroit, Michigan
Founder: W. D. Fard (or Wali Farad) **Other Leaders**: Elijah Muhammad (Elijah Pool), 1934 to 1975; Elijah Muhammad's son, Warith Deen Muhammad, 1975 to 1977; Louis Farrakhan, 1977 to present. **Prominent member**: Malcolm X (Malcolm Little)
Major Accomplishments or Involvements: an African American sect of the Islamic faith. The name Black Muslims is used by others to describe members of this movement, but its members reject this name. After Fard mysteriously disappeared in 1934, his chief lieutenant, Elijah Muhammad (formerly Elijah Poole), became the movement's leader. Muhammad claimed that Fard was Allah, and he was Allah's messenger. He continued Fard's teachings, which held three tenets: (1) the need for Blacks to establish a separate nation in the United States, (2) the need to recover an acceptable identity, and (3) the need for economic independence. In the 1950s and early 1960s, Malcolm X was the most prominent spokesman for the Nation of Islam. He converted to the movement while in prison in 1947. The years from Malcolm's release from prison in 1952 to his assassination in 1965 marked the Nation's greatest growth and influence. Malcolm left the Nation of Islam in 1964 and converted to Sunni Islam. After Elijah Muhammad's death in 1975, one of his sons, Warith (formerly Wallace) Deen Muhammad, was chosen as the next leader. He rid the movement of its Black nationalistic characteristics, announcing that Whites were no longer "devils" and could join his movement. He also made many changes to lead his followers toward Sunni Islam. Since 1976, the movement's name has changed from Nation of Islam to the World Community of Al-Islam in the West, to American Muslim Mission. Today, Warith Deen Muhammad's followers are known simply as Muslims, and this sect has decentralized into small groups in independent places of prayer called masjids. In 1977, Louis Farrakhan led a group of discontented followers in restructuring the Nation of Islam. This group has continued the Black separatist and nationalist teachings of Elijah Muhammad. Today, the term Black Muslims refers most appropriately to followers of Farrakhan's Nation of Islam.

Black Nationalist Party
Founded: March, 1964
Founder: Malcolm X, born Malcolm Little
Major Accomplishments or Involvements: Malcolm X declared that his new party would persuade Negroes to replace nonviolence with active self-defense against White supremacists. "There can be no revolution without bloodshed." Malcolm X was killed by gunmen from a rival religious faction on February 21, 1965.

Black Panther Party (Black Panthers)
Founded: October, 1966
Co-founders: Huey P. Newton and Bobby Seale **Leaders and Prominent Members:** Eldridge Cleaver, Fred Hampton, Stokely Carmichael, Bobby Rush, Rufus Walls, Jewel Cook. Their slogan was "Seize the Time."
Major Accomplishments or Involvements: "The Panthers" created free children's breakfast programs and free health clinics; they taught political education classes and conducted a community police control project, which monitored the actions of police in Black ghettos to keep them from violating the civil rights of citizens. The Panthers were greatly feared, misunderstood, and persecuted because of the formidable appearance of their uniform of black beret and leather jacket and because they often carried weapons openly, which was legal in California at the time.

Revolutionary Youth Movement (RYM and RYM II)
Founded: 1968
Founders, Leaders and Prominent Members: Mike Klonsky, Bernardine Dohrn
Major Accomplishments or Involvements: offshoot of the SDS and Weathermen.

Symbionese Liberation Army (SLA)
Founded: Spring, 1973. The word Symbionese was derived from the word symbiosis, meaning dissimilar organisms living together in harmony. Their symbol was a seven-headed cobra snake meant to symbolize black, brown, yellow, red, white, young and old. Their slogan was "Death to the fascist insects that prey on the life of the people."
Founders, Leaders and Prominent Members: Donald De Freeze (Cinque), Patricia Soltysik (Mizmoon or Zoya), Willie Wolfe (Cujo), Nancy Ling Perry (Fahizah), Emily Harris (Yolanda), Bill Harris (Tico), Angela Atwood (Gelina), Joe Remiro, Russell Little, Camille Hall, Patrica Hearst (Tania). It is still not known exactly how much involvement Patty Hearst had with the SLA. The SLA appeared to be dominated by the women in the group, notably Soltysik and Perry, although De Freeze was the figurehead as General Field Marshal Cinque. The SLA was associated with or evolved from a group called Venceremos, which was involved in breaking African Americans out of prison.
Major Accomplishments or Involvements: they killed Dr. Marcus Foster, Black Oakland Superintendent of Schools on November 6, 1973, and on February 4, 1974, they kidnaped Patricia Campbell Hearst, the daughter of Randolph and Catherine Hearst and heir to the Hearst newspaper fortune. On April 15, 1974,

the SLA robbed the Hibernia Bank at Noriega and 22nd Street in San Francisco. Patty Hearst was in attendance, holding an automatic weapon. On May 16, 1974, they shoplifted and shot up Mel's Sporting Goods in the Crenshaw area of Los Angeles. Patty was the shooter. On May 17, 1974, six members of the SLA were killed in a shoot-out and fire at a house at 1466 54th Street in Los Angeles. Killed were Donald De Freeze, Patricia Soltysik (Mizmoon), Willie Wolfe, Nancy Ling Perry, Angela Atwood and Camille Hall. Patty Hearst and Bill and Emily Harris were captured in San Francisco on September 18, 1975.

The New Years Gang
Founded: 1969
Founders and Members: Brothers Karl and Dwight Armstrong, friends David Fine and Leo Burt
Major Accomplishments or Involvements: on August 24, 1970, they ignited a car bomb in front of the Sterling Hall, Army Mathematics Research Center of the University of Wisconsin campus in Madison, killing a post-doctoral researcher and causing $6 million in damage. Robert Fassnacht was killed by 2,000 pounds of ammonium nitrate soaked in aviation fuel and packed into a stolen Ford van. The bomb was intended as a protest against the Vietnam War and was planted by the four young men known as the New Years Gang, two brothers Karl and Dwight Armstrong plus David Fine and Leo Burt. The conspirators did not intend to kill anyone, thinking the surrounding buildings would be empty on the Sunday night. The New Years Gang was named after a failed bombing of the Badger Ordnance Works outside Baraboo, Wisconsin, on December 31, 1969, by Karl and Dwight. Karl Armstrong also previously attacked the University's Armory Gymnasium (known as the Red Gym) and the UW Primate Research Center. The four young men fled to Canada after the bombing, but three were eventually arrested. Leo Burt has never been found. Karl Armstrong was released from prison in 1980; the others, being lesser participants, were released earlier. A documentary, "The War at Home," was produced about the Sterling Hall bombing, and at least two books have been written on the episode: *The Madison Bombing* by Michael Morris, and *Rads* by Tom Bates.

Up Against the Wall Motherfucker or the Motherfuckers
Founded: 1967
Founders: a group of artists from the Lower East Side of New York City
Major Accomplishments or Involvements: their slogan was "Armed Love," their logo was the face on the Zig-Zag cigarette papers, and they were associated with the SDS. They produced happenings, performances and conceptual plays, usually with some socio-political satire or message.

Weathermen (Weather Bureau)
Founded: violent offshoot of SDS started in 1968. The name came from a Bob Dylan song, implying that Weathermen "know which way the wind blows."
Founders, Leaders and Prominent Members: Bernardine Dohrn, Jeff Jones, Bill Ayers, Kathie Boudin, Cathy Wilkerson and Mark Rudd
Major Accomplishments or Involvements: Days of Rage, Chicago, October, 1969, was their major event. October 6, 1969, Weathermen blew up the nation's only

monument to policemen, located in Chicago's Haymarket Square. On March 6, 1970, three Weathermen members were killed while making bombs in a New York City townhouse on West 11th Street. Killed were Diana Oughton, Ted Gold and Terry Robbins. On March 1, 1971, Weathermen damaged the Capitol Building with a bomb. On March 6, 1970, three Weathermen members were killed while making bombs in a New York City townhouse on West 11th Street. In 1970, after the group was linked to these bombings, many of its members became fugitives, calling themselves the Weather Underground.

White Panther Party
Founder: John Sinclair
Prominent Members: Jim Fouratt, Lawrence Robert "Pun" Plamondon
Major Accomplishments or Involvements: their slogan was "Rock 'n' roll, dope and fucking in the streets." An offshoot of the Artists' Workshop of Detroit, and associated with The Translove Energies-White Panther commune in Ann Arbor, Michigan. Sinclair managed the bands MC5 and the Psychedelic Stooges, who performed at demonstrations during the Democratic National Convention in Chicago in August, 1968.

Yippies (Youth International Party)
Founded: during the Christmas holidays, 1967
Founders: Jerry Rubin, Abbie Hoffman and Paul Krassner
Major Accomplishments or Involvements: responsible for The Festival of Light and many of the demonstrations in Chicago, August 24-30, 1968, which precipitated the police riots during the Democratic National Convention. During the 1968 election campaign, the Yippies nominated a pig named Pigasus for President. The pig was "arrested" at one of the demonstrations during the Chicago Democratic National Convention.

Black Power and Revolutionary Leaders:

Angela Yvonne Davis (See: alphabetical listings)

Rennie Davis (See: **Rennie Davis, Chicago Seven** and **Chicago Democratic Convention** in alphabetical listings)

David Dellinger (See: **David Dellinger, Chicago Seven** and **Chicago Democratic Convention** in alphabetical listings)

Fred Hampton (See: alphabetical listings)

Tom Hayden (See: **Tom Hayden, Chicago Seven** and **Chicago Democratic Convention** in alphabetical listings)

Abbie Hoffman (See: **Abbie Hoffman, Chicago Seven** and **Chicago Democratic Convention** in alphabetical listings)

Elijah Muhammad (Elijah Poole) (See: alphabetical listings)

Huey P. Newton (See: alphabetical listings)

Jerry Rubin (See: **Jerry Rubin, Chicago Seven** and **Chicago Democratic Convention** in alphabetical listings)

Bobby Seale (See: alphabetical listings)

Soledad Brothers: George Jackson (1941-1971), John Clutchette and Fleeta Drumgo three Black prisoners at the Soledad Prison in California, who were accused of pushing a guard over a railing to his death. (See: **Soledad Brothers** in alphabetical listings)

Malcolm X (Malcolm Little) (See: alphabetical listings)

Free-Speech, Student Rights and Human Rights Events and Demonstrations:

October 1, 1964 led by Jack Weinberg, a group of University of California, Berkeley, students, discontented with compulsory ROTC and the impersonal bureaucracy, set up pamphlet tables against campus regulations at UC Berkeley's Sather Gate.

December, 1964 Mario Savio led 3,000 students, discontented with campus bureaucracy, to occupy UC Berkeley's administration building, Sproul Hall.

June 13, 1966 the Miranda Law was instituted; the Supreme Court ruled that confessions are invalid if obtained before a suspect is informed of his rights.

April, 1968 Columbia University students seized five campus buildings, including the president's office.

April 20, 1969 a 2.8-acre parcel of University of California, Berkeley, land became People's Park when it was appropriated and renamed by students and hippies. The Berkeley residents and street people laid sod, dug a pond and installed playground equipment.

May, 1969 People's Park demonstrations. (See: **People's Park** in alphabetical listings

January 27,1970 the US Senate passed "no warning entry" law for police on drug raids.

February 25, 1970 William Allen, Assistant Professor at UC Santa Barbara, was dismissed over issues of academic freedom; students rioting in his defense led to the burning of a local branch of the Bank of America.

June 22, 1970 Congressional bill reducing the voting age from 21 to 18 became law.

September 13, 1976 California approved the nation's first right-to-die law.

Free-Speech, Student Rights and Human Rights Groups:

American Civil Liberties Union (ACLU)
Founded: 1920
Founders: Jane Addams, Roger Baldwin, Clarence Darrow, John Dewey and Helen Keller
Major Accomplishments or Involvements: supplies legal aid in cases of civil

rights violations to any party, whether a member of the Ku Klux Klan or a member of the National Association for the Advancement of Colored People (NAACP).

Amnesty International
Founded: October 15, 1962, in London, England
Founder: Peter Benenson, a British attorney
Major Accomplishments or Involvements: exposes human rights violations internationally and reports the details to the United Nations. Amnesty International was awarded the Nobel Peace Prize in December, 1977.

Diggers
Founded: Mid-1960s
Founders: Emmett Grogan and a communal group of radical actors
Major Accomplishments or Involvements: fed, clothed and housed street people and hippies in San Francisco. They distributed food every day at 4:00 p.m. in Panhandle Park near Haight-Ashbury in San Francisco, California. They financed this effort by collecting donations from anyone who could afford to give. They pressured the drug sellers to contribute at least 1% of their profits to feed those to whom they sold drugs.

Students for a Democratic Society (SDS)
Founded: 1960, refined and defined at Port Huron, Michigan, in 1962. The SDS dissolved in June, 1969
Founders and Leaders: Al Haber, Sharon Jeffrey, Bob Ross, Dick Magidoff, Tom Hayden, Rennie Davis, Dorothy Dawson, Clark Kissinger, Jerry Rubin, Carl Oglesby, Carl Davidson, Bill Ayers, Mike Klonsky, Paul Potter, etc. The SDS actually evolved from one of the first student peace and freedom groups, the Student League for Industrial Democracy (SLID), an offshoot of the League for Industrial Democracy (LID), which actually contributed to the SDS financing through the years. The SDS was in actuality "The Student Department of the League for Industrial Democracy." The LID and the SLID were themselves offshoots of the Communist Party.
Major Accomplishments or Involvements: involved in planning the first national anti-war demonstrations in late 1964 to early 1965, notably the demonstration in Washington, DC, on April 17, 1965. In April of 1968 during a free speech demonstration, members of the SDS occupied offices of New York's Columbia University, including the president's office. The SDS was one of the most radical of the anti-war groups. In 1968, a number of SDS members, becoming even more radical, left to form the Weathermen (a.k.a: Weather Bureau). In 1970, after the Weathermen were linked to bombings, many of its members became fugitives, calling themselves the Weather Underground.

Free-Speech, Student Rights and Human Rights Leaders:

William Allen (See: alphabetical listings)

Daniel Cohn-Bendit (Danny the Red) (See: alphabetical listings)

Peter Benenson (See: **Peter Benenson** and **Amnesty International** in alphabetical listings)

Mike Delacour conceived the idea of the People's Park in Berkeley in April, 1969.

Art Goldberg a free-speech movement (FSM) leader.

Jack Greenberg (1924-) White civil rights attorney and director-counsel, NAACP Legal Defense and Education Fund, 1961-1984. He argued two of the five cases that led to the Supreme Court's *Brown v. Board of Education* (1954) decision holding racial segregation in public schools to be unconstitutional. In 1965, Greenberg launched a campaign for the expansion of prisoners' rights and for the abolition of capital punishment; in 1967, he founded the National Office for the Rights of the Indigent (NORI) to assert the rights of the poor in court. Greenberg joined the Columbia Law School faculty in 1984 and was named Dean of Columbia College in 1989.

Tom Hayden (See: **Tom Hayden, Chicago Seven** and **Chicago Democratic Convention** in alphabetical listings)

Mark Rudd (b. Mark William Rudnitsky 1947-) a.k.a. **Tony Goodman** an SDS leader who led the occupation of buildings, including the president's office, at Columbia University, in New York City in April, 1968. He was indicted for conspiracy to riot and eventually went underground with the Weathermen for a period of seven years. Mark Rudd is currently teaching at a community college in the Southwestern United States.

Jerry Rubin (See: **Jerry Rubin, Chicago Seven** and **Chicago Democratic Convention** in alphabetical listings)

Mario Savio (See: **Mario Savio** and **free-speech movement** in alphabetical listings)

Jack Weinberg (See: **Jack Weinberg** and **free-speech movement** in alphabetical listings)

Women's Movement (Feminist & Women's Liberation) Events, Demonstrations and Legislation:

July, 21, 1923 the Equal Rights Amendment (ERA) was first drafted. The amendment was not ratified by the states.

1960 women with full-time, year-round jobs earned 60.6 percent of what men earned; Black women earned just 42 percent. On the average, female college graduates earned less than men with only high school diplomas.

December, 1961 John Kennedy created a President's Commission on the Status of Women (PCSW), the "Kennedy Commission." Eleanor Roosevelt was its first chairperson. Although originally a device of appeasement for ERA supporters, it soon helped to solidify and generate the modern women's movement.

July, 1962 John Kennedy issued a directive requiring all federal agencies to hire, train, and promote all future employees equally, without regard to gender.

1963 upon the recommendation of the Kennedy Commission, John F. Kennedy established the Citizens' Advisory Council on the Status of Women (CACSW) just days before his assassination. It endured until Reagan dispensed with it.

1963 the Equal Pay Act was passed by Congress. It was the first Federal law forbidding sex discrimination by private business.

1964 the Civil Rights Act of 1964 was passed by Congress, prohibiting discrimination on the basis of race (and sex) in employment, public accommodations, publicly owned facilities, union membership, and Federally funded programs. At the suggestion of Martha W. Griffiths, a Michigan Democrat, the word "sex" was added to Title VII of this Act, thus opening the door to future job security for women.

1964 the Equal Employment Opportunity Commission (EEOC) was created as a result of the Civil Rights Act of 1964.

June 29, 1966 National Organization of Women (NOW) was founded by Betty Friedan, Pauli Murray, Kay Clarenbach, Catherine East, Mary Eastwood and Catherine Conroy.

1968 consciousness-raising (C-R) was developed and employed in the feminist movement. C-R sessions are gatherings at which women's issues are confronted and discussed. These sessions were influential in forming the direction of the women's liberation movement. The process was developed by the New York Radical Women.

1968 *The Florida Paper* was published in Gainesville, Florida. This publication questioned traditional goals of women, recommending celibacy and the forming of women's communes. Also, at the same time, members of the New York Radical Women (NYRW) produced *Notes from the First Year,* a radical paper about women's changing directions. These publications were distributed widely throughout the country's feminist population.

March, 1968 Chicago feminists published the first issue of *Voice of the Women's Liberation Movement,* a newsletter that reached radical women all over the country.

August 10, 1968 the Equal Employment Opportunity Commission (EEOC) released new guidelines barring the airlines from dismissing stewardesses for being "overage." Sometimes called "The Old Broads' Bill," this was one of the first tests of Title VII of the Civil Rights Act of 1964. The action was due to the lobbying and pressures of the Air Line Stewards and Stewardesses Association (ALSSA) led by ALSSA lobbyist Dusty Roads and ALSSA President of ALSSA Nancy Collins.

August 26, 1970 the 50th anniversary of the granting of women's suffrage in America. A historic Women's March for Equality was held on Fifth Avenue in New York City. NOW and Betty Friedan organized the event, Gloria Steinem was the MC, and most of the current feminist leaders were there. The turnout was so impressive that much of America awakened to the women's movement on that date.

September, 1970 the annual convention of NOW approved a resolution with this wording: "Be it resolved NOW recognizes the double oppression of women who are lesbians, and be it further resolved: that a woman's right to her own person includes the right to define and express her own sexuality and to choose her own lifestyle, and be it further resolved: that NOW acknowledges the oppression of lesbians as a legitimate concern of feminism."

January, 1972 *Ms. Magazine* was published in a preview issue of 300,000 copies and sold out; the first regular issue appeared in July, 1972.

March 22, 1972 the Equal Rights Amendment (ERA) was passed by Congress, yet in order to become law it needed to be ratified by a popular vote in two-thirds of the States of the Union. Later that year, it was put to the vote and fell three states short of the 38 states it needed to pass. The Equal Rights Amendment is still not law today.

1973 the U. S. military was integrated when the women-only branches were eliminated.

1973 the journal *Quest: A Feminist Quarterly* was started by members of the Washington, DC, NOW chapter. The organization was involved in developing utopian group collectives for women. Charlotte Bunch was a founder. The publication survived until 1982.

1973 the Boston Women's Health Book Collective first published the influential book for women, *Our Bodies, Ourselves*. It is still being revised and reprinted periodically.

January 22, 1973 the US Supreme Court decision on *Roe v. Wade* virtually legalized abortion by overruling all state laws that prohibit or restrict a woman's right to obtain an abortion during the first three months of pregnancy. The vote was 7 to 2.

November 7, 1973 the New Jersey Supreme Court ruled that Hoboken's Little League must accept girls on its teams.

1974 the Equal Credit Opportunity Act (ECOA) passed Congress through the efforts of a coalition of feminists.

December 15, 1975 the Food and Drug Administration (FDA) met to debate the risks of menopausal estrogens, deciding whether or not to inform women of the dangers of these products through the creation of Patient Package Inserts (PPIs). The National Women's Health Network (NWHN) also gathered in a demonstration and memorial service for all of the women who had died because of diethylstilbestrol (DES), the birth control pill, and estrogen replacement therapy. This protest was the first time the NWHN had ever demonstrated and also the first time anyone had ever demonstrated in front of the FDA. Questions concerning the safety of estrogens arose with investigations of DES and the pill. The discovery of the reproductive damage caused by DES led to its recall for use in pregnant women. NWHN founder Barbara Seaman exposed the dangers of oral contraceptives in her 1969 book, *The Doctors' Case Against the Pill*. Her work led to the Nelson Pill hearings, which resulted in the inclusion of PPIs with each prescription of birth control pills. Despite public warnings, many women were still being harmed by these drugs in 1975.

Women's (Feminist & Women's Liberation) Groups, Organizations, Publications and Administrative Commissions of the Era:

American Association of University Women (AAUW)
Founded: 1881
Major Accomplishments or Involvements: a national organization promoting equity and education for all girls and women, lifelong education, and positive social change. Distributed more than $3.5 million in fellowships, grants, and awards to graduate women in 2001-2002.

Boston Women's Health Book Collective
Founded: 1969
Founders: Nancy Hawley and a group of Boston women
Major Accomplishments or Involvements: in 1970, they compiled and published the influential health book for women, *Our Bodies, Ourselves.*

Bread and Roses
Founded: 1968
Founders: Nancy Hawley and a group of Boston women
Major Accomplishments or Involvements: taught skills, such as auto mechanics and carpentry, to women. The organization supported single mothers, helping women to achieve self-confidence and gain control of their own lives.

Cell 16, originally called Female Liberation Front
Founded: 1968
Founder: Rozanne Dunbar; **Members:** Betsy Warrior and a group of radical Boston women
Major Accomplishments or Involvements: they started the tradition of women learning karate for protection. Published *No More Fun and Games: A Journal of Female Liberation.* They advocated "free abortion and birth control on demand— communal raising of children by both sexes and people of all ages...."

Center for Women Policy Studies (CWPS)
Founded: 1972
Founders: Jane Roberts Chapman and Margaret Gates. Started with $10,000 seed grant from Ralph Nader's organization.
Major Accomplishments or Involvements: the first feminist group to receive a Ford Foundation grant; in December, 1972, the group received $40,000 to study sex discrimination in credit policies of lending institutions.

Center for the American Woman and Politics (CAWP)
Founded: 1972 at Rutgers University
Major Accomplishments or Involvements: Studied women's issues and organized politically motivated women.

Feminists, The
Founded: 1968
Founder: Ti-Grace Atkinson
Major Accomplishments or Involvements: on September 23, 1969, they invaded the New York City marriage license bureau armed with leaflets advocating the elimination of marriage and the raising of children communally.

Furies Collective
Founded: in Washington, DC, 1971
Founders and Leaders: Rita Mae Brown, Charlotte Bunch
Major Accomplishments or Involvements: a lesbian separatist collective involved in developing the basic lesbian social and political theories of the times. Analyzing heterosexuality, they defined it as a form of domination based on the assumption that heterosexual sex was the only "natural" way, and heterosexuals assumed that every woman was either bound to a man or wished she were. The Furies contended that women were viewed primarily as wives and mothers only, and the social order was based on the assumption that women would always put men first.

It Ain't Me, Babe (comic book/newspaper)
Founded: 1970, San Francisco Bay area
Founders Artists and Writers: Nancy Kalish (pseudonyms: Panzika, Hurricane Nancy), Trina Robbins, Lisa Lyons
Major Accomplishments or Involvements: the first all-female comic book.

National Organization of Women (NOW)
Founded: June 29, 1966
Founders and Leaders: First President, Betty Friedan; Pauli Murray, Kay Clarenbach, Catherine East, Mary Eastwood, Catherine Conroy
Major Accomplishments or Involvements: "To take actions needed to bring women into the mainstream of American society—now, full equality for women, in fully equal partnership with men." Organized after the Equal Employment Opportunity Commission failed to enforce Title VII of the Civil Rights Act of 1964, prohibiting discrimination on the basis of gender. NOW worked to pressure the Equal Employment Opportunity Commission (EEOC) to enforce Title VII of the Civil Rights Act of 1964 to ensure women's equality in the work place.

National Woman's Party (NWP)
Founded: 1916, Washington, DC
Founder: Alice Paul, radical activist
Major Accomplishments or Involvements: Alice Paul wrote the original Equal Rights Amendment and launched the campaign to gain the vote for women.

National Women's Political Caucus (NWPC)
Founded: July, 1971
Founders and Leaders: composed of many NOW members
Major Accomplishments or Involvements: promotes pro-choice women in elected and appointed offices, regardless of party affiliation. Supports other women's issues, such as equal pay and the ERA. Also supported the withdrawal from Vietnam, preservation of the environment, and the fight against racism.

New York Radical Feminists (NYRF)
Founded: 1969
Founders: Anne Koedt, Shulamith Firestone, and remnants of the Redstockings and the Radical Feminists.
Major Accomplishments or Involvements: in 1971, held a series of speakouts and a conference on rape and the treatment of women by the criminal justice system.

New York Radical Women (NYRW) originally known as the Radical Women
Founded: 1967
Founders and Leaders: Shulamith Firestone and Pam Allen
Major Accomplishments or Involvements: recruited women from the local Students for a Democratic Society (SDS). In January, 1968, they staged a funeral procession at Arlington Cemetery for a dummy representing "Traditional Womanhood," in defiance of the image of anti-war women as primarily "tearful and passive" wives and mothers of fighting men. The NYRW also organized the protest of the Miss America Pageant in Atlantic City, New Jersey, in the fall of 1968, where 200 demonstrators carried picket signs stating, "Women are people, not livestock," and asking "Can makeup cover the wounds of our oppression?" They also invited women to discard "objects of female torture" like hair curlers, girdles, bras and high heels. They developed consciousness-raising (C-R) among the feminist movement. C-R consisted of group discussions about women's issues. These sessions were influential in creating the direction of the women's liberation movement.

Parents Without Partners
Founded: 1957, New York City
Founders: two single parents, Jim Egleson, a noncustodial parent; and Jacqueline Bernard, a custodial parent.
Major Accomplishments or Involvements: organized concerned parents who felt isolated from society because of their marital status, forming a mutual support organization.

President's Commission on the Status of Women
Founded: 1961 by President John F. Kennedy
Leaders and Prominent Members: chaired by Eleanor Roosevelt
Major Accomplishments or Involvements: recommended 24 ways to combat sex discrimination, among them the installation of permanent government administrative departments. Created were: the Interdepartmental Committee on the Status of Women (composed of cabinet-level officials) and the Citizen's Advisory Council on the Status of Women (composed of private citizens.)

Quest: A Feminist Quarterly (newspaper)
Founded: 1973
Founder and Leader: Charlotte Bunch
Major Accomplishments or Involvements: a publication that explored the development of utopian group collectives for women. The publication survived until 1982.

Redstockings
Founded: 1969
Founders: Shulamith Firestone, Ellen Willis, and a group of New York radical feminists
Major Accomplishments or Involvements: one of the first of what could be called radical feminist groups. Influenced Gloria Steinem with their "abortion speak-out" at which women publicly described their harrowing experiences with illegal abortions. Disrupted the New York State Legislative Committee hearing on abortion reform.

Tits 'n' Clits (underground comic books)
Founded: 1972, Laguna Beach, California
Founders, Artists and Writers: Joyce Farmer and Lyn Chevely ("Chin Lyvely"), Nanny Goat Productions
Major Accomplishments or Involvements: the second all-female comic book and the first continuing all-female anthology, it lasted fifteen years. Also published *Pandora's Box*, 1973 and *Abortion Eve*, 1973.

Voice of the Women's Liberation Movement (a newsletter)
Founded: March, 1968, Chicago, Illinois
Founders, Leaders and Prominent Members: Chicago feminists
Major Accomplishments or Involvements: reached potential feminists and radical women all over the country.

Women's Comix Collective (underground comic books)
Founded: 1972, San Francisco, California
Founders, Artists and Writers: Ten San Francisco women

Women's Equity Action League (WEAL)
Founded: 1968, Cleveland, Ohio
Founders, Leaders and Prominent Members: Elizabeth Boyer and other disgruntled Midwestern NOW members
Major Accomplishments or Involvements: more conservative than NOW, it was ostensibly formed to fight sex discrimination in education.

WITCH an acronym from the names of several organizations: **Women's International Terrorist Conspiracy from Hell, Women Inspired to Commit Herstory, or Women Intent on Toppling Consumer Holidays**.

Women's Liberation Movement
The Women's Liberation Movement was never really an organization, as was NOW or the Redstockings; it was the description of the movement. For a time, FBI Director J. Edgar Hoover was actively pursuing a group that he called Women's Liberation Movement or WLM, but it was a quest for something even he could not identify.

Women's (Feminist & Women's Liberation) Leaders:

Bella Abzug (See: alphabetical listings)

Dolores Alexander in 1969, she became NOW's first national executive director. She was fired in 1970 due to a conflict with Betty Friedan over the lesbian involvement in NOW. Alexander was defending lesbian membership, although she herself professed not to be one. Along with Rita Mae Brown's resignation from NOW, Alexander's ouster was called the first NOW "lesbian purge."

Kathie Amatniek changed her surname to Sarachild in rejection of the tradition that children are always given the last name of their fathers, and their mother's maiden name is ignored. Her mother's first name was Sara, and she was her mother's child; therefore, Sarachild. (See: **Kathie Sarachild**)

Ti-Grace Atkinson (See: alphabetical listings)

Helen Gurley Brown (See: alphabetical listings)

Rita Mae Brown (See: alphabetical listings)

Susan Brownmiller journalist/author. Author of *Against Our Will: Men, Women and Rape*. Architect of the March 18, 1970, protest at which hundreds of women stormed the office of John Mack Carter, the male editor of *Ladies' Home Journal*. After a 9-hour siege, Carter agreed to publish a supplement written by feminists.

Charlotte Bunch (1944-) educator, writer. A leading member of the Washington, DC, NOW chapter, organizer of the Sandy Springs meeting and the Thanksgiving Conference. In 1970, she helped to start the journal *Quest: A Feminist Quarterly*, which explored the development of utopian group collectives for women.

Jane Roberts Chapman economist who co-founded the Center for Women Policy Studies (CWPS) in 1972 with Margaret Gates. CWPS was started with a $10,000 seed grant from Ralph Nader's organization. It was also the first feminist group to receive a Ford Foundation grant; in December, 1972, the Center received $40,000 to study sex discrimination in credit policies of lending institutions.

Shirley Chisholm (See: alphabetical listings)

Kay Clarenbach chairperson of the NOW Board of Directors in the late 1960s to early 1970s.

Nancy Collins president of Air Line Stewards and Stewardesses Association (ALSSA) in the mid 1960s. Helped convince the EEOC to draft its August 10, 1968, guidelines barring the airlines from dismissing stewardesses for being "overage." This was one of the first tests of Title VII of the Civil Rights Act of 1964.

Simone de Beauvoir (1908-1986) French author/philosopher, who wrote *The Second Sex*, the book that many say started "the second wave of feminism" or the "modern feminist movement." Jean Paul Sartre was her lover.

Catherine East originally a government civil servant working for the Kennedy Commission. Founding member of the National Organization of Women (NOW).

Mary Eastwood a Justice Department attorney working for the Kennedy Commission. Founding member of the National Organization of Women (NOW).

Jean Faust the first President of the New York Chapter of the National Organization of Women (NOW).

Shulamith Firestone a founding member of the Redstockings and New York Radical Feminists. Author of *Dialectic of Sex*, published in 1970.

Muriel Fox a public relations executive, she handled the PR for the National Organization of Women (NOW) in the early years.

Betty Friedan (See: alphabetical listings)

Margaret Gates attorney who co-founded the Center for Women Policy Studies (CWPS) in 1972 with Jane Roberts Chapman. CWPS was started with a $10,000 seed grant from Ralph Nader's organization. It was also the first feminist group to receive a Ford Foundation grant; in December, 1972, the Center received $40,000 to study sex discrimination in credit policies of lending institutions.

Germaine Greer (See: alphabetical listings)

Martha Griffiths (See: alphabetical listings)

Nancy Hawley originally a founding member of the first chapter of Students for a Democratic Society (SDS). She was important to the early women's movement in Boston and involved in the development of Bread and Roses and Cell 16, originally called Female Liberation Front. Hawley was a founding member of the Boston Women's Health Book Collective in 1970 and instrumental in publishing the bestselling book, *Our Bodies, Ourselves,* in 1973.

Aileen Hernandez (1926-) the first Black female member of the Equal Employment Opportunity Commission (EEOC) and the only woman at its inception. In 1966, she resigned from the Commission in protest over its reluctance to confront women's issues. Her resignation prompted the EEOC's decision to censor the airlines for sex discrimination because of their age limits for stewardesses. Hernandez was elected as President of the National Organization of Women (NOW) in 1971.

Flo Kennedy "ol' black Flo" (See: alphabetical listings)

Kate Millett (See: alphabetical listings)

Robin Morgan (1941-) author, writer, feminist, women's liberationist. Involved in the 1969 feminist takeover of *The Rat,* the new left, alternative newspaper in New York City, she has written many important feminist articles for that and other publications. Morgan was active in the New York City coven of WITCH—Women Inspired to Commit Herstory. She helped to compile the 1970 feminist anthology, *Sisterhood Is Power,* an important influence on many women and the women's movement. Morgan was the editor of the advertisement-free *Ms. Magazine* from 1990 to 1993.

Jean O'Leary (1948-) social activist and former nun. She led the Lesbian Feminist Liberation group out of the Gay Activists' Alliance.

Letty Cottin Pogrebin author of the books *How to Make It in a Man's World* and *Growing Up Free,* and the article "Down with Sexist Upbringing," which appeared in the first issue of *Ms. Magazine.* She was also a talented promoter of other people and their books, such as Helen Gurley Brown's *Sex and the Single Girl* and Jacqueline Susann's *Valley of the Dolls.*

Dusty Roads airline stewardess, unofficial lobbyist for the Air Line Stewards and Stewardesses Association (ALSSA). Spearheaded the fight to force the airlines to drop their age restrictions for stewardesses.

Kathie Sarachild a radical member of the New York Radical Women. Wrote the pamphlet "Sisterhood is Powerful," which was distributed at one of the first feminist women's marches and demonstrations, held at Arlington Cemetery in January, 1968. This was actually an offshoot of an anti-war demonstration. Sarachild co-wrote the book *Feminist Revolution,* published in 1975, and was influential in developing consciousness-raising (C-R) in the feminist movement. C-R consists of group discussions confronting women's issues. These sessions were influential in creating the direction of the women's liberation movement. Sarachild changed her surname from Amatniek in rejection of the tradition that children are always given their father's last name, and their mother's maiden name is ignored. Her mother's first name was Sara, and she was her mother's child; therefore, Sarachild.

Barbara Seaman a successful journalist for women's magazines, wife and mother of three who became the "confessor," telling of her youthful abortion at a Redstockings "speak-out," which was subsequently broadcast over New York City television. It was a pivotal moment in the fight for abortion rights. In 1969, she brought questions about the pill to the public when she wrote *The Doctors' Case Against the Pill,* linking oral contraceptives to blood clots, strokes and cancer. Her work led to the Nelson pill hearings, which resulted in the inclusion of Patient Package Inserts (PPIs) with each prescription of birth control pills, in 1975. Seaman has also written *Free and Female* and the 1987 biography of novelist Jacqueline Susann, *Lovely Me.*

Valeria Solanis author of the SCUM manifesto; SCUM stands for the Society for Cutting Up Men. Solanis shot and wounded artist Andy Warhol over a dispute about the making of a movie based on her manifesto.

Gloria Steinem (See: alphabetical listings)

Marlo Thomas (1938-) star of the "That Girl" television show, and one of the first celebrities to embrace the feminist movement. She and her friend Gloria Steinem once tried to collaborate on a script about women's self-awareness. With the help of her entertainment friends, Thomas eventually produced a series of songs that was the first in the genre of children's celebration of self and equality. Called the "Free to Be" series, it eventually spawned the Free to Be Foundation.

Gay & Lesbian Movement
Events, Demonstrations and Legislation:

Fall 1965 the Ritch Street Health Club (The Ritch Street Baths) opened in San Francisco, California, as a safe place for homosexual men to meet.

June 27-29, 1969 Stonewall Rebellion, a riot by gay men in New York City prompted by a police raid on one of their bars in Greenwich Village called the Stonewall Inn.

July 9, 1969 the first meeting of radical new Gay Power activists in Freedom Hall, New York City. Dubbed the "Mattachine Action Committee," it was initiated by Dick Leitsch, the executive director of the Mattachine Society, and held at their meeting place. Leitsch named Michael Brown to run the meeting, and the group that attended soon became more radical than Leitsch and the Mattachine expected. This was the beginning of the gay liberation movement. At one of the first meetings of this group, Martha Shelley proposed the Gay Power Vigil at Washington Square Park.

July 27, 1969 the first Gay Power Vigil held in New York City's Washington Square Park on the one-month anniversary of Stonewall.

January, 1970 the boycott and picketing of Barney's Beanery began. Barney's Beanery was a chili restaurant on Santa Monica Boulevard with a large after-hours clientele. Even though many gays frequented the place and were never discriminated against, there was a sign on the wall that read "Fagots Stay Out" [sic]. The homosexual community finally decided to make an example of the restaurant and picketed it for three months, eventually getting the owner to remove the sign. The sign soon reappeared and stayed up until it was removed in 1984 by the newly chosen Mayor of North Hollywood, Valerie Terrigno, a lesbian.

May 18, 1970 Jack Baker and Mike McConnell applied for a marriage license in Minneapolis, Minnesota, the first recorded attempt to obtain a same-sex marriage sanctioned by law. They were denied the license on the grounds that it would "result in an undermining and destruction of the entire legal concept of our family structure in all areas of law." Baker, student body president at the University of Minnesota, later tested same-sex tax laws.

June 27-29, 1970 the first Gay Pride Day. It began as the anniversary remembrance of the Stonewall Rebellion and soon became an annual event.

September 16, 1975 opening of the administrative discharge hearing of Technical Sergeant Leonard Matlovich, the first gay member of the United States military to fight discrimination in the service.

March, 1977 Christian singer Anita Bryant launched her crusade against gay rights. Her efforts were aimed at a gay rights ordinance in Dade County, Florida. Later in the year, the ordinance protecting homosexuals by giving them equal rights in jobs and housing was repealed in a referendum vote by the county electorate.

November 27, 1978 San Francisco Mayor George Moscone and City District Supervisor Harvey Milk were shot and killed in the City Hall by a homophobic ex-policeman and district supervisor named Dan White. White was disturbed by what he thought was the City's favoritism toward the gay community.

October 14, 1979 the National March on Washington for Lesbian and Gay Rights was held.

December 7, 1979 US Court of Appeals required the Defense Department to accept homosexuals unless the military offered some reasonable explanation for exclusion.

Gay & Lesbian Movement Groups, Organizations and Publications:

The Los Angeles Advocate (newspaper)
Founded: 1967; renamed The Advocate in 1970
Founders: Editor Dick Michaels and partner Bill Rand
Major Accomplishments or Involvements: one of the few national gay newspapers with any longevity. In 1974, it was sold to former Wall Street broker David B. Goodstein.

Alice B. Toklas Club (**Alice** for short)
Founded: December, 1971, San Francisco, California
Founder: Jim Foster
Major Accomplishments or Involvements: the first homosexual Democratic Party club.

The Chicago Society for Human Rights
Founded: December 10, 1924
Founders, Leaders and Prominent Members: in 1924, Rev. John Graves, President; Al Meininger, Vice-President; Henry Gerber, Secretary; Ellsworth Booker, Treasurer
Major Accomplishments or Involvements: the earliest documented organization dedicated to the emancipation of homosexuals in the United States. The Society published a paper called Friendship and Freedom.

Come Out (newspaper)
Founded: published from 1969 to 1970
Founders: published by the New York Gay Liberation Front

Daughters of Bilitis (DOB)
Founded: 1955 in San Francisco
Founders: Del Martin, Phyllis Lyon
Leaders and Prominent Members: Barbara Gettings helped to establish the East Coast chapter in New York City in 1958 and was its first president
Major Accomplishments or Involvements: published *The Ladder*, a magazine on Lesbian issues, from 1956 until 1972. *The Ladder* is said to be "one of the single most important manifestations of the organized Lesbian resistance move-

ment." The DOB's charter was "A Women's Organization for the Purpose of Promoting the Integration of the Homosexual into Society...."

Furies Collective
Founded: 1971, Washington, DC
Founders and Leaders: Rita Mae Brown, Charlotte Bunch
Major Accomplishments or Involvements: a lesbian separatist collective involved in developing the basic lesbian social and political theories of the times. Analyzing heterosexuality, they defined it as a form of domination based on the assumption that heterosexual sex was the only "natural" way, and heterosexuals assumed that every woman was either bound to a man or wished she were. The Furies contended that women were viewed primarily as wives and mothers only, and the social order was based on the assumption that women would always put men first.

Gay Activists Alliance (GAA)
Founded: Sunday, December 21, 1969, in Arthur Bell's apartment in the Upper East Side of Manhattan in New York City
Founders, Leaders and Prominent Members: Jim Owles was its first president with Marty Robinson, Arthur Evans and Kay Tobin as other founding members
Major Accomplishments or Involvements: a spin-off from the Gay Liberation Front, the GAA was created to be "completely and solely dedicated" to the fight for gay rights. Their first act was to petition demanding that the city council pass a bill prohibiting discrimination against gays in employment in New York City. For the next several years, this group, headed by the outspoken Robinson, actively confronted Mayor John V. Lindsay and the New York City government. This was the beginning of a new, proactive, more confrontational gay community. Within months after the first meeting in New York, GAA chapters begin showing up across the nation.

Gay Community Service Center
Founded: October, 1971, in Los Angeles
Founders, Leaders and Prominent Members: Morris Knight, Don Kilhefner and Sheldon Andelson
Major Accomplishments or Involvements: one of the first homosexual health clinics.

Gay Liberation Front (GLF)
Founded: July 31, 1969. The first meeting was held in an industrial loft in Greenwich Village, New York City, that housed the Alternate U, an alternative educational facility.
Founders, Leaders and Prominent Members: Jim Fouratt, Michael Brown, Martha (Altman) Shelley, Marty Robinson, Jim Owles, Lois Hart
Major Accomplishments or Involvements: the first organization of homosexuals that was really dedicated to protecting their civil rights. It grew out of the older and less contentious Mattachine Society and the Daughters of Bilitis. The organization was sparked by the Stonewall Rebellion of June 27, 1969. The use of the term "gay" was new to the established homosexual community, though it had been used on a social level. Incorporating "Liberation Front" was a direct refer-

ence to the North Vietnamese guerrilla forces "National Liberation Front" in an effort to identify with other oppressed people in the third world, Black Americans, women and workers. Groups using the same name popped up in other cities of America during the next few months. The organization lasted less than a year, but it was the start of an active, vocal gay movement.

Gay Rights Lobby, Gay Rights National Lobby
Founded: 1978-80
Founders and Leaders: Steve Endean
Major Accomplishments or Involvements: one of the nation's first national gay and lesbian political action committee.

Johnny Appleseeds
Founded: 1969
Founder: Steve Endean
Major Accomplishments or Involvements: individuals and groups of homosexuals who were sent out from New York City and Los Angeles to start new GAA and GLF groups in cities, towns and on college campuses around the country.

The Lesbian Feminist Liberation Group, (LFL)
Founded: 1973
Founders and Leaders: Jean O'Leary
Major Accomplishments or Involvements: a group that split off from the Gay Activists' Alliance in New York. The split was predicated on the belief that the gay movement at the time was male dominated and didn't address all of the needs and concerns of its lesbian members.

Mattachine Society
Founded: 1950 in Los Angeles
Founders, Leaders and Prominent Members: Henry (Harry) Hay, William Dale Jennings
Major Accomplishments or Involvements: the first real, modern-day organization of homosexuals in the United States.

Municipal Elections Committee of Los Angeles (MECLA)
Founded: 1977
Founders and Leaders: David Mixner, Rob Eichberg and Sheldon Andelson
Major Accomplishments or Involvements: one of the nation's first gay and lesbian political action committees.

National Gay Task Force (NGTF)
Founded: 1973
Founders, Leaders and Prominent Members: Chairman, Howard Brown; Bruce Voeller, Jean O'Leary, Nathalie Rockhill, Frank Kameny
Major Accomplishments or Involvements: a split from the Gay Activists' Alliance, the Task Force was accused of cultivating only the more affluent, professional homosexuals. The NGTF had as its primary goal the creation of a gay political power base.

One (magazine)
Founded: 1953; it was published until 1975.

Major Accomplishments or Involvements: one of the first homosexual emancipation magazines in the country.

Personal Rights in Defense and Education (PRIDE)
Founded: mid-1960s
Leaders and Prominent Members: Jerry Joachim, chairman in the late 1960s
Major Accomplishments or Involvements: in 1967, two of its members, Dick Michaels and Bill Rand, turned this small newsletter into *The Los Angeles Advocate*, later renamed *The Advocate*. It became one of the few national gay newspapers with any longevity. In 1974, it was sold to former Wall Street broker David B. Goodstein.

Society for Individual Rights (SIR)
Founded: San Francisco in the early 1970s
Founders, Leaders and Prominent Members: Larry Littlejohn, Jim Foster
Major Accomplishments or Involvements: one of the first organizations to lobby actively and seek legislation to stop police harassment of homosexuals in the bars and bathhouses of San Francisco.

Gay and Lesbian Movement Leaders:

Sheldon Andelson a gay Beverly Hills lawyer who supported and defended homosexuals arrested on morals charges. A millionaire with investments in real estate and an occasional gay bathhouse, he became one of the major political powers in the nation's gay community, giving support and money to Democratic candidates and liberal causes. Along with Don Kilhefner and Morris Knight, he helped to start The Gay Community Service Center in Los Angeles in October, 1971, one of the first homosexual health clinics.

Jack Baker and Mike McConnell the first couple on record who tried to obtain a license for a same-sex marriage. They applied for the marriage license in Minneapolis, Minnesota, on May 18, 1970. They were denied the license on the grounds that it would "result in an undermining and destruction of the entire legal concept of our family structure in all areas of law." They were, however, able to receive approval as a couple eligible to receive food stamps. Jack Baker, student body president of the University of Minnesota, later tested same-sex tax laws.

Michael Brown was assigned by Dick Leitsch, the executive director of the Mattachine Society in 1969, to run the "Mattachine Action Committee," whose first meeting was held on July 9, 1969, at the Mattachine meeting hall in Freedom House, New York City. The meeting and the group that attended soon became more radical than Leitsch and the Mattachine Society expected. Brown was a founding member of the Gay Liberation Front (GLF), which first convened on July 31, 1969, at Alternate U, an alternative educational facility in New York City's Greenwich Village.

Donald Webster Cory the pseudonym for an otherwise unknown person. Author of the book *The Homosexual in America*. Considered by many to be "the father of the homophile movement."

John D'Emilio (1948-) author of *Sexual Politics, Sexual Communities: The Making of a Homosexual Minority in the United States, 1940-1970,* a book considered the definitive account of the times.

Steve Endean founded the Gay Rights Lobby, later the Gay Rights National Lobby, in 1978-80. It was one of the nation's first national gay and lesbian political action committees.

Arthur Evans a founding member of the Gay Activists' Alliance (GAA). Wrote extensively for the gay newspaper *The Advocate* during the 1960s and 70s.

Jim Foster the first gay power broker in the Democratic Party. Started his Gay Democratic Party in San Francisco in December, 1971, and called it the Alice B. Toklas Club (Alice, for short). He died of AIDS.

Jim Fouratt originally a Yippie with Abbie Hoffman, Fouratt attended the second Gay Liberation Meeting held outside the Mattachine Society at a church on Waverly Place in New York City. He was instrumental in radicalizing the methods of the early group, thus achieving maximum attention for the burgeoning movement. Fouratt was a founding member of the Gay Liberation Front, which first convened on July 31, 1969, at Alternate U, an alternative educational facility in New York City's Greenwich Village. He was an Andy Warhol insider and was involved in the music industry.

Barney Frank US Representative from Massachusetts, elected in 1980. One of the first US Congressmen to announce that he was gay.

Barbara Gettings (1932-) helped to form the East Coast Chapter of Daughters of Bilitis in New York City in 1958 and was its first president.

David B. Goodstein a former Wall Street broker who purchased the gay rights newspaper *The Advocate* in 1974.

Lois Hart a former nun, she attended the first meeting of radical new Gay Liberation activists at Freedom Hall, New York City on July 9, 1969. A founding member of the Gay Liberation Front, which first convened on July 31, 1969, at Alternate U, an alternative educational facility in Greenwich Village, New York City.

Henry (Harry) Hay (1912-) co-founder of the original Mattachine Society in Los Angeles in 1950.

Don Jackson a journalist writing articles about gay issues for underground newspapers in the late 1960s. One of the founders of the Los Angeles Chapter of the Gay Liberation Front in December, 1969.

William Dale Jennings (1918-2000) author, co-founder of the original Mattachine Society in 1950 in Los Angeles. His arrest for indecent behavior in Griffith Park in Los Angeles sparked the formation of the Mattachine Society, considered the first modern gay organization.

Cleve Jones (1954-) AIDS activist, co-founder of the San Francisco AIDS Foundation, founder and custodian of the AIDS Quilt.

D. B. (Dorrwin Buck) Jones (1934-2000) gay rights activist, president of the Mattachine Society in New York in the 1950s. Advocate for the elderly and disenfranchised. Founding executive director of the San Francisco Foundation for Aged Colored Persons (now called the Sanderson Foundation) from 1964 to 1970. Founding executive director for Meals on Wheels from 1970 to 1987.

Franklin Kameny (1925-) the pioneering gay rights activist from Washington DC. Started the DC Mattachine Society chapter in 1961. Initiated the slogan "Gay is Good." Fired from his position with the US Army in 1957 for being a homosexual. Helped to start the National Gay Task Force in 1973 with Howard Brown, Bruce Voeller and Nathalie Rockhill.

Joan Kent head of the Daughters of Bilitis in New York City on June 27, 1969, the night of the Stonewall Rebellion. A leader of the old-line homosexual attitude in New York City, she was opposed to the revolutionary practices of the young gay and lesbian activists at the beginning of the "Gay Power" movement.

Jim Kepner gay activist in Los Angeles in the 1960s. One of the people who started the boycott of Barney's Beanery over its sign, "Fagots Stay Out" [sic].

Don Kilhefner from Amish/Mennonite background with experience in the Peace Corps. Along with Morris Knight and Sheldon Andelson, he helped to start The Gay Community Service Center in Los Angeles in October, 1971, one of the first homosexual health clinics.

Morris Knight an early peace activist, head of the Dow Action Committee, which demonstrated against Dow Chemical's manufacture of napalm. One of the founders of the Los Angeles chapter of the Gay Liberation Front in December, 1969. Was active in the January–March, 1970, demonstration of Barney's Beanery restaurant in Hollywood over its sign, "Fagots Stay Out" [sic]. Along with Don Kilhefner and Sheldon Andelson, he helped to start The Gay Community Service Center in Los Angeles in October, 1971, one of the first homosexual health clinics.

Tony Kushner (1956-) Winner of the 1993 Pulitzer Prize in Drama for his play, *Angels in America,* about politics and the AIDS epidemic.

Dick Leitsch executive director of the Mattachine Society in New York City on June 27, 1969, the night of the Stonewall Rebellion. A leader of the old-line homosexual attitude in New York City. Although he helped to facilitate the beginnings of the "Gay Power" movement, he was at first opposed to the revolutionary practices of the young gay activists.

Phyllis Lyon (1924-) a co-founder with Del Martin of Daughters of Bilitis in San Francisco in 1955. Co-author with Del Martin of the 1973 book *Lesbian and Liberation.*

Del Martin (1921-) a co-founder with Phyllis Lyon of Daughters of Bilitis in San Francisco in 1955. In a 1970 essay in *The Advocate,* Martin began a separation between the gay male and lesbian communities. Co-author with Phyllis Lyon of the 1973 book *Lesbian and Liberation.*

Leonard Matlovich (1943-1988) Air Force Sergeant dishonorably discharged after declaring his homosexuality in 1975.

Harvey Milk (See: alphabetical listings)

David Mixner along with Rob Eichberg and Sheldon Andelson, helped to form the Municipal Elections Committee of Los Angeles (MECLA) in 1977. It was one of the nation's first gay and lesbian political action committees.

Paul Monette (1945-1995) a Hollywood screen writer who created the movie "Borrowed Time: an AIDS Memoir," the story of the death of his lover, Roger Horwitz. He also authored *Becoming a Man: Half a Life Story* in 1992. He died of AIDS.

Elaine Noble (1944-) the first openly homosexual woman to be elected to state office when she became a representative in the Massachusetts House in November, 1974.

John O'Brien former radical member of Students for a Democratic Society at Columbia University, who became a recruiter for the Gay Liberation Front.

Jim Owles attended the first meeting of radical new Gay Liberation activists at Freedom Hall, New York City on July 9, 1969. A founding member of the Gay Liberation Front, which first convened on July 31, 1969, at the Alternate U, an alternative educational facility in Greenwich Village, New York City. A founding member of the Gay Activists' Alliance. He died of AIDS.

Tory Perry (1940-) Southern Pentecostal minister who started his first homosexual church in Los Angeles in 1969. Was active in the January–March, 1970 demonstrations at Barney's Beanery restaurant in Hollywood.

Marty Robinson attended the first meeting of radical new gay liberation activists at Freedom Hall, New York City on July 9, 1969. Was a principal speaker at the first major gay and lesbian rally "Gay Power Vigil" held in Washington Square Park, New York City, on July 27, 1969. A founding member of the Gay Liberation Front, which first convened on July 31, 1969, at the Alternate U, an alternative educational facility in Greenwich Village, New York City. A founding member of the Gay Activists' Alliance (GAA).

Craig Rodwell owner of the Oscar Wilde Memorial Bookshop on Mercer Street in New York City in 1969. Planned and organized the first Stonewall riot anniversary celebration, which eventually became Gay Pride Day.

Alma Routsong author of the 1960s novel *Patience and Sarah*, the revelation of a colonial American lesbian relationship.

Rand Schrader the public spokesman for the gay community during the January–March, 1970 , demonstrations at Barney's Beanery restaurant in Hollywood over its sign, "Fagots Stay Out" [sic]. He later became the first openly gay California judge. He died of AIDS.

Martha Shelley (the pseudonym of **Martha Altman**) a member of the Daughters of Bilitis in New York City on June 27, 1969, the night of the Stonewall Rebellion. Attended the first meeting of radical new gay liberation activists at Freedom Hall on July 9, 1969.   Proposed and organized the first major gay and lesbian rally "Gay Power Vigil" held in Washington Square Park, New York City on July 27, 1969. A founding member of the Gay Liberation Front (GLF), which first convened on July 31, 1969, at the Alternate U, an alternative educational facility in Greenwich Village, New York City. Is often credited with introducing the word "gay" into the mainstream by suggesting its inclusion in the name Gay Liberation Front.

Randy Shilts (1951-1994) reporter for the *San Francisco Chronicle* who covered the scene at gay bathhouses and sex clubs. Wrote *The Mayor of Castro Street: The Life and Times of Harvey Milk* in 1982, as well as *And the Band Played On: Politics, People and the AIDS Epidemic* in 1987. One of the first in the media to raise the alarm about the epidemic, eventually named AIDS. He died of AIDS.

Rick Stokes San Francisco gay community leader, co-owner, with David Clayton and a dozen other investors, of The Ritch Street Health Club (The Ritch Street Baths), which opened in the fall of 1965 as a safe place for homosexual men to meet in San Francisco.

Kay Tobin (pen name for **Key Lahusen**) a writer/photographer, pioneer gay activist; author, along with Randy Wicker, of the 1972 book *The Gay Crusaders*. A founding member of Gay Activists' Alliance, along with Jim Owles, Marty Robinson and Arthur Evans.

Randy Wicker writer, early gay leader in New York. Author, along with Kay Tobin, of the 1972 book *The Gay Crusaders*.

Native American and other Minority Rights Events, Demonstrations and Legislation:

1961 Declaration of Indian Purpose was given in Chicago at the American Indian Conference organized by the National Congress of American Indians. It began, "We... [have] a right to choose our own way of life. Since our Indian culture is slowly being absorbed by American society, we believe we have the responsibility of preserving our precious heritage...."

October 15, 1962 Amnesty International created.

May 9-12, 1964 American Indian Capital Conference on Poverty was held in Washington, DC, to lobby for new economic opportunities.

May, 1964 the Economic Opportunities Act included American Indians as a benefactor of its programs. For the first time, Native Americans were asked to administer their own programs.

September, 1965 César Chávez and his Mexican-American National Farm Workers Association went on strike in Delano, California. It was a show of solidarity with grape pickers. *La Huelga,* or the strike, had been started eight days earlier by Filipino workers organized by the agricultural Workers Organizing Committee of the AFL-CIO.

November, 1969 78 Native Americans from 50 tribes, a group called "Indians of All Tribes," took over Alcatraz Island in San Francisco Bay and occupied it until June, 1971.

November, 1969 Washington, DC, "American Indian Task Force" a 42-member group, converged on The Capitol to lobby for Native American civil rights.

December 4, 1970 César Chávez, leader of the United Farm Workers, was jailed for organizing a national boycott of lettuce in support of field workers.

September 9, 1971 Attica Prison inmates revolted against conditions; 10 hostages and 32 prisoners were killed. (I feel that prison inmates are sometimes an oppressed minority.)

1972 Raymond Yellow Thunder, a 51-year-old Lakota, was killed by US Army veterans in Gordon, Nebraska. American Indian Movement (AIM) leaders Russell Means and Dennis Banks and 1,000 members marched on the town and forced authorities to prosecute the guilty parties.

April, 1972 Dick Wilson, a right-wing, mixed-blood rancher, illegally took over control of the Oglala Sioux reservation in Pine Ridge, South Dakota. He suspended the tribal council and installed himself as a dictator, thus prompting the Wounded Knee occupation by AIM.

1972 Indian Education Act passed by Congress.

October, 1972 "The Trail of Broken Treaties," a caravan of Indian activists, left California for Washington, DC, to illustrate the Native American struggles.

November 2, 1972 500 Indians seized Bureau of Indian Affairs office in Washington, protesting poor reservation conditions.

1973 Menominee Tribe Restoration Act passed by Congress.

February 27, 1973 250 members of the American Indian Movement seized Wounded Knee, South Dakota. They asked for an inquiry into government treatment of Native Americans. The occupation lasted 71 days.

April 17, 1973 American Indian Movement (AIM) member Frank Clearwater was killed by heavy machine gun round at Wounded Knee. No investigation was conducted.

April 23, 1973 Eight to 12 individuals, names unknown, who were bringing supplies into Wounded Knee were intercepted by Goons (Guardians of the Oglala Nation) and vigilantes. None was ever seen again. An unsuccessful search was conducted for a mass grave after the Wounded Knee siege. No further investigation was conducted.

April 27, 1973 American Indian Movement (AIM) member Buddy Lamont was hit by M-16 fire at Wounded Knee and bled to death while pinned down by fire. No investigation was conducted.

April 27, 1973 American Indian Movement (AIM) supporter Priscilla White Plume was killed at Manderson, South Dakota, by Goons. No investigation conducted.

June 19, 1973 American Indian Movement (AIM) supporter Clarence Cross was shot to death in ambush by Goons or vigilantes. Although assailants were identified by eyewitnesses, no investigation was conducted.

1974 Indian Financing Act passed by Congress.

January 4, 1975 Indian Self-Determination and Education Assistance Act passed by Congress, releasing tribes from strict control by the Bureau of Indian Affairs and rejecting the termination policy, whereby government assistance for Native Americans, treaty rights, tribal sovereignty, and reservation lands were being systematically taken away.

June 1,1975 American Indian Movement (AIM) supporter Kenneth Little was killed at Pine Ridge, South Dakota, by Goons or vigilantes. Investigation still "pending."

June 26, 1975 a shoot-out between American Indian Movement (AIM) members and FBI agents on the Jumping Bull property at Pine Ridge, South Dakota, resulted in the deaths of Agents Jack Coler and Ron Williams, and Native American Joseph Stuntz Killsright. In 1977, American Indian Movement member Leonard Peltier, a Chippewa, was convicted of murdering the agents and was sentenced to two life terms. Two other AIM members, Dino Butler and Bob Robideau, were acquitted of the murder charges. No investigation was conducted to determine the killer of Joseph Stuntz Killsright.

July 28, 1975 Congress extended the Voting Rights Act seven years; Hispanics were added under this law.

1976 Indian Health Care Improvement Act passed by Congress.

January 30, 1976 Byron DeSersa, OSCRO organizer and American Indian Movement (AIM) supporter, was assassinated by Goons in Wanblee, South Dakota. Arrests by local authorities resulted in Dale Janis and Charlie Winters serving two years of five-year sentences for "manslaughter." Charges were dropped against two others, Manny Wilson and Chuck Richards, on the basis of "self-defense," despite the fact that DeSersa was unarmed when shot to death.

July 3, 1976 American Indian Movement (AIM) member Betty Means was killed at Pine Ridge, South Dakota, by Goons or vigilantes. No investigation was conducted.

1978 Indian Child Welfare Act passed by Congress.

1978 Tribally Controlled Community College Assistance Act passed by Congress.

August 11, 1978 American Indian Religious Freedom Act passed by Congress.

July, 1978 Several hundred Native Americans marched on Washington, DC, the "Longest Walk," to illustrate Native American struggles.

1979 Archaeological Resources Protection Act passed by Congress.

During the 1970s, many Native Americans were killed under suspicious circumstances relating to their fight for civil rights. The yearly murder rate on Pine Ridge

Indian Reservation in South Dakota between 1973 and 1975 was 170 per 100,000. By comparison, Detroit, Michigan, the reputed murder capital of the United States, had a rate of only 20.2 per 100,000.

Native American and other Minority Rights Groups and Organizations:

American Indian Movement (AIM)
Founded: July 28, 1968, in Minneapolis, Minnesota
Founders: Dennis Banks and George Mitchell, co-founders
Leading Members: Clyde Bellecourt, Pat Ballanger, Edward Benton-Banai, Russell Means, John Trudell and Leonard Peltier
Major Accomplishments or Involvements: formed to draw attention to Native American issues and promote better treatment for Indian peoples. AIM was responsible for the occupation of Alcatraz Island in San Francisco Bay in 1969 and the takeover of Wounded Knee, South Dakota, in 1973.

Council of Energy Resource Tribes
Founded: 1975

Native American Church
Founded: 1870
Major Accomplishments or Involvements: a religious organization of North American Indians teaching a doctrinal mixture of native religion and Christianity. Its rituals include ceremonies using peyote cactus, which contains the hallucinogen mescaline. Hippies learned of peyote through the Native American culture. At one time, the Native American Church was one of the only sources of the cactus, and people of the counterculture tried to join the church in order to indulge in the psychedelic plant.

National Congress of American Indians
Founders and Leaders: Earl Old Person, Blackfoot, president; Robert Burnette, Rosebud Sioux, executive director
Major Accomplishments or Involvements: brought together 70 tribes in Chicago in 1961 at the American Indian Conference and issued the "Declaration of Indian Purpose."

National Indian Education Association
Founded: 1969

National Indian Youth Council
Founded: 1961
Founders and Leaders: Melvin Thom, Northern Paiute, president in 1964; Clyde Warrior, president in 1967

National Tribal Chairmen's Association
Founded: 1971

Native American Rights Fund
Founded: 1970

National Interstate Congress on Equal Rights and Responsibilities
Major Accomplishments or Involvements: claimed Indian rights as a separate nation and owners of the land upon which the United States of America is built.

The United Farm Workers' Union (UFW)
Founded: 1962
Founder and Leader: César Chávez, founder and leader from 1962 until his death in 1993
Major Accomplishments or Involvements: this union was started to represent California's field workers, comprised largely of naturalized Mexican-Americans. The UFW began demonstrating and striking in 1965 and boycotted California grape growers in 1966. They also struck and boycotted the lettuce industry, eventually gaining better pay and conditions for its workers.

Women of All Red Nations (WARN)
Founded: 1974
Founders and Leaders: Lorelei DeCora Means, Minneconjou, Lakota; Madonna Thunderhawk, Hunkpapa Lakota; Phyllis Young, Hunkpapa Lakota

Native American and other Minority Rights Leaders:

Pat Ballanger mother of the American Indian Movement (AIM).

Dennis Banks Chippewa, co-founder and director of the American Indian Movement (AIM).

Clyde Bellecourt Chippewa, president and co-founder of the American Indian Movement (AIM).

Robert Bennett Oneida, Commissioner of Indian Affairs 1966-1969.

Edward Benton-Banai co-founder of the American Indian Movement (AIM).

César Chávez (See: alphabetical listings)

Henry and Leonard Crow Dog Rosebud Sioux, spiritual leaders.

George Groundhog Cherokee, director of the Original Cherokee Community Organization.

Ted Holappa Chippewa, executive director of the American Indian Cultural Center in Los Angeles, California.

Robert Jourdain radical tribal chairman.

Janet McCloud Tulalip, early fish-in activist.

Lorelei DeCora Means Minneconjou Lakota, co-founder of Women of All Red Nations in 1974.

Russell Charles Means Oglala Sioux, co-founder, American Indian Movement (AIM); led the 71-day takeover of Wounded Knee, South Dakota, in 1973.

George Mitchell Chippewa, co-founder of the American Indian Movement (AIM).

N. (Navarre) Scott Momaday Kiowa-Cherokee, Pulitzer Prize winner for his 1969 novel, *The House Made of Dawn.*

Richard Oakes (1942-1972) Mohawk, an AIM leader of the occupation of Alcatraz Island off the coast of San Francisco, California. Was shot and killed over tribal fishing rights by Michael Morgan, a White man, on September 20, 1972.

Leonard Peltier (See: alphabetical listings)

Earl Old Person Blackfoot, president of the National Congress of American Indians.

Jess Six Killer Cherokee, executive director of American Indians United.

Melvin Thom Northern Paiute, president of the National Indian Youth Council.

Madonna Thunderhawk Hunkpapa Lakota, co-founder of Women of All Red Nations in 1974.

John Trudell Santee Sioux, American Indian Movement member; participated in the occupation of Alcatraz Island off the coast of San Francisco, California, in 1969.

Clyde Warrior Ponca, president of the National Indian Youth Council in 1967.

Phyllis Yong Hunkpapa Lakota, co-founder of Women of All Red Nations in 1974.

Ecology and Environmental Events, Demonstrations and Legislation:

1960 President Eisenhower vetoed a Federal pollution control bill because he believed that polluted water was "a uniquely local blight."

May 9, 1960 the FDA approved distribution of "The Pill"; it became available in the spring of 1961.

July 12, 1960 Federal Hazardous Substances Act passed. A federal law stipulating requirements for labeling consumer products.

January 3, 1961 an overheated reactor core caused a steam explosion, killing three workers at the Idaho Falls, Idaho, nuclear plant.

July, 1961 the Federal Water Pollution Control Act was strengthened by passage of a bill from Congress called Public Law 87-88, signed by President Kennedy. One of its sections gave the Federal government authority to take action on interstate streams and waterways at the request of state governors.

July 10, 1962 one hundred citizens of Scottsdale, Arizona, appeared on the steps of City Hall wearing gas masks, holding signed petitions and waving placards protesting the sewage problem in that city. Other demonstrations, in cities such as St. Joseph, Kansas City and St. Louis, Missouri, erupted during the late 1950s and early 1960s as citizens in communities across the nation began complaining about water quality and the danger of disease from bad sewage systems. Massive fish deaths in rivers and lakes began to occur in the early 1960s.

1963 the Clean Air Act (CAA) passed. A Federal law stipulating requirements for the reduction of air pollution and giving government agencies the power to act on violations.

October 16, 1964 the Chinese government began nuclear bomb testing in the Lop Nor desert in western Xinjiang Province.

1964 the movie "Fail Safe" was released; directed by Sidney Lumet and starring Henry Fonda, it dramatized the story of a US President faced with nuclear war.

October 5, 1966 a partial meltdown occurred in a nuclear breeder reactor at the Enrico Fermi nuclear plant only 30 miles southwest of Detroit, Michigan. It was a near-disaster that could have contaminated much of the Detroit area.

1966 the French government began testing nuclear bombs on the Islands of Mururua and Fangataufa in French Polynesia. Between 1966 and 1977, they conducted 40 to 45 atmospheric tests, many of which were highly contaminating.

1966 the Animal Welfare Act (AWA) passed. A Federal law regulating the transportation, sale and handling of dogs, cats and other animals used for research. It gave the Department of Agriculture power to inspect facilities, seize animals and levy fines.

March 18, 1967 the tanker *Torrey Canyon* ran aground off Cornwall, England, spilling most of its 118,00 tons of crude oil cargo, causing a massive environmental disaster that fouled 175 miles of British and French coastline.

1968 the Wild and Scenic Rivers Act passed. A Federal law enabling the government to designate "outstanding and remarkable" free-flowing rivers as protected environments.

February 31 to February 8, 1969 an offshore oil well leaked an estimated 800,000 gallons of crude oil onto the beaches near Santa Barbara, California. The spill caused the death of hundreds of birds and the destruction of a great deal of marine plant and animal life. The disaster prompted the creation of new restrictions on oil drilling in the sea, and four oil companies eventually paid $4.5 million to settle claims.

October 1, 1969 seven thousand Canadians and 1,000 US draft dodgers and deserters blocked the Douglas Border Crossing between British Columbia and Washington State to protest nuclear tests on Amchitka Island, Alaska. Many original members of soon-to-be Greenpeace were involved in this action. The Canadians thought that the detonations might trigger earthquakes and tidal waves. Their slogan was "Don't Make A Wave. It's your fault if our fault goes. America is Death."

April 22, 1970 Earth Day celebration (See: **Earth Day** in alphabetical listings)

1971 the first major action of the Canadian ecology group Greenpeace. A successful protest of the underground nuclear weapons test on Amchitka Island in Alaska. The island was later declared a bird sanctuary.

1972 Marine Mammal Protection Act passed. A Federal law allowing the government to create restrictions on drift nets, require permits and levy fines on violators.

1972 Convention on the Prevention of Marine Pollution by Dumping of Waste and Other Matter (London Dumping Convention or LDC) held. An international conference to discuss ocean pollution and endeavor to create restrictions on vessels dumping waste, such as heavy metals, lead, copper and zinc.

1972 Clean Water Act (CWA) passed. A Federal law formally known as the Federal Water Pollution Control Act of 1962 was amended and strengthened. This did not deal with drinking water; that was covered by the Safe Drinking Water Act, which was not passed until 1974.

June, 1972 Greenpeace activist David McTaggart sailed his 38-foot ketch into the French atmospheric nuclear test site near Mururua in the South Pacific. He and his crew were attacked and beaten by the French military. This act brought international attention to the nuclear tests, and in November, 1973, the French Government decided to conduct future tests underground.

1973 Consumer Product Safety Commission formed. A Federal agency given the power to create standards, inspect facilities and enforce restrictions pertaining to hazards, such as hydrocarbon use. It took over some powers from the Food and Drug Administration.

1973 the movie "Soylent Green" released. Set in New York City in the year 2022, it dramatized the overpopulation and food shortages that were imagined to exist at that time. The lead character, played by Charlton Heston, investigates and reveals the production of an artificial food source made from recycled human beings. The movie is based on a novel by Harry Harrison entitled *Make Room! Make Room!*

1973 the Arab oil embargo. Gasoline became scarce in the US, and hundreds of thousands of motorists sat in long lines waiting to fill their gas tanks. It was thought to be a scenario created by all the oil companies, both domestic and foreign, to soften up the public in preparation for raising prices.

1973 United States Customs revealed the extent of worldwide animal species depletion when it intercepted just one shipment containing 250,000 pelts of animals on the endangered list. In one year, one furrier alone was found to have handled over 100,000 illegal skins worth a total of $5 million.

1973 Endangered Species Act created the Convention on International Trade in Endangered Species (CITES). By 1987, CITES officials admitted that their organization was effective in halting only 17 percent of the trade in endangered species!

1974 Safe Drinking Water Act (SWDA) passed. A federal law empowering the Environmental Protection Agency to set minium standards for drinking water safety. The designations were in Maximum Contaminant Levels or MCLs.

Ecology and Environmental Events

February 22, 1974 Sam Lovejoy monkeywrenched the Northeast Utilities Nuclear Power Plant near Montague, Massachusetts.

September 25, 1974 it was revealed that freon gases released from aerosol spray cans were destroying the ozone layer.

June 27, 1975 Greenpeace positioned three small, inflatable zodiac boats between the Russian harpoon ship *Vlastny* and a pod of sperm whales. A whale was shot and killed in spite of their efforts, but the incident was widely publicized and increased the public's awareness of the whaling industry's exploits.

December 15, 1975 the Food and Drug Administration (FDA) met to debate the risks of estrogen therapy for menopausal symptoms, deciding whether or not to inform women of the dangers of these products through the creation of Patient Package Inserts (PPIs). The National Women's Health Network also gathered in a demonstration and memorial service for all of the women who had died due to diethylstilbestrol (DES), the birth control pill, and estrogen replacement therapy. This protest was a first for both the NWHN and the FDA. Questions concerning the safety of estrogen therapy arose with investigations of DES and the pill. The discovery of the reproductive damage caused by DES led to its recall for use by pregnant women. NWHN founder Barbara Seaman exposed the dangers of oral contraceptives in her 1969 book *The Doctors' Case against the Pill*. Her work led to the Nelson Pill hearings, which resulted in the inclusion of PPIs with each prescription of birth control pills. Despite public warnings, in 1975 many women were still being harmed by these drugs.

December 15, 1976 the *Argo Merchant* ran aground off Nantucket Island, Massachusetts, spilling 7.5 million gallons (approximately 25 tons) of fuel oil, greatly damaging nearby New England fishing grounds.

May 12, 1976 the *Urquiola* ran aground off La Coruna, Spain, spilling 60-70,000 tons of crude oil, fouling 50-60 miles of the Spanish coastline.

1976 Toxic Substances Control Act passed. A federal law authorizing the EPA to monitor pesticide storage, transport and application.

1976 Resource Conservation and Recovery Act (RCRA) passed. A Federal law enabling the EPA to stipulate regulations for transport, storage, treatment and disposal of hazardous waste.

February 24, 1977 the oil tanker *Hawaiian Patriot* caught fire in the mid-Pacific, spilling 30 million gallons (approximately 100,000 tons) of oil.

April 22, 1977 oil well Bravo 14 blew out in the Ekofisk field, spilling 8 million gallons (approximately 27,000 tons) of crude oil into the North Sea.

May 2, 1977 over 2,000 Clamshell Alliance protesters were arrested for demonstrating against the nuclear power plant under construction in Seabrook, New Hampshire.

March 19, 1978 US tanker *Amoco Cadiz* ran aground at Portsall, Brittany, spilling its entire cargo of 226,000 tons of crude oil into the English Channel.

August 4, 1978 at Love Canal near Niagara Falls, New York, a birth defects cluster was discovered, and 740 families were evacuated. The area was a notorious chemical dump site used by the Hooker Chemical Company to dispose of an estimated 21,000 to 22, 000 tons of waste, including dioxin, between 1942 to 1953. In 1953, the company donated the land to the local school district, and homes and a school were built on the site. In 1980, the location became the first Federal environmental disaster area. In 1990, the government deemed the area safe for re-occupancy, but environmental groups dispute its safety.

1979 President Jimmy Carter put a solar water heater on the roof of the White House, turned down the heat, and wore a sweater to demonstrate to the nation the importance of energy conservation.

1979 the movie "The China Syndrome" was released. Directed by James Bridges, and starring Jack Lemmon, Jane Fonda and Michael Douglas, it dramatized a fictional nuclear power plant core meltdown disaster. Ironically, it was released just after the Three Mile Island nuclear accident occurred.

March 28, 1979 atomic reactor accident at Three Mile Island. (See: **Three Mile Island** in alphabetical listings)

June 3, 1979 the oil well Ixtoc 1 blew out, spilling 600,000 tons of oil into the Mexican Bay of Campeche in the Gulf of Mexico. It was the largest oil spill on record at that time.

July 19, 1979 the *Atlantic Empress* and *Aegean Captain* collided off the Island of Tobago, killing 27 and spilling 370 tons of oil into the Caribbean. It was the largest shipping spill on record at that time.

Ecology and Environmental Groups and Organizations:

Abalone Alliance
Founded: May, 1977
Founders: 70 California activists
Major Accomplishments or Involvements: dedicated to protesting the construction and use of nuclear power plants. It was initially formed over concerns about Pacific Gas and Electric's plans to build and operate the Diablo Canyon nuclear facility near San Luis Obispo, California. On August 6, 1977, the Abalone Alliance held its first blockade at Diablo Canyon; 47 people were arrested while 1,500 people showed support at a nearby rally. August 6, 1978, 487 people were arrested at the gates of Diablo Canyon, while 5,000 people attended a supporting rally. June 28, 1979, a statewide rally drew 40,000 people to San Luis Obispo, and Governor Jerry Brown spoke out publicly against Diablo Canyon at the rally. Thanksgiving, 1979, Alliance members held a 38-day sit-in at Governor Brown's office to protest continued operation of the Rancho Seco reactor, a duplicate of the Three Mile Island facility.

American Cetacean Society (ACS)
Founded: 1967

Leaders and Prominent Members: Patricia Warhol, executive director
Major Accomplishments or Involvements: focuses on protecting marine mammals, such as whales, dolphins, sea otters, seals and sea lions.

American Wildlands Alliance (AWL)
Founded: 1977
Leaders and Prominent Members: Sally A. Ranney, president
Major Accomplishments or Involvements: formerly called American Wilderness Alliance (AWA), works to promote responsible management and protection of forests, wildlife, wilderness, wetlands, watersheds, rivers and fisheries.

America the Beautiful Fund (ABF)
Founded: 1965
Leaders and Prominent Members: Paul Bruce Dowling, executive director
Major Accomplishments or Involvements: conducted Operation Green Plant, which distributed surplus seeds donated by seed companies.

Bolt Weevils
Founded: 1970s
Founders: George Crocker and a group of Minnesota vigilante farmers
Major Accomplishments or Involvements: in the 1970s, they cut down power poles belonging to the Northern States Power Company.

Committee for a Sane Nuclear Policy (SANE)
Founded: 1957, in poet Lenore Marshall's New York apartment
Founders: Norman Cousins, Clarence Pickett and Lenore Marshall
Leaders and Prominent Members: Norman Cousins, Clarence Pickett, H. Stuart Hughes, Donald Keys, Dr. Benjamin Spock, Edward U. Condon, Wayne Morse, Seymour Melman, Andrew Young, Trevor Thomas, Homer A. Jack and Sanford Gottlieb
Prominent Supporters: Dr. Albert Schweitzer, Eleanor Roosevelt, Norman Thomas, Bertrand Russell, Pablo Casals, Roger Baldwin, Paul Tillich and Erich Fromm
Major Accomplishments or Involvements: worked on disarmament in general and nuclear weapons systems in particular. Opposed the proposed antiballistic missile (ABM) system in 1970 and helped to defeat the B-1 bomber in 1977.

Committee for Nonviolent Action (CNVA)
Founded: 1958
Leaders and Prominent Members: A. J. Muste
Major Accomplishments or Involvements: an organization that sailed small ships into nuclear test zones in the Pacific Ocean, scaled barbed wire fences surrounding nuclear installations, and ventured out in rowboats, attempting to obstruct the launching of American nuclear submarines.

Committee for Nuclear Responsibility, The
Founded: 1971
Founder: Dr. John Gofman
Major Accomplishments or Involvements: a nonprofit, educational group organized to provide independent analysis of the health effects and sources of ioniz-

ing radiation. Dr. Gofman, Professor Emeritus in Molecular and Cell Biology at the University of California, Berkeley, was uniquely qualified to articulate the critical and essential health issues surrounding exposure to low-level ionizing radiation and its consequences.

Concern Inc.
Founded: 1970
Leaders and Prominent Members: Susan F. Boyd, executive director
Major Accomplishments or Involvements: concerned with household waste, pesticides and global warming.

Cousteau Society
Founded: 1973
Founder: Jacques-Yves Cousteau
Leaders: Jean-Michel Cousteau, executive director
Major Accomplishments or Involvements: created to fund marine research and document environmental changes. Maintained the research vessels *Calypso* and *Alcyone*.

Clamshell Alliance
Founded: 1976
Leaders and Prominent Members: Robert Cushing
Major Accomplishments or Involvements: formed in order to protest the construction of a nuclear reactor in Seabrook, New Hampshire. On May 2, 1977, over 2,000 Clamshell Alliance protesters were arrested for demonstrating against the nuclear power plant under construction at Seabrook, New Hampshire.

Earth First! (Rednecks For Wilderness)
Founded: 1980
Founders: David Foreman and Mike Roselle
Major Accomplishments or Involvements: fashioned after the fictitious eco-commando group in Edward Abbey's 1975 book *The Monkey Wrench Gang*.

Eco-Command Force
Active: in early 1970s in Florida
Major Accomplishments or Involvements: one night they planted bombs containing yellow dye in the sewage systems of eighteen Dade County, Florida, polluters. The result was that half the county's canals turned bright yellow with the harmless dye, proving dramatically to the citizens how extensive the region's pollution was.

Elsa Wild Animal Appeal
Founded: 1969
Founders: founded by Joy Adamson, author of *Born Free,* and her husband George Adamson
Major Accomplishments or Involvements: created an international campaign asking people to refrain from buying wild animals as pets or purchasing products made from such animals.

Environmental Action
Founders, Leaders and Prominent Members: conservationist Congressman

Gaylord Nelson, John McConnell, Dennis Hays
Major Accomplishments or Involvements: coordinated the first Earth Day celebration on April 22, 1970, in which millions marched and participated in rallies across the United States and around the world.

Environmental Defense Fund (EDF) shortened to **Environmental Defense** in the year 2000
Founded: 1967, Brookhaven, New York
Founders: Arthur Cooley, Charles Wurster and Dennis Puleston
Leaders and Prominent Members: Fred Krupp, executive director
Major Accomplishments or Involvements: involved in the first presentation of scientific arguments leading to the banning of DDT. In the process, the founders of Environmental Defense learned that DDT levels in human mothers' milk had risen to seven times the level permitted for milk sold in stores, turning attention to issues of human health. Part of the joint task force that convinced the McDonald's fast-food restaurant chain to stop using polystyrene foam sandwich containers. Instrumental in efforts to block the Two Forks Dam in Colorado in 1990.

Environmentalists for Full Employment
Founded: 1976
Leaders and Prominent Members: Richard Grossman, executive director, 1976-84
Major Accomplishments or Involvements: their goal was to build understanding between the labor and environmental movements based on anti-toxin campaigns and worker retraining programs.

Friends of the Earth
Founded: 1970
Founder: David Bower, founder and president from 1970 to 1979
Major Accomplishments or Involvements: their slogan is "The Earth needs all the friends it can get." Concerned with tropical rainforest loss, ozone layer depletion and global warming.

Friends of the River
Founded: 1973, California based
Leaders and Prominent Members: David Bolling, executive director
Major Accomplishments or Involvements: promoted better water management as an alternative to building more dams.

Greenpeace
Founded: 1971, Vancouver, Canada
Founders, Leaders and Prominent Members: Jim Bohlen, Irving Stowe, Robert Hunter, Ben Metcalfe, David McTaggart, Richard Grossman, Peter Bahouth. Offshoot of the British Columbia Sierra Club. Originally called the "Don't Make a Wave Committee," involved in blocking American nuclear tests on the Island of Amchitka, Alaska. The Canadians thought that the detonations might trigger earthquakes and tidal waves. Their slogan was "Don't Make A Wave. It's your fault if our fault goes. America is Death."
Major Accomplishments or Involvements: first major action was in 1971, a

successful protest of the underground nuclear weapons test on Amchitka Island in Alaska, later turned into a bird sanctuary. June, 1972, they sailed a ketch into the French atmospheric nuclear test site near Mururua in the South Pacific. In November, 1973, the French Government decided to conduct future tests underground. On June 27, 1975, Greenpeace positioned three small, inflatable zodiac boats between the Russian harpoon ship Vlastny and a pod of sperm whales. The hunters shot and killed a whale in spite of their efforts; yet, with this and many other confrontations with hunters of marine mammals, Greenpeace has created public awareness of the excesses of this industry.

Human Ecology Action League (HEAL)
Founded: 1977
Founders, Leaders and Prominent Members: Ken Dominy, president
Major Accomplishments or Involvements: involved in promoting a healthy lifestyle and improving the quality of life for all human beings.

Inform, Inc.
Founded: 1973
Leaders and Prominent Members: Joanna D. Underwood, president
Major Accomplishments or Involvements: examined businesses and pinpointed pollution violations.

National Audubon Society
Founded: 1886
Founder: George Bird Grinnell
Major Accomplishments or Involvements: originally devoted to the opposition of killing birds for their decorative feathers. Concerned with the protection and wise use of wildlife, land, water and other natural resources and the promotion of rational strategies for energy development and use. Committed to the protection of life from pollution, radiation, and toxic substances, and the solution of global problems caused by overpopulation and the depletion of natural resources.

National Recycling Coalition (NRC)
Founded: 1978
Leaders and Prominent Members: David Loveland, executive director
Major Accomplishments or Involvements: a coalition of recycling companies and municipal recycling centers that researches new ways to solve solid waste problems.

Sea Shepherd Conservation Society
Founded: 1977
Founder: Paul Watson
Major Accomplishments or Involvements: involved in saving whales and other marine mammals by disrupting hunting expeditions with their boat *The Sea Shepherd.*

Sierra Club
Founded: 1892
Founder: John Muir
Leaders and Prominent Members: David Ross Bower, president, 1952 to 1969

Major Accomplishments or Involvements: involved in educating the public about national wildlife and wilderness and in disclosing threats to the future of our natural resources.

Wildlife Management Institute
Founded: 1911
Major Accomplishments or Involvements: dedicated to the conservation and preservation of North American wildlife and natural resources.

Whole Earth Catalog: access to tools
Founded: 1968
Founder: Stewart Brand
Major Accomplishments or Involvements: published a catalog listing and advertising hundreds of sources for alternative lifestyle products, religious organizations and counterculture businesses. It weighed heavily toward ecological, spiritual and holistic interests.   Created by Stewart Brand, it was published by the Portola Institute in Menlo Park, California. The Portola Institute was established in 1966 as a nonprofit corporation to encourage, organize, and conduct innovative educational projects; it began publishing the catalog shortly thereafter. The Whole Earth Catalog was at one time published six times a year, twice in large, tabloid format, and four times in a smaller format.

World Wildlife Fund (WWF)
Founded: 1961
Leaders and Prominent Members: Kathryn S. Fuller, president
Major Accomplishments or Involvements: involved in monitoring the export, import and sale of wildlife and endangered species. Environmental education.

Ecology and Environmental Leaders:

Edward Abbey (See: alphabetical listings)

Joy Adamson (See: alphabetical listings)

Jim Bohlen one of the original founders/leaders of Greenpeace in Vancouver, Canada. An American, composite-materials researcher, once an associate of Buckminster Fuller and US missile systems designer.

Stewart Brand (See: **Stewart Brand** and **Whole Earth Catalog** in alphabetical listings)

David Ross Brower (1912-2000) one of the world's leading conservationists since the early 1950s, the architect and long-term director of the Sierra Club from 1952 to 1969, and founder of Friends of the Earth in 1969, serving as its president until 1979.

Rachel Carson (See: alphabetical listings)

Barry Commoner (1917-) biologist best known for work with "free radicals," short-lived, highly reactive chemicals that set up the destructive chain reaction involved in depleting the ozone layer. Commoner has written a number of books on the dangers that our chemical tinkering poses to mankind, including the 1966 publication, *Science and Survival.*

Jacques-Yves Cousteau (See: alphabetical listings)

Digit (See: alphabetical listings)

David Foreman (1947-) co-founder and leading member of the radial environmentalist movement, Earth First! The organization was patterned after The Monkey Wrench Gang in a book of the same name written by Edward Abbey and published in 1975. Foreman himself wrote several books, including the 1985 *Ecodefense: A Field Guide to Monkeywrenching.*

Dian Fossey (See: alphabetical listings)

"The Fox" (See: alphabetical listings)

Euell Gibbons (1911-1975) "the guru of wild foods." From his experience as a small child having to forage for food to feed his desperate family, GIbbons developed into an advocate of natural "wild" food. Author of *Stalking the Wild Asparagus, Stalking the Healthful Herbs,* and *Stalking the Blue-eyed Scallop.*

Group of Ten a group of environmentally concerned organizations that meets several times a year to compare notes and consider new ecological problems that need attention. These organizations are: Friends of the Earth, the National Wildlife Federation, the National Resources Defense Council, the Wilderness Society, the Environmental Defense Fund, the Izaak Walton League, the National Audubon Society, the National Parks and Conservation Association, the Sierra Club, and the Sierra Club Legal Defense Fund.

Robert Hunter early leader and former president of Greenpeace. A Canadian journalist, he wrote about Greenpeace in *Warriors of the Rainbow*, the definitive 1979 book on the beginnings of this important organization.

Stuart Leiderman ran for Congress from Missouri in 1976, on environmental issues relating primarily to the Meramec Dam project by the U. S. Army Corps of Engineers. A singer/songwriter, he wrote the song "Blackout Blues" about our electrical energy problems. Traveling in a 1946 Chevy with his guitar, Leiderman's "Free Rivers, Free People" campaign built public opposition that led to the defeat of the Meramec Dam project.

Sam Lovejoy monkeywrenched the Northeast Utilities Nuclear Power plant near Montague, Massachusetts, on February 22, 1974. He did this by loosening the turnbuckles on supporting guy wires for the 500-foot weather tower used to test wind direction at the site so that authorities would know which way the radiation would blow from the plant in case of an accident. The tower fell, leaving 349 feet of twisted wreckage. Lovejoy then turned himself in to authorities telling them in his written statement, "As a farmer concerned about the organic and the natural, I find irradiated fruit, vegetables and meat to be inorganic; and I can find no natural balance with a nuclear plant in this or any community."

David McTaggart (1932-) Canadian businessman, conservationist and social reformer. To prevent nuclear testing, he sailed his 35-foot ketch *Vega* onto the

French test site in the Pacific Ocean on behalf of Greenpeace, which was at the time a small Vancouver-based conservation group. McTaggart subsequently took part in other Greenpeace campaigns, and in 1979, he founded Greenpeace International.

Ralph Nader (See: alphabetical listings)

Gaylord Nelson (1916-) conservationist Congressman from Wisconsin from 1963 to 1980, who was instrumental in starting the first Earth Day celebration on April 22, 1970. This was one of the first nationally recognized ecological events, and millions of people marched and participated in rallies across the United States. Part of the pageantry was an effort to have people holding hands across the entire United States as a symbol of unity toward our environment. April 22 is now National Earth Day.

Earle Reynolds (1910-1989) holder of a PhD in Anthropology, he was hired by the Atomic Energy Commission in 1951 to research the effects of the atomic bomb. He worked in Hiroshima and Nagasaki, Japan, coordinating research for the Atomic Bomb Casualty Committee (ABCC). In 1954, Reynolds and his family, wife Barbara and three children, Tim, Ted, and Jessica, began an around-the-world-voyage on their hand-built sailboat, *The Phoenix of Hiroshima*. They stopped at over one hundred ports, and Earle presented lectures on conditions in Hiroshima. Young Jessica documented this trip in her book *Jessica's Journal*, which was later published. In 1958, the Reynolds' met the crew of the *Golden Rule*, Quakers who were on trial for attempting to sail into the nuclear test zone of Bikini Island to protest nuclear weapons and atmospheric testing. Earle and his family decided to complete the mission in their place. He was arrested and sentenced to two years in prison, but the verdict was eventually overturned. From that point on, Reynolds became dedicated to peace activism and anti-nuclear causes, using voyages on *The Phoenix* to spread his message. In 1959, a film called "The Reynolds Story" was made about the trip into the nuclear test zone. Earle also wrote about these events in *The Forbidden Voyage*, published in 1961. In 1962, Earle co-founded the Hiroshima Institute for Peace Studies (HIPS), affiliated with Hiroshima University. In 1967, Earle and a crew of peace activists sailed to Vietnam under the sponsorship of A Quaker Action Group. They delivered medical supplies to both North and South Vietnam as an expression of the Quaker principle of neutrality.

Karen Silkwood (1946-1974) a technician at the Kerr-McGee Cimarron Plutonium plant in Crescent, Oklahoma, who died in a suspicious auto accident on November 13, 1974, while driving to meet representatives of *The New York Times* to give them evidence of her employer's safety violations and negligence. The records she was carrying were never found.

Paul Watson commander of the ecology boat *Sea Shepherd*. Watson and the *Sea Shepherd* were involved in numerous confrontations with whale and seal pup killers throughout the 1970s. Watson founded the Sea Shepherd Conservation Society in 1977.

Computer Revolution Milestones and Events:

Many of you might think that the computer industry is an example of commerce, industry and greed, but you would be mistaken. The computer revolution was a creative explosion with commercial, industrial and economic repercussions on our society; yet, it was not greed, but art, that brought this new tool to life. Do you honestly think that thousands of dedicated people joyously worked thousands of hours so that you could play interactive games in your home, or so someone 10,000 miles away could steal money from you?

1935-39 the electronic digital computer was invented by John Vincent Atanasoff in Iowa. This was determined in 1973 by a United States District Court after years of litigation. It was called the Atanasoff-Berry Calculator, or ABC. Berry was Clifford Berry, Atanasoff's graduate assistant at Iowa State University. The ABC was the size of an office desk and used condensers and vacuum tubes. It was the first demonstration of speed and reliability by a binary mode electronic computer.

Early 1940s the "Bombe" computing device was built in Bletchley Park, England, designed by Alan Turing and other members of the Government Code and Cipher School. Its purpose was to decipher the German ENIGMA code machine.

1943-44 Colossus, the first programmable computer, was constructed by Tommy H. Flowers, a British postal employee. It was created to break the code from the new German Lorens coding machine.

1943-45 ENIAC (Electronic Numerical Integrator and Calculator) computer constructed by John W. Mauchly and J. Presper Eckert for use in US War Department efforts. The first program run in the winter of 1945 was preliminary calculations for the hydrogen bomb being designed at the time. ENIAC was huge, with thousands of vacuum tubes, resisters and switches.

December, 1947 the transistor (short for transfer resistance) was invented at Bell Labs. It won a Nobel Prize for inventors John Bardeen, Walter Brattain and William Shockley. A transistor is a crystal or "semiconductor" that controls the flow of electricity in circuits and amplifies the electrical signals.

1948 Claude Shannon published his concept of information theory, which became one of the most valuable elements contributing to the development of the personal computer.

1959 the silicon-based computer chip was conceived by Robert Noyce, the eventual founder of Intel.

1960 Ken Olsen was greatly responsible for the "minicomputer," or personal computer (PC), as the founder and president of Digital Equipment Corporation (DEC). In 1957, Olsen founded DEC with the goal of producing smaller, less expensive equipment than that existing at the time. In 1960, he hired Gordon Bell from the Massachusetts Institute of Technology (MIT). Bell brought his experience of creating the TX-0 at MIT and adapted it to create the DEC's PDP-1 in 1960. The PDP (Program Data Processor-1) weighed 250 pounds, a quarter of the weight of prevalent computers of the time, and cost only $120,000, much less than the $1 million or so cost for an IBM at the time.

1961 Advanced Research Project Agency (ARPA) was created by the Kennedy administration. ARPA was funded by the US Defense Department to advance America's defense-related technologies. Its major accomplishment was creating the ARPAnet, which was the predecessor of the Internet.

1964 BASIC, the first "simple" computer language, was created. It was developed in 1964 by two Dartmouth College professors, John Kemeny and Thomas Kurtz, through a grant from the National Science Foundation to help their students more easily use computers. This language was what made personal computers possible, when in 1975, Bill Gates and Paul Allen wrote a BASIC program for the MITS Altair 8080.

1965-69 ARPAnet was created during this period by engineers at Advanced Research Project Agency (ARPA). It was the predecessor of the Internet and was developed at ARPA as the link to a limited number of mainframe computers at locations around the United States.

1972 floppy-disk invented. Before "floppies," large, 2-foot diameter disks were used for mainframe computer storage from about 1956, and, before that, magnetic tape was used. Magnetic tape took scores of minutes to access information; disks took seconds. Eventually, the floppy would become the information storage system for personal computers, at 25,000 characters per second, but originally, PCs used paper tape at 10 characters per second.

1972 Pong was introduced to the public as the first major electronic video game. It was created by Nolan Bushnell, the founder of Atari. It was not a general-purpose computer and could function only for the running of the game, yet it helped to launch the personal computer revolution by putting computer-type devices in homes.

1973 Alto, the first actual personal computer (PC) was created in the early 1970s by Xerox Corporation's Palo Alto Research Center (PARC). It was built primarily for executives at PARC, where it was in use as early as 1974. Fifteen hundred of them were made, and some went to associates at Stanford Research Institute, Stanford Artificial Intelligence Laboratory, the US Congress and White House staff. It had most of the elements of the PC of today, including a bit-mapped, high-resolution screen and a mouse pointing device.

1973 John V. Atanasoff and John Mauchly fought in court for years to determine the true inventer of the computer until 1973, when Atanasoff was awarded that distinction by a United States District Court.

January, 1975 an article in *Popular Electronics* told of the existence of the Altair 8080 microcomputer, produced by an Albuquerque, New Mexico, firm called MITS (Micro Instrumentation and Telemetry Systems). That article prompted Bill Gates and Paul Allen to write a BASIC program for the Altair.

1975 Paul Allen, Monte Davidoff and Bill Gates wrote a BASIC program for the MITS Altair 8080. They wrote it while students at Harvard, on a PDP-10 computer funded by taxpayers' money through the Defense Advanced Research Projects Agency.

Summer, 1975 Bill Gates and Paul Allen formed Microsoft, an abbreviation for "microcomputer software." It was a 60/40 partnership between Bill Gates (60%) and Allen (40%), later changed to 64/36. The company evolved from Gates and Allen's original company called Traf-O-Data, which they started in high school to analyze automobile traffic patterns in small Oregon communities.

April, 1976 Apple I was introduced to the public at the Homebrew Computer Club. It was one of the first ready-made personal computers. Though it lacked a keyboard, video terminal, power supply and memory, for the hobbyists of the time, it was a unique toy. Its reliability gave Apple a reputation to start with and helped to launch that company when it introduced the much more user-friendly Apple II.

1977 Apple II was introduced to public. It was the first completely self-contained, ready-to-use, "user friendly personal computer." It had a bit-mapped monitor, 8K of memory, expansion card, Microsoft BASIC 6502, weighed 12 pounds and cost $1,350.

Computer Revolution Companies, Agencies and Groups:

Apple
Founded: 1976
Founders: Steve Jobs and Steve Wozniak
Major Accomplishments or Involvements: introduced **Apple I** in April, 1976. Apple I was one of the first ready-made personal computers. It lacked a keyboard, video terminal, power supply and memory, but for the hobbyists of the time, it was a unique toy. This computer's reliability gave Apple a reputation to start with and helped to launch the company when it introduced the much more user-friendly **Apple II**. Apple II was the first completely self-contained, ready-to-use, "user friendly personal computer." Introduced to the public in 1977, it had a

bit-mapped monitor, 8K of memory, expansion card, Microsoft BASIC 6502, weighed 12 pounds and cost $1,350.

Atari
Founded: 1971-72, purchased by Warner Communications in 1976
Founder: Nolan Bushnell; **Leaders:** Al Alcorn, Ray Kassar
Major Accomplishments or Involvements: produced Pong, the first major electronic video game. Invented by Nolan Bushnell and introduced in 1972, it was not a general-purpose computer and could function only for the running of the game, yet it helped to launch the personal computer revolution by putting computer-type devices in homes. The word "Atari" is used in the ancient Chinese game of Go as a warning meaning "Watch out or I'm going to get you on your next move."

Advanced Research Project Agency (ARPA), originally the Defense Department Advanced Research Project Agency
Founded: 1961 by the Kennedy Administration
Funded by: US Defense Department **Leaders:** Jack Ruina, J. C. R. Licklider, Bob Taylor
Major Accomplishments or Involvements: created the ARPAnet, the predecessor of the Internet. Made human-computer symbiosis a national goal. Mandated and lavishly funded bold projects to advance America's defense-related technologies. Bypassed the normal government peer review process and put research administrators in direct contact with researchers. Licklider, as director, started funding unrestricted research at 13 different universities and labs, including the Massachusetts Institute of Technology; University of California, Berkeley; University of California, Los Angeles; University of California, Santa Barbara; University of Southern California; Carnegie-Mellon University, University of Utah, Stanford Research Institute, System Development Corporation and Rand.

Digital Equipment Corporation (DEC)
Founded: 1957
Founder: Kenneth Olsen
Major Accomplishments or Involvements: greatly responsible for the "minicomputer," or personal computer (PC). Olsen founded DEC with the goal of producing smaller, less expensive computers than those currently in existence. In 1960, he hired Gordon Bell from the Massachusetts Institute of Technology (MIT). Bell brought his experience of creating the TX-0 at MIT and adapted it to create DEC's PDP-1 in 1960. The PDP (Program Data Processor-1) weighed 250 pounds, a quarter of the weight of prevalent computers of the time, and cost only $120,000, much less than the $1 million or so for an IBM at the time.

Digital Research
Founded: 1976
Founders: Gary and Dorothy Kildall
Major Accomplishments or Involvements: Kildall created the CP/M Control Program for Microcomputers in the early 1970s. It was the only operating system designed to control floppy-disk drives and for computers based on 8-bit microprocessors with 16K of memory and a 8080, 8085 or Z80 chip. CP/M was the

industry standard in disk operating systems until 1980 when MS/DOS was introduced.

Intel (from Integrated Electronics)
Founded: 1968
Founders: Robert Noyce and Gordon Moore, with venture capital from Arthur Rock
Major Accomplishments or Involvements: developed and manufactured the best silicon chips and semiconductors. Their employee, Ted Hoff, invented the microprocessor in 1971.

Microsoft
Founded: 1976
Founders: Bill Gates and Paul Allen
Major Accomplishments or Involvements: Bill Gates and Paul Allen wrote a BASIC program for the MITS Altair 8080. The creation of that operating system began the personal computer revolution.

MAC (MIT's Artificial intelligence Project)
Founded: 1960
Founder: J. C. R. Licklider
Major Accomplishments or Involvements: a group of computer programmers and engineers at MIT working on artificial intelligence, they called themselves hackers and created some of the first computer games, such as Spacewar and MacHack, the first chess-playing computer.

MITS, Micro Instrumentation and Telemetry Systems
Founder: Ed Roberts
Major Accomplishments or Involvements: produced the Altair 8080 (the people's computer) in 1974. It was a kit and became one of the first popular hobbyist (or personal) computers (microcomputer). The Altair 8080 used an Intel 8080 chip and ran a BASIC operating system programmed by Bill Gates, Paul Allen and Monte Davidoff. The Altair kit sold for $397; it was named by a twelve-year-old girl after the Forbidden Planet to which the Starship Enterprise was heading in "Star Trek." MITS was also the first company in the US to build calculator kits.

Palo Alto Research Center (PARC)
Founded: 1971 by Xerox
Administrators: Alan Kay, Robert Taylor
Major Accomplishments or Involvements: in 1973, PARC created Alto, the first actual personal computer (PC). It was built primarily for executives at PARC, where it was used as early as 1974. Fifteen hundred of them were made, and some went to associates at Stanford Research Institute, Stanford Artificial Intelligence Laboratory, the US Congress and White House staff. It had most of the elements of the PC of today, including a bit-mapped, high-resolution screen and a mouse pointing device.

Computer Revolution Leaders:

Paul Allen (1954-) co-founder of Microsoft with Bill Gates in 1975. In 1975, Bill Gates, Paul Allen and Monte Davidoff wrote a BASIC program for the MITS Altair 8080. They wrote it while students at Harvard, on a PDP-10 computer funded by taxpayers' money through the Defense Advanced Research Projects Agency. The partnership in Microsoft started as 60/40%, in favor of Bill Gates.

John Vincent Atanasoff (1903-1995) invented the electronic digital computer in Iowa during the years 1935-39. It was called the Atanasoff-Berry Calculator, or ABC. Berry was Clifford Berry, Atanasoff's graduate assistant at Iowa State University. Atanasoff fought for years in the courts with John W. Mauchly to determine the true inventor of the computer, until 1973, when Atanasoff was awarded that distinction by a United States District Court.

Charles Babbage and **Ada, the Countess of Lovelace** in 1833, Babbage, a British mathematician-inventor, constructed a prototype computing device he called the "Analytical Engine." Ada tried to use it to win a fortune at the horse racing track. She failed, but was history's first computer programmer. Babbage was the first computer designer.

Gordon Bell (1934-) a computer engineer greatly responsible for the "minicomputer," or personal computer (PC). Working for Digital Equipment Corporation (DEC) in the early 1960s, he helped to pioneer the PC by creating smaller, less expensive equipment. Bell helped to develop the TX-0 at the Massachusetts Institute of Technology (MIT) in the late 1950s and adapted it when he went to work for DEC into that company's PDP-1. The PDP (Program Data Processor-1) weighed 250 pounds, a quarter of the weight of prevalent computers of the time, and cost only $120,000, much less than the $1 million or so for the IBM at that time. Bell was also responsible for pioneering computer speech recognition when he interfaced speech input equipment to the TX-0 and wrote speech analysis and recognition programs in the late 1950s. It is called "Analysis by Synthesis," and it is still used today in speech recognition programs.

George Boole (1815-1864) invented "algebra of logic," which was used 100 years later to link the process of human reason to the operation of machines. The algebraic system was contained in his book *The Laws of Thought*.

Vannevar Bush (1890-1974) scientist and researcher at MIT, the head of US war-related scientific research during WWII. He was also involved with building high-speed mechanical calculators (analog computers) and was a close friend of Norbert Wiener, who conceived the idea of cybernetics. Bush, in 1945, was one of the first persons to conceive of and propose the use of computers as information resources for the public. At the time, the concept of personal computers seemed economically farfetched, and Bush's idea was for library use in which the public could come in and access information. In his 1945 *Atlantic Monthly* article, Bush urged men of science "to create a type of device to improve the quality of human thinking." He called this hypothetical machine memex because it extended human memory.

Nolan Bushnell (1943-) created Pong, the first major electronic video game, and founded Atari. Pong, introduced in 1972, was not a general-purpose computer and could function only for the running of the game, yet it helped to launch the personal computer revolution by putting computer-type devices in homes. Bushnell likes to think of himself as a 14-year-old mind locked inside an adult's body.

Doug Engelbart (1925-) one of the prominent forces in development of the personal computer by his concepts of displaying words and images on a monitor that could be manipulated with a keyboard, buttons and levers. Engelbart is directly responsible for the development of what we call today the "mouse." His reading of Vannevar Bush's article, "As We May Think," in 1945 prompted Engelbart's lifetime of effort toward information for the masses.

Bill Gates (1955-) co-founder of Microsoft with Paul Allen in 1975. In 1975, Bill Gates, Paul Allen and Monte Davidoff wrote a BASIC program for the MITS Altair 8080. They wrote it while students at Harvard, on a PDP-10 computer funded by taxpayers' money through the Defense Advanced Research Projects Agency. The partnership in Microsoft started as 60/40, with Gates (60%) and Allen (40%), later changed to 64/36.

Marcian E. (Ted) Hoff (1937-) invented the microprocessor in 1971 while an engineer at Intel.

Steve Jobs (b. Feb. 24, 1955; orphaned, raised by Paul and Clara Jobs) co-founder of Apple with Steve Wozniak. Jobs was the entrepreneur/salesman, and Wozniak was the engineer/inventor. Jobs answered a 1974 ad that stated, "Have fun and make money," and he became the fortieth employee at Atari, where he designed video games. Early on, his interests were vegetarianism, LSD, meditation, Eastern religions and India.

Alan Kay an original television quiz show whiz kid. Too mentally active for school and military service, as a graduate student he ended up at the US Defense Department's Advanced Research Projects Agency (ARPA), and then at Xerox Corporation's Palo Alto Research Center (PARC). Kay was demonstrating his own minicomputer, the FLEX, in the early 1970s. In the 1970s at PARC, he was a major contributor to the Alto computer project, which was considered the first personal computer (PC) even though it was limited to use by industry personnel. He is credited by some as coining the term "personal computer." Kay was instrumental in developing the bit-map concept. After 1980, Kay became associated with Atari Corporation; he became a research fellow at Apple Corp. in 1984.

Gary Kildall (1942-) created the CP/M Control Program for Microcomputers in the early 1970s. It was the only operating system designed to control floppy-disk drives and for computers based on 8-bit microprocessors with 16K of memory and a 8080, 8085 or Z80 chip. CP/M was the industry standard in disk operating systems until 1980, when MS/DOS was introduced. In 1975, Kildall also assisted Ben Cooper in creating the astrology machine. These computing devices were placed in various San Francisco locations, and for 25 cents, people could enter their birth dates and get a printout of their astrological chart. The dials were complicated, and the paper often jammed; so goes another cosmic money-making endeavor!

J. C. R. Licklider (1915-1990) American experimental psychologist at the Massachusetts Institute of Technology in the 1960s. As the creator and director of MAC (MIT's Artificial intelligence Project) he oversaw a group of computer programmers and engineers working on artificial intelligence who called themselves hackers and created some of the first computer games, such as Spacewar and MacHack, the first chess-playing computer. He eventually became the director of the Information Processing Techniques Office of the US Defense Department's Advanced Research Projects Agency (ARPA). Although Licklider and his associates were funded by the military, they all felt that their interactive computer projects were a social as well as technological contribution. His group looked upon their creations as a new kind of human communications revolution. Licklider was a visionary who enabled many to pursue dreams of unrestricted education and communication.

John W. Mauchly (1907-1980) creator of ENIAC (Electronic Numerical Integrator and Calculator) computer, constructed with J. Presper Eckert for use in US War Department efforts. The first program, run in the winter of 1945, was preliminary calculations for the hydrogen bomb being designed at the time. ENIAC was huge, with thousands of vacuum tubes, resisters and switches. Mauchly fought in the courts for years with John V. Atanasoff to determine the true inventer of the computer, until 1973, when Atanasoff was awarded that distinction by a United States District Court.

Ted Nelson a pioneer in text manipulation in the 1960s. Chose the word Xanadu as the name for his information processing system. He wrote *Computer Lib*, *The Home Computer Revolution* and *Literary Machines*. His pronouncements of the possibilities of the home computer helped to create the PC revolution.

Ken Olsen (1926-) greatly responsible for the "minicomputer," or personal computer (PC) as the founder and president of Digital Equipment Corporation (DEC). In 1957, Olsen founded DEC with the goal of producing smaller, less expensive equipment than that currently in existence. In 1960, he hired Gordon Bell from the Massachusetts Institute of Technology (MIT). Bell brought his experience of creating the TX-0 at MIT and adapted it to create DEC's PDP-1 in 1960. The PDP (Program Data Processor-1) weighed 250 pounds, a quarter of the weight of prevalent computers of the time, and cost only $120,000, much less than the $1 million or so for an IBM at that time.

Claude Shannon (1916-) American. Adapted Boole's algebra of logic to analyze the complex network of switching circuits used in telephone systems at the time and later, in computers. During WWII, Shannon created the mathematical foundation of information theory that, combined with cybernetics, created a new understanding of people and machines. His theories in *The Mathematical Theory of Communication* (1958) established information as a cosmic fundamental, along with energy and matter.

George Stibitz (1904-1995) a Bell Telephone Laboratory and General Electric employee who, in the late 1930s, combined telephone relays, the binary counting system, and salvaged junk, including a coffee can, to produce what he called the K-Model computer. The K stood for kitchen, the room in his house where he built it. His creation became the Bell Lab's Model 1, which demonstrated that binary systems could be used successfully to carry out long and complex calculations quickly and reliably.

Robert Taylor director of ARPA between 1965 and 1969, where he collected the most unorthodox and creative minds to produce the first Internet system, called ARPAnet. In 1970, Taylor again assembled the brain trust, this time at PARC, where he continued the advance toward the Internet and personal computers as we know them today.

Alan Mathison Turing (1912-1954) at age 24, he created the theoretical basis of computation. As a British code decipherer during WWII, he helped to crack the German code, an effort that many feel saved the war for the Allies. After the war, he developed the concept of artificial intelligence and created the fundamentals of the art/science of programming.

John von Neumann (1903-1957) born in Hungary/Germany, he moved to American before WWII and was deeply involved in US Atomic energy and rocket development. A physicist, logician and mathematician who helped to invent the first electronic digital computer. The leader of a group that created the "stored program" concept that made powerful computers possible. He created the "von Neumann architecture," a template that is still used to design most computers.

Norbert Wiener (1894-1964) Professor of Mathematics at Massachusetts Institute of Technology (MIT) who conceived cybernetics, the nature of control and communications systems in animals, humans, and machines. In his 1948 book entitled *Cybernetics; Control and Communication in the Animal and the Machine,* he described his theories as a general science of mechanisms for maintaining order in a disorderly universe. This was one of the most valuable elements of understanding that contributed to the development of the personal computer.

Steve Wozniak (1950-) co-founder of Apple with Steve Jobs in 1976. Jobs was the entrepreneur/salesman, and Wozniak was the engineer/inventor. Wozniak, called "The Woz," created the Apple I. He started his computer career making long-distance phone boxes used to circumvent toll charges. Founding member of Homebrew Computer Club in 1975. He designed the first simple floppy drive ROM for personal computers.

Media of Importance to the Era:

Alternative and Underground Newspapers and Magazines: (Only a few of the many)

Advocate

Ain't I a Woman, Iowa City, Iowa

Amazon Nation

Argus, Ann Arbor, Michigan

Armageddon News, Bloomington, Indiana, 1968

Avatar, Boston/Roxbury, Massachusetts, from June 9, 1967 to April 26, 1968; a bi-weekly newspaper that lasted 24 issues; founder, Mel Lyman

Berkeley Barb, Berkeley, California, from late 1960s to 1980; founder, Max Sheer

Berkeley Tribe, an offshoot of the Barb

Big Mama Rag, Denver, Colorado

Body Politic, leading gay newspaper in Canada; Toronto, Canada,1971 to 1987

Canadian Free Press, Vancouver, British Columbia

Chicago Seed, a Chicago underground newspaper involved in trying to get parade and festival permits for the Festival of Life, the Yippies' celebration that was part of the Chicago Democratic Convention anti-war demonstrations in August, 1968.

Come Out, New York City, from 1969 to 1970, published by the New York Gay Liberation Front

Daily Planet, Miami, Florida

Dock of the Bay, San Francisco, California

Door, San Diego, California

Earth Times, San Francisco, California

East Village Other (EVO), Greenwich Village, New York, New York

Fag Rag, from 1971; published in Boston by Prof. Charley Shively

Fountain of Light, Arroyo Seco, New Mexico, a communal living publication

Free Press, Washington, DC

Great Speckled Bird, Atlanta, Georgia, from late 1960s

Green Revolution, Freeland, Maryland, a communal living publication

Helix

High Times, New York, from 1974; founder, Thomas Forcade

In These Times, Chicago, from 1976

It Ain't Me Babe, from 1972; publisher, Trina Robbins

Kaleidoscope, Chicago, Illinois

Liberation News Service (LNS) alternative news syndicate

Los Angeles Advocate, from 1967; owned by David Goodstein still published today, dedicated to the advocacy of homosexual issues

Los Angeles Free Press, "The Free Press" or **"Freep,"** from 1964; founder, Art Kunkin

Modern Utopian, Berkeley, California, from 1966; publisher, Richard Fairfield, a communal living publication

Mother Earth News, Madison, Ohio

Mother Jones, San Francisco, from 1976

The Nation, New York City, from 1865

New York Free Press

Nolo Express, New Orleans, Louisiana

Notes From the Underground, San Francisco, California

Off Our Backs; **Open City Press**, San Francisco, California

Open City, Los Angeles, California

Prisoners Digest International
Progressive
Psychedelic Review, from 1965, edited by Timothy Leary
Quicksilver Times, Washington, DC
Rampart
Rags, from 1970; founders, Mary Peacock, Daphne Davis, Blair Sabol and Baron Wolman; counterculture fashion; supposedly the only fashion magazine devoted to street fashions. This magazine argued that fashions are not created by industry designers, but are "borrowed" from styles first seen on the street, thrown together by ordinary folk. I agree.
RAT, Subterranean News, New York, New York from 1960s, a new left, alternative-culture newspaper that split into the women's paper **RAT feminist,** founded by Robin Morgan and Jane Alpert
Realist, publisher, Paul Krassner
Renaissance, San Francisco, California
Rising Up Angry, published by Students for a Democratic Society (SDS)
Rolling Stone, San Francisco, California; from 1967; founder, Jann Wenner & Ralph J. Gleason
San Francisco Express-Times
San Francisco Goodtimes
San Francisco Oracle, from late 1960s;
Sappho, a lesbian/feminist magazine published in London, England, from 1972 until December 1981; the oldest consistently published lesbian/feminist magazine; founder, Jackie Foster
Second City
The Seed
Space City, Houston, Texas
Street Journal, San Diego, California
The Haight-Ashbury, San Francisco, California
The People's Republic of Berkeley, Berkeley, California
Village Voice, Greenwich Village, New York, from 1955; founders, Norman Mailer, Don Wolfe, John Wilcock, Ed Fancher and others
Washington Free Press, Washington, DC, from 1960s

Books of and About the Era, and Some That Helped to Create It:

I have not included the publishers names in this list, since so many of these books have been reprinted by new publisher, are out of print or the publishers no longer exist. To find these books ask your local independent bookstore or look on Ebay, Amazon, Barnes and Noble or the personal website of the author.

A Child's Garden of Grass, Jack S. Margolis and Richard Clorfene, 1969
A Confederate General from Big Sur, Richard Brautigan, 1964
Affluent Society, The, John Kenneth Galbraith, 1958
Age of Reason, The, Jean Paul Sartre, 1947
An American Dream, Norman Mailer, 1965
Anarchy, State and Utopia, Robert Nozick, 1974
An Essay on Liberation, Herbert Marcuse, 1968
Art of Loving, The, Erich Fromm, 1956

A Separate Reality, Carlos Castaneda, 1971
Back to Eden, Jethro Kloss, 1939
Barefoot in Babylon, Bob Spitz, 1979
Be Here Now, Baba Ram Dass (Richard Alpert), 1971
Being There, Jerzy Kosinski, 1970
Breakfast of Champions, Kurt Vonnegut, Jr., 1973
Bury My Heart at Wounded Knee, Dee Brown,1971
Catch-22, Joseph Heller, 1961

Lawrence Ferlinghetti at his bookstore,
City Lights in San Francisco, ca 1957

Cat's Cradle, Kurt Vonnegut, Jr., 1963
Choirboys, The, Joseph Wambaugh, 1975
Crisis of Psychoanalysis, The, Erich Fromm, 1970
Cultivators Handbook of Marijuana, The, Bill Drake, 1970
Demian, Herman Hesse, 1919
Dharma Bums, The, Jack Kerouac, 1958
Diary of a Mad Housewife, Sue Kaufmann, 1967
Don't Push the River, Barry Stevens, 1970
Don't Shoot— We Are Your Children!, Anthony Lukas, 1986
Doors of Perception, Aldous Huxley, 1954
Doctor Sax, Jack Kerouac, 1959
Dragons of Eden, The, Carl Sagan, 1977
Eros and Civilization, Herbert Marcuse, 1955
Everything You've Always Wanted to Know About Sex But Were Afraid to Ask,
David Reuben, 1969
Family of Man, Museum of Modern Art, Edward J. Steichen, 1955
Fear of Flying, Erica Jong, 1973
Female Eunuch, The, Germaine Greer, 1971
Feminine Mystique, The, Betty Friedan, 1963
French Lieutenant's Woman, The, John Fowles, 1969
Function of the Orgasm, The, Wilhelm Reich, 1940
Fugitive Days: a memoir, Bill Ayers, 2001
Greening of America, The, Charles A. Reich, 1970
Gestalt Therapy Verbatim, Fritz Pearls, 1969
Grow Your Own, Jeanie Darlington, 1970
Harrad Experiment, The, Robert Rimmer, 1965
Hobbit, The, J. R. Tolkien, 1937

How To Keep Your Volkswagen Alive: A Manual of Step-by-Step Procedures for the Compleat Idiot, John Muir, 1969
I'm OK—You're OK, Dr. Thomas A. Harris, 1967
Johnny Got his Gun, Dalton Trumbo, 1959
Jonathan Livingston Seagull, Richard Bach, 1970
Journey to Ixtlan, Carlos Castaneda, 1972
Knots, R. D. Laing, 1970
Liberator, The, Max Eastman, 1918-22
Living on the Earth, Alicia Bay Laurel, 1971
Looking for Mr. Goodbar, Judith Rossner, 1975
Lord of the Rings, The, J. R. Tolkien
Magus, The, John Fowles, 1966
Masses, The, Max Eastman, 1913-17
Media Monopoly, Ben Bagdikian, 1983
Medium Is the Message, The, Marshall McLuhan, 1967
Mexico City Blues, Jack Kerouac, 1959
Monday Night Class, Stephen Gaskin, 1970
Moon is a Harsh Mistress, The, Robert Heinlein, 1966
Mutual Aid, Peter Kropotkin, 1902/1955
Narcissus and Goldmund, Herman Hesse, 1930
Nobody Knows My Name, James Baldwin, 1961
Other America, The, Michael Harrington, 1960
Other Side of Haight, The, James Fadiman, 2001
On Death and Dying, Elisabeth Kubler-Ross, 1969
One Dimensional Man, Herbert Marcuse, 1964
One Flew Over the Cuckoo's Nest, Ken Kesey, 1962
On The Duty Of Civil Disobedience, Henry David Thoreau, 1849
On the Road, Jack Kerouac, 1957
Passages, Gail Sheehy, 1976
Poems of Nature, Henry David Thoreau, 1895
Population Bomb, The, Dr. Paul R. Ehrlich, 1968
Pot Shots, Michael Stepanian, 1972, illustrated by R. Crumb
Proposition 31, Robert Rimmer, 1968
Psychedelic Experience, The, Richard Alpert, Timothy Leary and Ralph Metzner, 1964
Rubyfruit Jungle, Rita Mae Brown, 1973
Satori in Paris, Jack Kerouac, 1966
Search for a Method, Jean Paul Sartre, 1963
Selling of the President, The, Joe McGinnis, 1968
Sexual Politics, Kate Millett, 1969
Sexual Revolution, The, 1974
Siddhartha, Herman Hesse, 1922
Silent Spring, Rachel Carson, 1962
Slaughterhouse Five, Kurt Vonnegut, Jr., 1969
Soul on Ice, (Leroy) Eldridge Cleaver, 1968
Spirit of Zen, The, Alan Watts, 1936
Steppenwolf, Herman Hesse, 1927

Stranger in a Strange Land, Robert Heinlein, 1961
Strawberry Statement, The, James Simon Kunen, 1969
Subterraneans, The, Jack Kerouac, 1958
Summerhill, A. S. Neill, 1960
Teachings of Don Juan, The, Carlos Castaneda, 1968
Vital Center, The, Arthur Schlesinger, Jr., 1949
Trout Fishing in America, Richard Brautigan, 1967
Troubled Sleep, Jean Paul Sartre, 1950
Two Cultures and the Scientific Revolution, C. (Charles) P. (Percy) Snow, 1959
Ulysses, James Joyce, 1922
Unsafe at Any Speed, Ralph Nader, 1965
Up The Organization, Robert Townsend, 1970
Walden, or Life in the Woods, Henry David Thoreau, 1854
Walden Two, B. F. Skinner, 1962
Way of Liberation, The, Alan Watts, 1983 (posthumously)
Way of Zen, The, Alan Watts, 1958
Zen and the Art of Motorcycle Maintenance, Robert M. Pirsig, 1974
"1984," George Orwell, 1949

Movies of Importance in the Era:

"Dr. Strangelove: Or, How I Learned to Stop Worrying and Love the Bomb," 1964
"Blow-Up," 1966
"The Trip," 1967
"Barbarella," 1968
"I Love You, Alice B. Toklas," 1968
"Easy Rider," 1969
"Bob and Carol and Ted and Alice," 1969
"Harold and Maude," 1971
"Everything You Always Wanted to Know About Sex, But Were Afraid to Ask,"
1972
"Slaughterhouse-Five," 1972
"The Paper Chase," 1973
"One Flew Over The Cuckoo's Nest," 1975
"All the President's Men," 1976
"Network," 1976
"National Lampoon's Animal House," 1978
"Up In Smoke," 1978
"Coming Home," 1978
"Apocalypse Now," 1979
"The China Syndrome," 1979

Comix & Underground Cartoon Strips of the Era:

Abortion Eve (1973), Nanny Goat Productions, Joyce Farmer and Lyn Chevely
All Girl Thrills (1972), Trina Robbins
A Teen Abortion, Wimmen's Comix, Lora Fountain

Big Ass Comics, Rip Off Press, R. Crumb
Bijou Funnies, Jay Lynch and Skip Williamson
Bijou Funnies, Denis Kitchen's Kitchen Sink Enterprises
Book of Raziel, Book of Thought, John Thompson
Come Out Comix, (1973), Mary Wings (the first lesbian comic book)
Dyke Shorts (1978), Mary Wings
Eternal Comics, John Thompson
Everyman Comics, (1979), David Taylor, Hobo Stories, Rudie Tute and Breezy
Fat Freddy's Cat Comix, Gilbert Shelton
Feds 'n' Heads, Gilbert Shelton
Gay Comix, Howard Cruse
Insect Fear; It Ain't Me, Babe (an all women's comic) (1972), Nancy Kalish (pseud-
onyms: Panzika, Hurricane Nancy), Trina Robbins
Mod Love (1967), She's the Hippest Girl in the World, Western Publishing
Moondog #1-4, George Metzger
Mr. Natural, Apex Novelties, R. Crumb
Mr. Natural, Kitchen Sink Enterprises, R. Crumb
Pandora's Box (1973), Nanny Goat Productions, Joyce Farmer and Lyn Chevely
Pudge, Girl Blimp (1973), Last Gap, Lee Marrs
Snarf, Denis Kitchen
Snatch Comics, S. Clay Wilson, R. Crumb
Tales of the Sphinx, John Thompson
Tits 'n' Clits (1972), Nanny Goat Productions, Joyce Farmer and Lyn Chevely
Truckin' #1 and #2, George Metzger
Wet Satin (Women's Erotic Fantasies), 1976, Denis Kitchen
Wimmen's Comix #1 (1972), Last Gap, Sandy Comes Out, Trina Robbins
Wimmen's Comix, Last Gap, Lora Fountain, Lee Marrs
Young Lust
Zap Comix # 1, Feb., 1968, Don Donahue's Apex Novelties, R. Crumb
Zap Comix #0 & #3, Print Mint

Comix Artists, Writers and Producers of the Era:

Michele Brand (artist/writer), It Ain't Me Babe
Joel Beck (artist/writer), Lenny of Laredo (1965), Marching Marvin (1966), The
Profit (1966) and Johnny Marijuanaleif
Vaughn Bode (artist/writer), Cheech Wizard (1967)
Roger Brand (artist/writer), Gothic Blimp Works
R. Crumb (artist/writer), Mr. Natural, Eggs Ackley, Vulture Demonesses, Johnny
Fuckerfaster and Valerie the Vegetarian
Joyce Farmer and Lyn Chevely ("Chin Lyvely"), Nanny Goat Productions, Tits 'n'
Clits, 1972
Bill Griffith (artist/writer), Mr. Toad, Griffy, and Zippie the Pinhead
Rick Griffin (artist/writer/publisher), Zap, Snatch, Bill Graham Productions, and
Family Dog posters
Doug Hansen (artist/writer), Little Bungo

Greg Irons (artist/writer), Dungeons and Dragons
Jack Jackson ("Jaxon") & Frank Stack, God Nose (1965), The Adventures of Jesus (1962), and Blood on the Moon
Denis Kitchen (artist/writer/publisher), Bizarre Sex #1, Grateful Dead Comix #6, Wet Satin
Jayzey Lynch (artist/writer), Nard, Patrick th' Cat
Lee Marrs (artist/writer/publisher), Wimmen's Comix (1972), Pudge, and Girl Blimp (1973)
Paul Mavrides (artist/writer/publisher), Furry Freak Brothers
Victor Moscoso (artist/writer), Zap Comix
Dan O'Neill (artist/writer/publisher), Air Pirates Studio, Odd Bodkins
Harvey Pekar (artist/writer), American Splendor
Trina Robbins (artist/writer/publisher), It Ain't Me Babe (1972), Wimmen's Comix #1, and Sandy Comes Out
Spain Rodriquez (a.k.a., Algernon Backwash) (artist/writer), Trashman, Road Vultures
Ed Romero (artist/writer), The Adventures of Artie Stick
Artie Romero (artist/writer), Everyman Comics
Gilbert Shelton (artist/writer/publisher), Wonder Warthog, Fabulous Furry Freak Brothers, and Fat Freddy's Cat
David Sheridan (artist/writer), Fabulous Furry Freak Brothers
John Thompson (artist/writer), The Book of Raziel, Book of Thoht, Eternal Comics, and Tales of the Sphinx
Fred Todd (publisher, cofounder), Rip Off Press
Larry Todd (artist/writer), Dr. Atomic
Ron Turner (publisher), Last Gasp Eco-Funnies Company (1970–present), Slow Death Funnies (ecology comics)
Reed Waller (artist/writer), Omaha the Cat Dancer
Lary Welz (artist/writer), Cherry Comics, Captain Guts
Robert Williams (artist/writer), Gizmo, Mr. Baldpubis
Skip Williamson (a.k.a., Flippy Skippy) (artist/writer), Snappy Sammy Smoot
S. Clay Wilson (artist/writer), the Checkered Demon, Ruby the Dyke, and Captain Pissgums
Mary Wings (artist/writer), Gay Comix

Comix Publishers of the Era:

Apex Novelties, Don Donahue, Zap and Snatch Comics
Bijou Publishing Empire, Bijou Funnies
Everyman Studios, Doug Hansen
Gothic Blimp Works, East Village Other (1969)
Kitchen Sink, Denis Kitchen
Naturally Curly Studio, Trina Robbins, Sharon Rudahl, Leslie Cabarga
Print Mint, Don Schenker, Bob and Peggy Rita (publishers, comix store owners)
Psychedelic Comix Inc., Skip Williamson
Rip Off Press (1968- present); cofounders, Jack ("Jaxon") Jackson, Dave Moriarty, Don Shelton, Fred Todd

Twisted Sister (1976), Diane Noomin
Wimmen's Comix (1972-1992), Trina Robins
Young Lust Comics (1970); publishers, Bill Griffith, Jay Kinney

Kelly   Moscoso   Griffin   Wilson   Mouse

Poster Artists of the Era: (psychedelic music art)

Jim Blashfield worked for Bill Graham; Fillmore, Hollywood Bowl
David Byrd worked for Bill Graham; Fillmore
Jack Hatfield worked for Bill Graham; Fillmore
Michael Chechik worked for Bill Graham; Fillmore
Lee Conklin worked for Bill Graham; Fillmore
Rick Griffin worked for Chet Helms; Family Dog, Bill Graham; Fillmore, Winterland
James H. Gardner, Toronto, Canada
Greg Irons worked for Bill Graham; Fillmore, Winterland
Alton Kelley worked for Bill Graham; Fillmore
Nicholas Kounjnos worked for Bill Graham; Fillmore, Winterland
Bonnie MacLean worked for Bill Graham; Filmore, Cow Palace
Stanley "Mouse" Miller worked for Bill Graham; Fillmore
Norman Orr worked for Bill Graham; Fillmore
Clifford Charles Seeley worked for Bill Graham; Fillmore
David Singer worked for Bill Graham; Fillmore
John Thompson, Berkeley
Randy Tuten worked for Bill Graham; Fillmore
Wes Wilson worked for the Avalon and Bill Graham; Fillmore

Communes and Religious Communities of the Era:

The term commune comes from the word community. The communes of the
hippie era came in all sizes and shapes. There were urban communes, consisting
of only a house and a few unrelated people, and farms with hundreds of residents. Communes were based on shared interests in a variety of areas, such as
religion, sex, music, ecology, food disciplines, etc., and some were no more than
crash pads. Most communes eventually had troubles from outside or from within,

and all but a very small number dissolved within a few years. I have listed neither the populations of most of these communes, for they fluctuated greatly, nor the ending dates, because those too were very arbitrary. Today, the new terms for commune are intentional community, eco-village and cohousing; there are numerous such nouveau-communes existing. Additional information on this way of life may be found in the *Intentional Community* magazine or at www.ic.org, which lists approximately 500 communities and communal houses in the world today.

Ammon Hennacy or **Peace Action Farm** located in upstate New York, it provided a place for disadvantaged urban children as well as families of jailed conscientious objectors against the Vietnam War.

Ananda Cooperative Community formed in 1967 on two parcels of 70 and 270 acres near Nevada City, California. It was started by Swami Kiyananda (J. Donald Walters), a disciple of Paramahansa Yogananda founder of the Self-Realization Fellowship.

Animal Farm located in upstate New York.

Auroville Pondicherry on the Bay of Bengal in India. A religious ashram started in 1909 by an East Indian Hindu spiritual leader and intellectual, Sri Aurobindo Ghose (1872-1950). This "religious commune" was an experiment in international living with a large following of American hippies and hundreds of devotees from all over the world. A French/Algerian woman, Mirra Alfassa (1878-1973), known as "The Mother," was with Aurobindo from 1914 until his death in 1950. She was responsible for the guidance and management of Auroville, and, after Aurobindo's death, she carried on his spiritual leadership. There is some history of the possibility that this international commune was The Mother's idea in the first place. Auroville still exists today and has grown to between 1,500 and 2,000 people from 35 countries, living on hundreds of acres of land along ten miles of coast. (See: **Aurobindo [Sri Aurobindo Ghose]** in alphabetical listings)

BLOSSOM (See: alphabetical listings)

Brook Farm West Roxbury, Massachusetts, formed in 1841, it was one of the first groups of Americans to study and practice the philosophies of Eastern religions.

Camphill Village a service community established in 1955 in Copake, New York, based on the Camphill Movement started in Scotland by Karl Koenig. The Camphill Movement was based on the work with mentally retarded adults done by Rudolf Steine (1861-1925). Steine's concept, called Curative Education, is based on the principle of accepting the retarded as individuals, concentrating on their potential rather than their liabilities. Camphill gave work and activities to mildly retarded residents. Another Camphill community was called Beaver Run in Pennsylvania.

Canyon location unknown.

City of Light, The first established in San Francisco and later near Santa Fe, New Mexico. Beliefs included flying saucers and New Age religion.

Cold Mountain Farm established in 1967 on 400 acres near Hobart, New York.

Cooperative Village established in 1968, near Nevada City, California.

Crow or CRO Research Organization a group marriage community in a large dome and a large house on 65 acres in Oregon.

Dog House the residence of members of the Family Dog. Located at 2125 Pine Street in San Francisco, California.

Drop City (See: alphabetical listings)

Earth Cyclers established in the 1970s by Huw "Piper" Williams, on land owned by his parents. "Things got wild and different at the Tolstoy Farm commune," Williams said, so he left and created this other community.

Earth People's Park over 200 people on acreage near Norton, Vermont.

Family of the Mystic Arts location unknown.

Farm, The (See: alphabetical listings)

Findhorn (The Findhorn Foundation Community) established in 1962 at the Findhorn Bay Caravan (trailer) Park in the northeast of Scotland.   Through the years, it has become the United Kingdom's largest intentional community "based on spiritual values." It is a center for adult education of "new ways of living that are appropriate for the world of today and tomorrow, founded on the basic belief in the underlying spirit and intelligence with Nature and all forms of life on our planet."   In 1984, the members purchased The Park, which was the original community site. Findhorn is today an eco-village.

Five Star in a large building with hot springs near Taos, New Mexico.   Short lived due to troubles with other area residents.

Fort Hill Community (See: **Lyman Family Community**)

Gorda Mountain established in 1962 in Big Sur, California. Considered the first open-land commune, it was on land owned by Amelia Newell. Its members were hassled by other local residents, and the commune closed in 1968.

Gould Farm near Great Barrington in western Massachusetts.   Created to help people with emotional stress return successfully to society. It had a paid staff, which is a phenomenon among communes.

Greenfeel a youth commune on 5 acres in Barre, Vermont. It was started by two young bisexuals and was short lived.

Harrad West a group marriage community established in 1968-69 in a 12-room house in Berkeley, California. It was a development of the Wednesday Night Group started by Richard Fairfield, who wrote *Commune USA* and published *The Modern Utopia* magazine. The Wednesday Night Group was a meeting intended for people interested in the possibility of setting up one or more intentional communities. The name Harrad West came from *The Harrad Experiment,* a book by Robert Rimmer, a foremost proponent of group marriages. A movie based on the book was produced in 1973.

Heathcote established in 1965 on 37 acres in northern Maryland. It housed the School of Living, which espoused the idea of self-sufficient existence. Mildred Loomis was the guiding force. Loomis also published the monthly newspaper *The Green Revolution.* "A community of friends and family who choose to live cooperatively and consciously create a better way of life striving to care for one another and for the natural systems that nurtures them." Members lived in a 150-year-old grain mill, a 100-year-old farmhouse, and several outbuildings.

Himalayan Academy in a large, deserted brewery in a historic ghost town near Virginia City, California, led by guru master Subramuniya and committed to a monastic lifestyle.

Hog Farm (See: alphabetical listings)

Juke Savages a California commune, location unknown. Associated with the Hog Farm and Hugh Romney.

Koinonia established in 1942 on 1,400 acres south of Macon, Georgia. Clarence Jordan was the guiding force. A Black and White interracial commune with Christian influence.

Krishna movement or International Society for Krishna Consciousness (See: alphabetical listings)

Lama Foundation established in June, 1967, on land at 8,600 feet in the Sangre de Cristo Mountains, 20 miles north of Taos, New Mexico. It was a semi-religious retreat and vegetarian oriented. The land was purchased by Steve Durky with $21,000 from an anonymous donor. The founders were interested in creating "environmental art" pieces. The community ran the School of Basic Studies, to which tuition-paying students came to live, experience Eastern disciplines and work during the summers.

Land of Oz near Meadville, Pennsylvania. Led by George Hurd, it lasted only four months due to harassment by the residents of Meadville.

last century location unknown.

Last Resort, The near Taos, New Mexico. Mickey Peyote, leader.

Liberty or **Libre** established in June, 1968, in northern Colorado. Led by Peter Rabbit, it consisted of geodesic domes and was an offshoot of Drop City.

Lord Buckley and Friends a group marriage community started in Berkeley, California, 1968. It eventually grew to 23 girls, 22 guys and 9 kids in a two-bedroom bungalow and a school bus near Taos, New Mexico.

Lorien (from Loth Lorien in *The Hobbit*), New Mexico.

Lower Farm near Placitas, New Mexico. "Not a commune, a village," said leader Ulysses S. Grant, self-identified reincarnation of the Civil War general and candidate for Governor of New Mexico.

Lyman Family Community established in Roxbury, Massachusetts, in 1965. Its leader was Mel Lyman, who was from the State of Oregon by way of California, where he was married and worked as a computer technician. In 1961, Lyman dropped out and traveled to Asheville, North Carolina, where he learned to play the banjo. He moved to Cambridge, Massachusetts, and eventually joined The Jim Kweskin Jug Band. Mel Lyman's amazing personality and profound knowledge of people made him a teacher, helping others with their emotional problems of life. In 1965, Mel moved his friends and "family" around the park on top of Fort Hill in Roxbury, Boston's Black ghetto, creating the Lyman Family Community in a number of old, Victorian mansions. At times, the family had communal homes in New York, San Francisco, Los Angeles, New Orleans and Kansas.

Magic Farm Oregon.

Morningstar East established in April, 1969, on 35 acres near Taos, New Mexico; an offshoot of Morningstar Ranch.

Morningstar established in 1966 on 32 acres in Sonoma County, northern California. Its leader was Lou Gottlieb, folksinger from The Limelighters. Based on the principle that all land should be available to those who wish to use it; known as LATWIDN, Land Access To Which Is Denied No One. Eventually, the County of Sonoma denied access to everybody except Gottlieb. They bulldozed all buildings except one, and, although Morningstar was officially closed, people continued to live there in tents. In the spring of 1969, Lou deeded the land to God, but the County, not being able to serve God with papers, continued to hassle Lou.

Messiah's World Crusade established in 1967 in a house on Oak Street in the Haight-Ashbury section of San Francisco, a house in Larkspur, and in Berkeley. Its members ran the Here and Now Restaurant, 798 Haight Street, San Francisco; and The Mustard Seed Restaurants in Sausalito and on Telegraph Avenue in Berkeley, California. Allen Noonan, a fifty-plus-year-old leader, was called "The Messiah." The Messiah talked a lot about flying saucers and the commune had a lot of troubles with drug busts.

New Buffalo established on June 21, 1967, on 103 acres in Taos County, northern New Mexico, Indian tribal alliance. Financed with $50,000 by Dick Cline; led by "Headmen" Justin and George Robinson.

Olympali established in 1967 on 750 acres north of San Francisco in an elegant, historic mansion with a swimming pool. Financed by entrepreneur Don McCoy. Lasted less than two years; besieged by legal and monetary hassles after McCoy's money was tied up in litigation.

Oneida established by John Humphrey Noyes near Oneida, New York. One of the longest lasting communes.

One World Family of the Messiah's World Commune (See: **Messiah's World Crusade**)

Oregon Family, The fundamentalist Christian. Bob Carey, leader.

Phoenix Family House, The located south of Hot Springs, New Mexico.

Packers Corner located in New York State. Established by Sam Lovejoy, famous for monkeywrenching a nuclear power plant. Sister commune to Total Loss Farm.

Pine Street Commune located at 1836 Pine Street, San Francisco, California. A house managed by Bill Ham, the famed Avalon Ballroom light show artist, it housed many artists and musicians during the heyday of hippiedom, 1966-67. It was Janis Joplin's first home in San Francisco when she arrived to join Big Brother and the Holding Company.

Ranch, The located in northern California, reportedly a hangout for the Brotherhood, who made and sold LSD, and financed by Billy Nellon Hitchcock, a counterculture millionaire. Nicky Sands, the premier acid chemist, hung out there, as did some friends of the Grateful Dead.

Rock Bottom Farm located in Strafford, Vermont.

School of Living (See: **Heathcote**)

Shiloh established in 1942 on 500 acres near Sherman, New York. A Christian ministry founded by E. Crosby Monroe. Monroe was an interior designer of ships, who served in the US Navy during World War II and opened his home to servicemen and others. In 1968, the communal family moved to 117- and 150-acre parcels near Sulphur Springs, Arkansas. This intentional community has developed and continues to distribute an extensive line of sprouted whole grain breads and other quality whole food products.

Synanon established in 1958 in Santa Monica, San Francisco and the mountains above Fresno, California. Originally a substance abuse rehab community founded by Charles Dietrich, it still exists in various forms.

Talsen a group marriage community in Oregon.

Taos Learning Center a youth commune and school 20 miles from Taos, New Mexico, across the valley from New Buffalo.

Tolstoy Farm established in 1963 on 80 acres (North 80) and 120 acres (South 120) in Mill Canyon near Davenport, Washington; founded by Huw "Piper" Williams. This commune exemplified the hippie ideals of peace and love, rejecting all regulations. They tolerated drugs, sex of all kinds, nudity, and any imaginable thought and behavior. Williams was involved in the early 1960s peace movement and the New England Committee for Nonviolent Action. Tolstoy was a nonviolent training center, had no electricity, no flush toilets, no gas for heat or cooking and no clocks. At its late-60s peak, the community had as many as 80 residents, including numerous children, with a cooperative alternative school and cooperative work projects. In 1970, a journalist wrote that this was a community of "serious, straightforward people who, with calculated bluntness, say they are dropouts, social misfits, unable or unwilling to cope with the world 'outside.'" Eventually, "Things got wild and different," as Williams says, so he left and moved to another community, which he called Earth Cyclers, on land owned by his parents 25 miles from Tolstoy.

Total Loss Farm in western Massachusetts. Its prominent member Ray Mungo, artists and writers were the subjects of the autobiographical book *Famous Long Ago,* about the founding of the Liberation News service and alternative press syndicate. Its famous nude softball games were attended by prominent people, such as Kurt Vonnegut. Total Loss Farm was a sister commune to Packers Corner.

Tivoli Farm part of the Catholic Workers Farm system, on 90 acres in the Hudson Valley of New York State, it was an offshoot of the Catholic Workers Movement in New York City in the 1930s. Dorothy Day of the Catholic Workers Movement was involved in some way. Originally a pacifist organization that published *The Catholic Worker* magazine, Tivoli Farm was dedicated to providing a place away from urban life where needy and sick people (in many cases drug addicts) could recuperate, learn and make changes in their lives.

Translove Energies-White Panthers, The established in 1967-68 near Ann Arbor, Michigan, by John Sinclair, a poet, jazz critic and supporter of marijuana and LSD. Sinclair previously had a performance venue in Detroit called the Artists' Workshop. He managed bands, including MC5 and the Psychedelic Stooges, both of which performed at demonstrations during the Democratic National Convention in Chicago in August of 1968. "Our culture, our art, the music, newspapers, books, posters, our clothing, our homes, the way we walk and talk, the way our hair grows, the way we smoke dope and fuck and eat and sleep—it is all one message, and the message is FREEDOM."

Twin Oaks established on June 16, 1967, on a 123-acre farm in Virginia. Original inspiration came from B. F. Skinner's novel *Walden Two*. Twin Oaks still exists as an intentional community of around 80 people living on 456 acres of farm and forest land in rural Virginia. "Based on equality and nonviolence, its goals have been to sustain and expand a community which values cooperation; which is not sexist or racist; which treats people in a caring and fair manner; and which provides for the basic needs of its members." The community continues to produce hammocks and swinging chairs from recycled polyester and rope.

Walden House established in 1965 in a house in Washington, DC; based on the book *Walden Two* by B. F. Skinner, in which one of the premises was group marriage. This community eventually evolved into Twin Oaks.

Wheeler's Free, Wheeler's Ranch or **Sheep Ridge Ranch** established in the winter of 1967 on 320 acres near Occidental, California, by Bill Wheeler.

Yellow Submarine established in 1968; a youth commune in Oregon.

Gurus and Religious Leaders of the Era:

Meher Baba (See: alphabetical listings)

Satya Sai Baba (India 1926-) a spiritual leader who resides in his ashram, Prasanti Nilayam, northeast of Bangalore. He claims to be a reincarnation of the Hindu Saint Shirdi Sai Baba. Sai Baba supposedly produces ashes (*vibhuti*) from thin air and gives them to his devotees. He is also reported to produce valuable jewelry and perform the healing of serious diseases. He preaches, interprets holy scriptures, and instructs devotees in the use of mantras.

Yogi Bhajan religious leader of the 3HO Foundation, which stands for Healthy, Happy, Holy Organization. A follower and teacher of kundalini yoga. Since arriving in the United States in 1969, he has become the "Chief Management Advisor" to 14 corporations worldwide, supplying goods and services to health

Yogi Bhajan   photo by Lisa Law ©

food, computer and security companies. Yogi Bhajan conducts annual business seminars and has authored several books guiding aspiring entrepreneurs and business executives.

A. C. Bhaktiveda (See: **International Society for Krishna Consciousness** in alphabetical listings)

Baba Ram Dass (See: **Ram Dass** in alphabetical listings)

Swami Vishnu-Devananda (India 1927-1993) a world authority on hatha and raja Yoga. A student of Sri Swami Sivananda. Swamiji, as he was called, was also known as the "Flying Swami" for the many peace missions he led to troubled areas of the world. He founded the International Sivananda Yoga Vedanta Centers and authored *The Complete Illustrated Book of Yoga, Meditation and Mantras*, a commentary on hatha yoga, karma and diseases. He created the first Yoga Teachers Training Course, which trained thousands of certified teachers.

Steven Gaskin (See: alphabetical listings)

Sri Aurobindo Ghose (India 1872-1950) a Hindu intellectual and spiritual leader, born in Bengal, educated in England. Jailed in 1902 by the British for his political activities in the cause of Indian independence. He experienced a spiritual awakening in jail, and, after release in 1909, he began an ashram in Pondicherry, East India. Aurobindo attempted to incorporate Eastern and Western philosophy through the theory of evolution; he developed "Integral Yoga," a system for teaching yoga in a way acceptable to both cultures. He called one of his primary philosophies Unity in Diversity. His "religious commune," Auroville, in Pondicherry, eventually became one of the largest international centers in India, with hundreds of devotees from all over the world, including a large following of American hippies. A French/Algerian woman, Mirra Alfassa (1878-1973), known as "The Mother," was with Aurobindo from 1914 until his death in 1950. She was responsible for the guidance and management of Auroville, and, after Aurobindo's death, she carried on his spiritual leadership. (See: **Auroville** in **Communes** list)

Mahara Ji (See: alphabetical listings)

Jiddu Krishnamurti (See: alphabetical listings)

Dalai Lama (See: **Dalai Lama** and **Esoteric Buddhism** in alphabetical listings)

Mel Lyman (USA 1938-1978) called "The Second Coming" or the "East Coast Messiah," he was a musician who garnered a following with his music, humor and publication of the irreverent, satirical *Avatar,* a short-lived newspaper in Boston, Massachusetts (June 9, 1967-April 26, 1968). He also started the Fort Hill Community in Roxbury, Massachusetts. Mel was from the State of Oregon by way of California, where he was married and worked as a computer technician. In 1961, he dropped out and traveled to Asheville, North Carolina, where he learned to play the banjo. Music became his new life, and he eventually moved to the Cambridge-Boston area and joined The Jim Kweskin Jug Band. Mel Lyman's amazing personality and profound knowledge of people made him a teacher, helping others with their emotional problems of life. To many people, Mel became God, and he fueled this image through his profound, yet sacrilegious, writings. In 1965, Mel Lyman moved his friends and "family" around the park on top of Fort Hill in Roxbury, Boston's Black ghetto, creating the Lyman Family Community in a number of old, Victorian mansions.

Reverend Sun Myung Moon (See: alphabetical listings)

Allen Noonan called "the Messiah," leader of the Messiah's World Crusade Commune on Oak Street in San Francisco. Proprietor of the Here and Now Restaurant, 798 Haight Street, San Francisco; and The Mustard Seed Restaurant in Sausalito, California. The Messiah talked a lot about flying saucers, and the commune had a lot of trouble with drug busts.

Swami Muktananda Paramahansa (India 1908-1982) a teacher of siddha yoga, Sampradaya and follower of Bhagawan Nityananda (d. 1961). In the early 1970s, Muktananda established the siddha yoga movement in the United States and guided its development during his three world tours—in 1970, 1974-76, and the third, in 1979-81. He was already a widely known master and spiritual leader when he came to America to establish a branch of the movement that had grown up around him in India.

Bhagwan Shree Rajneesh (See: alphabetical listings)

Swami Satchidananda (India 1914-) the founder of the worldwide Integral Yoga Institutes. An esteemed yoga master and spiritual leader, Sri Swamiji is regarded by many as an apostle of peace. He is often affectionately referred to as the "Woodstock Guru" because he was present at the Woodstock Festival and is credited with introducing the Woodstock generation to yoga. In 1966, sponsored by illustrator Peter Max, he toured America. He was the first person to receive an American visa under the title "Minister of Divine Words," and he eventually became a United States citizen.

Sri Swami Sivananda (India 1887-1963) a practitioner of karma yoga. He started the Sivananda Ashram in India 1932, the Divine Life Society in 1936, the Yoga-Vedanta Forest Academy in 1948. He convened a World Parliament of Religions in 1953, wrote over 300 books and attracted disciples, such as Satchidananda and Vishnu-devananda. In 1957, Swami Sivananda sent his industrious disciple Swami Vishnu-devananda to the West, where he established the International Sivananda Yoga Vedanta Centers.

Satguru Sivaya Subramuniyaswami (India 1927) the current preceptor of the Natha Sampradaya's Kailasa Parampara. A student and follower of Sage Yogaswami, Sivaya Subramuniyaswami was ordained by Yogaswami in 1949. Subramuniyaswami founded the Saiva Siddhanta Church in 1949. In 1957, Subramuniyaswami founded the Himalayan Academy. In 1970, he established his international headquarters and monastery complex, Kauai Aadheenam, on Hawaii's Garden Island of Kauai. In 1979, Subramuniyaswami founded the international newspaper *Hinduism Today*, a publication devoted to the advancement of the Hindu renaissance. Satguru Sivaya Subramuniyaswami urges his devotees to "Know thy Self" through self-inquiry, meditation, traditional temple worship, scriptural study and selfless service.

Daisetz Teitaro Suzuki (See: alphabetical listings)

Paramahansa Yogananda (India 1893-1952) "emissary of India's ancient wisdom." In 1920, Yogananda traveled from his native India to the United States and founded Self-Realization Fellowship to introduce worldwide India's ancient science and philosophy of yoga and its discipline of meditation. In India, the Self-Realization Fellowship is known as the Yogoda Satsanga Society. In 1925, Yogananda established an international headquarters in Los Angeles. The Fellowship grew in popularity, and, even after his death, his teachings drew many followers, particularly during the hippie era when many young people were experimenting with Eastern religions. In 1967, one of Yogananda's followers, Swami Kiyananda, started the Ananda Cooperative Community, a commune on two parcels of 70 and 270 acres near Nevada City, California.

Sage Yogaswami ("Master of Yoga") **(Sri Lanka 1872-1964)** one of Sri Lanka's most renowned spiritual masters, a Sivajnani and Natha siddhar revered by both Hindus and Buddhists. He studied and practiced kundalini yoga under the guidance of Satguru Chellappaswami, from whom he received guru status. Sage Yogaswami was in turn the teacher of Sivaya Subramuniyaswami, current master of the Natha Sampradaya's Kailasa Parampara.

Maharishi Mahesh Yogi (See: alphabetical listings)

Presidents of the United States During the Hippie Era:

Dwight David (Ike) Eisenhower (1890-1969) (President from 1953 to 1961) served two 4-year terms as US President.

John Fitzgerald Kennedy (JFK) (1917-1963) (President from 1961 to 1963) served 2 years, 10 months and 2 days, from January 20, 1961 until his assassination on November 22, 1963.

Lyndon Baines Johnson (1908-1973) (President from 1963 to 1969) as vice-president, he assumed the presidency on November 22, 1963, following the assassination of JFK, and completed JFK's term. He was re-elected in 1964, but declined nomination for re-election in 1968.

Richard Milhous Nixon (1913-1993) (President from 1969 to 1974) served one 4-year term, was re-elected in 1972 and then, due to indiscretions, was forced to resign on August 9, 1974.

Gerald Rudolph Ford (1913-) (President from 1974 to 1977) as vice-president, he assumed the presidency upon Nixon's resignation on August 9, 1974, and completed Nixon's term. He was defeated in his re-election bid in 1976.

James Earl (Jimmy) Carter (1924-) (President from 1977 to 1981) served one 4-year term and was defeated in his re-election bid in 1980.

Ronald Wilson Reagan (1911-) (President from 1981 to 1989) was elected November 4, 1980, and assumed the presidency on January 20, 1981.

Afterword

For the last 20 years, much of the idealism of the hippie era has been forgotten. Although the positive lessons of the era now lay dormant, the indulgences of that era were too much fun to be abandoned. The hippie movement gave some people the opportunity to break free, others an excuse to break rules, and still more, a license to get stupid.

Lessons of the hippie era have been misunderstood and misused. The search for self-realization has become selfishness. The expression of sexual joy has become debauchery. Experimentation with mind-expanding drugs has become, for many, indulgence in mind-controlling drugs.

It is true that no generation can pass on its lessons like mother's milk; each person, it seems, must learn through experience. But the wiser members of the species also look for a little guidance from respected sources. The more sources of reference to past excesses and successes, the easier it will be for future generations to make choices based upon knowledge rather than painful experimentation. Someday, hopefully, the lessons learned from the last 40 years will influence our judgment in positive ways.

History is a valuable reference to help us with today; yet, if we delve too deeply into the past for too long, it can become a glorification of our mistakes. We don't have to look back 100 or 200 years to study ourselves. To this point humankind has a habit of repeating everything over and over again. The hippie era had sex, drugs, social turmoil, war and religious conflict in as great a measure as any period of history. The time has arrived to begin studying the 1960s and 70s; it will teach us a great deal.

Many people thought that the hippie era was frivolous and that the people who indulged in the lifestyle were frivolous, but underlying everything that the true hippie did was a very serious effort to improve society and create a better future. This book is not merely a look back, but a reminder that we have a future to tend to; we cannot do it properly without learning from our past experiences and mistakes.

Our ability to communicate is what makes humans most unique from other creatures. This provides us with an opportunity to rise above the basic conflicts in which all other creatures indulge. Sadly, all words do not possess the same meanings for everyone. We must work harder to find common definitions so that we can discuss important issues rationally; it is the only hope for the future of mankind. Hopefully, this book will help to bring people closer to understanding one another.

The establishment was so threatened by the hippie counterculture that it did everything possible to trash it. The media focused on the bad parts and ignored the ideals of peace and love. They weren't listening to the messenger; always listen to the messenger even if you don't want to hear the news. Keep your options open by knowing every possibility of movement around you. That is the *Homo sapiens* way to act; pragmatism is the human beings' most valuable asset. If we are stagnant in the midst of changes, we will not survive.

Our society threw out the baby with the bath water when it rejected the hippie ideals. Sure, there were problems with the counterculture of the 1960s and 70s; we were experimenting. We were trying out all kinds of things, and many of the people who joined the counterculture didn't fully understand what it was really about; they did negative things and went to excesses.

The events of September 11, 2001, would not have taken place if our society had listened to the message of the hippies. A lot would be better today if the ideals of 1960s had been appreciated; even those in high and wealthy places, who conspired to suppress the liberal movement of that era, would be better off today.

Many people feel that liberal philosophy is the same as communist ideology and will somehow take away all their freedoms. That could not be further from the truth. Liberals want freedom for all, not just those who agree with them; conservative policies are what really suppress freedom. People must learn that there is a big difference between liberal ideals and communism (totalitarian socialism).

The hippie era was an experiment, a test of ideas and concepts. We learned a lot of lessons. We discovered that sex, drugs and rock & roll can be valuable parts of life with the proper education, moderation and protection. We learned that not everything about communism is bad, and not everything about capitalism is good.

Most aging hippies still believe in sex, drugs, rock & roll and socialist ideals. But we also believe in democracy and free enterprise. Not capitalism, the right of the rich to get richer, but, free enterprise, the right of everyone to be enterprising. True hippies believe in democracy, not totalitarian dictatorships, either fascist or communist.

The conflict between socialism and capitalism is mutually destructive. Capitalism and socialism can and must live together. Neither of them is going to go away, and so a mutually advantageous truce must be reached. If mankind is truly as intelligent as we say we are, we will cooperate; otherwise, we will self-destruct.

I do not hate capitalists; I think they are misguided, selfish and destructive, but I am willing to let them have their money and power if they will stop pushing the other 90 percent of the population around. I'm sure most people would be willing to let them keep their wealth if they would be kinder to our environment, stop engaging in wars and allow the rest of us to achieve just a bit more comfort and security.

As a liberal intellectual, I may not like the capitalist system as it is implemented today, yet I understand its value as part of a fruitful economy. A creative person can profit from a capitalist who exploits his creations and markets them. The creator never gets as much of a financial reward as the capitalist, but by working together, they can both reap benefits. Blue-collar workers can also profit from corporations who exploit them. If we could just get the capitalists to take a slight cut in profits and pay their employees a better living wage, then everyone would be happy.

The capitalists must start accepting the fact that without the ideas of the creative people and the work of the blue-collar worker, they would not be able to reap such large profits. And without that same majority of workers and consumers, there would be no market for their products. It should be a simple thing for them to start being just a little more benevolent.

If incomes don't start evening out a bit, there will be more revolutions. Unless the military-industrial complex starts respecting its workers and being more concerned about the poverty and struggle of people in America and the rest of the world, there will be more terrorism and wars. Our economy could be just as profitable making tools for peace and mutual prosperity as for war and superiority, and we would *all* be more comfortable in that environment.

The Enron collapse and its corporate management greed are fine examples of why most immigrants came to America. They came to get away from the feudal lords, who were collecting all the money as it trickled up to them.

We have no new worlds to emigrate to. If we don't place adequate controls on business practices and profits, eventually, 10 percent of the population will own everything. Then anarchy will prevail.

Changes never come willingly from the center of a society. Change emanates from the edges of a culture, the counterculture, the young people and students in society. People in the middle of society are too content with the status quo to want change. They are "invested" in things as they are, and are far removed from the problems of society at large, and the dailystruggle with the hard facts of life.

Those people at the comfortable economic top of a culture are usually exploiting society and are too corrupted by their power and comfort to want change. Yet often it is their oppression of the lower classes that creates the atmosphere that causes revolution and change. Will society ever learn this, so perhaps the world won't have to keep repeating the same struggles?

In the 20th century we made all the mistakes. The conservatives made monstrous mistakes, and the liberals made monstrous mistakes. In a few years, all of the leaders and perpetrators of those errors will be dead of natural causes. The people of the 21st century won't be able to blame others if they continue making the same mistakes. This book is a reminder of the mistakes and successes of the last great era of the 20th century. Learn from it, build on it and don't mess up your last chance.

We must tear down fences and build bridges in order to make a peaceful life for all of us. As John Lennon said, "Imagine all the people living life in peace. You may think I'm a dreamer, but I'm not the only one. I hope someday you will join us and the world will live as one."

John McCleary

Mr. McCleary is available for lectures and public appearances. Please make inquiries by E-mail at hippiedictionary@attbi.com.

Self-portrait, 1973

2001, photo by David Glover

About the Author John McCleary

Fifty-eight years old and what is commonly known as an aging hippie, John was born in San Francisco, California, and is a third-generation journalist. He attended Monterey Peninsula College, Santa Barbara City College and UCLA. He has worked as a writer, art director and photographer in the newspaper, music, publishing and advertising industries for the last thirty-seven years.

John was present at the Monterey Pop Festival and was a music industry photographer in Los Angeles in the 1960s and 70s; he was on stage and in the dressing rooms with The Doors, Jimi Hendrix, The Stones, Tina Turner and others. In the early 1970s, he produced a series of twelve posters and *The People's Book*, a photographic book of the counterculture of the era.

He participated in and photographed many anti-war demonstrations across the United States during the 1960s and 70s. John was at the Isla Vista, Santa Barbara, demonstrations and Bank of America burning, with photos to prove it. During the 1970s, he traveled to most of the hippie centers and many communes around the world, spending time in Amsterdam, Greece, Afghanistan, India, Goa, London, Greenwich Village, Big Sur and Haight-Ashbury.

John has a pierced ear and a severe reading habit. He has a daughter, Siobhan, from his first marriage. He is remarried and lives with his wife and editor, Joan Jeffers McCleary, in their home overlooking Monterey Bay.

"I do not regret anything I did during my hippie era, and most who lived that lifestyle will say the same. If the truth be known, it was a high point in our lives (no pun intended), and many of us would go back in a second if we could. I see photos of myself in my striped bell-bottoms, and I am not ashamed. I look at my pierced ear and feel pride. I think back on my drug and sexual experiences during that time and realize that I learned a great deal, and fortunately I didn't pay too great a price for the education.

"Though, in theory, I would gladly go back in time, I do not want to change today into yesterday. I don't want to hide from now and the problems of today. If we try to retreat to a more innocent yesterday, we will never solve the problems of today. If, as we grow older, we atrophy into our memories, then the new generations will lose our wisdom and must then continue to solve the same problems over and over again. I want us to build on yesterday, to reintroduce the precepts of that time into our lives today, and to evolve from our past discoveries.

"I am proud to be an aging hippie. I will defend to the very end our value system and continue to promote many of the concepts by which we lived then. I know I am not alone. The Dream is still alive."

"Oh yes, I'm a Pisces. What's your sign?"

John

About the Editor Joan Jeffers McCleary

A distant relative of poet Robinson Jeffers, Joan was raised in a literary family. Her father was a teacher and librarian, and her mother, a prodigious reader and grammarian. She was raised on the Monterey Peninsula, and lived in both the Boston area and the San Joaquin Valley of California before returning to Monterey seven years ago. She is an honors graduate of Katharine Gibbs School in Boston, and attended California State University, Fresno.

Joan has worked as a freelance editor for many years as well as a university administrative assistant. She has two sons, Sean and Ian, from a previous marriage and now lives with her husband, John McCleary, in their home overlooking Monterey Bay.

Acknowledgment of Artwork and Photography

Photography: David Glover, John Jeffers, Lisa Law, Jim Marshall, John McCleary, Jerry Takigawa.
Artwork by: R. Crumb, Bill Griffith, Paxton Mobley, Alicia Bay Laurel www.aliciabaylaurel.com.

Every effort has been made to acknowledge correctly and contact the source and/copyright holder of each picture. I apologize for any unintentional error or omission; any such error will be rectified in future editions of this book.

Acknowledgment of Others Who Have Helped

Phillip Butler for his recollections of the Hanoi Hilton, JT Mason for her women's issues insight, Tracy Valleau for his technical assistance, Irene Morris and Andrew White for computer wizardry, David Glover for his photography and "brain truss," Jorma Kaukonen and Jack Casady as musical and spiritual advisers, Country Joe McDonald as inspiration, the two intellectual giants Richard Miller and his brother John Miller, and Joann Way for proofreading. Also Tom and Carol Berg, Bryan Callas (photo subject), alter ego Jonas Candler (photo subject), Karl and Sandy Dobbratz (photo subjects), Steve Downey (photo subject), Blair Everett (photo subject), Steve and Bev Forker, Buzz Greenberg (photo subject), David and Linda Grubbs, Art Guerra (photo subject), Ian Heuston, Sean Heuston, Russell and Caren Hicks, Eileen Hurtt (photo subject), Joe Lubow, Neill Kramer (Hippie Museum), Siobhan McCleary (photo subject), Geri McComb (photo subject), Marianne Mangold (photo subject), Bill Minor, Bill Monning, Daniel Pantalone, Michael Peterson, Rainbow, John Random, Arthur Rogers, Sonja (photo subject), Kerry Sissem, Gordon Smith, Spade Phil (photo subject), Candice Tahara (photo subject), Patrice Ward (hand model) and many others.

For more counterculture information and a trip through the hippie era, logon to www.hippiemuseum.org or www.hippiedictionary.com

Disclaimer

The publisher, distributors and booksellers of this edition are not responsible for the political views expressed herein; they are the sole responsibility of John McCleary. As a history book, the intent of this publication is to examine the opinions and ideals of the hippie movement. The companies that helped to distribute these pages are to be commended for their patriotic adherence to America's First Amendment right of free speech.

I am in no way advocating the use of any of the sex, drugs or rock and roll defined or explained in this book. Nor am I condemning or glorifying this stuff; I am only expressing the opinions of certain segments of our society.

Artists' Relief Fund (ARF)

If this book is profitable, I intend to make donations to establish an Artist's Relief Fund. This is not a special bank account to ensure my own comfort in old age; it will be a *bona fide* foundation to assist artists of the Central California Coast who may be in need. America's creative people are among the most unappreciated and underpaid segment of our society.

JBMc

662

Suggestion:

In your automobile, always have a Jimi Hendrix tape or CD poised to play when radio advertising or life itself becomes just too much to handle.

This is a space where all you aging hippies can write down the words, terms and definition that I somehow missed. Some of the language of the time was
regional, and I didn't come in contact with all of it during the era or in my research. If you want to send me your entries for a possible update and reprinting, please E-mail. JBMc
hippiedictionary@attbi.com

_____
_____
_____
_____
_____
_____
_____
_____
_____
_____
_____
_____
_____
_____
_____
_____
_____

This is a space where all you concerned citizens can write down all the things that you think our government and business leaders are doing wrong and what should be done about it. You can also E-mail all of this to me and, above all, to your elected officials.

_____
_____
_____
_____
_____
_____
_____
_____
_____
_____
_____
_____
_____
_____
_____
_____
_____
_____
_____
_____
_____
_____
_____
_____
_____

This is a space where all you concerned spirits can write a poem to mother nature about how you think she should reprimand all the bad people who are destroying our earth.